ALICE
HAD A PALACE

Brenda Rae Schoolcraft

Alice had a Palace

Copyright © 2019 by Brenda Rae Schoolcraft

Tellwell Talent
www.tellwell.ca

ISBN
978-0-2288-1369-9 (Paperback)
978-0-2288-0494-9 (eBook)

W hen I was a little girl, I would ask Mom to tell me her childhood stories, over and over again. We didn't have a library of
children books, but I never missed a thing. The recollections
of her childhood stories was all I needed. There were so many things
happening to Mom at different stages of her life that fascinated me, as they
will fascinate you. I draw events from my mother's life, starting in her
childhood. I tell them to you, the best I remember. One thing for sure,
you will never forget Alice.

This story begins in the Great Depression, better known as the Dirty
Thirties.

Alice was born in 1924, in Nova Scotia, Canada, to Irene and William
Purple. Moments after her birth, the midwife announced, "The baby is
dead." Just as God reached his hand out to take his angel back, she loses
her grasp, falling back to earth.

An innocent soul, caught in the hands of fate.

Instead of fairy-tale characters in another Alice story, my Alice endured
real-life monsters and a life on earth symbolic of hell.

It hurts me to take her back to the events in this book. She was eighty
when I started to write this story.

This book is to celebrate my mother's life and to give her closure. It is the
healing of my soul, finally able to wash away the pain of a tsunami of tears.

A story that begged to be told, an epic multigenerational read that spans
my mother's life to my father's life and my life, Brenda Rae Schoolcraft.

I show you how abuse gathers speed and becomes a cycle, like a runaway
train. Many can never get off, and it manifests into a demon of hurt. The
children suffer needlessly, caught up in the cycle that resonates with them
the rest of their lives, sometimes destroying them as adults, turning to drugs
and alcohol to suppress the hurt that seems to never go away.

Warning! This story, based on true life is filled with explicit sexual content, abuse, and homicidal violence. It is not for the underage reader or the faint of heart.

You will see and feel the truth of this tale. Time lines and circumstances leading up to major events may have been changed. Names have been changed to protect the innocent.

Enjoy your ride...on the runaway train.

PART I

Alice

CHAPTER 1

Alice Goes to School

Alice didn't sleep much all night. The ritual of the first day of school unfolded at her house before bedtime. Everyone picked out their outfit, something passed down. Having waited in anticipation for this day, not only was this the first day back for the other kids, but for Alice it was also her first ever day of school.

It had seemed like forever to her, finally being able to escape the prying eyes of her abusive mother, Irene.

She did everything her mother asked of her with zealous enthusiasm to avoid the heartless punishments Irene inflicted. Alice feels small and helpless around her.

Her brothers ranged from three to ten years older. They had little time or consideration for this last addition to their large family. Eleven, since Pearl died of pneumonia at the age of ten.

The only ones who made time for her was her loving father, William, and the youngest of her brothers, Earl. She was the only girl now.

The boys kept busy with one another, doing boy things, competing for their hierarchy in the family. Meek as a mouse and the smallest of them all, Alice cowered at a raised voice or a loud noise. Her brother Skip nicknamed her Mouse.

It was a chilly September morning, the dew crystallized on the emerald grass blades catching the sparkle in her eyes. With her chin resting on the windowsill, her mind wandered to the excitement of the day ahead, a smile adorning her angelic face.

The simplest things made her happy. The animals. Her dad explained that they were God's creatures. Everything he told her about God resonated with her. A squirrel scampering up the tree or the chickens in the yard were the best things in her world.

William adored his little angel. She vied for his attention every second he was around her.

Irene found fault in everything she did, trying to make her look bad in her father's eyes.

William let Irene run the household, the children were her responsibility. The boys all seemed fine, but something told him Alice was being mistreated.

Today, the first day of school, was going to be the best day ever.

Everyone sat down to breakfast as usual.

"Why haven't you touched your porridge?" barked Irene, her eyes bulging as she stared Alice's way.

The boys' heads rose in unison, like jacks in a box.

Looking up, Alice finds her mother's gaze, then dropped her head, staring back into the white porcelain bowl.

Dragging her spoon through the thick porridge, Irene continued glaring, a swirl of brown sugar in the centre like the eye of a storm.

The milk pitcher made it to Skip, who sat two deep from Alice. Earl and Alice would do without milk this morning.

"It would be drier if there weren't any," barked Irene, her eyes following the circular movements, of Alice's spoon. "Were you going to eat it or just play in it? You are not hungry!"

"I was just thinking about school," she answered in a meek, high-pitched voice.

"Never mind the porridge," insisted Irene, "your brothers already have on their coats. Maybe, I should just keep you home. How would you like that?"

Earl looked back at his sister.

"C'mon, Alice, we got to get going."

Glancing fleetingly toward the door, like it is at the end of a long tunnel, her brothers are stepping out in single file.

Irene glares at little Alice, as she struggled to push in the chair perfectly squared in front of the table. Walking toward the sink with her bowl in her hands, her feet as though on an airy cloud that might burst through any second.

At the sink, she placed her bowl in as not to make a noise. Just steps from the door, she realized she has forgotten her sweater. Turning, she focused on the sweater as Earl stood watch, waiting.

Irene was looking the other way as she grabbed for the sweater and darts to the door, not even looking at her mother out of the corner of her eye.

During the last few steps to the door, she began counting in her head: one, two, three, four, and out the door. The cool air hits her face. Breathing a deep sigh of freedom, she runs to Earl grabbing his hand.

For the first day of school, Alice wore her dead sister's dress. Falling a little past her knees but fitting perfectly otherwise. It is white cotton. Big, bright, crimson flowers dot the white canvas of the dress like red paint.

A wide red satin sash decorated the waist.

While Alice struggled with the ribbon, trying to make the perfect bow in the back, the loss of her sister weighed on her mind.

"If only you were here, Pearl, you could help me with this bow and brush my hair and walk with me to school. Oh, how I miss you," she whined.

Thinking about asking her mother but changed her mind, just in case she told her not to wear the dress.

Pearl had a nice collection of things for her hair, precious keepsakes, and clothes that the Jeffersonses had given William for his daughters. Irene insisted that the hand-me-downs were too big for Alice or not proper for her. Either she was too young or too stupid.

The Jeffersonses' daughter Sarah was the same age and size as Pearl. Irene made sure that everything was given to Pearl.

Although Irene didn't want Alice to have the hand-me-down toys and clothes, Pearl shared everything with her little sister.

Alice had her sights set on inheriting all the dolls and things that were Pearl's. She would take good care of them. Pearl would want her to have them.

CHAPTER 2

Alice was five and a half when her sister Pearl died. On that fateful day, she watched them carry her out, a white sheet covering her stiffened body.

Before she died, the doctor had come every day for a few months to assess her condition. Irene would shoo Alice away from the room.

With her ear to the door, she heard the doctor say, "She isn't getting any better. I don't think she will be with us long." A dead quiet hung in the air, Irene not answering. Scrambling away, forlorn, Alice ran down the stairs. Standing at the foot of the staircase, she watched as the doctor started his descent with Irene close behind. The doctor nodded at Alice, then pulled on his hat and slipped into his overcoat, leaving without looking back.

Walking past Alice as though she wasn't there, Irene heads to the sink. Staring out the small window, she watched as the doctor pulled himself up in his buggy, grabbing the reins urging his horse on.

A stolen moment for Alice to go back into the room with Pearl.

Her feet were quick and light. From the top of the stairs she took one last look, then ran down the hallway to Pearl's room.

Lowering herself on the side of the bed she stares down at her sister. A quiet gasp, she holds her breath.

Pearl's eyes are closed, her white nightgown buttoned to her chin. Golden auburn curls rested on the pillow.

The silkiness of her hair caressed Alice's fingers as she stared hard into Pearl's face.

In a breathy whisper, she begged, "Please don't leave me alone, please." As she rests her head on Pearl's chest, her tears cascading down her cherub cheeks. A wet stain of sorrow spread across Pearl's nightgown.

The door opened abruptly.

Irene's eyes bulged in rage.

"You will get sick too, you stupid girl."

Rushing by her mother, almost tumbling down the stairs, she continued running out the door to the chicken coop. There she laid her head on a bale of straw, burying her face into her little hands, she cries and cries.

After they took Pearl away, Alice was scared to sleep in the room all alone. There was no light. Darkness fell through the sheer curtains on the windows, turning the room into a tomb. Tucked in under the blanket, Alice listened to the house breathing, the windows creaking, the floorboards settling.

In the middle of the night, she sat straight up, eyeing the silhouette of Pearl's empty bed.

The light of the moon cast shadows on the wall dancing back and forth like scary creatures. The cold air breathed through the weather-beaten window frame, awakening the curtains as they dance like ghosts.

Scared, she covered her head with the thin grey blanket, her heart beating hard and fast in her hollow chest, like bunny rabbits running in her heart.

Some nights, when the room took on its own life, Alice stole into her parents' room. The sounds of her mother's snoring, a clean break to get to her dad.

Quiet, she nuzzled in next to William. Like a motionless feather, she falls asleep, her own breathing becoming one with his.

If Irene awakened, she'd send her back to her room. Other times she didn't notice till morning.

"You spoil her. She will be rotten," she yelled at William.

Irene realized Alice's fears and used them as another way to torture her. For the least little thing, she'd send Alice to her room.

"Get to your room, and now," she'd order in her sister superior voice that rings in her head.

Alice would run up the staircase as fast as her little legs can carry her and fall into a heap on her narrow cot.

It seemed that Irene's patience would wear thin especially around supper-time. These were the nights Alice went to bed hungry, hearing the sounds of the chairs around the table, hunger pains racking her belly.

If only she could have just a little. Her brothers often leaving a few scraps for her, knowing she didn't have any dinner. Curling into a fetal position, she'd hold her bear and ragdoll close. Finally, sleep would take her.

William was often late coming home from the dairy. The table would be cleared, the dishes washed, the children in their rooms. He was oblivious to the fact that Alice didn't have any supper most nights.

The first few days after they took Pearl away, Alice spent as much time in her room as she could stashing things so Irene wouldn't take them from her. Expecting her mother to do an inspection any minute, she takes another swipe under the bed with the broom. No dust bunnies. There could be no dust bunnies.

One of Alice's daily chores is to wash the floor in the bedroom.

The worn wooden planks gave up splinters, the same way Alice's heart was shredded by Irene's hate.

Dragging the heavy mop, she'd pull it behind as she made her way up the stairs.

When her brothers offered to take the mop upstairs, Irene would intercede and insist she was a girl and needed to learn to do housework.

After going over the floor three times, four times, she'd drag the mop back down the stairs.

Irene had a pail of cold water waiting near the broom closet. The mop had to be rinsed, rung out, and put back in the broom closet in the emptied pail.

While rinsing the mop, Alice would get splinters in her fingers. The few times she complained about splinters, Irene goes for a needle, burned the end of it, digging at her little fingers, making her scream. Learning from the needle torture, she became very careful wringing out the mop, her fingers like specks in the wide springy mop head.

There were two brooms in the closet. One for inside, one for outside. Both made of straw. They were bound around the tops to the wooden handles with a heavy gauge wire.

Alice hid the pretty dresses under her mattress, surveying each, taking into consideration when she would be able to fit into them. Counting ten in all, tugging the thin stuffed matress over her treasures. Smoothing the sheet over the top, then the blanket. Irene is listening at the door, pushing the door open.

"Hi, Mother," said Alice, her voice quivering like an arrow penetrating a tree. "I was just folding some of Pearl's things, like you told me," pointing to a neat pile on the small table next to the bed.

"Is this all of her things?" barked Irene, glaring at Alice, her eyes iced over.

"Yes, Mother, but can I keep the bear and the doll? Please, Mother, Pearl would want me to have them. Please, Mommy?" Lowering herself on her knees in front of Irene, putting her little hands together as if in prayer.

"Fine," answered Irene, "but if you are bad, I will give them to some kids who deserve them."

"I will never be bad, Mommy," she said, crying now.

"You are always bad, child!" Irene shakes her finger in Alice's face. "Get up off the floor, girl, and stop that crying, before I give you something to cry about! And get this room cleaned and dusted. I will come back to inspect it before you get any supper."

Irene marched out, slamming the door behind her.

"Yes, Mother," she answered, wiping at her eyes.

Getting up, she goes straight to Pearl's bed. Grabbing up the doll and the bear, pulling them close to her, her little face buried deep in the love of them. She whispered, "Thank you, Pearl. I will look after them, you will see."

Just as Alice was setting them on the bed, Irene came back into the room.

"There are other kids who can use these things. By the time you are big enough to wear them, the moths will have eaten them," she hissed as she grabs up the pile of sweaters and things.

Alice searched her face, then lowered her eyes, staring at the doll. Irene left the room, pulling hard on the door handle.

Butterflies played in her stomach, a smile crossed her angelic face. She couldn't believe it! All of Pearl's very best things were hers now. She would love and cherish them the way she loved her sister, remembering the games they would play with Sally, the rag doll.

Alice would hide the bear from Sally and Pearl, then Pearl would have to find it. Sometimes Pearl would make Sally dance, and Alice would make bear dance. They laughed and sang songs till Irene would interrupt their play with orders of do this or do that.

A smile played on her face, the light in her eyes dancing as she watched Sally and bear sitting on her bed. They were her new friends now. Not alone anymore, she snuggled in close to the fuzzy bear. Rubbing his white tummy, she hums a tune. Pulling Sally and the bear close to her chest she falls asleep.

CHAPTER 3

Running to catch up to Earl, grabbing for his hand.

Her other brothers are already out of sight. Earl lagged behind to help his baby sister. Earl is eight, close in age to Alice.

William went in to talk to Earl before bedtime.

"You wait for your little sister, OK, son. Make sure she gets to school. I am counting on you."

"Yes, Father," answered Earl, looking deep into his father's caring eyes.

"How far is it to the school, Earl?" she asked, looking up at her brother.

"It is a long way. You have to walk faster, or we will never get there."

"OK, Earl, I will walk faster then." Alice getting into a running walk, as fast as her little legs will go. Laughing, she gets way ahead, then sits on the side of the road waiting for him to catch up.

School was a two-mile walk each way, and the Purple kids had to walk most days, even on the coldest days of winter. There was the odd day they would get lucky with a ride from someone, in a horse buggy. Only the fortunate had horses and buggies. The Purple family's only transportation was the shoelace express.

"Earl, what is the teacher's name again?" Holding tight to her brother's hand, peering up at him.

"Her name is Miss Ink, and she has hair the color of ink."

"You mean her hair is black?"

"Yes, it is," he answered.

He had told her that many times, but she just wanted to hear him say it again.

"Do you think she will like me?" she asked in a squeaky mouse voice.

"I suppose she will. She is nicer to the girls. Just don't get caught talking when she is giving a lesson. You could get the ruler over your knuckles."

Shuddering at the thought of getting her little fingers whacked, she said, "I will never talk when she is talking. Thanks for telling me. I will be the best kid, and she will never hit me with the ruler."

Earl looked down at his little sister in her pretty dress. Her golden hair hanging in ringlets around her cherub face. How could anyone ever hurt her, knowing deep in his heart, Alice bore the brunt of Irene's misery.

Skipping along the road, ahead of Earl for a while, examining the pretty fall wildflowers. The purple bell ones capture her eyes. Her teacher would like a few flowers. Earl watched his baby sister stop and crouch down, realizing what she was about to do.

"Oh no, come on. We have not time for you to pick flowers. Surely we are going to be late, then we will be in trouble."

Getting to her feet, she walked back toward her brother. Earl grabbed her hand, trying to pull her along faster.

"I can't go fast. My feet are hurting me now, Earl," she whined, a half cry. "My heel!"

Letting go of his hand, she pulled her white stocking foot out, red showing through the thin cotton.

"Oh no," said Earl, "your foot is bleeding."

"It hurts a lot," she said.

"Can I sit down for a spell?"

"Come along, we haven't even gone halfway yet. When we get to the big maple tree, it marks the halfway point."

"Oh please, I can't put my sore foot back in," she complained.

"Well, OK then," said Earl, thinking of the long road ahead. "I will just have to piggyback you. Hurry, get your shoes off and put them in my bag."

Wincing, she peels off the other shoe.

Bending he pulls her up on his back, her legs snake around his waist, her little arms around his neck.

"We were going to be in trouble, for sure. We are late," complained Earl.

Alice's brow furrowed in worry.

"Let's go faster then, Earl."

"I can't go any faster, I am not a horse." A giggle escaped her lips, making Earl laugh too, his legs weakening.

"I have to stop for a breather," he said,

bending over from the waist to help her down.

"Miss Ink will keep us after school if we are late."

Started to worry now, in her mind's eye, she can see her mother standing in the doorway of their clapboard house.

Irene's moods changed like the weather. Some days were sunny, others grey and cloudy, bringing tears, like rain.

Walking as though on broken glass, afraid to move the wrong way or say the wrong thing. It was a familiar sight not far from her mind: Irene standing over her, an off-white flour bag apron pulled tight across her bulging stomach, waving a thick finger in her face, her wide hips and thick ankles bearing down on Alice, like a dark cloud.

Irene wore her mousy brown hair pulled straight back off her face, a tight bun in the back. Her dark, beady, raven eyes sat back behind her swollen cheeks. The beauty of the young woman Irene had faded, like petals fallen from a rose. Now, burdened with eleven children, she had no time for herself, her girth increasing with each child that came.

William was merely half of his wife. Standing five foot four, a slight build, he was dwarfed by her five foot seven height and close to two hundred pounds.

Alice folded her little body against her brother like a jockey on a horse.

They trotted along, the schoolyard coming into view.

"Thank goodness," said Earl. "I thought we would never get here."

The schoolhouse is red with a steeple on the top. It had been a church at one time.

"A playground!" screamed Alice, excitement in her voice.

"Yes, but not now, let's go in," he urged, reaching for her hand.

"The others are already inside, hurry!"

Straightening her dress, Alice gazes down at her stocking feet.

"Oh no, I can't go in without my shoes on. I will show the teacher my bloodied foot," she said, "then the teacher won't be mad at us."

"Sure, let's just get inside," he urged.

Holding her shoes in her hands, walking in directly behind Earl.

Earl pushed the door open, exposing the big school room. Alice huddled in behind him, trying her best to hide.

All eyes are on Earl.

The teacher put down her chalk, turning to face Earl and what seemed to be a small person hiding behind him. The kids stop what they are doing, all staring their way.

"Well, well, said Miss Ink, folding her arms in front of her. "First day of school, Earl Purple. You are late!"

The teacher's sharp-tongued voice shook Alice's humble demeanour.

Nervous, thinking she had better put her shoes on, one of them dropping to the floor. Miss Ink eyed the white shoe, then she notices a little girl bending to put on the shoes.

"Owww," Alice cried aloud as the blister breaks open, the pain stinging her heel.

"Who is the small person behind you, Earl Purple?"

"Oh, ma'am, this is my baby sister, Alice. She is six years old."

"Come out here and let me have a look at you miss," said Miss Ink, her eyes fixated on Alice.

Stepping to the side of her brother she looks up at the teacher, folding her hands together in front of her dress giving Miss Ink a half curtsy.

"Hello, teacher," she said faintly. "My name is Alice."

"I am not your teacher yet, miss." A few chuckles erupted from the classroom. "You don't look old enough to be here at school?"

"Yes, Miss Ink," Earl interrupted. "She is really six. She is just small for her age."

Grabbing Alice's arm pulling her in front of him.

"That's enough, kids. Print my name twenty times, that will keep you busy," ordered the teacher.

A drawn-out moan hangs in the air over the classroom.

"We might just have to talk to your mother and find out how old you are."

"I am really six, promise," Alice said with a plastic smile.

"For now, Earl, you find a seat in the back row. For you, miss, you sit right up here, where I can keep an eye on you."

Miss Ink pointed to the first desk at the head of the row, right in front of her.

"Yes, ma'am," she answered, fitting her little body into the seat, wiggling around a minute, trying to find the perfect posture, then looking up to see if Miss Ink is watching.

All heads are down as Miss Ink starts her march up each aisle, staring at their papers. Then she walked back to the front of the class, like a captain at the stern of his ship. Stealing another peek at the cutest little thing, with her big ringlets and green eyes, she proceeded with the lesson at hand.

"Everyone take out a piece of paper, write your name on it, and draw a picture while I am getting this lesson ready," she said, peering over her small spectacles, Alice stealing a quick glance behind at all the kids.

Earl had told her that all the grades from one to eight were in the same class, noticing that as the rows went, the kids were taller and older. All of them in the same row as Alice were more her age. She was the smallest.

The classroom is bright yellow with green trim on the windows, like a warm ray of sunshine, she smiles sweetly.

A boy in the back row sticks out his tongue. Alice giggled out loud. Miss Ink spun around looking straight the way the giggle had come.

"Miss Alice, you must not disrupt the class! Sit straight in your seat, and keep your eyes on the blackboard unless I tell you otherwise. Do you understand, miss?"

"Yes, teacher, yes, teacher." Her eyes wide with fright, folding her hands together on top of her desk.

Miss Ink's big wooden desk interested Alice, with all the books and pens. She loved pens and couldn't wait for the teacher to give her some picture books to look at, anxious to learn how to read everything in those books.

Keeping her eyes on the blackboard, the teacher showing them how to spell her name. Alice copies the name onto her paper. The tall thin woman walks over to Alice's desk peering down at her paper.

"This is good writing, did someone teach you to write already?"

"Yes, my sister Pearl did, and my aunt Rita too."

Miss Ink's face grew sullen as she walked back to the blackboard. Pearl had been one of her favorite students. She missed her. Should she talk to Alice about Pearl? A bright light came on in her head. She would show Alice Pearl's artwork, displayed at the back of the class. That would be the best way to talk to her about her dead sister.

Keeping her eyes on Miss Ink, Alice watches as the teacher stepped from side to side at the blackboard on her thin, birdlike ankles. Just like Earl had said, the teacher was tall and slim, her pitch-black hair pulled straight back off her face, in a perfect bun in the back, not one hair out of place. The bright red on her lips looked like red paint.

It made Alice remember the day she was at the train station with her mom, when a lady with red lips walked by, Irene commenting that the lady looked like a whore. Alice didn't know what that meant but the way her mother said it, she knew it wasn't good.

When it came time to have lunch, Alice bolts outside to join the other kids in the playground, like a racehorse out of the gate. A few of them gathered around, looking her over.

"I love your dress," said a girl with long red braids tied with bright blue ribbons.

"Thanks," replied Alice, a show of pink cascading over her cheeks.

Playing a game of chase with a couple of kids near her age, asking them their names.

Miss Ink came through the schoolhouse door looking out onto the playground, her eyes scanning the yard for the pretty little girl in the flowery dress.

There was just something about this one that played on her heart strings. As she watched, Alice darted here and there like a firefly, trying to get in as much playing as possible. A smile crossed Miss Ink's lips.

Alice found her brothers. Whispering as she scans around. "Please, you won't tell, will you? I just have to come to school. Don't you see? If Mother found out what the teacher said, she will keep me at home, maybe for another whole year, then I'll be seven and too old to come to school."

The boys laughed, looking from one to the other. They agreed on their silence. Skip nodded.

"We won't say a thing, Mouse. Will we, boys?"

"Oh, thank you," she said, hugging him with a sweet smile.

"Please don't call me Mouse around my friends."

"Sure, fine," he answered.

Running back to where the other girls were playing noticing they were all eating their lunch. Her appetite hadn't coaxed her yet.

Turning away from them, rushing to the swings. A few pulls and pushes, she is flying, happier than she could ever remember, her spirit, like a bird that had been caged all its life finally free to fly.

This was the best day ever, new friends and a new teacher. She liked the tall skinny lady with the ink-colored hair.

Just then, Miss Ink walked over and stood in front of Alice. A bright red apple in her hand, she smiled.

"Just thought you might like this apple. I have an extra one. I see you didn't bring a lunch, Alice."

"Really, I am not hungry, teacher."

"If you were not hungry now, you soon will be, with all that playing you are doing."

"Ah, I just forgot my lunch today," said Alice, putting her finger up to her lips.

The hand movement told Miss Ink the little girl is fabricating a story.

The thinness of her arms and legs tells her what she knew already, Alice is malnourished. She had seen it a lot in her years of being a teacher in this small community, lots of families going hungry.

"You have this apple, Alice, and I'll get you half of my peanut butter sandwich."

"OK," answered Alice, her eyes dancing with excitement. A peanut butter sandwich was her favorite. "With jelly too?"

"Of course. What would it be without the jelly?" A big, loving smile on Miss Ink's face.

The two of them shared the sandwich, Alice munching the apple down to the core.

"Remember, now, to bring your lunch tomorrow."

"Yes, teacher. I was so excited to come to school, I forgot all about a lunch."

Really, she had watched the brown bagged lunches getting eaten up as her brothers picked them from the counter. They were all gone when she looked for one, not daring to complain, in case Irene kept her at home.

"I love apples. Thank you, teacher," giving Miss Ink a cutie pie grin.

The first day at school had gone by way too fast for her liking.

"Attention, class." Miss Ink standing in front of her theatre, looking at her subjects. "It's time to get your books together. Make sure you take your homework. We have ten minutes till the bell goes."

At that very moment, Alice's happiness drained through like the pink from her cheeks, her uncertainties tumbling down on her narrow shoulders. It was all too good, too much fun. Was it a dream?

It was time to go home.

Placing her reader in her schoolbag, looking down at her stocking feet. She would have to put her feet back in the tight shoes. The pain had subsided in her heel.

Walking to Miss Ink's desk, the teacher writing something on the blackboard, noticing the white of a dress out of the corner of her eye.

"Oh, Alice, I didn't see you there."

"Just wanted to say goodbye, teacher." A soft, seeking-love look, her deep green eyes searching into Miss Ink's dark eyes.

"We'll see you tomorrow."

That was all she wanted to hear, her heart swelling.

Skipping out the door of the schoolhouse, Earl waiting for her just outside the door.

"C'mon, we got to get going. Here, get on. We'll try and get home on time so mother doesn't punish you—I mean us," he said, looking down at his little sister.

Miss Ink showed in the doorway just as Alice is getting on her brother's back.

"Remember to wear comfortable shoes. Also, we'll let it go this time, but we do not tolerate lateness. You could be kept after school."

"Yes, ma'am," answered Alice, waving to Miss Ink as Earl took off like a donkey with his burden.

Miss Ink chuckled at the sight of Alice on Earl's back.

"I love school, Earl," Alice said, her voice celebratory.

"You will see if you like it so much, when you get lots of homework. Mom will be waiting for us to do our chores. We don't want to make her mad at us," said Earl.

As Earl trod along, she goes quiet, thinking of all the new things in her life, anxious to learn more tomorrow, like a dry sponge in a sea of knowledge.

Earl stopped only once to catch a breather, his sister feeling like a heavy load of wood on his back.

Once he made it to the yard, he bends to let her down.

"Oh, I just can't do this again tomorrow. Please wear shoes that fit you."

"I don't have any that fit perfectly, just too big and too little."

"Well, make a better choice. It was so hard carrying you all the way. Good thing you are just a bit of a thing."

"Thank you, Earl. You were just like a pony."

"Sure. Let's get in now, before Mom comes out, yelling," he urged.

"I'm as hungry as a bear," said Earl.

"Grrrrr," said Alice playfully, running ahead of Earl.

They went straight into the dining room to the big table, scanning for the fresh buns that usually greeted them before supper. There were no buns today.

CHAPTER 4

William had split a pile of wood, Skip and William Jr. helping to bring some in the house. With a towering armful, Skip can hardly see where he is going, heading towards the woodbox, when Alice comes running around the corner, straight into him.

"Watch it," he yelled. The wood tumbled with a thud to the floor. Irene's head shows around the corner.

"What happened here?" she demanded. Alice putting her hands over her face.

"It was just an accident, Mom," said Skip, "Alice and I collided."

"You stupid girl. See what you have done. Get over there now, and pile the wood perfectly behind the stove," pointing her index finger.

"Yes, Mother," she answered, cowering. Kneeling down to pick up the pieces, like her broken dreams, she worries about her pretty dress.

Irene ambled back to the kitchen, where she was doing some preparations for supper. William walked in with an armful of wood, straight to where his princess is kneeling in her pretty dress.

"Go and get your school clothes off. What are you doing? This is the boys' job," he said.

Irene turned from the sink, her mouth hardening, watching as William offered his hand to his little girl, then gently hugging her.

Turning on her heels, she mumbled something under her breath. William couldn't help but notice the hateful glare. Why was she so mean to the only girl child they had?

Although he didn't understand it, something was eating away at his insides, like maggots on rotting flesh.

In his heart he knew Irene was hurting his little angel every chance she got. It had gone too far. Where was his manhood? Why couldn't he stand up to her?

He had let her bully him for years now and would rather just walk away than cause a confrontation. Anything to keep her from nagging at him.

William heads back outside in the yard to finish cutting a few more pieces of wood.

Alice ran up the stairs to her room closing her door, as though closing out the sadness of her life.

Laying on her stomach, going over the wonderful day she had at school, a smile crossed her lips.

Stirring herself out of her daydream, she stepped into her overalls, ready to start her chores for the day.

Her favorite was feeding and watering the chickens. She never let on that she loved this chore. Chasing the bandy rooster with his bright feathers around the coop colored her world.

Careful, as though they were made of fine china, she carried the six brown eggs in her little plastic bucket into the house.

"We got six today, mom," she said, excitement in her voice. Standing behind Irene at the sink, she turned, a sneer on her lips.

"Well, how was school today?"

"It was nice," she answered, fiddling with the braces on her overalls. "I like the teacher. Her hair is the color of ink, and her name is Miss Ink," declared Alice.

"That is all fine and dandy, but right now, I need you to help. Peel those potatoes," ordered Irene, pointing to the big bowl sitting on the table.

"OK," answered Alice, heading to the table. Getting up on the chair, she sat next to the large silver bowl.

A paring knife is piercing one of the potatoes's heads.

Counting the potatoes as she worked. "Fifteen," she said out loud, picking up the last one.

"If you are finished there, you can go to your room, dust and wash the floor while you wait for supper," ordered Irene.

"Yes, Mother." Taking her eyes off what she is doing, the sharp knife slipped, cutting into the side of her finger.

"Owwww," she cried, as the blood from her finger drips onto the potatoes.

"What is wrong with you now? Can't you do anything right?" Irene screamed. "You will never make a good wife for anyone. Here, hold it tight," she instructed, shoving the dirty dish towel at her. "I will go and fetch the alcohol."

"No. Please! Not the alcohol," whined Alice. "It burns."

"Never you mind. It kills germs. Do you want your finger to fall off?"

Irene grabbed the bowl of potatoes off the table and plunks them in the sink, pouring fresh water over them, wiping the blood off as she goes.

Sitting with her finger in the towel, her face stained with tears, her eyes doe-like.

Irene is just dabbing the alcohol on the cut finger when William walked into the room.

"Owwwweeee," screamed Alice.

"What is wrong with the child?" he demanded.

"She cut her finger peeling the potatoes," answered Irene, a knife in her tongue, her voice sharp, decisive.

"Couldn't you have one of your sons do that? They are all sitting around, waiting to be fed."

"It's girl's work, William. Do you want to make your sons into sissies?"

Shaking his head in abandon, he leaves the room. Hearing the shrill cries make him sick to his stomach.

"Now, get over here," ordered Irene, holding up a large apron. Alice shuffled to her mom. Irene proceeded to wrap the apron around Alice's waist, twice around, then tied it in the back. The tightness of the apron makes it hard for her to breathe normally, her breath coming in short spurts. Trying to reach the knot in the back, her little fingers searching, trying to loosen the tight apron.

"Get busy now," Irene ordered, her lips pursed. "Never mind fumbling with that. Put those potatoes in the pot. We need to get supper on the table before nightfall."

Picking up a few potatoes off the top of the bowl, making her way to the stove. A tall silver pot sits on the front burner. The water rumbles at the sides in a full boil. Alice raised her little arms. The tight apron constricted her movements as she reaches the top of the pot. One of the potatoes slipped from her hand and splashed into the boiling water, sending a wave of scalding water over the side and onto her face.

Grimacing in pain, her little hand darted to her face, a piercing scream escaping her lips. Another potato rolls under the table. Irene's eyes darted to the floor now.

"Now look what you have done! You just can't do anything right, can you? Now you were wasting the little food we do have." Irene rushed to pick up the potato, her belly hanging toward the floor as she bent.

Placing the potato in the sink, Irene stomps to the broom closet. With one eye on Alice, she grabs for the outside broom.

Watching in horror the broom gets caught up in her mother's long dress, sending Irene sprawling face down on the wooden floor. Afraid to budge an inch, her eyes frozen on her mother.

Irene's dark eyes bulging, her face reddened as she struggles to get her body off the floor. Picking up the broom with both hands, she strikes Alice over the back. Alice dropped to the floor, bringing her little hands to her head. Irene pummeled the back of her legs and back, one, two, three, four, five times.

"No, Mummy please," she begged. Her muffled cries go unheard.

"I'll teach you to daydream when you were doing your chores!"

Blood dripped from her nose onto her hands. Whimpering, she tried to get up, but her legs wouldn't move. Urine pooled around her little body sprawled on the floor.

Just as Irene is going to bring the broom down on her back again, Earl comes running into the kitchen.

"Stop it! Stop it right now! Before I go and get Dad. I will tell him everything I know. Leave her alone, now!" ordered Earl, half crying. Irene stared, her eyes glossed over with hatred.

Bending, he picked up his sister and lifted her onto his chest. Whining, she rested her body on him. With all his might, he helps her upstairs to her room, laying her on the cot. Face down, Alice cries into her pillow.

"Are you all right? Mom has gone crazy. I can't believe she was hitting you with the broom. I don't know what to do."

Looking at his little sister, crying, he feels helpless. Thinking he had better find his dad, he pulls the scratchy, grey wool blanket over her, running down the stairs, and out the door.

Her face is stinging so bad a taste of bile in her mouth, she just pulls herself up in time to vomit over the side of the bed, crying harder now she can hardly move. The pain in her back and legs reminds her of the assault. Her face stained with sticky tears, she just lay there hoping Earl will find her daddy and bring him to her.

After a few minutes, she dragged herself to the bathroom at the end of the hallway. Pouring some water from the bucket into the basin sinking a washcloth into the cold water.

Irene had always bathed the kids' burns with cold water until the pain subsided.

Back and forth from her face to the basin, bathing her burn.

Stepping out of her blood-stained clothes slipping a long flannelette nightgown over her bruised body. Next she put her T-shirt in the cold water and swished it around, the blood staining the water pink. Now she just had to make it back to her room and clean up the vomit on the floor.

A stir of chairs around the table. Did that mean that daddy was home? Would Irene send someone up with something for her? Would she feel sorry for her? Did she feel bad that she had hurt her again? Really, her hunger had gone down below the horizon, like the sunshine.

The darkness stole the light in her room. As she lay awake in her bed, the moonlight dancing on the wall. Hunger pains racked her stomach. Tonight she would not be able to go and search for peelings in the garbage. How was she going to get down the stairs? The way her legs and back hurt, she could hardly make herself move. Oh no, how could she go to school tomorrow?

The tears flowed now like an endless spring, her cheeks tightening her cries on mute.

The pain in her face was like a hundred bee stings. Her whimpered like the beating of a dove's wings. Closing her eyes she prayed.

"Please, God, let me go to school tomorrow. Oh please, I just have to go."

CHAPTER 5

W illiam walks into the house. The pungent, gamey smell of moose roast ignites his taste buds, his mouth watering. Excited, he peers in the dining room.

Irene and the boys are at their designated places around the table.

"We were just waiting for you," said Irene.

William's eyes searching the table.

"Where is Alice?"

Irene couldn't meet his inquiring eyes, offering no explanation. Picking up the bowl of mashed potatoes, she passed it to her left.

Earl breaks the silence, like a china plate hitting a stone floor.

"Alice burned herself, Daddy. She is in her room."

"What are you saying, boy?" his voice loud.

"She did just that," added Irene. "Being clumsy as usual, that girl is always hurting herself."

At the thought of Alice burning herself, William's stomach tightened, his throat goes dry.

William glared Irene's way. Her eyes darted away from his breaking heart.

As he stared into his plate, as if into space, the bowls are passed to him. Without serving himself anything, he passed them on.

A moose roast, glistening in its own gravy, sits on a platter. Fresh golden buns and a bowl of yellowed, buttered mashed potatoes.

His favorite dinner. His appetite escaped him, like a fish released from a hook.

Glancing at Irene's helpings, he is further disturbed. Heaped with potatoes and meat, gravy spilled onto the table around her plate. Eyeing her in pity, and disgust he asked, "How can you eat, when your only daughter is burned? Where and how bad is it, Irene? Have you dressed it?"

No answer from Irene. William raised his voice.

"Irene, have you tended to Alice's burn?"

"No, I just sent her to her room. She dropped the potatoes all over the floor, then one of them splashed the hot water onto her face."

"What was she doing with the pot, Irene?"

"She was putting the potatoes in the pot, William. I can't do everything around here."

Getting anxious, his voice quivered. "You should not ask a small child to put potatoes in boiling water. What is wrong with your head?"

The air in the dining room is thick as a blanket of fog. All the boys stopped eating, stared ahead or at each other. Never had they heard their father raise his voice to Irene.

William pushed himself away from the table, walking to a cabinet in the kitchen, pulling out the first-aid kit. With a heavy heart, a glossy sadness in his eyes, making his way up the staircase towards her room.

Scared to see his little one, he stood still, his ear to the door, when he heard her talking. But who could she be talking to? There is no one in the room with her, not now, since Pearl died.

He opened the door.

"Alice, Alice it's Daddy. What happened to you, princess?" he said in little more than a whisper.

The grey blanket moved, Alice peeking her head out.

"I burned my face on the potato pot when I dropped a potato in, that's all."

William set down the lantern on the small table next to her cot.

"Oh my God, let Daddy see."

Pulling the wet cloth away from her cheek, exposing a large round area, reddened and blistered.

"Oh, my, you got a big burn, honey. Just sit still. I am going to put some salve on it, and it will take out the sting."

Moving her face toward her dad, he applied the salve with his index finger as she searches his face and eyes for the love, like a plant needing water.

His smiling eyes glossed over in sadness, kissing Alice on the forehead.

"I could have sworn I heard you talking to someone. Were you talking to yourself?"

Pulling Sally close to her, hugging her rag head and red yarn curls to her chest, peering up at her dad, her eyes big.

"Ah, I see," said William. "You were talking to the doll."

She nodded, a shy smile on her angel face.

William didn't ask any more questions. Taking his baby girl in his arms, covering the scalded skin of her cheek with a square of white cotton gauze, a few pieces of tape to hold it on.

"There, does that feel better?"

"Yes, Daddy, thank you. Much better."

The closeness and the love from her dad had taken the sting out of her burn.

"I will be more careful from now on, Daddy, I promise."

"It's OK, sweetie. No more putting potatoes into boiling water again for you. Not till you grow tall enough to reach it, OK?"

"Don't make me laugh, Daddy, my cheek hurts," she uttered, laying back on her pillow, Sally nestled in close in her arms.

"I bet my girl is hungry? You didn't have supper, did you?"

"No."

"OK, tell you what. When they are done eating, Daddy is going to bring up food, and we were going to eat together. Would you like that?"

"Oh yes, Daddy. That would be the best," she answered.

"Would you like me to read you a story, dear?"

William picked up a book from the small table next to her bed. "You've been reading this one?"

"Well sort of, just looking at the pictures really, trying to make my own story. Soon I will be able to read it. I love my teacher."

"That is great, I bet you are a good student."

"Yes, Dad, I am, and Miss Ink likes me too. She gave me a big red apple and half of her peanut butter and jelly sandwich at lunch."

William's stomach tightened, thinking of his little girl going to school without a lunch.

The book Will held in his hands had a picture of a boy with a stick over his back, a bag of his belongings tied to it.

29

"Things could be worse," said William. "Look at this boy. He doesn't even have a home. He is a hobo."

Thinking of reading the book to her, his appetite crept into the story.

"Hey, you just stay still. Daddy is going to go and get our supper."

Her little face lit up like a ray of sunshine.

"Yes, Daddy, just you and me, and Sally."

William tiptoed down the staircase, as not to arouse Irene's curiosity, when he reminded himself he was the man of the house.

Peering into the kitchen, it is empty, quiet as a tomb. The light of the moon through the small square window over the sink, shedding enough light for William to see his plate on the top of the stove, another plate covering his food. Grabbing another plate and two forks, he headed back up the stairs.

William put a share of everything onto a plate and placed it on Alice's lap. A smile that would warm the coldest heart crossed her face.

They sit quietly eating the meal, sharing in the love for each other. Alice forgets all her woes, a warmness spread across her chest.

"I'm really not that hungry, Daddy, and my mouth hurts too."

"That's OK. At least you had a little. Now you just lie down and get some sleep. School is tomorrow, and you have to get up early."

With renewed hope, Alice closed her eyes, a softened baby smile on her lips, drifting off to dreamland.

Will is listening to sounds of the sleeping house wafting down the hallway when he walked back into Alice's room. Sound asleep, her breathing like a lullaby to his ears.

Walking to his beauty, he tightened the blanket around her, tucking it under her small body. The brown soft bear is under her one arm, Sally's raggedy head sharing the pillow.

Bending, he kisses her forehead, taking one last adoring look.

CHAPTER 6

The alarm rings promptly at 5:00 a.m. William is the first one in the kitchen most mornings. Knowing Irene has lots to do with the kids, he doesn't depend on her for breakfast. Irene prepares his lunch for the dairy, at night, with leftovers from supper. The best part of his day was eating the fresh bread Irene baked almost daily.

The second alarm rings, sending its morning signal throughout the small clapboard house.

There is an instant buzz of activity. Boys' voices, mostly, each vying for the sink to wash their faces and brush their hair and teeth. One by one they arrived at the table, taking their places as though in an army barrack.

Irene stands at counter, buttering bread and organizing what she has to offer her children for breakfast. A tower of thickly sliced homemade bread stacked in front of her. A heady smell of burned toast in the air.

This morning she was working on a special plate for her only daughter. Freshly buttered toast and strawberry preserves, the ones she saved for special occasions.

Once she buttered the strawberry on two pieces of toast, she puts the jar back in the pantry. It would not even last one breakfast if she put it out for everyone to have.

Alice rolled over rubbing her eyes, the sting of the water-filled blister like needles through her skin. Pulling herself upright, the pain in her back and legs makes her whole body feel too heavy to move.

If she didn't make it down to breakfast, she knew that Irene would keep her home for sure. With that in mind, Alice puts the pain away.

In the bathroom she looked up but notices just the silhouette of a small white porcelain mirror that once hung there. Since Pearl died, Irene had removed it.

Tears filled her eyes. How could she go to school like this?

What would she tell the teacher?

"I burned myself on the pot," she rehearsed. Just part of the story; it wouldn't be lying.

While making her bed, thoughts of school transport her to the school-yard. Her pain rode on the swing and flew away from her as she smiled, remembering the kids and the playground.

Tucking the brown bear into Sally's raggedy arms, taking one last look at the bed. Not one wrinkle. Perfect.

Today she would wear pants to cover the bruises that peppered the back of her legs. And a long-sleeved pink sweater. Yes, it was good. Now only her burned cheek was showing. The blister on her face would be easy to explain.

"Goodbye. See you later, dolly, I am off to school."

Waving, she closed her room door.

As she neared the staircase, a buzz in the air, like a fully engaged beehive.

The staircase took forever this morning. One, two, three, four, five... twelve.

From the foot of the staircase, she peered into the dining room.

The sound of voices ceased. William stared toward her as she emerged. All her brothers watched her every step toward the table.

"Come over here and sit by your Daddy," said William.

Alice moved cautiously, not to bring on the pain. William noticing his baby girl laboring to walk.

Irene turned from the sink, watching. William opened his arms to Alice, who snuggled into his warm love, pulling out the chair for her to sit.

Settling in straight in her seat, she makes eye contact with each of her brothers.

All eyes on her at once made her feel shy, pink rising in her unburned cheek.

"The bandage fell off, Daddy, when I was sleeping."

Trying on a smile, she winced, pain burning her face.

Irene walked to the table with a big plate of scrambled eggs and a tall stack of toast.

"Everyone dig in. There is honey in the big jar," Irene said, pointing to the jar of bright yellow buttercup honey. "And for you, Alice, strawberry jam. I buttered your toast with it."

"Oh, thank you, Mommy," she answered in a high pitched voice.

Irene did not look her way but continued on as though talking to the boys.

They passed the plate of eggs around, each taking just a couple of spoonfuls.

William put some of the eggs on Alice's plate.

She tried to eat, but even chewing hurt her face.

"Daddy, do you think you could put a bandage on my face? I don't want the kids looking at my burn."

"You should really stay home from school until that burn heals," interrupted Irene.

"Oh no, Mommy, please, I have to go to school. I can't miss my lessons. And my face doesn't hurt at all," she said, her words falling fast, like a marching band.

William looked from Irene to Alice. Alice's green eyes begging.

"No, she is fine to go to school. It's just a burn, and it will heal. I will get some salve right now and a new bandage and fix it up good, OK."

Irene's jaw tightened, glaring at her husband, who is avoiding her eyes, feeling the animosithy of Irene in her silence.

Irene ambled from the table. Standing in front of the sink, she stares blindly out the window.

"Just keep spoiling her. See what happens."

"What did you say, Irene?" asked William, hearing his wife's mumbling.

"Nothing, nothing at all," she answered through clenched teeth.

"After all, Irene, she is only six years old, for God's sake. Have some consideration."

The boys looked up from their plates, waiting for the hammer to come down.

William didn't say another thing. Continuing on with his breakfast, keeping his focus on Alice.

Irene watched as William dressed the burn, covering it with fresh gauze.

"You kids had better be going now," said Irene, trying to get Will's attention.

William is holding Alice's sweater for her, putting her arm through one sleeve, then the other.

"You better hurry along now, Alice. Have a nice day at school." Bending, he kissed her on the forehead.

Irene's brow furrowed, her back teeth clamped together like a vise.

The boys walked single file out the door, Alice following.

Today she wore a pair of shoes that were a little big. At least they weren't pinching her toes.

Irene went to the door, watching, hating to let her go.

"Don't get any dirt in that burn," warned Irene. "You will get an infection."

"No, Mommy, I won't. I promise." Waving, she runs to catch up to Earl, floating as though an invisible wind force propelled her, the pain magically flying away.

CHAPTER 7

Earl, next in age to Alice, with similar golden blond hair, looked more like her than the others. Short for his age, he took after his father. When the older boys left him out of their games, he searched out his baby sister and loved to play the silly games she made up.

Usually they ended up in the barn with the chickens or playing catch, her favorite game.

That was close, she thought, realizing that her mother had planned on keeping her home from school. A deep sigh escaped her lips, nothing could erase the permanent smile on her cherub face. School was the best thing ever in her life so far, and Miss Ink was her angel.

Irene had made sure all the kids had a sandwich for lunch today, even Alice.

William's job was very demanding of him, keeping him some nights until long after suppertime. Those days, sometimes too tired to eat himself, he went straight to bed, not knowing Alice had gone to bed hungry.

William worked six days a week, eighteen hours a day.

There was only one other hired hand, Billy, who drove the milk truck to the small towns and into the city of Halifax. His wife and their four children lived in the other house allotted for the help. Spending time with Billy during lunch breaks and after work gave William some time to get his mind off his duties and his domineering wife.

William always has a kind word and a smile for everyone.

The Jeffersonses loved William's work ethic. They also appreciated his company and invited him to the big house for tea and sandwiches when he had a particularly long day.

Mr. Jefferson respected William's input on the productivity of the dairy, encouraging him to give any ideas.

On his day off, Sundays, William enjoyed some quality time with his only daughter.

On some Sundays he would take her up to the barns to show her the herd of cows explaining to her his various duties.

There was a black-and-white dog named Rex that Alice would seek out as soon as she got there.

Mrs. Jefferson looked forward to the little girl's visits, always inviting her to the house for milk and cookies and anything she wanted.

One Sunday Mrs. Jefferson couldn't help but notice the dark circles under Alice's eyes.

"My dear girl, I have just the thing for those dark circles under your eyes. I'll just fetch some tonic for you."

Alice watched as Mrs. Jefferson goes to a cupboard and brings back a brown bottle and a spoon.

"It is tonic. I think you need some of this."

"Sure, ma'am," answered Alice.

"It will taste bad, but just swallow fast," instructed Mrs. Jefferson.

Wrinkling her nose, Alice took the spoonful of tonic, washing it down with the smooth chocolate milk.

"That wasn't so bad. Thank you, ma'am."

"You can call me Anne. That is my first name. After all, I call you Alice."

"OK then, Anne," she said, trying out the new name.

Billy lived a stone's throw away from Will.

His two sons played with the Purple boys.

Billy's wife, Laura, had encountered Irene one afternoon. Irene was hanging some things on her clothesline when Laura approached her.

"Have you seen my boys? Its past suppertime, and they were over here earlier playing."

Irene turned to look at the pretty redhead. "I am not anyone's babysitter. I have enough trouble trying to keep up with my own brood."

Turning her back to Laura, she goes back to pinning her clothes on the line.

Laura walked back home and told Billy how rude Irene had been.

"She was downright miserable," said Laura.

"That explains a lot about Will. Sometimes the man just stares into space, and you can see that he is troubled about something. He is such a wonderful, kind man," said Billy.

CHAPTER 8

Oakfield, a rural community, is a half-hour train ride to Halifax. Every two weeks, when William gets his pay from the dairy, Irene planned a trip to Halifax for food and things.

The first week there seemed to be enough to go around, but by the second week supplies would dwindle to bare bones.

There was no money for new clothes, so the children passed down the things they grew out of to the next one in line, till they were threadbare. The best they had came from the Jeffersonses' two girls. Hardly worn dresses, shoes, and other things.

Soup, the main staple, was served with Irene's homemade bread.

Potatoes were the one food they had in abundance in the growing season.

The real advantage to William working at a dairy was he got to take home some of the milk and butter, and sometimes cheese that was close to expiry, and bags of apples from the Jefferson's orchard.

Irene would make everyone's favorite, apple crisp, when there were oats, butter, and brown sugar to accompany them.

The smell of cooked apples and cinnamon wafting into the yard led the kids by their noses, like an anesthetic, numbing the harshness of their world.

All through apple season, Alice would sneak a few, hiding them in her room for times that Irene sent her to bed with no supper.

Her chair was positioned to watch out the window, toward the barns, where she counted the black-and-white-spotted cows and watched for her father on his way home.

Irene insisted that there was not enough room at the big butcher-block table for everyone. There were ten seats and eleven people. "The odd one out," Irene said, ordering Alice to sit at the sewing machine table, between the parlor and the kitchen, blocking her view of the table that housed ten chairs, and her whole family. Patiently waiting around the corner, the aromas of the food, coming to her, teasing her hunger. One thing she could count on, the chore of cleaning the table, and dishes, sometimes a few scraps left by her brother's she would gobble while Irene wasn't looking.

When William was at home for supper, Irene made sure that Alice got a few things to eat.

With the depression in full swing, the Purpleses and countless other families were going without the bare necessities.

CHAPTER 9

Alice's Second Day
at School

E arl and Alice were no sooner round the bend, their house out of sight,
when she started whining.

"My back hurts so much. Can you carry my book bag, please?
Can you look and see if I have a cut on my back?"

Earl pulled up her blouse to expose red welts and blotches of purple
bruises.

"Oh my God," said Earl, tears welling up in his eyes, shaking his head,
hugging his sister to him. "I hate her. I hate her so much for hurting you."

He piggybacked her all the way to school. The bell rang just as the
schoolhouse came into view.

Miss Ink stood just inside, with her clipboard in hand, marking the kids
off as they came through the door. Delighted to see Alice and Earl tucked
into the back of the line, a smile crossed her painted lips.

Getting seated, Alice put her pencil in the groove at the top of her desk.
Folding her hands, she stared up at the blackboard, trying to guess what
Miss Ink had written.

Remembering the big gauze bandage, bringing her hand up to her cheek.
What would Miss Ink say about it?

The other kids shuffled around, getting their books out, starting into
their lessons. Miss Ink made her way to Alice's desk.

"My dear, what has happened to your face?"

Looked into the teacher's softened dark eyes, she whispered, "Well, teacher. I was helping my mom make supper, and I burned myself on the potato pot."

"Really? Well, today you should stay in at recess, and I will give you some pictures to color, OK?"

Miss Ink went silent for a few minutes, looked down at the little girl with the big ringlets, the redness of the burn spilled out from under the bandage.

Sitting at her desk she penciled in a report of the burn.

With the severity of the burn, the child should not have been sent to school. Suspicious, making a note of the date and time.

Looking over Alice's paper, Miss Ink realized that Alice could print better than some of the students in the grade three class.

She is a bright girl. She must be six years old, she concluded.

CHAPTER 10

Alice's Brothers

Her eight brothers ranged in age from nine to nineteen. Having learned their own survival skills, the older ones had plans of when they would leave their humble beginnings and make a life for themselves.

The oldest boy, Jack, a tall, slim, dark-haired boy of nineteen, had already enlisted in the army and was anxiously awaiting his deployment to France.

The next in line, Ralph, was also joining the army when he turned eighteen. He still had a year to wait. Then James, fifteen; Mark, fourteen; and William, thirteen, who looked most like his dad. Edward, the redheaded one, had freckles. Skip, ten, was the handsome one of the bunch with dark curly hair and blue eyes. And Alice's favorite, Earl, eight, was blond, blue-eyed, and looked most like her.

The Depression, a heavy burden, put a damper on the young men's hopes and dreams.

The army was the really only resource for a job and three square meals.

Earl's older brothers called him Baby Boy and left him to play with his little sister most times.

Earl would take Alice for walked in the meadow, letting her pick flowers and watch the little animals. Squirrels and the birds made her happy. His brothers teased Earl, calling him a sissy for always playing with their baby sister. He didn't care what they said, just went on playing, ignoring their comments. The favorite pastime, though, was going up to the dairy with their dad.

There were so many things there to play with. A dog and goodies. Earl and Alice loved it, especially when Mrs. Jefferson invited them up to the big house.

When Alice sought out her brother with a book in hand, Earl knew what that meant: quiet time. Sitting close, he smelled the sweetness of her nuzzled in next to him. She loved the stories that she could get lost in, feeling herself there and away from her own life.

At the young age of four, she already recognized some words. Following the pictures putting words to the story.

CHAPTER 11

Irene's Humble Beginnings

When Beth, Irene's mother, discovered she was pregnant, she started planning right away how to get rid of the baby. Her grandfather, a rich man, had his favorite granddaughter in his will to inherit his millions.

Her cousin Charles came to the big estate every summer. The two of them spent lots of time together.

Every time Charles came, he started noticing her, growing more beautiful, blooming into a woman. A forbidden love sparked like a germinated seed in thick, lush dirt.

One day, as they sat at the water's edge, they decided to take all their clothes off and go swimming.

A pink-colored sky caressed them as Charles fondled Beth.

They moved from the water onto the beach, where he laid her down gently and had his way with her.

She lay motionless while he did what they both knew was wrong.

When it was all over, she got up right away and put her clothes back on.

Sitting, looking out over the lake, contemplating what had just happened.

Charles and Beth never spoke of what they did.

A couple months later, Beth started noticing changes in her body. Her breasts became very tender, and they hurt, even when she tried to dress herself. Her stomach started to round out. Wearing bigger dresses, she tried to conceal the baby growing in her. Being a tall girl, no one noticed the changes, only her mother, who commented that she had gained some weight.

Six months later, Beth was in the bathroom. The pains of childbirth wracking her abdomen. Her mother had gone to the city for the day, and she was all alone in the house.

She delivered the baby herself, right on the bathroom floor, cutting the cord the way she had witnessed at other births. Sneaking out of the bathroom, leaving the screaming, bloodied baby on the floor.

Coming back with a soft blanket she sets a warm bath in a porcelain bowl.

Humming, she runs her wet hands over the baby, cleaning it of the blood and mucus.

Wrapping the baby in a swathing she hurried with it to the woodshed. Holding the baby quiet against her chest, she would wait till she heard her mother bring the horse and buggy back into the barn. Then she would take the baby away. No one could see her.

Finding a firm cardboard box, she laid the soft blanket in first, then tucked in the baby.

Getting into the buggy, Beth settled into the seat, still warm from her mother's body. When the coast looked clear, she heads out onto the dirt road.

A short ways down the road, the baby started crying, Beth urging the horse to the side of the road. Reaching into the box, she lifts out the baby. Holding it to her chest, a warm sticky feeling, milk seeping down the front of her dress.

Opening her blouse, bringing the baby's mouth to her breast, the gentle urgings of the infant's mouth. In a few minutes the baby's eyes closed in sleep.

Laying her back down in the box covering her with the soft blanket, staring down at a perfect baby. Rosy cheeks and wispy platinum hair. Looking away, tears filled her eyes.

"I just can't," she cried out loud.

The tears fall with the milk in one stain of sadness, covering the front of her blouse.

She would take the baby to the orphanage run by the Catholic nuns. Everyone knew that they took in babies, the ones people didn't want or couldn't care for. She would be safe there.

The large grey stone building with the black wrought-iron fence came into view. Beth pulled up the buggy. Lifting out the box, heading to the steps of the convent. A sign read St. Mary's Convent. Placing the box on the top step, one last pang of regret penetrating her heart, then looking both ways to make sure no one noticed her as she backed away.

Running to the buggy, she didn't look back. With no baby to cause her shame, she would return to her perfect life.

One of the nuns came out to pick up the day's milk and spotted the box. Opening the lid, a baby bundled in a blanket fast asleep. Carefully, she picked up the box and walked back into the convent.

"We have another one."

A few nuns came running down the corridor, the black and white of their uniform like a colony of penguins.

"It's a little girl," one of them announced. The mother superior came to give her blessing.

"We'll call her Irene Hazel."

By the end of the day, Irene was just another mouth to feed, in the ranks of the ten rows of babies.

Before long Irene learned her cries would go unheard, layin in her own excrement sometimes for hours before being attended to.

The babies were not the nuns' main priority. They took turned going in to feed them, propping their bottles up under a blanket. Rarely were they handled by them. The nursery, a white room, had an eerie silence.

Some of the children were adopted. The rest continued their lives at the convent, enduring the same rules of conduct that the nuns followed.

CHAPTER 12

The nuns made her work from the time she could hold a scrub brush. At six years old Irene was on her hands and knees scrubbing floors. They taught her the basics—to read and write and pray.

Prayer was an hourly duty. Having to kneel and say the same words over and over felt like punishment, like she was already in the hellfire, they threatened.

Her knees went from pain to numb, like the feeling in her heart.

"Go and pray. Ask God to forgive your bad thoughts," the mother superior would order, sending her to bed many nights with no supper.

Irene was ordered to keep her head covered at all times. The nuns assigned her daily wear. Long bloomers and an undershirt. Two identical grey dresses that were altered as she grew, that hung to the floor as grey as the mood in the cold convent.

Long hallways connected two sections of the large convent. The nuns passed each other, barely nodding.

"Speak only when you are spoken to," they ordered the children.

There were no mirrors; to be vain was a sin.

Irene was caught by the mother superior one day trying to catch her reflection in the window.

"What is it you were looking for? Reassurance of who you are?"

"God knows who you are. He reads what is in your heart and mind. He knows all. Now stop trying to see what others already see."

The little girl hung her head in shame.

CHAPTER 13

Irene never knew love. Only the invisible love of God, which she had a hard time understanding? Numb from the harsh punishment from the nuns, surely God didn't know her.

Irene was adopted when she ten years old. The family had another five children, all boys. A girl child would come in handy for a family that needed help raising of the boys.

Conditioning by the nuns had made her the perfect addition to the family. Without complaint she washed floors and dishes till her hands were raw and blistered. They tried to love her, but Irene showed no happiness even when she was included in outings. Seven hard years of working as a maid.

One day at a church function, Irene meets William. Six months later, Irene and William are married in the same church. Finally, Irene was free to do as she liked.

Slender, dark hair, and blue eyes, Irene had grown into a pretty girl.

William and Irene settled into the small clapboard house on the Jefferson plantation.

It wasn't long before the children started coming. Every nine months, Irene was with child. By the time her fifth child came along, she had lost her girlish figure. With no time for anything but the children, her own looks and self-esteem soon plummeted. Work and more work.

Losing track of time and the children, Irene had six more. Consumed by her mounting responsibilities, she started to become disconnected, her mind far away, sometimes just going through the motions.

When Alice is born, the doctor announced "the baby is dead." The midwife is wrapping the baby up when she comes back to life.

A squeak from the blanket, like a loud scream to Irene's ears.

The midwife unwrapped the baby, handing her to Irene, who refused, turning her face away.

"No, not another one," she said under her breath.

As the pink returned to the baby's cheeks, the color drained from Irene's face, biting down on her lip drawing blood. Another mouth to feed.

CHAPTER 14

Bread was the one thing the Purple family rarely went without. The smell of fresh buns wafted out to the yard around their humble abode. It was the highlight of William's days.

Irene kept William at arm's reach, especially lately, not wanting to get pregnant again.

"William Purple, you see that room down there—the pantry. I have cleaned it out so you can put a cot in there. I just can't have you sleeping in my bed anymore."

Listening, but saying nothing, William takes his things to the small windowless room.

Following him to the pantry standing in the doorway, Irene glaring in at William.

"Can't you see what all these children have done to me? I barely have time to comb my hair." Grabbing a handful of hair in each hand. "I can't do this much longer," she whined.

William turned to look at his wife. He was concerned but didn't know how to answer her.

One day after school, Earl and Alice rushed in the door of the house with buns or fresh bread on their minds.

With no sign of the golden heads or freshly buttered loaves, Earl goes to his room. Alice peeked in the dining room. Irene is bent over the big silver bowl she makes the bread in.

Pulling and pushing the dough back into the bowl with a fury of tugs and punches, each stroke growing stronger and fiercer. Alice backed away just enough so one eye could watch what was happening.

Lost in the sea of white, she catches a glimpse of Alice in the doorway. A sliver of a smile crossed her face, like a demented clown. In horror, Alice is shocked, watching Irene's tears dripping into the bowl. With a slight whimper, Alice frightened at what she is witnessing. Irene turned her focus back on the mixture, punching and pulling at the raw dough with a renewed vigor.

With Irene lost in her bread making, Alice retreated to the yard. Her stomach heaved, as she runs to the side of the woodshed throwing up.

Finishing up the loaves, shaping them in perfect, bread-pan-size mounds, Irene covered them with a clean linen dishcloth.

That wasn't the only bread incident that stuck out in Alice's mind.

Another day, Alice happened to come along when Irene was in the midst of making bread, ripping and tearing at the dough as though it was her worst enemy.

Alice watched as the bowl went flying off the chair, a big mound of white dough landing in the corner of the room, picking up the dust and dirt off the floor as it rolled.

Hiding around the corner, Alice can see Irene on her hands and knees crawling toward the white mound. Picking it up, raising it in the air with both hands like some sacrifice to the bread gods. Looking around at her whitewashed floor, flour strewn about like talcum powder. Rubbing both of her hands in the flour, Irene brings her hands to her face, rubbing it into her face and hair. Her tears started falling, mixing it into a paste. Her eyes beneath look like two piss holes in the snow.

A blood-curdling scream infects the airwaves. So frightened now, Alice runs out of the house, looking for one of her brothers. Two of them came running from the field, worried for Alice.

"Mom is making bread and fell on the floor. Now she is crying and scaring me."

The boys hurry into the house, Alice close behind. Irene is sitting, her back propped up against the wall. The white of the flour spread around her, a disconnected look in her eyes. A plaster of white covers her hair and face, scaring the boys too. They too run out of the house.

By the time William gets in from the dairy, the little clapboard house is filled with the wonderful aroma of fresh loaves. The warm buns with their buttered headed welcomed him home. No one uttered a word to him about what they had seen.

The buns are being passed around the table. When they reach Alice, she hesitates, then passes on the plate.

"You aren't hungry tonight, Alice?" asked William.

"No, Daddy, I had a big lunch at school. Miss Ink shared hers with me."

William is about to take a bite out of a shiny headed bun, feeling all the boys eyes on him, he puts it back on the plate.

"What seems to be the issue? Haven't you ever seen me eat bread before?"

Irene bites down on a buttered bun.

CHAPTER 15

Pearl, Alice's older sister, had been gone for about six months. The sadness of her absence hit Alice hard. Crying herself to sleep for days on end, asking God to please take her where her sister had gone.

"Please, God, give me back my big sister. I need her, God."

Irene's abuse has intensified since Pearl died.

Alice misses everything about Pearl. The way she brushed her hair every night before bedtime, laying with her in the small bed, reading her a story.

She helped her pick out the best things to wear, always telling her how pretty she was and how much she loved her.

Pearl was born sick and anemic. One sickness after another plagued her body till she died. Irene never mistreated her.

Alice rarely got sick, even when her brothers had a cold.

Nights that Irene sent Alice to bed hungry, she would wait till all the sounds of the household quieted, then steal down the stairs into the kitchen.

The sound of Irene snoring was Alice's green light to hunt for whatever she could find to eat. Scraps from the garbage or an onion from the pantry. Usually there were a few of them, and Irene wouldn't notice or think that Alice would eat an onion like an apple.

The biggest treat of all were the apple peelings. Stealing them out of the garbage, she would wash them, and eat them like candy, the sweetness making her heart glad.

The sight of a big bowl of apples spelled comfort for Alice and her brothers. It was either apple pie or apple crisp, Alice's favorite. As long as they had oats and brown sugar to accompany the apples. The apple desserts were like painkillers in a way, the smell alone anesthetizing the kids' brains. Baked apples brought feelings of a wholesome home.

From the moment they walked in the house to the welcoming smell of apples and cinnamon, the kids were hypnotized by the combination, aromatherapy, awaiting their dessert anxiously. Irene used the sweet treat to cajole them into whatever she had in her devious mind.

"Do you want a big bowl or a bite?"

The large rectangular silver pan sat in the middle of the table like a sacrificial offering of sugared apples with buttery, crunchy oats. Quite often they had cream to drizzle on it. Expired cream from the Jeffersonses' dairy.

Everyone took turned passing their small white ceramic bowls to Irene for their share. Alice's eyes were bright, hopeful, begging. She waited until the last bowl was dished out, then hers. If William was home, Alice would always get her share, but those nights when he was late from work, Alice got a few spoonfuls or maybe none at all.

CHAPTER 16

School: A Safety Zone for Alice

Miss Ink couldn't help but remember Pearl now that she had Alice sitting in the front row, just a few feet from her. They looked a lot alike, thought Miss Ink, only Pearl was taller. A really pale girl, her blue eyes hauntingly beautiful, her skin the color of a whitish pearl. She missed her very much and had kept Pearl's artwork. It adorned the wall at the back of the classroom.

One afternoon, as Alice buzzed around the classroom putting out fresh chalk on the blackboard, helping Miss Ink dust some books, Miss Ink had an idea.

"Come with me, Alice. Let's have a look at some of Pearl's pictures."

"My sister Pearl, ma'am?" asked Alice, excitement in her voice.

"Just look here," she said, pointing to a row of pictures on the wall. "These were your sister's pictures. Look at this one, Alice."

There was a small girl with golden curls bending down in a grassy meadow, picking daisies.

"Do you think that little girl is you?"

"I think maybe it is. It sure looks like me, and I have a dress like that with butterflies on it. It is me! Oh, my goodness, thank you, God," she said, her voice on high octave. "Pearl needs to be in this picture, Miss Ink. We use to pick flowers together."

"Well, I'll tell you what. When I take the picture down, I will give it to you so you can color your sister into the picture. That is a great idea, Alice. Then I will put it back up for the whole classroom to see."

Miss Ink walked away, tears coming to her eyes. Alice moved closer to get a better look. Reaching up, she traced the picture of the little girl with her index finger. *It really is me*, she thought. In the right-hand corner of the picture was a pencil of her name. Pearl, the name illuminated.

"This picture is going to be yours, Alice. I just want to share it with the class for a while. Everyone here misses her. You and Pearl are almost the same, only she was taller. Now that we have you, you have brought back a part of us we had lost. I don't know if you know what I mean, but we loved Pearl too. The kids lost a friend, and I lost a student I loved. Thank you, Alice," said Miss Ink, walking away.

When Alice was in her room, she missed Pearl the most. The empty cot spelled the absence. All she had left of her sister were the memories, the big rag doll, and the teddy bear.

When Alice hugged them and loved them, she could feel the love of her sister. Remembering Pearl rubbing the bear's belly and braiding the doll's hair. She would love them the same way.

The school days were going too quickly for Alice's liking. She kept watch on the big wooden clock that hung on the wall over the blackboard.

Miss Ink pondered the thought that she had never met the mother of the Purple children. The father had come to pick them up a few times, and she liked the kindness and gentleness she felt from him. The Purple kids were well behaved and only spoke when spoken to.

She couldn't help but notice that the kids were doing without but making the best of a bad situation. Since she had met Alice, there was something else about the family she just couldn't put her finger on.

CHAPTER 17

A Birthday Party

Alice had overheard some of the older girls in the classroom talking about someone's birthday and the party they were planning. The words *games*, *balloons*, and *cake* ignited a fire in her. It sounded like lots of fun. She had never been to a party. The girls' voices bellowed in excitement, their eyes wide with anticipation. Alice inched forward, trying to hear every word about the party. One of the girls noticed Alice.

Everyone in the class already knew her name. She was Pearl's baby sister. All eyes were on her; everyone wanted to know her.

Sarah, a blue-eyed, dark haired girl with pigtails, approached her.

"Would you like to come to a party, Alice? We were planning a surprise party for Jenny. She is going to be turning ten real soon."

"You mean you want me to come? Come to a party? I've never been to a party before. But it sure sounds like it would be lots of fun, with cake and balloons." Her voice grew squeakier as she spoke.

Other girls had gathered around now, all eyes on the little girl with the golden ringlets and the big green eyes.

Giggling, they surround her with open arms and a group hug.

"You would have to arrange a ride," said Sarah. "It's about twenty miles from here."

Alice's happiness drained from her like the blood from her cheeks.

"I'll have to ask my mother, and if she doesn't have any chores for me that day, she might let me come."

Her head bowed, turning she walked away from the girls.

Pondering the thought all day about going to a stranger's house for a party. The only houses she had been to other than her own, were the Jeffersonses' and her Aunt Rita's, who would take her in the wagon about ten miles down the road.

Maybe the girl lived near her aunt Rita, and she could ask if she could take her the rest of the way? All the possibilities swirled around in her head like a dust storm before a hurricane. She knew deep down, in her heart of hearts, Irene would deny her any happiness and dreams of going. She would find some excuse to not let her go, a party would be like a dirty word to her mother.

One day Irene walked in on Alice with a handheld mirror she had found in a box with some hair ornaments.

"I'll beat that pride and vanity out of you," she threatened. "Where did you get this mirror? There are no mirrors allowed in my house." Ripping the mirror out of her hands, she grabbed at the front of Alice's dress with her soot-covered hands.

"Get those fancy clothes off. Go outside and look after the chickens, then get back in here and wash the floor." Pointing her index finger to the floor, her eyes bulging, like she just saw a giant spider, foam gathered at the corners of her mouth.

Tossing the thought of the party out of her head, knowing she shouldn't fool herself into thinking she would be going. Her eyes filled with water, a quiet whimper escapes her lips. Thinking of the bandy rooster waiting for her in the coop brought back her smile.

As much as she tried to bury the thought of the birthday party, it kept coming back in her mind. Would it really hurt to ask Irene? Maybe she would question her mom, about a party of her own for her seventh birthday, and if the girls from school could come to her house?

As soon as the thought arrived, Alice chased it away. Mother would never let her have a party. But if she asked her father, maybe with his help, there might be a slight chance.

With renewed confidence, she decided that was what she would do.

St. Jude Children's® Research Hospital

Finding cures. Saving children.
ALSAC • DANNY THOMAS, FOUNDER

stjude.org/givehope

9A1

April ninth. The birds were just started to build their nests, singing their songs of spring. William always did something nice for Alice on her special day, even if it was just a walk in the meadow.

A special fantasy was growing in her mind. She would invite a few of the girls from school. Maybe. Everything was a maybe, just like that elusive bunny rabbit that couldn't find their house at Easter time. There must be lots of kids the Easter bunny couldn't find, surely not just the Purple kids.

CHAPTER 18

The winter had been a long, cold one. Many days Irene kept Alice from school, but not until Alice suffered frostbite to her fingers. In blizzard conditions, the boys would fight their way through, baring their faces to the bitter cold winds, better than dealing with the ice queen at home.

A letter came home to Irene from Miss Ink.

Please keep Alice home on extremely cold days.

The days she kept her home, Irene made sure she didn't have a dull moment. Wash this, wash that, iron this, iron that, do this, do this some more, until Alice didn't know if she was coming or going. Numb from the orders and the back-breaking work, she went about her chores. So exhausted by the time Irene bellowed bedtime, the call to end her torturous day.

Stealing to her room, she'd count the stairs as she went, her head down until she reached her sanctuary. Closing the door, she stands against it, breathing a sigh of relief, closing out her tormentor.

She'd fall into her narrow cot and pull the thin grey blanket over her, bringing teddy and Annie into her arms, the sandman taking her into her dreams as soon as her eyes closed.

One afternoon Irene asked Alice to go with her to the train station to pick up a parcel. Excited, Alice dressed in her best wool coat that had belonged to Pearl. It was a soft pink color, just a little too long but warm and pretty, with two rows of big round white buttons running down the front.

While they stood waiting in line, a tall black woman came up behind them, Alice catching sight of her out of the corner of her eyes. Turning right around, taking in the beauty of the ebony lady, with the bright multi-colored scarf wrapped around her head. Her large almond, bright smiling eyes gazing down on little Alice.

"Hello, miss," she said in a soft angelic voice. "And what is your name?"

"My name is Alice," she answered quietly. "What is your name?" Alice asked shyly, looked deep into the dark, loving eyes. Taking her in, Alice felt the warmth of her smile into her heart.

"My name is Sadie West."

Irene turned, noticing Alice talking to the black woman.

"Come over here, Alice, and don't make yourself a bother."

"Oh no, she is no bother. What a sweet little girl. You didn't mention you had another daughter?"

Feeling shameful, Irene tugged on Alice's arm.

"We have to get along now."

Alice kept looking behind as Irene pulled her away.

"You need to stay away from that nigger wench. She pulled a cougar's tongue right out of its head. She will bite you too, so don't get too close to her."

Alice wrinkled up her nose. The love she felt from a stranger was more than she had ever felt from her own mother. She loved the dark lady with the beautiful eyes and sweet smile. That lady would never bite her. Plus, wasn't she the same black woman, that Irene had said, was her real mother, and had just left her with Irene?

Sadie couldn't take her eyes off the precious child, walking toward them again she approached Irene.

"Hello, Missus Purple."

"A good day to you," answered Irene, ushering Alice toward the door. Sadie followed them.

Alice turned again to look at Sadie, noticing the raised scar that ran like a pink snake from her face down her neck and into her blouse.

"Stop your staring. Just because she is black is no need to stare."

"Oh no, missus," said Sadie. "The child is looking at the claw marks from the cougar. A big cat was going to kill my grandchild, and I fought it to save my grandson."

"That was very brave, ma'am" said Alice, her eyes growing wide.

"I'll tell you the whole story when your mom has more time. I have to get going now too. It was so nice to meet you."

"You too," answered Alice.

"Bless you, child."

Staring deep into Alice's bright green eyes, taking her to the many forested paths she had ridden her buggy.

"Take care now. My horse awaits."

Alice watched as Sadie walked by them out the door, her long skirt flowing like a gentle breeze blowing it.

When Sadie was out of sight, Irene turned to Alice and grabbed her arm.

"You mustn't talk to strangers, girl! What is wrong with you?"

"She was talking to me, Mommy."

Irene shook her head, no reply.

Down the snow covered road, she walked ahead of her mother, thinking of the black lady with the pink scar running down her face. She would never forget her. How she wished she was her mother and hoped she would see her again soon. All the way home the story of Sadie ran over and over in her mind. Before she realized how tired and cold she was, they were walking into the yard, the chickens scratching in the snow around their coop.

Sadie had worked as a maid for some millionaires who had given her the horse and buggy to get to and from their house.

When the old couple passed away within days of each other, they left the horse, Mozart, and buggy to Sadie. Loving the Lord, Sadie decided to give the horse a bible name, Moses.

Sadie had been their servant for twenty years. They had long decided that the beautifully carved wagon and horse would be hers one day. Sadie had been everything to them. Without her, their lives would have not been so full of happiness. A blessing that was what they'd called her.

CHAPTER 19

Birthday Thoughts

The birthday party idea was as bright as a light that wouldn't go out. If she did her chores extra well, maybe Irene would say yes. Just maybe she would let her make cookies all by herself. Invite a few girls from school. Oh, how it was coming together in her mind like a real party. A smile on her lips, Alice's mind far away.

CHAPTER 20

William would walk in on Irene forcing her discipline on the children.

"Don't interfere, William. I bore these children, and I will raise them the way I see fit!"

Her threats were like broken glass underfoot. William always just walked away, shutting her out, his authority over his family dwindling.

The bullying had gone too far, and now he didn't know how to change things, trying to keep the peace, his heart heavy.

Alice wore the scars from the burns she acquired while ironing her brothers' shirts and pants. Since she was five, Irene had given her this as her first job to do with the boys' clothes. Watching as her mother would stir the shirts in a big cast-iron pot on top of the stove. Then she put them into a tub with cold water, rinsing and rinsing till they came out clean.

The cast iron was heated on top of the woodstove till the sides of it glowed with redness.

It took all of Alice's strength with both hands to move the iron along the cotton shirts.

"Be careful. Why are you so clumsy? Pay attention, and you won't burn yourself," chastised Irene. Eventually, Alice saw it for what it was. A danger to her. If she was careful and smart, she could do the ironing without burning herself.

Most nights after Alice was done with her outdoor chores, she would spend a couple of hours ironing the boys' shirts.

Never good enough, Irene complained. Alice could never do anything right.

After a long day at school, she wished she could just go straight to her room, to her friends. But she learned early that dreams were just that—dreams.

When the long day was nearing an end, she would wearily trudge up the staircase to her private heaven.

Diligently going about her chores, humming as she went with the desire to do the best job she could, so maybe Irene would praise her, even just once.

If someone else commented on Alice's behavior or mentioned how adorable she was, Irene would take the credit.

Once when she was at the train station with her mother, she overheard her talking to a lady.

"She is my only girl child now that my other daughter, Pearl, died. Sure happy to have her. All my other children are boys. Eight of them."

Maybe she really does like me, thought Alice.

Her dad found every opportunity to tell her what a good girl she was and how much he loved her.

There was a worn place in the yellowed linoleum in front of the sink, where Irene spent countless hours washing dishes, staring out into the world that held no promise for her. From the first thing in the morning till the last thing at night. Too bad Alice was too short to reach the sink yet. Even if she stood on a chair. Then she would be too tall to reach the sink and the dirty water.

The Purple kids looked forward to the days that Irene was gone all day in the city. Earl and Alice chased each other around the house and up and down the stairs. Laughter, a delicacy to them, like music to their own ears. They could relax without the warden watching their every move.

CHAPTER 21

Water Duty

There was one chore in particular that none of the kids wanted anything to do with. Irene decided that Alice could handle the job, and that was it.

She had to carry four pails of water every day, except for weekends, when her dad took on the chore.

"Mom, why can't the boys get the water? They are bigger and stronger than me."

"Because I said you will get the water, that's why. And don't question my authority again."

This was the ultimate putdown for Alice, making her feel like a lowly creature that didn't deserve any better treatment.

"Go and get it, and stop complaining," Irene ordered, pointing her index finger toward the well.

As her brothers watched, perched up against the shed like crows on a wire, Alice bowed her head in submission walking to the shed where the pails waited.

It didn't matter how much she pleaded, her cries went unheard.

Irene shut out her own emotions. No love was able to get in or out of her heart's bindings.

Struggling with the water, most times she spilled half of it, going back again and again, until the four pails were delivered into the house. Stopping every few minutes, her shoes soaking wet, Alice would whimper. Earl would sometimes go to his sister's aid when his heart would overflow with sadness for Alice, hoping his mother wouldn't see him, and punish him too.

One day after school, as Alice is on her way to the shed to start her water duty, a bright light came on in her head. The boys used a wagon to pull cut wood to the house. If she could figure out a way, the wagon would be a big help.

Pleased with her idea, Alice put two pails on the wagon and headed to the well, anxious to see if she could get the water to the house, without spilling much.

Irene watched, her teeth clenched, as Alice maneuvered the wagon with two pails of water at a time.

"Stupid girl," she muttered under her breath.

CHAPTER 22

The sun beamed a warm ray into Alice's room, settling on the side of the wall. Waking, pushing her curls away from her face, heading to the chair facing the window. Today, her dad had said, she could accompany him to the dairy, and he'd told her to dress up.

"Mrs. Jefferson wants you to join her kids in some fun and games." William put his finger to his lips. "Shh, we don't want anyone else to know, OK?"

Her eyes widened, sparkling like stars in the night.

"We will have to sneak by your mother. Put on one of your pretty dresses."

With a nervous feeling in her stomach, Alice smiled. A party at the Jeffersonses', just like the party she was dreaming about.

Her dad had said to have breakfast, then excuse herself to get ready. Then she would walk outside and wait for him behind the shed.

"When I see you at the top of the stairs, I will distract your mother till you get outside."

"Yes, Daddy," she answered.

So much joy overflowed, her eyes watering like a pail that had been filled to the brim.

After breakfast of toast with strawberry jam, Alice helped clean the table and waited for Irene to busy herself when she started up the stairs. One, two, three, four, until she reached the top, heading to her secret place where she kept her pretty dresses. Finding the perfect one, a pink chiffon with an overlay of lace. A wide rose-colored ribbon adorns the waist, tying in the back.

Holding the dress up to her, she saunters to the window, trying to get a glimpse of what it would look like.

Pulling the dress over her head, a sudden sadness, missing her sister. If only she was there, she would help her dress and fix her hair. Tears filled her eyes, and she started to cry.

No, she told herself, wiping at her tears. She just couldn't cry now. It was a happy day. And Pearl was with her; she would always be with her.

Trying to shake the sadness, she thought of the party. It had been just a dream, but now it was real. The dress hem fell below her knees, her ankles barely showing. The body of the dress was perfect. As she struggled with the bow in the back, she thought about asking her dad to tie it.

Dressed, she sits on the little wooden chair looking off into the meadow, the barns, and the dairy in the distance, excited to go to the big house, to see Anne and the kids.

There would be some surprises too! It had to be a party. Why else would her dad say to dress pretty?

Thinking of Anne and how beautiful she was, like an elegant swan. She always had a big smile for Alice and special things. Little sandwiches and a big glass of chocolate milk. Secretly, she wished Anne could be her mother.

As she nears the top of the staircase, she eyed her dad. He waved to her without words. Just as she is about to go out the door, Irene comes through from the dining room, a pair of knitting needles in her hands.

"Where do you think you are going? All dressed like you are attending a funeral or something."

William stands behind Alice, a lump rising in his throat. He had to be a man and stand up to her. Alice spoke, feeling the tension in the air.

"Anne invited me to the big house today to play with her kids. So Daddy and I were going to the dairy. Right, Dad?"

"That's right, Alice. Yes, we are going to the Jeffersonses' today for lunch. They told me to be sure and bring Alice. And Anne's girls always have dresses on, so I just thought Alice should wear one too."

"And just where did you get that dress, Alice? I've never seen it before." Glaring her up and down.

"Anne sent it home with me for Alice, Irene."

"Oh, I see how it is. Now you two are keeping things from me."

"Well, I think it's time that Alice did something fun instead of work, work, work. After all, Irene, sometimes I think you have no heart at all for our little girl."

"Irene stood speechless, her knitting needles clicking together, her jaw set, her eyes bulging. Turning, she walks away from them. William holds the door for Alice.

As they neared the big house, the black-and-white dog came bounding out toward them. His tail straight in the air, he runs to Alice rubbing his head on her.

"Sorry, Rex, but today, I have a party to go to. You will just have to wait till I visit you next time to play, OK? I just can't get my dress dirty," she said, staring straight into the dog's eyes.

William had a chuckle hearing Alice talk to the dog like he understood her. Watching them, the love swelled in his chest.

His perfect little angel made him cry and laugh. A princess forever.

"Is it lunchtime yet?" she asked, following her dad around the barns.

"Anne will come down and get you when she is ready," he answered.

"OK then." She smiled.

Sitting on a tall upside-down milk can, she waited, her eyes peeled on the big barn door.

The heavy door squeaked open.

"There you are my dear," said Anne. "It's nice to see you, and you wore your pretty dress."

"Yes, ma'am, my dad told me to dress up, so here I am." Curtsying she holds the edges of the hem of her dress.

"C'mon up to the house. The kids are awaiting you."

"Waiting for me? Reeeeally, my goodness."

Walking next to Anne, reaching for her hand. Anne looking down at Alice, smiling, love radiating from her like warmth from sunshine.

Leading Alice into the foyer of the grand house, the long windows run the length of the wall on one side. The shiny, pearl-colored marble floor catches Alice's eye.

"I like your house," she said, smiling at Anne.

"Thank you, Alice. Go into the dining room. The kids are in there."

Anne walked away, secretly watching from around a corner.

Her heart went out to the tiny girl, knowing that she was doing without many things her children had in abundance.

Life could be so unfair, she reasoned, shaking her head, heading upstairs to her room.

Alice stood alone in the marble foyer. Putting down her bag, she takes off her boots, slipping into the shiny white doll shoes.

Suddenly, a whole new feeling comes over her, like she is in a fairy tale.

Brushing off her insecurities, loving her dress, taking in everything in the beautiful house. A princess, that's what she was. It wasn't a dream; it was real. At least for a while, came back the voice.

Anne sat pensive, overlooked the rolling hills beyond.

What could she really do to change the little girl's life? Having met Irene on a couple of occasions, she hadn't made a connection with the woman.

Once she had walked down to the Purple house with a few extras from her own kitchen. Flour, butter, sugar, and some other things she had in abundance.

Knocking on the door, after standing there for at least five minutes, she leaned in trying to hear if there was anyone inside, her ear to the door.

Not a sound, and no movement in the yard except for a few chickens scratching.

Sitting the box down, heading back toward her house. When she had walked a little way, she turned and noticed the corner of the curtain come up, a finger holding it in place. Strange, she thought to herself.

Another time, William had brought Irene up to the Jeffersonses'.

Anne answered the door and invited them in for tea.

"Oh no, we need to be going," answered Irene. "The kids are alone at home."

William shrugged his shoulders and said nothing.

They waited outside the door till Mr. Jefferson brought out William's pay.

Following the sounds of excitement, getting closer to the dining area. They had just started singing "Happy Birthday" when Alice poked her head into the grand dining room.

There was a long wooden table. A bright crystal chandelier hung over the room.

Alice's eyes darted around the room and then to the cake. The light on the candles and the glint of the chandelier catch the sparkle in her eyes.

A tall slim girl seemed to be the centre of attention. Anne walked up behind Alice and led her in.

"Come over and meet everyone. This is Jenny, my oldest girl. She goes to school in France and has come home to celebrate her birthday with us."

"A birthday party. Oh my goodness, a real birthday party," she whispered as though it would all disappear if she said it too loud. Happiness spread through her whole body, a smile brightened her face.

"Pleased to meet you," said Alice, holding out her hand to Jenny.

Alice looked deep into her big doe eyes. Jenny recognized the dress, her dress from years gone by. She smiled and thought of how cute she looked. And the shoes too. Jenny's heart overflowed seeing her things on this little angel girl.

"Hello, Alice, glad that you could come. Go and get some cake from the kitchen and some ice cream too."

"She can go with me," piped up another girl who Alice had never seen before.

"Hi, my name is Beth. I'll show you where all the goodies were." The girls walked hand in hand toward the kitchen. A spread of cakes and cookies, sandwiches, ice cream, and more food than Alice had ever imagined adorned the counters.

Beth handed Alice a plate as she got busy helping herself to cake and ice cream. Afraid to make the wrong move, Alice just stared and couldn't seem to move her feet toward the feast. Anne came in to see how things were going.

"Oh my, Alice. Let me help you."

Anne took the plate from her and pointed to everything, asking Alice what she wanted. *A princess didn't eat much*, she kept thinking to herself. After choosing just a couple things, Anne walked the plate back into the dining room and sat Alice at the big table.

Just a little of this and that. Then she giggled as she dug into the cake and ice cream.

The laughter and the sights took Alice to a faraway place. Could this really be happening? A birthday party, just like she had imagined?

A few of the girls are dancing around, twirling their dresses. Without hesitation, Alice joined in. Her dress floated through the air; her feet as light as on a cloud.

A clown appeared out of nowhere, bouncing into the room. Going from one girl to another, giving out shiny wrapped presents as he goes from one child to another.

Jenny is busy unwrapping her table full of gifts.

Anne's eyes were on Alice. How precious she was. The happiness that radiated from her had cast a spell on the party. A princess had arrived.

When the clown came around to Alice, she looked deep into his eyes. Eyes she had seen before. She realized he was just a man in a clown suit. Staring deeper, she started to giggle. It was her Daddy. The same height and eyes couldn't disguise the clown.

"Daddy," she whispered.

"Shh," he answered, handing her two brightly wrapped presents.

Alice took her two presents to a corner of the room, where she could unwrap them without anyone noticing. After carefully undoing the shiny red bow, she opened the small box to reveal a charm bracelet. A heart and an angel hung from the fine gold chain.

Holding it up, taking in the beauty, slipping it around her tiny wrist. It was so pretty, and it wasn't even her birthday. Who had really bought it for her?

The birthday party went on for two hours. A few of the kids sprawled out on the long couches that ran along the wall. Some of the parents were coming in, searching the big room. Anne stood at the door, thanking them for coming, greeting the parents.

When the last girl had left, Alice looked around the big room. She was the last one.

It was time to go and look for her dad in the barn. Time to go home, the dream coming to an end. The party was over and so was her fun. Back to her life.

"Daddy, Daddy," she bellowed, her echo reverberating through the tin barn.

William stepped out from behind a pillar, the clown suit still on. At first Alice was startled until William spoke.

"Hello, little girl." He bent down to shake Alice's hand.

"Daddy, is that you? I just knew it when I looked in your eyes. You make a great clown."

"I love you," she said, hugging him.

"Well, I suppose I should get this thing off. If your mother saw me, she would think I totally lost my mind. I have a few more things to finish up. Alice, you can fetch some milk from that vat over there." William pointed to a round barrel with a spout.

There was a cork stuck in a hole just up from the spout. Picking up a milk bottle, she pulled on the cork instead of the spout. A rush of milk spilled out, knocking her to the barn floor, spraying her in the face and eyes, she struggled to get her breath.

Her hands were blackened now, the dirt of the barn floor stuck to her like glue.

Starting to cry, she stared down at her dress, the bottom of it brown with dirt.

William rushed over to the vat and put the cork back in the hole. Going over to her, picking her up off the floor.

"Oh my goodness, look what you have done." Trying to wipe her milk clumped hair from her face, shaking his head.

"How will we get you past your mother without both of us getting yelled at? Stop crying now," he urged.

William couldn't help but laugh at the sight of her. Alice stops crying and started to laugh too. Hugging her close to him. "Never mind, sweetie. That was something that the clown should have done, not you. But I want to tell you something, my angel." Looking deep into her soft green eyes. "You were the belle of the ball today. A princess if I ever did see one."

"Oh, my Daddy, you really mean it, me a princess?"

"A beautiful princess," he recanted.

Giving her another big squeeze, then taking her hand, he leads her out of the barn through the field toward their house.

William walked in first, trying to get Irene's attention, as Alice sneaks behind him, headed up the staircase, when Irene spots the tail of her dirty dress.

"Hey, where are you going so fast, girl? What are you hiding?" Just as her foot hit the top step, Irene bellowed again.

"Get down here right away, young lady!"

William just watched, his tongue stuck to the roof of his mouth, his voice muted.

With a sigh of relief, Alice noticed William standing right behind Irene.

"What kind of lunch date did you have? You look more like you had a lunch with a bunch of pigs," said Irene, spit flying from her clenched teeth. "This is what you call a party?" she said, turning now to glare at Will.

"Mother," said Alice nervously," it had nothing to—"

"Oh, just shut up. What do you have to say, Will?" Don't just stand there looking stupid."

"It was just an accident in the barn," he answered, hanging his head. "It was my fault. I asked her to get the milk from the vat."

"Sure, take the blame for her stupidity. Get out of my sight, Alice," Irene ordered, pointing her finger up the stairs. Alice's eyes shot to the ground. Making her way slowly at first, then quickening her pace till she is out of sight.

CHAPTER 23

The Big Rag Doll

Scampering down the hallway, pieces of straw falling on the floor. Turning the room door handle, looking back just once, she steps in. Going to her small bed sinking to her knees, her hands together. "Dear God, could you take me where my sister is? I miss her so much, and it is lonely in this room without her."

Salty tears trickle down her cheeks as she waited for God to answer. No answer.

Peeling off her milk-soaked clothes, her hard bottomed shoes sticking to the wooden floor. Getting to the bathroom, she washes her face and hands, taking off her dress, submerging it in the pail of water.

Wrapped in her too-big flannelette nightgown, Alice walked to the chair that faced the window. Losing herself in the landscape, she begins to count the black and white cows dotting the field beyond, her mind far away.

Thinking back to the birthday party and the princess in her. Her real life was forgotten, left at the door. The kids had been so kind to her, kindness she never knew. And with all the fun she had, a guilty feeling taking over, like it was wrong. Wrong to be happy? To be a happy little girl? Tears formed in her eyes. Staring out the window, she let her mind go blank, back to counting cows.

She couldn't tell her brothers or else Irene would find out about all the fun she had. They just couldn't know it was a real birthday party.

Sprawled out on her bed on her stomach, Alice stared at the big rag doll with the long red braids.

Pearl would undo and braid them again, tying bright yellow ribbons on the ends. Sometimes she would let Alice tie the ribbons. Big blue eyes and cheeks with a circle of pink, freckles dotted them like ink spots. The biggest smile spread across her red plastic lips.

A bright light flooded Alice's mind.

"OK, dolly, I have a plan, and it's just between me and you. From now on, your name will be Pearl." Putting the doll on her lap, she stared into her eyes.

"I want my sister back."

The doll stared back with the same plastic smile, her eyes bright with excitement. Alice goes quiet for a minute.

"So, you just won't be the big rag doll anymore, now you are my sister. Listen," she said, bringing the doll's head close to hers. "I want to tell you about the party today."

Recalling all the events of the day, she told the doll everything. The doll listened and stared, without blinking.

"Can you believe it? Me, the princess of the ball. And you are a princess too, Pearl. I love you."

Kissing the top of the rag doll's head, she hugged her close, falling asleep.

Minutes later, Alice is in dreamland. There she was again. A real princess with a palace of her own. Everything a little girl could want and a mother who loved her. The mother looked like Anne. She wore the same pink lipstick Anne wore at the party. Twirling Alice round and round, dancing and dancing. Her party ended with a bang at the door.

Waking, she rubbed her eyes and looked over at the rag doll.

"Good morning, Pearl." She sat the doll up on the pillow. Getting busy, she readied herself to go down and join her family for breakfast. As she walked around her room, she glanced at the doll and smiled at the thought.

"I will see you later. Take care of Bear. When I get back, we will go over everything I did at school. Goodbye, Pearl. I love you."

Walking out the door, pulling it gently, as to not disturb the inhabitants.

Miss Ink had given Alice a thick pair of red mitts and a hat that she said another student had left behind. Alice put them on right away, her face lighting up.

"I love them, Teacher, and I love you too," she said, her voice getting higher and thinner.

"It is great to be loved by you, Alice. Now run along and get some of your homework done." Heading to her desk right away, Alice gets busy finishing her homework in short notice.

On the way out of the schoolhouse, Miss Ink was waiting, saying her goodbyes to the kids, making sure they were all accounted for. Putting her arms out to hug Alice, who lingered in the hug, laying her head against Mrs. Ink's thin body.

CHAPTER 24

Winter was started to lose its bitter fury, the ground showing in places. There were brown muddy spots in the yard, exposing the softening ground, free from the throws of winter.

It was always around this time of the year that Alice would start thinking of her birthday, and especially this one, now that she had been to a party already. Every little girl had a birthday party, didn't they? Even though she couldn't remember ever having a birthday party.

Miss Ink had whispered, "You will soon have a birthday, Alice. Are you going to have a party?"

"Mom is too busy all the time and probably won't let me have one," answered Alice, looked into her dark loving eyes almost as black as her hair. "My birthday is in twenty days," she announced.

Even Miss Ink thinks I deserve a party, she thought to herself. She would ask her Daddy to see if he would talk to her mother about it.

The birds sang in a chorus; squirrels scampered up the trees. The ground warmed, incubating the grass seedlings. In a bright show of color, flowers reached out their petal hands to the source of all of life, God's face, the sun.

Feeling the warmth of the sun, she tilted her face toward the warmth, like God's kisses.

Lately, Irene hadn't hurt her physically. As with all the other assaults, she hid her pain away in the dark recesses of her mind, trying to send the memories deep, deeper, hidden.

Wishing Pearl was with her to help her plan the party. Her sister's face, always in her mind's eye, angel-like platinum hair. Pearl had never seen a party either. It seemed like she was always sick, spending days on end in her bed. Alice would stay with her as much as possible, even while Pearl slept. Curling up next to Pearl, she could still feel the warmth of her breath on her face.

Spring for Alice meant more time spent outside, away from Irene. Earl and Alice played outside as much as Irene would allow. Earl had been helping her with the water now, since Alice had found an easier way to get it to the house and Irene hadn't scolded Earl for helping her with the wagon.

Wandering in the meadow behind her small wooden house, she picked a few crocuses and violets.

Could she possibly melt the ice from Irene's heart, the way the sunshine was warming hers?

With a big bouquet of yellow and purple crocuses and violets, Alice admired the collection. After arranging them perfectly, pleased with her choices she stepped up to the door, pushing the door in. Irene is standing in front of the sink, suds stuck to the sides of her thick arms.

"These are for you, Mommy," said Alice, holding them straight out in front of her with both hands, searching deep into Irene's cold eyes, the sparkle faded, like the dead flowers she had picked out of the bunch.

Irene raises her arms out of the sink, without wiping the soap from them, grabbing for the bouquet. Already worried about her offering, Alice backed away.

Staring into the flowers, a glazed look in her eyes, Irene spoke. "What do you want me to do with these flowers? You should have left them where you found them. They will just die, and then what?" Shoving them toward Alice, she loosened her wet fingers on them. The flowers fell, scattering on the floor.

Love falling, love shattered.

Bending down on her hands and knees, Alice's tears fall like soft raindrops. Picking each flower up putting the love back together. Holding them gently between her little fingers, she eyed a few loose petals on the floor. Realizing Irene could punish her for the mess on the floor, she bends scooping them up. Keeping her eyes straight ahead, she headed for the staircase to her room.

When safely in, she laid them gently on her bed and headed back downstairs to get a glass to put them in.

Arranging the flowers in the glass, bringing them to the doll to see.

"I brought flowers for you, Pearl. Do you love them? I love flowers," she said, smiling.

Although the bouquet hadn't worked to soften her mother's heart, Alice never stopped trying to win her love.

CHAPTER 25

Miss Ink had the kids doing a project at school. Everyone had to make something to bring home. Alice decided to make knitted cotton squares that could be used for dusting or dishes. Perfect squares of white cotton.

She would wrap them in the silk scarf that Anne had given her. It would be a perfect present for her mother.

"I think your mom will love them," said Miss Ink, looked over Alice's shoulder. All day at school, Alice envisioned the scenario that would unfold, like the scarf being unfolded by Irene. She might say, "Go and do the dishes with them." All kinds of things were going through her mind.

After supper that night, Alice waited until the kitchen was cleaned and Irene had settled into the parlor for some relaxation and a piece of apple cake.

Standing in the archway, between the kitchen and parlor, she held her present like a peace offering.

Approaching Irene, seeking out her mother's eyes.

"I made something for you, Mom, and…"

"Oh, come over here. Let me see," she said, her lips becoming a straight line, with a hint of a smile. Eyeing the blue silk scarf, she unfolded it as Alice watched, holding her breath. The white cotton squares were exposed like fluffy cumulous clouds.

"You made these?"

"Yes, I sure did," answered Alice, waiting nervously.

"First of all, what were they?"

"Well, you can use them for anything,"

All of a sudden she didn't want to tell Irene they were dishcloths.

"They are beautiful," said Irene, holding one to her cheek. "Soft too. Thanks."

"You mean you like them?"

"Yes, yes." Pulling Alice to her bosom she kissed her on the forehead.

Shocked, Alice's eyes widened. Had she really just kissed her?

Before the happiness could drain away, she walked, as if in a trance, toward the staircase.

Irene went back to her cake before she realized that Alice has walked away.

Sitting on the side of her bed, Alice turned to look at the doll.

"Pearl, I just can't believe it. She kissed me, as she put her finger on the spot on her forehead. Maybe she loves me?"

Excited, she grabbed the doll in her arms, hugging her close, putting the rag arms around her neck, she gets up, twirling and twirling around.

The next day after school, she thought it might be a good time to talk to her mother about her birthday and a possible party. The kids came through the door in single file, heading into the dining room straight to the big wooden table. Hungry as jackals, they are looking for the buns with their buttered headed.

"As you can see, children, I am still making the bread you are looking for. Go outside and play or find something to do. The bread will not be ready till the morning."

Alice stopped at the counter and looked up at her mother, elbow-deep in the flour as though she has long white gloves on.

"Now is not the time, child. As you can see I am busy. What is it? Spit it out."

"I just wanted to ask you about my birthday, Mom. It's in a few days."

"And another year older, what?"

"Just go and do your chores. That's what you need to do."

With a deep sigh, Alice walked toward the door, her head hanging. How was she ever going to be able to ask for a party?

After walking back into the house with seven eggs in the small basket, Alice set them on the counter next to where Irene is moulding some dough into biscuits.

Standing behind her mother now, her head cocked to the side.

"Mommy," she said, placing her finger to her lips. "Could I have a… birthday party? Mommy," Alice pleaded, her eyes growing smaller, wrinkles appearing on the top of her cheeks. "The teacher said that all little girls have birthday parties."

Irene's eyes grew wide, staring deep into Alice's forest-green eyes. She said nothing, lost for a few moments, like she was walking into a dense forest.

"Absolutely not, and just why do you think that you somehow deserve a party? Young lady, life is no party. No party for me, never was, never will be. We can't afford the fancy things like the Jeffersonses. See what your dad has gone and done now, put stars in your eyes."

"Shoo, now get out and wait till suppertime." Pointing her index finger, toward the door.

Running straight to the chicken coop, Alice threw herself on the straw bales in the corner of the small shed.

Tears cascaded down her face like raindrops on a windowpane, without sound.

Why had she even asked? The answer was already written in stone, as hard as Irene's heart. "Why doesn't she love me? I am her only little girl. Doesn't she like having a little girl? I'm a good girl too. Oh God, please… please…make her love me," she prayed out loud.

The bandy rooster flew on top of one of the bales, making his soft coooooing sound. Straightening up, wiping the tears from her cheeks.

He fluffed his feathers and looked straight at her as if to say, "I love you."

The dark cloud of sadness started to lift, bringing back her smile. She picked up the pitchfork and started to clean the coop. The rooster showed he loved her, and she would make his house clean and nice for him.

Just then her Daddy poked his head in, looking for her.

"Would you like to go to the dairy with me while I finish up some chores?"

"Oh, yes, Daddy. It will only took me a few minutes, and I'll be right there."

William waited in the yard, busying himself with cutting some wood.

Irene was peering out the small window over the sink. She watched as William held Alice's hand, as they took off toward the barns. Her stomach tightened to knots. She hated the love William showed Alice. There was no love for either of them, or for herself for that matter. She hated herself and her life.

When they made it back from the dairy, Irene and the boys were already sitting at the table, the hungry eyes all staring at their father and sister. Irene didn't pay them any mind but continued to pass the bowls of buttered potatoes and green peas.

"Come and sit next to Daddy," William ushered, motioning to Alice.

"But that is Skip's seat. He is still in the shed getting wood," interrupted Irene. "Where will he sit then? Alice has her seat at the sewing machine. That's where she always sits."

"No, Irene, tonight she sits next to me, Skip can sit there."

William surprised even himself. He had found his voice. Clearing his throat, he picked up Alice's plate and started to put her supper together. Mashed potatoes, a spoonful of green peas, and a slice of moose meat with brown shiny gravy. Next he picked one of the golden biscuits and placed the plate in front of Alice.

"There you are, princess. I want you to eat everything, OK? We don't waste food around here."

All the boys had slowed their eating, looking at each other then back at their father and mother. Irene, her head down cutting up her moose meat into small pieces. When she heard the word *princess*, the knife scraped the bottom of the plate, like fingernails on a chalkboard.

"And I think we should thank the Lord for this meal," said William.

Everyone put down their knives and forks. Irene's head rose, making eye contact with Will. Bowing his head, he began.

"Please, Lord, keep this family in your embrace. Show us how to love each other more."

At this point Irene pushed her chair from the table and walked to the sink, staring out.

As he finished the prayer, Amen was passed from the boys like a thank you to their dad for stepping up.

Without paying any attention to her, everyone digs into their meal. The room is silent but for the lip smacking.

"Thank you, Daddy, for letting me sit next to you, and I love the supper."

"You need to thank your mother for that. She is the one that does all the work preparing the food."

"Thank you, Mom," said Alice, looked over at Irene, who is still standing with her back to them. No answer.

Coming back to the head of the table, Irene digs into her meal.

Alice and William exchanged a few smiles. The love in the air was giving Irene's supper a bitter taste.

Just then Alice piped up, her voice on high.

"Daddy, Daddy. I was wondering…" Irene's eyes darted to Alice, shooting arrows her way. William had stopped eating and was looking at Alice, waiting for her to finish what she was saying.

"My birthday is in a few days, and I would really like to have a birthday party."

The room took on a dead silence, all movement to the lips stopped.

Looking deep into Alice's soft, moss green eyes, he said, "I don't see why not. A girl has to have a party once in a while. I don't recall this house ever seeing a party. Maybe it's time it did. What do you say, Irene? It would be good for the kids, and I can get some ice cream from the dairy."

Irene's eyes lowered from Will as she pushed herself hard away from the table. The boys get back to eating, a heaviness, like a wool blanket in water, stilled the air.

Irene headed towards her room. Alice heard the thud of her footsteps on the wood floor. Stewing mad, she sat on the side of her bed. How dare she go over her head to ask her father about this stupid birthday? *She will pay. I will show her who is boss,* sweat beading on her forehead. When she could gather herself, she went back to the table and picked up some of the dishes to take them to the sink.

Alice is talking to her brothers circled around her.

"Ice cream, cake, and cookies, and balloons. It will be a great party."

They stare at each other and then back at Alice, each parting their separate ways.

CHAPTER 26

The Birthday Party

"So, you are going to be seven," the teacher mentioned. "Are you having a party? Are you inviting some of the kids from school?"

"I really don't know," answered Alice.

A look of concern crossed Miss Ink's face. "Don't eat too much cake. I think you are sweet enough already."

Alice chuckled, getting back to her school work.

It seemed like Sunday would never come. The days dragged.

Just having her brothers and her dad at her party was good enough. When it came time to ask the kids from school to come to her house, she decided against it. Her house was too small and other reasons.

Sunday morning arrived. Awakening, the sunshine greeted her through the window, casting long shadows on the wooden plank floor.

"Wake up, Pearl, it's my birthday," she sang, picking up the big doll in her arms. "I will bring cookies and milk for you and me, and we will have our own party."

She never took her doll outside of her room. She wanted to keep her safe, where no one could hurt her or steal her. The doll meant everything now: love, comfort, and the best friend in the world.

As she readied herself, making her bed perfectly, brushing her hair, she nervously continued to talk to the doll, who sits on the pillow listening to every word.

Today she would wear one of the pretty dresses she had inherited from Pearl. With her ear to the door, listening, to make sure, no one was near, going back to her bed, she pulls up the side of the mattress.

Choosing a baby blue chiffon, with a bodice of eyelet lace and a satin ribbon decorating the waist. Holding it up against her thin body she eyed the doll.

"What do you think, Pearl? Do you like this one? I think it will be perfect for a birthday girl." With nervous chatter, she continued talking to the doll as she dressed herself. Slipping on the doll shoes and white anklet socks she surveyed herself.

"Just like a princess," she said out loud.

The doll smiled.

Sitting down at the window, overlooked the meadow. The sun beamed its warmth into the day and into her heart, taking her back to her dream.

Hearing a stir of chairs around the breakfast table, the alarm for her to get ready to make her entrance downstairs. Would they all be waiting for the birthday girl? Would they sing "Happy Birthday" to her as she descended the staircase?

Starting her desent down the stairs in her shoes, *clack, clack, clack.* Alice counting in her head. One, two, three, four, five… When she hit the tenth stair, she looked up, expecting all her brothers, mother, and dad to be waiting for her. No one in the kitchen but Irene.

Taking the last step down, Alice let go of the banister and headed to the kitchen. "Good morning, Mom," she whispered. Irene standing with her back to her.

"What's so good about it?" she scowled, turning around. "You are all dressed already? Going nowhere. What are you doing? Get your head out of the clouds. Have you lost your mind? Get back upstairs, and get your overalls on," Irene ordered.

Turning on her heel, holding the edge of her dress, she hurried up the stairs as fast as her hard-bottomed shoes could take her. When she gets into her room, she gasped for breath.

Why didn't I remember, even if it is my birthday, I still have chores to do? No one is going to do my chores just because it's my birthday.

Had her daydream of being a princess as she dressed, taken her into a trance? Wasting no time, she takes the dress off, replacing it with her overalls and a sweater.

Hoping she hadn't already upset her mother. Nothing could go wrong today, her special day, straight to the door and out into the yard. The sun kissed her face. Taking in a deep breath, the fresh smell of spring in the air. The chickens were happy to see her, following her as she scattered the feed on the ground. Her dad passed her with an armful of wood.

"Good morning, princess, do you feel older today?"

"Oh no, Daddy, not older, just smarter. Miss Ink tells me I am smart for a little girl."

Will smiled at her quick comeback and kept on going. A few of her brothers passed her on the way to the coop.

"Happy birthday," said Skip as he went his way. Her heart swelled. Everyone was being so nice to her today.

The smile seemed glued in place as she diligently finished up her chores. Earl joined her in the water duty, holding the pails while she pulled the wagon.

"Are there any other kids coming?" he asked.

"I didn't ask any of them, just in case Mom was not in a good mood."

"I understand. I suppose we will have enough of us to have a party anyway," he commented.

"Yes." She smiled.

With her chores completed, she goes back upstairs to put on her party dress one more time, then back downstairs to seek out Irene, who is busy with her hands in the sink.

"Mommy," she said quietly, cocking her head to one side. "Can we make cookies and cake? I can help."

Irene spun around on her heel.

"Look at you. Dressed like you are going to church or something. And where did you get that dress? It's way too big for you. Suppose Anne gave it to you. We are not rich like them. How dare she put things in your head?"

"But, Mommy, it's my birthday. I want to look special and feel special too."

"Here it is, nine o'clock in the morning, and you are dressed like you think you are a princess or something. There are no princesses in this story. Have a good look around. This is no palace, and you are not a princess."

As her heart sinks, just staring at Irene as the words coming out of her mouth go on mute.

And this is the story of the wicked mother, a forbidden thought.

Irene is shaking her finger in Alice's face now, grabbing her arm, digging her fingers in, leaving red marks on Alice's tender skin.

"Get outside now. And don't come back in till I call you, do you hear me?"

Before Irene could get the last words out, Alice runs out into the yard, across the meadow, into her dream world.

Sitting down on a dry piece of fallen tree, she can see her shanty house in the distance.

"Alice has a palace, Alice has a palace," she said out loud. A blue bird flew by, catching her eye.

"Today you won't make me sad, Mommy. Today is my day, my birthday." The birds are singing, the beauty abounds around her, the sun kissing her face, under a spell of happy her mind far away.

After a couple of hours of playing in the yard, talking to her brothers, with no sign of Irene coming for her, Alice decided it was time to find out about making cookies and things. If there was going to be a party, they had to get busy.

Hurrying into the house, there is no sign of Irene in the kitchen, Alice finding her in the parlor, a needle in her hand, mending a shirt.

"Mommy, can we make cookies now? I have done all my chores," giving Irene a crooked half smile.

"OK, just give me a few more minutes while I finish this mending, then we will get started. Go to the kitchen, find a big bowl, and get out the oats, brown sugar, peanut butter, and some eggs."

"Sure, right away," she answered, running into the kitchen.

When she had everything on the table, she hurries outside to tell Earl.

"Mom is letting me help make peanut butter cookies. And we are having ice cream and cake too. Oh, Earl, I am so excited," she said in a high-pitched voice. "OK, got to go." Waving at him, she runs back into the house.

Irene is standing at the table, waiting for her.

"Here, put this on. Don't want to spoil your pretty dress. Hurry now, I am in the middle of ironing a heap of shirts and things."

The apron strings are long, and she struggled to tie them, Irene coming up behind her.

"Here, let me help you." Grabbing the ends, Irene catches two of her fingertips. "Owww," squealed Alice.

"Oh, come on now," answered Irene.

Irene ties the ends tightly in a knot, the whites of her eyes showing, her teeth clenched.

Going to the cupboard Irene takes out the baking soda and salt, bringing them to the table.

"Count out six eggs, and break them in a bowl. Can you do that?"

"Yes, Mother," she answered. Irene goes back to her ironing, keeping one eye on Alice, a white heap of shirts sit at the end of the ironing board.

Eying the ingredients like a chess game, waiting for Irene's orders, ready for the next move.

"Put the butter in the bowl. Now add one cup of brown sugar, just a couple of handfuls. For your hands, four will do." The sugar jar was a wide-mouth glass jar with a tin top.

Her little fingers dive into the sugar, the round brown beads sticking to her hand, a strong smell of molasses wafted out.

"Drop the sugar into the butter and use the big wooden spoon to stir them together. Now put in the eggs. Then beat them, and beat them until the whole thing is smooth like butter. Next put in five big spoonfuls of peanut butter. Lastly a pinch of soda and salt, then three cups of flour. Add a cup of milk, then mix it and mix it."

Sitting beside the big silver bowl, Alice stirred with both hands. The thickness of the batter made it hard to do, but she uses all of her might, watching Irene out of the corner of her eye.

Irene was also watching every move of her only girl child, her eyes seeing, her heart blinded.

Going back into the kitchen, Irene reached into a bottom cupboard and pulled out a flat pan, placing it on the table next to the bowl.

"Butter the pan now. Just use your fingers, and make sure there is a little butter everywhere, so the cookies don't stick. Now make little round balls and then put them on the cookie sheet. You should have twenty round balls. Then use a fork to smash their little heads down, leaving the print of the fork on their heads."

An uneasy feeling crept into Alice's mind. Why would her mother say it that way? Making cookies wasn't supposed to be scary.

Her head raised, she looks straight at Irene. The instructions taking on a new tone. Searching her mother's face for clues, Alice gets busy with the job at hand. Smashing down all the heads, all bearing the print of the fork.

Admiring her handiwork, she walks toward Irene with the cookie tray in her hands. The cookies are spaced all the way down, with one left over, crowded between two others.

"Put them in the oven now," Irene instructed, pointing to the woodstove. A heavy cast iron sits on top, an ember glow around the edges.

Opening the oven door, Alice is careful to put the cookie sheet in the middle and closed the door.

Irene heads toward the door, pulling on her sweater.

"I am going up to the dairy to talk to your dad. See about getting that ice cream he promised." Giving Alice a plastic smile like the one on the clown face. A frown crossed her forehead. The door banged shut.

The wonderful smells of peanut butter and sugar filled the board house. Alice looked over the table settings, eleven sets of knives and forks and spoons.

Irene had set the table. A glass vase in the middle of the table, with one single plastic yellow rose.

Mmm, thought Alice. *Wow, she did this all for me?* Her brow furrowed, her mind blank.

The smell of the cookies is teasing her appetite. She'd missed breakfast with all the fuss about changing and chores. Irene had everything cleared from the table by the time she finished. Her belly rumbled, the smell of the peanut butter makes her mouth water.

Carefully, she slid the cookies out of the oven with the two large mitts. Just then, Irene comes back in through the door, watching as Alice puts the hot pan on the table.

"Be careful now. Don't burn yourself," Irene warned, her voice reaching a higher octave.

"No, Mommy, I am being careful."

"There is a platter over there you can put the cookies on. Leave them until after dinner. Do you hear me? No eating the cookies. They are for your party."

"My party. Right. Don't worry, Mom, I won't eat any," she answered, swallowing hard.

Arranging the cookies, perfectly spaced, exactly five in each line, and four lines of five. It equalled... She quickly counted to twenty.

And one extra one, she registered, as she put the last one on the platter. Surely she wouldn't miss just one.

Keeping her eyes on the door, she puts the cookie in her pocket. She would go somewhere and eat it where no one would see. Nervously, she rearranged the cookies again so they looked perfect when Irene comes back through the door. The frightened look on Alice's face told of the deceit.

"What have you done, Alice? You look like the rat that swallowed the mouse." Her mouth is thick with guilt; her eyes like a scared rabbit.

"You little thief. Just how many have you eaten?"

"Oh no, Mother. You see there was..."

Irene runs her hands down Alice's sweater into her pocket and pulls out the cookie.

"What did I tell you before I left? Didn't I tell you not to eat any of the cookies!" Screaming into Alice's face. "You just had to go and disobey me."

As Irene's tone of voice grew harsher, Alice's eyes wide with fright.

Cowering, she tried to back away from the table.

"But, Mommy, really, I didn't eat any. I just took the extra one. I..."

"Never you mind," said Irene. "Just for that your birthday party is cancelled, as of right now."

Alice slid down the wall, her world crumbling around her. Sobbing holding her face in her hands.

"Get up off that floor now! You look so stupid sitting there in your fancy dress. Guess you aren't worried about it now. Some princess you are. No princess at all. You are nothing but a thief. Get up to the table, sit there, and wait for your punishment."

Scared, Alice gets up going to the table. Pulliing out a chair she watched as Irene goes toward the woodstove. Grabbing the heavy iron, its bottom glowing hot, rushing towards her.

In horror, her screams escaped her lips, trying to alert someone. Almost breathless at first, then growing into a high-pitched siren. Trying to get away from the table, slipping under, one of her little hands still on the table, when Irene brings down the hot iron onto Alice's fingers. A scream that could peel the paint, bounced off the walls and into the yard, over the rolling hills, settling on God's ears. With the smell of burning flesh, Irene comes out of her state of madness, running back to the stove, she drops the iron.

Earl was outside whittling when he heard the screams that were undoubtedly from his sister. What had she done to her?

Dropping his pocket knife and the piece of wood he is carving, he runs into the house. Irene is standing near the stove, a blank look on her face. Then he notices Alice, curled into a ball under the table, still screaming.

"You are nothing but a lowly thief, Alice!" screamed Irene when she noticed Earl now trying to get to his sister.

"Oh my gosh, what is wrong?" Staring at his mother now, his eyes narrowed. "What have you done to her, Mother?" he cried.

"Nothing at all. She burned herself on the hot stove, taking out the cookies. I told her to be careful. She is careless, that is all. And don't you yell at me, young man, before you get a whipping in the woodshed!"

Bending down to pick up his little sister, the front of her dress wet with tears. Putting her little shaking hand out to him, red raw flesh on all four of her fingers, a large water blister on the top of her hand.

"Oh my God," Earl cried now, his own tears melting into hers. "We have to get Dad. Let's get you out to the block of ice in the shed." Almost carrying her, he struggled to get her to the door. Just then Skip came through the door.

"Help me get Alice out to the ice block. She has burned herself badly. Where is Dad? I don't see him yet."

"I think he is still at the dairy," answered Skip, a frightened look on his face.

"Please, run and get him now," begged Earl.

Skip brushed his thick red hair off his forehead and wasted no time, taking off at a full gallop toward the dairy.

Irene is staring out the window over the sink, a glazed look in her eyes, blankness on her face, like a blackboard without any chalk marks. She watches Skip running towards the dairy.

Alice held her little hand on the ice block, whimpering, her eyes closed tightly. She goes limp in Earl's arms, her eyes closed.

"Oh my God, please, someone help me," he cried. Unable to move, her head on his chest, realizing Alice has passed out.

Skip comes flying into the shed. "Dad will be here as soon as he closes up the barns. What happened to Alice?"

"Mom burned her. Oh my God, her fingers are raw. Just look. She said Alice burned herself taking the cookies out of the oven, but there is no way she would have gotten such bad burns."

Shaking his head, his eyes wide, Skip eyed her fingers.

"What do we do? Just wait for Dad and see what he says, I guess. I sure don't want to go into that house."

Skip paced up and down and kept looking out the shed door.

After about ten minutes, Alice started to come to.

"Alice, Alice, are you OK? Skip and I are here with you. We are waiting for Dad to come from the dairy. You are going to have to tell him what really happened. What happened? You can tell us. We are not going to tell Mom."

"Mommy burned me with the iron. She said I was a thief and put the iron on my fingers. Owwww," she cried.

"OK, just be still and keep your hand on the ice."

Earl chipped away at the block of ice, getting half a pail full.

"You have got to keep your hand in this ice. I know it will hurt at first, but it will take away the pain."

Wincing, she puts her hand in the pail while he gently gathered the ice shards around her fingers. Looking deep into her sad green eyes, Earl is saddened deeper. His poor little baby sister.

"No, no, you can't tell Dad. Then she will punish me more. No, Earl, you have to promise not to tell. Like she said, I burned myself on the stove."

Earl shakes his head, his eyes red. "I just can't believe she did this to you. And today is your birthday. I hate her so much. She is a bad mother. I hate her. I hate her so much!"

Bringing her head to his chest, he runs his hand over her hair, trying to wipe the tears from her face. Turning her face to him, she manages a glimmer of a smile.

"It's started not to hurt, Earl."

Earl has a good look at her little hand. It is swollen, to double the thickness. The skin is brown and crusted. Her reddened flesh shows through on all her fingers that are swollen together.

"We will have to stay here with your fingers on the ice so the pain doesn't come back. When Dad gets home he will know what to do."

"And she said my birthday party is cancelled." A faraway look in her green eyes.

Deep in the forest, there were lots of places to hide. Beautiful birds to see and flowers to pick.

Her hand slipped out of the pail, the pain coming back in waves. Staring down at her hand, the skin on her fingers wrinkled and red. Blisters starting to form on her fingers too.

"How will I print now? How will I go to school? The teacher can't see my fingers like this. I have to go to school, I…" She started crying now, an elongated whine. Her whines turned to whimpering as she immersed her hand back in the bucket of ice.

The other boys all came running to see what the commotion was. Irene is standing on the steps, talking to them.

"You boys come in soon for supper. There is no party going on here. Your sister burned herself on the stove taking the cookies out of the oven."

They glanced at each other, then back at Irene, saying nothing, filing into the house, heading to the table.

Earl walked with Alice, carrying the pail she has her hand in. Irene is watching out of the corner of her eye when they come through the door, standing squarely in front of them. Earl met her stare, glaring into her hard, cold eyes.

"Don't worry, Mother," he whispered. "Your secret is safe with me. But God sees everything."

"Who asked you, you stupid boy? Just like your sister. Both of you get out of my sight. And just for that, no supper for you either, Earl."

Without answering, he walked beside Alice, getting her to the foot of the stairs. Being careful to not spill the bucket of ice, they climb the stairs together, into her room, to her cot.

Sitting down next to her placing the bucket of ice close to her feet.

"Just put your hand right in here when it starts to hurt too much. I am going to find Dad and get him up here to wrap your hand, OK? I love you," he said putting his skinny arm around her shoulder. Alice looks at him adoringly.

"I am going downstairs now to wait for Dad, OK?" Heading out he gently closes the door.

Upon getting to the bottom of the stairs, he notices his brothers around the table, Irene passing around the bowls. Walking out of the house, he goes into the shed. Supper was the last thing he wanted anyway. The sadness had taken his appetite. If his baby sister wasn't eating, neither was he.

The seven boys sat at their designated places at the table. They weren't the hungry bunch that usually greeted Irene. A sadness had settled over the dining room table, robbing them of their appetites. They just stared at one another, then back at their empty plates.

Irene had placed a few bowls on the table. Mashed potatoes. Coined buttered carrots and a plate of meatloaf, ten pieces cut.

There were no takers. Irene stared at them now.

"What, my food is not good enough for you? Don't look so forlorn. It was just a stupid birthday party. And your sister is a thief, and so careless, burning herself." They say nothing, just started to pass around the food, their eyes expressionless.

"That is what happens to a thief," said Irene, not making eye contact with any of them. "Just make that a lesson for all of you." Trudging away from the table, going to stand near sink, Irene staring out the little window.

Just then the door opened. William enters the house. There is a chill in the air. Dead silence. No birthday sounds, no laughter, like a circus without children. Irene didn't turn to greet him. He looked from her back to the boys at the table. No sign of Alice. A knot winds in his stomach, something is terribly wrong.

"Where is everyone? Did you guys have the party without me?"

"There will be no party here tonight, William, sorry to tell you," said Irene, her hands on her wide hips.

"Your daughter is a thief. She has been sent to her room. She burned herself badly on the stove."

"What are you saying, woman? How did she get burned?"

"On the stove, as usual. She is never paying attention, always has her head in the clouds."

"No, Irene, I want the truth! What happened?" he demanded. The boys all focused on their father, not the meek one they all knew, his voice loud, accusing.

"She is upstairs," said one of them.

William stared up the staircase, worried for his little angel. Scared of what he would find, he started up the wooden stairs, his head hanging in sadness.

With every step he took up the stairs, his heart broke apart a little more, leaving it hanging in shreds, afraid to see his little girl.

Grabbing for the handle, William heard Alice talking.

Everyone was downstairs. Who was in Alice's room with her? Putting his ear to the door, he could hear her high-pitched voice.

"Yes, it is true. Mommy did this to me. She burned my fingers with the hot iron on the woodstove. I don't know why she hurts me, Pearl." She started to whine again, a cry ripping through William's broken heart. His eyes filled with tears. Quietly he turned the door handle and stepped into the room. Alice was holding up her burned hand, showing it to the big rag doll, who is staring straight at Alice.

"Oh, gosh, Daddy." Her tears started to fall harder now.

"What have you done, child?" Alarm written on his face.

He walked closer. Taking her little hand in his, he looked down at the skin peeled off most of her hand with water-filled blisters, her little fingers three times their normal size. A quiet whine escaped his lips as he hugged her to him.

"I—I burned myself, Daddy," she started.

"Never mind, princess, I know what really happened. I heard you telling someone before I came in the door. Who were you talking to? You called her Pearl."

"Yes, Daddy, I just miss her so that…"

"Don't say another thing," he said putting his finger to her lips. "Sit still while I go and get some bandages. I'll be right back."

"OK, Daddy," she answered, her eyes glued to his like she never wanted to let him out of her sight.

Hurrying, William ran down the staircase, straight to the cupboard, pulling out the first-aid kit. Irene noticed him but didn't look his way, just kept stuffing her face with the potatoes and meatloaf.

Back with Alice in her room, he dressed her hand and fingers with a thick salve, wrapping fresh white gauze bandage over the whole hand, right to the wrist. Pulling her close to him, he wrapped his arms around her, wishing he could never let her go. Feeling so insecure now about how to protect his little angel, looking deep into her compelling green eyes.

"You know, Alice, sometimes we can't change a thing about our lives, as much as we would like to, but be reassured that those who are hurting God's people, the ones he loves, will pay dearly one day. They will feel the wrath of the Lord. God does not like bad people, and he is watching all the time. If we could change the hand we were dealt, we would surely ask for another. In which case, everything would be perfect. But this is not a perfect world and never will be. I am so sorry that Mommy is mean to you, my angel. I believe your mother has something wrong in her head." He pointed to his own head. "I will make sure she never hurts you again."

"No, no, Daddy, don't say that. You mustn't tell her that you heard me telling the doll. I know she will punish me more, please…please."

"Just don't worry your pretty head, princess." Hugging her tight, he stared into her eyes streaked with red lines. The sadness of her eyes made him think of the injustice Jesus had suffered at the hands of the ungodly.

"I'll tell you what. I will bring my supper up here, and we will share it. How does that sound?"

"Oh yes, Daddy, I would love it." Her eyes brightened.

Sitting perfectly still, she pulled the big doll over to sit on her lap. Hugging the doll, she lay down and pulled the thin grey blanket over them.

Her father's footsteps descending the staircase, the heaviness and his gait telling of his despair.

He went straight to the table, where the boys and Irene were finishing up their supper. Staring at Irene at the head of the table, William took his seat at the opposite end. Not making a move, he continued to stare her way till she finally had to meet his gaze.

"You are a wicked woman," he said. "If I would have known that my life would have turned out like this with you, I would have kept walking and never looked back. You are a disgrace for a mother. I can't believe…"

His voice grew deeper and the words more mechanical. "I can't believe that you would burn a helpless child, your only daughter."

Irene gets up from the table, picking up her plate walking toward the sink, where she stays with her back to everyone.

"May God have mercy on your soul? You think that you would have learned better behavior being brought up in a convent."

"Just a minute," she said, spinning around. "Before you get ahead of yourself, she is lying, I did nothing of the sort. The girl burned herself on the oven. Earl was here when it happened. Weren't you, Earl?" She met Earl's eyes now, and silence fell like a frozen lake over the room.

"Mother, I didn't see anything. I just walked in the house and heard Alice screaming. I don't know what happened."

"Not only that," said Irene, "I don't suppose she told you she was stealing cookies. The very ones she was baking for the party."

In disgust, William shook his head. "You are pathetic. Just shut up now! And just for the record, Alice didn't tell me anything, I heard her talking to her doll through the door. I know the whole story. And I think it's time your sons all know what you did to Alice. Burned her with the hot iron. Her little hand is three times the size, and all the skin is burned, her flesh raw."

Irene's eyes grew larger with every word.

All the boys hung their heads, already knowing the wickedness of her.

She had lashed out at all of them on occasion, but Alice had become her chosen victim.

Standing at the sink, her hands on her squared wide hips, she squinted her eyes in hate and guilt. No more words came from her, watching as William fixed two plates of food.

Filling them both with mashed potatoes, coined carrots, and meatloaf with gravy. Reaching for two buns, he put one on each plate with a dollop of butter on top. Pouring two glasses of milk, he placed it all on a silver platter they had received as a wedding gift. Never had he seen Irene use it for anything but a decoration. Swallowing hard, Irene had to turn before she started yelling or ripping out her hair. How dare he use her silver platter? It had never been used for food.

Walking into Alice's room, William announced with a smile, "We are going to have our own birthday party, Alice, just you and me."

"Wow, Daddy, let's put it down over here," she said, beckoning him to a small table near the window. "Here, Daddy, you sit here."

"Oh no, you sit there, princess, I will have mine sitting on your bed."

Alice started to eat her birthday supper. Bringing up her bandaged hand, she realized she could not butter the bun or cut her meat, looking helplessly at William. He smiled.

"Oh my dear, Daddy will do that for you."

They ate in silence, Alice staring out the window to a faraway place.

William picked at his food, his appetite taken by the sadness of his heart.

"I'll be right back. Going to get us some cookies."

Just as he entered the kitchen, Irene was finishing up the dishes. The platter of cookies was on the counter. About half the cookies are left.

"I'll be taking these," he said. "After all, Alice did make them, and it is her birthday."

"Do as you will. You just keep spoiling her. She will end up to be nothing."

"What, just like you, Irene?"

What? Had he really just told her she was nothing?

Grumbling under her breath, she got back to the dishes, her feet planted like a deep rooted tree, her jaw set in hate. A hissing sound escaped her lips, like a snake ready to strike. She just couldn't believe he had just said she was nothing.

The day had ended horribly, with everyone retiring to their places, trying to erase the events of the day. William made himself a bed on the threadbare couch, the lumps and bumps made his sleep come in intervals. His mind was on Alice and how she was sleeping with the bulk of the bandages he had put on her hand.

The alarm woke the household. A steady stream of boys into the bathroom and then downstairs. They congregated at the table, waiting for the offerings of their mother.

This morning Irene had fixed the only staple they had in the house. Porridge. There was a bowl of brown sugar sitting in the middle of the table and a pitcher with milk. After stirring the thick porridge in the pot, she then transferred it to a big silver bowl. She put a wooden spoon into the centre of the bowl. The spoon stood on its own.

Without words, William took his place at the foot of the table, then greeted each of his sons with a smile and a nod of his head.

"Good morning, Father," they all said in unison.

William kept his eyes focused on the bottom of the staircase that he could see from where he sat.

This morning William had gone to the shed and brought in a stool.

He'd sat it just to his left, between him and Earl. Staring down at the stool, Earl could feel the thickness of the air in the house. He knew his dad had brought it in for Alice so she could sit next to him.

"We will be waiting for my daughter this morning," William announced, looking straight at Irene, a stern look in his eyes.

"We always wait for her. What other lies has she been telling you?"

"None whatsoever," he answered watching toward the staircase.

Everyone was now staring, as the pitter patter of hard-bottomed shoes sounded on the wooden steps.

In her head she counted one, two, and three…until she reached the bottom. Appearing in the archway, Alice searched out her father's eyes. A big smile for him, brightened the day, William's heart swelling.

"Good morning everyone," she said, in a voice as though an angel had descended as she came in full view of the big table where her brothers and father were seated.

"Good morning," the boys all said, as though in announcement to Irene's keen ears.

"Good morning, Alice," said Irene, not looking at her daughter. "You look older today."

William shook his head at that comment.

"Good morning, Mother," she answered, hanging her head.

"Well, now that the princess has honored us with her presence, can we have breakfast?" Irene said sarcastically. "William, don't you have to be going soon? I thought you had some early things to take care of today?"

"I will be going shortly," he answered, not looking her way.

"There is only porridge for breakfast," Irene said. "The chickens haven't been laying."

"We will be fine with what the good Lord has given us. And we all love porridge, don't we boys? And Alice too," he said with a big smile for her.

"Would you like to stay home today, Alice?" asked Irene. Everyone rose their head to see where this was going. "I am making some apple pies today and could use your help."

Alice looked her mother in the eyes, a look of wonderment on her cherub face.

"Mother, I would love to make pies, but…"

Just then she brought up her bandaged hand and put it on the table, only the tips of her pinkies showing. There was an aww from her brothers. Irene eyed the bandaged hand, and then her eyes met William's.

"You should just be more careful around the stove, Alice."

William stood up, pushing his chair away from the table.

"That is just enough from you, Irene. I won't sit here listening to your lies anymore! Don't think you can fool the boys, neither. We are all wise to you."

"It's OK, Daddy," Alice spoke up in a little voice, looking her mother's way. "My hand feels much better today, and I am sure in a few days it will be just like new."

Irene hung her head in guilt, her eyes widened, staring into the floorboards.

"My hand hurt me all night, and I couldn't go to sleep, so I am really sleepy now. Do you think I could go back to my room and stay there all day?" she asked, looking from her mother to her dad. William eyed Irene.

"Yes, Alice, that is fine. I will call you for supper, and you can have some of the apple pie," answered Irene. William watched with a half smirk on his face at the unfolding deception of Irene's acceptance of Alice's request.

Getting up from the table, Alice addressed her brothers.

"Please tell Miss Ink I burned my hand and that I will be to school tomorrow." Waving her good hand at everyone, she curtsied and headed toward the staircase, to the peaceful serenity of her make-believe world, her doll, and God.

From that day on, William promised himself that he would not stand by and watch Irene hurt his little girl anymore. He loathed her. Coming straight home from work, eating his supper in silence, then to his room to shut her out.

He thought about all the telltale signs he hadn't paid attention to. Too busy with work, he'd let her take charge of the children.

What damage had she already done to the child? He wondered.

The power to rule with a fist was effective and so damaging to a child's mind, frightening Alice so, that she never let on that Irene was abusing her regularly.

Alice rested, played with her doll, and looked out the window to the outside world.

"God, one day could you please make this life better, and can you deal me a different hand? God, that's what my daddy said, we have a bad hand. Well, really now I do have a bad hand. Mommy burned me, God. Well, I guess you already know, because Daddy said that you see everything. I love you, God, and I know that you are looking after Pearl. Just don't tell her that I call the rag doll Pearl. There will never be another Pearl, but I just miss her so much, I am just pretending. Make it all better, God, so I can print and play again."

Holding her doll close, she slept in her small cot all afternoon.

CHAPTER 27
The Day Alice Was Born

The doctor took the naked baby, immersing her in warm water and then into cold water, but there were still no cries, no breath. Rocking her back and forth for a few minutes, then putting his lips to the little rosebud mouth, he tried to blow the breath of life into the baby, again and again. Still no cries. "Mrs. Purple, I am sorry to tell you that your baby is dead." He laid the naked, lifeless baby on the bed.

"Wrap the baby in a blanket," he ordered the midwife. Carefully swathing the baby in a soft pink blanket, tucking the triangle of cloth down over her head, she handed the baby back to the doctor.

Just then, a tiny squeak came from the bundle.

"My God, I think she is alive," he announced. Unraveling the baby from the tightly wound blanket, staring into her little face, the pink returning to her cheeks, the baby starts to squirm and cry.

"Your baby is alive, Mrs. Purple. A beautiful baby girl," he announced.

Irene turned her back to the doctor, mumbling something under her breath.

CHAPTER 28

Alice Was Ten Now

Alice grew prettier every day, learning new survival skills. Still dressing in Pearl's hand-me-down clothes as she hadn't grown much taller.

They fitted her perfectly now. Wearing the dresses and things made Alice feel a closeness to Pearl. Sometimes she thought she could feel the warmth of her sister's breath on her face. Just like when they lay in the bed together at night, when she read stories to Alice.

The big rag doll was still her best friend and confidante.

The doll had a few new things Alice had knit for her. Miss Ink let the kids do projects that they could take home. A pink pair of slippers, a sweater, and a hat to match. They looked lovely on the doll. Alice didn't talk to the doll quite as much these days, just a few things, like good morning, goodbye, and love you.

Irene continued to punish her for little things. She made her do most of the housework, the dishes, mopping the floors. After walking to and from school, then home to start the grueling housework, exhausted at the end of the day.

One good thing was her aunt Rita was coming around more often, inviting Alice to spend some weekends at her place. Irene ran out of excuses for why she couldn't go and gave in once in a while to cover up her abuse. Rita lived a twenty-minute ride down the road. She had a horse and buggy, which was such a treat for Alice.

One sunny afternoon Alice is sitting in the grass behind the house brushing her hair and singing to herself when Irene interrupted her peace.

"Alice, you need to have your hair cut today. Skip said there is lice at school, and everyone will be getting their hair cut. We don't have the money for the fancy stuff to kill them, and the eggs they lay in your hair."

"Oh no, Mommy, I don't have any bugs in my hair. I brush my hair one hundred times every day, and no bugs could stay in my hair."

"You heard what I said, girl, you will be getting a haircut, and that is final."

Turning, Irene walked back to the house, the inside of her fat thighs rubbing together, her movements labored.

Tears run down Alice's face, staining her cheeks.

Watching her mother from behind, her drab grey dress swaying from side to side.

How could she possibly be spared this hair cut? She would run away to her Aunt Rita's house, but surely Irene would send her brothers to get her.

"Oh, why, God?" Couldn't he just show himself and come and help her? Running the brush through her hair, feeling the silkiness of her curls, counting as she brushed, one, two, three, four...

Irene, appeared in the doorway, her head stuck halfway out.

"Come and get it," she hollered. The boy's heads came into view, each coming from a different way. Settling in single file, they marched into the house.

The sound of the screen door slamming like a heavy gavel into her heart. The call of the beast had come to pass. She would have to succumb to the torture at the hands of Irene.

Watching for her mother's face in the window, she trods toward the house, her brush in one hand. Her dad had told her he was working late tonight. That's why Irene had chosen tonight to give them haircuts. There was no way she was going to get out of this.

Things wouldn't be much different for the boys, who always had a close cut. But taking her hair would be like stealing her pride. No, the hair would grow back, she could never take her pride from her.

Irene watched Alice, the absence of her father in her eyes.

"You can help me take the food to the table, Alice."

"Yes, of course, Mother."

Irene got busy carrying the food from the stove. A roast of some kind, thick, dark brown gravy, mashed potatoes, and apple crisp.

One by one, Irene brought a plate or bowl, Alice followed behind with another.

The boys' jubilance was evident in the sound of mmms coming from their lips.

"Everything looks delicious, Mother," said Alice. "Are we waiting for Dad to get home to eat?"

"No, your father works late tonight. We will be eating without him."

A lump rises in Alice's throat.

Irene sat at the head of the table giving a nod to start eating.

Alice watched, thinking of the prayer that usually accompanied a meal when her dad was at the table. Not daring to ask for a prayer, she closed her eyes and said a quick thanks to God.

The stool was in the same place it had been since William had brought it in from the woodshed, it had been Alice's seat at the table since then. No more sitting at the sewing machine table, out of sight and out of mind.

Tonight there was even warm buns, their buttered heads waiting for the anxious, hungry fingers to pull their heads apart. But the best of all was the apple crisp, Alice's favorite thing in the world.

Her brothers filled their plates, digging in. As the bowls were passed Alice's way, she just looked at the food, then passed them on to Earl, who sat beside her. Irene was busy filling her plate, not noticing that Alice had taken no food and was just sitting staring at her plate with watery eyes. As each of her brothers realized she had taken no food, their forks also went down, one after another.

"What is wrong with you, young lady? You aren't getting any apple crisp if you don't eat your dinner."

"That's OK," answered Alice, her head hanging. "I am not really hungry tonight."

"Go to bed hungry then. Think you can waste food around here?"

Not looking her mother's way, Alice gets up from the table, started to clean around the sink and the counter. Maybe, just maybe, she could make Irene happy, and she wouldn't cut off her hair.

"Lice. Just think, if we didn't cut everyone's hair, we could have them running all over the house. In no time they would be in every cupboard and in everyone's beds. We just can't have that."

The whole conversation about lice had severed the appetites of all.

Irene had positioned a chair between the parlor and kitchen and had set up a pair of clippers, and scissors, waiting for the kids to finish up their supper.

"OK then, let's get this started. I don't have all night. You boys get in line right here." She pointed to the chair.

"Alice, get out of the sink and get over here now." Turning around, Alice eyes the chair set up like an execution, threatening.

The weapon of Irene's choice was a long pair of steel-nosed scissors. And a fine-tooth comb sat on a white towel, with some electric clippers next to the comb.

"We will start with you, Alice. Get over here," she ordered.

The command from Irene sounded like it came through a long tunnel.

Without hesitation, Alice bolted for the door like a frightened colt.

Stumbling and falling hands down into the hardened graveled yard, she scraped her knees and bloodied her palms, specs of dirt in the scrapes.

Holding up her hands now, streaks of blood showing in the pink of the creases of her palm, she starts crying.

"Bring her back in here, right now," Irene ordered. Jack and Skip picked her up from the dirt and carried her back into the house by her arms. Irene walked directly to Alice, raising her fat arm slapping her hard across the face, the fat of her arm swaying.

"You think you can run from me? I will teach you to disobey me! Go and get me some rope from the shed, Jack, and hurry up."

"What?" answered Jack, the tallest of the boys. "Rope for what?"

"Never you mind, just go and get it before you get a whipping. You are not too big to go to the woodshed," she threatened through clenched teeth. "Go get it now," she bellowed, wildly shaking her head like a crazy person. Jack came back in the house, the rope in his hand.

"Get on the chair, Alice," ordered Irene, her dark lifeless eyes glaring.

"No, no, Mother. No, please," she cried. Irene grabbed her arm, leading her screaming to the chair.

"Now, James, you tie her to the chair. That way she won't be trying to run away again." The boys are all staring at each other now, wondering exactly what Irene was up to. And why was she trying to involve as many of them as possible, like this was some kind of game of torture?

Squirming to try and get away, Irene digs her fingers into the soft flesh of Alice's bare arms.

"Sit here and shut up," she ordered, her back teeth clamped together like a vise grip, her eyes wild. Spittle flew from her tightly pursed lips, and a wet circle spotted under each of her arms, showing on her grey dress.

James tied her hands behind her back, making sure not to tie it too tight to hurt her.

"Now tether her legs to the chair legs," she ordered like she was talking about a sheep for shearing.

"Sorry, sorry, Mom, I wasn't running away," she pleaded. The outline of Irene's handprint showed pink the side of Alice's face. Screaming louder now, hoping there was some chance of William hearing her.

"Shut up," said Irene, slapping Alice on the other side of her face. Her brother's watch in horror as Irene went for the bucket of cold water, heaving the whole pail in Alice's face.

The coldness of the water is shocking, Alice gasps for breath.

"Now you will do as I say."

Grabbing up the scissors, she started taking chunks of Alice's hair, dropping them to the floor, each handful like the hatred she had for the child. The boys watched as each of Alice's locks fall. Irene's eyes are popping out of her head as she takes more chopping motions on Alice's hair till there is nothing left to grab. Reaching for the clippers, four rows of cutting, Alice is completely bald.

Watching the last of her curls hitting the floor like the last piece of her broken heart. Almost breathless, with no movement, silent tears fall like rain on a windowpane.

"Next," she yelled as Alice picked herself off the chair ambling to the staircase.

Going up, one, two, three, four, five, counting her way to the top.

Along the hallway and into her room, shutting out the world.

Grabbing the big doll, she squeezed her tight.

"Mom cut all of my hair off, Pearl. Oh my God." As the pain from the haircut subsided, her hands started stinging, forgetting that she had scraped her knees and hands when she fell. Wiping at her tears, she lay back in her bed pulling the blanket up over their heads.

Closing her eyes, she prayed.

"God, can you please take me out of this place? God, can you please take me where Pearl is? I know she is with you, and I want to be with you too."

Falling into a deep sleep, God's angels covered her with their wings.

She dreamed that she lived in a palace, and she had servants and everything a girl could want, and a mother who loved her. She dreamed that Pearl was still alive. They were playing with the big rag doll, Sally, and Bear. Pearl was brushing her hair and singing a lullaby to her when…the alarm woke her.

Placing her hands on her head, a soft, feeling under her fingers. A wisp of silkiness was growing in already.

Sitting up in her bed, she glanced at the alarm clock that sat on the small wooden table beside her bed. Five o'clock, it read. Her daddy would be up by now, sitting at the kitchen table, probably having his morning coffee and toast.

Getting into her housecoat, sliding into her slippers, she walked out into the hallway, listening for voices. No sounds of anyone yet. She would go downstairs and see if her father was at the table.

Spying around the corner, her heart swelled. He was there, drinking his morning coffee.

"Daddy, Daddy," she cried, running to him, burying her head in his chest. He tried to pull her away from him now. "What is the matter with you, child?" Holding herself tight against his chest, he puts his hands on her shoulders, looking into her eyes. The lids are swollen, her eyes bloodshot. "What is wrong? Tell Dad now." Having a better look at her now, at the scarf on her head and her skinned knees showing red against her light, pearl-colored skin. Feeling her head now, he realized she had no hair. "What happened to your curls?"

Knowing what he was about to hear, that it had something to do with Irene, he kept a stiff upper lip waiting for Alice to tell him the story.

With a sudden marching down the stairs, the boys descended into the kitchen. All fresh haircuts. Ah, he knew right away what had happened. Forced haircuts could only mean one thing. Lice.

Just then Irene walked to the table. "Before you start asking, William, there is lice at school, and everyone needed to get a haircut. And just because you think you are a princess, Alice, do you think the lice would just fly by you?" A few giggles from the boys, who all took their places at the table.

"It's OK, Alice. Your hair will grow back, and prettier I bet," said William.

A lump rose in Irene's throat. The word *prettier* was like a knife in her neck. Walking away to her spot, staring out the little window over the sink.

Straightening out her room, she takes one last look at the doll.

"Goodbye, dolly. Wish me luck today. I have to go to school with no hair."

CHAPTER 29

Changes

The last time she had been to her aunt Rita's, Alice had taken a good look at herself in a long mirror on the back of her aunt's bedroom door. Admiring what she saw, her beautiful blonde curls framing her pretty face, her body, lean and muscular. Her dad had said she just kept getting prettier, blushing at her reflection. Her green eyes the color of new spring grass, and her rosy porcelain skin reminded her of her sister Pearl. They looked more alike all the time. Moving away from the mirror, she felt guilt creeping into her chest. Her mother had always said vanity was a sin. Was it a sin to look at yourself in the mirror and like what you see?

As soon as Alice walked through the schoolhouse door, Miss Ink noticed something different about her. She hadn't walked over to her desk, like she usually did, to say good morning and give her a smile.

Miss Ink walked over to Alice, who sat quietly, a bright scarf on her head. Her eyes met Miss Ink's questioning eyes.

"My mom gave me a haircut," said Alice shyly.

Miss Ink scanned the classroom for the Purple boys, who also looked like they had fresh haircuts.

"Oh, I see your mother cut everyone's hair."

"Yes, ma'am," answered Alice.

There was clearly something bothering Alice this morning. She was not her usual happy self, sullen almost, hanging her head, trying to avoid eye contact with Miss Ink. Losing her hair had taken her happiness?

113

The kids all settled into their desks. Miss Ink put a lesson on the board and asked Alice to put some fresh chalk on the blackboard. Noticing a few purplish blue marks on Alice's pink flesh, an alarm goes off in Miss Ink's mind. The apparent signs of abuse. Having a closer look, she saw scraped knees, her eyelids swollen, and the sadness in Alice's eyes telling a story. And the burned hand. It was all making sense now.

Taking Alice aside, Miss Ink whispered in her ear, so no other kids could hear.

"Is someone hurting you, Alice?" Her green eyes grew large.

"No, no, I am just clumsy," answered Alice.

"Are you sure?"

"Yes ma'am," she answered, lowering her gaze.

Miss Ink didn't have to ask any more questions. It was clear to her that the child was being abused. Going back to her desk, she made notes of the extent of the child's injuries and also the time and date.

"Alice, you know that I will do anything to help you. Would you like to talk to me sometime about what is happening to you?"

"I am all right. My hair will grow back in. My dad said it will be thicker and prettier."

"That is right, Alice, you are cute with or without hair."

"Thank you, ma'am," she said, a show of pink on her cheeks.

There had been numerous things that Miss Ink had noticed since Alice first came to school. Bruises, and many days with no lunch. She had grown to love the child and shared her lunches with her, packing an extra apple most days, and had gifted Alice with a few pairs of shoes, and other things.

The day after her seventh birthday, she went to school with her hand bandaged to her elbow.

There was a big parcel sitting on Alice's desk wrapped in shiny silver paper, a white bow adorning the top.

"Oh my," said Alice. "This is for me?"

"Yes, go ahead. It is from the whole class," said Miss Ink. Everyone cheered as Alice pinched through the wrapping paper. A brand new pair of shiny red shoes. Grabbing them out of the box, she gently brought them to her feet as though they were made of glass.

CHAPTER 30

Her mother could cut off her hair, beat her, hurt her feelings, but she couldn't take her pride. Strangers would walk up to Irene and remark how well behaved Alice was or how pretty she was. These comments landed on deaf ears.

The sweetness of Alice was like the last sun-ripened peach at the top of the tree. No one would have ever guessed the sadness that lay just below the surface.

As Alice grew stronger, Irene was failing fast. Swollen from her ankles to her neck, her body bore the heavy burden of her overweight frame. She looked more like Alice's grandmother.

Always having to use a walking stick now to steady her heavy body or to strike out. The hatefulness was sucking the life out of her, like a heavy rain cloud, stealing away a sunny day.

Alice would be turning twelve soon. She loved school, and things had settled down a little at home. Irene mostly yelled these days, Alice dodging her slow hand. She could get out of Irene's reach quick and had taken to running down the road or into the meadow.

It was Alice's last grade at school, and Miss Ink had been discussing what she wanted to do after grade eight.

"Why don't you go to Halifax to college there? Think about your future. You would make a wonderful nurse."

"Yes, that is what I would love to do." The thought of helping others really appealed to her. Living away from Irene was the ice cream on the strawberries. It was sounding more glorious all the time.

Irene was getting increasingly miserable. William was not working steady these days. He had taken to coming home in the middle of the afternoon with splitting headaches keeping him in bed sometimes all day. With little to no appetite, some days only eating toast. The doctor came to visit him often, trying to assess the problem.

With William home a lot now, and less money to provide, things started getting very tense and the food sparse.

Irene ordered Alice to start making bread and preparing most of the meals. Potatoes were the one staple that they still had lots of. The Jeffersonses sent down fifty-pound bags, having ten acres planted in potatoes.

The boys were sent out to hunt for whatever they could catch, but still there was hardly enough.

Two of Alice's brothers had enlisted in the army.

One day after school, Alice was in the kitchen helping her mother peel some vegetables when she looked over at her and made an announcement.

"Mother, I am..."

"What? Spit it out girl," Irene interrupted, staring at her deeply, as though into her soul.

"I am going to Halifax to go to college there to become a nurse." An urgent, quickening pace in her voice.

"Really," answered Irene sarcastically.

Alice kept her eyes on the peeling, waiting for the ax to drop.

"It is true that you should start earning your keep around here. You could surely get a job and make some money, but who has the time for you to go to school? Maybe for two years, and where in God's name do you think you will be getting the money to live in the city and go to some fancy school? Really, Alice, get your head out of the clouds."

"But, Mother, Miss Ink knows someone I could board with, and she said..."

"Whatever," her voice bellowed. "I don't really care what Miss Ink said, I said no, no, no! You won't be going anywhere to school. School is for the privileged, and the last time I checked, we are poor, in case you haven't noticed, always walking around with your head in the clouds."

The tears start to fall as her dreams are

washed away. It was no use to try and make sense to Irene.

Why would she dare to think that she would want anything for her, especially if it meant happiness? Like a caged bird, Irene would not let her go free.

"As a matter of fact, Alice, I have been thinking that we would find you a job. We sure do need some help around here, and there are a few domestic jobs out there."

"We might as well talk about it now that you brought up this job thing. I overhead a few ladies saying a well-to-do family, the Olsenses, were looking for a housekeeper. Actually, I spoke with the lady, Gladys, I recall is her name, a tall pretty lady, well groomed. I would say, a rich look about her. I told her I had a hardworking girl for the job."

Her eyes brightened, excitement in her voice. "Mother, you mean you already promised me for the job without telling me about it?"

"Yes, with your father sick and all. I just forgot to mention it to you. I've been so worried about William. They live in the countryside, just outside of Halifax. They have ten children, and the word is they have a chef, a gardener, and a driver. And two housekeepers who live right there in their mansion."

Trying not to seem too enthusiastic, her eyes widen.

"Gladys is eager to meet you Alice."

A bright blue sky emerged out of the stormy skies. Did she really just hear her mother properly? Was this some kind of trick? Would Irene really let her go to live in a mansion?

"You will live right there and come home once a month to bring me your pay. I will need all of it to keep food on this table. I'm sure you will get all the food you need to eat there and a nice place to sleep, maybe even your own room."

To quell the excitement building in her mind, she needed to safeguard this dream.

"But, Mother, you want me to go and live with strangers? I don't want to go."

Secretly she wished that they would come for her right now, tonight. She could get her things together fast…

"Listen here, young lady. It has already been decided. You have no say in the matter."

Turning her cheek, a stolen smile on her lips, her heart filled. A scream tried to escape her lips, butterflies playing in her stomach.

"Oh, I just remembered, they are coming for you the day after tomorrow. Pack your things and make sure you are ready," she ordered, ambling away.

Without another word spoken, Alice hurried to her room.

Going straight upstairs, not even counting. Scanning her room, her eyes settled on her doll.

Oh no. The doll couldn't come with her to a mansion where she had to work as a housekeeper. She would have to leave her. It tore at her heart. Separated from her best friend and confidante. She was too big now for a doll.

"Oh, Pearl, I might have to go away and leave you. I am going to be a maid, and I don't think I should be taking a doll, to work with me. I will leave you to take care of Bear." Bending, she kissed the doll on the head. "I love you."

She hadn't been talking to the doll for a couple of years now, just found comfort in tucking it into bed with her. Her little room, her doll, and her things. Her prison, her sanctuary.

William had taken to spending his whole day in bed. He couldn't work anymore. The doctors diagnosed him with a brain tumor. Daily, William felt sicker and had lost all hope, just laying in bed waiting for the good Lord to take him home. The strong medicine was making him sleep most of the day.

Looking in on him, Alice sat on the side of his bed, running her hand over his face. Talking in a whisper, she professed her undying love to him. If only he could just get better, but she knew that was not going to happen. Things were changing in her life, and she had to be strong, for her mother and her brothers. They were counting on her now. She would work and bring every cent home to help. Getting away from the only home she had known was scary and exciting all at once.

The morning she was leaving for the Olsenses', she stopped by her father's room. "Daddy, I will miss you. Please get better. I will be back to see you soon." Bending down, she kissed him on the forehead, a long adoring look, pulling the blanket up to his chin.

Alice would never see her father again.

She wouldn't get to finish her eighth grade, and she had to tell the teacher that she would not be going to college. Her dreams of being a nurse were squeezed out like the dirty water from the mop.

She explained to Miss Ink about her father having a brain tumor, and that she had to go to work right away, to help out the family.

The teacher listened to Alice's story and could only wish her the best.

"Don't worry, dear," she said, holding both of Alice's hands in hers. "You never know where fate will lead you, but one thing I do know is that you will be a great help to anyone you work for. Make sure you write me a letter, and tell me how things are going. Just address it to the school. I will really miss you, Alice," her dark eyes glossing over. The sadness in Miss Ink's eyes brought down her own tears. Miss Ink reached her arms out to Alice and they embraced in a loving hug.

Their friendship had grown over the years, and they loved each other. Realizing that she maybe wouldn't see Miss Ink again for a long time, maybe never, sent Alice's tears overboard, openly sobbing.

"Life goes on, and things change. You are a fine girl, Alice. The world is yours for the taking," kissing her on the cheek.

"Thank you. I love you." Turning, she headed for the classroom door, knowing if she looked back she would never stop crying.

It would be the last time Alice would see the classroom or the wonderful teacher she had grown to love like a mother.

On her walk home that day, her mind a buzz of activity, the possibilities of a start of a new life for her, working away from home. The happiness she felt for herself was overshadowed by the sadness of her dying father. Why, why did life have to be so hard? Too much sadness in such a young life.

Was her mother really telling her the truth about her leaving to go away to work? Nothing had ever been straightforward with Irene. Why should she believe her now? Always some kind of darkness lurking, like a scary monster waiting around the corner. Being able to just pack a bag and leave the wicked witch of the… What fairy tale was that again?

CHAPTER 31

Today she was leaving for her new job. After awakening early and freshening herself, she sits looking out the window into the meadow. As she brushed her hair, she envisioned her father walking in the green grass and the spotted cows in the meadow.

No, today she had to be happy. No sad thoughts. Just then, she peered over on her bed at the big rag doll.

"Pearl, you know I love you. I just have to go away to work for a while, and I can't take you. You understand, right? And anyway, I can't leave Bear here by himself."

Staring the doll in the face, she kissed her on both cheeks, then set her back on the pillow, stuffing the bear in the crook of her arm.

"I will tell you everything when I get back."

Just then she realized it was done. Talking to dolls was silly. She was growing up now into a young woman. But she could still love Pearl and always would.

Irene had given her an old brown suitcase that had been in the family forever. She packed all her special things and finally kneeled on it to pull the zipper around.

Irene said they would be there at noon to get her.

By nine o'clock everything in her room was perfect, and she was ready to leave. Instead of going downstairs, she decided to sit and look out the window. Memories good and bad flooded her mind. Mostly, she kept trying to suppress the sadness she felt about her sick dad. Every time she went in to see him, he was sleeping. She wouldn't get to talk to him before she left. All she could hope for was a miracle that he would get better.

Just a quick peek in at him before she left. She had to say goodbye and kiss him one more time. Just as she was about to touch the doorknob, Irene came up behind her.

"Your father is dying. He is in a lot of pain. Leave him alone. No sense in going in bothering him."

It was too close to her escape time to rile Irene. Backing away from the door, she hurried back upstairs to watch for her ride.

A horse and buggy ride sounded like great fun. Today was a happy day, feeling like it was really someone else in her shoes.

At ten to noon, Alice decided it was time to get herself and her suitcase downstairs. A couple of her brothers were lingering around, but if she asked them, and they somehow dropped the suitcase and all the contents spilled, she feared Irene would take her precious things. All the keepsakes from Miss Ink, her aunt Rita, and the special things that had belonged to Pearl. No, she just couldn't let her see any of them.

Managing to navigate the suitcase, she gets it to the bottom of the staircase. With no sign of Irene, deciding to go in quick to say a last goodbye to her dad. Sitting on the side of the bed, bending to his ear, she whispered, "I am going away to work, Daddy. Please get better." Tears fall on his checkerboard flannel shirt.

He moved slightly, his cloudy distant eyes staring at her.

"Thought I was being awakened by an angel. I am not well, Alice, I am dying. I am going to see Pearl. We all have to go sometime," he said, his voice straining. "If I don't see you when you come home, I will see you when you get to heaven. Always remember I love you."

Just then his eyes closed, his breathing shallow. Wincing, she feels his pain. Reaching her hand to his face, she touched his sallow grey skin. The thinness of it like tracing paper. Waves of sorrow wash over her, as though she would drown. Her own breath now coming in spurts.

"Oh my God, how can I go away? What if I never get to see you again?"

A shrill sorrow-drenched cry assaulted the quiet of the house. Hearing the wails, Irene came thudding down the hallway, death beckoning.

Pulling on the door abruptly, Alice, holding her dad's hand in hers.

"What is the matter with you now? You know full well that your father is sick. We can't change that. Get out of here and wipe your face. They will be here to get you soon. You had better not mess this up."

Bending, she kissed him one last time on the forehead, a faint smile on William's lips. Wiping at her own tears, heading out the door, past her mother.

Bringing her suitcase and her little purse, she stands at the door looking out periodically, like she is waiting for a train, trying to block out her mother, who is standing at the sink, mumbling something to herself.

"Just don't stand there looking stupid, girl, come over here. We need to have a little talk."

Turning to face Irene, she walked to the table and sat down. Irene sits across from her.

"Let me make myself clear, girl. You are not to spend a penny of the money you will make. We need it now more than ever to put food on the table and buy your father medicine. Go to work, and do the best you can do. No time for foolishness anymore. You are a grown girl. Soon you will be having babies."

"Oh no, Mother, not me. I will wait a long time to get married. Not all ladies get married, Mother. Miss Ink is not married, and she is happy."

"Well, don't get ahead of yourself. You are only twelve years old and still under my care. You will do as I say, do you understand me? Also, if I get any complaints about your work, you will come back home here and work for your keep. No school, no college."

Staring deep into Irene's bottomless black eyes.

"I will make you proud of me, Mother." Irene froze, raising her eyebrows as though she just stepped on a nail.

"Proud, you say?" Just then there was a knock at the door.

Getting up from the table, Alice goes to open the door. A tall, thin, older man in a uniform standing there. Alice gasped.

"I am here to pick up Miss Alice?"

"Yes, yes, that is me," answered Alice with a suspicious smile.

"I will just gather your things for you then, if you would like to just wait by the car. I will be there promptly to get you settled in, miss. I am your driver. My name is Orville."

"Pleased to meet you," answered Alice with a slight curtsy.

Transported to another place and time, Alice did not turn to look at her mother, who was peeking out the little window over the sink, her mouth ajar.

It was the longest car Alice had ever seen, even in pictures. As she stepped closer, a smiling Orville waited, holding the door for her. *Don't look back, don't look back,* she kept saying to herself in her mind, for fear that her beautiful chariot would turn to dust and her wicked mother would...

Sliding into the middle, she felt the softness of the leather seats under her fingers, leaning back into the embrace of the chariot, heaving a comforting sigh. The stuffed seat was hugging, welcoming. Staring out the opposite window from her house at the green meadow and the spotted cows. Where was she going again? Away, away, as far as she could go.

Irene watched as the man in the suit put Alice's things in the trunk, holding the door for Alice.

"Just imagine, my Alice riding in a fancy car. Going to live with millionaires," she said, a sly smile crossed her face.

Alice keeps her eyes on the back of Orville's head, his starchy hat and his grey haired neck. When his eyes caught hers in the mirror, they sparkled with warmth, smiling back at her. She liked him already. Sitting back in her seat, she relaxed every muscle, leaving the driving to him.

Watching out the window was almost like a dream she had, the car taking her away from her tormented life. What awaited her?

Butterflies played chase in her stomach.

The landscape changed from familiar to nothing she had seen before. There were more buildings and wider roads, watching intently, not wanting to miss a thing. The car pulled up into a circular driveway, Alice staring out the front window at the biggest house she had ever seen. Everything is white except for the large wooden door with an ornamental golden handle.

"We have arrived, miss," Orville said, looking at her through his rear-view mirror. He privately chuckles at the young girl with the wide-eyed amazement.

"This is where I am going to work?" Her voice getting higher, squeakier.

"Yes, miss, this is the Olsen residence. The whole family is awaiting your arrival. So you go ahead in. I will bring in your bags promptly."

"Thank you, sir," she answered, straightening her dress, smoothing down her hair with her hands. Scanning the grounds around the house, watching to see if anyone was coming out, inching her way across the seat, stepping out onto the paved driveway.

Orville stood waiting for her with an open door. Smiling, Alice walked past him into the most beautiful house she could have ever imagined.

Gigantic crystal chandeliers hung from soaring ceilings. Her eyes followed the winding staircase to the top floor. A tall lady descending.

"Oh my," she said, looking at the girl standing in the foyer. "You must be Alice. We have been expecting you. Orville will take your bags to your quarters." Starting to kick off her shoes, Gladys spoke, "Don't worry about your shoes, dear. It is dry outside. The children await you in the dining room. Come along," she urged, touching Alice on her arm.

When they reached the dining room, Gladys stared at Alice. "My goodness, dear, I didn't know you were so young. Your mother said you were thirteen going on fourteen."

"Well, actually, ma'am," answered Alice, looking up into Gladys's soft blue eyes, "I am twelve going on thirteen. My mother has so many ages to remember, she forgets how old I am sometimes."

Already worried about her position in this household, there was no way she could lose this job, not before she'd even started.

"I see," said Gladys. "Well, let's go in and meet the children. By the way, we weren't officially introduced. My name is Gladys. You can address me as Mrs. Olsen, as the other staff do. And my husband you will address as Dr. Olsen, as he is a doctor and a very busy man. He is a heart surgeon and in great demand. Also he travels extensively and is rarely home, so when he is, we want to take the best care of him. Always curtsy when you see him."

"Yes, ma'am, of course."

Listening to the beautiful lady was like music to her ears. Platinum blonde hair swept up the back of her head, a few tendrils on the side, an elegant long neck and bright pink lips. Holding her head high, she reminded Alice of a beautiful swan she had once seen, her complexion bright and clear like cream.

Alice liked the way she looked and the kindness in her voice.

"Oh, before we go in, let's go to the library. That is where you can spend your free time, enjoying all that it has to offer." Opening a large oak door to expose a library, the smell of lemon oil and leather in the air. Sitting in the middle of the grand room is a large dark-colored wooden desk with oversize claw feet, like it is part animal.

A big black leather chair on a swivel behind the desk.

Books and more books, thought Alice, travelling the walls with her eyes, like she had just been dropped into a magical place.

"Can I read all of them?" she asked.

"You can read as many as your heart desires. Of course a lot of them are doctor's books, but you go right ahead. Reading is knowledge, and you can't have too much of that. The kids do their homework in here. This is called the study.

"The children have tutors who come in for special lessons, and you are welcome to join in their classes," pointing to the long leather couches lining the walls and a few overstuffed chairs near the windows. Examining a few of the pictures of old men in cloaks, Alice wondered who they were.

An overwhelming feeling of joy made her feel like she would start crying any minute. Biting the inside of her lip, she felt the pain to stop the tears.

"I love everything, Mrs. Olsen. Thank you, thank you," she said again, curtsying.

"OK then, now are you ready to meet the kids?"

"Sure, I am," answered Alice, following Gladys down a long hallway, a shiny grey stone floor.

As they walked into the dining room, a hush fell around the table, all eyes on Alice. Two chandeliers hang over the long wooden table. Ten faces staring back at her. Girls and boys, five of each. They all looked at Alice inquisitively.

There was so much silverware on the table, Alice wondered what they did with it all, eyeing the golden candleholders, and long, white slender candles in each. Smiling eyes and faces awaited the introduction.

"Children," Gladys said, "this is Alice, our new housekeeper." Trying to straighten up, Alice stood on her toes a little.

"Hello," they all said in unison looking from one to another.

A blonde-haired girl who sat close to where Alice was standing spoke up.

"Mommy, she is the same size as me, and I am only nine. How old are you?" she asks, looking at Alice.

Gladys watched Alice, who was thinking hard what to say.

"Never mind right now. That is not important. You two can discuss all these things when you get to know each other."

Just then the little girl walked up to Alice standing next to her.

"Hi, my name is Lucy. See, we are the same height," she said with a big smile.

"Look, dear, Alice is almost thirteen, just short for her age, that is all."

"OK, but I think we can play together, right, Alice?" she said, grabbing her hand.

"Yes, of course, dear, when Alice is done her chores for the day. Chores before playing, Lucy, you know that."

Lucy and Alice exchanged glances and smiles.

"Your duties don't start till tomorrow."

A foreign-looking lady with a tray of desserts entered the dining room, noticing Alice sitting next to Lucy.

"This is our new housekeeper, Jackie. Meet Alice," said Gladys.

"She is so young, ma'am," Jackie said, staring at Alice.

"It doesn't matter how old she is. She is here to help this household run smoother and give you a break with your workload. Her duties will include helping Pierre in the kitchen, laundry duties, and other odd jobs around the house. That will free up your time to do the more important ones."

"I see," answered Jackie, putting the platter with the desserts down.

"Welcome," she said in her Spanish accent, smiling at Alice.

"Will see you later to help with the dishes," she said.

"Excuse me, Jackie, but I will be assigning Alice to her chores. And today she has other things to do, so as usual the dishes are your duty."

Having said that, Gladys turned and walked out of the dining room.

"Yes, ma'am," answered Jackie, turning on her heel heading to the kitchen.

The kids all started in again, asking Alice questions.

Lucy was so taken with Alice, she kept her eyes peeled on her, listening to every word she said.

Gladys appeared in the dining room doorway.

"Come, my dear, I will take you to your quarters. You can get settled in, then I'll give you a tour of the house. Afterward you can have a snack before bed."

A nighttime snack sounded so good to Alice. She hadn't eaten all day. The food on the dining room table had made her mouth water. Looking away, she swallowed hard, hoping they didn't see the hunger in her eyes.

She was sure the special things she saw were no doubt just for the family, not the maids.

"Your job will start officially tomorrow. You will have a good night's rest after all the travelling, and you need to get familiar with your new home." Alice tried not to seem too happy. Did Mrs. Olsen really say, it was her new home?

Following Gladys along a wide corridor to a door at the end of the hallway, just past the kitchen. There was no doorknob. Gladys just pushed in a panel in the wall.

"It is a secret staircase to your private room."

"Wow," said Alice, looking in at the light streaming down from the wide open space.

"Just go straight to the top and you will see your things there. Make yourself at home. Come back down to the kitchen when you are settled in. We can wait till tomorrow to show you everything and describe your duties to you. I'll meet you in the kitchen later. Enjoy your new room."

"Oh, thank you, ma'am, I will be down in a while."

Keeping her eyes on the narrow steps, she took her time climbing the staircase, counting as she climbed. One, two, three…thirty two, as she climbed the last step.

Entering the ivory-colored room, the first thing that caught her eye was the large windows overlooking the grounds of the property. Rolling hills and a group of four long white buildings with red tops. A circular ring and wide open pastures, fenced and cross fenced. A few horses leisurely eating grass.

"Wow, this is amazing," she said out loud.

Haven taken in the beauty outside her window, Alice turned to focus on her new room.

A large bed, bigger than she had ever seen before, a white fluffy comforter and lots of pillows. And how was she going to get on the bed that was so far off the floor? This bed made her one at home look like a mat on the floor. It was just unbelievable!

Giggling, she leaned on the bed, then put one leg up, then another.

Burying her face in the deep plush pillows, like floating on a cloud. It was so good, it almost felt sinful. *If Mother only could see me now*, she thought to herself.

Sitting up on the bed, all of a sudden she felt alone, like she was missing something. Her doll. If only she had put the rag doll in her bag, she could have hidden her away in her private place.

It was too late now. The next time she went home she would sneak the doll back.

Her eyes basked in the beauty of the room. There was a large wooden dresser with an oval mirror and a stool covered in red velvet. Brushes and bottles of colognes and bathwater adorned the dresser.

Slipping off the side of the bed, Alice walked to the dresser sitting down on the plush-covered stool. Running her hand over the finished wood, she catches her reflection in the mirror. Not a fuzzy reflection caught in a window, but her true reflection.

Bright green eyes, porcelain skin, her blonde curls framing her face. The sight of her own image excited her. She was happy to realize how she really looked to others. A rosy glow spread over her cheeks. Looking away, like she had stolen something.

"Alice has a palace that is what they will say. Who would believe little old me, living in a real palace?"

Getting up from the dresser, she walked around her room, entering another room. Her own private bathroom. A big white enamel tub with claw feet sat in the middle. Alice smiled, running her hands over the smoothness. Brightly colored towels and various soaps in special dishes decorate the shiny counter. A black and white gleaming tiled floor.

"I am dreaming. Alice has a palace. Alice has a palace," she chanted playfully. "Please don't let me wake up if this is dream. Not from this one."

Hugging herself, spinning around and around till she stumbles drunk with happiness, to the big bed, face down into the softness, giggling, the smile frozen on her cherub face.

My room is as big as my whole house at home. Mother would never believe it, and she couldn't ever know. A faint dizzy feeling, her belly grumbling to her made her realize it was time to take Mrs. Olsen's offer of a bedtime snack.

From the bottom of her staircase, just out the narrow door, the kitchen is right there. Tiptoeing in, she spied a plate with a dome cover. Beside the plate was a large glass of chocolate milk. Her favorite. How did she know that she loved chocolate milk? Lifting the dome, a plate of small sandwiches on brown bread. Ham and cheese, and cucumber and cream cheese. A cinnamon bun with nuts on the top, caramel and white icing drizzled across the top.

Sitting at the counter, amazed at the beauty and order of the white kitchen, with the black and white diamond floor. Enjoying her food, then washing her dish and glass she makes her way back to her room. Full from the milk and sandwiches, she wrapped the cinnamon bun in her napkin, deciding to take it back to her room, for when she was hungry again.

Running a bath, enjoying a peace that comes over her. A dream; it just had to be a dream. Relaxing, she then dressed in a cotton nightdress that had been left over the headboard. Eating the cinnamon bun was like heaven with icing. It was the best thing she had ever eaten in her life. Licking her fingers, she then washed her hands and face and gets into bed, pulling the lush blanket over her, closing her eyes, and prayed.

"Thank you, God, for bringing me here." No sooner had she said the silent prayer, she drifted off.

Upon awakening, she realized it is not a dream. She is still in the palace. Running her fingers through her hair, she swings her legs to the edge of the bed, yawning, stretching her arms in the air. Her bags are at the top of the stairs. Realizing she had to unpack and put her things away in the closet. Opening the panel doors to expose a large walk in closet. Shelves lined either side for her shoes, and lots of overhead hangers for her clothes.

The round clock on the wall said six o'clock.

As soon as Gladys awoke, she decided she would go to Alice's room and give her a rundown of the day's events.

Knocking gently, she walked up the staircase. "Good morning, Alice," she said at the top stair, peering in.

Sitting at the big mirror, brushing her hair, turning to look at Gladys.

"Good morning, ma'am. I am so excited to start my first day. I've been awake since six o'clock. I sure hope this is my uniform. There were two of them in the closet, and this one fit me the best." Looking down at her white-and-blue uniform with its scalloped collar and blue piping.

"It looks very nice on you, Alice, and there is another one for you downstairs. Just give them to Jackie to wash. She does the kitchen laundry.

And of course, you only wear them one day, then they must be laundered. So I'll leave you now and see you in the kitchen at seven thirty sharp. After breakfast duties, you clean and dust the children's rooms, then you have time for yourself before the dinner duties. After that, you are free to do what you like for the rest of the evening."

Gladys turned, heading back downstairs.

"Oh, thank you, God, for these blessings." Gazing around her massive room with all the luxuries she had never known.

Walking over to the window, a beautiful glow of orange and pink showcasing the horizon. Horses grazing. Just then she spotted someone on horseback. Watching until they disappeared into the meadow.

"What a wonderful day..." she sang in a lullaby tune.

Taking her time on the staircase, she headed downstairs, through the narrow door into the corridor. She looked left, then right. Which way had she come from? For a minute she didn't know which way to go, until she heard the laughter of children, a buzz of activity leading to the kitchen.

A slender man with a tall white hat stands at the stove, Steam rising from large pots and a few small ones.

Jackie is bending over, putting some bread in the oven.

Gladys is making fresh coffee.

"Here she is," said Gladys, looking around as though a princess, had just entered. "Everyone welcome Alice."

"Good morning, Alice," the kids all said in chorus. Pierre turned a good morning smile on his face. The welcoming smells of sausages and maple syrup filled the air. A big jug of orange juice sits on the counter.

"Alice, for starters, you could make the kids' lunches, Lucy will tell you what they usually have. Actually, Lucy, you help Alice with the lunches today."

"Yes, Mother, I will," answered Lucy.

"It would be nice to have tea with you after breakfast, Alice. We will take it in the garden room."

"Thank you, ma'am," she answered.

Breakfast went without incident. Jackie not uttering one word the whole morning.

Gladys sat in the garden room, a lot of things going through her mind. The morning had come together wonderfully. With Alice taking over lunch duty, it freed up her time to read and have her coffee in the study. Her early morning ride on her horse, Sabre, a tall black gelding, had been especially enjoyable. Henry had bought her the Arabian quarter horse cross for their last anniversary. They rode together a lot when she first got Sabre, but lately it seemed Henry was too busy. It had become her morning ritual, no matter what the weather, to spend a couple hours in the barns or riding.

This morning while riding, her mind had been on Alice, wondering about the child's life, thinking of how to talk to her without offending her.

First of all, what kind of mother sent her daughter to work when she turned twelve? Shouldn't she still be in school? Feeling guilt at haven taken her in as a maid, but at the same time, there was something telling her that she was rescuing this girl from a bad life.

Sneaking a peek in at Lucy and Alice when they all first met her, made Gladys realize what a child Alice still was. They looked more like sisters, Lucy's hair just a little redder. They stood the same height and body size. With that in mind, she could give Alice all of Lucy's hand-me-downs. Usually she donated things to the church, but now she would pick out the best and give them to Alice.

The kids went regularly to the city to shop and go to the theatre.

I will make a difference in this child's life, thought Gladys. *I will give her easy tasks and make sure she gets some schooling. She will be like one of my own*, she decided.

Glancing at her watch, expecting Alice to arrive at any time. Noticing Alice coming down the hallway, standing Gladys greeting her.

"Come over and have a seat. We will have a nice cup of tea and a chat. So how do you like your new job so far?"

"Oh, I like it very much. Just wondering, though, does the other maid not speak English? I asked her a few things, and she answered me in another language. I think it was Spanish."

"Really, well, yes, of course she speaks English. She speaks three lan-guages and is teaching my children to speak Spanish. She speaks French, as well. That seems odd that she wasn't speaking English to you. She might have been having a bad day. Jackie has been with the family for five years now, and I don't know how we would manage without her. She is of great value to me."

Sitting down, Alice listened intently.

"I wanted to say that I was very pleased with your work this morning." Reaching her long fingers toward Alice's hand Gladys embraces her.

"I see you were helping Pierre."

"Yes, ma'am, I had to do a lot of cooking at home lately since my father has been sick, and my mother is not well neither."

Gladys remembered meeting Irene that day at the store. A long grey dress, a hand-crocheted shawl draped over her rounded shoulders. Sharp tongued, asking right away how much money Alice would be making.

Everything about the woman spelled misery. Not once during their visit did she smile.

"I will give you a week as a trial to see if you can handle the work. You will be making lunches and helping prepare breakfast. Then after you have had your own breakfast, you can start upstairs in the bedrooms. All the children's rooms are your responsibility. Dusting, making beds, and putting their things away. Some of them are better than others, but you know children. I don't like to burden them with things like housework. Their main focus is their education, and they all play instruments. They have a busy schedule, just like the rest of us. This household run like a well-tuned piano. You can skip the children's rooms today. Tomorrow, following breakfast duties, you can get busy cleaning their rooms. When you are finished with the bedrooms, you can have time for yourself until dinnertime. You will be helping Pierre clean and cut vegetables, or whatever chores he might have for you. Between now and dinnertime you have some time for yourself."

"I can do all those things. I have worked hard ever since I can remember. I am the only girl in the family since my sister Pearl died. My mother made me do lots of housework."

"I see," answered Gladys, "I'm sure everything will work out fine. Most important, be on time for things, whether it be at the breakfast table or the dinner table. Keep your mind on your work. It's fine to talk to the other maid, but don't get involved in her private life. Also, keep your private life to yourself. It's not that I don't want the children to know you, but I need them to focus on their own lives and not be burdened with other people's issues."

"Yes, ma'am," answered Alice. The word *burdened* shook her demeanor. Did Gladys know about her horrible life?

"Thank you, ma'am. I will do the very best work, you will see."

With a slight curtsy, Alice walked out of the garden room, heading outside.

Her head down, she stares at her shoes, white with white laces.

The cobblestone walkway led around a few sheds and down to the long barns where the horses were corralled. Getting closer to the barns, she noticed large open doorways. Just then she spotted the two older girls, each leading a horse on a sawdust pathway. They wore black velvet hats and tall black boots. Examining their attire, Alice had never seen anyone dressed like that.

The girls looked her way, smiling gently, mounting their steeds and galloping off through the meadow.

She decided to go back to the house and to her room for a while. Maybe she would go to the library to get a good book and relax in her room. A fairy tale room, she thought. A real palace for Alice. She chuckled, walking quicker toward the big house.

Everywhere she looked beauty spilled over in abundance. The smell of fresh cut grass, taking in a big breath. She loved it here. Had God landed her in this special place because she had pleaded for him to take her away? Oh, how she wished that Pearl could be here with her.

Maybe that was too much to ask right now. She was grateful for the new hand and a renewed faith. Remembering her father's words. Just talk to him. Throw your burdens on him. Be humbled by the Lord. God had really listened to her.

Dinner was underway, Alice hanging close to Pierre, getting all the information she could about the soup he was making.

"It is bouillabaisse, a fish zoup," he said. Aromatic smells wafted from the big pot. "There are mussels, clams, lobster, shrimp, and some white fish in a tomato broth, with a finish of saffron," he said with the emphasis on saffron.

She'd never heard the word before, but she didn't want to look stupid. "It smells amazing."

"I like having you in my keechen, Alice. We will make great things togeder."

Alice chuckled, getting back to peeling some carrots.

After waiting until everyone was served, Pierre fixed Alice a big bowl of soup with a piece of French bread with butter.

Taking her food into the maid's quarters, Jackie already seated there. As soon as Alice sat down, Jackie got up with her bowl, heading back into the kitchen.

For a minute, Alice felt the cold shoulder Jackie was giving her. Maybe she really didn't like her?

Savoring every bite of her soup, Alice finished up, then took her bowl into the kitchen, washing it, putting it back in the cupboard.

Heading down the corridor to her room, watching on both sides. Arriving at the dining room before she realized she totally missed her door. Walking back slowly, she finds it, but not without really looking for the break in the wall. It was a hidden passageway that just looked like another panel in the wall. It thrilled her. More fairy tale stuff. Giggling she pushed her door in, then glances up her narrow staircase.

Thinking back to the first time Gladys showed her the room, it was not this way at all but a door just behind the kitchen. There had to be two ways to get to her room. Wow, this was amazing. Just as that thought escaped her mind, she turned to see Lucy standing behind her, "C'mon, Alice," said Lucy. "We have lots to see."

Taking her by the hand, Lucy led Alice around the big house, showing her the wine cellar, the pantry, all the bedrooms, except where her mom and dad slept, which was off limits to everyone. Once the tour was over, Alice was more confused than ever.

Lucy's room really intrigued Alice. It had all the things she would have loved to have at Lucy's age. A big bed, stuffed animals everywhere, brightly colored curtains dressing the windows. Everything spelling beautiful.

"I share my room with my baby sister," said Lucy. "Her name is Molly, and she is one year old. She is a baby still."

Confused, Alice wondered where the baby had been all along. She hadn't noticed a baby, and Gladys didn't mention she had a baby.

After the tour, Lucy stopped and looked deep into Alice's eyes.

"Molly is just my make-believe baby sister. Don't tell, OK?"

Alice smiled, thinking of her own secret playmate.

"Let's go to your room now, Alice. It has a secret passageway. It goes up here, through the pantry door. And there is another entrance in the corridor. All mansions have them, especially for the maids. So if you were needed quickly you come straight down into the kitchen. And the other door before you get to the dining room, so you do not disturb us when we were having dinner." All of a sudden, the fairy tale drained from Alice cheeks. They were hiding her away. It was like a private prison of sorts. Not a princess at all. Just a maid in a palace. How could she have fooled herself? Thinking more about it, her smile returned, her happiness renewed. She was a princess in a fairy tale, hidden away in a palace. There was everything a girl could dream of, and she had never felt love like this before. Two doors and two staircases to her private space. It was a special, heavenly place.

"I love your room, Alice. All the maids who come from abroad stay in that room. Are you from abroad?"

"Not that far away, from the countryside."

"Can I come to your house sometime? I would really like to."

Thinking fast, and not knowing how to answer, Alice said, "Well, I suppose so, but you will have to ask your mother."

She was afraid for Lucy to meet the evil mother in her fairy tale life. No, not ever. Irene would scare Lucy. There was no way she would ever take her home.

"I am living here now," said Alice.

"Really, so you are never going home again?" asked Lucy.

"I hope I can stay and live with your family forever. I really love being here."

"Oh, I am so happy, Alice, I hope you stay forever," said Lucy, wrapping her arms around her.

"Thank you for showing me everything, but I need to go and do some reading now. I will see you at breakfast, OK?"

Lucy started down the stairs. "Good night, Alice, see you tomorrow."

Lying in her bed, Alice thought over all the things she had learned. The kids' names, which she had forgotten already. Gladys had told her that in time she would remember them and not to worry.

All of a sudden, a weary, tired feeling came over her. Stretching her legs out, her muscles feeling tight, her back a little sore. Going from one bedroom to another, with so much to see, the work didn't seem hard until now.

Ten bedrooms to clean and kitchen duties. The dream was not so vivid anymore. The shiny floors worried her, hoping she wouldn't slip and fall with an armful of food.

The round alarm clock woke her promptly at six. She had set it an hour before she had to be in the kitchen.

After a good long soak in a hot bath, toweling herself off, her body feels relaxed and strong for another busy day. Slipping into her uniform, she heads down the staircase into the hallway. A strong waft of coffee coming from the kitchen, but there are no sounds of children.

Stepping in, she didn't see anyone but Jackie, who was mopping the kitchen floor. Worried now that she'd missed the breakfast duties, Jackie spoke.

"Gladys and the kids were up earlier today and are already headed into the city. Seeing that I did your duties already, I have left the dishes for you."

A pile of dirty dishes filled the sink.

"I have slaved for these people for years now. And you are just a maid around here. Don't go thinking anything else. Just because you get to sleep in that fancy room and eat their food doesn't make you more important than me. And don't think you are going to be taking my job. You would never be able to handle the workload they give me!"

"Oh no, Jackie. Mrs. Olsen hired me to make your job easier. That's what she said. I am just supposed to make the house run more like a fine-tuned piano."

Alice thought she would throw in the humor to break the ice that had formed since she had arrived.

Just then Pierre walked into the kitchen with an armful of fresh herbs and lettuces.

"Why are you washing the floor already, Jackie? I need you to do the dishes first so I can have my counter space for my cooking."

Flashing a mean look at Alice, Jackie put the mop back in the broom pantry.

"Don't you have your rooms to do now, Alice? The house needs to be in perfect order before Gladys and the kids get back," said Jackie.

"Yes, of course," answered Alice, smiling at Pierre.

Just as she turned to leave the kitchen, Pierre spoke.

"There is French toast and sausages for you in the oven, Alice. You could have your breakfast, then get to your duties."

Flashing Jackie a stern look, he pulled out the plate with the steaming sausages and browned French toast.

"Thank you, Pierre," she said as she took the plate from him.

"My pleasure, my dear," he replied.

Jackie angrily rattled the dishes in the sink.

Alice walked out of the kitchen to the back of kitchen, near the pantry sitting down to enjoy her breakfast.

Ten bedrooms, five on each side. Spending quality time in each, dusting, vacuuming, making beds, and hanging up stray clothing.

All the children had books in their rooms, making it hard for her not to want to have a quick peek inside.

One day, while in Lucy's room, she picked up a book. One familiar to her. The little girl in the story was so much like herself as a young child.

On the inside flap, a girl sat in front of a shack, chickens running in the yard. A trail led to a meadow with flowers on either side. The little girl had blonde curls and a handful of daisies. The sun was beaming down on her. Staring closer, the little girl had a white dress on with big crimson flowers. It was almost the exact picture that Pearl had drawn that Miss Ink had showed her. Remembering now, she forgot to ask for the picture before she left. Tears cascaded down her cheeks, closing the book she wiped at her eyes.

CHAPTER 32

J ackie was feeling secure again about her role in the family. Alice was taking care of the children's rooms, giving her more time for her breaks. Going up and down the stairs carrying linen, gave her a sore back every day.

Alice was young and capable of climbing the stairs daily.

One morning, a few weeks after Alice's arrival, Jackie strikes up a conversation.

"You are a good worker for your age, Alice. Did you say you are twelve? I was doing hard work when I was twelve too. Sometimes in this life you just don't have a choice. Only a few are lucky like this family. I had to work or go hungry. You just have to do what you have to do to survive."

Her heavy Spanish accent was like music to Alice's ears.

Not knowing how to respond to her, Alice nodded her head.

"I am thirty years old," said Jackie. "It's so hard for me to realize you are only twelve years old and already such a good worker."

"Thank you," replied Alice.

At the end of the day, Jackie made it a point to say goodbye to Alice. It was better to feel good about the girl, anxious to find out Alice's story.

Retiring to her room at night was the best time of the day for Alice. She loved a hot bath in the arms of the beastly white enamel tub, lavishing in aromas of lavender and vanilla.

Gladys had brought Alice a basket of bath salts, different soaps, and body spray made from real lavender flowers. Alice felt guilt accepting such luxuries, but Gladys would not take no for an answer.

Reading until her eyes could no longer stay open, comfy under the soft feathers of angel wings, such blessings after a day of hard work.

One morning Jackie walked into the kitchen, handing Alice a dress.

"Here, this belonged to another girl who worked here. Margarite. She was tiny like you. She was from Poland."

"Thank you," said Alice, examining the uniform. It was exactly like Jackie's uniform. Red piping around the sleeves and a rounded scalloped collar.

Rushing into the pantry, Alice slipped into the dress and walked back out to Jackie.

"We look like twins now," said Alice, smiling.

"It fits you perfectly," said Jackie, admiring Alice's slim, tight figure.

The maids took their lunch breaks together now.

"My name is really Jakita," she said, lowering her voice. "I don't want the Olsenses to know everything about me. Can you keep a secret?" Oh no, not another secret, thought Alice. Pulling another file from her brain's storage, she opened it, waiting to put the secret safely away.

"Yes," answered Alice, her eyes wide.

"I am from Mexico, and my mother met a sailor from Nova Scotia. They got together in Mexico. You know what I mean, right?"

Alice nodded, not really understanding, but she didn't want to appear naive.

"Anyway, the rest is history. The ones who knew my mother say she was a whore from Mexico. The story started going around, and then before long, that was the big gossip. Oh, why am I telling you this anyway? Sometimes I forget you are still a child."

Starting to feel uncomfortable with the conversation, Alice stood up.

"I really should be getting back to my chores."

Just then Gladys walked in, a questioning look on her face.

"I see that you girls are getting along fine. That's what I like, when everything is smooth and sweet, just like beautiful music."

The girls looked at each other and giggled. "You are both a big part of this family. You hard work will not go without gratitude for your servitude."

The next day after breakfast Gladys asked Alice to meet her in the garden room for tea.

It was time to have the talk to Alice about Jackie.

"I don't want you getting caught up in Jackie's life. And it's best not to discuss your life with her either. There is a saying that goes don't mix business with pleasure. What she doesn't know, won't hurt her."

Alice scrunched her face, not understanding what Gladys was saying. Not wanting to appear stupid, she answered, "I understand."

That relieved Alice's mind, anyway. Why would she want to tell anyone about her life?

"Also, some people in town say things about Jackie and her mother. It is none of my business, and she does a good service to my family, and that is all that matters to me."

After their tea, Gladys gave Alice a tour of the house and filled her in on a bit of the history of the estate.

"This mansion was built by a diamond merchant. It was bought by my husband's family and passed down when we first married. We have lived in this house twenty years now."

Getting close to the barns, Gladys pointed to the horses.

"There have always been horses here. Some show horses, some race horses, and a few Arabians. The children all love riding. Would you like to ride sometime with Lucy?"

"Oh no, ma'am, I am scared of horses. They are so big." Her eyes grew wide.

"You aren't the only one. Some grown men are afraid of horses. They can be dangerous if you don't know how to handle them."

Getting back up to the house, Gladys pointed to the ornamental door knocker. "It is solid gold," she said. "As well as all the fixtures in the house."

Throughout the tour, Alice kept saying, "Wow."

Everything was so amazing and beautiful that was the only word that would come to her mind.

Alice was spending lots of her free time in the garden room, usually with a book and a snack. Gladys had never told Jackie she could spend time there. It was another reason for the jealousy that was growing silently, like a virus. Jackie never had that much free time that she could stop to read a book. Every time she noticed Alice in the garden room, she was irritated.

Although Alice tried to avoid any personal conversations between her and Jackie, it seemed that she was always trying to spell her life out to her, like coffee spilled on a white tablecloth, seeping into the delicate whiteness of it.

"I have two children," confessed Jackie. "They live in Mexico with my grandmother. I wasn't able to care for them there, so I came here to work, and that's when I met that useless husband of mine. Biggest mistake I ever made. Fat assed bastard, he is."

Alice put her hand over her mouth, her eyes wide.

Jackie continued to spread out her life like a map for Alice to read and connect the highways.

"Work, work, work. That's all I get out of this life." Holding her face in her hands, she stared deep into the well of her teacup.

"Yes, I have made mistake in my life, and I've had to pay for them dearly. I am so tired; some nights I fall asleep with my clothes on. I leave here and go home to cook and clean some more for that lazy husband of mine. Said he hurt his back working on the railway. Didn't do a damn thing anymore. Never took me anywhere. Just orders me around, like I'm his maid too."

Alice was sad for Jackie. She just listened, saying nothing. What could she say that would make things any better? Feeling sorry for Jackie; her life did not sound happy.

"Oh my, why am I telling a child my story?"

Jackie started laughing almost hysterically, causing Alice to start laughing too.

"Thank you for listening, Alice. I have no one to talk to. So tell me, Alice, what is your story, now that you know all about mine?"

"I don't have much of a story," answered Alice. "I have only lived twelve years, and I have eight brothers, and my sister Pearl died. My father is sick, with a brain tumor, and my mother needs me to work to help out. That is my whole story. Like I said, I haven't lived long enough yet to have much of a story."

"What about school, Alice? Do you even know how to read and write?"

"Of course I do. I am going to be sitting in on the children's lessons. I am so excited to learn everything."

Those words were like a knife going through Jackie's chest. Twisting her mouth, she got up from her seat.

"I have some things to do. I will see you later."

Feeling like she had been punched in the stomach, Alice got up from her seat and went into the kitchen to see how she could help Pierre.

The next morning, Alice thought she would break the ice again by saying something to Jackie.

"You know what, Jackie? We both have terrible lives. My story might be a little different but much the same."

"Thank you, Alice. You are a sweet kid."

With a big smile for Jackie, Alice walked away.

Alice had only seen Mr. Olsen a few times since she arrived, at the breakfast table giving the kids a news flash, or in his study with his nose in a newspaper. The couple of times Gladys had asked her to take him coffee in his study, made Alice a bit nervous. The air about him seemed strained and intimidating, the way he commanded his children's attention. Gladys had told her not to bother him at all, unless she was asked, in other words, speak if spoken to. And it seemed like the kids were always standing at attention when he was addressing them.

Watching the children interact with Gladys and their father reminded Alice of what she had missed out on. The love hung in the air like a sticky toffee apple, sweet and infectious, like they were wrapped in a blanket of love.

Mr. Olsen carried himself like a king. He seemed to always be dressed in a suit or in his silk smoking jacket. Alice had noticed him in the library on occasion when she was in selecting a book. He would just look at her over his spectacles and then go back into the book he was reading. Sometimes there would be a big waft of cigar smoke hanging around his head. She liked the spicy, woodsy smell.

Alice's dad had never smoked anything. Mr. Olsen was nothing like her father. Cigars were probably just for the rich, she concluded.

One day Gladys sent Alice down to the barns to get Mr. Olsen. He was riding a horse over some jumps, sitting high in the saddle. Alice watched, admiring his outfit. Tall black boots and jodhpurs, as they called the tight pants, and a black velvet jacket and helmet to match. She couldn't understand why they had to dress up just to ride a horse.

He looked rather handsome, thought Alice.

It was the way he held his head, finely groomed, just like the well-tuned piano, Alice thought laughing to herself.

Lucy had told her the tight pants were called jodhpurs.

CHAPTER 33

The first few weeks at the Olsenses', Alice enjoyed a little of everything that was offered in the kitchen. She loved all the good food and ate as much as she wanted, on a few occasions going to bed with a bellyache, not used to eating three square meals a day. Watching the Olsen children, how they ate a little of this, a little of that, and sometimes Gladys would have to encourage them to eat their food. Imagining her brothers with so much food, they wouldn't leave a scrap, starting to wonder how they were doing. Wanting to stay happy, she chased those thoughts out of her mind. Gladys had said, to be cheerful.

Lately Gladys had encouraged Alice to sit in on the tutoring, and it had become her favorite time of day. Listening intently to the lessons, making notes and then studying them at night, almost like she was sneaking in something forbidden, feeling good about learning.

The instructors were pleased with her interest, and the kids were enjoying her joining in, answering questions, and asking more, like a hungry sponge, anxious to tell he brothers about all she had learned.

Any time the thoughts of her father came, she would try to erase the sadness right away. The way she had seen him last made her heart heavy.

Gladys had found Alice deep in thought one day, tears in her eyes. Putting her hand on her shoulder, asking if everything was OK. Alice replied that she was just thinking of her father.

It had been almost a month now. She'd grown accustomed to the rigid schedule, having time for herself, and learning lots in the kitchen. Pierre was letting Alice cook some things while he watched and coached her.

"The zoop is very good," he said. Jackie and Alice giggled at the *z* in soup.

Gladys was teaching the girls how to crochet, and Alice had started a dress for her rag doll. It was purple with pink flowers on it.

Everyone loved the dress, asking Alice who would fit such a small dress.

"It is for a doll. Actually it is my sister's doll, and I am looking after her now."

"I'm sure she will love it," said Lucy, giggling. Not even a smirk from Alice.

Always a buzz in the air when the children were home, all the kids going in different directions.

On Saturday the Olsenses were always astir with plans for the day. A few of the kids were getting ready to go riding. Gladys was in the corner of the study, talking to a couple of them. Lucy is all ears and excitement, looking Alice's way every few seconds, like a secret was brewing. The playful look on her face told Alice they were talking about her. They smiled, excitement on their faces, and Gladys laughed and smiled Alice's way. She strode with her kids in tow toward Alice.

"We were going into the city today for some fun and shopping. Would you like to come with us? Everyone would love to have you along." For a long minute, Alice went silent. It was like she had just stepped into their world, their perfect forbidden world. "Oh yes, sure. Why, yes, ma'am," answered Alice, her face lighting up like a sunburst.

"Go ahead and get ready then. Just wear comfortable shoes. We will be walking around the city and going to the museum of art today."

"Yes, of course," she answered, running toward her secret passageway.

Everyone standing straight, Gladys examining her clan. They are all dressed in fine clothes, their hair perfect and their shoes shining. Gladys wore a yellow tweed suit with a soft butter-yellow blouse. Alice looked her over from head to toe. She looked like a lady in a magazine, so pretty, like a field of buttercups, dainty and beautiful.

Orville pulled up in front in the long black car with the silver grill and the bird that lead them on their journey.

Watching in awe, she didn't realize how long the car was. The first time she rode in it, from the time she entered she had gone into a dream state. Was it real? Was it really happening? Where would the road take them?

Everyone piled into the car carefully as not to wrinkle their clothing.

They sat perfectly still and quiet, five on either side, Alice sitting between Lucy and one of the older girls, Beth, a tall, fair-skinned beauty with a few freckles over her nose. Gladys reached back from the front seat.

"A little something for you, Alice." Handing her an envelope. The kids watched the exchange, smiling.

"Thank you, ma'am," she said, clinging to the envelope.

That day in the city was one Alice would never forget. Gladys included her in all the fun and shopping. They spent the whole day going from the museum to a movie and then shopping, until the kids were getting tired of all the walking and fun. They made it home before dark, everyone retired to their rooms, Alice with a permanent smile on her lips.

What a day, right out of a dream, she thought, lying back in her plush, comfortable room.

Gladys secretly eyed Alice all day. Her laughter, like an angel's wings beating. This was no ordinary child, she thought to herself. She was an angel. Had this child ever had a happy day like this before? God had been good to her family, and she had lots to share. It would be her duty to bring as much happiness as she possibly could into this girl's life.

One whole day Gladys spent going over her girls' things they didn't use anymore, clothes that were too good to throw away, carrying armfuls of clothing to Alice's room, displaying them all on her bed.

When Alice walked into her room and saw all the things on her bed, she put her hands over her face. Tears of joy poured down her cheeks uncontrollably. These things were all for her. Looking through the clothes and hair things and a few pieces of jewelry, sitting on the floor, taking in all the blessings. It must be a dream, she decided. How could all these things be happening to her? A mere poor child who had never known such happiness?

Handling every piece of clothing as though they are fine china, she hangs them in her closet. Lining up the shoes, she counted twenty pairs.

Dresses and more dresses, her whole closet full. One complete wall of clothes and fancy things. Standing back, she admired her newfound treasures.

"I am the luckiest girl in the world," she said out loud, looking up to her savior. He was always with her, never out of her sight. Going to her bed, she gets down on her knees. She prayed.

"Thank you, God. Thank you for all blessings you have bestowed upon me." It was the prayer she had heard her father utter so many times.

The next few days after the trip to the city, Jackie dismissed Alice like the plague. Gladys couldn't help but notice the way Jackie was avoiding even looking Alice's way. It made Gladys feel as though she should replace Jackie, who was showing signs of jealousy of a child. But she had been a part of the family for years now, and the language tutoring took centre stage. Jackie was almost irreplaceable at this point, almost like a vital organ.

Alice was feeling the rift that was growing between her and Jackie, wondering if she thought Alice had told her secrets to Gladys. Without any conversation with Jackie, it had been a hard couple of days going through their paces in the kitchen, to and from the dining room like two ships passing in the night, making Alice feel uncomfortable and unhappy.

Jackie was walking by her without even as much as a glance her way. It had been three days when Jackie finally had to get something off her chest.

The maids were both in the pantry, straightening out some canned goods, when Jackie spoke.

"Look here, Alice. I see you are getting special treatment around here. They have never taken me shopping for a day in the city."

Gladys had walked by and decided to stand outside the door to hear what was being said.

"Maybe because I am still a child. And Lucy asked that I come along. It didn't mean a thing."

Just then Gladys stepped into the pantry. Jackie with an alarmed look on her face.

"Jackie, I have noticed that you are not very talkative to Alice. And now I know it's because she came to town with us the other day. This is sure childish of you, Jackie. After all, Alice is just a child herself. I want you to get over your jealousy towards her before I have to take things into my own hands. I will be watching to make sure that you are not being unkind."

"Of course, ma'am," answered Jackie, turning to put a few cans on a shelf.

Gladys winked at Alice and walked out of the pantry.

"I am sorry, Alice." said Jackie.

"It is OK," said Alice. "I just hope that we can be friends because I was sad when you didn't want to talk to me. After all, we are the maids, and we need to work together and help each other."

Gladys was still listening outside the door and was pleased with what she had just heard. And proud of Alice for being such a grown-up.

"Mrs. Olsen told me that you help her family to run like a well-tuned piano. And I know that means that you are a big help. Also, I could never do all the hard work you do, Jackie."

"She really said that?" answered Jackie.

"Yes, she did," said Alice.

"Thank you, Miss Alice. Forget I ever said anything, OK? I will see you later. Got to get busy and make some bread for dinner."

It was almost two months since Alice had arrived. Gladys and Alice were having a tea break.

"I think it's time you maybe go back home for a day or so to see your family. Your mother said she would need your wages, and she made a point of telling me you were not to spend any of it."

Alice's smile turned sullen.

"Yes, ma'am," answered Alice.

"I'll see if Orville can take you this week and pick you up the next day."

Alice breathed a deep sigh of relief when she said he'd pick her up the next day. It was as though her chariot was turning to dust, right before her eyes.

Walking out of the kitchen, Alice headed down the corridor to her secret door. One, two, three, four, she counted all the way to the top. Stepping into her room, she breathed in the smell of lavender in the air. A large vase with fresh lavender displayed on her dresser. Taking in another deep breath of the essence, she relaxes on her bed. The visit home was inevitable. No matter what, she didn't want her mother to come and take her back home.

The next morning at the breakfast table, Gladys had some announcements to make.

"We are going to take Alice home for a day to see her mother." Looking Alice's way, she said, "You can either go tomorrow or when the kids and I get back from visiting the grandparents in Manson Ville. We will be gone a week."

Tomorrow was just too soon, thought Alice.

"I would rather wait until you return. There are just so many things I have to do before I go."

Gladys looked deep into Alice's eyes. A scared little girl. She really didn't want to go home.

"Fine, Alice. We will arrange it for the day after we get back. Mr. Olsen will be home. With the kids gone, both you and Jackie will have an easy week. It will only be Mr. Olsen who will need taking care of."

"Yes, of course," answered Alice.

CHAPTER 34

The first couple of days, the house seemed ghostly, no voices, no footsteps on the marble staircase. It felt like her own private palace. How beautiful everything was, twirling around in the foyer.

With all the kids gone, there wasn't much to do. Mr. Olsen was taking his breakfast and dinner in the library. Jackie said she would take care of serving him his meals and that Alice could find other things to do or just help Pierre in the kitchen. That was fine with Alice. More time for her to read and just explore the grounds and the mansion.

Jackie seemed extra nice to Alice. She dismissed her altogether the first morning after the kids and Gladys had left, saying she would take care of Mr. Olsen.

"This will be like a week off for you. Do whatever you want," Jackie said.

Gladys hadn't said anything about the week off. Something just didn't seem right. How could Jackie tell her that she could just do whatever she wanted?

Sitting at her window at the top of the house, she noticed Mr. Olsen going toward the barns, his whip in his hand, dressed in his usual riding gear. Not too long afterward she noticed Jackie walking down the same way, entering the same barn where Mr. Olsen had gone. She watched for a while, and when there was no sign of either of them, she wondered if he was taking Jackie riding, since neither of them came out of the barn. Curiosity got the best of her, and she had to go and see what they were doing.

Following the cobblestone pathway to the large white barns, pushing in the big heavy door. The door creaked, a waft of horse manure and strong sticky molasses. Standing in the middle of the shed row, she looked down the length of the barn, many heads of horses showing from the top of their shoulders, they all stared Alice's way.

Searching the barn, she found no sign of life except for the horses and a sparrow flying low over her head and out the door. Walking slowly between the horses' heads, on either side, close to her, their big eyes rolling around. Some bowed, some shook their heads, one shook his head from side to side, one sidestepped from one side to the other. A big white one stuck his head way out and grabbed Alice by the sweater.

"No, let go," she said, her eyes wide, his long, yellow teeth showing.

Almost knocking Alice off her feet, he finally let go.

"Don't do that, you stupid horse," she said, giggling.

Treading carefully the rest of the way up the aisle of the barn without incident. Noticing a door leading to what looked like an office, she could see Mr. Olsen and Jackie bending down, facing him.

She was doing something, maybe tying his shoelaces. Just then, Mr. Olsen noticed Alice standing there.

"Go back to the house, Alice," he ordered, trying to conceal his bare skin, his jodhpurs open in the front. Jackie was startled, stood up straight, her back to Alice.

"Make me some lunch, Alice. We will be at the house in a bit."

"Yes, of course," she answered, turning and walking back down the shed row and out of the barn.

Getting back to the house, straight to the kitchen, where she sat at the maid's table. Pierre was nowhere to be seen. What was she supposed to make for Mr. Olsen? Worried now, he had yelled at her. Was she in trouble? And what had she seen? It looked like Jackie was rubbing Mr. Olsen. But his naked privates? It wasn't right.

She would never speak of it, not to a soul. Some things were better unsaid. Another secret to tuck away.

The day the kids and Gladys came back home, there was a flurry of activity in the house. Excitedly, Alice watched and welcomed everyone home. It felt good to have them all back. The house without the laughter and constant activities seemed lonely. And a week of having most of her time to herself gave her too much time to think, a constant worry about having to go home to her mother soon. The rest had been good. After studying the lessons and reading about ten books, Alice felt renewed and ready to get back to her normal schedule.

After dinner, Gladys called Alice out to the garden room.

"Let's have some tea and a little talk."

Always excited to spend alone time with Gladys. Alice had grown to love her, like she had never felt for her own mother.

Sitting across from Gladys adoringly, she waited, anticipating her instruction.

"Orville has fit you into his schedule. Tomorrow you will leave at nine sharp to go home. You will stay two days, and he will be there to pick you up on the morning of the third day at nine sharp. I am sorry I have other engagements, or I would take the journey with you. The next visit home I will go with you so I can have a chat with your mother. I want to tell her what a great job you are doing and how we love having you in our family."

Not knowing what to say, the last part of what Gladys said worried Alice. Her mother couldn't know that they loved her. Anything that showed she was having a good time or was getting too much attention could signal to Irene that Alice was too happy with her new job.

Staring at Gladys, all these worries going through her mind, draining away her happiness, her expression showing her insecurities.

"Are you OK, Alice? Did I say something wrong?"

"Oh no, just that if my mother thought I wasn't working and having too much fun, she might make me come home for good. It's just she wants me to work hard."

A concerned look crossed Gladys's face. Sitting without saying a word, just watching Alice, the love radiating from her.

"You are dismissed, Alice."

"Yes, ma'am. I will go and prepare a bag for going home tomorrow."

Getting up from her seat, she pushed in the chair. With a curtsy, she backed away, then turned and walked back into the main house and down the corridor.

With every step toward her private place, she felt a heaviness coming over her. Her dad. She had to think of him now, and she had to see him. Following the lines in the marble floor reminded her of the veins she had seen in her father's eyes. Trying to keep from worrying about him, she changed her mind-set and started thinking of how happy he would be to see her. Yes, her daddy needed to see her.

After dinner duties, she retreated to her private place. Going over her clothing, she picked out a few things she had arrived with. A couple pairs of trousers, two blouses and a sweater. That was all she would need for two days. The only new thing was the pretty blue sweater with the cables on the front. It had belonged to one of the girls. A camel-colored pair of canvas shoes also belonged to one of the girls. With her small bag packed, placing it at the top of the staircase, tucking herself into her dreamy bed, she lay quietly. All her insecurities were coming to her mind. Tears fell without sound. Frightened of the possibilities, she decided to take it to the Lord.

"Please, God, let everything be OK with my daddy. And I need to come back to my new family and my job. Don't let my mommy keep me at home. Please, God, I sure hope you have time to hear my prayer. And thank you, God, for all the blessings. Good night."

The round clock spoke with a loud alarm. Sitting up, it is seven o'clock. Lots of time to have a bath and get ready to leave. Sitting at the dresser, she brushed her hair stealing glances at her reflection in the mirror. The shine of her curls like a new copper penny, staring deep into her own forest-green eyes. She says, "Mirror, mirror on the wall. Can you please tell me, does my hand stay the same or forever change? Where, oh, where will the road take me? To another world, and then back again. My chariot will arrive and depart. Alice has a palace," she said, smiling, her eyes softening. A smile crossing her lips.

"I think I've been reading too much."

Orville arrived at the front of the house waiting for Alice, holding the door open for her.

"Good morning, Miss Alice. I will put your bag in the trunk."

"Thank you, Orville."

Settling into the comfy seat, her eyes wide, she stared straight ahead.

Taking his seat behind the wheel, Orville's eyes searched out Alice in the back. Her pink sweater and her rosy cheeks like candy floss, the sweetness of her, infectious.

"Is everything fine, Miss Alice? You didn't forget anything?"

Her eyes meet his in the rear-view mirror.

"I'm really fine, Orville, and no, I didn't forget anything, thank you."

He watched her as he started up the big car, navigating it around the circular drive out onto the road.

With her book propped up in her lap, Alice escapes into the story.

It wasn't not until Orville hit the pot-holed driveway to her house that she was jolted back to the reality of Irene's hard, cold heart.

Staring straight out the front window now, no sign of anyone in the yard, just a few chickens running around the outside of the coupe.

Orville pulled up to the steps and turned off the car. Just then two boys stuck their heads out the door, staring at the big black car.

"It's Alice," yelled Skip, Earl coming to have a look.

Irene came up behind the boys, wiping her hands on her apron.

"Oh, I see the princess has arrived finally. She better not have messed up that job."

Irene went to the window over the sink, holding the side of the curtain with one finger, spying as Orville gets out, opening the back door. Giving Alice his hand, he helps her out of the car. Watching as Alice surveyed the house and yard like she had been away a long time. Orville was saying something to her, but Irene couldn't make it out. Then he went around to the back of the car and took out a bag, handing it to her. Alice smiled and said something, heading towards the steps when the big car started its retreat out of the driveway, backward.

Just then Irene went to the door, sticking out her head.

"Thought you had forgotten you have a family here waiting for you."

Earl and Skip run to Alice to hug her. Skip took her bag and brought it in the house. They both waited for her to get in the door, then the questions started flying like a thousand sparrows in a tree.

"What's it like, living with rich people?" asked Earl.

"Bet you get lots to eat there," said Skip. "You look different, Alice."

Irene was all ears waiting for Alice to answer her brothers.

"I am a maid. I work from the time I get up at six in the morning till the end of the dinner duties. Always busy doing chores. They have ten children, and I have all the bedroom duties as well as kitchen duties. It is hard work, but I don't mind. Everyone is kind to me, and I do get good food to eat."

Bile rises in Irene's throat at the sound of good food to eat.

"I can see that you are eating well. You have filled out a bit, and your cheeks are rosy. Things have not been so rosy around here. We scarcely have food on the table. It's been almost two months now. You were supposed to come home a month after you started. If I didn't see you in a few days, I was coming there to bring you home."

"I had to wait for them to fit it into their schedules to bring me, Mother. I didn't have any say in when they would have time."

"Don't try any fancy talk with me, miss. So get your wages now and give them to me. I've been waiting so I can go and get the staples we need around here."

Before Alice could even sit down or go to her room, she digs in her bag and pulled out a white envelope that Gladys had given her just the night before.

Handing it to Irene, she rips it open, pulling out the bills.

Irene's eyes widened as she counted the money, stuffing it into the pocket of her apron. Without saying anything more, she walks away, back to the sink where she is washing some vegetables.

"How long are you staying home?" asked Skip. "I missed you a lot, Alice."

"I miss everyone too, but I really need to work to help out. And the family wouldn't be able to go on without Jackie and me."

"Who is Jackie?" piped up Irene.

"She is the other maid. Much older than me. She does most of the hard work. I'm staying for two days, then I have to go back to my job."

Just then Alice regretted having said that. There was no way that Irene should think that her work was easy.

"What I mean is, she helps Pierre, the chef, make bread and do things like that. I don't do any of the cooking. Just cleaning and serving meals. At the end of the day I am so tired, sometimes I go to sleep with my uniform still on."

Oh no. She immediately felt guilty at that white lie.

Waiting for Irene's reaction, who has turned her back to Alice, her hands back in the sink.

That was a close call, thought Alice. She would have to be careful to choose her words carefully, like walking on glass.

"They have two maids and a chef? Wow, they must be rich," cried William.

"I am working all the time, so I don't get to enjoy all the things they have. I am just happy to have a job."

The boys kept on bantering Alice, question after question. Afraid to say the wrong thing, she grabs her bag and headed up the stairs to her room.

"Where do you think you are going, Alice? The boys have taken over your room now that you don't live here anymore. While you are here, you will have to sleep on the couch. And where did you get those clothes you are wearing? Ah, new clothes. You better not have spent any of your wages on new clothes."

Alice turned on the step and walked back down. Standing at the foot of the staircase, with her bag in hand, she wanted to run out the door. But, no, she had to answer Irene and make sure she said the right thing.

"No, Mother. Gladys gave me some of Lucy's used clothes that she didn't fit into any longer. Just a few things."

Irene walks away toward the pantry. Walking into the parlor, Alice puts down her bag sitting on the couch. The threadbare arms showed some of the stuffing, the seat cushions sagging. Not wanting to show her disappointment, she settled into the couch. A shock to the senses, unreal how the fortunate lived, compared to the poor.

The first thing that came to her mind was her doll. If she had no room anymore, where were her doll and teddy bear?

Walking back into the kitchen, she stood near Irene.

"Mother. Where did you put my things that were in my room, like the rag doll and teddy bear?"

"You are kidding me! What is a grown girl like you doing with a doll in the first place? I gave those things to some kids who needed them. You are almost a grown woman. You will soon have children of your own."

Alice's eyes grew wide and shiny, the tears ebbing.

"No, Mother, I am not having any children till I am grown up and a lady. I am just a child yet."

Realizing there was no sense in arguing about the doll or teddy, she swallowed her sadness and stopped the tears from flowing.

Taking a discriminating look at her mother, her dingy white apron pulled across her buldging stomach, the same drab grey dress hanging over her heavy body. Dark, receding eyes and listless hair. How different she was from the lady of the house, Gladys, who looked like a queen, compared to her. Really she felt sorry for her mother. The next important thing: How was her father?

"How is Daddy? Can I go and see him?"

"Your father is not getting any better, Alice. He sleeps most of the day. I don't want you bothering him. Your father is dying."

All the tears that had been held back, like a dam holding back rushing water, came running down her cheeks. Holding her hands to her face as the tears soaked her sweater. Trying not to wail, she runs to the parlor burying her head in her hands.

Irene just shook her head and walked away.

When suppertime came, Irene did not make a place for Alice at the table, nor did she offer her anything.

Alice sat in the parlor, hearing the boys settling in around the table. Covering herself with a grey wool blanket Irene handed her, wondering if it was the one she always had in her room, since she could remember. Wishing that the time would be over soon, closing her eyes, she falls asleep.

When the boys are finished eating their potatoes and bread, Irene goes to the parlor doorway, shouting in at Alice.

"You are not a guest in this house. Get in the kitchen now and do the dishes and clean up. I work all day long around here, and since you've been gone, I have all the work to do. It's a good thing for you that we are in such need that you have to stay at that job, because I would bring you right back here."

Breathing a sigh of relief, Alice gets up right away, pushing the blanket aside, like casting her doubts and sadness away, heading into the kitchen. Without hesitation, she washed the dishes, straightened up the kitchen, even washed the floor without Irene demanding she did. Nothing could get in the way of her going back to her job, whatever Irene wanted, Alice would do willingly.

The shanty kitchen gleamed from the bleach Alice used to wash the counters and the floor that was mostly all wooden slats now, in and around the sink area. Whitewashed to boards, the linoleum cracked around the cupboards.

Irene has an eagle's eye on Alice, as she wrings the heavy mop in a pail of water. Just as she put it in the broom closet, Irene comes up behind her.

"Get out of my sight. You are too high and mighty for me these days. Look at you, the way you have changed. In a short two months I can hardly recognize you."

"Changed, Mother, what do you mean?"

"The way you walk around here and look at us like we are dirt under your feet."

"Oh no, Mother," answered Alice in a high-pitched voice. "I don't think like that."

"Anyway, get out of my sight. Tomorrow is another day. We will talk more tomorrow."

Walking away toward the parlor, she turned. With love and sadness in her eyes, she spoke.

"Good night mother."

Taking the bow, she disappeared into the parlor like a mouse scurrying away.

The first night back home, Alice tossed and turned trying to get warm.

Making a nest in the threadbare couch, curling into a fetal position, she finally fell asleep.

Thrust into a dream, Alice is running in a meadow, a flock of butterflies overhead, the sun kissing her face. Not far from her, another girl is picking wildflowers, bent down in the grass. When she stands up, she turns to Alice and started running toward her with wide-open arms. They hold each other, the warmth of Pearl's breath on her face. Pearl kissed her on the cheek, looking deep into her grass-green eyes, a longing love look.

"Breakfast is served," Irene bellowed from the kitchen.

Pushing aside the grey wool blanket, Alice sits up. Reliving the dream, a smile crossed her cherub face. How wonderful it was, the best night ever. It had been a long time since she had dreamed about Pearl. Nothing could make her sad today. Pearl had hugged and kissed her, Alice touching her cheek with her index finger, deciding not to wash her face in that spot all day.

Pulling on her housecoat over her nightgown, Alice shows in the doorway.

"Good morning, Mother. Can I help with anything?"

"What's so good about it? As you can see we only have toast and jam for breakfast."

Alice's eyes scan the table. Her brothers sit quietly, exchanging glances with Alice. She smiled, a heartfelt warmth to all of them. Her dream had made her so happy, she wanted to share it, but she knew that Irene would have something negative to say so she kept it to herself. Remembering the thickness of the envelope, Gladys had given her for her mom, the poor us story not sitting right. Irene would have lots to put on the table, as soon as she went into town, realizing her mother was trying to make her feel guilty, for the abundance of food she now had.

There was an empty seat at one end of the table—her father's.

Wondering how he was, she wanted to go to him right now.

A stack of white bread toast in the middle of the table, and a big jar of strawberry jam. No butter, milk, or eggs. *Things have sure been sparse around here*, she thought to herself.

Irene watched as Alice took a piece of toast and buttered it with the strawberry preserve. Her appetite had flown out the window like a scared bird. Forcing the dry bread into her mouth, she knew Irene was watching. All the boys were watching Alice too. Trying to appear grateful, she finished her piece of toast and pushed away from the table. It was all too much. Feeling guilt and sadness at not wanting to be there or any part of her old way of life. If only her chariot would come now to take her back to her new life, away from all this sorrow.

"Well, princess. See what we have to eat in this house. I'll bet you haven't spent a hungry minute since you have been gone."

Searching Irene's face, trying to find a hint of love or at least something. Nothing. Just threatening, hurtful eyes. Eyes of a stranger, not a mother. The misery hung in the air like a looming grey cloud, ready to burst its fury onto the earth.

"OK, Alice. I have a few things for you to help me with today. You will be gone tomorrow, back to your new family. Your brothers have been cutting wood, and it is all strewn about around the shed. It needs to be piled in the shed so it will dry out. I'm going up to the dairy to beg them for their milk and cream that they would be throwing away."

It was her chance. Her mother was going to the dairy. Time for her to sneak in to see her dad. Waiting and watching for Irene to leave out the door, then she would go to him.

Irene was pulling on her coat and slipping into her boots when she looked back to see if Alice was still standing in her housecoat.

"What are you doing, you stupid girl? You are just standing there, watching me? Get your clothes on and get out to the shed!"

"Yes, Mother, of course. I will get dressed and get out and pile that wood right away."

Turning, she walked away from Irene into the parlor. Getting dressed, coming out to the kitchen, Irene is gone. Looking out the door, she can see Irene's red coat in the distance, perfect timing to sneak into her dad's room.

Scared but excited to just see him, kiss him, and tell him how much she loved him.

She reached for the doorknob, pushed the door in, holding her breath.

William is lying with his back to her. His white dressing gown is pulled tight around him, his bone-thin legs milky-white.

"Daddy" she said, sitting down gently on the side of his bed. He turned slightly, his eyes still closed. Looking at his face, she hardly recognizes him. His cheekbones are like mountain peaks showing through his thinning, sallow, yellow skin. Running her hand over his face, she stopped to linger her fingers on his cheeks and then on his lips. She couldn't see him like this. The tears started to stream down her face, whining softly, planting a forever love kiss on his forehead. Getting up from the bed, walking out of the room, his face etched in her mind.

Getting back in the kitchen, hoping some of her brothers were still around to talk to. Just then Earl came running toward Alice.

"I miss you, Alice. I wish I could come and live with you too."

"Sorry, I can't take you, Earl. It is my job, not just a place for me to live. It's work and more work. Ten kids to help look after. I have to clean all their rooms every day. And kitchen duties, helping to make lunches and meals."

"My goodness," he replied. "Maybe I'll just go in the army. I want to get away from here. You were so lucky you don't have to live here anymore."

"What do you mean?"

"Mom has taken to fits of crying. She goes outside to the woodshed and screams, sometimes ripping at her hair. It is scaring me. Daddy doesn't wake up anymore. He is just lying there waiting to die."

"I am sorry, Earl," she said, hugging him close to her. "I am leaving tomorrow. I don't know when I will see you again. Earl."

"I will miss you Alice, but you are so much better away from here."

Getting close to Earl, she whispered in his ear. "It's like living in a fairy tale. I never want to come back here. I am so happy there. All the work is like play to me, but please don't tell Mom."

"I won't, sis. I know how mean she is to you."

By the end of the day, with her hands in the sink, Alice is daydreaming about Orville picking her up in her chariot. Would Irene be watching out the little window like she always did? Would her brothers surround the long car and wave goodbye to her, like their sister turned princess?

Irene came up behind Alice.

"So, when will you grace us with your presence?"

Deep in thought, she didn't hear what her mother had said.

"I beg your pardon, Mother."

"I said, when are you coming back again? I want you here every month. Do you understand? If not, you will be losing that fancy job of yours."

"Of course, Mother," she answered.

Irene sits down at the table with a cup of tea.

Watching her mother out of the corner of her eyes, she pitied her. Irene would never know any happiness. It had eluded her, like water in a desert.

What had really happened in her life to make her the way she was?

The bandy rooster trumpeted his five o'clock alarm, a good morning to the world.

Stretching, she gets up from the couch, folding the grey blanket. It had been a cold night, and she had woken up intermittently. A smile formed on her lips. Her chariot would come for her today.

Holding her hand out as though someone was going to kiss it, she realized she had better wake from the dream before the evil mother entered her fairy tale. A few wrinkles formed on the top of her nose, chuckling to herself. A rush of happiness pulsed through her mind, placing her slippers and housecoat back in her bag.

In the kitchen, everyone is seated at the breakfast table.

"We have eggs today, Alice," said Earl. "Come and sit next to me. Look, I already fixed your plate."

"Thank you, Earl."

Not making eye contact with Irene, but she can feel her mother's hateful gaze, like it is piercing her heart.

Two eggs sunny side up and a piece of homemade bread with butter.

"Thank you, Mother, for the lovely breakfast."

"May your day be as sunny as your eggs," answered Irene.

With her fork in hand, staring at her mother, wondering what she meant by that.

"Thank you, Mother."

"What time are they coming for you?" asked Irene.

"At nine, so if there is anything you want me to do, I am at your service."

Before the last word came out of her mouth, she realized she had said the wrong thing.

A scowl crossed Irene's face.

"Don't speak to me with your fancy way of talking, before I slap it right out of your mouth. I should just keep you right here to do all the work in this household. You are lucky we need the money. Get the dishes done and clean the kitchen is what you can do," she ordered.

"Yes, Mother, right away."

Standing at the sink, she had the same view her mother has every day. A few jersey cows dotted the meadow and the forest beyond. That same view she had from her bedroom window. The one thing missing from her view was her father. Remembering how she saw him yesterday brought tears to her eyes. No, she couldn't let Irene see her crying. She wiped at her eyes with the dishtowel.

This house no longer felt like her home. Life was changing for her. Soon her chariot would arrive to take her away...far away, getting lost in the bubbles in the sink.

"Your car and driver is here, Alice," announced Irene, holding the door for Orville. He stepped in, his eyes on Alice just wiping her hands on the dishtowel.

"Oh, sorry, Orville. This is my mother. I was just finishing up here. The time got away on me. You can take my things out," pointing to her bag and red purse sitting near the door.

With her mouth ajar, Irene stood in amazement. She had just ordered him to take her things? Shaking her head, she watched as Orville picked up the bags and headed down the stairs toward the big black car.

Slipping out the door as she is pulling on her sweater, she looks back at her mother.

"I will be home in a month, Mother. Hope everything is OK with Daddy. Tell him I love him."

Orville held the door for her, as Alice slips into the seat, closing in his passenger.

Standing back now, Irene examined the situation. Her Alice was not the same wretched, abused child. She had grown into a young lady. Shiny hair and clear complexion, her cheeks rosy, healthy. And the way she spoke to the driver like he was her slave. She almost wanted to take the credit for giving her daughter a chance at a new, wonderful life. But no, it wasn't her intention at all. Things had just taken on a life of their own.

Slamming the door behind her, she goes to the little window, her finger holding the lace curtain, watching until the long black car is out of site.

Numb from the hectic couple of days, Alice relaxed every muscle, settling into the comfort of the plush leather seats. The yard is quiet in an eerie way. Watching out the side window as Orville tried to turn the big car around.

Onward driver, she chuckled to herself.

God would take care of her brothers. She had to look ahead now, not back, never back. The end of the bad dream was over. She had awakened to a new wonderful day.

> *My chariot takes me.*
> *It saves me.*
> *From a life of sorrow and pain.*
> *Far away.*
> *Wash my tears away, like a walk in the rain.*
> *Happy faces. Love in the air.*
> *Back to my palace. My name is Alice.*

Watching out the window, larger houses wider roads.

Never looking back once, her mother far out of her mind, thinking of the kids that needed her, and her lessons.

Gladys was planning a party and had asked her to help her with everything, saying Alice should wear one of her pretty dresses. A party. She couldn't wait. Orville soon pulled into the circular drive. Alice did not wait a second once the car came to a stop. Opening the door, she hurried out. Orville was just coming around the side of the car.

"My, my, Miss Alice, are you anxious to get in?"

"Oh, I'm sure that Gladys is awaiting me. There are things I need to get doing right now. Don't want to keep her another minute."

"OK then, I will get your bag."

"Thank you, Orville. You are the best driver."

Curtsying, she turned and hurried toward the door.

Standing in the foyer, magic in the air. The brilliance of the overhead chandelier catches the light in her eyes. Turning round and round, she stretched her arms out.

"I am so happy to be home." she said out loud, pirouetting.

Gladys had just showed up at the top of the stairs. She was just about to announce her hello when she sees Alice turning round and round. How wonderful. The happiness in the air around Alice, like strawberries and whip cream. Gladys turned, walking back down the hallway. The moment was too endearing to interrupt.

Getting to her secret door, she stepped in, closing it quietly behind her.

"Oh, thank God I am back. Twenty nine, thirty...she counted the last stair. Entering her room, looking around, everything is in the same place she left it. Taking a deep breath, she runs to the bed, abandoning all worries, pulling the comforter up around her, like nothing could hurt her now, falling fast asleep.

In a few minutes she is thrust into a fairy tale dream. She is the princess, riding in a golden chariot. Four white horses galloped through a dense forest, as the trees pass in a blurr, faster and faster the horses went, until they reach a furious, bubbling river. Scared, she clutches her seat. Just as the horses reach the river's edge, she awakens.

"Miss Alice, I have your bags."

"Oh, thank you. I just lay down for a minute and fell fast asleep. I guess I was pretty tired."

"Yes, I would say you were. We've only been back a short time."

Sitting on the side of the bed, her mind goes back to the dream. Wow, she was really taking this fairy tale life too far. Now she was dreaming she was a princess? Could there really be any harm? Even weirder, was Irene had taken to calling her a princess too. After all, it was all just make believe.

163

And her life was sort of a fairy tale. Giggling, she slips off the side of the bed, to put her things away.

It felt so good to be back. Thinking of those two days at what used to be her home, felt like an eternity. The not knowing if Irene would let her leave ate at her, like limestone being eroded by vicious water. Her mother would have the last say, her future lay in her caloused hands. The hands that scrubbed, baked, wrung out clothes, worked, and cooked every day, from sun up till sun down. The hands that beat her and controlled her life. The uncertainties of what her mother had in store for her was the one thing that could take the fairy tale out of her life.

There was no point in worrying about her mother now. She was back in her palace, and every minute counted. The heavy weight that had followed her from the time she walked in the door at home was now lifted. She was happy to put on her uniform, to be in the kitchen, helping with the breakfast duties.

Walking into the kitchen, tying her apron as she went. Gladys is sitting having coffee.

"Great to have you back, Alice."

"It's great to be back. Thank you, ma'am," she said, exchanging smiles.

"Yes, and I missed your help too," said Jackie, smiling.

"Oh, thank you. It is great to be missed," she answered.

"Qui, qui," said Pierre, peeking his head around the corner. "I will need your help in the keechen later, Alice. I missed you too."

"At your service," she answered, a big smile on her pretty face.

It was all so wonderful to be wanted and loved. Was it all just a dream?

One day a few weeks later, Alice and Gladys were sharing a cup of tea in the garden room, when Gladys started asking Alice about her home life.

"So, I hope your visit home was nice?"

"My mother is a very sad lady. I have never really seen her happy. Now my father is dying, and she will be left alone. My brothers can't wait to get away from home. She is just not right. I don't know how to explain it," she said dropping her gaze. "My mother was raised by the nuns in a convent. She never felt love."

Searching deep into Alice's forest-green eyes, Gladys is lost in the depth.

How sad Alice's life must be at home. It made her appreciate her own life and realize how different the lives of her children had been. Privileged.

Dance lessons, piano lessons, tutors, and their own driver.

CHAPTER 35

A Birthday Party in the Palace

Counting her way down her staircase. One, two, three… hitting the bottom stair. Dressed in a fresh blue-and-white-pinstriped uniform and white rounded toes, like doll shoes. Walking down the corridor to the kitchen, the click-clack of her shoes on the marble floor, passing the dining room. Voices wafted out to her ears. Gladys's high-pitched voice sounds excited, the kids are laughing and talking. Alice overheard what Gladys was saying.

"Let's make it the best day of her life."

That could only mean one thing. The party was for her. Oh my God, it was her party! Oh no, it could mean anyone. Suddenly feeling selfish, she hangs her head. How could she be so foolish? After all, she was only the maid. Why would they want to have a party for her? This whole fairy-tale life was making her think crazy thoughts. She would have to start getting more realistic, so she wouldn't be disappointed.

Deciding she could just go and listen closer to the door. She just had to know if it was her party.

"We will make Alice the happiest girl in the world," said Lucy, a high-pitched fever in her voice.

Her eyes widened. A smile, no sumani could wash away, adorned her pretty face, she hurries back down the corridor, into the kitchen.

Humming a tune as she worked, cutting up vegetables.

"What is it? You seem so happy today, miss," asked Pierre.

"Today is a wonderful day," she exclaimed.

Jackie noticed too, commenting on how happy she looked.

"Is it your birthday or something?" asked Jackie, who had overheard Gladys discussing the very fact.

"Not until next month. I will be thirteen."

"Surely that thing will happen to you soon, Alice."

"What thing?"

"Oh, it's not something we should talk about in the kitchen. We will talk later," said Jackie.

Happiness came and left like the sunshine. All day after that comment, Alice's uncertainties made her uneasy. What could Jackie be talking about?

Pierre noticed the instant change in her.

"We are making crepes this morning, Alice, all kinds. What kind can I make for you? Strawberry, raspberry, chocolate?"

"Ah, I don't think I am hungry this morning, but thank you, Pierre."

Not even the art of flipping the flour disks out of the pan could take her mind off of what Jackie had said.

Gladys stopped Orville on his way out the door with the children in tow.

"Can you make time to take me to Alice's house in a month from now? We can just make it a day to drive around the countryside and stop in to see Alice's mother. It's so beautiful out there. All the wide open spaces."

She would take Irene the wages. That way, Alice wouldn't have to go home. It seemed to her that would make her happy, wanting to get a feeling for herself about Alice's home life and an insight into Irene.

"Be glad to be of assistance, ma'am." He tipped his hat.

CHAPTER 36

Alice Has a Palace

One morning after breakfast duty, Gladys asked Alice to meet her in the garden room for tea.

"We are having a bridge club meeting. There will be at least twenty women coming. You and Jackie will prepare the luncheon, little sandwiches, and desserts."

"Mmm, I would love to help make all the goodies."

The day of the party, the kitchen is abuzz with laughter and excitement. A tender love feeling was in the air. The joy was felt throughout the house, everyone smiling and exchanging hugs.

Jackie had mentioned to Alice that she would not be staying for the party. She had to go home and prepare dinner for her husband.

Gladys was sitting at the piano, the classic sound penetrating the air waves.

Walking toward the music, Alice peeked her head into the parlor. Gladys with her head held high, straight back, a beautiful scroll of blonde hair in the centre of her head. Regal, like a queen.

Alice stood by watching as Gladys placed the dinnerware and the golden candle holders on either end of the long table. Golden rimmed cups, plates, and saucers. Everything was exquisite.

"Is there anything I can help you with?" asked Alice.

"Oh no, everything is almost done. You could just go and take some time to get yourself prettied up. And wear the best dress you have, OK?"

"OK, yes, ma'am, I will go and get ready."

Taking one last look in the kitchen to see if Pierre needed her help.

A large beautifully browned turkey displayed on a white porcelain platter. Pierre is just pulling a roast of beef out of the oven. Dark gravy and a sprig of rosemary decorate the top of the roast.

"Everything looks so good and smells amazing," said Alice. "Can I help you with anything before I go and get dressed?"

"Oh no, Alice, we are just about ready. It's a feast for a princess," he said, standing back admiring his handiwork."

At that very moment, she knew for sure it was her party. Butterflies played in her stomach, a warm glow spread over her cheeks.

"I had better go and get ready then. See you in a while, Pierre."

As she walked away toward her room door, she reminded herself her birthday was not for another week. Of course, this was a surprise party!

Yes, I won't let them down. I will be the princess of the ball. Holding her bottom lip with her teeth, she chuckled to herself.

A surprise, she thought. She would just pretend that she didn't know, so as not to spoil it for the kids, and Gladys and Pierre, who were all caught up in the moment.

Feeling so blessed. *I will wear my prettiest dress and be the princess of the ball.*

Just then, she heard Jackie say to Pierre, "You guys have a great birthday party." Then the door slammed.

Lucy was just going into the kitchen as Jackie was leaving, looking behind to see if Alice was anywhere to have overheard what she said. There was no doubt in her mind, but hearing Jackie say that, made her feel the jealousy.

Just then, there was a knock at her door.

"It's just me, Alice. I wanted to tell you that the necklace in your bathroom is a little present from me. You can wear it today."

"Oh, thank you so much, Gladys." Running into the bathroom, a string of mauve pink pearls with a gold clasp lay in a purple velvet box.

Picking up the pearls as though they are fragile, like a robin's egg, Alice's eyes glinted with happiness.

"They are beautiful, thank you so much!"

Coming out with them falling between her fingers, Gladys is nowhere to be seen. Bringing them to her lips, she kissed them, gazing at the delicate beauty of the pearls, setting them back in the velvet-and-silk-lined box.

Walking into her closet, she fanned through the dresses. Picking a pink one with the tag still on, she takes it down. A pink chiffon with a tight bodice and full skirt. Pearls adorned the edges of the skirt.

"It is truly fit for a princess," she said.

Laying it gently on her bed, she placed the pearls around the neck of the dress. Nothing could be more perfect or beautiful.

Steam infused with the intoxicating aroma of lavender, rises from the enamel bath tub, its animal like claws, planted firmly on the tiled floor. Slipping out of her uniform, she stepped into the water. The warmth caresses her, transporting her into a fantasy daydream.

Sitting at the dresser, she gazes into the gold-embossed framed mirror. The girl who looked back at her is happy, and beautiful.

The dress was a perfect fit. A white pair of shiny soft slippers on her feet.

Staring deep into the glass, her green eyes like emeralds.

> *Mirror, mirror, on the wall.*
> *I am going to a ball.*
> *Will my slippers fall?*
> *Will my chariot turn to dust?*
> *Please tell me, you must.*

She started to giggle uncontrollably.

"If only Mother could see me now. She would wear a frown. I am a real princess, and I will wear a crown." Her lips pursed in a kiss.

Taking one last look; everything is perfect.

Piano music made her heart glad. Turning round and round, her dress floated like her spirit, high and free.

"Alice really does live in a palace," she uttered.

Taking one last look around her special place, she looked up.

"Thank you, God," she whispered. "Thank you for this special day. Princess for a day."

Heading down her staircase, she counted. Stepping light and carefully on the narrow, steep, staircase.

Slowly, she pushed open her doorway. A steady stream of laughter and chatter coming from the dining room. Stopping at the doorway, she took a deep breath, anticipating the surprise. Holding her head high, her eyes wide. All eyes on her now, she searches their faces, smiles and love thick in the air.

"Surprise, surprise," they all shouted.

Lucy runs to her. Streamers hang from the high ceiling, a warm glow of candlelight on the long table. Balloons adorned everything. All colors. People, lots of people. Must be the bridge club ladies Gladys had mentioned.

Everyone was making their way toward her. Standing perfectly still, one by one, they embrace her. Hugs and kisses, enough to make up for the years of doing without. Her head starts to feel light. Going to the nearest seat, Lucy practically sits on her lap.

"Ae you OK?"

"Oh, yes, just the excitement, I guess."

Lucy is fingering Alice's curls and touching her cheeks.

"You sure do look pretty today, Miss Alice. Just like a real princess."

"Thank you, Lucy. That is the nicest thing anyone has ever said to me." Leaning into Lucy kissing her on the cheek.

"Happy birthday, Alice. It's your day. Let's have lots of fun. No work for you today."

"C'mon." Grabbing Alice's hand, Lucy leads her to a table against a wall in the dining room. A three-tiered birthday cake, with swirled icing, like cumulous clouds. Red baby roses sit at the feet of a princess sitting on top of the cake. Next to the cake sits a plastic jeweled crown, Lucy reaching for it, placing it on Alice's head.

"It's kind of like a game. You are the princess for the day. We all do it when it's our birthdays."

"Of course, I would love to."

Around the edges of the cake, A L I C E is spelled in pink icing.

"I just love it so much!" Tears started to pool in her eyes. But no, she couldn't cry now. They were tears of joy, but they would ruin her dress. No tears today. Only laughter and smiles.

The party is in full swing, Gladys makes a grand entrance in a long red gown, a row of white pearls around her neck and white gloves up to her elbows. She looked more beautiful than Alice had ever seen her. Running to her, Alice wraps her arms around her. "I love you, Gladys."

"I love you too." Staring deep into Alice's eyes, a cute wrinkle at the top of her nose.

"Attention, everyone!" she shouted. "It is time for the cake and the candle ceremony." A rush of *yaaaahhhhs* floated through the grand ballroom.

Pierre makes his appearance in the doorway.

He has a white apron on, a white linen cloth hanging from his arm.

Everyone stands in line. Pierre is cutting the cake and asking each one what kind of ice cream, strawberry or vanilla.

"And for you, princess, strawberry or vanilla?"

"Thank you, Pierre." A rosy blush spreads across her cheeks. "Thank you for the beautiful cake. Vanilla for me, please."

"Such a pleasure for you, Miss Alice."

A single candle in the middle of her piece of cake.

Gladys walked up beside her.

"Make a wish, dear, then blow it out."

"I wish that everyone in the world could feel as much love as I do right now."

Everyone giggled. The first time they had heard someone say their wish out loud.

"OK now, you must blow out the rest of the candles before I cut any more of the cake," said Pierre, lighting the last twelve candles.

Blowing hard, all but one of the candles stayed lit.

"This one is for you, Pearl," she whispered as she blew a gentle breath. The candle extinguished.

There is a loud, thunderous clapping, everyone staring at her. Blushing, her cheeks are rosy as her dress. Curtsying she walks towards the garden room, needing some alone time to gather herself.

It was all so over the top. And being the centre of attention made her feel uneasy. Never before in her life had she felt such caring and love. This was what she had been missing her whole life.

"Oh, God, thank you for such a wonderful day. I would love to ask you to never let it stop, but I know you are busy doing lots of things. But I do wish that I never had to leave this life, God."

Staring out, looking over the horizon, the sun just setting. Cotton candy clouds, strokes of orange and mauve, painted into the most beautiful sunset.

How was everything so beautiful today? Her special day. Tears of joy spilled down her cheeks.

Just then, Gladys comes into the sun room.

"Are you, OK? Everyone is missing the princess of the ball."

Wiping at her tears, she stared into Gladys's eyes.

"I am just so happy, tears of joy. I am the best I could ever be. This is the happiest day of my life."

Gladys pulls her close in a loving mother hug.

"That's what we were going for, Alice. I guess we succeeded. Everyone is so happy today. You made this day so special, and we were honored to have shared your day with you. Oh, I have a little something from Mr. Olsen. He couldn't be here today, but sends his best birthday wishes to you."

A flood of emotions through her like electric current. She just couldn't open the box in front of Gladys.

"I just love surprises, but could I open it later?"

"Of course, Alice. Well, come back into the party soon before everyone thinks there is something wrong with our guest of honor."

"Yes, I will be right in."

Straightening herself out, she walks back into the parlor, where everyone is busy eating or talking, Lucy is eating ice cream, waving Alice over.

"Aren't you going to have cake?"

"Oh yes, of course."

Going to the table against the wall, Alice picked up her piece of cake, a few bites out of it, sitting the red box down with the gold ribbon on the table.

"You haven't opened any of your presents," said Lucy. "There are so many it will take you days to look through all of them. Here, I'll take this one in and put with the others.

"C'mon, Alice, I will show you where they are. There are so many Mom put them all on a table in the study."

"Really, oh my." Feeling a blush coming over her cheeks.

Getting up to go and see, Lucy tagged behind.

"I will help you take them to your room, Alice. There are lots."

"Wow!" exclaimed Alice. The whole desk is full of all different colored boxes, spilling off to a table full of bows and ribbons every color of the rainbow.

Staring at all the presents, she is spellbound. No words. *It must be a dream,* she kept thinking. *I have taken this fairy tale thing too far.* Tears streamed down her face. Lucy is worried.

"Are you OK? Aren't you happy?"

"Oh, I am so happy." Wrapping her arms around Lucy, hugging her hard. "These are all mine? Oh my! Let's get busy and take them to my room."

Making four trips up and down the stairs, some of the boxes spewing into the corridor and down the stairs. Laughing as they went, back and forth, until the last one is sitting on the big bed.

With the presents all in her room, Alice doesn't want to go back downstairs, but she realizes it would be rude to leave the party that is in her honor. So back down the girls go to search out everyone.

The games were on. Pin the tail on the donkey and bobbing for apples. The kids' laughter and song took Alice to a place children should be. For her, a temporary heaven.

Gladys stood holding Alice hand as the bridge ladies exited. Finally, a hug and kiss from Gladys sent Alice to her room with the biggest smile, he cheeks hurt. Happiness like she had never known or could believe could happen to her. Heading back up the stairs to her room and all her presents. Never wanting to wake from the dream, she stands beside the bed, the whole top of it, displayed in shiny colors and satin ribbons. All for her.

One by one, she opened ten presents, finding trinkets, books and clothes, everything a girl of thirteen could ever ask for. One box had something in it that puzzled her. White oblong pads, she rubs them on her face, and with them, some other feminine smelling things. Putting them aside, she would ask Gladys what they were for. Reading the tag. From Gladys. Overwhelmed, and tired all of a sudden from all the excitement, deciding to put the rest of the presents in the closet, and maybe just open two a day, until she had discovered all of her treasures. Slipping off her dress, she gets into her night clothes and turns off her bedside lamp, getting cozy under the angel feathers. Early morning Alice goes into a dream.

She is flying above the tree line, her arms outstretched but not moving, just floating. That was what it must be like in heaven, she thought. Just then, she sees Pearl walking to her on a path. Everything feels light, a foggy mist hanging in the air. Just as she was getting close enough to touch her, she is awakened by her morning alarm.

A beautiful spring morning, Gladys is in her garden, kneeling, rubber gloves on, she fingers the earth around a few of her beloved perrenials. A few purple and yellow crocuses pushing their little heads out to the world. It was her time to connect to the earth and the flowerbeds she loved. Gladys made it her duty to plant a few new perrenials every year.

Today she would go see Alice's mother. When she told Alice she didn't have to go, Alice seemed so pleased, saying she needed the whole day to finish cleaning and rearranging the pantry. Gladys didn't expect an explanation, knowing she didn't want to go home. She had told Orville they would leave at ten sharp.

Glancing at her watch, time to put her gardening away.

Going back into the house she readied for her trip.

"Good morning, Orville," said a high-pitched familiar voice. Gladys appeared around the corner in a baby blue two-piece suit, tailored jacket, and skirt to match. In her hand is a pill box purse, the same color, white piping around the edges. The shoes are also baby blue.

Yesterday, her beauty assistant had given her a facial and a massage. Feeling like a million dollars she looked the part.

"It's a wonderful day for a drive in the country," she commented.

The long Cadillac limousine rode softly, Gladys pensive, thinking of her day ahead, anticipating the meeting with Irene. Today, she would cover for Alice, saying she had work that was unfinished.

Orville turned off into a narrow, pot-holed road that led up to the Purple house. Gladys noticed the grey board house with the cinder block steps, a few chickens running in the yard.

"Just wait a while, Orville. I don't expect to be more than fifteen minutes."

"Yes, of course, ma'am."

Getting out, he holds the door for Gladys giving her a hand out. Walking toward the house, she carefully navigates the cement steps. Knocking gently at first, no answer, then she takes off her right glove, knocking again, this time harder. The door opens slowly, a rounded, ruddy face showing. Dark circles around her eyes, a few stray strands of hair hang around her face, the rest pulled back in a bun.

"Oh my, wasn't expecting any company," said Irene, eyeing the familiar black car. "You must be Gladys. Well, come in then," pulling her house coat over her dress.

"Where is Alice? Is she OK?"

"Yes, of course. There were just some chores she had to finish up, and I had time to come today to bring you her wages."

"I see," answered Irene, examining Gladys in her fine clothes. "You dress mighty nice. Don't mind my clothes, we are poor and..."

"Look, I didn't come to see if you were poor," Gladys interrupted. "I am here to talk about Alice."

"What, has she gone and done something stupid?"

"No, on the contrary. She has proved herself to be a valuable asset to my family, and we would love to keep her as long as you want her to work for us. My children all love her, and so do I."

Handing Irene an envelope.

"And there is a little something extra there. Alice told me about your husband not being able to work anymore." Irene nodded her head, her eyes dark, glossy.

"He won't be with us much longer. He is dying."

"So sorry," said Gladys, wanting to leave the house soon.

"I have a whole day planned and have to be going now. Alice will come next month. Orville will bring her."

"Fine, thanks," said Irene, shoving the envelope into the pocket of her robe.

"Goodbye for now," said Gladys, walking out the door. Orville was standing at the back door of the limousine. Irene closed the door behind her, then rushed over to the small window to peek out, watching until the end of the long car disappeared down the dirt road.

Her visit had been a success, feeling good about helping Alice's family, wanting to do more.

"Just drive, Orville. Take me to some beautiful places. Let's just sit and enjoy the day. I brought a couple of sandwiches and some tea."

"Sure will," answered Orville, finding a place high on a cliff, overlooking the ocean. Gladys gets out, finding a spot on the rocks. Sitting down, she takes in the beauty, as she counts her blessings. The stillness of the day calming her mind and body.

CHAPTER 37

Remembering the Dream

S itting quietly on the corner of the bed. Lucy had been so helpful, carrying some of Alice's presents up the stairs to her room. She counted them; in all, she had fourteen gifts plus the ten she had opened already. Looking them over, wondering what was in each box and whether there was a thought that went with each box, a note. She always loved notes. Notes to kids at school. Notes to the teacher, special thoughts. She decided she would open just one present a day, every night before bed.

It would be like a blessing from that day. As she lay back on her bed, going over the events of the birthday party, remembering now that she had dreamed the whole event. She was seven when she dreamed of a party where she was a princess. The same pink dress. Loving faces, kids, and balloons. Oh God, she had lived the dream. Wishing that she could dream everything that would happen to her, but maybe not, came the voice of reasoning.

"Thank you, God, for making my party, the most amazing day of my life on this earth." Laying back on her pillows, she fell fast asleep in her palace.

Good night, Alice.

CHAPTER 38

The Unexpected

One morning Alice wakes feeling a bit anxious and frightened. Sitting up, in her bed, queasy, her stomach upset. Sharp pains from her back straight through to her stomach, like a knife cutting through her. Doubling over in pain, not knowing what is wrong. They were expecting her downstairs in the kitchen in twenty minutes, and she didn't feel like she could get out of bed. Slowly, she tried to free herself from her sheets and blankets. As she threw back the blankets, she noticed a big red stain on the white linens.

"Oh my God!" She gasped. "What is happening to me? Am I dying?" Whimpering softly now, tears running down her cheeks.

Her legs feel stuck together at the top. Taking a better look, she almost fainted. "It's blood. Oh my God." Her panties and legs are stained with bright red blood. A shrill cry of alarm rang through her room.

Gladys heard the cries from Alice's room and hurried up the staircase.

"Alice, are you all right?"

"No, ma'am," she said in a small voice. "No, no." Gladys made it to the landing, looked in at Alice standing there. Blood stained her legs and hands, her eyes wide in fright and panic.

"I don't know what happened," she said, frozen, holding her stomach.

"Don't worry, dear. It's probably just your time. You know, your menses."

Staring with a blank, scared look, she said nothing.

"Oh no. Nobody has told you about your period?"

"No, ma'am." A shameful feeling comes over her.

"It's OK, dear. It happens to all girls. It's a sign you are becoming a young woman. Sometimes there is pain with your period, but it is worse the first two days, and then the last three days it subsides. Usually you will bleed for five days. And during that time, you will wear these." She handed her a box of pads. "I did give you a little present of them already. I will show you how to chart your period. It comes every twenty-eight days, so you will be ready for it before it shows. Also your body will let you know with signs, like bloating and pain."

Oh my goodness, thought Alice. Life had enough pain already. And now this. How would she be able to manage? The whole thing sounded disgusting.

A piercing pain shoots through her stomach, doubling her over, she holds her breath.

CHAPTER 39

Transitions for Alice

I t had been eight months since Alice had come to work for the Olsenses, which seemed like a lifetime already. Every moment so dear to her, Alice marked every month off on the calendar.

It was December, and all the talk was about Christmas coming. There would be celebrations and parties. Gladys had discussed a real bridge club party for her friends. She wanted Alice to be the hostess for the party. All the ladies knew her already and had asked about her constantly since they had met her.

The last two months when Alice visited her mother, Irene had been distant. More than a couple of times, she had hinted that Alice would be coming home soon to help care for her father. Torn between her new found happiness and going home to look after her father, who she loved more than her own life.

Just like Alice suspected, the next time she went home, Irene announced that this would be the last month she would be working for the Olsenses. It was November, which meant that Alice would be there for the last party, Christmas.

In shock, but she knew nothing she could say would change Irene's mind. Her heart started racing, a loud drum beating in her ears, somehow she just had to try to change her mind.

"But, Mother, they need me. And they pay me good wages. Why, Mother? I love being there."

"That is just my point. You think you can just adopt another family. Like we are not good enough for you anymore, now that you live in a fancy mansion. That is my final word on it. You are coming home."

"Please, please, no, Mother," she begged, falling on her knees, her arms around her mother's legs.

"Get away from me. Up off the floor, you stupid girl. Those people don't love you. All you are to them is just a maid."

Running from the kitchen up the stairs, then back down into the yard. No, no, this couldn't be happening. It must be a bad dream, and she would wake up any minute in her palace. Shutting her eyes hard, holding them shut a few minutes, opening them, she is still in the chicken coop, sitting on a bale of straw, a few chickens scratching at her feet.

Mulling it over in her mind, she would have to tell Gladys she was leaving them. Her heart is broken. How would the pieces ever come together?

She would have to find the right time and place to tell Gladys, wanting to be composed, her voice steady. Having gone over the scenario all day long, Alice broke down in her room. Tears, like steady rain, poured out her pain. This life was just not fair. Nothing she could say or do would change her mother's mind, which was set like cement.

Making toast for breakfast and some lunches for the kids, building a dam of protection from the children, Pierre, and Jackie.

Pierre noticed, and so did Jackie, who tried to make some small talk with Alice but got no answer. It was so hard to disguise her feelings, her heart in the pit of her stomach. Everyone knew by the end of the day there was something terribly wrong. No sunny good mornings or eye contact, trying to keep busy, a wall erected to keep them out.

Finishing up her kitchen duties, she hurriedly went upstairs to get the children's rooms cleaned. It was mostly alone time, and she would have to think about how to tell Gladys.

The raw emotions were sitting on the surface. Unable to contain them, she sat down on the side of Lucy's bed and started whimpering. Tears cascaded down her face. Covering her head with her hands, Gladys was just walking by Lucy's room when she heard the whining.

"Oh my goodness, Alice, what is it?" Sitting down next to her on the bed, Gladys pulled her close.

"I have something to tell you, Gladys," she said, still weeping. "I have to go back home to my mother." Just then the crying got louder. "I have to go back home to help look after my father. That's what my mother announced when I was home. I don't want to go back, Gladys, but what can I do? I am just a child still." Turning her face into Gladys blouse, she buried her head, the tears streaming.

"Oh no, Alice. I am very saddened by this too. Maybe I can go and see your mother and help to change her mind. We will see. Don't cry now. It won't help matters any. When exactly did she say?"

"After this month is over."

"Well, that gives us until the New Year. Which means we will still have you for Christmas. It's the favorite time of the year around here for everyone. We will make it the best Christmas ever, and you will help me plan it all, OK? So wipe your tears now, dear. All the crying won't help. And I don't want the kids to know right away. They are all going to be saddened by these new events too. Especially Lucy, who loves you like a sister. She told me she wants you to stay with us forever. But nothing is forever, Alice, nothing." Kissing Alice on the cheek, Gladys gets up and walked out of the room.

Going straight to her own room, she lay on her bed crying silently into her pillow.

Wiping her tears, Alice walked to the big picture window. Gladys had shown that she loved her back. The heavy burden she had carried all morning was lifted now.

Time to get on with the tasks, with the feather duster in hand.

Gladys wanted to show a brave face for Alice. More than once she tried to go back downstairs, but she just couldn't face the day. Feeling helpless and hopeless for Alice drained her own happiness out of her, like a gloomy sky painting out the sun.

Meeting up with Alice later in the day, Gladys came up behind her, hugging her, whispering into Alice's ear. "I have watched you bloom into a beautiful young lady, Alice, just as if you were my own. I will go and talk to your mother and try to change her mind."

"I don't know if that is a good idea, Gladys. It might make it harder on me. She gets angry if anyone challenges her."

"Like she would hurt you? Is that what you mean?"

"Yes, Gladys, in one way or another. She always hurts me," she confessed. All the sadness of her whole life seemed to be pouring out, down her face. Holding Alice tight, Gladys started crying too, her heart breaking.

"The kids will be devastated to hear this news. I am not ready for them to know. When the time is right, we will announce it, so please, dry your tears now. The kids all love you, and I love you like my own. This is truly a sad day, Alice. But for the kids, we have to stop this crying and try and find a way to get through this. Go to your room, and get freshened up for dinner. I have some things to do right now. Remember, no more tears, OK? We will find a way."

A heavy burden settled on Gladys's shoulders, like Alice's world had settled there. Why had she let herself get so emotionally involved with a maid? But Alice wasn't just a maid and would never be to her. She had to realize you don't plan on loving; it just happens. Now she had to find a way to tell the children. And the sadness would follow them around too. It just wasn't fair. Nothing about this whole thing made any sense. Then again, there was something very strange about Alice's mother. Unpredictable. Everything that Alice had told her she had seen for herself. This woman was not in her right mind. She had never let on to the kids that she knew Alice was abused by her mother. They had their own lives and couldn't be burdened by Alice's life. It seemed selfish, but she had to protect her own.

After a whole day of pondering when and how, she decided that she would break the news at the breakfast table in the morning. No sense in carrying this heavy burden around. It was just too much. The children would be told in the morning.

Gladys retired early that night. Mr. Olsen was away on a business trip. In a way, she wouldn't want to confide in him the love she had for Alice. He wouldn't understand how she could get so involved in the life of a maid. He said he liked Alice, but he also saw her as a servant for his family. And he had expressed that to her, a few times, asking why she took Alice on the children's outings.

"What a day," she said out loud, laying back in a hot scented bath. Tomorrow morning she would take Sabre out for a ride in meadows. It was so beautiful in the mornings now. Cool air, a renewed freshness. The trails carpeted with a fresh layer of orange and red leaves. The beauty of the fall a softening to the winter that lay ahead. Fall was her favorite season. After a long ride, her mind was always cleared and ready for the day ahead.

She wasn't too worried about the boys or the older girls, but Lucy would be heartbroken.

Peeking her head into the kitchen, a buzz of children, arms going, lips going, smiles, and chuckles, Alice is standing at the counter, making sandwiches. Pierre is flipping pancakes, and Jackie has an armful of wash, going into the pantry.

"Good morning, everyone."

"Good morning," came back at her in a symphony.

"I have some news this morning, children. One of our own is leaving us."

All movement in the kitchen stopped.

"Alice will be going home to look after her father, who is very sick. We hope that she is not gone long, but we will just make out without her. I am not hiring anyone else in her place. We will wait for her to come back to us."

Then a chorus of *ahhhhhhhhhs*. Lucy runs to Alice, wrapping her arms around her. "I can go with you, Alice. Let's just ask my mother."

Instead of tears, Alice started giggling. Lucy had made her so happy!

"I wish I could take you, Lucy, but we have lots of people in my house, and not enough room. I have to sleep in the parlor. My bedroom was taken over by my brothers."

Having heard what Gladys had said gave her renewed hope that she would be able to come back when the time was right. Everything would work out, that is what she had to believe. To have hope and faith would get her through this hard time, and she shouldn't be selfish. Her father needed her now more than ever. She needed to be home for him.

That night when Gladys was tucking Lucy in after a bedtime story, she asked if they could adopt Alice. Gladys just laughed and said ten children were enough for her.

Before Gladys retired, she went upstairs to talk to Alice.

"The rest of the time you are with us, you can just do the kids' rooms. The kitchen duties can fall to the children, Jackie, and Pierre. They managed before you came and will again."

"Thank you, ma'am that is so nice of you. I love cleaning the kids' rooms."

Jackie smiled, a sly look in her eyes. "I will have this family all to myself again." She was happy that Alice was leaving. Walking quickly into the kitchen, getting busy with the lunches. Alice was off duty. She had heard it all. Gladys sure did like her, never treated her like that—time off with pay. Hmm, she thought.

"Well, I guess it is just you and me in the kitchen again, Pierre," said Jackie. Pierre turned around to face her. "I know. I am going to miss little Alice. She always brought the sunshine into my keetchen. And what a good helper too. I suppose her father needs her more than we do. I sure will miss her, though."

"Yes, and so will I," said Jackie, realizing her workload had just doubled.

Gladys told the kids they would be planning the best Christmas ever. Kind of like a going away party for Alice too, as she would leave at the end of December. The mansion had never seen a party like the one they were planning.

Days seemed to be going by way too fast. It seemed hard to put on her best smile when underneath she was devastated. She had nothing to look forward to, only her mother, never knowing her moods that changed like the tides in the ocean.

Counting the steps every time, even though she knew there were thirty. She didn't know why she counted. She just did, on the way up and on the way down.

"You have until the end of this month," Irene had warned. It was December 20, five days till Christmas, all excitement and planning. Getting caught up with decorating the tree and helping to bake special cookies and cakes, took her mind off the inevitable. It was when she was alone that reality hit her. The fairy tale was taking on a new twist.

With the days shorter and the nights colder, she thought of the work ahead of her. Carrying wood, cleaning the ashes from the stove, sweeping the splinters, and washing floors. Wasn't there a fairy tale that had the same scenario?

If only that was all she had to endure, the work itself she could handle.

Tomorrow was Christmas morning. She helped to wrap gifts for the kids, a whole mountain of presents under the tree.

"I don't want any gifts, Gladys. You and your family have given me so much already. The best gift was letting me come and stay with you this long. I just don't know how to thank you, but I am hoping that I will be able to come back."

"Yes, dear, and so are we."

Sitting at the breakfast table, Alice tried her best to eat her soft boiled egg and toast.

Tomorrow she would start packing her things. Her hand was changing again. Like the scenery that would inevitably turn from sunny to grey skies, her mind was weary, her heart heavy.

Questioning thoughts about her mother were invading her thoughts. What were the real reasons she was bringing her home? Things were never that simple with Irene. There were undercurrents in her decisions, like a dangerous pull into deep dark water. All the negative thoughts, like sinking into quicksand, stealing her smile.

Where will I put all my special things? Will I ever see the Olsenses again? I will have to hide my things in the chicken coop. Irene never went there. Good thing she was afraid of spiders. A stack of straw lined against the wall, spider webs fanned the corners, like nets to catch their next meal. The spiders, became her ally, standing guard over her precious things.

Just then, Gladys called from downstairs,

"Alice, wear your best to dinner tonight."

"Yes, ma'am," she answered.

Not in the mood for festivities, she could hear the kids' laughter and happiness wafting through the house, like the smell of apple pie. Today she would stay close to her room. They all knew she had to pack and get ready for her departure. Knowing her regrets would be written on her face, she didn't want to take any happiness from their special day. Already having bared her soul to them, she felt naked with emotion.

As she pulled her things out of the closet, five bags opened on the floor, taking special care to fold her things perfectly. A flood of emotion spilled out of her, like the wrath of a storm.

"No, no, I just won't go," she cried out loud. "Not back to Irene and her hell. I will run away far away." She cried.

Slumped over on the floor in a flood of tears.

The whole day in her room had been wonderful. She laughed, she cried, she sang. Every emotion she had ever known came to the surface.

Pulling the blankets up over her head, tired and weary from crying, she fell asleep.

Thrust into a familiar dream. Standing in a field of flowers, bending to pick a handful, admiring the colors and softness of the petals. There is another little girl there too, picking flowers, she recognizes it is Pearl, running to her now, the petals fall from the flowers, strewn on the grass, just as she is putting her arms out to her, Pearl reaching for her.....when she is awakened.

CHAPTER 40

The Party and Parting

After a long soak in the hot water infused with lavender salts, her mind on the dream. Pearl always came to her when she needed her most. Just seeing her made her feel so much better. Really, she had never left her. Getting ready to go and join the family, Alice wore a white dress with a tight bodice and flowing skirt, choosing a pearl colored pair of ballet slippers to match her pearls.

Sitting at the mirror, gazing at her image, one of a princess. Sauntering over to the big picture window gazing over the rolling meadows. A show of white, with a fresh powder of snow, trying to climb out of the dark place where her mind had taken her. These last few days, she would make the best of. The worry that was consuming her, robbing her of her smile, she would put out of her mind. Pearl had given her renewed hope. Today was going to be wonderful.

The children had decided they would drop the Christmas theme and make it, Alice's going away party. The lights on the tree and the feeling of celebration in the air.

As Alice came through the doorway of the grand ballroom, she heard piano music. Love and happiness, thick as chocolate pudding. Lucy rushed to Alice, taking her by the hand.

"This is your surprise going away party, and Christmas too. We all worked to make it the best party ever."

After a lunch of everything Alice could have ever imagined, with the finest chocolates for dessert, she is drunk with happiness. Her cheeks hurt from the permanent smile that had taken over her lips. Tomorrow was forgotten; today was all that she wanted. If only it could go on and on. Fairy tales didn't have to end, did they?

One by one, the children fell by the wayside, turkey sleepiness taking over. There were no chores today for Alice. Jackie came in and out of the ballroom in her blue-and-white uniform, not making eye contact at all with Alice.

Jackie had just walked out with a handful of dirty dishes when Gladys stuck her head into the dining room.

"You girls do whatever you like. Jackie will take care of the cleaning up."

Like a knife stabbing her in the back, Jackie felt anger pulse through her body. Sure, just leave all the mess for the maid. That was how Gladys thought of her, just a slave for her and her brats.

Before her chariot turned to dust and her beautiful clothes into tattered rags, the princess in her would live on.

Paying special attention to everything around her, etching it all into her brain. A place she could go when she needed times of memory to help her get through her days.

The last day before her parting, the uncertainties crept into her mind, like bugs that would just not go away. Darkness inked out the happiness of the princess. What plans did the evil mother have for her now?

One more night in her palace. She smiled and looked at her reflection in the mirror. Whispering softly, she stared into her own forest-green eyes.

> Mirror mirror, on the wall,
> I don't want to leave the ball. Will my chariot turn to dust?
> If you must, take me,
> To another place and time.
> I know not where I tread,
> I dread my hand has changed again.
> Where do I go from here?
> God only knows,
> And the river flows where it might. An innocent soul
> Caught in the hands of fate? I can't be late, twelve sharp.
> I can't be late, never late. I must go now. My chariot awaits.

Taking one last look around the room, not a wrinkle in the bed, not a speck of dust anywhere. It was perfect, just like she had found it. Ambling slowly by her own private bathroom, knowing she would miss the big claw foot bathtub that soothed away her tired muscles. Heading now to the staircase, her staircase to heaven, starting her descend to find Gladys. Looking forward to the morning with Gladys, hoping Lucy would be tagging along.

Finding her smile that was trying to hide away, she had only love for them. Gladys met Alice halfway down the corridor.

"Alice, I thought you and me would take our breakfast in the garden room. Lucy and her brothers have gone to the city to the library there. I thought it would be nice to have some alone time with you. The kids would barrage you with too many questions. Today I want you all to myself."

Feeling the tears just behind the eyes, she tried her best to stop them.

"Jackie will be bringing in our breakfast. We will sit and watch the sun come up. Lucy has been sullen the last few days knowing you are leaving. I just want to spare the children this parting. We are all sad that you are leaving us."

Not wanting to let Jackie see her crying, she straightened up and put on her happy face. Breakfast with Gladys. She would find her bravest face and leave without breaking down. Time to leave the dream, and be strong for her father. Pearl was with her and would help her through all the times she needed her.

Jackie appeared in the doorway with a silver platter with a dome cover.

"Good morning. I have brought your breakfast. French toast for Alice. Pierre made it special for you, with maple butter. Two eggs sunny side up and rye toast for you, ma'am."

"That will be all then," said Gladys. Jackie turned and left them alone.

Looking at the last offering of her palace, Alice digs in to the warm, moist French toast. This breakfast she would remember for the rest of her life.

Taking small bites, she tried to make the moment last forever. Gladys watched every move, taking in the beauty of Alice. She didn't know what to do to change things, feeling helpless. Privately she was really worried for Alice, like she was turning her out to the wolves.

Finishing her last bite, she excused herself, leaving Gladys with her coffee. She just wanted some alone time. One last time, into the ballroom, twirling around and around, the sun catching the light of the crystal chandelier, casting stardust on the marble floor.

"Alice really did live in a palace," she said.

Just then, Gladys walked in, watching Alice caught up in the moment.

"You are indeed a princess, Alice, and always will be the princess of this palace."

Feeling a warm blush coming over her cheeks, she stopped.

"Really, really?" she asked, tears coming to the surface.

"Yes, Alice. You have been an angel for this family. We would have kept you forever. We all love you."

"I love all of you too," she replied, her eyes soft, humbled.

Orville climbed the staircase to Alice's private space, locating her red suitcases lined up in order of size. Five of them, he counted, making two trips up and down the stairs.

He put them all in the trunk and headed back into the house, to the kitchen for a cup of coffee. There is steam rising from a cup and a plate with French toast, a pool of butter, and maple syrup dressing the browned egg toast.

"This is my lucky day," said Orville. "French toast is my favorite."

"Bon appetite," said Pierre, walking into the dining room. "Its Alice's favorite too."

Orville stood at attention, holding the door for Alice. Gladys and Alice were coming out the door together. Pulling Alice close to her, she kissed her on the cheek.

"I don't want this to be a sad goodbye, Alice. Write to me and let me know how your father is, and if and when you can come back. You will always be welcome in my home. I love you, Alice."

"Thank you for everything. I guess I had better not keep Orville waiting."

Orville held her hand as she slid into the car seat. Closing the door, Alice hung her head. She just couldn't look at Gladys. Her heart was breaking, the tears welling up in her eyes.

Getting the big car out of the driveway, Alice stole one last look. Gladys was waving from the palace in its white splendor.

"Goodbye" she whispered, looking down at her folded hands, her tears falling like silent raindrops.

Gladys stood watching until the car was out of sight. Going back into the house, she went straight to her room, needing some time alone to reflect on the girl child, Alice.

No one saw Gladys the whole day. She had her dinner brought into her, staying in bed, she read, and cried.

The next morning she goes to Alice's room. Everything was in its place, left perfectly. There was a book on the side table. Turning it over, the book of Cinderella.

CHAPTER 41

Where Will the Road Lead?

Watching straight ahead, the scenery changing from wider roads to narrow ones. The familiar places along the way brings her back to her humble roots, realizing she had to face whatever it was head on. No time for yesterday. Today was a new day, the fairy tale falling by the wayside.

Sitting quietly, she eased back now, trying to relax and enjoy the smooth ride of her chariot. Would her brothers all run out to greet her?

Would Irene be peeking out the window when the car came into the yard? How was her dad? She tried to erase the vision of the way he looked, his emancipated body, his hollow cheeks, his skin the color of milk.

Her mind took her back to the palace and the beauty she had enjoyed, even this morning at breakfast. Gladys's pretty face etched in her mind, her smile, and her bright, loving blue eyes, hoping against hope, she would see her again.

Shaken back to earth, the big car hit the pot-holed road up to her house. At attention, watching for any sign of life in the yard.

"We have arrived," announced Orville, looking around at Alice. The kitchen curtains are pulled, a few chickens in the yard, near their coop.

"Can you please wait a few minutes, Orville?" Alice asked. "Can you just let me check and see if anyone is here? And can you please put my bags over there, near the woodshed?"

Confused, but with no time to wonder why he would put them there.

"Yes, just a few minutes, Alice, I have scheduled pickups in the city today."

Getting out of the car, Orville goes to the trunk to retrieve her bags, setting them near the shed, getting back in the car. He watched Alice now, who was standing at the door, knocking and knocking? He rolled down the window.

"I really have to be going now, Miss Alice."

Without waiting to see what she had to say, she watches as the big car backed down the driveway, leaving deep tire marks in the snow.

Taking a look around the yard, no signs of life. The chickens march towards her, with their familiar greeting sound. It was good. No one could see her hide her suitcases. Irene could never know of all her treasures in those bags.

Tugging at the two largest ones, she walked toward the shed. Digging a space between the straw bales she wedges them in. Going back for the other two, also fitting them in tightly. Pulling two bales of straw down around them, covering the red of the suitcases completely. Happy with her hiding spot, she walks back out toward the house. Maybe her mother and brothers were at the dairy. Staring off toward the dairy, with no sight of anyone, only a few jersey cows dotting the snow laden pastures.

It was the first day of the New Year. Irene had said the end of the month. Wasn't she expecting her? And where could everyone have gone? Walking around the yard now, rubbing her hands vigorously together, up and down her arms. A few hours of being outside in the cold had chilled her mood, her body shiverering uncontrollably.

Close to a breaking point, she mustered all her will not to start crying.

Looking over the horizon, the sun started to set. Pink strokes of color are faded out quick by the darkening sky. Her heart is pounding in her ears, and her fingers and toes are hurting. Cold, ice cold, like Irene's heart.

Grey sky turned to black, still no sign of anyone.

Her resolve dampened, tears start falling. Whimpering now, she goes back into the shed. She would have to bed down until her family came home. Worried about herself, but where was her family?

Pulling out her biggest suitcase from the straw, she rifled through the clothing. Finding a wool coat and a couple thick sweaters, she spread them over the straw. She put three sweaters on and another pair of pants, looking down at herself. There was so much thickness of cloth, it made her look swollen. The tears stopped, a smile formed on her lips. Feeling warmer, she tucked herself into another straw bale and pulled the coat over her for a blanket. Settling into the nest, she fell into a deep sleep.

Thrust into a dream, Pearl is there. Her daddy is there too. His smile warmed her everywhere. Beckoning to her, she sat on his knee. Pearl was sitting on the other knee. They started playing patty cakes. Happiness filled her dream. There was a bright light over them both. Just then a shiver up her spine wakes her.

A bright ray of sunshine showed through the cracks in the board shack, casting itself onto the straw floor. Sitting up, she peered out the cracks in the wall at an orange pink sunrise. Reflecting on the dream, it was so good to see her daddy in her dream. And Pearl was there too.

"Oh, thank you, God."

Opening the shed door, she looked out. Still no sign of anyone.

Going to the door she knocked. Still no answer.

"Oh God, where is my family?"

Tears started falling again. Sitting on the step, holding her head in her hands. The warmth of the sunshine on her gave her hope. She would just wait, that was all she could do, wiping the tears from her face.

The sound of movement, voices, wafted to her ears.

Getting up from the steps, she stared down the driveway. Two people were visible in a wagon. As they came closer, she realized it was her mother behind the steed and her aunt Rita sitting next to her. A few dark heads behind them, and William, his red hair showing like a light. Running now toward the wagon, waving her arms in the air.

"I'm so glad you guys are here. I came yesterday. Had to sleep in the woodshed."

Irene just stared Alice's way but said nothing, her hands wrapped up in the leather strapping of the reins, a damask scarf wrapped around her head.

No one spoke. All eyes on Alice.

"We buried your father yesterday," balked Irene.

"Oh my God, noooo, nooooo," she cried. Turning, she ran toward the woodshed as fast as her legs would take her.

Throwing herself into the indent of the straw nest, she curled into a fetal position, holding her eyes tight. It must be all a bad dream, hoping she would open her eyes and be back in her palace.

Limp in the straw, she thinks back to the dream. Of course her daddy was with Pearl in the dream. That is what he had told her. He was going where Pearl was. They were together. That made her so happy, she stopped crying.

Feeling lost, cold, and helpless, laying back on the straw, hoping it would all just go away.

"Well, let's get out of the wagon and into the house. Life doesn't stop for us because the princess is grieving."

"You shouldn't be so hard on Alice," said Rita. "She just found out her father is dead. It's going to take her some time to get over it."

"Yes, yes," said Irene. "You boys take the horse to the shed and give him some hay and water. We are going in to get some tea on."

The house is cold, the warmth of their breaths causing a light fog in the air.

"We will need to get a fire going right away," said Irene. "It's like icicles in here. Go get that stupid Alice from the shed and tell her to carry some wood in here." She forgot that only Ruth was standing behind her.

"I will go get some wood," said Ruth, "and I'll see if Alice is OK."

Shaking her head, Irene ambled towards the wood stove, bending to pick up a few pieces of kindling, arranging them in a loose pile in the belly of the stove.

Anxious to hug Alice and give her some comfort in her sadness, Ruth hurried to the shed. Seeing Alice tucked into the straw, tears at her heart strings. Knowing how much her brother loved his only daughter, she had a feeling that she needed to help protect Alice against her tyrannical mother.

Ruth had never agreed with the way Irene mothered her children. William just told her to mind her business. There had been another time when she was visiting her brother and noticed Alice carrying heavy pails of water in the house while her brothers frolicked in the yard. Things just didn't add up.

"Alice, dear. We have to get some wood for the house. Your mother is going to make a fire. It's so cold in there."

Ruth's soft loving voice coaxed Alice from her straw bed, turning to see her aunt, with her arms outstretched toward her. Auburn wavy hair, big watery, blue eyes displaying the love and compassion that Alice craved.

Hungrily Alice invited her aunt's embrace, resting her head into her ample chest.

"Oh, Aunt Ruth. I am so sad my daddy is gone. I've been here in this shed since yesterday, freezing cold. Luckily I had some warm clothes and I made a bed in the straw. Are you going to be staying here with us tonight, or are you taking your horse and buggy home?"

"Oh no, dear, that is your mother's horse and buggy. A friend of your dad's gave it to her as a present to help out now that William is gone.

"It's my mother's horse and buggy, for real? What a kind man he must be. Do you know who gave it to her?" A puzzled look crossed her face.

"Just that his name is Charlie. Your mom didn't say much more about him."

"I never met a Charlie," said Alice.

"Maybe your dad worked with him at the dairy. So let's both take an armful of wood in. Your mother is waiting. Your dad is better now, honey. He was suffering a lot, and now he is at peace. You will see him again when it's your time. William went to heaven. He was a good, kind man. Now that your mom has her own horse and buggy, maybe you will get to visit me more. It sure would be nice to spend some time with you, Alice."

Thinking she would tell her aunt about the dream, she decided against it, just in case her mother got wind of it and turned it into something with teeth.

Rita helped Alice bring in five armfuls of wood. Stacking it neatly into four piles, then watching as Irene put a couple of pieces gently on the already lit kindling. When the sides of the pieces caught, Irene closed the cast iron door.

In no time, there was a roaring fire, the warmth spreading through the board house.

"C'mon, Alice," said Rita. "Let's sit and have some nice hot tea. It is time for us to come together. Everyone is sad about losing your dad."

"No sense is crying," said Irene. "You can't bring back the dead." Irene putting down three cups on the table, the steam rising from the tea pot.

"Your father's suffering is over, and ours still goes on. We will all die one day. The ones who go are the lucky ones," Irene went on.

"Here, a little sugar will go a long way. Have some tea and cookies, and then you can get settled into your new room."

"My new room, Mom?" Alice asked.

"Yes, your father's room."

Rita was shocked at what she just heard.

"You know William would not approve of that. Surely, you could give her somewhere else?"

"There is nowhere else. The boys have taken over her room, and I can't have her bunking down in the parlor. It's final. She will sleep in William's room."

"Mother, I just can't believe that you want me to use that room! It isn't even a room; it's a pantry. There are no windows in there, Mother. I can't. I just can't. I would rather die!"

"Maybe the woodshed suits you better. This is no palace, Alice, or haven't you noticed? Still have your head in the clouds?"

"I have to go," said Rita, standing up, tightening her sweater around her. "Could you have Skip take me home?"

"You just got here. I see how it is. That Alice, always causing some bad feelings."

"No, Irene, I just can't seem to get through to you. I won't stand back and watch you treat your only daughter like she doesn't matter to you. Really Irene, sometimes I think you are heartless."

"I'll go get the boys to take you home then, if that's how you feel."

Standing at the kitchen counter, a faraway look in her eyes, the floor in front of the sink, showing more wear, the bare boards coming thru in places, the yellowed linoleum turned up at the edges. There was nothing that said, this was a happy place. No family pictures on the walls. Even the ghosts had left Irene with her misery. *I will get away from here, if it's the last thing I do*, thought Alice.

"God show me a way, please," she prayed, walking down the hallway toward her new dungeon. Opening the door, the cot perfectly made, a small table next to it. Taking in the whole of the room, it was hardly enough to turn around in. Nowhere to put her things. Determined, this would be temporary, she would pray and ask God to deal her a new hand, take her away from this hell.

Thinking of the closet at the palace, it was the same size as her room.

I will only sleep in here, that's all, she decided. She would read in the parlor, till her eyes were too heavy to stay awake. Just as she was about to turn and walk out, a breeze blows through her hair. Picking up the pillow where her father had laid his head in his death bed prison, a warm love feeling, like he was there with her. Lying face down in the bed, she cries.

"Daddy, Daddy, please don't leave me here with her. She doesn't love me, Daddy. She hurts me. Please come back."

Whimpering and crying into the pillow, a sense of calm comes over her, falling into a deep sleep.

CHAPTER 42

Alice Settles In

With only six of them now, she would at least get to sit at the table.

The next morning, while preparing breakfast, Alice watched her mother with an eagle eye. Her movements are labored, her knees and back riddled with pain. She said she hurt all over and just wanted to sit down, while Alice fried eggs and buttered bread.

"You will be doing all of the housework now, Alice. There are fewer mouths to feed, and clean for. Soon you will find a husband and move out on your own."

"I don't want to find a husband."

"Really," said Irene, "you have high hopes. You have no education. Those people filled your head full of dreams."

Deciding it was better not to talk back, she walked out of the kitchen to her room. Opening the door, the big red suitcase sitting on top of her bed. Before Alice could close the door behind her, Irene comes up behind her.

"I see where all of your money went, buying new things. Don't think you can wear that fancy stuff around here. I will burn it all," she bellowed, hobbling away, back toward the kitchen.

The threat of Irene was still present, but the way she was so crippled up gave Alice some hope. She couldn't run after her, nor could she swing a broom over her back or beat her with her walking stick.

"Come out here now, and talk to me," screeched Irene from the table.

"Mother, what is it?" asked Alice, her eyes wide, waiting for the poison to spew from her lips.

"You bring twelve dollars a month home here, and you were living like some princess. How long did you think your fairy tale would last?"

"Mother, it was your idea that I go and work there. I don't understand why you are angry."

Irene extended her hand to slap Alice across the face. Alice moved out of her reach, Irene gritting her teeth.

"Don't get smart with me, you, you..."

Getting up from the table before more hatefulness spewed out, Alice walks out the door.

Taking in a deep breath, the air soothed her mind, closing the door behind her and Irene out of her space. Not a threat; she was too slow, too tired, and too old to hurt her anymore. Sunshine started to creep through the dark clouds of despair.

The next morning Alice is awakened by the bandy rooster saying his good morning to the world.

She would make crepes this morning for her brothers and get to talk to them before they went off for the day. George and Jack both worked at the dairy. Going out to the chicken coop, she picked some fresh eggs from the nests. This would be a surprise for her brothers. Pierre had shown her how to make the wonderful, airy, thin pancakes. Deciding on scrambled eggs and crepes on the side.

As she looked through the cupboards, she found a big jar of Irene's strawberry preserves, perfect for the crepes. Could it be too much to imagine maybe Irene would be bowled over, loving them too?

One by one, her brothers' heads showing in the doorway. Their eyes searched the counters and the butcher block table. A smell of fresh coffee wafted through the board house. Pierre had given Alice two jars of his special coffee to take home with her.

"Good morning, Alice," came her brothers' voices. Earl went straight to her, peering in the big silver bowl.

"What are you making, pancakes?"

"Yes, I guess you could call them the French version of pancakes."

"Wow," he answered, licking his lips. "How long before breakfast is ready?"

A stack of the crepes already on a plate, Earl eyes them curiously.

"Just take those to the table. I am making more, so you guys can start eating if you want." Just then she remembered she hadn't seen her mother all morning.

"Has anyone seen Mom this morning?"

"Ah, sometimes she stays in bed till the afternoon. We have to pretty much look after ourselves. She is not well," answered Jack, a tall, dark haired boy.

"Can you see if she wants to have some crepes brought to her room?"

Just then Irene showed in the doorway, pulling her robe around her.

"What is this? Don't have the decency to wait for your mother?"

Irene heads to her seat at the head of the table. Alice put five crepes on a plate and walked to the table, placing them down in front of Irene.

"What on earth are these?" Picking up one of the crepes, it goes limp around the fork.

"They are better than pancakes," piped Earl.

"Who asked you, big mouth? Eat and shut up."

The boys all looked up, a couple of them grinning, Alice watching the exchange as they looked at one another in a mocking manner. They too were over Irene bullying them. The room goes quiet, everyone enjoying the new confection.

Closing her eyes she counted the stairs to the top of her room. She was there, lying back in the big claw-foot tub with the smell of lavender. So many wonderful memories, she falls asleep.

Awakened by the bandy rooster's five o'clock alarm, sitting up she slipped out of the bed. Just then, she realized how much she had missed the bugle call of the rooster.

She didn't spend any time in the room. It was only for sleeping. After making the bed, she closed the door and went out to the kitchen. There was a chill in the air. She walked to the woodstove and opened the latch door. No embers, no heat. Having watched Irene make the fire, she was sure she could manage. Just then George walked toward Alice.

"I was just going to start a fire, Alice. You can make the breakfast, I'll take care of this. Jack and I have to be at the dairy at seven, so it's better if we all share the chores around here."

Wow, her being away had made her brothers more independent too. And with their dad passing, they really had to help with everything. Things were feeling so different now.

Looking over at the wood box, she saw only a few pieces of kindling left. Without waiting for Irene to tell her, she would go and bring in some wood.

Put on her boots, she headed outside to the shed. A few freshly cut pieces of wood scattered around the dirt floor, and a stack of wood piled against one wall. Picking up a few pieces of kindling, and cut wood, taking a whole armful, the wood blocking her sight, taking time she makes it back into the house, letting the wood fall gently near the woodbox. Meticulously, Alice stacks the wood in the box.

Deciding she would go back out to the shed to stack the rest of the cut wood.

Inhaling deeply, the smell of the freshly cut wood reminding her of when she would join her father there. Tears welled up in her eyes. She could see him swinging the ax, his red checkered shirt, and his work boots. They would meet in the shed and talk over their next strategy against the evil mother. A sad realization takes over her. There would be no more talks or hugs from him.

Lately, Irene was getting the boys to bring the horse and buggy around to the door so she didn't have to walk far, complaining that her knees hurt so much she could hardly walk. "Going to visit Rita," she would say and take off down the road. It was great for Alice to have the house to herself while she worked without her mother over her shoulder, complaining.

Amazed that someone would give her mother a horse and buggy, Alice questioned Irene about the gift. The answer she gave Alice made her feel like Irene was trying to hide something. Not wanting to ask the question again, she just let it go.

"I don't have to tell you anything, Alice. Since when are you my mother?"

She missed the Olsenses so much, like they had been ripped away from her. Thinking too much about her life there made her sad, not knowing if she would ever be able to go back. Life was so cruel. How would her hand play out next?

The housework was down to a science, leaving lots of time for Alice between breakfast and supper.

Now with her two brothers working at the dairy, the Jeffersonses were sending a box of food home every week, as well as the cream and butter and milk that was close to expiry date. Things were more abundant, Alice noticing more food in the cupboards.

"If it wasn't for the Jeffersonses, we would be going hungry around here."

"I think you will have to go back to work soon, Alice."

"Yes, they are waiting for me to come back, Mother. Gladys told me she wouldn't hire anyone to take my job."

"I didn't say you would be going back there."

Just as Alice was going to argue the point, she decided not to say another thing. Why was her mother so against her going back to work there?

"Things are going to change around here, real soon," threatened Irene.

"What is it, Mother? What are you trying to tell me?"

"I overheard a few ladies at the station talking about the candy factory in Halifax. They are hiring young ladies. You could be a candy wrapper. Twice the amount of money you were making working for those rich people."

"But where would I live, Mother? That's a long ways away."

"I've got that figured out already. I got you a second job too, Alice. You are going to live and work for Charlie. Your father's friend. The one who gave us the horse and buggy."

Wide eyed at what she had just heard, her mouth agape.

"No, no, Mother. I don't want to be an old man's maid."

"It's really too bad. You will be making two wages and helping out around here. And how do think we are going to pay for this horse and buggy?

"Mother!" She yelled, "You said it was a gift. So that's how you are going to pay for it, by making me go and work for him? That is so unfair, Mother. You never asked me," she cried.

Falling to the floor, face down she doubled her fists. No! Pounding into the floor, losing all sanity. This wasn't really happening. Her mother was selling her for a horse and buggy.

Just then Skip and Earl came through the door, each with an armful of wood. Both of them shocked at seeing Alice on the floor. Earl tripped over his brother and the armful of wood, hit the floor, thud, thud, thud, shaking Alice out of her hysteria.

Irene started screaming and waving her arms. Alice gets herself up from the floor. She couldn't hear anything, just watched her mother's arms waving, her mouth wide open, her eyes buldging, her hair wild.

The insanity of Irene was causing Alice to act out too, no she couldn't bear it one more minute, running outside, going into the woodshed to her nest that still held her impression.

Tired and weary from the whole day of non stop chores, scrubbing her brother's clothes on the washboard, carrying wood, peeling potatoes, and washing floors, she lay there quiet.

Just after lunch, Irene ordered the buggy brought around. Watching from the window over the sink, her mother, reins in hand, headed down the road. Happy for her, probably going to her Aunt Rita's, she thought.

Lying on her narrow cot, she fantasizes of the big tub, her stress washing away, her eyes heavy. Just as she is drifting off, a slight breeze over her face, then a feeling of lips on her forehead. Frightened, she sits straight up in the bed, pulling her blanket to her chest. Staring into the darkness, a twinkling of star dust. Laying back she falls fast asleep. There was no need to question the magic in her life.

In the early morning hours, Alice goes into a dream. She dreams that she is at the dairy with her dad, who is standing next to a big black-and-white jersey cow. He is holding on to one of its ears and smiling, trying to tell her something, his lips moving, but no sound escaped. The first word his mouth was wide, the second one, his tongue was showing, and the third one, his mouth pursed in a kiss.

All day she kept going over the dream in her mind, thinking of her father's smiling face and what he was trying to say to her. Finally she decided on three words. I love you.

Irene watched Alice's every move, humming as she went about her chores, her spirit unbreakable.

As Alice is on her way to the butcher block table with a platter of eggs, their heads sunny side up, she heard Irene talking to the boys.

"It's a job at a candy factory."

"It sounds good to me," said Alice. "I don't mind the thought of working with candy all day. Is it for real, Mother?"

"Yes, it's been decided," Announced Irene in her captain's voice, "and you will take a job as a maid for Charlie in exchange for your room and board. His wife has been dead for a few years now and he has been looking for a helper. He lives in a big house just a short walk from the candy factory. It's perfect. Remember the day the old fellow brought your father home in his buggy? Your dad had a terrible headache and had to come home from work? He had two horses. Do you remember him?"

Staring into her mother's lifeless eyes. "Mother! That old creepy man, with the hair all over his face?"

"Ah, he is a harmless old man. You will be leaving in a week. I saw him the other day at the general store. He said he would be here to get you next Monday morning."

Alice's brothers all but dropped their forks, staring from Irene back to Alice. The color drained from Alice's cheeks, her eyes wide, frightened.

Turning, walking slowly away from the kitchen, she headed down the narrow, dark hallway, to... No, out the other way, out the door, down the steps, across the dirt yard, into the snow-dusted meadow. Heading toward the barns, the cows, the spotted dog, Mrs. Jefferson, running and running until the cold air shakes her out of her distress.

The boys all make their way out of the house too, in single file, grabbing their coats off the wooden coat tree near the door. It was terrible what she was doing to Alice, and they couldn't do anything to stop it, leaving Irene alone with her misery.

Irene is fighting mad, spewing harsh words, as they all walk away from her and her madness.

The snow, against her bare ankles, a stinging, numbing her pain, realizing she had better go back to the warmth of the shack. Having a hard time making sense of it all, her mother sending her only daughter to live with an old man, to cook and clean for him, made Alice's stomach turn somersaults. "Why oh why God, how can this be?"

With her mother, there was always a catch, like she was setting a trap for a mouse? Deciding to go out to the road now, she just couldn't see her mother, her arms swinging at her sides, the run a dance of rebellion, wishing she could just keep on running and running.

Yes, she was happy to get out of Irene's sight. Thinking of two jobs tired her mind. Why couldn't she go back to the Olsenses'?

By the time she made it back home, she had it figured out.

Just make the best of a bad situation. No point in being sad. Changes.

She prayed her mother wouldn't change her mind again, like the shifting sands in the desert or the wind on a winter night whipping at your face.

Going back into the house. She would confront her mother again for more details.

"Mother, how many girls work at the candy factory, do you suppose?"

"I would imagine there are many girls, just like you," she said, a strained smile on her thin lips.

"So next Monday, Mother, was that the day?"

"Yes," answered Irene, the *s* elongated into a hissing snake sound. "One week from today."

"I will get all the cleaning done for you, Mother, before I leave,"

Irene turning from her, heading towards the parlor. "You just might take a likeness to the old guy," said Irene.

"Are you kidding, Mother? I don't think so." Wrinkling up her nose, she remembered him well. A long stringy grey beard, a fat belly that rounded up and out, like a big hard rock. Short, thick torso, big bulbous nose, and small beady eyes.

He had made it a point to stop on the way out the door, talking to her mother, but with his eyes fixated on Alice, who is sitting at the kitchen table.

When he had first come in, Irene introduced him to her daughter. A big cheesy grin, yellowed teeth, a few missing, and strands of grey beard hanging over his top lip, into his mouth, disgusting. A short, thick neck, with folds of fat.

Walking away, a foul smell of cigar smoke mixed with bad body odor infecting the air around him. Yuck, she thought to herself, trying not to inhale the stench.

The candy coating of Irene's story was taking on a sour note. Something sinister she wanted nothing to do with.

"I don't understand, Mother," she said staring into Irene's cold, dark eyes. "I don't want to go and live with an old man, Mom. Why do you hate me so much, Mother?" Her voice cracking, tears forming in her sea green eyes.

"Go," she said, pointing her finger. "Pack your bags, Alice, there is no argument here. It has been decided. I won't hear any more of it! Charlie will bring you home once a month to bring me your wages. Remember you are working for him. You cannot live under my roof anymore, Alice. Time you made your own way in life. I have nothing to offer you, just misery, like my life. Hope something good comes of you."

The way she spoke of Charlie, like he was a good friend of hers?

"I wish I was never born," yelled Alice, running toward the door. Down the steps, a cold wind slapped at her face, taking a deep cleansing breath. When her fingers and toes start hurting from the cold, she has to go back into the house. Opening the door, apprehensive, looking in. No sign of Irene.

The night before her departure, Alice pondered the things ahead. Where did he live? Irene had said it was a short walk to the candy factory, which could have meant an hour's walk or more. Nothing Irene said was set in stone.

Her destiny was changing again. Would they like her and hire her at the candy factory? Would she be old enough to work there, having just turned thirteen? Trying to imagine a candy factory, the intoxicating smell of chocolate in the air. Mmm, she loved chocolate. On that sweet note, she falls into a deep sleep.

Monday morning came. Up early, she dressed, packing her things in her big red suitcase. Today, the ogre would come to take the princess to a faraway old castle. Cobwebs and dark places, keeping her there, as his prisoner. Where had that story come from?

Giggling at her thoughts, a fine young prince would come and rescue her, taking her away on a white horse, with wings. Never would she see the evil mother or the ogre again.

"Don't get caught up in the fairy tale," she said out loud.

Dressed in the blue-and-white uniform she wore at the Olsenses', she looked the part of the maid. Slipping on the white shoes with the soft soles, she runs her brush through her hair, pulling it back in a ponytail. With no mirrors in the house, she had mastered the task, by feeling, then tying it with a ribbon.

When she was ready, she took one last look around the room. It felt like she was leaving her father, again. But now it was time for her to leave the nest, as Irene had stressed to her. Time to grow up.

Opening the woodshed door, she goes in, straight to the corner, where her luggage is hidden. Four red bags, strands of straw caught in crevices. Dusting them off, she lined them up in order of size.

This morning she had planned a decadent breakfast of French toast and fresh brewed coffee. A platter of browned egg toast stacked high. Butter pooled around the plate, strawberry jam to sweeten the morning.

One by one, her brothers take their place at the table. A fresh pot of coffee sits in the centre, cream in a bottle next to it. All eyes are on the French toast.

"This is great, Alice," said Earl. "Mom never cooks us anything fancy like this."

"Shh," said Alice. "Don't say that. It will make her feel bad."

"Can we eat now? Mother doesn't seem to be coming to breakfast this morning," said Skip.

It just dawned on her she hadn't seen her mother all morning.

"Wait, I will go and see if she is coming." Getting up from her seat going to Irene's door. Listening, she opened the door slowly peering in. A whining sound coming from a large mound in the bed, the blankets covering her head.

"Are you all right, Mother?" she said quietly, going to the side of her bed.

"I am in a lot of pain today. I won't be coming out for breakfast." Alice goes back out, closing the door quietly, back to the table and her brothers.

They ate quietly, exchanging smiles. No one asked her about her new job or where she was going to live. Their thoughts are apparent from the looks in their eyes. There was nothing they could do to change things.

CHAPTER 43

Charlie's

Her brothers licked the platter clean of the French toast. One by one, they thanked her and went their way. Irene still hadn't shown her face in the kitchen. Just finishing up the dishes, she glanced at the square clock on the wall. Fifteen minutes to nine. Walking back and forth to her mother's room three times, but deciding not to go in. Pulling on her coat, she navigated her large suitcase down the cinder block steps, bringing the other four from the shed, lining them up from smallest to largest.

At the sound of a hurrying of hooves, Alice looked down the beaten road. A buggy with two horses coming up the drive.

Her eyes widened as she saw the man. Charlie. The brave face she had put on fell away, her biggest fears realized. Her stomach churned like a heaving sea, bile rising in her mouth. With a drumming in her ears, her heart beat fast in her chest. Running back into the house, straight to the bathroom, vomiting up her French toast.

Heavy footsteps coming toward the bathroom, Irene peering in at Alice.

"What is the matter with you now, girl?"

"It's him, Mother, he is coming up the drive."

"You knew he was coming. I don't know why you are making such a fuss," she said, running her thick fingers across her apron. Ambling to the door, Irene sticks her head out. The buggy pulled up to the steps. Charlie got down.

"Good morning to you, ma'am," he said, flashing a yellowed smile.

"Come on in for a cup of tea while she gets her things together."

Just then Alice ran by them on her way out the door.

"Probably just going to feed the chickens. She won't be long."

"Yes, of course, I've been up since five this morning. Too busy to fix myself any breakfast. I can't stay too long."

Taking her bags one by one, she lined them up on the other side of the wagon so her mother wouldn't see them, stopping to say hello to the big horses, one black and one brown. Leather straps snake up the sides of their faces, attached to their mouths by large rings, a steel rod through their mouths. The big eyes of the horses, bright, dark, and scary.

Going back into the house. Charlie and Irene are sitting at the table, a cup to his hairy lips, Irene eating a cookie.

"Come over here and say hi to Charlie."

"Yes, Mother. We have already met."

"Well, get your things ready. He can't stay long."

"Yes, we want to get home before the sun goes down. It gets cold in the wagon," said Charlie, watching Alice, his eyes peeled on her rounded behind.

Coming back out with a bag with her toiletries, her robe, and slippers.

"That's all you have to take, Alice?" asked Irene.

"No, Mother, I have already taken my bags out to the wagon."

Irene shook her head. She hadn't seen her walk by with any bags.

Walking past the table, Alice pulls her coat around her. Getting to the door, she turned to look back at her mother just as she is bringing the tea cup to her mouth, her dark eyes peering over the rim.

Standing next to her bags, she waited for Charlie.

With a brave face, she watched as Charlie approached her, with a quarter moon grin.

"Let me help you, my dear." Putting out his hand to her, hoisting her into the wagon. Wide eyed, she stared straight ahead. Her heart is beating like the wings of a small bird in flight. A quick glance at him. He was definitely the ogre, not the prince, laughing at herself.

Charlie looked over the five suitcases. "These are all yours?"

"Yes, they are. Can you please put them in the back of the wagon?" Nervous about Irene seeing them, wringing her hands.

"Looks like you are leaving home for good," he said. "All these things?" he said again, grumbling under his breath.

Just as he is hoisting the last suitcase into the buggy, Irene comes to the door.

"Goodbye then, Irene," said Charlie, picking up the leather reins. The large steeds thrust their heads back, fighting the bits.

The wagon lurched forward.

Alice didn't look her mother's way.

"Go fast," she ordered. "I never want to see her again. Please, driver, onward."

Charlie wasn't sure of what she had said. All he heard was please, driver.

Irene went back in, closing the door behind her, going straight to the window pulling back the curtain with her index finger.

Charlie slapped the reins against their backs, as they pull the wagon, out of the snow laden trail.

"Good riddance," Irene mouthed. "Girls are no good anyway. Too much trouble."

Alice watched Charlie out of the corner of her eyes. His large grey wool hat is pulled over his head, a heavy grey wool coat, like a big hairy mammoth.

"Is it all right if I sit in the back with my things?" she asked.

"Go right ahead. Just crawl over there and put the blanket around your legs."

A red, itchy looking blanket, thinking she would rather be cold.

Settling in behind Charlie, she has a bird's-eye view of the back of his head. His neck looked like a stack of bologna. Weather beaten, leathery skin. Watching his movements with his thick, knobby, nicotine-stained fingers, long blackened fingernails. Wide, short hands, nothing like her father's.

Silence, except the heavy breath from the horses' mouths, steam rising from their nostrils, a clanging of the wagon wheels, against the axel. Charlie spoke. "We will be making lots of fires this winter. They say it's going to be colder than last year."

Alice didn't know what to say to that, or even if she should answer. The air stirring around the wagon was cold, she pulled the scratchy blanket around her legs. The drumming of the horses' hooves takes Alice into a daydream.

"Yeah, we will be coming up to the old homestead soon," he said, looking around at Alice.

The old homestead? Thought Alice.

"What are your horses' names?" Trying to change the subject.

"Ned and Sally. They are brother and sister and ten years old. They are a good pair, take me everywhere I need to go." Sitting up now, watching, not wanting to miss anything close to where she would be living. They had come a long way. The scenery was visibly different. The road was wider, with more houses.

Charlie turned up a long narrow road, a big red barn coming into view.

Just left of it a small greyish brown bungalow with a veranda, not much bigger than her childhood home. Two rocking chairs on either side of the door. Three wooden steps.

A sick feeling in her stomach, staring hard at the house. *Oh no, Mother! You lied again*, she thought.

Heaving a heavy sigh, her face forlorn.

"We have arrived, my dear," he said, turning around, a big toothy grin, like he had just brought his bride to her new home. "You are just a little bit of a thing, aren't you, fourteen?"

Another lie. Wonder what other lies she had told Charlie?

Frightened, she stared straight into Charlie's hungry eyes.

"Yeah, this is the old homestead, been in the family for a hundred years."

Oh no, thought Alice. A house that old probably had ghosts. Getting down out of the buggy, she walked begrudgingly toward the house. Standing at the steps, holding her hands in front of her, watching Charlie as he takes her bags out of the wagon.

"Just go ahead in," he said, pointing to the door.

Walking up the stairs, she turned the doorknob walking in. A waft of stale air infecting her nostrils.

"Go in and get yourself acquainted," he said, coming up behind her.

"Get acquainted with who? Is there someone else here?" she asked.

"No, not that I know about," he answered with a deep, menacing laugh.

Just inside the door she watches as Charlie toted her suitcases upstairs and down a hallway to a door on the left.

A musty, pungent smell hangs in the air. Dirt-caked boots sit at the door. A trail of dirt and dust led through the house. Clothes and horse things strewn all over. Two rocking chairs sits on either side of the woodstove. Taking a peek in the parlor, an old couch, its middle bowing like it is praying to be replaced.

A helpless, frightened feeling comes over her, tears in her eyes. How could she live in this pig house? The chicken coop was even better.

Spellbound, she watches Charlie coming back down the stairs, taking off his coat.

"Here," he said, thrusting it at her. "Hang it up for me. Might as well get used to having a maid as of right now. The house doesn't look like much, but you are exactly what it needs, a cute young thing to take care of it. Hasn't been cleaned real well since my wife died. Poor thing died of cancer. She was only fifty-five. Anyway, we won't go into my sad story. It is great to have you here, Alice. Maybe you can make some magic in this house. It is yours to explore," he said, pointing up the staircase.

"My room is across the hall from yours, and the bathroom is next to your room. You can have that bathroom as your own. I will use the outhouse."

Noticing the kitchen through an archway, Charlie walked in ahead, beckoning to her. Timidly, she stepped through into the kitchen, her eyes scanning the room, a putrid smell of sour milk, dirty rags, and black slime around the faucets. Putting her hand to her face, holding her breath, the stench turning her stomach. Heading back to the front door, looking around, for somewhere to sit down. Everywhere she looked nothing looked safe. Everything, disgusting, dirty. Where would she start? This house was not fit to live in, not until she had spent days cleaning it. Yes, her workload at home had been heavy, but having to clean layers of dirt off everything she looked at made her want to get to the front door and bolt like a runaway horse. There was nowhere to go, and Irene had said she had to make a way for herself in life. Despair and every sad emotion filled her mind. Why was life being so cruel to her? This creepy old man was sleeping right across the hall from her. How would she sleep at night? This just had to be a bad dream.

Walking back to Alice, getting too close, Alice taking a few steps back, as he stares her up and down.

"I know the house is in rough shape right now, but after a good cleaning, it will look a lot different." Spittle forms in the corners of his mouth, making her want to gag, and run somewhere, anywhere.

"It's going to take days to clean this place. Especially the kitchen. I hope you don't expect me to cook for you too?"

"You just look here. I gave your mother a horse and buggy for you to come and help me out here, plus you get a free place to live. So don't start giving me any of your smart talk, cause I could just take you right back to your mother. And by the way she speaks, she doesn't care much for you. Well, what I mean is, she gave you away for a horse and buggy."

Alice stared hard at him, digesting what he had just said. Tears flowed down her cheeks. Trying not to let him see her crying, she wiped at her eyes, heading to one of the rocking chairs sitting down to gather herself.

Losing herself in the warmth radiating from the woodstove, her mind goes blank.

"I'll just put a couple pieces of wood in the fire," he said, coming close to her, reaching out to touch her arm, she moved just in time, his hand falling to his side.

"I won't hurt you. Didn't your mother tell you about me?"

"No, my mother didn't tell me anything about you. How long have you known my mother?"

"I knew your father. Sorry for your loss," he said, walking into the parlor.

"We can relax in here after supper. I like coffee and cake. My wife always made cake for me. You make cake, Alice? Apple pie is my favorite," he said, his pink and grey tongue showing as it grazed his moustache.

A shiver runs up her spine.

"Yes, I can make all those things. I was taught by the best," she said, walking away from him toward the staircase.

Feeling his glare on her, she continued to the top of the stairs and down the hallway to the door on the left.

Opening the door, her suitcases lined against the wall. No dirty boot marks, just a smell of old things. A queen size bed in the middle of the room. A dark wooden dresser with a big oval mirror, and a small wooden stool sitting in front. A large picture window overlooking a dark green tree line beyond. Billows of soft, sheer, ivory curtains framed the window. A light dust covering everything, she runs her fingers over the windowsill.

A grunt from the doorway.

"Sorry to interrupt your thoughts. I shared this room with my wife for twenty years. Then she turned me out to the room across the hall. You know what happens to women when they reach a certain age. They don't want anything to do with you in the bedroom."

Why was he telling her all these things? Still standing with her back to him, hoping he would just go away. Walking up behind her, he rests his wide hand on her shoulder. Feeling violated, she turned and backed away, her eyes wide.

"Everything will work out, Alice. Don't be afraid of me. I won't hurt you. OK, I will leave you to get settled in. And the bathroom is just down the hallway. I have some chores to attend to, so I'll be in the barn, if you need me."

Yikes, she never wanted to need this old creepy guy.

Timid and scared in a new, dirty place, she just wanted to curl up in the bed, and hope to wake up in her palace.

Knowing the room had been closed up for a long time, she would start by opening the windows to air it out. Then she would pull the covers off the bed and hope there were some clean blankets and sheets. That thought went right out the window as soon as it entered her mind. There probably wasn't anything clean in the whole house. Hoping against hope that he had a wringer washing machine, oh please God.

Pulling down the top comforter, iron lines in the sheets, perfectly cleaned and starched.

Deciding she would just take them off and air them out, then it would be OK to sleep on them.

Carrying all the blankets and sheets downstairs, her arms full, peeking around the side, to watch where she is going, she makes it to the outside porch. A clothesline is strung from the side of the house to a tree beyond. Finding a can with clothespins, she hangs the sheets and blanket, then walks back into the house. Apprehensive, deciding to take a look in the bathroom, she heads back upstairs.

Turning the doorknob, afraid of what she will encounter, she peers in.

A sharp smell of urine burns her eyes. Covering her mouth with her hand, gasping. Taking a few steps in, a tall call, with shit floating on the top, "oh yuck," she exclaimed. The stench of urine, strong enough to make her vomit.

"Oh my God," she said, bile rising in her throat. Oh, oh…

"Yuck," she said. "I can't clean this. I think I will be sick."

Pulling the door hard, she closed out the stench, backing away from the door.

"Oh God, why is this happening to me, God?"

Holding her stomach, she goes back to the top of the stairs looking down. Where was he? She would rather die than have to clean that bathroom. There was no way!

Maybe she would just run away. Steal the wagon and horses and go far into the countryside. Just go as far as she could and hope that… No, it was not smart, not in the winter. No money to get a place to live, and what if he caught her stealing the horses and wagon? Would he beat her or kill her, or take her back to her evil mother?

She couldn't figure out what would be worse.

Counting the steps, she descended to the main floor. No sign of Charlie.

She was just about to walk into the kitchen when she heard him at the door.

The door slammed. Alice turned.

"Please, Charlie, can you clean the bathroom for me? I don't mind doing the kitchen and the rest of the house," she asked in a pleading, whispery voice.

"Yes, I suppose I could do that if you get busy and fix a hungry old man a sandwich or something. There is some roast beef in the cooler and some homemade bread your mom gave me. That is some bread, I tell you, Alice, the best I ever had."

She had given him bread too? Irene had done lots to pawn her off on this man, feeling worthless, like something she wanted to get rid of, like a sickness. Tears filled her eyes just to the brim, not falling over. No, she couldn't let Irene hurt her anymore. This was better than being with her mother. Anything was better, and she would make the very best of the situation.

"Yes, of course, Charlie. I will have to clean some of the table off and the counter, so it might be in an hour. I can't make anything in there until I clean it."

"And some tea with that sandwich, OK? I am going now to empty the pail and clean up the bathroom for you, miss. I want you to feel at home here, and hope you will come to like it and maybe me too. One thing I know you will love is the big claw-foot bathtub. You can warm water on the woodstove, fill it, and sit in it as long as you want."

Hurrying down the hallway to the kitchen, looking behind her. He was saying weird things, like about her liking him. Never. She wouldn't ever like him. The way he looked when he talked about the bathtub—he'd had a sneaky grin on his face. He had kidnapped the princess and was holding her in an old rundown shack. If she didn't do what he asked, he might tie her up in the cellar? No one would know. Irene was the only one who knew where she was. Or did she even know?

Thinking of sleeping in that room, where he and his wife, had slept for twenty years, makes her wonder, how old is the bed? And with him right across the hallway from her. Oh my God. She would have to check to see if there was a lock on the door. There just had to be. Before she could start cleaning the kitchen, she had to go and see.

Charlie had gone up there to clean the bathroom, Alice hoping she wouldn't rub elbows with him. She would try her best to avoid even walking near him.

The air around Charlie was strained. Dirty, foggy, sweaty. His house was disgusting, and so was he. She wondered when he had actually had some kind of a bath.

Running up the stairs, she counted fast to the top. Opening the door, walking in, then closed it behind her. Staring at the handle, no lock of any kind. But just above the door handle is a hook-and-eye closure. *Ahh, great, at least I have some way to lock the door.*

Charlie comes up behind Alice startling her, she screamed loud enough to wake the ghosts.

"I don't know what is the matter with you, girl. I was just checking to see if Mildred's wedding ring was in here. Maybe you would like to wear it? Diamonds in gold," he said, a twinkle in his dark eyes, wrinkles fanning out to his temples.

"No, noooo!" she screamed. "I don't want to wear your wife's ring, and please, don't come in my room anymore. I need my private place to be just for me."

Without saying anything to her, he walked out, heading down the hallway to the bathroom.

The kitchen needed more than Alice could ever begin to give. Just the surface was all she could fix. Years of dirt and grime had infected the place.

The linoleum that looked originally white and black was mostly black.

Searching the room for a mop and broom; she would need both. There was not one inch of clean space to prepare a sandwich and cup of tea.

Four of her mother's signature loaves in brown bags sat on the table. Remembering now that she hadn't had anything to eat since she threw up, her stomach grumbled. Happy now for her mother's bread, had her mother possibly have sent some of the bread for her, the thought making her heart glad. Possibly, but not likely.

Cleaning half of the table off, she gets busy with the job at hand. Two roast beef sandwiches for Charlie, and one for her. After filling the tea kettle with water, she continued cleaning.

No sooner had she finished pouring the tea, Charlie shows in the kitchen.

"Ah, that looks good. I'll have mine in the parlor, and you can join me, if you are not too scared to sit with an old man."

"I want to get settled in my room. If it is OK, I would like to have mine in my room."

"Sure, you do that. That will be all for today then. Tomorrow is a new day. You can be up bright and early and get a good start on this house. Everything will be waiting for you."

He talked so weirdly. What would be waiting for her? Not wanting to get into any deep conversation with him, she set his tea and sandwich down, turned, and walked back into the kitchen.

As she walked away, Charlie watched her tight body, licking his lips like she was the dessert.

"Mmm," he murmured.

She turned to look at him, just biting into the beefy sandwich.

At the top of the staircase, her sandwich and tea in hand, a strong disinfectant smell was in the air. She tried not to breathe in, her eyes stinging. Getting into her room, she set down her tea and sandwich, going right away to the door, putting the hook in the eye.

It was the only room in the house that was close to being livable, almost like it didn't belong to the rest of the house. With a welcoming feeling, she sat on the freshly aired bed. All she had to do was dust the cedar plank floor, which still had a slight shine to it. From her second largest suitcase, she pulled out the wonderful feather down blanket. Although it was so big and fluffy, she easily had stuffed it in.

So grateful that Gladys had given it to her, like the wings of angels covering her, she pulled it close to her chest.

Remembering the wonderful times at the palace now made her sad, almost not able to go there in her mind, better to think it had just been a dream. Wow, she had quite the mind that could take her anywhere she wanted to go. The room was cool and fresh, pulling the window shut. Heavy clouds darkened the sky as nightfall approached.

Sitting on the side of the bed, eating her sandwich. Charlie's wife, Mildred, came to mind, wondering if they had any children. Would he expect her to eat with him? There was no way she could. Just looking at him made her lose her appetite. Thinking of his wife, feeling sorry for any woman that had to share his bed, a slight breeze blew past her. The curtains moved, as in a slow dance. Weird. Now she was imagining things. Charlie seemed too happy that she was there. Did he need her for company too? That was the feeling she was getting. Ugh, just looking at his yellowed mustache around his mouth made her put down her sandwich. Another cold breeze and a shudder passed through her.

Hearing the thudding of footsteps, pulling her down comforter around her. Just then she saw the door handle turn. It opened just a slit, with the hook holding it closed. His ruddy cheek and part of his lips and mustache showed, she held her breath.

"Why, you don't have to lock yourself in. There is no one here but you and me. Hope everything is to your liking. Just wanted to mention that we get up early around here, six o'clock."

"That is fine with me," answered Alice.

"Good night. Don't let the bed bugs bite," he said with a devious laugh.

The sandwich sat half eaten, her appetite out the window.

What a creep, she thought. And thank God she had that lock on the door. He would have barged right in. Oh God, please.

Finally, with the angels wings wrapped around her, she falls into a deep sleep.

The rooster crowed its morning alarm. Sitting straight up, she looks out the window. A ray of sunshine sneaking through the pulled curtains, a pool of light on the cedar plank floor.

"Mmm, it's going to be a nice day. And if there is a rooster, there are probably chickens too." Happy about that, she gets dressed to head downstairs. Tomorrow she was going to the candy factory. Today was all about getting the top layer of dirt off everything, so she could feel better about being in his humble house. Considering, she would have to ask Charlie to take her to the candy factory in the morning. Another ride in the buggy. This time she had something to look forward to. A ride in the buggy, with the big horses at the helm.

Irene had said it was a nice lady who run the candy factory, and she was expecting Alice for an interview and orientation.

Hoping she wouldn't think Alice was too small for her age, wondering what age her mother had said she was. *Oh no, God. Do I have to lie about my age?* Would it just be a little white lie? She needed this job, and it sounded like it would be fun and easy. Excited, thinking of meeting new friends. Irene had told Charlie she was fourteen, so she would just say fourteen too. Just small for her age. *Please understand, God, I just need to get the job.*

Wearing her overalls and an old thick wool sweater, she heads downstairs, anxious to go out to the barn to see if there were any fresh eggs for breakfast, already thinking of what she would make for Charlie.

French toast made with Irene's famous bread. Surely, he would have jam or something sweet to put on it.

Getting on her hat and jacket, she walked out to the barn. As she opened the heavy wooden door, she was hit with the sweet smell of hay and molasses. Walking farther in, she could see the back of Charlie's jacket. He was picking up one of the horses' feet, digging at it with a sharp metal pick. Hearing her, he turned, and put down the horse's foot.

"Good morning, sunshine. Sure nice to see a pretty thing like you first thing in the morning."

"Ah, well, I was just wondering if you have chickens. I heard a rooster this morning."

"Yes, of course. They are in a shed behind the barn. And the chicken feed is in the room, just over there, Charlie pointing. You can take them some scratch, and pick up the eggs. I'm going to be good and hungry when I come in. I like four eggs in the morning."

"Yes, I was thinking the same thing," said Alice, walking away, out the barn door.

After spending an hour wiping, scrubbing, sweating over the kitchen that looked like pigs had lived in it, the linoleum started showing through, the bleach effect taking place.

She had found a bottle of bleach and used it straight on a cloth to wipe down everything. Her fingers felt dry and sore, just examining them, when Charlie walked into the kitchen.

"I have just the thing for your fingers, miss. Udder cream. We used to have dairy cows, and we used it on their teats." He gave a giggle and a sly grin. Oh, I will go and get it for you right now. And how long do you think before breakfast is ready?" Scanning the table.

"It won't be long. Do you have any jam to go with some French toast?"

"Ah, fancy stuff there, little miss. I have just the thing. We make maple syrup every year from our maple trees. There is lots of it in the cellar. The cellar door is just around the corner from the pantry. You will see a square cut in the floor. Just lift that and go down a few stairs, and you will see it lined against the wall. We keep perishables down there and other things."

Oh no, thought Alice. There is a cellar. Just what she was worried about. There was no way she was going to the cellar. And why is he talking like there is someone else living in the house?

"Can you please fetch it for me, Charlie? I want to get this breakfast on the table here, almost ready."

Other things? What other things would be in a cellar? Afraid to ask, she just carried on getting two plates from the cupboard. Feeling like someone is watching her, she turned. Charlie is standing there with his cup of coffee, staring at her behind. A short thick torso, broad, rounded shoulders, a red-and-white-checkerboard shirt, the elbows tattered.

It sure wasn't the picture Irene had painted. Deceit, lies and hate were all she could offer. Before she could let that emotion take over her day, she wiped it away, like the dirt with the bleach rag. Today was going to be a productive day. In the morning, she would be fresh and ready for her new job at the candy factory.

"Things are looking mighty good in here. Hasn't been anything like this since Mildred was alive. We can have some decent meals together."

The together thing was really bothering Alice. Why did he keep talking about them like a married couple? Why did he have to ruin her appetite, just when she was about to sit down and eat her French toast?

Just as Alice was about to take her plate to her room, he looked up at her.

"Why are you making me feel bad, Alice, always taking your food to your room? I want you to sit right here and eat with me. I'm a lonely fellow. Your mother said you would be good company for me. I won't bite you," he said, showing his yellowed and brown stained teeth.

Feeling defeated and betrayed once more, she sat back down, staring at her plate. Deciding she had better eat; there was so much work to do, and she would need the energy. Staring into her plate, she ate, not looking at him once. Charlie took a bite, then stared at Alice, like he wanted to eat her.

By the time breakfast is over, she was mentally weary. Picking up her plate and his, she gets busy with the job at hand.

Working hard all day, going from the kitchen to the parlor, mopping the stairs and the hallway upstairs and all the floors downstairs, Alice stands back, admiring her handiwork. She was pleased. Charlie had been in for lunch, and she prepared him two roast beef sandwiches. At least he said it was beef, but to her it smelled gamey. Reluctant to eat the meat herself, she resorted to peanut butter on her mother's bread.

For supper Charlie said he was killing a chicken and would bring it in for her to make a stew or soup. He said he would cut it up and wash it outside; that way, all she had to do was cook it. Deciding on soup, Alice cut some vegetables.

"All this house needed was some tender loving care. Everything looks so good, Alice. You are a hard worker. Your mother didn't lie about that. Makes coming in the house much nicer, having a sweet young thing like you cooking for me. What else could a man ask for?" Out came a deep belly laugh, his long horse teeth showing as he dribbled the hot soup onto his beard, wiping his face with the back of his hand.

If only he could just stick to business. Why was he always trying to involve her in his life? There was no him and her, never would be. She was the maid and the cook. Nothing else. Afraid to make him mad, she swallowed her pride and didn't say anything rude. What she wanted to say could have caused some hurt feelings and maybe more problems for her. He had agreed to take her to the candy factory in the morning for her interview.

Pleased with herself, a new day to look forward to, Alice settled in for the night, after cleaning up the kitchen after dinner. Just as she was about to go up the stairs to her room, she glimpsed out of the corner of her eye one of the rocking chairs moving by itself, deciding she must be seeing things now, tired from a long day.

Tomorrow would be the only day she asked Charlie for a ride, unless it was raining or snowing heavy. A long walk in the fresh air was great. Especially if the sun was shining. She loved being outdoors, taking in all the beauty of her surroundings.

As Alice is walking away up the staircase, Charlie called to her.

"It's your home now, Alice. Have a good sleep, and if you need anything, I am right across the hall. Even if you just want to talk."

Did he really think she was living with him forever? As soon as she could move out on her own, with her own money, she would go far away from this old man and never back to her mother. To talk to him about what? They had nothing in common except her mother.

Cozying up under her feather down, her mind strays to the palace, Gladys, and the kids. How she missed them so much. They wouldn't believe what was happening to her. Sadness coming in waves now, she starts whimpering.

"Oh God, I don't want to be here. Couldn't you just somehow help me to get back to my family, the Olsenses? They really did love me, God. I'm a good girl, God. Why are these things happening to me?"

She cries herself to sleep.

Going into a deep sleep, she dreamed of her palace. She was in the ballroom, twirling round and round, the crown on her head. All the kids were watching her, the balloons like colored moons. Gladys is waving and smiling at her. Then she went into another dream, like she had passed through into a different room. On her hands and knees with a scrub brush, the smell of bleach in the air. There are a few raw potatoes scattered under a table. Her hair hangs in strands over her face, scrubbing furiously, the dirt seems glued to the floor, pouring more bleach. Tired, weary, feeling herself going under.....then she awakes.

It wasn't the rooster's crow but heavy footsteps going down the hallway. Charlie must be up and heading to the barns. Today she was going to the candy factory. Did he expect her to make breakfast before they left? Yes, came back the answer in her head. Getting up, she stretched and started getting dressed. What would she wear today? Her blue-and-white uniform would probably be the best choice. That way, if she was to stay and work, she would be dressed appropriately. Going down to the bathroom, she poured water into the basin from the pitcher. Cool water refreshed her, reviving her from her terrible dream. There had been a couple of dreams, but the last one, she couldn't wait to wake from.

Charlie headed straight out to the barns to feed and water the horses, still thinking about Alice walking up those stairs last night watching her tight buttocks. Something was growing hard. Going over to a corner, between some straw bales, unfastening his belt, he let his trousers slip off his hips. Taking his fleshy member in his hand, stroking it up and down, thinking of her naked, stroking and stroking, until…a low growl escaped, his body jerking a few times, like a fish out of water. Putting his limp sausage back into his trousers, pulling up his pants.

Whipping up some eggs, Alice made an omelet for Charlie, with toast made from her mother's offerings. Sitting at the table, resting her feet, when Charlie comes through the door.

"Good morning, sunshine," he said, jubilant. "Nothing like fresh air in the morning to give a man an appetite. I sure do love having you in my life. And I see you got my breakfast all ready?"

"Yes, sir," she answered. "All ready, and we have to go to the candy factory right after."

"Indeed, I got the horses and buggy ready. Now, what is this? Mildred never made me anything fancy like this. Half-moon eggs?"

"It's called an omelet. When I worked for the Olsenses, Pierre the chef taught me to make lots of great things. This is eggs with onion and cheese in the middle. Hope you like it."

"It sure does look good," he said, as he picked a piece up with his fork, a string of cheese landing on his beard. Looking away before she lost her appetite, keeping her head down trying to eat her egg in a hole.

All through breakfast, she kept wanting to get up and take her breakfast with her. The slurping noises that were coming from him were like some kind of animal. Wheezing and sniffling between big bites of toast and egg.

"I tell you, girl. Your mother didn't lie when she said you would be good for me."

There it was again. The mention of her being good for him. Sure enough, her mother had sold her out to this old man. She would never forgive her for this.

With lots of hope for better things, going to a new job, made her happier. She would just stay out of his way as much as possible. The job at the candy factory was everything to her right now. That way she would only be around Charlie half the day, letting out big sigh.

"What is it? Are you troubled Alice?"

"Oh no, just thinking about my new job today."

"Well, I will just stay around until I know if you get hired. If you don't get the job, you can still live with me and be my…ah, I mean, I hope you get the job, Alice. You know what they say, a way to a man's heart is through his stomach." Giving her a cheesy, greasy grin.

Oh, how she wanted to tell him, nothing to do with his heart, knowing she had better watch her tongue. The cellar with its latched door came to mind. No one would ever know.

Getting up from the table, her breakfast only half-eaten, she heads to the sink with her back to him.

"I am actually already tired today, Charlie. Yesterday I scrubbed and cleaned all day. Tonight when I get back from work, can I just retire to my room? Could you fix your own supper tonight? Just tonight?"

"Yes, Alice. That will be fine for today. I know you worked hard yesterday."

"Thank you, Charlie."

Going back in her room, sitting on the side of her bed, she lathers her hands with udder cream. Thinking back to her dreams, there is another dream coming back to her in segments. A dark haired lady sitting in a big claw-foot bathtub. The white enamel of the tub is bright white in the dream, illuminating the room. The dark haired lady is staring at Alice, her eyes wide, frightened, her mouth open, but no sound coming out. It scared her so much that she shook herself out of that dream.

"Oh my God, I wonder if that was Charlie's wife. Dark hair framing a wide face, her complexion light, contrasting the dark hair. She would ask Charlie later to see a picture of his wife. Staring out the window, the room bathed in sunlight.

"Oh God, please let me get this job today. I love you, God. I know you haven't forgotten me. And say hello to Pearl and Daddy for me. Love you. Amen."

Pulling on a blue sweater, a blue ribbon holding back her hair in a pony, she took one last look in the mirror. Smiling back at herself, pleased, she looked professional and pretty.

Charlie sits at the helm of the wagon, his back straight, watching as Alice comes out of the house. As she is getting up in the wagon, he steals a peek at her legs getting a glimpse of her white cotton underpants, a warmth spreading through his groin. That was the way he liked to get his day started. The horses eyed her, as she slipped into the seat beside Charlie.

CHAPTER 44

The Candy Factory

Charlie wore his navy hat and coat to match. He wanted to look important this morning, in case someone saw him dropping Alice off. He knew the lady who ran the place, Mrs. Watkins. His wife had worked at the candy factory for a few years, and he knew everything about the place, not letting on to Alice. "You will get on fine there, Alice. There are a few young ladies, like yourself. You can make some new friends."

"Great," she answered. "I hope they like me."

"They will like you. There is a lot to like about you, princess," he said, grinning.

"OK then, if you say so, Charlie, thanks."

The buggy plugged along, the horses walking at a steady gait, Alice's mind wandered off to another place. Remembering Lucy's smiling face, Gladys's loving hugs.

"We are here. It is right there, Alice," said Charlie, pointing. "See the big red building with the white trim? And the dresses the girls wear are white with red trim."

"How do you know that, Charlie?"

"Oh, I just know," he said, catching himself. "So you will come straight home after work. I will expect you at five thirty every evening, six at the latest. Is that clear, miss?"

"Yes, sir, I will walk home promptly after work."

Getting down out of the buggy, he walked over to the other side, giving Alice his hand, helping her down.

"Thank you," she said, avoiding eye contact, walking away from Charlie, hoping no one would see him.

Heading toward the building, she opens a white door stepping inside.

In the foyer, a dark haired lady, sitting at a desk, a telephone to her ear. Making eye contact, she motioned for Alice to sit down, pointing to a row of chairs along the wall.

Getting up from her desk, she walked to Alice. "How can I help you, miss?"

"I am here about a job. My name is Alice."

"Yes, Mrs. Watkins is expecting you. She will be right with you."

White walls, black-and-white-checkerboard floors. A rosy cheeked lady with reddish brown hair walked toward Alice.

"Good day to you, dear. You must be Alice?"

"Yes, ma'am," answered Alice. Standing up, she held her hand out to the lady.

"My name is Mrs. Watkins, and that is how you will address me. You are fourteen? Your mother did tell me you were small for your age."

"Yes, ma'am. I am a hard worker. I worked for a family with ten children as a maid. My dad was sick, and I had to go home to help look after him. He died, and now I need a job."

"Well, with that attitude, you will fit right in around here. Go ahead into the hall and keep going down that way." Pointing to a conveyer belt that ran the length of the building. "Go along each side until you find an open spot with a letter on the floor. Keep walking till you find one, then fit yourself in. Get acquainted with the operation and the conveyer belt. Watch what each girl on either side of you is doing. By the end of the day, you will understand most things. You will become part of a tradition. At Mayer's Candy Factory, we have been making the best candies and chocolates for over a hundred years. We demand excellent work skills from all our candy girls. Within one week, you will know what makes this factory tick. All the ins and outs. Any chocolates that fall on the floor can be eaten."

"Yes, ma'am. I will do my very best work."

"That's all for now, Alice," said Mrs. Watkins, her face flushed from the speech.

When Charlie got home, he went straight to Alice's room. Moving the dresser exposing a hole big enough for him to look through when she was in the bath. He would wait until she was settled into the bathtub, and then watch her and play with himself. No one would ever know. Taking the hook and eye off the door, he would just say it fell off. He had been jerking off regularly since Alice had arrived, his sexual appetite heightened.

Sliding the dresser back over the hole. Rummaging through Alice's big suitcase on the bed, he finds a pair of her cotton underwear. Bringing them to his face, he inhales deeply. Putting those ones back, he looked around the room. Surely, she had a pair that she had worn already. Finding a few things in a basin, a pair of worn underwear. Holding them to his face, his penis hardened. Pulling his pants down over his hips, he started jerking off, back and forth, back and forth, till he spilled his semen on the floor. Pulling up his pants he wiped up the off white congealed sperm with his handkerchief, stuffing the panties and handkerchief, in his back pocket.

Mrs. Watkins had thick legs, and what was apparent in the smallness of her waist, a big bottom, taking Alice on a full tour of the factory. The assembly room, the cold room, and the chocolate room, explaining all the steps that went into making candy.

Finding an open spot between a younger looking girl with dark hair and big blue eyes and on the other side a middle aged woman with brown mousy hair who didn't flinch or look her way.

Mrs. Watkins comes up behind Alice.

"I see you found a spot. And look, it has an A for Alice on the floor. It was made for you, dear. Suzie will give you some pointers, won't you, dear? This is our new girl, Alice."

"Yes, ma'am, I would be delighted to." Looking deep into Alice's moss green smiling eyes.

Instantly, the girls take a liking to each other.

As soon as Mrs. Watkins disappeared into another room, Suzie spoke.

"My name is Suzie with a z. It's nice to meet you. I will show you everything you need to know. I have worked here for two years. Don't eat too many chocolates, though. When I first started I had to take a couple days off, I got real sick. Had to run to the bathroom every few minutes," she said, chuckling.

"Thank you for telling me," Alice answered with a big smile.

The girls spent the day together, like best friends already. They took lunch in the candy girls' lunch room. There were sandwiches, tea, and milk for the girls, provided by the candy factory.

"They take a few cents off our pay every month. It's great, then you don't have to carry a lunch," said Suzie. "We get two fifteen minute breaks and forty minutes for lunch. Do you want to take your lunch with me, Alice?"

"Yes, I would like that very much," answered Alice, feeling so happy to have met a nice girl already.

"We will have lots of time to get to know each other. I've been waiting for a friend around my own age. A lot of the women here are over twenty. How old are you, Alice?"

Hesitant at first, she answered, "Fourteen."

"I am fifteen, going to be sixteen in April," answered Suzie.

"So is my birthday in April," answered Alice.

"What day?" asked Suzie?

"The ninth. What day is yours?"

"The thirteenth," answered Suzie. "That's wonderful. We will celebrate together. Do you live around here?"

"Yes, not far," answered Alice, worried about the next question that would follow.

"I live the other way, about a half hour walk. We don't live far from one another. I think we are going to become very good friends, Alice. I am so excited to meet you."

Back at the conveyor belt, she watched Suzie wrap chocolates in shiny blue, green, and gold wrappers, Alice trying her hand at a few until she started to get the hang of it.

The day flew by, faster than the chocolates on the belt. Alice did not realize it until Suzie pointed to the large round clock behind the girls on the wall.

"We only have another half hour, Alice, and our work day is done."

"Amazing," said Alice. "It seems like I've only been here a short time. It was so much fun. Of course, it's because I met a new friend, and I am so excited about this job."

The girls talked every chance they got, watching for Mrs. Watkins. Alice ate a few chocolates, heeding the warning. Her cheeks hurt from smiling all day, at the other ladies who ran up the other side of the conveyor belt, and with Suzie, counting fifty women, including herself.

Steady, quick fingers wrapped and sorted the delectable candies and chocolates, the air thick with sugar and chocolate.

Just think, me, working in a candy factory.

A bell went off.

"That means our day is over, Alice. C'mon, let's go."

Heading to the door, Alice noticed Mrs. Watkins standing there. She was nervous now of what she would say to her. Did she get the job? Butterflies played in her stomach.

"Could I have a word with you in my office?"

"I will wait for you in the locker room, Alice," said Suzie.

Mrs. Watkins pushed open a door, motioning for Alice to sit across from her at a desk.

"Just have a seat, Alice. I just want to say you came with the highest recommendation from Mrs. Olsen. You have the job. I was a little concerned with your age. She said you were just like family to her. Is that right?"

"Oh yes," answered Alice. "I worked for them as a maid."

"You will do just fine around here, Alice. You are officially a candy girl. It's up to you to be a diligent worker and be on time. Lateness is not tolerated. As you know, this factory depends on the women to make it run. So having said that, we will see you bright and early tomorrow morning. The uniform you wore today was fine, but tomorrow you will find one in your locker like the ones all the girls wear. Have a nice evening now, Alice."

"Thank you, ma'am, I had better be going." Glancing down at her watch.

Twenty minutes to get to Charlie's.

In the locker room, Suzie was waiting to hear the news.

"I got the job. Oh, I am so happy, Suzie."

Suzie stood up and the girls hugged.

"I am happy too, Alice. We are going to have so much fun together. I've been waiting for a girl just like you. Someone my own age."

"I really should be going now. I have to get home," said Alice.

Waving as she left, wasting no time, quick as she could go, on the road to Charlie's house.

On the walk home, Alice thought about everything new that had happened at work.

Suzie talked a lot about a boy named Roger, the excitement climaxing when she mentioned the dances they had once a month. When they were deep in conversation, she confided in Alice that she had kissed him. That made Alice feel flushed. Suzie was fifteen, and really, she was just thirteen. Irene had lied to everyone about her age, forcing her to continue on with the lie, making her feel bad. Then Suzie told her that Mrs. Watkins had never hired anyone younger than sixteen. That made Alice feel really special and under more duress to keep her secret and her job. Gladys must have really spoken highly of her, for Mrs. Watkins to give her the job. A smile crossed her lips. How she missed the pretty lady.

She recounted the conversation with Suzie, when she was asking her about her home life.

"Do you live with your mother?"

"Actually, no. I live with my uncle right now because, he lives close to the candy factory, and my mother…and my father just died of a brain tumor. Can we just talk about something else now? It makes me sad."

Walking briskly, swinging her arms, thinking of how much fun she had today. Now she had a friend. Wondering where Charlie would be when she got there, hoping he wasn't sitting at the table, waiting to be fed.

At the sound of horse hooves behind her, Alice turned to see a buggy and a single black horse coming closer. It was a fancy black and gold trimmed buggy, with a tall black person holding the reigns. As the buggy edged closer, the horse slowed from a trot to a walk. She stood aside the road until the buggy was right in front of her. A smiling black face showed bright white teeth. This lady looked so familiar, Alice sure that she had met her somewhere before? Of course, she was the famous lady who fought a cougar and pulled its tongue out of its head.

"Hello," said Alice, staring into Sadie's dark almond eyes. A brightly colored scarf tied around her head. The telltale pink raised scars run down the side of her face.

"Good afternoon to you, miss," she said, pulling her horse to a stop. "Can I offer you a ride, dear? How far are you going? Were you coming from the candy factory?"

"Yes, ma'am, I just started working there today. I just live down the road a way. I can walk."

"No, I insist, get in. I will take you right there. I am going that way anyway." Leaning toward Alice, she extended her hand. "I would love your company."

"This is a beautiful wagon," said Alice, "and you have a beautiful horse too."

"Why, thank you, dear. His name is Moses."

"Moses, like from the Bible?" asked Alice.

"Indeed," she answered, turning to give Alice a big loving smile.

"I do remember you now, chile. You are Irene's daughter, Alice. We met when you were just a little girl. You haven't changed much, just prettier than ever."

"Thanks, ma'am," answered Alice, staring straight ahead, growing anxious, knowing she was getting close to Charlie's.

"I just live up here a bit," said Alice, pointing. "With my uncle Charlie."

"Your who? Charlie Mason is your uncle?"

Immediately getting the feeling she had better tell the truth, she said, "Actually he is just a friend of my mother's, and because he lives close to the factory, I am living there for now."

Sadie's brow furrowed, staring over at Alice.

Nervous now, Alice continued. "Yes, my mother arranged for me to work for him as a maid and also got me a job at the candy factory. My dad just died."

Sadie's eyes widened, she replied, "Oh, so sorry to hear about your father."

Sadie's hands tightened around the reins, her mind going fast. She wondered how Alice could come to live with the likes of Charlie Mason. It was probably better she didn't say what was on her mind right now.

"We haven't been officially introduced, Alice. My name is Sadie West."

"Yes, and my mother told me all about how you fought a big cougar to save your grandson. You are so brave," said Alice, smiling sweetly. "Every time my mother would see you walking by, she would tell me the story over and over."

"That is so cute, Alice. I am flattered. Do your mom and brothers still live on the Jefferson place?"

"Yes, they do."

Sadie, pulled up her horse. "We are here, Alice. I won't go in the driveway, not good for the wagon."

"Thank you so much for the ride. It was sure nice seeing you again, Sadie. Hope I will see you again soon."

"Of course you will, dear, now that I know you work at the candy factory. Anytime I'm in the area at this time, you can get a ride with me."

Getting down out of the buggy, Alice grabbed her bag. Waving at Sadie, she walked on the side of the road, turning right into the driveway. The red barn came into view.

Sadie continued on her way, deep in thought about Alice. How on earth would her mother send her to live with Charlie Mason? Everyone in the county either knew or had heard something about him. His wife, Mildred, was found dead in the bathtub. Drowned, he said. No one was able to prove otherwise. The gossip swirled and grew, like a tornado gathering speed and dirt.

Her head down, watching for the pot holes, her mind on the beautiful black lady. Looking ahead now, she notices Charlie walking briskly toward her, a stern look on his weathered face.

"I see that you took a ride from that Sadie West. Haven't you heard what they say about her?"

"Yes, of course. That she is a brave, strong woman who fought a cougar to save her grandchild."

"Well, you just heard half the story. Everyone knows she is a witch. Supposed to have pulled the cougar's tongue right out of its head. Then she probably went home and ate it for supper. Lots of those black people are into witchcraft."

"I just don't believe that. She is kind and good."

"Until she turns you into a toad or something," he said, opening his mouth wide, throwing his scruffy head back, a devious laugh infecting the air.

"I still don't believe it," argued Alice.

"Fine, don't matter. But I believe that there is a moose roast waiting to be cooked. It's sitting in the sink. I will be in about an hour or so. Could you get busy and make me some supper? Haven't eaten since you made me that breakfast this morning."

Getting into the house, Alice put down her bag and thought she would go upstairs and change her uniform but decided she might as well get the roast in the oven first.

She put it in a pan, with a little water and an onion cut up, then put the top on the roast pan and put it into the oven, then wandered upstairs to her room.

Back in the kitchen, it didn't take her long to get the supper ready. Mashed potatoes, coined carrots, and dark moose gravy. Pierre had shown her how to make it with a roux.

The door slammed. Alice looked up. Charlie is standing at the doorway, bending down, untying his mud-crusted boots.

"Smells mighty good in here."

Walking toward Alice sitting at the table, he pulled out the chair next to her. Feeling too close for comfort, she gets up, walking to the stove.

"Would you like your supper now? It is ready."

"Yes, of course, I am starving."

Setting his plate in front of him, Charlie gazes deep into Alice's eyes, making her look away. Grey clouded eyes, white stuff in one of the corners, Alice's stomach turned. Just the sight of him was gross. The big nose and the grey scraggly mustache hanging over his invisible top lip. There was no way she could eat with him, deciding she would just say she wasn't hungry.

"Well, where is your supper? Or did you eat too much chocolate today?"

"Yes, I guess that's what it is. I did eat a lot of candy. I am just going to retire to my room now. I am really tired. I might take my dinner to my room, in case I get hungry in a while."

"What about my cake and coffee?"

"I didn't make a cake."

"Well, before you go running off, just bake me a cake of some kind. I'm not fussy."

Disappointed that she couldn't just walk away and go to her private place, Alice goes to the kitchen. Taking out a big silver bowl, she begins by breaking in six eggs.

CHAPTER 45

Her New Life Unfolds

Sitting her supper down on the small table next to the bed, she ate a bit of the moose meat, the gravy and potatoes already cold. After taking a few bites, she pushes it away, going over to the dresser to sit down. Deciding to brush her hair, one, two, three, four.....looking down at the dresser. Another brush sits there, dark hairs throughout the spines. A chill runs down her spine, it must have belong to Charlie's wife. Just then she takes a quick glance in the mirror, a dark silhouette behind her, frightening her, looking around, no one standing there?

Sounds coming from the kitchen, a chair scraping across the floor. Charlie moving around.

Noticing the front of her sweater, her bumps showing. They were growing, definitely looking bigger, a blush running over her cheeks. *That was weird,* she thought. *I could have sworn I saw someone standing behind me.*

Before long, Alice lay down on her feather blanket, recanting the events of the day at the candy factory. Her new friend Suzie made her smile. Life might just turn out all right after all. Must go to sleep now, she told herself, looking over at the alarm clock on the table. Nine o'clock, it read. Tired from a long day of excitement and making new acquaintances.

Good night, Alice.

It had been a week now. Alice settling into a routine with her job at the candy factory and her chores for Charlie, mostly cooking and keeping up the cleaning. He seemed to be stayed out of her way.

He was watching her without her knowing every night when she ran her bath and relaxed in the tub. The best was when she got out of the tub. His hole was right on the target. Sitting at the hole, like a greedy little gremlin, watching the girl getting happier, singing as she bathed, towelling off her body, in full view of him. When she had put her housecoat on, ready to leave the bathroom, Charlie would push back the dresser and get out of her room without her noticing.

After a week's worth of cleaning every night after supper, the house started to breathe again, the layers of dirt scrubbed clean. Alice with her scrubbing brush and Javex. *Kill the germs, kill them all*, she said to herself, swiping at the floor.

One morning Alice is watching out the window toward the barn. She noticed Charlie bringing out the horses, harnessing them up to the wagon. Walking out to where he was, she asked him where he was going.

"Just into town for some supplies and food. Won't be too long. Can I bring you anything special?"

"No, thanks," she answered, wondering what he meant by special.

It was perfect. She could have some time to look through his room, maybe find pictures of his wife.

There were no family pictures on the walls of the parlor or kitchen. Surely, he would have a picture of his wife somewhere.

Pushing open the door to his room, a foul odor of dirty socks and body odor invade her nostrils. Covering her mouth and nose, stepping in. The floor is covered in socks, clothes everywhere and a pile of dirty towels in the corner. Pulling at a few drawers, she looked for anything that could tell her more about him. Under some sweaters, she found a glossy picture of a girl in a bathing suit. Oh my, thought Alice, quickly covering it again going to another drawer. After rummaging through the drawer, she found a framed picture of a dark haired woman. Wide faced, ivory complexion, she looked like the lady in the dream that had frightened her. Her hair stands on end, Charlie's wife. Fumbling now, she slipped the picture back in the drawer. Hurrying to get out of his room, she caught her shoe on a pair of beige grey underwear, a brown streak running down the crotch area.

"Yuck, yuck," she said out loud, kicking her foot. The underwear goes flying through the air, landing on the other side of the bed. Giggling now, she hurries out of the room, closing the door.

Back in the kitchen, staring out the little window over the sink, a slight breeze blew by her cheek. Looking around now for an open window, no open window, the feeling she wasn't alone in the house, dawned on her.

CHAPTER 46

Betty

Suzie and Alice were spending their days off together. Charlie complaining that she wasn't around enough.

"Your mother wouldn't like it, Alice. You were left in my care, and if you don't listen to me, I will send you back to her."

"I come home every day from work to cook and clean for you. On the weekends I would like to spend some time with my friends. I don't have to work on the weekends at the candy factory."

"You still are not to stay overnight. You must come home every day. I am responsible for you, and your mother wouldn't like it, not one little bit," he said, froth gathering at the sides of his mouth.

"I will go to your mother and tell her about your escapades," he threatened.

"Fine then, I will not stay away."

Really, she was thinking she wanted to pack her bags and never come back. The ogre was holding her in a faraway castle. When would her prince come to rescue her? Chuckling at her fairy tale thoughts.

The girls hurried along.

"You will like my mom, Alice. She is sweet, just like you."

"Why, thanks, can't wait to meet her."

Suzie pushed in the door into the foyer. There was a staircase to the right, leading to upstairs.

To the left of the staircase, a parlor with couches and a big chair, an archway leading into the kitchen. Suzie stuck her head through the archway, "Mom, where are you? Mom, we are here," she said with a song in her voice.

"Hi, you guys," said Betty, sticking her head around the corner.

"You must be Alice. Suzie has told me so many good things about you." A warm smile with dark brown wavy hair framing a pretty face, with big brown eyes. She was not a tall lady, almost the same height as Irene. A little thick through the middle, with thin legs.

"Suzie, dear, how was your day at work?"

"It was great, Mother. Ever since Alice came to work there, my days go by without me really noticing that I am working."

"The same for me," said Alice. "I really love my job at the candy factory."

"Looks like it is working well for both of you. Finally Suzie has a girl her own age to work with. You girls come and join me. I've got some fresh blueberry muffins, right out of the oven."

"Mmm," they both said at the same time, then started giggling.

"I just want to show Alice my room, and we will be right down."

Suzie led the way up the staircase to a room on the right side of the hallway.

The way Suzie's mom spoke with song in her voice, the love radiating from her golden brown eyes, made Alice realize even more how loveless her mother was to her. A stabbing feeling hit her heart. Why couldn't she have a mother who loved her?

Suzie opened her room door, "This my room. There is enough room for you too," she said, pointing to the two single beds. "My sister used to share this room with me, but she is away at school. If you stay over some time, like a sleepover?"

"Oh no, I don't think I can. My uncle wouldn't let me. He said if I don't come straight home from work every day, he will tell my mother."

"I could maybe come and ask him with you," answered Suzie.

"I don't know about that," answered Alice, her voice growing thin at the end of the sentence, looking away from Suzie's inquiring eyes.

Weird, thought Suzie. There was just something about Charlie that wasn't sitting right with her. The look in Alice's eyes when she said his name. A frightened look almost.

Sitting in a big comfy chair near the window, deep in her mind, gazing out into the front yard, a big willow tree bowing its branches to the ground, in prayer. A light frost dusted the ground like icing sugar. She had to get going back before dark.

Suzie's room was girly, bright pink frilly curtains and a bedspread to match. Stuffed toys, dolls, lots of books, and a big wooden desk near the window. One single pink rose in an ivory vase sat in the middle. There were two beds, one in the corner of the room, and the other on the other side of the room.

"My sister's name is Sarah. She is tall, beautiful, and three years older than me. She is studying to be a doctor. My dad is in the army, and he comes home for a week out of every month. We don't see him much."

"I had a sister too, but she died of pneumonia when she was ten. I miss her so much," Alice said, sadness in her eyes.

"I am sorry," said Suzie, hugging Alice. "I will be your sister, OK?"

The girls shared a tender moment, staring into each other's eyes, their souls connecting.

The girls spent an hour in the room, looking through picture books. Suzie showed Alice a love letter that she was writing to Roger, then hid it under the desk pad.

"My mother comes into my room to clean and bring in my fresh clothes. I can't let her see these love notes."

"I love books," said Alice, trying to change the subject. She knew nothing about this love thing and felt as though she didn't know how to answer.

Examining a large collection of books on a wide shelf, running her fingers over them lovingly. "Do you think I could read these books sometime?"

"Of course you can. I'll ask Mom if you can borrow a couple each time you come, as long as you bring them back. A lot of them belong to my sister."

"Oh, thank you so much. I would bring them back when I am finished reading them. I won't be able to stay too much longer," said Alice glancing at her watch.

"OK then. Let's go and have blueberry muffins with Mom. She wants to get acquainted."

At the thought of getting acquainted, Alice started to worry about the questions that would follow. Starting to sort out her secret files in her mind to make sure to pull out the right answers when the questions started flying.

The girls walked into the kitchen. Betty was at the stove, stirring a big silver pot. Alice had a seat at the table. Suzie went to her mother, peering into the pot. "What kind of soup, Mother?"

"Beef barley," she answered, continuing to stir. "Alice is welcome to stay for dinner if she likes."

"Oh no, her uncle Charlie said she has to be home before dark. Can we still have some of those blueberry muffins?"

"Yes, dear, they are on the counter with the dishcloth over them. Put two on a plate for Alice, with some butter. I'll be joining you girls in a minute. How about some tea to go with those muffins?"

Suzie pulled down a couple of small plates, placing two muffins on each plate. The blueberries poked their heads out of the browned crusted tops.

Placing one plate in front of Alice, Suzie sat down next to her. Alice waited till Suzie started buttering her muffin to do the same.

Betty pulled a chair at the head of the table. Reaching for a muffin, she cut it and spread butter on the inside. Everyone started eating the chewy muffins. "These are really good. Thank you, Betty. I wish I could stay for supper, but my uncle Charlie will be mad if I don't make it back before dark."

"Do you have to cook his meals every day, Alice? Suzie mentioned you have to do the housework and cleaning too."

"Yes, I do," she answered.

"Suzie said you worked for millionaires and lived in a palace?"

"Yes, I was their second maid. Really, I loved working for them. They were like my own family. It didn't feel like work, living and being in the most beautiful house you can imagine. There was another maid there, Jackie, who worked for them for a long time before I came."

"My, your life has already been so interesting. Your father just passed away? I am so sorry, Alice."

"Yes, I really miss my father," she answered, hanging her head.

"Sorry, didn't mean to bring up sad thoughts. Enjoy your tea and muffins."

"Charlie is not really Alice's uncle," said Suzie. "Her mother told her to tell people that in case they wondered why she lives with an old man."

A concerned look crossed Betty's face, and she didn't say anything for a few minutes.

"Your mother, Alice. Where does she live?"

"Just outside of Oakfield. My brothers and her live on the Jefferson place, the dairy farm. I have to get going now. Suzie."

Before any more questions could barrage her, Alice gets up, grabbing her coat and bag, heading for the door.

"Thank you, Betty, it was nice meeting you."

"Yes, Alice. You are welcome to come to visit any time. I am happy Suzie has a new lovely friend."

The sun is sinking into the dark hills, the evening cooling off quickly, hastening her pace, to get home to Charlie, in good time.

Stumbling in the doorway, a fishy smell in the air, looking toward the kitchen, Charlie is standing at the stove, flipping something in the big cast-iron frying pan.

"Thought I might as well go ahead and fix my supper, not knowing when you were going to show. What has kept you, Alice?"

"I told you I would be at Suzie's today. Her mother wanted me to stay for supper, but I said no, that I had to come home to cook for you."

"What exactly did you tell them, Alice?"

"Nothing. I have new friends now."

"Don't make any mistake around here. I warned you already, your mother would take you right back home if she thought you were running the roads. She doesn't care one bit about you. I'm the only one who cares about you right now. You live here, don't you? You eat my food and sleep in my bed."

The last statement made her want to scream. The fact was, he had slept in that bed for twenty years. It was not news to her that her mother didn't care about her. Was he trying to hurt her by saying that?

"Anyway, as you can see, I am frying the fish tonight. Can you make some potatoes?"

"Yes, Charlie. Just let me put down my bag and change my clothes."

"Fine then," he said, getting back to flipping his fish, smoke rising from the hot pan.

Taking the fish out of the pan, with a wide faced spatula, setting them on a plate on top of the woodstove. The fish is crispy and whole. Going for his cup of coffee, sitting at the table, waiting for her. As she is walking towards him, he notices the bumps in her sweater, her tight small body, enticing him.

Charlie's eyes are fixated on Alice as she peeled the potatoes. In his mind, he is peeling off her clothes.

His eyes glued to the bumps in her sweater, it seemed they had grown bigger in just a few days, his imagination running wild.

Feeling his eyes on her, catching him staring at her chest. Turning her back to him, she slipped the potatoes one by one into the boiling water. This chore always took her back to that frightful day when she was little.

Placing the dry, fried trout on the plate, she spooned a heap of yellowed mashed potatoes with a dollop of butter on the top, next to the crispy fish, its head crusted over, the eyes still intack. Never had she seen Pierre cooking a fish with its head still on. It seemed barbaric to her, but keeping with the orge theme, it didn't surprise her.

Bringing the plate to the table, he is sitting there with his fork and knife in hand. Not meaning to, she brushed up against his shoulder, he looks up at her, a sneaky smile on his ugly face.

His mouth runs water at her sweet breath on his cheek.

"Here is your supper, Charlie. Hope you like it."

"I would like it better if you would join me. I'm a lonely man, Alice. Sure would be nice to have your company tonight. What do you say?"

"Well, I guess I could," she said, going to the counter bringing back her plate to the table. Cutting the other fish in two, she leaves the head part sitting on the platter.

The air around Alice is strained as they sit quietly. Taking small bites of the fish, picking at the flesh of it, her appetite waning, his smacking and licking his lips as he ripped into the meaty fish, turning her stomach.

Looking up from her plate, Charlie holding half of the fish from the head down in his thick fingers, stuffing the whole head of the fish into his mouth, as he stared into Alice's eyes.

Shocked, she had never seen anyone eat the head of a fish, just thinking of the eyeballs, and all, her stomach flips, she gags, puts down her fork, and picks up her tea cup. Trying not upset him, she swallows hard.

Taking his last bite, he scraped the fork across the plate and pushed himself away from the table, heading into the parlor.

"Would you like to relax with me in here?" he asked, pointing to the couch.

"No, no, I would like to go to my room now, if it is all right with you?"

The girl was giving him a cold shoulder. He didn't blame her. She was young and he was old. Why would she want to sit with him? Only the ghosts didn't mind his company.

The next day at work, the girls talked about a get together at Suzie's house.

"My mom thought that you were really nice and told me to invite you for supper some time and a sleepover. It was her idea," said Suzie, excitement in her voice. Her bright blue eyes, against her pale skin and black hair, doll-like, thought Alice.

"You are so pretty like a doll," said Alice, trying to change the subject.

"I was thinking the same thing about you," answered Suzie. The girls share a hug.

"All you have to do is get permission from Charlie."

Quiet, thinking hard, Alice answered, "That would be fun."

"Yes, we could play games in my room all night. Hot chocolate, cake, and ice cream. Girl things."

Before the end of their work day, Suzie had convinced Alice to just come home with her. He would understand. It was Friday anyway, no work tomorrow.

"Saturday, I will walk you home," said Suzie, helping Alice to make up her mind. Knowing she would pay the consequences of this decision, it was just too delicious to pass up. A night away from the creepy castle, having fun, not having to look at the ogre, or cook him food. Really, he needed her now, and wouldn't send her back to her mother.....then who would cook and clean for him?

"Oh no," answered Alice. "Don't want him to get angry. I would have to ask first before I brought anyone home."

Betty was overjoyed to see Alice and Suzie coming through the door.

"Great to see you, Alice. Are you spending the evening with us?"

"Yes, thank you, ma'am."

"Did you ask your...I mean, Charlie?"

"No, I didn't know I was going to come today, but he will know that I am here. He knows Suzie is my only friend."

"I would be glad to talk to him for you if you need me to," answered Betty. "You girls can help me with supper. How about you make some coleslaw and some kind of cake, Suzie."

"Right away, Mother. Alice will help me. She was taught by a real chef from France."

"That is amazing," answered Betty. "At the Olsenses', I gather?"

"Yes, ma'am," answered Alice.

They made an apple cinnamon cake and coleslaw with creamy dressing. Betty made pork chops, mashed potatoes, and green peas.

"That was an amazing dinner, thank you," said Alice.

"You are very welcome, Alice, any time," answered Betty.

The girls finished up their supper, cleaned the table, and washed the dishes, leaving Betty to enjoy a cup of tea and the apple cake.

Spending a few hours in Suzie's room, the girls bonding like real sisters.

"I am writing Roger a love letter. Do you want to see it?"

"Sure," answered Alice, feeling a little uncomfortable with the subject.

Suzie pulled out a writing tablet from under her desk pad. Alice huddled close.

Roses are red,
Flowers are blue,
I have to say, I'm in love with you.
Your pretty brown eyes,
Sparkle, like a dark lit sky,
Dreaming of you,
What can I do?
Sweet kisses for you,
Your new friend, Suzie.

"That is just the cutest poem," said Alice. "Do you really love him?"

"I don't know, but something happened when he kissed me." As she closed her eyes, Alice watched Suzie's face. The emotion flooded the room like some uncharted territory.

Remembering the kiss. They had walked outside for some air after a couple of dances. He led her around the other side of the building, where no one could see them. Leaning her up against the building, he pressed his lips to hers, his tongue searching her mouth. It was strange at first, but she liked the feeling, sending sensations to other parts of her body. A whole new set of emotions flooded her. Since that day, she hadn't been the same, thinking of it over and over again.

"I can see it in your eyes that you really like him a lot. Maybe I will find a boyfriend too, someday." A cute smile crossed Alice's lips.

"The next dance is coming up in a month. There will be boys standing in line waiting to dance with you," said Suzie.

"Really, you think so? Just think, me dancing." Her excitement is short-lived, realizing she would have to get permission from the ogre, her demeanor changing.

Suzie noticed right away. "I thought you were excited about the dance?"

"I am."

"Why so forlorn then?"

"Oh nothing, just worried about Charlie."

"I've never been kissed," said Alice, lying on her side on the bed.

"I'm sure you will get your first kiss soon, Alice." The girls share a hard giggle, their eyes heavy. The clock reads 1:00 a.m.

It had been a night of fun and friendship. Growing up, life starting to be more interesting now that she had a special friend. Looking forward to every day now, work, and hopes for the future.

Just before the girls fell asleep, in the quiet of the room, Suzie asked Alice to tell her about her life with the Olsenses. Alice told her about the beautiful things in the palace, the fun things she did with all of the kids. The birthday party, when they made her wear a tiara and everyone told her she was a princess for a day. Dancing and laughing till dawn, her chariot came and left, her life flashing before her eyes.

"Just like in the storybook, my chariot turned to dust."

"Oh my gosh!" said Suzie, sitting straight up in the bed, staring into the darkness of the room. "I could see it all as you told it to me, Alice. You are a great storyteller. Is it really true?"

"Well, most of it, I guess. My life is like a storybook. I can make it into whatever I want. Since I was little, I was into make believe to help me deal with my life. Really, Suzie, you only know a little bit about it. One day I will tell it all to you."

"It's so exciting and scary too, Alice. I just can't wait to hear everything! Good night, my new best friend. I love you."

"Good night, Suzie. I love you too, and I'm so happy you love my story."

"Alice lives in a palace," she said laughing. "It rhymes too. You really were a princess, Alice. Good night."

Just as the sun rose, Alice awoke. Walking to the window, she looked out over the back yard, then back at Suzie, still cozy, under the covers. Feeling anxious and a little scared now, she dresses. Pacing around the room a few times, then decided to wake Suzie.

"I really need to get going. Charlie will be waiting for me."

Stretching, Suzie looked at the round clock. Five o'clock.

"OK, Alice, but I don't want to get up yet. Is it OK if you just let yourself out? Are you going to come back later?"

"Oh yes. I just have to check in, probably make him breakfast and do some cleaning up, then I'll walk back."

"OK then. I'm going back to sleep right now," she said, pulling the blanket up over her head.

The cold morning air bites at her face, pulling her scarf up around her mouth. Keeping a brisk pace, she walked on, hoping he was still sleeping when she got there.

A quick glance around the yard found no sign of Charlie. The barn doors were closed. When he was up and around, the barn doors were always open. It looked good so far. Edging into the house, closing the door behind her slowly, quietly.

A loud snoring coming from the parlor. Peeking in, she notices a bottle of golden liquid sitting on the table. Liquor. A pungent smell of sweat and foul body odor infected her nostrils. Mouth open, his grey woolly face like steel wool.

Tip-toing up the stairs and into her room with a deep sigh of relief. Thank God he was sleeping, she thought. Slipping out of her clothes, she put on her flanelette nightgown. Walking by the dresser, she catches a glimpse of a dark haired lady with red lips staring out at her. Putting her hand to her mouth, a silent scream. Was she just imagining this stuff? Why were these strange occurances happening? Of course, no, it was the lady, the one in the picture in Charlie's room, his wife. The ghost of the house. The fairy tale taking on a whole new feeling, making it scarier. Realizing now, she needed to get away from this place and the creepy old man. This place was worse than an old castle with cobwebs and dark places. She hated it, all of it!

Lying down, pulling her comforter over her, closing her eyes tight, falling into a light sleep, directly into dreamland. The lady again. On the porch, rocking back and forth, her mouth wide open, as if in a scream, but no sound escapes. Frightened, she wakes herself, realizing she had just dozed off. Getting out of bed, putting on her fuzzy slippers, pulling her housecoat tight around her.

Not knowing if he had realized she hadn't come home, scared now to lie to his face. Oh God, how she hated this lying. Why should she have to? She was changing into a person she didn't know.

In the kitchen there was still no sign of Charlie. Easing around the corner, peeking in the parlor, he is not there, thinking he must be out in the barn. Deciding she would try to sweeten him with his favorite, strawberry crepes. If he said anything about her not coming home, she would tell him the truth. Betty and Suzie had asked her to stay. By the time they had finished supper, it was dark, and Betty insisted she stay, saying she would talk to Charlie if he wanted. After all, the story was true.

Staring out the little window over the sink, spying the back of Charlie's red checkered shirt, just as he is walking to the barn, then he turned and headed back toward the house. Getting busy, she stirred the flour and the milk together, wanting to appear busy with her back to the door.

The door creaked open.

"My goodness, look who just appeared like a ghost. Didn't see you all day yesterday."

"Yes, I like to spend alone time so I can read and relax when I'm not working. I am going to spend the day with Suzie and her mom. I will clean up here after breakfast, then I'm going."

"I want to know where your friends live, Alice. That way I could always pick you up instead of you walking home in the dark."

"It's OK, I can walk. I don't mind."

Squinting his small snake eyes, he said, "Fine then, if you don't want to tell me, I'll have to tell your mother you are spending a lot of time away from here, with people I don't know."

Not knowing how to answer that, she just continued cleaning off the table.

Feeling his presence behind her, his hot breath on her neck. Trying to move out of his way, he pushes himself up against her.

"Move please," she said, her eyes wide, squirming to get out of his reach.

"Your mother said you would keep me happy. I can't say that you are trying too hard."

"My mother said I was to clean and cook in exchange for my room and board."

"I bet your mother didn't tell you she traded you for that horse and buggy I gave her. Said that maybe you would be ready to have a husband soon."

The things that came to mind she couldn't say to him, not wanting to make him mad. How could her mother tell him that? Nothing surprised her anymore about Irene.

"No, Charlie, she didn't. I will take that up with her. Like I said, I am here to cook and clean only. So if you don't mind, I am going to my room now to get ready."

Turning, she headed to the staircase, up and out of sight.

Wait until she tells Suzie what the old man had said. It was just unbelievable.

The girls had planned to spend the day making cookies and reading to each other. Suzie had found a friend who liked to read as much as she did. Alice mulled over the shelves, picking books out, glancing through them and the inside flap of their jackets.

Most of the stories that Suzie liked were romance novels, a pretty woman on the front of the jacket and a man and a woman in an embrace. Love in the air.

When she spoke of Roger, it was like she was floating on a cloud, stars filling her eyes.

The day after the sleepover, Suzie was in the kitchen with Betty, helping her make bread, when Suzie started talking to her mom about Alice.

"Do you think that Alice could come and live with us? I know I just met her and all, but she is scared living in that house, with a ghost that keeps showing up in her room. One night she heard someone crying, and she has seen her in the mirror. The worst part of it is that Charlie seems to think that Alice is going to become his wife someday. That is what he told her."

"Oh my God, it sounds terrible. Who do you suppose is the ghost?"

"The ghost of Charlie's dead wife," answered Suzie, her eyes filled with concern.

"Mmm," said Betty. The story keeps getting more interesting. "Do you think that Alice might be just telling you this stuff so you will ask me to let her live with us?"

"No, Mother. I don't think that at all. Alice is very honest in her feelings and what she tells me about her life. I'm really worried about her, Mom."

"Well, dear, we will see how your friendship grows and when we get to know her a little better. We would have to talk it over with her mother, of course."

"Really, Mom? Oh, thank you. Alice will be so happy when I tell her what you said.

"Don't get ahead of yourself. I said we will see how things go."

"She is my very best friend in the world, Mom. I love you."

Betty pulled Suzie in for a big mama bear hug. "You are such a good friend to Alice."

Pacing around the house like a caged wolf, Charlie talked to himself. "Going to spend the whole day with her friends. What will I fix for dinner? That is supposed to be her job. Nobody said she only had to cook for me five days a week."

His ranting turned to grumbling. Finally he sat down in the parlor, staring off in the distance.

Fantasizing about watching her in the bath, he would lie down as soon as he heard her coming in, pretend he was sleeping, and wait until he heard her going in for her bath, to make his move.

Today, the road home seemed lonelier. Going back, a saddened lost feeling of hopelessness. All the happiness of her new job, and a new found friend to spend time with, laugh and enjoy girl things together, was being washed out, by the ogre, and his dirty castle, holding her hostage from her happiness, and the ghost that lived in her room. The fairy tale taking on new horrors every day now. If only she didn't have to go back…

Just as he had thought, she came home just before nightfall. Stepping into the house, she looked both ways, no sign of Charlie. A faint sound of breathing coming from the parlor. Sticking her head in, his head cocked to one side, his eyes closed. Great, she thought. He was sleeping. She could go to her room and relax, maybe have a bath. After warming a couple pails of water on the woodstove, she poured them in the enamel tub. Walking into to the bathroom with her soap and towel on her arm, Charlie watching through the hole behind her dresser.

Everything was clean and neat, just like she had left it. Charlie didn't use this bathroom. She was happy about that.

She had no sooner got in the tub, when the bathroom door burst open, Charlie standing there holding out his hands, full of black grease. "Just have to use the sink a minute," he said as he looked Alice from head to toe. Alice covering her breasts with her hands.

"Get out, get out!"

"Sorry, didn't know you were in here, didn't know you came home."

"Get out!" she screamed again. Charlie grabbed a towel and walked out of the bathroom, taking one last look before he closed the door behind him.

Oh, that had been the best look yet. He saw her little rosebud nipples, hard, rounded titties, still blossoming, he thought. His member was getting hard. Going straight to his room, closing the door, laying down on his bed. Pulling out his glossy picture and a pair of Alice's underwear that he kept in his pocket. Wrapping the panties around his penis, stroking, stroking, stroking...

I can't believe he saw me totally naked, she thought, a sick feeling in her stomach. The way he looked at her, hunger in his beady eyes. No, she had to get out of the tub now and get back to her room to gather her thoughts. Had he really not known that she was home and walked in accidentally? She supposed that could have happened. After all, he was sleeping when she came in. It was her fault for not slipping the lock on the door.

There was no lock on the bathroom door. Alice had noticed that the first day that she had come to Charlie's. It made her feel vulnerable right away. Oh no, he will think of me naked when I am cooking for him. He is a dirty old man.

Getting into her room quickly, she put a few things up against the door just in case. Somehow, the hook and eye had disappeared, when she asked about it, he said it fell off. Placing the stool from her dresser and a few boxes stacked on top of each other in front of the door. It took hours before she was able to drift off to sleep. The way he stared at her, the lust in his eyes, imprinted on her mind.

Trying to erase the thoughts of him, she goes over all the wonderful things her and Suzie were doing, spending time with Betty baking a chocolate cake, then helping make spaghetti and meatballs. They had an early supper together, knowing that Alice had to leave before dark.

The girls laughed and sucked up their noodles, getting sauce on their faces, having the greatest time, just the three of them.

The alarm clock struck five o'clock. Anxious to get up and out of the house before Charlie woke up. After him seeing her naked, it was almost unbearable to be in close quarters with him.

She would tell him she was needed early at the candy factory, just a little white lie. They had to stock some shelves, or...she would think of something. She would make him boiled eggs and leave a couple of pancakes on a plate.

Everything was set at the table: three boiled eggs, three pancakes, butter melted into the top, a spoonful of strawberry jam on the side. His cup sat next to the plate. He should be happy with it. Quickly, she went back to her room, grabbed her bag, and stepped lightly out of the house. When she was a way from the house, she looked back at a lone window at the top of the house. A white face, dark haired... *Oh my God, it's her! I have to tell Suzie about this.* The ghost of Charlie's wife watched her as she was leaving. Turning, then looking back again, the face is gone. Running now to get as far away as she could. If only she could just keep running and never come back.

All the thoughts clouding her mind like the light snow falling. Before she realized it, she was at the candy factory.

Suzie's face showed, just as Alice came up to the door.

"I was waiting for you, Alice."

"Hi, Suzie. I know I am early today. I have something to tell you."

"C'mon, let's go to the locker room. We can talk in there."

Alice put her bag and things down. Sitting down on the bench, holding her head.

"What is it, Alice?" asked Suzie, putting her hand on Alice's shoulder.

Alice sighed heavily. "It is Charlie, Suzie. He...walked in on me when I was in the bathtub and wouldn't leave. I was screaming, and he just stood there, staring. It was terrible. He saw me naked. Said he didn't know I was in the bath."

"Just like my mother said. There are rumors about him, Alice. Scary ones. Some people think he killed his wife."

"Oh no!" answered Alice. "How? Mother would send me there?" Holding her face in her hands, she started crying now. "I am so scared now, Suzie."

"Don't cry, Alice. Mom said that you can come and live with us, but she has to talk to your mother first. And she wants to go to Charlie's too, so he knows that you have friends who care about you."

"Really?" she said, her eyes brightening, wiping at her tears.

"That would be great, but...my mother and Charlie... Oh no, my mother probably won't let me move in with you."

"Shh now, everything will work out. My mom and I love you, and we will be there for you."

"Pinky swear that you won't tell anyone about what happened. It is embarrassing, Suzie."

"I understand. I will always keep your secrets, Alice, and you mine." The girls twisted their baby fingers together, kissing each other on the cheeks and hugging. "We are sisters now, Alice"

Sharing a laugh, they dress into their candy store uniforms. "Suzie, I forgot to tell you, I saw the ghost of Charlie's wife again. She was in the window, watching me when I left the house today."

A chill runs up Suzie's spine, the ghost story more believable.

Everything was quiet around Charlie's for the next few days. Charlie ate in the parlor, his guilt getting the best of him. Alice tried to avoid him like the plague, putting his food out like she was feeding an animal.

All week, she took her food to her room. If he spoke to her, she answered quiet, fast, short. Yes, no, maybe, tomorrow.

"Your mother is expecting you to visit her soon. She will want a progress report from me too."

"Really, Charlie, I wonder if we should tell her everything. Like about your wife?"

"What are you talking about, child? Have you lost your mind? What do you mean? The woman is dead."

"She might be dead, but she never left this house. I have seen her a few times in my room, and heard her crying too. One day I saw the rocking chair going by itself. My dreams are filled with her."

"That is just foolishness, Alice, and I don't want you to bring up my wife again. Do you hear me? Life is for the living,"

The ghost of Charlie's wife was not letting up. She was trying to warn Alice of impending danger. Covering her head one night, a storm brewing outside. All of a sudden, a gust of wind raced through the room, the curtains dancing. Sitting up straight in the bed, Alice stared into the darkness. A faint screaming at first, peaking with one loud one, then a thud at the door. Why wouldn't she just leave her alone and stop scaring her?

"Please, God, make her stop scaring me," she said, finally dropping off to sleep.

The next morning, as she is dusting the room, a loud grunt in her ear.

It really wasn't scaring her anymore, but the presence of a ghost was interesting. The way Suzie got so excited when she talked about the ghost made Alice chuckle. After all, the ghost hadn't hurt her. Was she trying to tell her something? She couldn't tell Irene. She would just say she was lying, and with the way Charlie denied the ghost, she would say Alice was losing her mind. Wow, she was caught up in a real nightmarish story. How much more interesting would her life get?

It was getting worse, the ghost interrupting her sleep, waking in the middle of the night, finding herself tired at work. The chocolates going by in a blur, missing a few, Suzie picking up the slack.

"Alice, you don't look well these days," Suzie commented.

"Not enough sleep," said Alice. "I hate living with a ghost that doesn't sleep at all."

"I would too," said Suzie. "Sorry, I am not coming to your house for a sleepover."

The girls giggled, wrapping chocolates in tiny golden squares.

"You see, Suzie, there are a lot of things you don't know about my mother. She really never loved me and made my childhood unbearable. You are so lucky, you have a great mom. Even the way she looks at you with love in her eyes. I was born dead, and when I came back to life, it became my mother's mission to destroy me and hurt me. You don't have enough time to hear the whole story, Suzie."

"What an awful story. It's good then that you don't live with her anymore."

"Yes, it's actually better living with Charlie than with her. You will see when you come home with me. I have to take my wages to her soon."

"I will ask my mom. I am sure she will let me go with you."

Her new friends were giving her confidence that she could endure whatever was coming her way. Confiding in Suzie about her mother and Charlie, gave her some artillery in her fight against them or their fight against her. She needed to get far away from her mother and farther away from Charlie. *Give your burdens to the Lord*, her dad would say. *He will make them his own, and…* She had faith in God; her dad had taught her. After prayer, she always felt relieved, as though he was really there, listening to her. Her holy father, her daddy called him. *God does everything in his own time. Be patient,* he had said, Alice knew patience. She loved God.

Charlie didn't insist on Alice sitting with him. Something had changed between him and the girl. There was no harm in what he had done. He hadn't laid a hand on her.

As much as Alice didn't want to go back to Charlie's every day after work, she had no other choice. The happiness she felt at work drowned out the doldrums in her mind. Her smile waned the closer it came to five o'clock.

It was only a week until the dance, the girls busy planning what they would wear, how they would do their hair, and mostly how she was going to ask him if she could spend the night.

The closer the dance date came, the more Suzie talked about Roger.

"I know you must get sick of me talking about him. It's just that I really like him, Alice."

It was a love story, thought Alice. Boy meets girl. They fall in love and live happily ever after. Or like in the fairy tale, a Prince Charming sweeping her off her feet, flying through the air on a white steed. Chuckling now to herself, she could see Suzie flying through the air. How silly.

"Time to go home, Alice."

The conveyor belt stopped. Everyone gets up from their spots, heading to the locker room. Single file, the candy girls take off their nets, getting into their day clothes.

Eyeing each other as they are changing, a few exchanging smiles, a buzz of laughter and conversation.

They made their way to the front door of the candy factory.

"Good night, Alice. See you tomorrow, and don't forget to ask Charlie if you can stay the night."

"Yes, of course."

The Friday night before the dance, Alice goes straight to Charlie's. Getting out of her day clothes, putting on her overalls and a sweater, heading to the kitchen. She would make him his favorite, pork roast with baked potatoes and corn on the cob. Charlie walked into the house a few times, buzzing around her like a hungry hornet.

"I am making your favorite," she said.

Charlie bent, peeking his head in the oven. "Mmm, looks good. You know the way to a man's heart."

Yuck, she thought. She didn't care one bit about his heart.

This was a perfect time to ask him about tomorrow and staying at Suzie's for the night. Just as he was bringing the fork to his mouth, Alice spoke.

"Charlie, is it all right with you if I spend the night with Suzie and her mother? They want me to go to church with them in the morning. Betty said she would come and talk to you about it, but I told her that it would be all right with you."

"Now that you have put it that way, I suppose you can stay, but you get home here right after church. Maybe we could have supper together? What do you say, you could sit with an old man? I don't hardly see you around here anymore. You are either coming or going."

"I have another job, Charlie. I am tired when I get here and have to start working all over again. When I get to my room, I fall into bed, my feet and body are so tired."

"You are young, Alice. And tough too, if you survived a tyrant like Irene. The way she talks to strangers tells me a lot about that woman. Supper on Sunday, don't forget now."

If that was the only way, then she would sit and eat with him. Excited, Suzie's and her plans for the dance were coming together.

"One other thing," said Charlie, his eyes squinting. "Do you think you could sit on my knee in the parlor? Just a little hugging?"

"No way," answered Alice, her eyes wide.

"Fine, just kidding, kiddo," he said, showing his yellowed horse teeth.

That last comment killed her appetite for Sunday.

"I have lots of dresses, Suzie. Maybe you would like to choose one of mine? I can bring a few of them for you to try on."

"You have that many?"

"Yes, remember I told you that Gladys gave me so many dresses, some of them brand new. Some are too long for me or too small around the bust. Lately, I think they are growing. The last time I tried on one of my favorite dresses, I could really notice these bumps," Alice said, laughing. Looking at Suzie, who barely had any showing.

"Don't know what happened to mine," said Suzie, looking down at her sweater. Her bumps were covered by a bra that gave them the appearance of being larger than they were.

"A bra, that is what you need, Alice. It could make them look smaller or bigger, like in my case."

The girls had the biggest laugh, pointing to each other's bumps.

It was getting closer to two months now since Alice had left her mother's house, wondering every day whether or not Irene would just show up at Charlie's door, looking for her money. Knowing she had to go back home to see Irene, but taking Suzie would be the buffer to soften the encounter. She hoped Betty would agree for Suzie to go with her.

Suzie, couldn't keep Alice's secret about Charlie anymore, Betty had to know that Alice was in danger, living there with him.

"Mother," she said. "Charlie isn't Alice's uncle. He tried to press his body against hers when she was in the kitchen the other day, and he walked in on her while she was having a bath, and just stood there glaring at her, while she screamed for him to get out."

"Yes, you have already told me he isn't her uncle. I understand it must be terrible for her living with an old man who thinks he is grooming her to be his wife. Irene must have something wrong with her head or be just plain hateful to send her lovely daughter there. I just don't get it at all. I am angry and sad for Alice. Not even going there to see if she is all right. It doesn't sound good, Suzie. We need to look into this. We will have to go to Charlie's and meet him, and let him know that Alice has friends who care about her, and suggest that she come and live with us."

"Really, Mother? You would do that?" Her eyes widen. "Thank you, Mother," she said, hugging her around the waist. "Thank you so much!"

The thought of going to live with Suzie sat close to the surface of her happiness. Could it really happen?

No, came back the answer in her head. Who would cook for him then? He would not want her to go, and her mother would insist that she stay there to pay him back for the horse and buggy.

Deciding to be extra nice and make Irene see that it was better for her to live with Suzie. Closer to work, and they would offer her the same agreement, free room and board in exchange for cleaning. That was it. She would offer her services to Betty, that way she would be paying for her keep.

Smiling to herself, she had Betty and Suzie now, and hope for better things.

Charlie thought about spending all day Sunday with Alice, wishing she would find something else to wear other than that bulky sweater she had taken to wearing. Surely she could relax a little around him now. He wasn't a stranger anymore.

CHAPTER 47

Suzie, Alice, and Irene

I t had been decided. The girls were going to see Irene. The dance started at seven. They had lots of time to get back and prepare. They would catch the train and head to Oakfield.

"Good morning, girls. Breakfast is served," said Betty, her voice carrying up the stairs.

"C'mon, Alice, let's go have breakfast. Mom makes the best. I think I smell bacon and pancakes."

"That sounds great," answered Alice, pulling on her housecoat.

Running down the stairs, Alice right on Suzie's heels, the girls giggling. Betty is flipping a pancake, gazing back at them, hearing their laughter, happiness thick in the air.

"You girls can get started, blueberry pancakes and real maple syrup."

Once they are seated, Suzie passed the plate of pancakes, Alice taking one. Betty joined the girls, sitting at the head of the table.

"OK, so don't waste time, eat your breakfast and go get ready. I will do the cleanup today. You need to be on that train for 10:00 a.m., then you can take the two o'clock train back. That will give you lots of time for us to have a nice supper, then you guys can get ready for the dance."

"Yes, Mother."

"Yes, Mother," repeated Alice. They all have a chuckle.

Finishing up, they thanked Betty and hurried up the stairs to get ready, making it to the train platform just in time. The conductor sticks his head out announcing, "Next stop, Oakfield."

Settling into seats, one on either side, they stare at each other.

Sitting quietly, both of them peering out the small window, the train rattled, picking up speed.

"Will your mother be home, Alice?"

"She is always there. She has nowhere to go. Sometimes my aunt Rita comes and takes her to her house for the afternoon."

Just then, Alice remembered Irene had her own horse and buggy now. Thinking it was best not to bring it up as it would bring an avalanche of questions she didn't know how to answer.

"Must be a boring life for her."

"Yes, you will see. She is a grumpy, unhappy person. That's all I remember, my whole life she has been that way."

The train whistle sounded as they came to a jerking stop. Both girls looked out the window.

"Oakfield station," the conductor announced.

They get up quickly, making their way down the steps to the platform.

"It is just down the road this way," said Alice, pointing.

"Nice horses," commented Suzie, looking at a group of horses standing at a fence, looking their way.

"We had lots of horses at the Olsenses'. One day, when I went into the barn to find Mr. Olsen, I saw him and the other maid doing something weird. First of all, I thought she was tying his shoelaces, but when I looked closer, he was naked from the waist down, his jodhpurs down around his boots."

A puzzled look came on Suzie's face.

"What are jodhpurs?"

"Just a fancy name for riding pants. They didn't know I was standing there watching them. Then I saw Jackie put his thing, you know, his private part, in her mouth and was running her tongue on it like she was licking it. It was gross."

"Yuck," said Suzie, laughing. "That is a funny story. Your stories of the palace just keep getting better. Do you think she was washing it with her tongue?"

The girls started laughing so hard, they are doubled over.

"C'mon, Suzie, it's just up here," said Alice, running ahead.

Making her way to the steps, she looked back, beckoning Suzie to hurry. A few chickens scratched in the yard.

Stepping up to the door, Suzie now examining the small clapboard house.

"The dairy is over there." Alice pointed at the red rooftops of the barns. My brothers' work there, and my dad worked there his whole life, until he died."

Knocking softly, Suzie stands at the foot of the stairs. The door opened slowly. A bloated face appeared, a brightly colored scarf over her head. Wearing the same drab brown dress, not much different from the heavy damask dress she wore in the convent. An off white flour bag apron, her staple for her afternoons in the kitchen, pulled tight across her ample stomach.

"Wasn't expecting any visitors, Alice. You bring strangers to my house?"

"Suzie is not a stranger, Mother. She is my best friend." Before it had come out of her mouth, Alice realized admitting that Suzie was her friend wasn't the right thing to say. "What I meant to say is, she works with me at the candy factory." Suzie gazed at Alice, then back at her mother. Alice grabbed Suzie by the arm and walks into the house, past Irene.

"All right then, seeing you girls came a long way, just go and sit at the table. I will get some tea and cookies."

"It's OK, Mother, I will make the tea," said Alice, following Irene to the stove. It just felt wrong for Irene to wait on the girls.

"I almost sent your brothers to look for you. It's been two months now. Food is scarce around here. Where is the money you made?"

"You mean, you don't know where I live?"

"No, Alice, I don't know where Charlie lives, or I would have come myself. Don't have time to be running all over the countryside looking for you."

The girls eyed each other, a look of alarm on their faces.

Catching the exchange angered Irene.

"Does it really matter anyway? You do not live here anymore." Shooting a cutting look at Alice.

Before Irene could ask Alice for the money again, she pulled it out of her pocket, handing her an envelope, Suzie watching every move.

"How much is here, Alice? For two months, now let me see. There should be thirty-five dollars, seventeen fifty a month makes thirty-five dollars," she said as she opened the envelope, shaking the money onto the table. Straightening up the bills counting them now. "One, two, three, four...twenty five, and that is all?" she said, looking under the envelope.

"Where is the rest, Alice? You are not lying to me, are you?" Her eyes growing wide, her voice threatening.

"Mother, they take money out of my pay for my uniform and lunches that they provide for the girls there. Three dollars for each."

"Six dollars. Plus twenty-five makes thirty-one. Where is the rest?"

"Mother, I had to use the rest to get my train ticket here. Suzie paid her own way."

"Oh, never mind. You seem to have an excuse for everything. Maybe I just will keep you here."

Tears come to her eyes.

"No, Mother, please," pleaded Alice.

"Just kidding," said Irene with a plastic smile. "You need to keep on working. So, Alice, why didn't Charlie bring you home last month? You are still living with him? Are you doing a good job looking after him?"

"Looking after him, Mother? You mean cooking and cleaning for him? That is all I do, Mother."

"Oh, shut up. Don't have time to listen to you complain. You look like you are doing just fine. Your candy factory job is working out, and you have a place to live."

"Yes, Mother, I love my job."

Another big mistake. Watching Irene's face contorting, her beady eyes narrowing, as she turns walking to the window over the sink, her portal to her madness.

For a few long seconds, no answer from Irene, like she had gone into another world, staring out at the whiteness of nothing.

Alice beckoned to Suzie, pointing at the coats and the door. Shaking her head, she mouthed the words, "Let's go," her eyes wide.

The blank whiteness of the snow takes Irene back to the convent. Lost. Kneeling at the altar, her knees numb with pain. When would they come for her?

Looking up at the cross, Jesus nailed to it, the blood dripping from his hands onto her head. Couldn't they just let her do something else? Even scrubbing on the washboard was better. With Irene lost in her nightmare, the girls put on their coats and make a clean break to the door.

After closing the door, quietly, Alice started running, holding her bag at her side.

"C'mon, hurry, Suzie. Let's get out of here. Don't look back, Suzie, hurry."

Suzie did not quite understand why Alice was running. Catching up to her, she stared into her face.

"You are that scared? I kind of see why. Your mother is rather strange."

"Just like I told you, Suzie. I just knew what she was thinking. She was going to try and keep me there." Tears filled Alice's eyes. "I can never go back there again to live, Suzie, never, I would rather die! Did you see her walking stick? I wore the bruises from that stick, but the bruises on the inside never go away. I hate her!"

Tears cascade down her face, she starts whimpering, turning away from Suzie.

Reaching out to Alice, Suzie hugged her tight.

"You never have to go back there. Mom is ready for you to move in with us. The thing is, though, I think she wants to discuss it with your mother."

They make it back to the train station in lots of time. Sitting on a bench, their breath in front of them like steam from a hot spring.

"Here comes our train," announced Suzie, getting up, Alice following.

The conductor sticks his head out. "All aboard!"

The meeting had given both Suzie and Alice something to think about.

Exchanging a few glances and smiles, they sit quietly, waiting for their stop.

Once off the train, they hit the road, walking a fast pace toward Suzie's. It was a good half hour walk, if they didn't dilly dally.

At the sound of horse hooves behind them, both the girls looked around at the same time. For a minute Alice worried that it might be Charlie, ordered to take her back to her mother.

Having a better look, it is Sadie West and her horse, Moses.

Sadie pulled the wagon alongside the girls.

"Hello, Miss Sadie," said Alice. "This is my friend Suzie. We are just coming from my mother's. Now we are headed to Suzie's house, just down the road a ways."

"Come on, get in. Won't have you walking when that's the way I am going already."

"Thank you, Sadie. You come along when I most need you."

"Thanks, ma'am," said Suzie, looking at the side of Sadie's face, the raised pink scars running down into the top of her coat."

The girls jumped into the back of the buggy, Suzie still staring at the side of Sadie's face.

"Did Alice tell you the story? The scars speak for themselves. Fought a big cat."

"Yes. Alice told me you are famous," replied Suzie.

"I didn't know that I was famous," said Sadie with a big smile. The whiteness of her teeth was apparent in the ebony of her skin.

"Pleased to meet you, ma'am," said Suzie, trying not to stare.

"Suzie is my best friend. We met at the candy factory," said Alice.

"I think about you often, Alice," said Sadie. "I'm happy you have a nice friend."

"Thank you, Sadie. I have a story to tell you. Whenever my mom saw you on the road, she would call me to look out the window. She told me that you were my real mother and had left me with her. I prayed that one day there would be a knock at the door, and it would be you. She was always so mean to me. I really did believe you were my mother."

"Oh my God, child, that is some story. Well, I would have loved to have a daughter just like you, Alice. Maybe in another lifetime, but right now I think our differences are a big reason to believe that I am not your mother."

Sadie pursed her thick lips, lacing the leather straps through her fingers. As she urged Moses on, he throws his head back, leading the wagon out onto the road.

Suzie's house comes into the clearing,

"My house is right there." Suzie pointed.

"Whoa, Moses," she said, gently pulling on the reins. The girls hopped down, Alice and Sadie exchanging smiles.

"Thank you, Miss Sadie. It was great to see you again," said Alice.

"Thanks a lot, ma'am," said Suzie. "Was great to meet you."

"Look after each other now. God bless the both of you."

The girls stood aside the road, waving as Sadie urged the beast, a special sound escaping her full lips. Moses raised his head to the call, guiding his precious cargo back onto the road.

"We're home," announced Suzie from the doorway, Betty decending the staircase with an armful of clothes.

"How was your trip to Oakfield?"

"I met Alice's mom. We weren't at her house very long. Almost missed the train going there. Lots of fun until we met Irene. She is a miserable, odd lady, don't mind me saying so Alice. Then when we got off the train in Springfield, the famous lady picked us up in her wagon. Sadie West. She is Alice's friend."

"Who is Sadie West?"

"You just wouldn't believe it, Mom. There are scars running right down her face. Pink scars against her black skin, Mom. A really beautiful lady. Her story is written on her face."

"What story?"

"She fought a cougar and pulled its tongue right out of its head to save her grandson."

"Oh yes, I heard that story years ago. So she is your friend, Alice?"

"Yes, I have known her since I was a young girl."

The girls started giggling. Betty was confused at the joke.

"You know what? Irene told Alice that Sadie was her mother and had left her at Irene's."

With a deep sigh, Betty shook her head in disbelief of the madness of Irene, deciding to keep her comments to herself.

"What would you girls like for supper?" asked Betty.

"Nothing for me, Mother. We have to get ready now for the dance."

Before Betty could say a thing, the girls disappeared up the staircase into Suzie's room.

Doing each other's hair and makeup, walking back and forth to the mirror till they found perfection. Both wore tight dresses showing their slim figures and their hair in the same updo. With one last look in the mirror, they smiled at each other, pleased.

A pretty girl looking back at her, a total stranger. Rouge on her cheeks, the black kohl eyeliner turning the green of her eyes like emeralds. Holding the French cologne Pierre had given her for her birthday, she sprayed Suzie, then herself.

"Oh my, Alice, it's the best smell ever!"

The excitement of the dance showed in their eyes, the sparkle of a young woman's life.

"C'mon, Alice, let's go show Mom."

Suzie walked into the kitchen first, Alice coming up behind her, feeling self-conscious in the tight dress, her breasts rounded at the top.

"My goodness," said Betty, "you girls look great but rather sexy, I might add. Suzie, I know you are fifteen, but dressing Alice like she is your age?"

"I have never worn a dress like this," said Alice, looking down the front of her. Betty's eyes on her cleavage.

"Well, you girls be ready for anything. When you stimulate the boys, things could happen."

"Oh, Mother, we are not trying to stimulate anyone."

"Just saying, boys will be boys. Don't let any of them disrespect you. Just have fun and come straight home after the dance. What time is it over?"

"Eleven o'clock, Mother, just like before."

As the girls pulled on their coats and boots, Betty came back into the kitchen.

CHAPTER 48

The light of the moon showed the way. The coldness of the night encouraging the girls to walk briskly. They settled into a half trot, making it to the candy factory in less than fifteen minutes.

"Looks like we are almost the first ones here," said Suzie, looking around. Pulling open the door, they walk in, shaking off the cold they hang up their coats.

"Don't stare, Alice, but the band is setting up their instruments," whispered Suzie in her ear.

Four guys, all dressed in black, one of them sitting on the edge of the stage tuning his guitar.

"That really cute guy sitting down is the lead singer. His name is Elric. The band is called Elric and the Wanderers." Commented Suzie.

The girls stand against the wall, watching as more people arrived, the hall filling up quickly.

"This band is so good, Alice. They can really get the crowd going."

Glancing at her friend, Alice has her hands almost tied in front of her, her cheeks rosy, her eyes wide.

"Don't look so scared, Alice. It's just a dance."

The girls started giggling as a few guys walked by, sizing them up like they are prize fillies.

Nervously, Alice looked around at all the people. Glancing at the band, she happened to catch the lead singer eyeing her. Looking away, then back again in a few minutes. He was staring right at her. Black hair, tall, and handsome.

Surely, he must be close to twenty, she thought to herself. Why would he be looking at her so hard? She was only thirteen and shouldn't be at this dance at all.

"Let's go to the ladies' room," said Suzie.

Following close behind, just before they entered the bathroom, Alice glanced back at the stage, his eyes still following her.

Pulling a candy apple red lipstick out of her purse, Suzie puts it to her lips. Alice watched as she applied the red lip stain, announcing, "I am sexy."

"Do you want to put some on, Alice?"

"Oh no, thank you," she answered, thinking she would look like she was playing dress up.

There were lots of girls and boys coming into the hall, everyone taking off their coats, some going a soda. Suzie and Alice stood along the wall, not too far from the stage. They are deep in conversation when the lead singer walks by them, taking time to turn his head, looking the girls up and down. The blackness of his hair matched his outfit. His grey eyes stare hard at Alice's, then a smile that lights up his face.

"That's him, Alice, the lead singer. He really stared at you, I saw that."

"Whatever," answered Alice. "He looked at both of us."

Suzie kept eyeing the door. "Are you waiting for Roger to arrive?" asked Alice.

"Yes, but don't worry, I won't leave you alone. I will be close to you, even if we dance. I'm sure some guy is going to ask you to dance."

"Oh no, I hope not. I don't know how to dance."

"Sure you do. Just follow the lead of your guy."

The thought of dancing with a boy sent a blush over her cheeks, nervous but excited now at the thought.

"There's Roger. He just walked in," announced Suzie. The girls stared at the door.

Glancing at her friend, Suzie's eyes lit with a brightness of the stars.

"I have to go to him, Alice. Just stand here, I'll be right back, OK? I'll bring him over to meet you."

Sauntering away toward Roger, Alice watched as Suzie put a little swing into her walk. Oh my, she thought, Suzie changing right before her eyes. Alice keeps her eyes on Suzie, as she saunters over to a tall boy, leaning into him.

Feeling vulnerable, she looked down at her own bosom, the tight dress accentuating her breasts, the feeling that everyone was looking at her. A few guys went by, staring straight at her chest. "Please come back, Suzie," she mouthed under her breath.

A tall thin redheaded boy approached Alice.

"Do you think I could have the next dance, pretty girl?"

"Ah, um, actually, I'm just waiting for my friend to come back. Maybe later, OK?" she said, walking toward Suzie and Roger.

The boy came up behind her.

"Oh, by the way, my name is Russel. Thought I should ask you first before you get danced off your feet, a pretty little thing like you." Alice walks away.

Suzie turned to see Alice approaching.

"Sorry I left you there alone. This is Roger," she said, pointing to a dark haired boy with blue eyes, a Roman nose, and a warm smile.

"Hi, Alice, pleased to meet you. I am Roger," he said. Putting his hand out. Alice shaking it, smiling. "Hi Roger, Suzie told me nice things about you."

Trying not to stare at them, Alice looks from one couple to another, a buzz in the air, spirits flying high, in a frenzy of sexuality. The band played a fast tune, the dance floor coming alive with movement.

Just like mating peacocks, thought Alice. Prancing around, displaying their pretty costumes, attracting the males, who flirted around the girls, teasing and enticing the dance of courtship. *Oh my goodness, I think I read too much.*

It was amazing, and beautiful, opening up a whole new world for Alice, starting to enjoy the attention she is getting. Boys were taking notice. Some just walked by and smiled. A few groups of girls took notice too. Some smiled; others just looked her up and down, giving Alice mixed feelings.

"We are going outside for a few minutes, so just mingle and maybe have a dance. Don't be shy. Look at all the guys who are staring at you, Alice."

Suzie and Roger walked away, leaving her standing alone. The same red headed boy came back over to her.

"What do you say, can I have this dance?"

Better than standing here, looking lost, she thought, taking his arm. Leading her to the dance floor, the band playing a slow tune. Pulling her close to him, her head barely coming to his chest, she looks up at him. He was so tall, like a giraffe, she thought, giggling. Looking back down, trying to concentrate on where her feet were going. *Just follow his lead*, Suzie had said. Alice getting the groove of the waltz.

Roger had walked Suzie to the wall pressing his body against hers, kissing her full on the lips. Alice is lost in the dance, trying to keep up, when she notices Suzie and Roger stuck together in a lip lock. Looking away, feeling as though she is invading her friend's privacy. The song ended, the red headed boy leading Alice back towards Suzie, who is now standing alone.

Hurrying to Suzie, Alice hugged her friend.

"I danced. It was fun," said Alice. Suzie's mind far off.

"Roger came here with his friend. Do you want to meet him?"

"No. I don't want to, Suzie. I would like to just hang out with you."

"We came here to dance and have fun, Alice. So try to enjoy yourself. I am going to dance with Roger, the next slow dance."

The lead singer was talking to the crowd.

"Sure good to see so many of you out to join us tonight. For those of you who are new, we are Elric and the Wanderers, and of course I'm Elric."

A loud cheer went from the crowd, he takes a bow, picking at the side of his collar, the girls all hooting.

"So, for the rest of you who came to party, we will be back in ten minutes. Get your sodas. Grab your girls. Let's party while the night is young. Now to introduce my band. We have Dean on guitar." Pointing to a sandy haired, medium height handsome fellow, his thick hair hanging down over his forehead. Dean strummed at his guitar strings, delighting the crowd. "We got George on drums." A short thick fellow with black hair. George beat the drums hard for a few minutes. The crowd went crazy. "And Johnny on guitar." A tall, handsome dark blonde haired fellow giving the crowd a few deep strums on his guitar.

"Now, without further ado, let's get this party started!" Elric yelled, his voice reverberating off the walls. Scanning the floor, seeking out the prettiest girls, he jumped down off the stage.

"Oh my God, where did you go? I am not feeling good standing here all alone, too many boys stopping to talk to me, I am starting to feel nervous. A group of girls were pointing at me and laughing. Why would they do that?"

"You look so beautiful tonight, Alice. They are jealous, that is all."

Another boy grabbed Alice's arm, pulling her onto the dance floor. Trying to keep an eye on Suzie, she disappeared again.

After three dances, Alice was started to get the hang of it. When the last song was done, it was intermission time. The band members, all getting down off the stage, started to mingle with the crowd. The lead singer, Elric, jumped down off the stage into a group of girls who surrounded him, vying for his attention, circling him. Alice watched as the girls all tried touching him. He was indeed handsome, like Suzie had said. There wasn't another fellow in the whole dance that stood out like he did. The way he held himself, his head high. The swagger of his walk. Tall, lean, and gorgeous, Alice gets a bird's eye view of him. Steel-grey eyes, long dark lashes, black shiny hair combed back off his forehead, and a cleft in his chin. The voice just brought the whole package together. He had talent and looks.

More and more girls surrounded him, like he was a prize fighter or a movie star. Finally, he pulled away from them, Alice watching as he headed back toward the stage.

Standing against the wall, but definitely not a wall flower, the lead singer was coming toward her again.

Nervous she tries to turn her back to him, feeling shy, trying to avoid the attention.

She could feel his presence as he walked by her, a string of girls following close behind.

On his way back up the hall, he stopped right next to Alice, talking to two girls. One had her hands all over him, the other one flirting, laughing. Walking up to Alice, he motioned for the girls to give him a minute.

As he stared in her eyes, Alice tried to shy away. Placing his hand on her shoulder, she turned to face him.

"I would like to talk to you sometime, angel. You are sure a beauty, fresh as the morning dew," he said in a low, sexy tone.

"Thanks," she answered shyly.

Taking one more look at her, from head to toe, giving her a winning smile, sauntering back toward the stage.

Relieved that he had walked away, Alice scanning the hall for Suzie.

Heading toward the door now, she noticed Suzie and Roger just walking in, waving at Suzie, relieved to see her friend.

"Are you having fun, Alice? You sure do look like you are, up there on the dance floor. You wouldn't have guessed you never danced before."

"Oh, thank you, Suzie, I did get the hang of it quickly, I guess. There were too many boys trying to talk to me, and they kept pulling me onto the dance floor. I bet I danced five songs in a row. Just guess what? The lead singer came over to me. Said he wanted to talk to me sometime. Suzie, he said some nice things to me, and then gave me a smile that made me feel all woozy. He is so cute, Suzie, and I think he likes me. There were girls all over him, and he came to talk to me."

"Wow, the first dance, and you get the prince. You are sure lucky," said Suzie. "You know how many girls try to talk to that guy? He's a real actor. Just watch his antics. He's the star of the show, and he knows it. So do all the other guys."

Taking a second look at Suzie, her cheeks rosy against her pale skin, her hair messy.

"We were necking," said Suzie. "It was wonderful!"

A questioning look was on Alice's face.

"Necking, you know, like kissing. Lots of kissing. I love him, Alice. Just look at him. Isn't he handsome?"

Alice nodded, watching the stage.

The band announced the last dance, a waltz. Roger came for Suzie, taking her to the dance floor. Alice watched them, Suzie nuzzling into his neck, Roger holding her close. Just then a tall dark haired, handsome boy approached Alice.

"Can I have this dance?"

"Sure," she said, giving him her hand, walking to the dance floor. He pulled her to him, his breath warm on her face. She looked up at him. Dark almond eyes, full lips, long lashes. Warming up to him, they waltzed close, Alice lost in his embrace. No one had ever touched her like that.

The dance finished. Suzie and Roger went to a spot on the wall in an embrace.

"The guys are going to drive us home, Alice. Isn't that great? We won't have to walk."

The boys waited until the girls came out. Suzie got in the back seat with Roger, the two of them in a pretzel, before John even got the car started. Alice looked back at them, chuckling.

"So how far from here?" asked the driver.

"Go that way," said Alice. "I'll tell you when you are getting close."

They drove, no one talking, Suzie, and Roger deep French kissing in the back seat.

"We're

here," said Alice, looking over the seat. Suzie tried to straighten her dress, wiping her lips with the back of her hand.

"Thanks for the ride," said Suzie. The girls jumping out of the car.

Quietly, Suzie switched on the light in foyer. Taking off their coats and boots, Suzie put her finger to her lips.

"Shh," she said, walking on her tiptoe. "Don't want to wake Mother. We are quite late."

Getting into bed, they said their good-nights and turned off the light.

Alice lay awake, thinking of her Prince Charming. He said he wanted to talk to her again sometime. The way he looked at her made her feel like he wanted to do more than talk to her. His eyes roamed her body. She couldn't forget his beautiful smile and his eyes, grey like a stormy day.

Falling asleep, dreaming of her prince singing to her, holding her in his arms...

Good morning, girls." Betty standing at the door, looking in.

Alice's head is covered. Suzie's eyes opened.

"See you guys in the kitchen," said Betty, closing the door.

"I was having such a good dream," said Alice. "Didn't want it to end."

"Suppose you dreamed about that guy, the singer, ah." Suzie laughed, sitting up.

"How did you know? He was taking me away on his white horse with wings," she said, laughing.

"You are such a romantic, Alice. That is so cute."

"What about you? I think you are in love with Roger. Your cheeks were rosy all night."

"Really," said Suzie, bringing her hands to her cheeks.

They share a laugh, getting up, putting on their slippers and housecoats, heading down the hallway toward the stairs.

In the kitchen, a spread of bacon, eggs, and toast.

"Mmm," said Suzie. "I'm hungry."

"I bet you are. Neither of you girls had any supper last night. How was the dance?" Betty asked, turning she walks to the table.

"The guys kept pulling me onto the dance floor. I danced all night," said Alice, smiling.

"And you, Suzie, where were you when all of this was happening?"

"I was busy dancing too, Mother," she answered sheepishly. "Alice had so many fellows trying to dance with her, even the lead singer was smitten by her."

"Well, that must have been some night. It's great that you guys had fun. The last time I danced was at my wedding."

"You are welcome to spend the night with us, Alice. You and Suzie can go to work together in the morning. It would be nice to have you girls help me make a nice supper. I was thinking lasagna."

"Wow, Alice, let's do it. Thank you, Mom."

The girls looked at each other, stars in their eyes. Their friendship was blooming, like crocuses in the spring.

Walking away from the kitchen into the parlor, Alice sitting down in one of the comfortable overstuffed chairs, near the big picture window. Starting to worry about the consequences, if she denied him the supper he wanted to have with her. Sounded more like she was going to be the dessert, the way his beady eyes twinkled as he talked of having her company. More than anything, she wanted to stay, but what if Charlie was mad? He might go and tell her mother, and she could make her go back home. Oh no, that could never happen, she reassured herself.

Finally deciding she had better not stay the night. He had specified he wanted to have supper with her She had agreed, in exchange for that one sleepover night.

Getting busy in the kitchen, the girls helped Betty make the sauce for the lasagna. Before long, Alice noticed the darkness looming outside.

"Suzie, I really think I need to go home after supper. I am scared of what will happen if I stay away another night. Charlie made me promise to come home today."

"She is right," said Betty. "We can't make Charlie mad, or he might not let Alice stay overnight again. I really just have to make some time to go and see your mother to talk to her about you moving in with us."

"Oh, thank you so much, ma'am. I would be so happy, not having to go there to Charlie's anymore. The thing is, Charlie gave my mother a horse and buggy, and somehow that is in the whole deal with me working for him. I have to pay that debt before she will let me leave there."

"Oh my," said Betty. "This story gets more complicated all the time. Your mother traded your services for a horse and buggy? That is really strange, first of all."

"I am ashamed to admit she did," answered Alice, hanging her head.

All the while they prepared supper, Betty kept asking questions about the dance. Never once did Suzie bring up Roger, making Alice feel like she was lying the whole time.

When they finished cleaning, Alice heads to the closet, putting on her coat and boots, taking up her bag.

"Well, I really need to be going now. Thank you for having me. It's dark, but I know the way. I will see you at work tomorrow, Suzie. Good night."

All during supper, Betty had talked about her dreams for her daughter. She wanted her to go to college and get a degree of some kind. Suzie said she wanted to go to beauty school to learn hair and makeup. It was what she enjoyed, and she wanted to make a lifelong career of it. Alice agreed that would be fun and a good way to make a living. When Betty asked her what she wanted to do when she grew up, she just didn't see any light at the end of the work day. The candy factory was all she had in mind. What else could she do? Her dreams of being a nurse were all but squashed by Irene, who said that education was only for the privileged. Would she be able to still go to college one day?

Glancing at her watch: eight o'clock, hoping that Charlie would be sleeping when she got there, and she could sneak in and go straight to her room, and not have to see him.

Charlie had waited all day for the girl to come home to do something, cook supper, wash and sweep the floors, so he could sit in the parlor watching her from behind, his hand in his pocket. Where was she? He would have to find out where Suzie lived. If he knew, he would go and demand she come back with him. He didn't want to seem too pushy, not knowing what Alice might have told them about their living arrangement. They didn't know him, and maybe he would just wait until she came back. Pouring himself a double whiskey, talking to himself. "We will see," he said under his breath.

By the time his stomach started rumbling, he glanced at the grandfather clock. Seven o'clock, the girl was still not back. He would have to put some fear in her. She seemed to be doing her own thing, not taking care of his needs as her mother had promised. Going to the parlor, the whiskey bottle sitting there, he had one more drink. The alcohol coaxing his hunger, fixing himself a sandwich, leaving the plate and crumbs on the table near the couch. Laying back, his eyes bloodshot from the whiskey.

Making her way to the snow covered roadway, the imprint of the wheels that had formed in the hardened snow guiding her footsteps. A clear dark sky, a mocking sliver of a moon, hanging overhead, showing its illuminated smile.

Walking along briskly, the sharpness of the cold cutting into her face, her thumbs numb. Her cheeks were so cold, she stopped to warm them with her hands, then continued down the road. Charlie's house wasn't far now. The corner in the road was Alice's landmark.

The porch light gave the house a muted glow. She hoped that Charlie would be sleeping; otherwise she knew he would want to talk to her. She just wanted to go to her room and get settled in for the night. Oh my God, she remembered, she was sharing the room with the ghost. *Oh no, I don't want to go in.* If only she could turn and never go back. As she steps up to the door, her happiness drained from her, like water down a sink.

Trying the handle, the door is locked. Oh no, she would have to go around and try the kitchen door. Her hand hit the doorknob, turning. The door came flying open, Alice goes sprawling across the floor, her bag flying the other way, its contents scattered across the floor.

On her hands and knees now, Charlie standing over her.

"So, here you were finally. Trying to sneak in too? What have you been up to, Alice?"

Picking herself up, she scurries to get her things back in her purse.

"I was not sneaking in. The front door was locked."

"What, you think I should leave the front door open all night, waiting for you to come back?"

Turning, Charlie in her personal space, she tries to back away from him, a strong smell of smoke and whiskey on his breath. Unsteady on his feet, almost falling backward, his words slurred. What was wrong with him? Just then, Charlie grabbed her by her arm, applying pressure.

"Just what do you think you are doing? Coming in here all hours of the night."

"I was with my friends," she answered. A fear comes over her, his red eyes, a thick white substance in the corners of his mouth. Pulling away from him, she runs up the stairs, down the hallway to her room, frantic to just get in and close him out.

Her heart is beating so fast, her eyes wide, standing with her ear to the door.

Was he coming? There are no sounds, deciding he must have gone to his room. After about ten minutes of listening at the door, Alice settled into her room, taking off her coat and boots lying on the top of her covers, still wearing the clothes she'd had on all day. Thinking about getting into her nightgown but changing her mind, tonight she would sleep in her clothes, feeling insecure, and scared to undress now, not with him out there.

Holding her blanket against her chest, she falls asleep on top of the blankets. Awakened at the sound of something falling, she gets up from the bed and goes to the door, opening it slightly. Wondering what had caused the loud bang, she sits on the side of the bed, scared now. Could it have been the ghost? He had probably passed out, she reasoned.

With no sounds coming from downstairs, she decided it was probably safe to change into her nightgown and get a good night's sleep.

Just as she is slipping out of her sweater, the room door swings wide open. Charlie is standing there, his feet planted wide apart, steadying himself, weaving back and forth.

"Get out of my room!" she screamed, pulling her blanket to her chest.

"It won't do you any good to scream. It's just you and me here. I waited for you all day." His words slurred.

"How dare you! Get out!" she shrieked.

Grabbing for her sweater on the bed, he lunged at her, pulling her sweater away from her. Screaming now. "Get out, you stupid drunk!"

"You can scream all you want. No one will hear you."

Her heart is beating out of her chest, her legs weary. What was he doing?

Coming closer to her, he reached his arms out, trying to kiss her.

"Get away from me!" she screamed again.

Charlie slaps her across the face. "Shut up, you stupid brat. I am going to teach you a lesson. Think you can just come and go as you like. You want to live in my house, eat my food, and sleep in my bed without giving me what I need. I will just take what I need." Spittle flying from his mouth. "Your mother said to give you some time to warm up to me. Well, this is enough time."

Wide eyed, scared, she tried to push past him. Grabbing her hard, he pushed her back on the bed. Falling on top of her now, his whole weight bearing down, rendering her helpless. Alice screams louder now, he coveres her mouth with his broad scratchy hand. Alice bites his hand, he slaps her across the face again. Turning her face now, helpless, giving up the struggle, the density of his barrel chest, making it hard for her to breathe.

Shoving his hand down her leg, pressing roughly against her groin, ripping at her nightgown now, pulling off her underpants. She realized the most horrible thing was happening to her. Reaching down to his own pants, unbuttoning his trousers, his flesh making contact with Alice's stomach, laying his body fully on hers now. Her face turned, her eyes shut tight, heaving, bile coming to her mouth. Feeling his flesh, then the worst pain stung her between her legs. A shrill scream escaped her lips, separating the air waves.

The pain was intense, Alice biting at her own lips, bringing blood. Charlie was now heaving up and down, staring into her face, his big hand on the side of her face, rocking his body on hers, breathing heavy, like a crazed animal. Whimpered, her tears staining the pillowcase, realizing there was no use in struggling, it was just making him more aggressive. Trying to pretend this just wasn't happening, the sick rocking of his body heightening. A few more pumps, then one last hard thrust into her private place, then a low growl escaped his chapped lips. Then no movement at all, his full weight bearing down on her.

The iron metallic taste of her own blood, hate, sorrow, and everything unjust settling on her heart.

Lying still, holding her breath, she pressed her face into the pillow, away from him. Staggering away from the bed, he looked back once and pulled up his trousers.

With her back to him, her heart in her mouth, she pulled her blanket over her naked body, like the wings would take her to another place.

She could hear him at the door, now closing it behind him. Charlie headed to his own room. With the bang of his own door, staggering, he fell into his bed, clothes and boots still on, passing out facedown into the mattress.

Removing her blanket, she looked down at her blood-stained legs, her white comforter bloodied. Crying out now. "Oh my God. What happened to me? Why God, why?"

Standing up now, her legs stuck together at the top, her groin throbbing in pain. Going to the doorway, opening it, peering down the hall. No sign of him.

Vomit filled her mouth. Running now to the bathroom closing herself in, projectile vomiting into the bathtub, crying, she staggers. Just the light of the moon through the small window, casting shadows on the white tub. She just needed to get clean of the disgust in her mind, pouring cold water from the pitcher. A full pail of cold water, she would just have to use it. Frantic to get his germs off of her, she didn't even notice how cold the water is. Soaping her hands and face, she used a washcloth to clean her body, her groin her legs. Weeping now, a steady whine; her tears falling, like an overflowing spring. Scrubbing and scrubbing the lye soap burning her face and groin. Shivering, shaking so hard, she loses her balance, falling to the floor, hitting her face on the side of the tub.

An hour passed, time standing still. Opening her eyes, her hand to the side of her face, realizing she must have passed out. Pain. Her face is swollen on one side. Pulling herself up, she gets back to her room, crawling into the bed, pulling the covers over her head. Curled into a fetal position, the tears flowed uncontrollably. Silence. The house is dead quiet. She falls asleep.

Charlie woke early with the sound of the rooster. Pain behind his eyes, his head throbbing like it is in a vice grip. Water, he needed water and a cigarette.

Going down to the kitchen, he looks for his bag of tobacco. Sitting at the table he rolls himself a cigarette. Bits and pieces of his assault on Alice started coming back to him. Oh no. What had he done? If only she had come home when she said she would, he wouldn't have started drinking, then drinking too much and getting carried away. That was all. Before she came home, he had wrapped a pair of her soiled underwear around his cock.

Masturbating, he had walked from room to room, the urges to have her, rising to a frenzy.

It was the damn whiskey, he decided. It had made him crazy. Just like that day when he wanted his wife to have sex with him after nothing for months. Instead she went to the bathroom and ran herself a bath. After drinking himself into madness, he went in to confront her. When she told him she never wanted to have sex with him again, he drowned her.

It had been twenty years, a long time ago, forgotten. He had to make sure that Alice would not speak of what had happened. Waiting for her to show, he sits at the table smoking a hand-rolled cigarette, watching the staircase.

Hearing a door close. She must be coming downstairs. Watching and waiting, Alice showed in the doorway, her coat and hat on already.

"Charlie, I am not making breakfast this morning, I need to go to work early today." She said in a monotone voice.

"Oh no, you come over here right now. Sit down. We have to talk."

"What about?" Asked Alice. "What you did to me, Charlie?" Moving closer toward the door.

"Come here now, and sit down, young lady," he ordered, pointing to the chair next to him. "Your mother came here yesterday and demanded that I pack your things and take you back next week."

"I will run away," said Alice, crying, tears filling her eyes now.

"I saved you, Alice, don't worry," he lied. "I gave your mother some extra money, and she was glad to let you stay with me."

No, thought Alice. He couldn't buy her, but what choice did she have right now? Was he really telling the truth? There was no way she was going back to her mother. She would rather die. Even living with the ghost was better.

Today she would tell Suzie what Charlie had done to her, and surely Betty would insist that she move in. Regardless, today she was taking her things and getting far away as she could from Charlie and the ghost that had been trying to warn her all along.

"Don't worry, Charlie. I will keep your dirty little secret. Mostly because I want to forget it ever happened. I am not going back to my mother's house, and you will make sure of it, or else I will tell everyone what you did to me. You are an awful man, Charlie. I hate you! I wish I never knew you!"

"I don't hate you, Alice," he said with a cheesy, yellowed smile. "Even if you did tell anyone, they wouldn't believe you. They would think you were just trying to get away from here and your chores. Now you can go,

Alice. Have a nice day at the candy factory. I will have a good day after all that sugar I got last night. I am going to town today for supplies. Can I get you anything special?"

"No, I don't want anything from you," she retorted.

Did he really just say what she thought he said? This man was out of his mind.

Running to the door and down the steps out to the road, not looking back at the house, or to see if the ghost was watching her.

With every thrust, Charlie tore away at her fragile being, like the beating of waves crashing into limestone cliffs, the soft rock breaking away. Everything that had ever given her hope drained away from her. She was drowning, going under, her whole life flashing in and out of her mind, weak, helpless, alone.

Every step sent tears down her face.

How could she go to work today? Everyone would see. The happy Alice everyone knew had gone away, her smile faded. She needed to be alone somewhere where she felt safe. The only place was Suzie's.

Should she tell them everything? Would they scorn her and turn her away?

No, came back the voice.

Trying to put the assault out of her mind, but it lingered close to the surface. She could see his face over her, feel his skin on hers, making her want to get sick over and over. Could she ever wash it all away, make her mind forget?

So much uncertainty, sadness, like a heavy dark cloud overhead about to burst its fury onto the earth. Her tears fell like silent rain.

Walking right by the candy factory without even noticing, her eyes fixed on the road ahead, hoping she would pass Suzie on the way to work, unless she was already there. If it was just Betty at home, she would tell her she had her monthly and was in too much pain to go to work. Then Betty would tell her to go to Suzie's room and lie down for a while. There she would feel peace. Staring straight ahead, her mind a blank page, her palace comes into her mind's eye.

Lucy is standing at the top of the marble staircase, running down towards her, her arms outstretched. "I love you Alice," she said. Oh how she missed seeing her and Gladys, who had loved her like her own. The three tiered birthday cake with the crown on top came back to her. Smiling through her tears, a little sunshine breaking through dark clouds. She was happy there, happier than she had ever been.

Even the thoughts of the palace, which seemed like light years away, weren't helping right now, she needed to see her friend and confide in her. Suzie would understand and help her to deal with what had happened.

"I never knew a sick man named Charlie," she said out loud. "It was all just a bad dream."

Never, she didn't want to ever go back to that house again, or the sick orge that lived there. Her friends would see the urgency, and move her in, "oh please God.

"Please, God, help me. I can't live there anymore."

The straight line of poplar trees stood like soldiers, guarding the home of Suzie and Betty. Walking closer, she wiped at her face, trying to dry her tears. Just as she is walking up the stairs to the door, Betty opened the door.

"Oh my, Alice, are you all right?" she said, noticing her reddened eyes, her lids heavy and swollen.

"No, ma'am, I am not really," she said, collapsing into Betty's arms.

"Come in, dear. I will get some tea. Sit in the kitchen. I will be right in." Betty took off her coat and went straight to Alice, bending down over her shoulder. "What is it, dear?"

"I just don't feel very good, ma'am, lots of pain with my monthly, and I just couldn't go to work." Her eyes started to fill, softly whining now.

Noticing a black and blue bruise on Alice's cheek, the side of her face swollen. What did you do to your face Alice?"

"I slipped and fell in the bathroom, hitting my face on the tub," she whined.

"Oh, dear, don't cry. Let me get you something. We will have tea, and you can go and lay in Suzie's room until she comes home. I'll get you the hot water bottle. It usually helps with cramps. I have to go to the city. You got the whole house to yourself," she said, hugging her.

"Thank you, ma'am," smiling softly, hope bleaching out the darkness in her mind.

"There are blueberry muffins on the counter. Enjoy your tea, and have a muffin. Help yourself. I will see you later when I come home. We will all sit down and have a talk. Suzie and I have been thinking of asking you to move in here with us. You would be closer to the candy factory, and Suzie loves you. The way you girls get along just like sisters. Suzie has been so happy since she met you."

"Really," said Alice, crying again. "That would be great." Her eyes widened.

"We'll all talk about it later and figure out the details. I am happy to have you, dear," she said, giving her another hug.

Betty slipped on her coat and walked out the door.

The warmth of Betty's hugs was melting the ice that had formed over her heart. She wouldn't have to go back there to stay, not one more day.

"Thank you, God," she said under her breath.

Slipping into Suzie's bed, she lay quietly, motionless, staring at the ceiling. She would tell Charlie if he told her mother she had left, she would tell everyone he had raped her, using it as an advantage over him now.

Her things were already packed, hidden behind the door. She would ask Suzie to go with her. No, she should go and take her bags out of the house right away. He said he was going to town. It was perfect. She could get her things out while he was gone. She thought hard about where she would hide them, maybe in the woodshed or chicken coop, or in the barn under some straw. As soon as Betty was out the door, Alice put her coat and boots back on, hitting the road, wasting no time, towards Charlie's.

About twenty minutes into the walk, Alice hears the familiar sound of horse hooves. Turning, a smiling Sadie West with her ebony horse, Moses.

"Oh my goodness, Alice, isn't it nice to see you. I was just thinking of you, and here you are. Get in," she said, leaning, giving Alice a hand into the front seat. "Miss Alice, where are you going at this time of day?"

"I was just at Suzie's house. I'm not going to work today. I am kind of sick. I was just heading back to Charlie's...to take my things out of there."

"You look mighty sad Alice. Are you all right? And your face Alice, what happened?"

"I.....I just slipped in the bathroom, hitting my face on the big tub, and passed out, and.....and....no, I'm not alright Sadie," starting to cry again.

The dam of tears broke open, Alice crying hard now. Sadie pulled the wagon to the side of the road, pulling Alice to her, so worried about Alice now, knowing, surely it had something to do with that Charlie Mason her blood starts to get hot.

"Now, now, stop crying. It won't help. Tell me, what is it? Did he do something to you, Miss Alice? That animal, Charlie Mason, they suspected him in his wife's murder too. Did you know, Alice, they found her in the bathtub, drowned?"

"What? She drowned in the tub in his bathroom?"

"Yes, so the story went. He said he was in the city that day, came home and found her dead in the tub."

"Oh my God, Sadie, do you know what? The ghost of Charlie's wife is still in the bedroom where I was sleeping. A couple of times when I was looking in the mirror, brushing my hair, she was standing behind me. I had a scary dream of her in the bathtub too. Now I know she was trying to warn me about him."

"You have to get out of that house, Alice. If you want, you can come and stay with me for a while. I won't have you going back there."

"He raped me, Sadie." Then she started crying hard again, holding her head in her hands. Sadie wrapped her long arms around her, like a loving mother would.

Maybe that is where the story of her being Alice's mother came in, thought Sadie, and how she just happened to come along at the right time, when Alice needed her.

The Lord worked in mysterious ways, Sadie knew that. She would do whatever was needed to keep this child safe from Charlie Mason.

"OK, Alice, dry your tears now. I am going to take you to get your bags, and don't you worry, that old coot won't mess with me."

"My friends, Suzie and her mom, Betty, invited me to live with them, so I just want to get my things and get back to their house."

"I will help you, and I will take you to Suzie's house, OK? Don't you worry your pretty head. After all, I am your mother from another place and time."

Sadie looked deep into Alice's sea green eyes, their souls connecting.

"Oh, thank you so much, Sadie. I still wish you were my mother."

"I really do believe that Irene is not right in her head. Do you know what I mean? She is not all there, so we can't really blame her."

"Miss Sadie, that makes a lot of sense."

Alice goes deep into thought. That could explain all the terrible things her mother did to her. She wasn't to blame. It felt better to think about her mother just as a sick woman.

"My mother is mentally ill?"

"Yes, I would say that, in all honesty. Only a sick woman would send their child to live with Charlie Mason."

"Thank you," said Alice, with a hint of a smile. Sadie returning a big loving smile, her eyes on the reins of her life.

"I will go in ahead," said Alice. Sadie pulled the wagon close to the porch.

"I'll wait right here, and watch for that old geezer. If he gets in the way, I'll have to straighten him out." Watching Alice go up the stairs, opening the door, going in.

Everything was just the way Alice had left it. Going to the window, she looked out at the barn. No sign of Charlie, the barn door closed.

One by one, Alice hauled out her suitcases, in size from smallest to largest. Watching as Alice struggles with the bags, Sadie gets down out of the wagon, hoisting the bags into the back of the wagon.

"Just get in the wagon. I will take care of these," said Sadie.

"Oh no, Sadie, here comes Charlie!" said Alice, alarmed.

Looking down the narrow road, two horses, pulling a wagon, Charlie at the helm.

"You just sit right there, and let me take care of him. Don't say a word. I will do the talking."

Charlie pulled the wagon up behind them.

"Well, if it isn't Charlie Mason," said Sadie.

"And to what do I owe this visit?" he asked.

"You don't owe me anything, and I am taking my friend Alice away from here."

"Oh no, you are not doing any such thing! Her mother left her in my care," he said, his voice loud.

"Yes, Alice told me how much you care about her."

"What lies did she tell you? She tells lies all the time. That's why her mother sent her here, so I could straighten her out."

"I don't believe one word you say. You can fool some of the people, some of the time, but God sees and knows everything. Like how your wife really died. You sicken me. You are a despicable man!" Sadie spewed.

Mad, squinting his small eyes into an ugly face, as though it was frozen in place, his lips pursed into a straight line.

Sadie laced the reigns through her fingers, urging Moses on. Passing Charlie, she gives him a stern look, his mouth agape, Alice with her face turned away from him.

"Get thee behind me, Satan!" she spat, vile in her voice. "He is an evil man. He will burn in hellfire," said Sadie, handing down the judgment on him.

"That's right," answered Alice, safe in Sadie's company, envisioning Sadie pulling Charlie's tongue out of his mouth, Alice chuckling to herself.

As the chariot rumbled on, Sadie and Alice deep in thought. Moses held his ears forward, his head high, Sadie sitting tall and regal. With sadness for what had happened to Alice, she wished she knew how to make it all better for her young friend.

"Just throw your burdens on the Lord," said Sadie. Alice closed her eyes and prayed.

The farther they got away from Charlie's, her burden started to lighten. Looking behind her at her five red suitcases with all her treasures, then taking a long look at Sadie. She had come along just when she needed her. Had the Lord sent her? Of course he had. Sadie was an angel.

The love from Sadie, warmed Alice's heart, giving her renewed hope. The sun came through the clouds to kiss her face. It was going to be a wonderful day. A large bird with a wide wing span flew overhead.

"It is a sign," said Sadie. "The eagle is God's heavenly bird. The Lord's messenger bird. It means God is with you."

"Thank you, Sadie, I feel so much better now."

"It won't be long now. We are almost at Suzie's house."

"Yes, you will see a line of poplar trees along their driveway."

Sadie urged Moses into the driveway.

Suzie ran out into the yard.

"Hi, Sadie, hi Alice." She waved, her arms high, staring into the back of the wagon. "Those are all your things?"

"Yes. Sadie came with me to get them, and Charlie showed up just as we were leaving. I'll tell you all about it."

"Mom told me you came here. Sorry I went to work early this morning, hoping for us to have some time together before we started working. I'm so happy, Alice. Mom said you are going to be living with us."

Sadie got down out of the buggy. One by one, taking Alice's bags out, setting them near the door.

"Thank you, Sadie," said Alice starting to take her bags in the house. Suzie grabbed one of them, coming up behind Alice. "Let's just leave them at the foot of the stairs. I'll help you with them after supper. Mom is waiting on us. She made spaghetti and meatballs again."

"Great, answered Alice. "I just have to say goodbye to Sadie."

Going back out the door, the back end of the ornamental wagon just going out of site. Wishing she would have had time to thank Sadie again before she left.

The first night in her new home, Suzie and Alice cuddled up, reading, until the lights went out. When Alice confided in Suzie about what Charlie had done to her, Suzie started crying.

"Sorry for telling you that story, Suzie. I don't ever want to tell it again but thought you should know the truth. The worst part of all is Sadie told me that Charlie really did kill his wife. And you know where? In the bathtub where I used to bathe. It is so freaky, thinking that I bathed in there. I really believe she was trying to warn me about him. There was nothing I could do, and I never thought he would do that to me."

"That is the worst story ever, Alice. I blame your mother for sending you there."

"You know what else? Sadie told me that my mother is mentally ill."

"That does explain why she is not a good mother. I guess you are really happy to not have to live with her again."

"No, I will never go back to live at home again. I will run away, so far away."

The girls go quiet. Alice going back to the palace in her mind. Suzie, cried herself to sleep, sorry for her friend.

The ghost of Charlie's wife slept in the bed and sat at the mirror, looking at her reflection, brushing her hair. No reflection looked back. The room was quiet again, the way she liked it. The poor girl, where had she come from?

The mornings in the Redford household came like clockwork. Betty waited on them in the kitchen, breakfast on the table. While they ate, she directed the day, what she wanted the girls to do in the house, allotting the chores. With Alice staying with them now, things would run smoother, the workload lighter.

Her little girl was growing up. She couldn't help but notice they would go to Suzie's room for secret talks, guessing it was probably about boys. All teenage girls talked about boys. She just hoped that she had taught Suzie to keep perspective.

At suppertime Betty dropped a bomb on the girls.

"We have to do the right thing, and go and talk to Alice's mother. She has to know that Alice is now living with us. I will come along so she will know that I am the adult in the household."

Suzie and Alice share a secret look, Betty watching their faces.

"What is it? Are you girls hiding something from me?"

Suzie gave Alice a reassuring look, then looked back at her mother.

"Mom, Charlie raped Alice."

"Oh my God! I will take you to see the doctor. I am so sorry, Alice."

Hanging her head, Alice didn't know what to say.

"Alice just didn't know how to tell you, Mom."

"Well, I have some choice words for Irene. Can't believe she would put her daughter in such a place."

"My mother is mentally ill," said Alice.

"Sadie told me so. She knows my mother. I guess it explains a lot about her."

"Oh, I see," said Betty. "It gives me a better idea about her."

Alice goes quiet, her mind far away. Irene's face was etched permanently in her mind. Her plastic smile, waiting in the tea pot, for anyone who came to visit. The way she addressed Alice when strangers were around. *Dear* and *sweetie*, words that sounded like a foreign language, watching Irene struggle with the muscles in her face, the smile muscles untrained, the corners of her mouth turned downward naturally. The permanent frown leaving deep furrows in her unforgiving brow, showing the traces of her misery.

The child Irene came to mind. She saw her scrubbing floors on her hands and knees. Kneeling at an altar till she couldn't feel her knees. The mother superior beating it into them, to suffer, to be worthy of God's love.

Praying for hours on end. Going to bed hungry. Never any love, only orders, and prayers, and more prayers. Her mother's childhood mirrored her own, but worse.

"Forgive her, Lord, for she knows not what she has done."

The day she had beat her for looking in the small handheld mirror.

"Your vanity will get you in trouble. I was never allowed to look in a mirror. All that pride you have, Alice, I'll beat it out of you."

What was wrong with being proud?

"You have to accept disappointment," Irene said. "Do you think life is some kind of party?"

Thinking of a party. Yes, she was going to a party next weekend, the candy factory dance.

The three of them brainstormed every night at supper about the visit to Irene. They discussed the fact that Irene was indeed, out of her mind. They would handle her appropriately.

"Just be nice, Alice, and helpful. Show her that you love her. If she asks you questions, just answer truthfully. The truth is always the best," instructed Betty.

Watching Alice, the way she reacted every time they spoke of the trip, Betty could see she was scared and worried. The look told the story of a child abused, fright spelled on her face. Betty needed to know more and to finally confront Irene.

Settling into a routine with her new family, finally feeling safe again. Suzie and Alice talked and giggled until Betty ordered lights out.

Suzie talked about Roger mostly, and her dreams that included him. Alice entertained Suzie with stories of the palace and the ghost at Charlie's house.

"Tell me another ghost story," Suzie would say, until Alice ran out of them.

"That's all, I can't tell you anything more. That's all the ghost stories I know." The girls giggled uncontrollably.

"Can't imagine sleeping in the same room with a ghost," Suzie said. "Wooooooo." The girls laughed.

"Good night Alice."

"Good night Suzie."

Betty watched Alice. A proud girl, she showed her daughter how to walk balancing a book on her head. She taught Suzie some French words that she had learned from Chef Pierre and taught Betty how to make a French version of fish soup called bouillabaisse. It had all kinds of fish and shellfish in it. The girls helped make the soup. Alice made garlic bread, spreading the baked garlic and butter on French bread.

Everyone raved about the soup. Betty told her bridge club ladies about it. All of them looked over at Alice, sitting with Suzie at the kitchen table.

"She lived in a palace," said Betty. "A chef from France taught Alice to cook French food." They were amazed. All of them going to Alice to introduce themselves before they left. It was as though she was famous or something. Betty did not let on that she was one of the maids in the palace.

The girls were getting along royally. The next dance was just days away.

At night they shared their intimate thoughts about the boys. Suzie about Roger, and Alice about her newfound charmer, Elric. Suzie kept insisting that she could tell he was really interested in Alice. Contrarily, Alice told Suzie that he was everyone's boyfriend, the way the girls all flirted around him. She had watched him talking to a lot of different girls. She didn't feel special at all.

CHAPTER 49

Betty Meets Irene

One morning at breakfast, Betty started talking about Alice's mother.

"Your mother hasn't tried to contact you, Alice. I find that a bit confusing. Do you think Charlie would go and tell her that you have moved?"

"No, I don't think so, Betty. Charlie would not tell her anything now that he has a dirty secret to hide."

"So we will go on Saturday to see her."

A scared, sad look crossed Alice's face. Who wouldn't love Alice? The beauty with the soft golden curls and the green eyes that could take you to another place and time.

"All she wants is the money I make. She doesn't love me. Maybe she didn't know how to love. The nuns didn't teach her love, just how to scrub floors and pray."

"Your mom was brought up by the nuns? Well, that explains a lot. What a sad life she must have had too. When was your last monthly, Alice? Do you remember what day it started?"

"Yes, it was the same day that Charlie did that to me."

"OK then. If it was in the middle of your cycle, we would have to worry about other things, like whether you were with child."

"Oh no," cried Alice, her eyes wide.

"It's OK, Alice. It is impossible if it happened on the same day your monthly started. I'll explain it to you another time. We will stop in to see Doc Thompson sometime this month to make sure everything is OK"

Saturday morning, the girls are up early. Betty entered the kitchen to a spread of French toast and maple syrup. "Wow, you girls are amazing. Thank you so much." They all sit at the table.

"So, let's go over what we need to say to Irene, without stressing her. We will keep it brief and not give her time to say no. Just let me do the talking," instructed Betty.

Wasting no time, they made it to the train station. "Ten o'clock to Oakfield," the conductor yelled. "All aboard!"

The girls sat on one side, Betty on the other.

Deep in thought, Alice watched out the window at the snow-laden fields.

What would her mother be like today? Would she be mad that they came unannounced? Would she even be home? With that horse and buggy, Irene was no longer a prisoner of her own home. What would a child look like, with Charlie for a father?

The last thought sent a shudder through her being.

"Is something wrong, Alice?" asked Suzie.

"Just thinking. What if mother tells me I have to stay? I will run out the door, fast as I can, and down the road back to the train station. I will meet you there. I would rather die than spend another day with her."

The three of them dismounted the train, heading down the road toward Irene's.

Running ahead, the girls threw a few snowballs at each other. They came to the narrow road to the house.

Waiting for Suzie and Betty to position themselves on the steps, Alice knocked. In a minute, the door opened slowly, Irene sticking out her head.

"Well, if it isn't the lost one. Oh, you brought her again." Taking a better look, Betty stared her way. "And who are you?"

"Hi, my name is Betty. I'm Suzie's mother. Hope you don't mind that we came, but I thought it was important that we meet."

"Come in then," said Irene, brushing her hair away from her face, taking off the flour bag apron, hanging it on a hook on the back of the door.

"Should I make some tea, Mother?"

"Yes, that would be good," answered Irene, glaring daggers. "If I knew I had company coming, I would have dressed better," said Irene, looking Betty over.

"Come in and have a seat at the table. Alice will bring the tea."

Betty and Suzie pulled out a chair next to each other. Irene took her seat at the helm.

"It is fine," said Betty. "Let's get down to why I came today. We have taken Alice in to live with us. Where she was living was not fit for a young lady. She is such a bright, kind girl, who is years beyond her fourteen. The girls set a high standard at the candy factory, and Mrs. Watkins loves their work, but with Alice having to work for Charlie too, it is too much to expect from her."

Irene tried to butt in. "But, but…"

"Mother, there is no sense carrying on with that lie. He is not my uncle. And he raped me, Mother," she whined, tears in her eyes now. "How could you send me there?"

Irene swallowed hard, her eyes large.

"We will get to that," said Betty, leading the conversation again.

"I just got her that place to live because it's close to the candy factory," answered Irene.

"Our house is closer to the factory, and Alice does not have to be our maid. We are living together, and she is much happier. We all share the chores, and it's our pleasure to have her in our home."

Wide eyed, Alice stared from Betty to Irene, then to Suzie, who was sitting stone still.

Alice ran out the door and straight down the road. When she got to the end of the driveway, she looked back. Betty and Suzie were just hitting the last cinderblock step. Waving at them now, her heart glad, beating joy through her veins. Waiting and watching, Suzie runs to her, the two of them standing together, holding hands. Still watching her house, she sees her mother standing outside now, shaking her fist and mouthing something.

"What was that, Mother that you said? I just couldn't hear you."

"What? Who are you talking to, Alice?"

"Oh, just my mother. But she can't hear me."

The girls started laughing hard. Betty looked at them, wondering what the joke was.

Betty had felt the heaviness of hatred in the air, seeing for herself that Irene did not seem right in the head. When she got to the door, she turned and spoke to her.

"It was nice meeting you. I will take good care of her."

Irene stared past her, not making eye contact. She didn't say a word, just waited until Betty left, going to the little window over the sink, staring out blankly, into the blinding white beyond.

"All aboard," the conductor yelled.

Everyone is quiet. Private thoughts running rampant through their minds. Betty thought of how strange Irene was. It was a great escape for Alice and Suzie, just happy to be going back home with her best friend.

The talk for the whole week was the dance on Saturday. Betty took the girls to get hot pink material to make matching dresses. Black satin trim around the neckline and hemline, a black sash around the waist. A slit up the back. "Not too high up," said Alice, her modesty showing.

Suzie was admiring her dress. "I love it," she declared. Alice looking her over.

"It's beautiful," said Alice. "Your mom is a great dressmaker. The boys are going to get crazy." Sharing a giggle, Alice wiggled herself into her dress.

Just then Betty showed in the doorway. "Well, don't you two look beautiful? The dresses turned out great."

"Thank you, Mother."

"Thank you, Mother," repeated Alice.

"How about we surprise your mom with a special supper for making these dresses?"

"Sure, what did you have in mind?"

"How about a vegetable quiche, with a side of scalloped potatoes and some chocolate mousse for dessert?" Said Alice.

"Eggs and vegetables, potatoes, milk, onion, and a little flour, for the roux," Alice said. "Cocoa, cream, sugar, and cornstarch is all we need for the best dessert you ever had."

Getting all the ingredients on the counter, Alice started to break the eggs, into a bowl. The girls talked and laughed, working together on the supper. Everything turned out perfectly. The quiche sat on the counter, cooling. The scalloped potatoes were almost ready, the chocolate mousse in fancy glass bowls, with whipped cream on the top. "This is great," said Suzie. "Mother will be pleased."

The girls waited, anxious for Betty to see their creations. Betty returned through the door, bags of groceries in her arms. Alice hurries to take one of them. Betty noticing the spread of food on the table.

"My goodness, you two have been busy. Look at that. Wonderful, let's eat."

"My goodness, Alice, you are sure a good cook."

"Thanks, Suzie helped with everything."

"You girls did a wonderful job. Delicious."

"He really likes me a lot," said Suzie, brushing her hair looking in the mirror. Alice sat on her bed, listening to Suzie talk about Roger…and talk about Roger some more. So happy that she would be seeing him in one more day, so she could stop telling her about him. "Are you excited to see the lead singer, Alice?"

"No, not really. I do like the way he sings, though, and he is the star of the band. Just watching the way he was carousing around was entertaining. It's probably all part of the show."

"You are right. I never thought about it like that before. He is the star of the show." Commented Suzie.

"I suppose you and Roger will be doing the giraffe thing," said Alice, chuckling teasingly. "Necking, that is." The girls shared a laugh, getting back to wrapping chocolates.

"Oh my God, the dance is tomorrow," said Suzie, grabbing her coat and hat. The girls headed out the door of the candy factory, heading home.

Betty had prepared a lovely supper for the girls, grilled cheese sandwiches and hand-cut French fries. *I know how to make something French*, Betty thought to herself while she dipped the potato wedges into the hot oil. Giggling to herself, she wondered if they were really a French invention.

Excitement, hormones accelerated to high, the girls dressed for their big night, helping each other with the finishing touches on their hairdos and makeup.

"We look like twins, Suzie. I love these dresses. The guys will think we are sisters."

Betty stood in the doorway, watching the two of them. Her little girl was growing up fast.

"You girls will be a hit with the guys. Make sure to stay in the hall. You two are not allowed to go in anyone's car or leave the dance hall."

"Of course, Mother, we know that. We can still accept a ride home, though? We did last time."

"You didn't tell me that, Suzie. Who drove you home?"

"Roger, a friend of mine," answered Suzie, not knowing how to get herself out of the question.

"Oh, I see. Keeping things from your mother now? You never mentioned him before, Suzie."

"Ah, he is just a friend, Mother. Don't worry."

Betty left the room shaking her head, walking back down the stairs into the kitchen to make herself a cup of tea. *You just have to trust young people to make the right decisions.* All her advice to her daughter had made her a responsible young woman. Suzie would keep Alice safe from stupid boys.

She could hear the girls coming down the stairs, Betty meets them in the foyer.

"Try to make it before twelve this time, Suzie. I know you girls were quite late the last dance."

"Sure, Mother," she answered, following Alice out the door.

It was a cold, bright, star-filled night.

"We had better hurry," said Suzie, starting to run a little. They made it to the hall in less than fifteen minutes, freshened by the night air, rosy cheeked and invigorated.

There was heightened sense of sexuality in the air. Boys and girls holding hands and stealing kisses.

A group of single guys were already mulling around them, like a pack of hungry wolves.

"C'mon, Alice, let's go in."

The band was setting up on stage. The tall lead singer was talking to the drummer. He turned just in time, his eyes zoning in on Alice. She didn't notice him staring her way, talking to Suzie, who had her eyes glued on the front door of the hall.

The hall was filling up, with more and more couples congregating near the stage.

"Good evening, ladies and gentlemen. Welcome to the best party in town. If you aren't familiar with the band, we are Elric and the Wanderers.

I am Elric." He takes a bow. The girls get wild, hooting and yelling, some extending their arms to him. Looking over the crowd like they all belonged to him, he starts singing.

"When my blue moon turns to gold again..." Throwing back his head, his voice sweet, like an angel just dropped from the sky.

Changing the pace, the band goes into a slow song, the couples getting close. With the girls' attention on the band, they didn't notice Roger, until he slipped in beside Suzie, kissing her on the cheek.

Cozieing up to him, they exchange some whispers. "I'll get you a soda, Alice. I'm just going outside with Roger for a few minutes, OK?"

Handing her the soda, Roger and Suzie walked away toward the door.

Feeling vulnerable again, Alice stands against the wall, sipping her soda.

Guys are walking by slowly, looking her up and down. Not knowing if she should smile or turn her face from them making her feel uncomfortable.

A boy Alice had danced with the last time was walking toward her. Glad that she had already met him, she started to relax.

"Hey, nice to see you again. Can I have the next dance?"

"Sure," she answered, a blush running over her cheeks. The bright pink of her dress giving her cheeks an accentuated glow.

"I'm going for a soda. Would you like one?"

"Yes," she answered, just finishing the one Suzie had brought her.

Elric just happened to be watching when he noticed the exchange of glances. A suitor talking to the girl he was interested in. When he got a break, he would go to her.

The band was getting wild with a fast song, everyone doing the twist, shaking and rocking on the floor.

"We are going to slow it down now," said Elric. As the song started, everyone tried to find the one they wanted to hold close. Roger pulled Suzie onto the floor, Alice watching from the sidelines.

John had just got back with the soda for Alice handing it to her. "Thank you," she said.

"Here, put it down. Let's have a dance," he said.

"Sure," she answered, John taking Alice's hand, leading her to the floor. Pulling her close, her breasts resting on his chest, the closeness making her feel stifled. His breath is hot on her cheeks and neck. Bending he forces his mouth on hers, reminding her of the assault by Charlie, she tries to push him away.

Elric is watching the action. Motioning to the guys to keep playing, he jumps down off the stage. The dance floor opened like the parting of the sea.

The tall singer headed straight to where Alice was, his stride long and strong. Elric pulled on John's shoulder, turning him, punching him square in the jaw, knocking him out cold. John falls hard onto the dance floor. With no movements from him, his head falling to the side.

"I saw what he was doing to you, Alice," said Elric. Everyone stared their way now. Grabbing one of John's legs, he motioned to another guy to grab the other. They hauled him off to the sidelines.

Alice stood in shock, her hand over her mouth, everyone watching her. Elric was headed back her way.

"Alice, let me know if anyone else bothers you. A little thing like you, I'll be watching," he said, walking away now, back toward the stage.

Roger and Suzie ran over to where Alice is standing.

"Are you all right?" said Suzie, staring into Alice's glossy green eyes.

'Yes, I am. He was just holding me too tight, trying to kiss me. I didn't want to kiss him, and I was trying to shove him away. I guess Elric saw it all. I never told him my name, and he called me Alice."

"Who called you Alice?"

"The singer did."

Everyone was back to partying, John came to and stood up, a little wobbly on his feet. His jaw hurt, putting his hand to his face now.

"Fucking bastard. She didn't say he was her boyfriend. Who the fuck does he think he is?"

The band was working on the last song before intermission. Suzie and Alice heading toward the stage. She didn't look up but could feel his eyes on her. Raising her head, his grey eyes caught hers. Smiling at her, he showed his perfect white teeth in a Cheshire grin.

"I'll see you later," he mouthed to her. A few girls near the stage turned to see who he was talking to. A couple of them pointed at her, making Alice feel self-conscious. The same thing had happened at the last dance. They stared straight at her breasts, then back at their own, barely there bumps.

After finishing up the last song, the band put their instruments away. Elric jumped down off the stage. Noticing him coming her way, Alice looked away. He stopped to talk to a few guys and girls, but he was so close now, she could feel him. With a coke in his hand, he positioned himself behind Alice, putting his arm around her shoulders.

"Hey, little one. Sorry for earlier, but I just can't have a guy manhandling my girl."

Turning to face him now, feeling uncomfortable with him touching her. Staring into his stormy grey eyes now. "He wasn't hurting me, just…"

"Never mind, I am watching you, and no guy better get out of hand. Anyway, sugar, I'll be back later to talk to you." Sauntering away, down the hall, his fans taking the opportunity to follow and stop and talk to him, some girls reaching out to touch him, others blowing him kisses.

A few friends of Roger's were standing around now. Reggie moved closer to Alice.

"My name is Reggie. Could I have a dance when the band starts again? Is that lead singer your brother or something?"

"No, he is just a friend, is all."

Reggie, a nice looking fellow, with bright dark eyes and dark hair, kept Alice engaged in a conversation for a while.

Roger and Suzie noticed Elric perching himself on a speaker, not far from where Alice and Reggie were talking, watching as he stared them down, Reggie not budging. When he had seen enough, he made his way over to them.

"If you don't mind," said Elric, staring Reggie directly into his eyes. "I believe I have the next dance with this princess." Pushing his way between them, Reggie backed off, a perturbed look on his face.

Her heart beat fast in her chest, like a frightened sparrow. A strange warm feeling crept across her breasts. What was this effect he was having on her? Her Prince Charming was claiming her as his own, and he had called her a princess. Holding her hands together in front of her, she looked up into his eyes. Elric bent down, whispering something in her ear.

"You will be mine. Do you hear me? Don't go far. I'm coming back to talk to you after the next set."

"OK," she answered shyly, turning her face from him.

In the excitement of it all, Alice hadn't noticed Suzie and Roger had left the hall.

Roger had told Suzie he wanted some private time with her, taking her to the car.

The car was parked alongside the back of the factory, with no other cars around. They climbed into the back seat and wasted no time, Roger pulling Suzie to him, deep French kissing her. The heat of their bodies rose, steaming up the windows. Before long, he had pulled her dress over her head. Without thinking of the consequences, her body did the talking. She wanted him closer. Loosening his belt and his pants, his cock long and erect.

In the heat of her own wanting, she didn't try to stop what was happening. They helped undress each other. His hot body on hers, the coldness of the air stiffening her nipples.

Roger lay on top of her, his penis hard against her stomach.

"Can I, Suzie? I really want you, all of you." There was no answer from Suzie, who was panting, her breath coming in short bursts.

Pushing his penis against her privates with a hard thrust, a deep moan, and a quick cry. Roger put his hand gently over her mouth as he rocked back and forth on her. Pain mixed with pleasure. Suzie held her eyes shut tight. Locked in the sex dance for about ten minutes, Roger let out a loud grunt.

His body slowed, finally resting on her, his head on her chest.

Coming back to her senses, she pushed him off her, started to put her clothes back on.

"That was not the right thing to do, Roger."

"I asked you, and you didn't say no. Anyway, it was bound to happen at some time or another. It's just what lovers do."

"I know it is my fault too for not stopping you. I just don't know what came over me. We had better go back in before people start realizing we are missing." A terrible guilty feeling coming over her, like the worst shame of her life. Pulling her dress back on, she straightened her hair, and they get out of the car.

As they walked through the door, the singer announced the last dance. Alice is standing next to the stage. Suzie noticed her watching the lead singer's every move, in a trance, like a spider's catch, enchanted.

The way his body moved, his voice, his swagger, falling under the spell of her knight in shining armor. It didn't seem right, but her body was defying everything that made sense.

The song finished, Elric jumped down off the stage, standing directly in front of her. A few girls tried to get his attention on the sidelines.

"Hope you don't mind, but I asked someone your name. Ever since I first saw you, I haven't been able to keep my mind off you. The band plays all over Halifax, and we are here every month. You are like an angel," he said. Alice bowing her head.

"There are lots of girls, but you are the most special. You are beautiful. How old are you?"

"Fifteen," she lied. "Just petite for my age," she said.

"I'm nineteen. A little old for you. But the fact is, in a few years you will be old enough for me." They both laughed at that comment.

"Anyway, I got to get going now." Bending down, he put his big hand under her chin, bringing his full lips to hers, kissing her softly then deeply pushing his tongue in her mouth. Pulling away, the tongue gross and wet, the rape coming back to her mind.

"I'll look for you here next month, OK? Don't go falling in love with anyone. I am going to make you my girl. Do you hear me?"

"Yes," she said, looking deep into his mysterious grey eyes.

Suzie and Roger had just walked in, noticing Elric standing over Alice. Suzie wondered what she had missed.

"OK. I got to go, sweetie, got another gig tonight at the Halifax hotel. See you next month," he said as he walked away from her, jumped on the stage putting his guitar in its case. As she watched, he hoisted the guitar over his shoulder, following his other band members out of the hall. Her eyes stayed glued on him till he was out of sight.

It had been a memorable night for both of them. Suzie lost her virginity, the sensations in her private parts reminding her all night.

What had she done? It wasn't the right time or place. Why did she let it happen? Regret and shame. How could she tell her mother? Thinking hard about it, she decided she could not.

Betty had warned her about giving into boys and ruining her chances of a career. They talked about Suzie going to beauty school in another year. The plan was to save money from the candy factory and in due time, start a home based beauty business, something Suzie loved. Every chance she got, she practised her skills on Betty, doing her hair and makeup.

Same thing, day in and day out, she had nothing to look forward to, only more and more chocolates. It was only Alice who had taken her mind off how much she hated the job, her back sore every day after sitting at the conveyor belt for hours.

Roger had arranged a ride home for the girls with one of his friends. Suzie was surprised when he told her that Phillip would drive them home, as he was going that way anyway.

Something had changed. Suzie wasn't talking about Roger, not wanting to say the wrong thing, Alice didn't bring him up either, keeping her private thoughts to herself about Elric, feeling as though it was a secret that she was going to be his girl, and she had agreed.

They went to work every day, home to make supper and clean up, then spent hours reading. One day Alice just had to ask her friend.

"Is there something wrong, Suz? It's just a week till the next dance. You haven't mentioned what we are going to wear. Are we even going? Did something happen between you and Roger. You haven't even mentioned his name?"

Looking at her friend, Suzie's eyes softened. "I have a big secret to tell you."

Alice's eyes grey large, staring, waiting for her friend to spill out the secret.

Just as Suzie was about to share her secret, Betty called the girls into the kitchen.

"I have an exciting announcement. What do you girls think? Let's have a big party for Alice's fourteenth birthday. It will be great fun. I would like to invite all my friends from my bridge club. They were so impressed by Alice's creations. You girls could make an amazing French feast."

"Wow, Mom, that sounds great. What do you think, Alice?"

"Oh my, I would love it!"

Her mind went back to the palace and the grand birthday party they had in her honor. Nothing in her life could ever compare.

"It's a date then," said Betty. "You girls could invite some friends if you like?"

"Mother, actually, I have a friend I've been meaning to talk to you about. Roger, the boy who drove us home from the dance. I really like him mom."

"That brings to mind, you girls haven't been talking about the dance this month. Are you not interested in going? Did something happen the last time?"

Suzie swallowed hard, a quick glance at Alice, then back at her mom.

"No, I just don't feel like going this time. It's all the same thing. The lead singer punched a guy in the face the last time, knocked him out cold."

Before she finished what she was going to say, she decided against telling her mom that Alice was the reason for the fight.

Watching the exchanged glances between her daughter and Alice, Betty knew there were some secrets brewing. Better to wait till the girls wanted to tell her. After all, they were teenagers.

"Mom, just wondering, could I bring Roger to Alice's party? When we saw him the last time at the dance, he asked me to be his girl."

With a sigh of relief, Suzie smiled, anxious for Betty response.

Betty is shocked but knew this day would come.

"Yes, of course. I need to meet this boy."

"Thank you, Mom. We are not going to this dance, but next month we will go. That will be a month from Alice's birthday. It will work out perfect."

That night, when the girls were settling into their beds, Suzie started to tell Alice the secret.

"We did it," Suzie said.

"You did what?"

"Well, you know what Charlie did to you."

Alice gasped.

"Sort of like that, only I wanted to."

"You mean you did that? Oh no."

"Yes, but it has to be our secret, Alice. Mother warned me about what could happen. It went from heavy kissing to something I didn't have any control over. At first it hurt a lot, then the pain turned into something else I can't explain. But since that day, it has become a worry for me. I regret doing it and don't know if I can tell Mom, ever."

Silence. Not knowing what to say, Alice said nothing.

"I know you have a crush on the lead singer. I could see it in your eyes when he was singing to you. Better not tell Mom that you caused the fight."

So many secrets to keep. Growing up was fun, but the new things that were happening were not. Afraid and sad for Suzie, the guilt and shame Suzie was carrying around had changed her from a happy carefree girl, to one she didn't know.

"It's all set then, girls. April ninth. Is that right, Alice?"

"Yes," answered Alice.

"You girls will plan the menu. I want my friends to meet my new daughter."

Putting her arms around Alice, she kisses her on the cheek, Alice looking up at Betty, love and longing in her eyes. There was nothing better than to feel real love from her new family.

"I want you to thrill them with your culinary expertise. Just let me know what I will need to get for the feast."

It was nearing the end of the month again, time for Alice to get paid and get it to her mother somehow, deciding she would not go back there, and if her mother wanted it, she would have to come for it. Realizing the assault by Charlie, had given her some artillery against both of them. Irene didn't know where Betty's house was, only that it was not far from the candy factory. Mentally, she was ready to face her mother if she came looking for her, and give her the money to help her, like she had promised, minus a few dollars she needed, for toiletries and things.

Going back home was not an option, not anymore, not ever.

Payday came and went, no sign of Irene. Two weeks into the next month, Betty asked Alice if she was making the trip to see her mother.

"No, I am not going there. She can come to my workplace. She knows where I am if she really needs to see me."

"Suit yourself," Betty said, not volunteering to go back there either.

Maybe things were better at home. Both of her brothers were working at the Jeffersonses' dairy. Surely they were making enough to keep them without her money. Secretly Alice wished that her mother would never come. *I don't live there, and I don't eat there,* Alice concluded.

Sadie's words were ringing in Alice's ears. The things she had told her about Charlie. In the quiet of her mind, the assault came back to her again and again. Remembering the day he walked in on her in the bathtub, the same bathtub where he killed his wife. Bile rising in her throat, her stomach wretched, her ears feeling like she is in a deep tunnel, the sounds coming muffled.

Go away, Alice would tell her mind. *I never knew a man named Charlie. It was all just a bad dream.*

If she couldn't chase away the demons of thought, she couldn't go on. How could she find her smile? She had to forget, put it far away in the deep recesses of her mind, never to think of it again. The love and happiness she was feeling squashed the sadness of it all.

The next time she saw Sadie, she would tell her what Charlie had said about her being a black witch. No, on second thought, she wouldn't want to hurt Sadie's feelings. *Too bad she isn't a witch,* thought Alice. *She could turn him into a toad.* Laughing to herself, she thought he really did look like a big toad.

"What's so funny?" asked Suzie, listening to her friend giggling to herself.

"Oh, just a fairy tale I read once."

If Sadie was a real witch, she would have known all of Charlie's dirty little secrets. That's why he didn't want Alice to talk to her. It all made sense to her now.

CHAPTER 50

A Birthday Party

The girls couldn't be happier, planning for the upcoming dance and Alice's big bash. They had an extensive menu, all French food: chocolate fondue, bouillabaisse, even French wine. The girls chipped in their money and bought all the special things to treat the ladies of the bridge club and a few of the single girls from the candy factory. Ten ladies from Betty's bridge club and five girls from the candy factory, plus Suzie and Alice, made seventeen.

Brie cheese and liver pate with crackers. French bread, camembert, and a bottle of sauvignon Blanc from the Bordeaux area of France. Suzie was fascinated at the knowledge Alice had absorbed living in the palace.

"Pierre always seemed to have a glass of wine going when he was cooking, using some for his cooking and the rest for him. How about chicken Cordon Bleu as the main meal?" asked Alice, Suzie nodding in agreement.

"Sure to whatever that is," answered Suzie. The girls having a good laugh. The menu was planned.

Excited at all the people coming, Alice decided to put on one of her dresses she had never worn. They were so full of giggles and talk of the dance and party, almost laughed out, permanent smiles on both of their faces, the happiness casting a warm glow around them.

They made new dresses for the dance. Listening to her mother, extending the hemlines, and the necklines higher.

Choosing a lemon yellow silk, with a slip up the side but not far up. While the girls were modeling them, gazing in the full-length mirror, a shocked look crossed Suzie's face.

"What is it, Suz?"

Suzie was staring at her profile and touching her waist area, then ran her hand over her stomach.

"Oh my God, my stomach. I never thought about it till now. I am thicker in the waist too. My stomach never looked like this before. My breasts are tender too, I can hardly touch them. My monthly hasn't come now since we were at the dance two months ago."

Falling onto her knees on the floor, whimpering now, her hands to her face, tears falling onto the floor.

"Oh no, Suz, do you think, you are...with child?"

"Yes, I must be. There is no other explanation. Oh God, how will I tell Mom about this? Nooooo," she cried, running to her bed.

"Please, Suz, don't cry. You make me want to cry, then if your mom walked in and we were both crying, it wouldn't look good." Placing her hand on Suzie's shoulder, she rubbed gently. "It's not the end of the world, Suz. There has to be a way. Pull yourself together. Sit up. Let's talk."

Betty had spent the better part of a day finding the perfect present for Alice. She had heard her complain that she couldn't find her red watch that Mr. Olsen had given her for her birthday. Alice said she might have left it at Charlie's house in the bathroom, and there was no going back there.

The one thing that was bothering Betty, but she didn't want to tell anyone, was that she had noticed Irene with a red watch on when she the girls first went in. Irene went to the parlor and came back without it on. The fact that she took it off made Betty feel suspicious. Was that Alice's watch? That would be the worst possible answer as to where Alice's watch had gone. Wanting to spare Alice any more unhappiness, deciding she would just keep it to herself.

She'd asked the store clerk to show her the card of watches she had in her cabinet. "I am trying to find one for a young lady of fourteen," she said, finding the perfect one—a silver one, shaped in a heart, with a red face and large Roman numerals. "She will love this one," said Betty. "I'll take it. Can you wrap it in red paper with a big silver bow?"

"Yes, ma'am," answered the clerk, walking away with watch in hand.

Betty was pleased with her well-thought-out present. *Alice will get lots of presents,* she thought to herself. She could just see her now, smiling as she opened each of them.

Suzie had bought Alice a gold locket with two hearts, one representing hers and one for Alice's heart. Inside, there was an inscription. Friends for life. Love always, Suzie. A picture of Suzie's pretty smiling face was in one of the heart's petals.

It was the best present she could give her. Everlasting friendship and love.

Suzie realizing more every day how important Alice's friendship was to her.

Right now, she had to find a way to break the news to her mother. She was going to have a baby.

Oh my God, what will Roger think? I don't even know his parents, and I hardly know him. Oh, God, what have I done?

Finishing up her shopping, Betty was anxious to see how the girls were doing with their party preparations. She walked into the house, her arms full of packages. Alice ran to help her. "How did you girls make out?" said Betty.

"Just come in and see," said Alice with a bright, proud smile.

Suzie was standing at the sink, her apron pulled tight around her, looking out into the field. Most of the snow was gone now, a few fresh patches of green. The sun was shining. What was she going to do? Was she really pregnant? There were so many little things she hadn't put together until now. Going to the bathroom through the night—she had never done that before, and the way her nipples hurt. She thought she had gained a little weight, but some months she was thinner than others. She had always had a flat stomach, though, and the way it was rounding out was the main sign that there was a life growing inside of her.

"How are you, dear?" asked Betty, coming up behind Suzie, who hadn't noticed her mother come in.

"Oh, you are home, Mother. Sorry, I was just deep in thought."

"Thinking of that boy, I bet," said Betty, Suzie's eyes growing wide.

"Come in the dining room," ushered Alice, taking Betty's hand. The table was filled with the French delicacies the girls had spent all day preparing. There were balloons and streamers hanging from the ceiling, and a big vase sitting on the table filled with wild flowers.

"It is absolutely beautiful," said Betty, hugging the girls to her. Suzie felt afraid to have her mother hug her, in case she noticed before she was ready to tell her.

All of the worry and deceit was hurting her feelings. She would have to take Roger aside and tell him the news. How would he react? Would he be happy or angry? Surely he didn't have plans for a baby after just doing it once. It was important for her to tell Roger. The girls would have to go to the next dance.

"You can get pregnant from just one time." Her mother's words came back to haunt her. That was what had happened, she was sure.

"I am going to tuck in now," announced Alice after the dinner dishes.

"Big day tomorrow," said Betty. "I think I will do the same." Everyone went to their private rooms, each with their own thoughts.

Betty had noticed a change in her daughter. She had become quiet, pensive, not like her usual giggly self, almost withdrawn even when she had come in, not even noticing her or hearing her talk to Alice. She hoped her daughter was not falling in love with the boy she had asked to bring to the party. Love came with many side effects and a disconnecting feeling from the ones who love you. That must be it, she was falling in love, and Betty knew she had better watch for signs of other things, like intimate relations, she thought. She had taught Suzie about boys, what to watch for, and what not to do. Surely she would listen to the guidance she had given her. Why should she worry? Suzie had always been a good girl, always listening to the advice of her mother.

The girls had spent two days getting Anne's old room ready for Alice to move into. While sharing Suzie's room, it had been like a pajama party every night, but they stayed up way too late. Betty mentioned it would be better for Alice to have her own room.

They all helped paint the room a light lemon yellow, cleaning and dusting until it was perfect. A long walk-in closet was on one side, perfect for all of Alice's clothes.

Standing at her closet, running her hands through the dresses of many colors. She hadn't grown out of any of them, and some were still too big for her, some with the tags still on. Picking out a white one with a lace top and silk underskirt, a rounded neckline, and silk ribbon running around the waist. It was the perfect dress for the event. Searching through her secret pocket in one of her suitcases digging out the emerald necklace Gladys had given her. Too beautiful for words. Holding it up to the light, the green stones enrobed in gold. Only a princess should possess such a gem. A few times she wanted to show it to Suzie but felt guilty for having something so beautiful.

Suzie would ask Alice to tell her about her life in the palace, as though it was a fairy tale. She chanted teasingly, "Alice had a palace." the girls giggling uncontrollably. She was saving the necklace for the right moment to bring the stories all together. Surely Suzie would believe them when she saw the amazing jewels.

Sometimes Suzie would say, "I think you have been reading too much."

When Alice was unpacking her clothes, Suzie stood back in amazement, then asked if she could try on some of the things. She told Suzie she could borrow anything, anytime. Suzie was so grateful. Since she had noticed her waistline expanding, she was afraid to try on any of Alice's special things.

She would wear the necklace for her party, letting the princess come out. Taking the dress down out of the closet, she laid it on her bed, placing the emerald necklace where it would fall around her neck. It was exquisite. After all, it was a special day.

Her mind went back to her birthday party in the palace. It had been the best day of her life. She wanted to live it again. Searching through her many pairs of shoes, finding a pair of pearl-colored ballet slippers.

Suzie lay quietly on top of her blankets, staring into the darkness of her room, her mind far away, full of doubt and regret. Why had she disobeyed her mother's advice? "There will be a right time for these things," Betty had told her. "You'll get married and settle down and have as many children, as you like, but there are other things I want for you, Suzie. Get an education. Go to college." All of those possibilities had just been banished from her.

Tears formed in her eyes. All alone, with her secret, she cried herself to sleep.

Alice woke early and sat up, stretching, smiling. The sun beaming in her room, casting long streams of light showing on the shiny wooden floor, going to the window, a beautiful day, a great day for a birthday for a princess even, she thinks, then giggles.

Sitting down at the dresser, running the brush through her curls. Staring deep into her own emerald eyes, she chanted.

Mirror, mirror on the wall,
Am I the princess of the ball?
Will I be so fair?
Will my chariot take me there?
Will my chariot turn to dust?
Enough with the chariot already.
I am the princess of the ball.
My slipper will not fall.
My prince will come one day.
Right now, I cannot say.
Another place and time.
He said, you will be mine.

"Good morning world. It's a beautiful day." Twirling around on one foot.

Walking out of her room, going to Suzie's door. Listening, then knocking gently, pushing the door open.

"Suzie, are you awake? Let's make strawberry crepes for breakfast, and surprise your mother."

Suzie poked her head out of her covers. "Oh, I don't feel very good."

Jumping out of the bed, she ran past Alice, straight to the bathroom, wretchng into the toilet.

Following her in, Alice stood back, watching. "Are you all right? Should I go for your mom?"

"No, no…" She was crying now, wiping at her face.

Frightened, she runs from the bathroom down the stairs, with the strong smell of coffee wafting out from the kitchen, hurrying in, Betty is sitting at the table, just about to take a drink of her coffee….

Alice's eyes large, not knowing what to say.

"What is it?" asked Betty.

"You had better come. Suzie is getting sick."

Getting up from the table, Betty hurried up the stairs to the bathroom. Suzie is bent over the toilet, dry heaving and crying.

"Oh my God, are you all right?" Helping Suzie up off the floor, taking a wash cloth, rinsing it in cool water, running it over her face.

A deep stare into her daughter eyes, she knew right away.

"Mother, I've been keeping a big secret. Just didn't know how to tell you." Suzie whined, putting her hands over her face.

At that point, Alice realized she should leave and let them have some private time, not wanting to hear Suzie's pleas.

"What are you saying, Suzie?"

Standing back now, she takes a good look at her daughter up and down. "What is it?" she screamed. "No, don't tell me. I'll tell you. You are with child, aren't you?"

"Yes, Mother," Suzie answered in a low whine. Betty raised her arm, slapping her across the face, Suzie's starts crying louder now, all of her worries and frustrations, running down her face.

"That is what you have gone and done after everything I have taught you!"

Suzie slumped down on the floor, Betty continuing her verbal assault.

"You will move out of my house before this baby is born. I am not going to look after a baby." Her voice was loud, trembling. "You will have to marry the guy. What is his name again? Roger, some guy that you met at the dance. Does he know what he has done? I want to talk to his parents. This is a disgrace! Does Alice know of your antics? What kind of example are you setting for your friend?"

Betty backed away from her now. Suzie still on the floor crying, hunched over.

Sitting on the side of her bed, Alice listened for any door closing or footsteps. Betty stormed past Alice's room and down the stairs. Waiting until she is downstairs, Alice goes back out toward Suzie's room.

Betty went straight to her own room and shut herself in, just wanting to lock herself away all day. Throwing herself on her bed, face down, she prayed.

"What is happening to my family, God? Please help us."

Just then she remembered the festivities of the day and Alice's birthday party. "Oh my God. How will I do this now? Give me strength, please, God." There was no way she could cancel. Seventeen women had already planned their day around Alice's birthday. *I will just have to put on my brave face*, thought Betty, wiping at her tears. *It is Alice's day, and nothing should ruin it.* How would Suzie enjoy the festivities now? She was saddened that she had slapped her daughter. They would have to pick up the pieces and go on.

Alice rushed back to the bathroom and looked in the door. Suzie was standing at the mirror, running a washcloth over her face. The right side of her face holding the imprint of her mothers slap, her cheek redenned.

"Oh, Alice," she said quietly. "Can you come here? I need a hug. Mommy hates me now. I told her everything."

"Oh my gosh what did she say?"

"She said I have to move out if I am having a baby," she cried. "What will I do? I am only fifteen."

"No, Suzie, that is not fair," said Alice, starting to cry now too.

"No, Alice, no tears. Remember what day it is?"

"Oh no, and now everyone is upset. No, we will just cancel it," said Alice. "Your mom won't want to have guests now."

"I am so ashamed, Alice," said Suzie, starting to cry again, Alice hugging her hard.

"It will be all right. I will be with you. I will help you with your baby too. Suz, your mom will change her mind."

"Do you think so?"

"She loves you so much, Suz. I just imagine that her heart is broken right now, but a mother's love like hers will mend quickly. She's just in shock. I just hope she is not sad," said Alice.

"C'mon now. We've got things to do, dry your tears. We have lots of guests coming, and your mom wanted the house shining from top to bottom. Let's try and put this all behind us. I just wish it wasn't my birthday today. Everything is all wrong," said Alice, a saddened look in her eyes.

"I am so sorry for spoiling your special day. It's all my fault."

"I still love you," said Alice. "I would cancel everything for you, Suz."

"I haven't seen Roger to invite him, so until I go to the next dance, there is no way I could possibly tell him. I can't go to any more dances either. I am showing already. Look," she said, running her hand over her rounded stomach. "How will I see him again? How will I tell him if we don't go to the dance?"

"I want to go to the dance at the end of the month, Suz. Can't we please go?"

"Yes, we will. I have to see Roger and tell him he is going to be a father."

"Suzie, Suzie," called Betty, her voice on high. "Meet me in the kitchen for a cup of tea. You too, Alice, seeing this involves you."

The girls look at each other, wide eyed.

"Yes, Mom, we'll be right down."

Alice led the way, Suzie coming up behind her, shame written on her face. In the kitchen, Betty is sitting at the head of the table, a pot of tea in the centre, three cups in three places and a saucer with three butter tarts.

"Sit down, girls. I have a few things to say. Thought we would have something sweet while we discuss a few things.

The girls eyed each other as Betty poured the golden tea into the cups.

"First of all, it is Alice's birthday, and she shouldn't be denied her party because one individual was so selfish in making decisions that would ultimately affect everyone." Suzie hangs her head.

"You did wrong, Suzie, and you will be punished for it. I don't want you to feel in any way responsible for Suzie's actions, Alice, and I hope that it won't affect you in any way. You are welcome in the house, no matter what. You pay your way here. Suzie, for you, there are other rules that apply. You have been deceitful, and it hurts me. Now is no time to talk about the past. Right now, we need to think of the future and the future of the baby that is growing in you."

The thought of Roger's baby growing inside of her, a warmth spreading over her chest. A stolen moment of happiness galloping through her mind.

"The other thing is I will be a grandmother, and that is a blessing," Betty went on. "So, for the baby's sake, and our happiness, we will go about this day like nothing has happened. I want to see smiling faces. Tomorrow, Suzie, we will spend the day together, and go see Doc Thompson. Alice, you will tell them at work that Suzie is sick."

"Yes, ma'am," answered Alice, smiling softly.

"Both of you come here," ordered Betty, standing now.

Glancing at each other, the girls approached Betty, who pulled them into her embrace.

"Love will always prevail. God will help us to conquer whatever it is to make this all right. I love you, Suzie. So dry your eyes now."

"I am so sorry, Mom. I love you," she said, hanging her head.

"Right now we will have some breakfast and get busy shining this house. Everyone is set to arrive at two o'clock, which gives us lots of time. I want the both of you to put on your finest."

With renewed hope, the house took on a spanking penny kind of clean, floors shining, everything dusted.

Standing back, the girls take in their handiwork, it was perfect, the house proud to accept its visitors.

"One o'clock," said Betty. "Time you girls went and polished yourselves up for this party. I'll take care of setting up the table and getting the appetizers out. This is going to be a day to remember."

The girls hurried up the stairs to their rooms and shut the doors. Alice's outfit was set out perfectly, laying on her bed, the gold and emerald necklace pulling it all together. *I know it is a bit much, but what is wrong with me wearing it? Just because others might wonder how I, a lowly maid, would have such a gem. I will wear it proudly. I will dress like a princess because I am a princess, he even thinks so….a stolen thought of her prince charming.*

Sitting at the mirror, she pinned up her hair with the pearl pins Gladys had given her. Today, she would be princess for a day. It was her party, and she would not disappoint.

Dressed, she sprayed herself with the fine French cologne, slipping the necklace around her neck, fastening it in the back. Her green eyes picked up the emerald hue. Pulling the ribbon tight around her tiny waist.

The final touch. As she slipped into the pearl ballet slippers a warm fuzzy feeling all over. The princess had arrived.

Looking into the mirror, just about to recite a poem, when Suzie walked into the room.

"Oh my God, Alice. You look like a princess out of a fairy tale! You are beautiful! Wait till Mom sees you." Her eyes catching the magic of the emeralds.

"Wow, I have never seen anything so beautiful, Alice. Is it emeralds? Real emeralds and gold?"

"Yes, Suz. Do you think it is too much? Gladys gave it to me for my going away present."

"I believe everything now, Alice. There were times when I thought you were just making up stories of living in a palace. Not that I didn't like them, but it just seemed so unreal. You are the princess, Alice."

"Thank you, Suzie."

"I am sorry I doubted you. You really did live in a palace."

"Yes, Suzie. Why would I lie about such a thing? It really was just a mansion, but to me it was my palace. I have been a poor waif all my life, and when I worked there, it was like God had given me the best gift ever. If I could make up all those stories, I should write storybooks."

"I guess you are right about that." The girls shared a giggle.

"Stand up, Alice, let me see your dress."

Getting up from the mirror, she turned to face Suzie, giving her a curtsy. Suzie looked Alice up and down.

"All you need is a tiara to look like a real fairy princess."

Bowing her head in humility. "You are too kind, Suz."

"If only your mother could see you now. She just wouldn't believe it."

"No, she never could see me like this. She would want to hide me away, in a dark cellar, until I was dead."

They started laughing uncontrollably.

Suzie wore a dark blue loose fitting dress with empire sleeves. Taking a last look in the mirror, she felt good. Her eyes were bright, her cheeks rosy.

"You look beautiful, Suz."

"Thank you, princess. Should we go downstairs now to see what Mom is doing? I can't wait for her to see you."

As the girls are descending the stairs, a stream of chatter met their ears.

"Sounds like some of the ladies have arrived," said Suzie. "You go ahead of me, Alice. You are the birthday girl."

Holding the sides of her dress, she took every step as though walking on water. Her head held high, she stepped lightly toward the voices.

Betty turned just in time, watching the girls come into the room. A light illuminated around Alice, everyone stopped and looked her way.

"Ladies, I would like to introduce our guest of honor, our birthday girl, Alice."

"My goodness, how beautiful you look," said Betty, her eyes wide.

"Thank you, ma'am," she answered with a slight curtsy.

The strangers all turned to Alice, wishing her a happy birthday, handing her their present. Suzie took them as they came, placing them all on a table in the parlor.

Each of the ladies took time to fuss over Alice's dress and the necklace, the star attraction. It was as though it had a life of its own, given the compliments on the beauty of it and how Alice's eyes were the same emerald color.

With so many compliments and presents, Alice started to feel like she was in a story book again. How could she be getting all this love from strangers?

Thanking them all, and answering their questions, Betty and Suzie stood back, letting Alice have the stage. They watched how her friends were treating Alice, like she was truly a princess, with her golden curls and her emerald eyes.

"If everyone would like to go into the dining room, we have a French feast awaiting."

Betty stood at the dining room entrance, watching and waiting until everyone had found a seat. Although the table had ten chairs, the girls brought in a couple of chairs from the veranda.

"Alice, if you would take the seat at the head of the table today."

With the buzz of laughter and happiness the room was warm and fuzzy all over.

Everyone complimented the food, amazed at the French creations.

Betty was dishing out the strawberry ice cream when there was a knock at the door.

"Mmm, wonder who that could be?" Taking an inventory of the guests, opening the door, and a tall black lady with a small boy next to her.

"Hello," said Betty. "Can I help you?"

"Yes," answered the black lady. "We came to see Alice. Is she at home?"

A few of the ladies poked their heads around the corner to see who had arrived.

"Yes, of course. I will call her for you."

"Alice, you have company," announced Betty.

"We are just having a birthday party for Alice. Would you like to join us? There is lots of food and cake and ice cream." Betty smiling at the little boy, holding Sadie's hand. "How old is he?"

"He is three," answered Sadie.

"I bet you would love a piece of cake with ice cream," said Betty, bending towards Jacob.

Alice comes around the corner.

"It's my friend Sadie West." Betty watched as Alice embraced her, resting her head on Sadie's chest before pulling back with a soft, adoring look.

"I'm so happy you came. How did you know this was my birthday?"

"I didn't know, chile. I was passing through and wanted you to meet Jacob. I might say, you do look like a princess today, Alice. So beautiful, almost sinful, a girl could look so pretty. Angelic, I mean to say."

"Thank you, Sadie. I am so happy you are here to share my special day." Bending to his child level, Alice grabbed both his hands.

"Hello, Jacob, pleased to meet you. I bet you would like to have some cake and ice cream?" Large, watery almond eyes stared into Alice's own emerald ones, the boy getting lost in the green pools of water. Hugging his grandma, shying away from Alice, then looked back at her with a bright, loving smile.

"He is so cute," said Alice. "I would love it if you could stay, Sadie. Is it OK, Betty? Sadie is like my mother from another time. I've known her since I was a little girl."

Betty went quiet for a few seconds, wondering if she heard right what Alice had just said.

"Of course they can. There is lots of food. Let me take your coat. You can go in and join the festivities."

Sadie took off her long black wool coat, handing it to Betty. "Thank you, ma'am." Smoothing down her high-necked black blouse with white scalloped edges and her long black ankle length skirt, she took Jacob by the hand, following Alice into the dining room.

"C'mon, Jacob, let's go get you some cake," said Alice, taking his hand, leading him into the kitchen. There were a few ladies mulling about with tea and small plates, a buzz of chatter and laughter. Just as Alice entered with Jacob, the laughter came to a standstill, as though the music had been turned off. Everyone stared now at the little dark boy in a blue pants and shirt with a white V-neck sweater.

"This is Jacob, everyone." Just then, the elegant tall black woman showed in the doorway, watching Alice. Her magenta head dress was regal, for a queen. The guests were all taken aback.

Fidgeting now with their plates, some put down their tea cups, some looked away, with a few smiles for Jacob.

"It is my birthday, too," said Jacob in a sweet, little boy voice.

A few giggles, but not enough to explain a beautiful little boy imagining it's his birthday too.

Immediately, Alice felt a chill come over the gathering. Why? What had changed? Then she realized that some of these women probably had heard the stories of Sadie being a witch. How stupid. There had to be some way that she could explain her friend was a God-loving woman, and such talk was just nonsense.

Sadie too felt the coldness from the revelers.

"Maybe Jacob and I should go, Alice. It's not right to just come to a party without being invited."

"No, no, I insist. It wouldn't be a fun birthday for me if you left without some of the wonderful things Suzie and I made. All French food. And the cake. Come, wait till you see the cake. Betty spent all day making it."

Sadie held Jacob's hand tightly while Alice walked them over to the counter with the three tiered cake. A white cake with thick cloud icing and raspberry preserves in the layers of white. Plump red raspberries spelled out Alice in a beautiful red against the purity of white. Jacob's eyes lit like the candles on the cake.

Betty handed Sadie a plate.

"Help yourself. We have more than enough to go around. Here is a plate for Jacob too." Handing her a smaller plate.

Sadie dished herself out a few small servings on her plate, then fixed one for Jacob, who she sat next to her. Sadie looked up to see a few frozen faces watching, turning her eyes from them. Alice was spreading joy to some of the women when she walked back around the table and sat down on the other side of Jacob. A happy little boy, loving his cake.

The air was thick, the laughter and chatter quieted, Betty noticed now too the change in the women. Trying to ignore the chill, she got up and put on some music. With some piano music, everyone got back to eating and talking.

One of the ladies from the bridge club walked over to the table, near where Sadie was sitting. She had reddish brown hair, heavy, bloated cheeks, and deep furrowed lines in her forehead, setting down her half eaten piece of cake near Sadie.

"Well, nobody told me there would be a nigger coming to this here party, or I sure wouldn't have come. Let's go, Hazel," she said, turning to her friend, another heavy set, dark, curly haired woman, who plunked down her plate, the cake eaten, just a few crumbs, like her thoughts left.

Shocked at what she had just heard, Alice spoke up.

"What was that you said?"

Sadie stiffened, glaring her dark eyes at the woman who spoke.

"Let not you judge me! You don't know me. God is my only judge. I only serve him, not humankind, and surely not you. Alice is my friend, and she invited Jacob and me. God forgive you for your ignorance."

"So now you are calling me ignorant? I'm not taking that from no nigger wench," the fat lady spat. Picking up her piece of cake, she plastered it into Sadie's face. Jacob's white of his eyes bright, scared.

"Oh my God," screamed Alice.

"Enough, what are you doing? Get out! Get out of this house!" The white cake slid down the side of Sadie's face, where the visible pink scars showed on her dark skin. Alice wiped at Sadie's face, crying now.

"I am so sorry, Sadie. I don't even know this woman and don't want to ever know her." The cake was smeared onto Alice dress now, the raspberries like blood on the front of the bodice.

Betty came over to the table now, her eyes wide.

"What in God's name? What is going on here?"

"This woman threw cake in my friend's face." Alice in tears now, mixing with the redness of the raspberries, smeared on her dress.

"Get out of my house, and never do I want to see you again!" ordered Betty, pointing to the door. The fat lady and her friend were already halfway to the door. They put on their coats, went out, slamming the door behind them.

"Alice, go and wipe down your dress before it stains. Sadie, come to the bathroom. You can clean yourself up there. I apologize for that stupid woman. So much for her in my bridge club. Not anymore. I will quit before I sit down to tea with her again. Just goes to show you how ignorant some people can be."

"Don't worry, ma'am. If that is all that happens to me is I get a little cake in the face, I am hardly saddened. It was sweet, and we were able to rid the party of the negative energy that was trying to ruin Alice's party. The air feels lighter in here now." Sadie got up from the table and walked toward the bathroom, with Jacob in tow.

Everyone got back to eating and talking. The laughter returned, lighting up the room. Smiles and love were restored. The party went on. Alice got the stain out of her dress with a little bleach and soap.

"That was the rudest thing I have ever seen," said Betty.

Standing, she looked at her guests and addressed them.

"I would like to properly introduce Sadie. She has been Alice's friend since Alice was a little girl. There will be time for a story after we have our cake. Sadie, would you be so kind as to do the honors?"

"Yes, indeed."

All the women, excited at a story, stared at the beautiful ebony-skinned Sadie. The magenta scarf around her head her crowning glory. A few of the ladies came closer to shake Sadie's hand and give their respect. The raised pink scars of a warrior. She would recite the story that was written on her face. One by one, they retreated to the parlor for story time.

With the last lady seated, and Jacob and Alice sitting together on an overstuffed chair, Sadie took the stage.

"If it wasn't for the Lord Almighty, Jacob would have been lunch for the big cat." A loud ahhhhh went through the ladies. "A huge cougar, about two hundred pounds, pounced into the wagon from a tree above. We had just started on our journey, Jacob in his basket in the back of the wagon. He was a mere babe of two months. My daughter died giving birth to him. He is my grandson, and God's son. The cat landed almost on my head, digging its teeth deep into my scalp, ripping the flesh from my face, as you can see from the scars on my face." Opening her blouse, she showed the scars running down her chest. All mouths fell open.

"I jumped on top of that cat. I reached down deep into its throat, and I pulled its tongue straight out of its throat. I called out God's name, and the strength he gave me, I cannot explain." Stretching her arm out, she displayed the scars of disturbed flesh running down her arm.

Wows and amazement filled the room, everyone listening and watching the storyteller. "I had just lost my daughter, and there was no way I was going to lose my grandson." Jacob watched his grandmother with pride and love in his eyes, Alice hugging him close.

Sadie stood, taking a bow, everyone clapping, sending love and admiration to the amazing warrior woman.

"What a wonderful story," said Betty. "Thank you, Sadie, for telling it to us. This has been the best part of the party, and of course the cake. Anyone for seconds?"

A few women followed Betty back to the kitchen, where the cake was sitting in testament of celebration. Jacob came up behind them, everyone clearing a way for the little boy with his plate.

Suzie came up behind Alice. "Have you forgotten? You have a whole pile of presents in the parlor."

"Oh, I will get to them later," she answered, keeping an eye on Sadie, who was heading toward the door.

Walking to the door now, Sadie put on her coat and Jacob's. "Thank you for making this a special day for Jacob. Although we had a little drama, it was still wonderful, Alice. You never know where the Lord will lead you, and today he brought me to you."

"Yes, Sadie, thank you for coming, and I hope I see you soon." Betty walked toward the door now too to say her goodbyes.

"Sadie, I want to apologize for the incident. It was an eye opener for me about that woman. It was wonderful having you and Jacob. Please, anytime you are going through, come and join me for tea."

"Thank you, Betty. I will take you up on that offer. Goodbye, Alice."

"Goodbye, Sadie. Goodbye, Jacob. Oh no, wait just one minute."

Running into the parlor where the presents were stacked, she saw a brown bear with a red ribbon around his neck and moveable arms. Grabbing up the bear, she ran back to Jacob and handed him the fuzzy brown bear.

"It's mine?"

"Yes, it is," said Alice. "You can call him whatever name you want." Everyone's eyes were on the little boy, his eyes bright.

"I will call him Baby Bear, answered Jacob, a proud look on his child face.

"That is a great name. How about a big hug, and I'll see you soon, OK?"

Jacob clung to the bear, hugging Alice with his other arm.

"Take care now, Alice. God bless and watch over you. And you and your family, Betty."

Thank you Sadie, have a safe trip."

"When you have the Lord, you fear nothing. He rides along with me. The best passenger you could ever have in life."

"Yes, indeed," answered Betty, with a big hug and smile for the beautiful black woman.

The women slowly dispersed toward the door, saying their goodbyes. Betty, Alice, and Suzie bid them all a good day.

The house seemed odd, with the buzz of chatter and the laughter gone out the window, like the abandoned ark of Noah. The house had become a spiritual temple, God coming to the party in so many ways.

"I will go and get changed now, Suz, and we will get busy and clean the house."

"Just wait one minute, Alice. Would you open just one present?"

Betty handed Alice a small red box. "Hope you like it."

Taking off the ribbon and bow, Alice held her surprise as though it was a new robin's egg. Carefully, she opened it. It was a silver heart-shaped watch with a red face and silver numbers.

"I know you missed your watch, Alice. Here, let me put it on you."

"I love it so much, Betty, thank you. I love you."

She hugged Betty, who kisses her on the cheek.

"I love you, Alice. Sadie is an amazing lady. You said you have known her a long time?"

"Yes, since I was a little girl. She has been like an angel to me. Comes along just when I need her, and gave me hope as a child that my life would change. When my mother told me, Sadie was my real mother, I would sit and watch for her to go by, sometimes for hours. That was long before she got the horse and buggy. I would see her walking down the road, and always wondered when she was coming back for me. When I grew older, I realized it was just another one of my mother's lies.

"Well, that is quite a story in itself. Just don't get why your mother would deny you, Alice? The truth of the matter is I believe your mother has mental health issues. She didn't seem right."

"C'mon Alice, let's get changed and get this place cleaned," urged Suzie.

"Yes, right away," answered Alice, following Suzie up the stairs to her private room.

Getting out of the dress and slipping the jewels off her neck, she put it back in the green velvet box. She thought over everything that had happened. Wow, she thought. What an amazing day it turned out to be. She had a private chuckle at the little boy, Jacob.

Alice put on her overalls and a sweater, then hurried back downstairs into the kitchen. Betty and Suzie were taking dishes to the sink, putting things away.

"No, dear, said Betty. "This is your day, Suzie and I will handle the cleanup. You can take your presents upstairs and have some private time for yourself."

"OK then, if you insist," said Alice. "Thank you for making my day so wonderful."

"Suzie and I need some private time."

"Yes, of course. See you later, Suz," she said, walking away toward the parlor. Gathering an armful of presents, she took them up the stairs to her room. Three trips later, they were all spread out on her bed.

Deep in thought, she realized strangers could be anything. Today she had learned that you couldn't trust them. Life was unfolding for her like a new card game, her hand changing again. Suzie's hand had changed drastically, she thought, upsetting the whole security of the life she knew. She would learn from Suzie's mistake. That brought thoughts of the lead singer. She wondered if he had been looking for her at the last two dances, anxious to see him again, hear his voice. How would her cards be dealt?

Would she win or lose to a wild card?

The cards were dealt, and the game of life would go on.

Oh, darling, save the last dance for me.

Dancing was the only thing on the girls' minds now, tomorrow, Saturday, the big night. Betty had thought long and hard about Suzie's predicament, feeling bad about how she had reacted. There was no way she could banish her daughter with her baby, but she needed to meet Roger and his parents. They had to decide what would happen to the young couple. Should they marry? Who would look after the baby?

If Suzie remained at home, she and Alice would help her raise her child. Betty imagined a little one running around, bringing a smile to her lips. Her grandchild. Surely Suzie would have learned a hard lesson from all of this. She just had to take her to the doctor to get the details on when and how far she was along.

Saturday morning, the girls and Betty met in the kitchen for breakfast together. Up early, Betty had made a special breakfast for the girls. Crepes, the way Alice had shown her. Fresh strawberries, whipped cream stuffed into the weightless pancakes that melted on your tongue.

Suzie was searching her mother's face for clues. Did she still love her? Would she give the girls permission to go to this last dance?

"Good morning, darlings," she said as the girls entered the kitchen, pulling out a seat.

"Mother, this is fabulous," said Suzie.

"Yes, mmm," said Alice.

"Well, you girls eat your breakfast, then I want you to go over this house with a fine-toothed comb. Clean and polish everything. We will be having guests soon."

A questioning look came across the girls' faces.

"I will need to see Roger's parents. We have to go over the details of everything."

"Yes, of course, Mother. That brings to mind, Alice and I need to go to the dance tonight so I can tell Roger and have him tell his parents that they have to come and see you."

"That is fine, but this is the last dance. You have things to do now in preparation for your new baby. It won't be about you anymore. A child has many needs. Tonight you must be home before twelve. If you are not in by the strike of twelve, your chariot will turn to dust, and your horses into mice."

The girls laughed so hard, till their bellies hurt.

"I love you, Mother."

"I love you, Mother."

"I love you both back. Now get busy, and I'll see you when I get back from town."

For tonight's dance, the girls would dress differently. Alice chose a cream colored dress, tight to her slim figure, and a wide red belt announcing her tiny waist. Suzie chose a loose fitting navy dress. She was still slim, and the dress camouflaged her baby bump. Her cheeks were rosy, her eyes sparkling like the blue of an ocean.

It had been a beautiful spring day, the evening warm and inviting. They finished up their makeup and hair, taking time to look each other over, making everything perfect.

Hurrying out the door and down the road toward the candy factory. Alice has butterflies in her stomach. She couldn't wait to see him. Suzie was thinking of how she would tell Roger about the baby. What would he say?

The girls walked along, quiet, Alice staring into the clear night sky. Spring was in the air, she had a happy skip in her walk. "You are excited to see him, aren't you, Alice? I can see it in your starlit eyes."

"Yes, I am anxious," said Alice, thinking of her prince.

Before they knew it, they were there. A few cars were in the parking lot, bunches of girls and boys standing here and there. Alice and Suzie made it to the doors, with Roger running toward Suzie. "Oh, my, I thought you would never come back. I have missed you." Staring deep into her blue eyes. "Come, we have to talk," he said, pulling her aside.

"I will go in and wait for you," said Alice with excitement and longing.

"Fine, see you shortly," answered Suzie.

Roger walked Suzie over to a tree, leaning into her, trying to kiss her. She turned her cheek.

"What? What is it? Didn't you miss me? Has something changed since I last saw you? Aren't you my girl?"

Staring deep into his brown eyes, she said, "Yes, something has changed. Roger, I am with child." Tears started to pool in her big blue, glossy eyes.

"You are what?" answered Roger, standing back now, looking her up and down. "You mean?"

"Yes, Roger, the one time we did it, and now I am pregnant. It's almost cost me my mother's love."

Roger stiffened. "Just a minute. So you say that you are carrying my baby? This is all wrong, Suzie. I have been deployed to France to fight on the front lines. I cannot help you with a baby. I am leaving next month, and who knows if I'll even come back at all."

"Oh no," said Suzie. "I don't know what to say. Only that I am sorry, but it wasn't just my doing. We did this together."

"Are you sure of all of this, Suzie?"

"Yes, I haven't seen my monthly since I last saw you. My mother wants to meet your mother and father, and share the news. She said we need a plan, like you and me getting married."

Roger stood quiet, a shell-shocked look on his face. "My father was killed in the war. I only have my mother."

"I am sorry," answered Suzie, looking sympathetically at her lover.

He hugged her to him now. "I have missed you so much, Suzie. It's going to be hard to be away from you. I don't' know when I'll be back. Will you still be my girl, Suzie?"

"Yes, Roger, I will miss you so much. I will probably look different when I see you again."

"You are beautiful to me, and now that you are having my baby, you will be mine forever."

He bent to kiss her, a loving, intimate bonding.

Then, getting down on one knee, he looked up into her blue pools of love. "Will you marry me, Suzie?"

"Yes, of course, Roger. Ah, I am so happy." They held each in a forever embrace.

"Everything will work out, Suz. I love you."

"I love you, too, Roger."

CHAPTER 51

Alice's eyes scanned the hall. No sign of Elric. The other guys in the band were walking around, talking to some of the revelers. Her eyes finally spotted him, face to face, with a girl up against the wall. Just then, she watched as he bent into the blonde girl, kissing her. His body was pushed up against her, his hands holding her around her waist. Then he extended his hands to her behind. *Oh no*, she thinks, disgusted. How could she have been so stupid, to think that he was really her guy? He was everybody's guy, just like she had first told Suzie. Feeling like such a fool, she starts to walk the other way. *Forget him*, she told herself, feeling stupid.

Just then a boy walked up to her.

"Hello, Alice," he said, making eye contact. "Remember me? My name is Anthony. We danced before."

"Of course," she said. "I would love to." He put his arm around her waist, leading her to the dance floor.

Elric had pulled himself away from the blonde girl and was now walking back toward the stage, when he spotted Alice with a boy. Walking right by them, he looked back, making eye contact with her.

"Remember, angel. Save the last dance for me." A charming smile for Alice and a look that said *I'll take a bite out of you* for Anthony.

Walking back to where they were standing, Elric glared at Anthony.

"Hey, buddy, that is my girl, so easy with her."

"Sure, man, just dancing."

"He is your boyfriend, Alice?"

"Not that I know anything about. I think he is crazy. He thinks all the girls belong to him."

The dance went on, Alice and Anthony sharing a few quick beat tunes. The Wanderers delivered as usual, the revelers in high spirits. The lead singer put them all in a trance, his voice intoxicating.

Roger and Suzie had come into the hall, deep in conversation.

"When should I bring my mother?" asked Roger.

"How about in a week next Saturday. Come for lunch. Mother and I will be waiting for you."

"OK, Suzie, I don't feel like being here. I will head home now and find a way to tell Mother."

"That's fine," answered Suzie. "Alice and I have to be going soon too." Kissing her long and soft, he walked away from her, heading to the door. Looking back once, Suzie staring his way.

Spotting Suzie standing by herself, Alice made her way to her.

"Are you all right, Suzie? Where is Roger?"

"He left, Alice. I told him everything. He asked me to marry him! Oh my God, I am so happy now, Alice. Do you believe it? He has been enlisted to fight in the army and is leaving soon for France. We will get married when he comes back. Mother will be happy."

Her friend's happiness was important to her, but now it meant a new hand for Alice. Suzie would be leaving the house, and she would be alone with Betty. How things could change so fast when you didn't expect it?

Suzie noticed Alice's sullen demeanor. "Aren't you happy for me?"

"Yes, of course, it is just that it will mean changes for my life too. Will your mom still let me live there?"

"Of course, Alice. Mother loves you. Can't you tell? I'm sure you could stay with her till you are old."

The girls started laughing uncontrollably. The happiness for Suzie, the sex in the air, the confrontation with Elric, all of it presented itself in hysteria.

"How's it going with lover boy, Alice?"

"Never mind. He is not my lover boy. And the nerve of him. I was dancing with a fellow, and he came by us and told Anthony that I was his girl. When I first came in, he was necking with a girl. She was up against the wall, his hands all over her. He is sickening. I don't want anything to do with him."

"Can't believe he thinks he owns all the pretty girls," answered Suzie.

"Whatever, I am not his girl. Let's get out of here before he bothers me again."

The band stopped their set just as the girls started heading toward the door. As they were going through the door, a hand touched Alice's shoulder, turning her around. Elric stared hard at her.

"Not so fast, young lady. I want a few words with you. If you don't mind," he said, looking at Suzie.

"We were just leaving," said Suzie, giving him a stern look.

"This will only take a minute," he said.

Putting his hand on Alice's arm, he ushered her back into the hall. Suzie came back in too, standing not too far, watching her friend. Leaning up against the wall, he pulled Alice to him. "Where have you been? I thought I had lost you. I am going away for a while, and I needed to see you before that happens." He applied a little pressure to her arm, as she stared into his stormy grey eyes.

"When I come back, you will be old enough to leave with me. It might be a year or more. What I want to say to you is you must stay at the candy factory and continue living with Suzie and Betty."

Concerned and interested, she listened to every word. How did he know Suzie's mother's name?

"I am coming back for you. Be ready, darlin'. You will never wrap another chocolate. I'll be your candy, I'll be your sugar daddy, sweetie." Leaning into her, he kisses her, the fullness of his lips the sweetness of his breath, made her dizzy. He kissed her long and gently, a firm hand behind her head she couldn't pull herself from the kiss. Giving into the embrace, she kissed him back.

"You will wait for me. Say you will," he demanded.

"Yes, I will," she answered in a provocative whisper, all of her senses, turned on.

"That is all I need to know right now. So I got to go, get back to the city. Got some things to do. I just needed to see you one more time and confess my love for you. This is the last dance for me here. I will just surprise you one day and sweep you off your feet."

Giggling at his quick wit, charming too, but the prince part she couldn't quite envision.

"Another thing: save yourself for me. You are a virgin, right?" She nodded, no eye contact.

"Look at me," he ordered, staring into her innocent green eyes. "I have staked my claim on you. You are mine."

Staring into his eyes, no depth, just grey clouds, a shudder running through her. Kissing her one last time, he led her over to where Suzie was standing. "Take care now. I'll be seeing you."

Sauntering away toward the stage, Suzie staring at her friend, a blank look on her face, like she is lost in a storm.

"What just happened, Alice?"

"I'm really not sure, Suz. Let's just go home."

On the walk home, the sky is bright, the girls both enamored with their thoughts. Alice thought of her Prince Charming, swooping down on his white horse, taking her to a castle far, far away.

Suzie's mind was on Roger, their baby, and a wedding. It was all so overwhelming, she didn't know if she should cry or laugh.

In a blink, the girls were at the house, walking up the stairs to the door.

Suzie smiled, following her friend in. The girls made their way up the staircase, both heading in their room directions.

"Good night Alice."

"Good night, Suzie."

CHAPTER 52

A buzz in his head, the whiskey in his blood turned to firewater, lighting something in him.

He went straight to his car, parked alongside the back of the hall. The pretty blonde girl is there waiting for him.

There is a nervous excitement in his mind. He had watched her at almost every dance. She was a tease, going from one guy to the next. Fluttering around like a butterfly, landing on different suitors. Tonight, he would taste some of that nectar. Getting into the driver's seat, he reached for her right away, grabbing at her breasts. She moved into him, kissing him. Finally, her main conquest, the lead singer. Every girl wanted a piece of him, and he chose her.

"Let's drive a little," he said. "Just out a ways from this place. Go somewhere private."

"No, I can't go anywhere, I came with friends, and they will wonder where I have gone," she answered with a teasing smile.

"We won't be gone long enough for them to miss you," he said, pulling out onto the road. Before she could rebel, he pulled in behind an old abandoned farmhouse.

"C'mon, let's get in the back seat, where it's more comfortable." Grabbing for her, he pushed her into the back seat and moves in next to her, pulling the door closed.

Before she knew what was happening, Elric had pulled her clothes off and was undoing his pants. He bit at her nipples and forced her down on the seat. Pushing and pulling at her panties, he covered her naked body with his. Pushing her legs apart, he wasted no time ramming his hard penis into her private place.

Thrusting at her with no mercy, she started screaming.

"You are hurting me. Let me go!" As he continued his assault, she tried biting his face, grazing his ear with her teeth. Slapping her hard across the face, he pushed her face to the side, holding her head with his big hand, he continues raping her, rocking on her body till he stiffened, shooting his sperm into her. Getting up off her, he pulled his pants back up.

"Fuck you, you bitch, you know you liked it. You are nothing but a cock tease. You got what you deserved," he said, vile in his voice. "Get the fuck out of my car."

Crying, her hair in her face, she tries to wipe at her face. Pulling her clothes back on, opened the back door, stumbing out, almost falling face first. Picking herself up now she looks behind, was he coming back for her? Running down the road now, in her stocking feet, not taking time to put her shoes back on, trying to get as far away from the madman as she could.

Pulling the car out onto the dirt road, he raced away, billows of dust left behind as he fled the crime scene.

In the early morning hours, during her rapid eye movement sleep, Alice dreamed of her Prince Charming, but he wasn't on his horse, he was leaning into the blonde girl, kissing her.

Waking herself from the dream, she sat up. "What a stupid dream," she said out loud. Lying back down, she could feel his full lips on hers, her fingers to her lips, she falls back asleep.

Saturday, the day of Roger's visit, with his mother, came and went.

Suzie dressed in an appropriate loose fitting top and skirt. She was watching, pacing back and forth like a caged animal. Betty watched her anxious daughter, feeling her sadness, biting down on her own lip. As the darkness bleached out the dream of seeing him and the hopes for closure with his mother, Suzie excused herself, running up the stairs to her room, shutting herself in with her private thoughts. Uncertainties came down over her, sadness, feeling rejected and alone. In the darkness of her room, she cried herself to sleep.

The next morning, Alice met Betty in the kitchen. Suzie was still in her room. They discussed the disappointment of Roger not showing. Betty assured Alice that they could be Suzie's support system and that they could handle it together.

"Just give her some time today, Alice. She was sad yesterday. With a wonderful friend like you, and all the love we give her, she will be fine."

Roger never did come. He was killed in the war at the French port of Dieppe.

He had sent his mother a letter from France, telling her about Suzie and the baby, professing his love for her and his intent to marry the girl.

The Saturday they were supposed to go, he got cold feet. Being deployed to the war was heavy on his mind and all he could handle.

Six months after his departure, a letter came announcing his death. Feeling helpless and alone, her only son was dead.

When the immediate shock and sadness settled around her heart, Cindy decided it was time to go and find Suzie and give her the news. The excitement at seeing the baby shook out the sadness, like sand from a blanket. Roger had left her a piece of himself in a child. Not all was lost, giving her renewed happiness. She was going to be a grandmother. What a joy a child could bring.

The burden of grief started to lift, like a heavy fog being burned out by the bright sunshine of a child.

Doing the math, she decided to wait, until the baby was born. It would give everyone time to adjust to the loss of her son.

CHAPTER 53
Preparations for Baby

With the baby more and more apparent, there was no room for sadness. There was painting the baby's room, buying baby clothes, excitement in the air for a baby coming to the world in less than a month.

In the back of her mind, Suzie couldn't give up on the thought that he would come to her and the baby. Betty assured her that she would help her raise the little one, and they would be a big happy family.

"You can still go to college, Suz. It's not the end of the world. A new life, your baby, my grandchild."

Smiling, Suzie, cradled her hand over her rounded stomach, feeling the baby kick.

Two weeks before the due date, Suzie went into labor in the middle of the night. Screaming, Alice and Betty were awakened, running to her bedside. "I think it's time, Mother. They are coming every twenty minutes."

"We have no time to get the doc. Alice, you and I are going to have to deliver this baby. Get me some towels and a basin with warm hot water."

Suzie was screaming now, "It hurts, oh, God, it hurts so bad." Grabbing for her mother's hand she squeezed hard.

"It's OK, it won't be long," assured Betty. "Push hard when you feel the contraction."

A few more screams and more contractions, and the baby slid out, covered in yellow mucus and white fluid. Betty washed the baby, Alice's eyes are wide as Betty cut the umbilical cord, placing the crying baby on Suzie's stomach.

"It's a boy," Betty announced, jubilance in her voice.

They hadn't noticed Alice had passed out and was slumped over in the chair.

"Wow," said Betty. "Looks like it was too much for Alice. I'll get the smelling salts. She passed out."

After running the bottle under her nose, Alice came to, staring toward the bed. "Oh my, your baby, Suzie," she said. Excited, she came closer. "It's a boy, Alice. Isn't he beautiful? He looks just like Roger."

Everyone in the household adjusted to the new member of the family. The women had it down to a science, the care of the little boy, Roger Amour Williams.

Cindy, Roger's mother, couldn't wait a day longer to meet the baby, waiting for Suzie, one day after work, at the candy factory.

Watching as the girls came out, one by one, she knew when she saw Suzie. She was exactly how Roger had described her. Beautiful, wavy dark hair, and blue eyes, medium height.

"You must be Suzie," she said, extending her hand to her.

"Yes, ma'am, and you are Roger's mother." Recognizing the same golden brown eyes.

"I came to see the baby, Suzie. Would it be all right for me to come home with you today?"

A questioning look on her face, she waited for her to tell her where Roger was and when he was coming.

"I have some bad news, Suzie. Roger was killed in France."

The women held each other and cried out their love for him.

She showed Suzie the letter he wrote, professing his love for her and his intention to marry her. It gave her back her happiness and willingness to raise his child with love.

"We both lost him, but now we have—what did you call him?"

"Roger Amour Williams. He will carry my last name."

"I love his name, Suzie. Thank you for honoring my son."

Staring into her grandson's eyes, tears of joy ran down her face, a loving grandmother smile. "Oh, Suzie, he is beautiful. I will help you any way

I can to raise this little boy. Thank you for giving me a piece of my son back." The women embraced, Suzie and Cindy sharing in their loss and love of their blessing.

Within a few days of baby Roger's arrival, Alice noticed her life was changing again.

Their usual time for gossip, reading books, and makeup was interrupted by the care of the baby. Alice involved herself as much as she could. Missing out on her special time with her friend, she started to daydream a lot, keeping her private thoughts to herself.

Betty couldn't keep her hands off her grandson, vying for his attention and smiles. Baby Roger brought Suzie and Betty together in a whole new capacity of love.

There was more private time for Alice, and her hopes for her own life, not living in the shadows of the new baby. The things he had said gave her reason to dream. The way he has said he would take her away, she didn't doubt him for one minute.

His insistence of her staying with Betty and Suzie, until he came for her. And how did he know she lived with Betty and Suzie? He had made it his point to find out everything about her. Truly, he must be in love with her.

As the months flew by, she grew weary, with too much work and no play, wanting more for her life. Her job was still great, but doing the same thing every day was wearing on her demeanor. Wrapping chocolates and more chocolates, sitting at her spot with the big A.

If he never came along, she would not have wanted anything more for herself. He had instilled a dream in her she couldn't put out of her mind, telling her self she was in love with him too. No, she wouldn't confess this emotion to her friends. The way he squeezed her flesh when he said it meant he was coming back.

Her mother never came looking for her. She didn't know what happened to her brothers. Going home was not in her future. Never. She wanted a life of her own, and it didn't include her insane mother.

PART II

Elric

CHAPTER 54

With a name like that, you would think he was famous or something—something being the right choice. My father, Elric, did inherit great genes, down the line from his forefathers. Great men trickled down from that blood line.

Elric had a lot in common with others, who ruined their lives with alcohol, never coming to realize their greatness in all its glory. Genius ran in his blood. With no one to guide his brilliance, it found its own niche in life.

Choosing the wrong road, the road to destruction of his own life and anyone who had the unfortunate timing of contact with him.

I remember asking him some mathematical questions. He fired back the answers to me, many times without a pen or pencil. He could build anything without a plan. It was the way he ran his life.

His father found out quick that he was a bad seed after Blanche, Elric's mother, ran away from Earl and her children.

The alcohol became his excuse and his crutch to lash out his madness. Mom, my three siblings, Roderick, Lilly, Gwen, and me, bore the brunt of Elric's anger. It's nothing short of a miracle that any of us survived to tell this story. By the Grace of God.

This is where the fairy tale ends.

I will take you through my father's childhood, into his adult life, up until he met my mother, Alice, and started a family with her....my family.

Elric was born to Blanche and Earl Schoolcraft in rural Quebec in 1929. He had a twin brother. They called him Jack.

The boys looked nothing alike. They nicknamed Elric Widdy. Jack looked more like his mother, stout and shorter. Elric favored his father, taller and handsome to a fault from the day he was born.

A cunning look in his eye, charming, smiling. From day one, he knew he could use his good looks and talents to get whatever he wanted.

My grandfather Earl was a tall, dark haired, nice-looking gentleman. Well-spoken and successful. With two businesses, a car lot, and a logging business, he didn't have much time to spend with his children. He met Blanche at a barn dance. After the dance, he took her home to his house and presented her with a proposition of being his wife. Within days, Blanche moved in.

A woman to cook his meals and a bed partner made Earl very happy.

Within months of Blanche moving in, she was showing signs of pregnancy. She didn't tell Earl until she missed her period a couple of months. Earl was happy about having a baby. Blanche had other feelings, it hadn't been in her plans.

Blanche gave birth to twins. After a hard time in childbirth, she resented them quickly. Her once-slim figure ballooned, and she hated the feeling of her breasts filling with milk. She couldn't find the motherly love for them. The babies kept her up all night. With regular breastfeeding, her nipples cracked. Getting through the days after their birth, she was tired and sorry she had let herself get into this predicament. Blanche became very depressed, leaving the babies to cry for hours instead of going to them. While Earl was away at work, she would just walk out of the house, the babies eventually knowing she was not coming, leaving them in their cribs for hours unattended, sore red rashes developing on their bums.

Earl came home a few times to find his children wet, dirty, and hungry. "What is wrong with you, Blanche?" Noticing his babies' red blistered bums. "Aren't you changing them enough?"

Truth was, she didn't want to care for them. They had become a burden, her happy days gone. Her own milk dried up the first week after their birth. Blanche refused to breast feed them. Earl bought cow's milk for them, the babies developing a bad case of colic, crying for what seemed like all day.

Earl was becoming agitated at her. What kind of mother was she? He yelled at her a few times. "Get the children some milk, do something, stop them from crying."

It was no use; she couldn't find the love for them. Earl realized something was terribly wrong.

One bright sunny day, in August, the twins were eighteen months old.

Blanche dressed them in their diapers and a white T-shirt, put them in the yard with a ball to play. The boys frolicked in the sun, kicking the ball back and forth between them.

Blanche appeared in the doorway, a suitcase in her hand, a car came toward the house, stopping at the porch. Blanche walked to the car, put her bag in the back.

She never looked back. The boys stared her way, watching their mother leave them for good.

Before long, wet, hungry, and alone, their tears mixed with the dirt in the yard. After what seemed like forever, the twins cuddled up to each other, sucking their thumbs, their faces caked in dirt, tears, and snot, hardly a white patch on their faces.

Lucky for the twins, Earl came home that day for lunch. Pulling up in front of the house, he settled the big black Cadillac. Getting out, he noticed his boys right away. The state of the children told him something was terribly wrong.

Dirt embedded in their hair and their faces, their little eyes red, swollen. "Oh my God," he said, running to them. "Where is your mother?" Picking up his boys, he peeled off their dirty clothes and ran a bath, putting them both in there. Fixing bottles, he warmed them, handing each of them one while he washed the dirt and crust off their bodies. Leaving them in the tub, he ran through the house screaming her name.

"Blanche, Blanche, where are you?" Searching the whole house and yard, no sign of her anywhere. Going to the closet, he noticed the blank space where her clothes had hung. She was gone. He knew now she had run away from them.

Dressing the boys in clean diapers, he combed their hair and fed them settling them into their cribs. What would he do now? How could he care for them and run his businesses? He needed to figure something out, and quick. Maybe she would come back? That idea came and went like a hail storm. How could a mother be so irresponsible? To just leave two babies in the yard and take off? Shaking his head in disbelief.

She had become disconnected from them, and ignored his needs as well. After the twins came, Blanche was not the same woman.

Maybe he should go to the neighbors and ask if anyone had seen her. Had something terrible happened to her?

All of the possibilities swirled around in Earl's head like a twister picking up velocity.

Watching his sons, now warm and fed, looking out of their cribs at him. If only they could talk to him and tell him what had happened, to their mother.

Deciding he would go through the neighborhood, he dressed the boys and sat them in the back of the big Cadillac. They stared straight ahead, not a peep out of them. "We are going looking for your mother," he told them, looking back at his perfect children. Who could just walk away and leave them? She must be heartless, he concluded.

He pulled up outside of his neighbor to the right, an old gray haired gent was just coming out of his house.

"Hello, Earl. What can I do for you today, sir?"

"When I came home today from work, I found my boys in the yard and their mother nowhere to be found. Just wondering if you or your wife might have seen her earlier today?"

"Just a minute. I'll ask June if she knows anything."

The grey haired man went into his house, coming back out with his wife in tow.

June, a tall, thin, woman, was wiping her hands on her apron, she approached the Cadillac.

"Yes, I did see her, two days in a row now, getting into a Chevy. There was a younger man, I would say in his twenties. Yesterday they all left together, the boys and her. I thought he might have been your brother. Today when he came, I noticed that she had a suitcase. He got out and put it in the trunk, and I didn't think any more about it till now. Oh no, you mean she didn't come back at all?"

"Left the children in the yard," said Earl. June put her hand to her mouth, staring at the little boys in the back seat.

"Well, that kind of solves the puzzle. I suppose she has gone and left us."

"Thank you then," said Earl, pulling away from the curb. Looking back at his sons, he told them, "Your mother is nowhere to be found." No sounds came from the children.

"Gone with another man. That bitch," he said to himself, heading back to the house. Thinking of all the possibilities now, he had to attend to his business. He would have to find someone to tend to the boys. When he got them home, he fed and changed them, put them in their cribs with a bottle of milk. They were good boys, he thought. He hadn't heard them cry once.

After a few days of caring for them, and trying to go to work, Earl became very frustrated. Tired, the boys weren't getting the care they needed. With his mother having arthritis in her knees and back, he couldn't even think of asking her to care for them. With no other options, he decided he would ask her.

Delores loved the boys and agreed she would try to care for them. Within less than a week, she confessed to Earl she just couldn't care for both of them, but she would keep Widdy. "You can take Jack to your brother. I'm sure Ellen would take him. She doesn't have any children to care for. I think they have been trying to have a baby. It's perfect," she said. "Just go and ask," she suggested.

The house was eerily quiet now, Blanche missing, the children gone. Thinking hard about his predicament, Earl couldn't sleep, deciding his only option was to separate the twins and take Jack to his brother's house.

Putting all of Elric's clothes and toys, dropping them off the next day. Picking up little Jack, taking him toward the door. Elric had his hands up to his father, crying now, as the door slammed, his twin brother gone.

A welcoming Ellen scooped little Jack up in her arms, kissing his cheeks. "I will raise him as my own, Earl. All we need is a little help with money around here."

"Yes, of course," agreed Earl. "I will give you a monthly allowance to cover things you will need for him." Satisfied that little Jack would be well cared for, and he could come to see his son any time, Earl left happy.

CHAPTER 55

Delores did the best she could to raise Elric. He would grudgingly go to school, skipping out when he felt the urge. His grandmother couldn't do anything to make him listen to her. Elric did what he wanted, when he wanted. Delores sheltered him and covered for his shortcomings. He hid his failing grades from her. In her eyes, he could do no wrong.

Elric took advantage of his grandmother's illness and her love for him.

When he asked for pocket money, and she didn't give in, he would steal it from her purse. Near his fifteen birthday, Delores died in her sleep. He was heartbroken, with no mother, and now no grandmother. Earl decided he could take the boy in now that he was older, thinking of putting him to work at the car lot, cleaning cars.

"Listen, boy. If you don't want to go to school, you can come to work at the car lot. There are a few things you can do there. Keep you busy and out of trouble. You can start earning your keep."

The thought of working around all those new cars excited Elric. Right up his alley. He agreed to go and live and work for his father.

At fifteen, Elric was nearing six feet tall, with chiseled features, dark black hair combed back off his high forehead, grey eyes, and full lips. Everyone commented on the dimple in his chin. Surely he could sell cars for his father, he reasoned with himself, especially if there was a woman he could use his charm on.

Within days of Elric washing cars and cleaning up the lot, Earl realized that his son could possibly learn to sell cars. Everyone who stopped by looking at cars couldn't help but notice the tall handsome boy, walking around the lot, a towel in hand, dusting and cleaning the cars.

"Get up, boy," Earl yelled from the doorway. "Today you start working the lot. No sense in you going to school. You only go half the time, anyway."

"I get bored," said Elric, sitting up in his bed. "They can't teach me anything I don't know already. I can read and write, think that can take me through this life just fine."

"Really," answered Earl, shaking his head. Why should he waste his breath on his know-it-all son? If he could learn to sell cars, it would all work out.

Kicking his covers off, he gets out of bed.

"Get yourself cleaned up. Put on a nice pair of black trousers and a white shirt." Elric looked up at his father, knowing he didn't own such items.

"Just look in my closet. We are the same size, son."

Excited, he would wear his old man's clothes, whatever it took to get him on the stage and let him show his dad he could sell cars better than him.

"Fine, Dad, I'll meet you at the breakfast table. Eggs, sunny side up, bacon or sausage, and rye toast," he said.

"You will make mine and yours, boy. Get your ass in gear. I won't spoil you the way your grandmother did. You will work for everything you get from me."

Making his way to the bathroom, he took a fresh white shirt from his father's closet, a pair of black pants, black shoes he had shined up a few days earlier. Watching his reflection in the mirror as he dressed for his big day, he turned his jaw, admiring his handsome face. "This face will get me anything, I want," he said out loud. "Damn, I'm good looking," chuckling to himself. Singing as he headed down the hallway toward the kitchen. Shit, he had forgotten that Earl wanted him to make breakfast.

"What took you so long, Widdy? I won't be waiting for you like this every morning. How long does it take to throw on a pair of pants and a clean shirt?"

"But, Dad, I want to look my best," he said as he straightened out his collar. "You want me to be a good salesman, don't you? I got to look good."

Earl looked his boy over. Fine looking, no doubt. Reminded him of himself when he was young.

"You got your looks from your old man. Your mother was nothing to look at."

The hair stood up on Elric's neck. Fuck, why was he bringing up his stupid mother, who was never a mother to him? Bitch. He hated her with a vengeance.

On the way to the car lot, Elric sat in the back seat of the big Cadillac, his father at the helm. "Can I take this baby for a spin, Father?"

"No, you will need a license before you take any of the cars off the lot. Today you will watch and learn how to sell cars. I still need you to shine and clean some, until you have a potential buyer.

"I'm ready to sell cars today," argued Elric. "I didn't dress up to wash cars, Dad, come on now."

"Don't get ahead of yourself. You have to learn the ropes and everything about the cars. You can't sell them if you don't know the guts about them."

Pissed off now, he tried to shut his father's words out. He was going to make him wash cars in this fucking monkey suit. Stupid bastard, he thought.

Whatever, it was still better than going to school. Swallowing his pride, he would do as his father asked. He needed this. It was perfect.

"I'm going to be a singer, Father. This selling cars is just for now. I have big dreams for myself. Everyone says I have a sweet voice," he said, starting to sing a tune for his father.

Impressed and proud, Earl spoke. "You have talent, son, there is no doubt."

"I play guitar too, Dad. Some kid stole my guitar. Do you think you could spring for one?"

"We will see, son. Let's see how good you do this week on the lot, OK?"

The first day at the car lot, Elric washed cars half of the day. Earl was walking the lot with him, pointing to different features on the Cadillacs.

"These are top of the line," said Earl, running his hand over the hood like he was petting a dog. A shiny black Cadillac, with a silver grill and white walled tires.

"This one is a babe," said Elric. "I'm going to have me one of these for my own."

"You will be selling cars a long time before you could have one of these," said Earl, looking at his ambitious son.

"Well, the way I see it," said Elric, "I'm just going to become a famous singer, and I'll have one in no time, you will see."

By mid-afternoon, he had washed down ten cars, wiping out the interiors. After stopping for a sandwich and tea for lunch, he was back out into the car lot. Earl watched, impressed at his willingness for the job. It was a great idea, he determined. Maybe he could take over his business one day when he retired.

While Earl was throwing out a sales pitch, Elric would walk up behind him, his ears sharpened, listening to everything his dad was saying.

"Oh, this is my son. He is learning the business," Earl said to a customer.

"Good day, sir," said Elric.

A few of the potential buyers mentioned to Earl his son was polite and handsome.

At the end of the first day, Earl had sold three cars. It had been a long time since he had been that lucky, wondering if Elric might have had something to do with it. The way he spoke to the people, smiling, encouraging, his youth glowing. Probably that smile of his, thought Earl.

The following week, Earl decided that he would watch and see if his son had picked up enough skills to actually seal a deal.

"I got this, Dad, piece of cake."

Putting up his collar, he runs his hands on the sides of his black hair, sauntering out onto the lot, like it was a stage. There was a man and woman walking around, looking at the cars, when Elric walked up behind them.

"Good afternoon," he said, putting his hand out to the gentleman. "And a good day to you, ma'am," said Elric, smiling his perfect white teeth. "What kind of car would you have in mind?" Elric asked, looking at the man, noticing a fancy gold watch on his arm. "Sporty, conservative—for work or play?"

"We were thinking of something for the spring and summer, maybe a convertible," she answered.

"Follow me, I'll show you the best we got. Let me tell you, there is no other like this baby," he said, heading toward a pale yellow Cadillac coupe with a soft top. "Have a good look at this one." Running his hand over the sleek body of the car with love. "This top comes down," he said as he pushes a lever, the top rolled back to expose a butter yellow interior with a silver chrome radio.

"It is sure a beauty," said the auburn haired woman.

"Of course, just the car for a pretty lady like you," he said, looking her over. "What do you say we take it for a test run? I got the keys right here," he said, opening the passenger door, the lean, pretty lady getting in.

As her husband is sizing up the Cadillac, Elric gets into the driver's side, putting the key in the ignition. "We'll just go a few minutes down the road, see how you like it." The woman nodding her head.

Earl was watching from his office when he noticed the yellow coupe, Elric at the wheel, driving off the lot. Before he could stop him, he came out, just watching now, not wanting to alert the gentleman, who they had left standing there.

"So do you like it?" asked Elric,

"I sure do. What is there not to like?" Taking notice of how gorgeous Elric was, staring at his profile.

Pulling over onto the side of the road.

"Do you want to drive it back?"

"Sure," she answered, excited.

As she settled into the driver's seat, Elric moved over, a little close to her.

"Just think of taking this baby to the beach in the summer. Why, you would have the nicest car in the whole countryside. Not to mention, look at all the space this baby has." Glancing in the back seat, thinking of the possibilities. "Hope you don't mind me saying, you look great behind the wheel."

"Why, thank you, young man. Just call me Mrs. Smith. What was your name again?"

"Elric," he answered, smiling seductively at her, stealing a peek at her long, slim legs. "Well, Mrs. Smith, what do you think?"

"I think you have made yourself a sale. I just couldn't live without this car. It's the nicest one I've seen since we started looking. Might I say, you are quite the salesman? I like your style," she said, smiling.

"My father owns the car lot. I am his new recruit. I am a singer too, just going to sell cars for a while till I can get myself one of these."

As the Cadillac made its appearance, Earl is standing in the doorway of the sales office, Mr. Smith standing next to him, both eying the Cadillac, Mrs. Smith behind the wheel.

A confident, smiling Elric sits comfortably, his arm resting on the back of the seat. He had just made the best sale of the day, or possibly the month. *Dad will be so surprised*, he thought to himself.

The car pulled to a stop, Elric getting out, closing the passenger door gently. The pretty lady, a big smile on her face, gets out of the driver's side, walking up to her husband.

"Bill, I would really like this car. You know my birthday is coming next month? Please, I just want this car, I love it! Please, please." Nuzzling into her husband, gazing into his eyes.

Earl is amazed, eying Elric, who gives him a slight nod.

"Yes, OK, it's your birthday present."

Kissing her husband on the cheek, following him into the sales office.

Walking into the office, Elric stands in the doorway, listening to his father and watching the paperwork being passed to the new owners.

"Elric, you could go and find something to do while I finish up this deal here," said Earl.

Without hesitation, he walked out back into the lot. What the fuck, the old man didn't have to treat him like an employee. He was his son, not his slave. Today was a happy day, and his father would not take that from him. As soon as the couple left, he would go see his dad and demand his cut.

Surely, his father would give him at least a hundred dollars. With that, he could go and buy a new guitar and some new clothes.

He had a secret passion he needed money for too. He had acquired a taste for beer, and whiskey was his favorite.

The days he skipped school, he found other wayward boys. He played his guitar and sang, sharing a few drinks with his new friends. Now, he was a car salesman. Not bad for fifteen, he thought to himself. This car business was going to be a snap for him.

He watched as the happy couple get in their new car and head out of the lot. The woman waved to Elric, and he waved back, smiling.

Standing in the doorway, he rested his arm on the door frame, his head cocked to the side.

"That's what I call beginners luck. I am proud of you, son. You are proving to be a good salesman. Just let me ask you a few questions. What did you really do to that woman? She couldn't stop talking about how great you were. Said you carried yourself like a professional who had been selling cars for years."

"Really, she said all that?" said Elric, walking to an armchair, proud as a peacock showing his feathers.

"I see, you are quite the charmer, Elric. Not that it's a bad thing. Just don't think it will be so easy every time. You just got lucky today. Regardless, you did great, and I have a twenty-dollar bonus for you," he said, handing Elric four five-dollar bills.

Staring at the twenty dollars, he looked up at his dad.

"Really, this is all I get for selling the best car on the lot? I was figuring more like fifty dollars. I got my heart set on a guitar, and I could use some new digs."

"You will get a paycheck every two weeks, and a ten percent bonus on any cars you sell. Just keep up that kind of work, and you will be able to buy anything you need."

Realizing it wouldn't do him any good to argue with his old man, Elric gets up from the seat, walking back out to the lot.

Earl sold a second hand car that day, bringing the total sold to two. He was quite pleased at how the day turned out as he gets ready to leave for the day.

Getting bored waiting for his father to close up, he headed to his father's car to relax and go over the day's events. Pulling open the back door to the Cadillac, he slipped in on the butter soft leather.

Earl approached the car, noticing Elric in the back seat. *Now he thinks I'm his chauffeur.* Without any complaint, Earl gets in the driver's seat and headed out onto the road.

"We got a couple of steaks waiting for us at home. You cook the dinner, Widdy."

"Sure," answered Elric. "You got potatoes?"

"Yes, we do," answered his father.

Going straight to his room, he takes off the white shirt and black pants, putting them over a chair. Changing into his black T-shirt and jeans, then heads back out to the kitchen. He would make steak and mashed potatoes.

By the time Earl walked into the kitchen, the steaks were in the frying pan, a pot with boiling water, steam rising from the top. Sitting at the table, with his paper, he watches his son out of the corner of his eye.

Elric is cutting up the potatoes, then dropping them into the boiling water. Taking the steaks out, he put them on a plate, then cutting up an onion, tossing it in with the oil and butter in the pan. Making a pan gravy, with a little flour and water, stirring until it was smooth.

Draining the water off the potatoes, he put in a big tablespoon of butter and some cream, mashing them until they were smooth and creamy.

Two plates were waiting for the meal. Setting one steak and some of the onion gravy on top, he put a few clumps of the mashed potatoes, then another dollop of butter on the top. Walking to the table, setting his dad's plate down in front of him.

"Enjoy," he said, walking back to get his own plate, a knife and fork in his hand.

"Where did you learn to cook like this, son?"

"Grandmother taught me everything. It was hard with her arthritis to do much in the kitchen, so I had to learn to cook or go hungry. I love cooking, Dad."

"This looks great," complimented his father, digging into his steak.

They sit quiet, each with their own thoughts. Glancing up from his meal, Earl watching his son.

When Elric was done his food, he pushed himself away from the table, leaving the dirty plate.

"No, before you go anywhere, you wash your dishes. As long as you are in my house, you do the dishes. You can get mine here in a minute."

What? Thought Elric. Now he had to do the dishes too? Not too happy about his new assignment, he went ahead and did them, wiping the stove and counter, then walking out of the kitchen without as much as a word to Earl, who was making himself a cup of tea.

Going back to the room, he sits on the side of the bed. Pissed that his father wouldn't give him more than twenty dollars. If he bought the guitar, he wouldn't have any left for beer or new clothes. He just couldn't get the guitar today. He would have to wait for his paycheck in two weeks.

Fuck, a whole two more weeks of following orders, cleaning and dusting cars, being his father's gopher. Laying on his bed, he thought back to the day's events. *Wonder how they paid for the car? Probably cash,* he decided. That's why Earl wanted him out of the office when they were settling up everything.

He hadn't noticed his father taking his briefcase to his room. He'd just set in on the coffee table in the parlor then gone into the kitchen. If the money was in there, he wouldn't have left it just sitting there. Ah, he must have left it in the office at the lot, he decided.

If he went back there in the dead of night, he could sneak in through a window, take the money, and fuck off. *He just wants to use me to wash his fucking cars,* he thought the promise of the wages not sitting right with him. What if his old man decided that he wasn't getting paid after all? He had mentioned a few times that he was under his roof, eating his food. Now was his chance to get the hell away from him. He could get that new guitar and everything else he wanted, he reasoned. There must be a lot of money in the desk.

The more he thought of it, the more, he wanted to rob his father. He waited until he heard him turning off the lights, walking down the hallway, past his room, turning in for the night. Elric lay still, fully clothed, thinking of the possibilities. Should he or shouldn't he? Came the voice of reason.

Yes, he would. Fuck it. *Opportunity knocks,* he told himself. Why should he live under his father's roof like he was his prisoner? Do this, do that, wash the dishes, clean, take orders. No fucking way. Not his idea of a good time.

Waiting and listening, he put on his comfortable shoes and a few of his things in a pack. He would walk to the lot. The summer night was bright, warm, inviting.

After an hour or so, he walked down the hallway toward his father's room. No light under the door. The old man must be sleeping. Putting an ear to the door, a light snoring. Stealing back down the hall and out the door, closing it, quietly.

CHAPTER 56

Walking with conviction, knowing it was a long walk, the thoughts of all that money in his hands, the excitement firing in him. It was five miles, Earl had told him, walking along the side of the road at a brisk pace.

The lights of an oncoming car showing, he slipped behind a tree until the car passed. No one could see him going there. He would do what he had to do and get back to his bed, Earl not any the wiser.

Approaching the office, all the lights are off. First he checks the door, grabbing the handle. Pushing his right shoulder into it, trying to force it open no give. Walking around the building, he notices a small window just big enough for him to climb through. Looking around on the ground, he finds a stick. Slamming the wood against the glass, a loud sound of shattering glass, a spray of shards onto the ground. Sheilding himself, his arm up in front of his face, then taking the flat screwdriver out of his pack.

Hoisting himself up, he leaned his body in, a glass shard ripping through his cotton shirt,

Sparing no time to worry about it right now, he worked on. Knocking the few stray pieces of glass out with his foot, jumping down into the dark office.

With a few prying jabs at the drawer, it springs open. Putting his hand in, he felt it. A big stack of cash. Wow, it was his lucky day. Stuffing the money into the inside pocket of his jacket, taking off the shirt, using it to wipe down the desk drawer, then going to the door, opening it, wiping at the handle of the outside, wiping off any prints.

Putting his hand inside his jacket, double checking for the money. The thickness of it made his heart go faster, excitement rushing through his veins.

Hoisting himself back up through the window, a stray shard of glass digging into his side, stinging pain, a warm wet feeling on his ribs. Running his hand down his left side, his hand sticky with his own blood, he wipes his hand on his pants.

Now that he had the money, what should he do next? If he didn't go home, and just went to the city, the cops would surely be on his tail. There would be no doubt as to who stole the money. No, he would go back home, hide the money somewhere, and just settle back into bed, like nothing had happened. Tomorrow when Earl discovered the break in, he would think it was just some thief. Elric had been at home in his bed all along. It was perfect. He would hurry and get back to the house.

Settling into a half running gait, he made it back to his father's house in no time. Everything dark and quiet, he gets in, back to his room, closing the door, his secret in with him. When passing his father's room, he heard a light snoring, giving him extra confidence.

The alarm wakes Elric, he sits up in the bed. Seven o'clock. Time to, wash up, put on the monkey suit, and do some serious acting. A pinch of his flesh, he looks down at his side. A long gash runs from just under his ribs to his belt line. A red irritated line, pain when he moved.

"Good morning, Father," he practiced, smiling at his reflection, a devious, happy face. Getting into the bathroom, he hung the black shirt on the back of the bathroom door, still thinking of where to hide it. The bathroom door left ajar a bit. Earl was walking by when he noticed Elric running a razor over his left cheek.

"Hey, you are up early today. That's what I like to see," he said as he looked in at his tall lean son. Bare back, a towel around his neck.

"Just cleaning up," answered Elric, watching his father in the mirror. Shit, he hoped his dad hadn't seen the cut.

Earl looked away, thinking he noticed a long red scratch on Elric's side, deciding not to pry.

Getting back in his room, he dressed in his black pants, pulling on another of Earl's white cotton shirts. Today he would even put on a jacket, making him look like the perfect gentleman that he wasn't. Having a look in the mirror; the jacket made him look like a preacher. Too much, he decided, putting the jacket back in the closet.

Taking a last look at his reflection, running the comb through his black hair. Looking good, he assured himself. Today was a great day. Feeling like a million bucks, Elric strode into the kitchen.

Earl was just putting on a fresh pot, the smell of freshly ground coffee thick in the air.

"Mmm, nothing like the smell of java in the morning," said Elric.

His father took a second look at his son. He was fresh, happy, and ready for a new day selling cars. He liked what he saw, bright eyes and great attitude. Why had he been so worried about taking him in? The boy was growing into a fine young man.

"It looks like a nice day, son. Are you anxious to sell another car today?"

"You know I am," answered Elric, a sly smile on his face.

"I'll fix some bacon and eggs," said Elric, going to the counter. Earl headed to the bathroom to clean up. Elric's black shirt was hanging on the back of the door. Taking a closer look, he saw one side of his shirt ripped to the armpit. Then he saw what looked like blood.

"What the hell?" he said, holding the shirt, examining it.

Walking back into the kitchen, the shirt held in one hand.

"What happened here?" asked Earl, staring at Elric, who has his back to him, standing at the stove.

"What, Father?" He turned to see his father holding his shirt.

"Oh, I just got into a bit of a scuffle, that's all," he said realizing how stupid he was to not have hidden the shirt.

Earl had a puzzled look on his face. Seemed to him, he had seen Elric wearing that shirt yesterday, and when had he got into a fight?

"I see," said Earl, putting the shirt over the back of one of the kitchen chairs.

"Bacon and eggs is served," said Elric in an announcer's voice, putting his father's plate down in front of him.

"Thank you, son," said Earl, trying to make eye contact with him. Elric walking back to the counter.

Sitting down opposite his father, he ate his breakfast, thinking of the stupidity of not throwing out the shirt. When his father wasn't looking he would take and dispose of it.

The money was hidden outside under a pile of bricks that sat next to the house. Would he suspect him? Whatever, he would have to prove it, and when the timing was right, he was getting the hell out from under his father's roof, reasoning he would have enough money to get a fresh start in the big city. The best guitar money could buy, and the finest clothes. A star singer had to have nice things, he conceded.

"Are you ready, son?"

"Right away, sir," he said, going for his fedora. Earl put his hat on, walking out the door to the awaiting Fleetwood. Today, Elric sat up front. Earl got in, wasting no time pulling the big black Caddy out onto the road toward the car lot. Earl was optimistic about his boy, looking over at him. Things were going to work out.

Pulling into the lot, parking next to the office. Earl goes to the door first, using his key, unlocking the door. Elric comes up behind him. Earl notices the drawer to his desk on the floor, the papers and things on his desk in disarray.

"What the hell happened here? Oh my God, we've been robbed! The money from the sale of the cars yesterday. All of it. There was over eight thousand dollars. I have to call the police right away. Don't touch anything, Elric, stay out of here," he ordered, panic in his voice. Glancing around the office, Earl noticed the broken window. "Ah, that's how they got in," he said. "Fuck, there is glass everywhere."

"I'll clean it up, Dad."

"No, leave everything. Go out in the lot. Keep yourself busy until the cops come." Earl ordered.

"Sure, Dad, whatever you say," he answered, hanging his head, pretending to be upset at the robbery.

Slipping on a pair of overalls over his clean white shirt and pants, choosing a few cars away from the office, he put his pail and rags down, watching the office for any sign of the cops. Shit, he hoped they didn't want to talk to him.

He had barely started washing one of the cars when he noticed a black-and-white cop car pulling up in front of the office. Two officers going to the door, then disappearing inside, thinking he recognized the one detective in street clothes.

"Good morning. My name is Detective Scott. My partner, Peterson. What happened here?" asked Scott, noticing the glass sprayed on the floor.

"As you can see, we had a break-in here. My son and I just got to work and came to the office. The first thing I noticed was the drawer of my desk on the floor, then I noticed that the window was broken," said Earl, pointing to the window behind the desk.

"When were you last in your office, Mr. Schoolcraft?" asked Scott, a notebook and pen in his hand.

"We left yesterday and went straight home after work, at five o'clock."

"Who is we, you mean your son?"

"Yes, my son, Elric. That's him out there washing cars," he said, pointing out the window. Elric is pretending to keep busy, wiping down a car, his back to them.

Scott looked out the window, staring at Elric.

"Thing is, my son made a big sale yesterday, sold the best Cadillac on the lot. The customer paid in cash, over eight thousand dollars. Not wanting to bring that much cash home with me, I decided it would be fine here in my locked desk. How stupid was I, not thinking I would be robbed the very day."

Scott, a tall man in his thirties, wore a grey trench coat, grey fedora with a black band. He was talking to Earl, while not taking his eyes off Elric. He thought he had seen the kid hanging out with a bad bunch, down near the river.

"How long has your son been working with you?"

"He just moved in with me about a month ago now. His grandmother was raising him, but she died."

"Sorry to hear that. Your mother?"

"Yes," answered Earl, hanging his head.

"Did your son happen to see you put the money in the desk?"

"No, he didn't know anything about the money. He was busy in the lot when I put it in there. He was at home with me all night. We live about five miles from here."

"I see," said Scott. "Well, sir, we will do some fingerprint work on that broken window. We'll let you know if we turn up anything. There has been a few break and enters in this area lately."

Going back out to the cruiser, Scott returned with a brush and the fingerprint kit. After about twenty minutes, he came back out to Earl with his thoughts.

"Well, sir, we were unable to detect any fingerprints on the window, mostly because it is smashed to bits. As far as the frame goes, there are no fresh prints on there."

"Let us know if you get any leads on this robbery, I'll go back to the precinct and compare notes on the other robberies in his area. I'll be in touch," said Scott. Nodding his head, he headed out the door, his partner following.

Scott looked over at his partner. "I know that kid. Let's just say, he's not the Ivy League type. I would have never guessed he was Mr. Schoolcraft's son. He hangs out with that bad bunch under the bridge. We arrested a couple of them a few weeks ago. This kid saw us coming and ran like hell."

Elric could feel their prying eyes on him. Why the fuck were they still sitting there? Rubbing the shining rag over the same area, the paint glistening.

"That kid's friends are all thieves and drunks. The Riverside Gang. I'll bet you anything it was him who robbed his father. Do you notice how cool and collected he looks? Don't think he didn't know we were watching."

"Thing is we got to prove it," answered Peterson, a heavy set dark haired guy.

"Pretty bad when your own kid would rob you. I hope we can find the thieves, and prove me wrong." Commented Scott.

Elric washed ten cars before he headed to the office for his lunch break. Earl was sitting at the desk, looking over some papers, eying his son as he walked through the door.

"You wouldn't happen to know anything about what happened here, Elric?"

"Really, Dad? How would I know anything more than you? Are you trying to blame me? You think I stole your money? I was home with you all night," he said, his voice irritated, accusing.

"No, I'm not blaming you, but the detective seemed really interested in you. Asking me a bunch of questions. The cops dusted for fingerprints on the windowsill.

"Really," said Elric, a lump of guilt rising in his throat.

"Can you get that glass cleaned up? We will get a new pane at the hardware store."

"Sure," answered Elric, walking to the broom closet.

Earl weighed the possibilities of Elric stealing the money. Maybe he came in the middle of the night? He would have had to walk. Then the torn shirt—he was sure that he had seen him wearing it yesterday. Then the blood on the shirt...the broken glass, the ripped shirt...hmm.

He decided when they got home today, he would go to Elric's room and tear it apart. If he stole the money, it would be hidden somewhere in his things.

Not many words were exchanged all day, Elric staying out of his father's way. He didn't want to answer any questions, the air thick with uncertainties. Earl finally spoke.

"That Detective Scott was really interested in you, Elric. He seemed to know you from somewhere. Have you been in any trouble in the city you are not telling me about? I'll tell you one thing. If I find out you robbed me, you will be out on your ass, and don't ever darken my door again!"

No point in trying to defend himself or get belligerent, he said nothing, just eyed his father as he spoke. His plans were set already, and now that he was being blamed for the robbery that would be the reason he split. Nothing was going to stop him now.

"When we get to the house, you can watch while I rip your room apart," said Earl, almost convinced that he would find the money in his room.

"What?" answered Elric. "Whatever, go ahead, then you can finally stop blaming me for your fucking money."

"Look here, boy, don't use that kind of language around me. Save it for the streets."

Storming into the house, Earl heads straight to Elric's room. As his son stands in the doorway, Earl tears the room apart. Pulling everything out of his bags, clothes strewn all over the floor, a couple black shirts, just like the one he found ripped.

"Well, you satisfied now?"

"I just don't know what to say," answered Earl, rubbing his head. "If you are innocent, I am sorry."

Walking past Elric, he heads into the kitchen and sitting down, feeling remorse for accusing his son.

Picking up his clothes throwing them all on the bed. Fuck that old bastard, he thought, trying to find the right to feel violated.

The air in the house is disturbed. Earl didn't want to sit and eat with Elric at the same table, after everything that had gone down during the day, his appetite none to nil.

Making himself a sandwich and a cup of tea, he sits in the parlor with the paper.

All night, he didn't see any sign of Elric, who stayed in his room making plans.

Really, he didn't know the boy, who had been raised by his grandmother. Could he ever trust him again? The working relationship was strained. Tomorrow, he wouldn't take him to the lot in case the cops came back. He didn't want him around, while the case was still hot.

Morning came, Elric awakened by his alarm, wondering what the vibe would be in the kitchen this morning. After washing up and dressing, he walked into the kitchen. His dad is seated at the table, pungent Arabica beans in the air.

"Good morning, Father."

"Good morning, Elric."

Getting out the breakfast things, he started to fry up some eggs and sausages.

"Should I make you some breakfast, Father?"

"Sure. But today you will be staying close to home. I don't want you at the lot when those cops come back. Let me deal with this, and you can come back to work in a few days. Clean up the house, and find things to do around here. We will figure this stuff out," he said, getting back to his coffee.

Perfect, thought Elric. Today would be his chance to get the hell out of his father's house. With his dad gone, he could pack up his stuff, dig out his treasure, and hit the road. It was like his father had just handed him his freedom.

Earl finished up his breakfast, pushing his plate away from him. Getting up, putting on his fedora and his overcoat.

"I'll see you at dinnertime, son. Make sure to keep yourself busy around here. This house could use a good cleaning."

"Yes, Father. I'll do just that," he said, picking up his father's plate heading to the sink.

Back to his room, his door ajar, listening for the sound of the door and Earl leaving. Making his bed, rolling up some of the clothes, he stuffed them into his backpack. Knowing he would have to travel light, a suitcase would be too much. He would have to hitchhike into the city and get himself a place to stay.

When he finished packing his clothes, he realized he didn't need to take everything. He could buy new digs. Taking half of them out, he threw them on the bed, taking only his nicest pair of shoes, two black shirts, two pairs of pants, and one sweater.

The door slammed shut. His father was gone.

Earl had just arrived at the office when the same two officers showed up at his door.

"C'mon in," Earl said. Detective Scott walking in first.

"Good morning, sir. We would like to have a few words with your son. Is he here today?"

"Actually, he isn't here today, after what has happened. I blamed him, tore his room apart, found nothing. I feel terrible, blaming my own son."

"Well, Mr. Schoolcraft, we would like to tell you that there was a robbery not far from here a few months ago, same sort of crime, break and grab at a gas station in the night. There was a description of a boy, much like Elric, but they didn't get a good enough look at him."

"Oh no, don't try to tell me anything about my son. No speculation anyway."

"Whoever robbed you was not stupid. We didn't find any prints. As far as the blood went, we can't tell anything from that. Sorry for your loss, Mr. Schoolcraft. You must have insurance on your business here?"

"Yes, I believe there is partial coverage. I will be contacting them today. I will need a police report from you."

"Yes, of course. It is right here," he said, handing Earl the paperwork. "In the meantime, don't be leaving any cash around here. These are hard times."

"Thanks for your help," said Earl, getting up from his chair, escorting them to the door.

The detectives sat in their cruiser, jotting notes on the investigation.

"I still think it was Elric," said Scott, looking over at his partner. "The old man just doesn't want to believe it could be his own son. Neither would I. I'll be keeping an eye on that kid."

"I didn't want to tell Mr. Schoolcraft his boy has been in the drunk tank a few times already. We will be hearing more about Elric. He's got a bad eye in his head."

The cop radio blared. An assault with a weapon at the Quebec Hotel. Spinning out of the lot, the cops left, hot on the trail of a gunman.

Bewildered, Earl looked around his office. Maybe he should have some bars put on the window? That was the last time he would leave money in the office, he thought, realizing it was stupid on his part.

The insurance company would reimburse him for most of it. After all, he paid his insurance dues every month, which was a pretty penny. Life went on. This had taught him a hard lesson.

Elric buzzed around the house, thinking of all the possibilities with that much money. He wouldn't have to steal or beg for a long time. Going back into the kitchen, he finished his breakfast, put his dirty plate and his father's in the sink. The old man could wash his plate too.

Taking one last look around his room, he would write his father a note.

Sitting at the kitchen table, he penned the message. "Sorry, Dad. I just couldn't stay under your roof, thinking that you blamed me for stealing your money. It's better this way. I'll find my own life. Thank you for everything. Your son, Elric."

Hoisting the pack over his back, his fedora cocked to the side, money safely put away, he headed out, locking the inside of the door handle.

Once outside, he decided to take off the hat. Too flashy, and he didn't want to attract any more attention to himself. Better to keep it as low key as possible, until he found a place to hang out and stay out of the way of the cops.

Walking a ways, a few cars passing him on the road, the sun shining down on him, a lift in his step, not a care in the world.

Sticking out his thumb out a few times, a car finally pulled over, a single man in a business suit, probably in his late forties, with mousy brown hair and glasses. "Going into town, are you?"

"Yes, sir, going into the city."

"Great, get in," he said. Elric hoisting his things in the back seat.

"Oh, you are quite young," said the man, taking a good look at his passenger.

"Going on sixteen," answered Elric.

"From behind, I would have thought you were much older."

"Been living on my own for a while now. My Granny died, left me alone."

"Sorry for your loss, son."

"I'm going into show business. I'm a singer, and I play guitar."

"Really, well, you got the looks. If you are talented too, you are well on your way."

"What's the name of your band?" asked the man.

Thinking fast, he answered. "Elric and the Wanderers."

"So, you'll be playing in the city then? Why don't you give me a song right now? If you can sing without a guitar that is what makes you talented."

"Sure, man," answered Elric, sitting up straight, staring out at the road ahead, his life in the balance.

"I got a feelin'called the blues, oh, Lord
Since my baby said goodbye
Lord, I don't know what I'll do
All I do is sit and sigh, oh, Lord
The last long day she said goodbye
Well, Lord, I thought I would cry
She'll do me, she'll do you she's got that kind of lovin'
Lord, I love to hear her when she calls me sweet Daddy..."

"Hey, kid your pretty damn good. Just keep at it. I really like your voice! The girls will be crazy for you. Just play the hand you were dealt, son, you've got what it takes."

"Thanks again, appreciate that," answered Elric.

Relaxing now, deep in thought, what would be the first things he would do? Get a room so he could relax, have a hot shower, and get ready for a night on the town.

When he had the money safely hidden, he would go down to the river to see the guys, maybe share a bottle of whiskey with them. He liked the way the whiskey warmed his blood and made him fearless. Just thinking of it made his mouth water. After all that stress he had to put up with, the drink was well deserved.

"Thanks again, man," said Elric, putting on his fedora, now, hoisting his bag over his shoulder. The man drove off, leaving Elric at First and King Street, just a few minutes from the Quebec Hotel.

"Rooms five dollars a night, with breakfast in the morning," the clerk told him.

He pulled out a hundred-dollar bill. The clerk stared at the bill, then back Elric.

"We can't change that. You will have to go to the bank."

"How much is it for the whole month?" he asked.

"Seventy-five dollars," answered the clerk.

"OK then, I'll take it for the month."

"Sure thing then, Mr.....?"

"Schoolcraft," answered Elric.

"Fine, here is your room key. Have a nice stay."

Taking the key, he looked at the number: 410. Great, he thought, on the top floor, so he could look out at the city.

As he settled in, he remembered the guitar shop was not far from the hotel, just down the street a bit. Showering, he got ready to go get the best guitar his money could buy him. Taking five hundred-dollar bills, he tore a small place in the side of the mattress and stuffed the rest deep in toward the middle of the mattress. No one would look in there, he told himself.

Strolling down the street, he pulled his fedora down on his forehead. Didn't want those detectives to recognize him. They had nothing on him, but better they didn't see him at all.

CHAPTER 57

A Star Shines

Only the best guitar would do. Standing outside the guitar shop, he noticed a black shiny one with a pearl colored panel and gold strings. He looked closer. Fender. That was the best name in guitars, and he was going to have it today. Excited, he walked into the shop.

He was just about to try and take it out of the display when the store clerk walked up to Elric.

"Hi there. Can I help you with something?" He looked at the boyish looking man.

"Yes, I would like to take a look at that Fender you got there. The black and pearl one."

"You got good taste. That's our best guitar in the whole store. It's not cheap, let me tell you that now."

"How much is it then?" asked Elric.

The clerk turned over the price tag. "Two hundred and seventy," he answered. "You got that kind of money?"

"Yes, I do. My grandmother just died and left me a little money. I'd like to see how it sounds."

A wide eyed, robust man, with long stringy hair, moved past Elric, picking up the guitar handing it to him.

Eyeing the guitar, feeling the smoothness of the neck of it, he strummed a few chords. "I love it," he said. The clerk keeping a close eye on him.

Deciding he would showcase his voice a little, he sang a few lines of a hit song.

"Man, you are good! Do you sing here in town? Do you have a band?"

"Yes," answered Elric, happy that he had a name for his band that didn't exist yet. "Elric and the Wanderers."

"Are you new in town?"

"Ya, you might say that," he said, holding the guitar like it was a beautiful woman.

Standing at the counter, the salesman wrote up the receipt.

"Is your band playing in town here?"

"Yes, we should be getting some gigs around here soon."

"Great, I'll be watching for you. I know you are going to make that guitar sing. The best we got."

"Thanks again, man," he said, walking out of the store, guitar in hand.

He had merely sung a few notes, and the guy recognized a star. And the guy who'd picked him up—how he'd praised his voice. He had it all going on, and now in the big city, he was going to own it. Throwing his head back, he walked proud, and happy back to his room.

Just like that. *That's what I call happiness. You want it, and you get it. Now, to celebrate with a little drink. Maybe go down to the bridge and look up the guys.* He would get the older one to get them a big bottle of whiskey.

They were probably all wondering what happened to him since his father had taken him in.

Earl opened the door, looking in. No sign of Elric. He must be in his room, he thought, taking a look around the kitchen. Noticing the note at the head of the table. "Dear Dad, it read." What the hell?

The boy is gone? Run away. *What have I done?* He asked himself, holding his head in his hands.

Walking down the hallway toward Elric's room he opened the door. The bed was perfectly made, a few pieces of clothing strewn on the top. A pair of black shoes showed under the bed. Looking in the closet: two black shirts and two pairs of black pants. Realizing Elric owned more than one black shirt, all the same.

Maybe he planned on coming back. Why wouldn't he have taken all his things?

Where the hell did he go? Should he go to the police, report him missing? Would that bring reproach on his business? Schoolcraft Auto Sales.

He could ruin everything he had worked so hard for. An upstanding citizen of the community. Maybe it was better that he had left on his own so he didn't have to kick him out.

If the cops came back again, asking about Elric, he would just tell them he disappeared. Left him a note and split.

Deciding he would lay low, stay away from the bridge and the guys. If they figured out he had that kind of money, they would all be begging him for this and that. Dressing in his best, fedora cocked to the side, his shirt open to the breastbone, he headed to the bar, to put back a couple shots of whiskey.

Picking up his new guitar, slinging it over his shoulder.

Fuck the old bastard, he thought. *Thinks he can just come for me when he has no other options. Didn't fucking want me from the beginning. Nobody fucking wants me,* he said to himself. *Who the fuck cares?* Came back the voice in his head.

"So, what really brings you to the city, young man?" asked a middle aged man sitting next to Elric at the bar.

"My mother lives on the outskirts. I'm planning on looking her up. My grandmother raised me, and she just died. I don't remember my mother."

"Are you a singer? I see you have a pretty nice guitar there. Why don't you get up there, and give us a tune. I'm sure the management wouldn't mind a little entertainment."

With his renewed confidence, and the best guitar money could buy, why not give it a shot.

He walked up to the stage, all eyes on him. Sitting down on the stool, he looked out at a few people staggered around the bar. A couple were just coming through the doors.

"Good day to all you fine folk out there. Just thought I would give you a tune, try out my new guitar here."

As a silence fell across the room, he takes one last look out at his audience.

"My name is Elric," he said and started to strum out a tune.

"I'm losing my mind over you," he sang.

When the song was done, he stood and took a bow. There was a loud clapping sound and a couple of hoots. Someone from the bar yelled, "Give us another."

Then another patron yelled, "Ya, give us another."

Excitement fueled, whiskey brave, he sang another song.

A furious clapping rounded throughout the bar, as more people came in.

Taking his guitar in hand, Elric dismounted the stage, taking one last look at his audience. They loved him. One woman was staring at him hard. She was a looker too, a little too old for him, but she was beautiful.

Going back to his place at the bar, a shot of whiskey was waiting for him. The bartender walked over facing Elric. "Hey, this one's on the house. The owner loved your singing. Said you could come back anytime."

A few other patrons walked by, trying to make small talk with the handsome man child. Not wanting to answer their questions, Elric took his guitar and left the bar, all eyes on the handsome crooner.

In his room, he reflected back to the love they gave him after just a couple of tunes. He did have what it takes to be a star. They couldn't get enough of him, making him feel fabulous. The whiskey had warmed his blood.

In the glory of the moment, he didn't want to be alone. He would go down to the bridge and look for the guys. Tell them about his gig. Get a bottle of whiskey to share with them.

They would be happy to see him, he thought, especially bearing gifts, making his way out of the hotel, down the road toward the bridge.

Nearing the bridge, he can see sparks flying from the top of the barrel. Their darkened silhouettes holding their secrets, the forgotten boys of the night.

Walking with a swagger, his overcoat pulled around him. Looking down at his father's long overcoat. They would think he was playing dress up.

Whatever, it was keeping him warm, disguising him as an adult. With his fedora pulled low over his forehead, he wasted no time getting down to river.

"Hey, buddy," came a yell from way down near the river.

"Where the fuck you been, man?" asked Johnny, a tall good looking guy, head of the Riverside Gang.

"Ah, shit, I was working for my old man. Quit after one day. Fuck that old bastard. Sold the best car on the lot, and he gave me a hundred bucks. I am not no fucking beggar." He immediately felt bad for his choice of words.

"Sure, man, so you got two bucks? I'll go get us a bottle."

"That's just what I was thinking," said Elric, handing Johnny a twenty-dollar bill. Taking a double take at the twenty, he jammed it in his pocket, thinking Elric made a mistake. Catching the deceit, Elric decided not to let on. Whatever, he had lots.

A few of the other guys were coming out of darkness, slowly inching their ways toward him, like gruels of the dark.

"Good to see you, man," said another thin boy, dark circles under his eyes, long stringy hair, a toque pulled down over his head.

"Got anything to eat, man? Haven't eaten in two days now."

Elric looked at Jim, his cheeks sunken, hunger in his eyes.

"Sure, man, would never say no to a hungry man if I got it, man." Feeling in his pocket, he pulled out another twenty-dollar bill. Jim's eyes widened, his smile lighting up his face. "Really, you just gave me a twenty?"

"Yes, go and get some food to share with everyone, and don't ask me for anything for a long time. My grandmother died and left me a little money. So thank my grandmother, man."

"Thanks, that is mighty kind of you."

"Sure," he replied, bowing his head, happy to share his jackpot.

Heading toward the river, he saw five more sad mongrel looking men, their eyes deep in their heads. Their hands out to the warmth of the barrel, like some kind of worship. A dark sky, the sparks melting into the night.

Johnny showed up, hoisting the bottle into the air with a whoop, whoop from the others. Breaking the seal, he passed it to his left. Elric took it from him and put it to his head. He passed it to his left, then the bottle got around to the last one. Not a drop was left by the time it got back to Johnny.

As they all looked toward Elric, Johnny pulled another mickey out of his pocket. More cheers went off in the night. As the bottle got passed, the guys all feeling the warmth. The one thing in their lives that made them feel like family, even if it was just for the moment.

"From now on, man, when it's my bottle, I get the first drink," said Elric, looking at Johnny.

"Sure, sorry, buddy, just the first one. I didn't get a drop."

"Where's the other guys?" asked Elric.

"Dean, Roger, and George are in jail. Got caught breaking into a warehouse. They been in for two weeks now, waiting to go to court."

"Shit, you see, you got to be slick. They fucked up. Stupid bastards," a loud hearty laugh.

"Yeah, glad I wasn't in on it," answered Johnny. "My uncle has been letting me hang out at his place lately. Gave me an apartment over his garage. Man, if you got a little change, I could talk to him about you staying too."

"I might just take you up on that, brother. Right now I'm staying at the Quebec Hotel for a bit."

With a questioning look from Johnny, Elric had to think fast.

"Ya, my old man didn't want me staying with him anymore, so he put me up in the hotel for the month. After that, I will need a place to stay."

"Sure, sounds like a deal." The boys shook hands.

When Elric had first met the Riverside gang, Johnny brought him in. Elric had been hanging out around the general store, waiting to ask someone to get him a bottle. Noticing Johnny approaching, Elric walked up to him.

"Hey, buddy. Can you get me a bottle of whiskey?"

That bottle of whiskey had brought them together. A friendship started blooming from that day.

"You want to come and meet the boys? I don't know if you heard of us, the Riverside Gang. The fucking cops gave us that handle, and it kind of stuck."

Elric had heard a lot of bad things about them. Bad guys, everyone knew they were a band of beggars and thieves.

They all took to Elric like bees to honey. The tall, handsome kid who always seemed to have money and some booze to share with them. It became his regular crowd anytime he could steal from his grandmother's purse and play hooky from school.

Ten in all, like a big happy family. Only thing, they weren't happy at all, nerves on edge. Hunger and loneliness, their families having abandoned them. They fought like dogs to determine their places and to gain respect. They had their own code of ethics they lived by. Live, or die trying. Whatever it took.

"You see," said Johnny, the gang standing around the hearth barrel. "We are like a big family here. We look after each other. What I mean is if you fuck one of us, you were fucking with all of us. Do you get what I am saying?"

"Sure, I know what you mean," said the barely fifteen-year-old Elric. Since then they had become his family too.

Elric left the boys early that night, thinking of his stash of money and his new baby, his guitar.

The whiskey buzzed in his head like a swarm of bees, a dizzy feeling coming over him. Shit, he didn't feel good at all. Running to the river's edge, he puked into the dark water. Kneeling down, he washed his face in the cold water. "Fuck, I didn't eat anything all day."

"You going to be all right, man?" asked Johnny.

"Oh, ya, just drank too much, is all."

"I'm going to get going. We should get some practicing in. I got me a new Fender."

"Fuck man, where did you steal that?"

"I didn't. My granny died, left me a little money."

"Shit, well, my guitar is in the pawn shop again."

"I'll fix you up, man. I just got to go and get a good sleep."

Walking up the hill toward the bridge, Johnny follows behind.

"OK, man, I'll see you soon. You going to come down here tomorrow?"

"I'll see how I'm feeling. But I'll see you soon, OK?"

The booze usually made him feel better. Eased his loneliness. But today it had made him sick. He felt terrible, cold chills run up his back. Wasting no time, he made it up the hill in long strides to the road.

His coat pulled around his lean body, his fedora cocked to the side. Even at this time of the day, he looked and carried himself like a well-to-do gentleman.

Earl's days were consumed with where his son had gone. He had another visit from the same constables, asking for Elric again.

"No, actually, he got mad and packed his bag. Haven't seen him," said Earl, concern in his voice.

"We'll keep our eyes out for him," said Scott. "By the way, there was one thing I wanted to mention. Whoever broke into your office was wearing black cotton. We got back a few strands from the lab from the broken glass."

Just the word *black* filled Earl's mind with dread.

"Does that mean anything to you?"

"No," answered Earl, having already filled out the insurance claims. Might as well leave it alone, not bring reproach on the business, came the voice of reason.

"You have a nice day now," said the constable, holding the door for Detective Scott.

All day after their visit, Earl thought about the deceit. Elric had stolen the money and taken the first chance to get away with it. He remembered the black cotton shirt ripped up the side. With the long scratch he had noticed on Elric's side, it was all coming together perfectly now. *Fuck that kid. He can stay the hell away from me.* The cops were looking for him now. The way that one cop was talking, the way he had looked at Earl, told him he knew Elric was the thief. That was it; his door was closed to him. He would go and clean out his things and put them in the shed, change the locks on the doors, too. Suppose he sneaks back, trying to move back in? He didn't know the boy, couldn't trust him now. What had gone so wrong with the kid?

Elric got up a few times through the night to vomit. His head feeling like it didn't belong to him, the room spinning when he lay down on the bed. "Fuck," he said, passing out.

The morning sunshine crept through the window. The sun's rays splayed on the hardwood floor, Elric shaking himself out of his stupor.

"Oh, fuck, my head hurts," he said out loud. Getting up quickly, he heads into the shower, the steam from the hot water rising, "Ah, ah, yes, that feels good," he said, putting his face to the hot water, showering until the water went cold. Stepping out, he wrapped a towel around his waist, walking to the window, looking out on the city streets, buildings, people walking, men and ladies in hats. The city was waiting for him. It was his to do with what he liked. He had better get dressed, get some food in his belly, bacon and eggs, and rye toast, his favorite.

Dressing quickly, he stood in front of the mirror, combing his black hair off his high forehead, his grey eyes piercing, his square jaw, the dimple in the chin. "Sweet, swweeeeetttt," he said, taking a good look at his profile before leaving the mirror.

Today was his first day in the big city. Some new clothes, maybe new shoes, and…fuck, no. *I had better not spend any money right away,* came the voice in his head. Maybe the old man had gone to the cops, and they were looking for him right now. That was the likelihood, he reasoned.

It was great that Johnny had offered to let him stay at his place. He could lay low for a while, get a few tunes together. He was going to give Johnny some money so he could get his guitar out of hawk. Lots of money to chill for a while, maybe find a pretty girl to have some fun with, lately girls were interesting him more and more.

First things first. Elric walked down the street, looking for somewhere to eat. Finding a diner, just a few minutes away. "Bacon and eggs, toast, and jam," he told the waitress, "and coffee too, please and thank you," he said, his stomach growling. "And make that rye toast."

He hadn't noticed how cute she was until after he had eaten, asking for another cup of coffee. "Hey, what's your name?" he asked when she came back to fill his cup with steaming coffee right from the pot.

"Sarah," she answered, looking into his eyes, smiling.

"Can I take you out, sometime?" he asked, putting on his sexiest smile.

"Oh, maybe some time," she answered, walking away, her tray in her hands, Picking up some dirty dishes from another table.

Noticing the curves of her body under her skirt and blouse, undressing her with his eyes. Mmm, dessert, he thought. He would come here to have breakfast often, leaving her a five-dollar tip, making sure she had a good look at him before he left, bowing his fedora to her.

Back on the main street, doing a little window shopping when two constables coming towards him, he drops his head, not making eye contact. They both take notice of him.

Enjoying his freedom, carousing, and the attention he was getting from everyone, including the coppers. Heading back to the hotel, sitting at the bar, downing a couple shots of whiskey.

"Hey, buddy, gonna give us couple of tunes later?" asked the bartender.

"No, not today. My band wants to play here. We just gotta put in some practice time."

"Sounds good. We'll let you guys play one night, and if we like you, you'll get paid. We get a band in here once a week," said the dark haired bartender.

"That's a deal," said Elric, walking out of the bar to his room.

Laying down on the double bed, resting his hands behind his head, deep in thought.

All alone in the world, a free spirit. He liked that part of it, didn't have to take no shit from anyone, make his own way in life. *I don't need my old man,* he thought, closing his eyes.

By the time the week was ending at the hotel, Elric was ready to get going. That small room was driving him. Stopping by the desk, he told the clerk that something had come up, and he would like the rest of his money back, he would only be staying for the week. Packing up his bags, hanging his guitar over his shoulder, he walked down the steps of the hotel, heading toward the bridge.

Noticing a tall, older man, standing at the corner with his coat opened showing two men something. He had to see what the guy was selling.

Watches, rings, and gold chains hung inside the heavy overcoat. "Buy one, get one," he kept saying. An old weather beaten face, the wrinkles deep, like the stories behind the lines, at least seventy years old.

"Hey," said Elric, "show me the best watch you got."

"Yeah, buddy, in a minute. Show me some money first, kid," he said as he sold a watch to one guy and a gold money clip to another, stuffing his money into his top pocket of his gray overcoat.

"This is the best money can buy, right here," he said, holding up a watch in his nicotine stained fingers. "Gold with diamonds," he said.

"Let me see it, said Elric putting his hand out. The old man has a keen eye on Elric. "How much again?" he said, pointing to another watch. "Let me see that one too. This one is too big, for me, and how about that one there? Let me look at all of those. I got the money right here," said Elric, holding up two twenty-dollar bills.

"OK here, two for twenty," said the man, handing Elric the two smaller watches he had chosen.

"Thanks a lot," said Elric, picking up his bag, walking away quickly. Heading straight to the river, not looking back once. When he is well out of sight of the salesman, Elric pulled out the best watch, the first one he had shown him. He probably fucking stole this one anyway. "Wow, what a beauty," he said, fastening the gold and diamond watch to his wrist. The other two he would give to the guys, one for his new best friend, Johnny.

The city was providing for him already. It was great. He had met a pretty girl, got a new watch, and a job offer at the Quebec Hotel. Things were looking up. He couldn't wait to tell the guys.

It was a bright summer night, the boys hanging around like fireflies. A few of them throwing dice, some played cards. Heading down the hillside, toward the action and his newfound family.

A few guys huddling around the cement pillars, throwing dice, everyone's eyes are glued to the white squares dotted with black eyes.

"Seven come eleven," yelled Elric as the dice rolled in front of him. "Eleven, yeah," said the guy, rolling. "Want in on this game, man?"

"Five dollars? Sure why not," said Elric, putting his bag and guitar down. "Let the game begin," he said, grabbing up the dice, the excitement of the gamble making his heart beat faster.

Playing cards and dice all night, the first hundred dollars he started with dwindled to just a few dollars. Fuck, he said to himself. The wolfish eyes of the other guys watched his every move. Now he felt like drinking.

"Hey, Johnny, let's get a bottle of whiskey. Fuck these guys, took all my money."

"Whatever, Elric, the way you throw money around, I don't think you will miss it," laughed Johnny.

Pretending he didn't hear that comment, he walked away from the crowd of guys to get into his bag without anyone noticing.

Taking out two twenty-dollar bills, he handed Johnny one. "Here's a down payment on my room. Go and get a bottle of whiskey. On you today, man."

"Sure thing, Elric, see you in a bit."

Johnny went to a guy who was selling whiskey out the back of a wagon, put the bottle under his jacket, and ran back to the bridge.

The guys were still gambling, a few sad faces just looked on. Elric got back into the game, working on his second hundred, when he rolled a seven and then an eleven, taking the pot twice. The next roll, he rolled a seven again, with the dice rolling out of the seven, Elric already taking his money.

"No so fast there, buddy," said George, a short, stout fellow, with a dark grey suit on, a fedora on his head.

"What do you mean, I won it fair and square," said Elric.

"No," said George, grabbing Elric's arm.

"Look, man, it's not a seven, it's a nine."

"Fuck off," said Elric. "Get your paws off me," he said, turning, punching George straight in the face. Blood gushes from his nose.

"Don't fuck with me, man," said Elric, walking away, back to where Johnny was standing.

"Fuck, man, did you have to go and do that? He's one of us, buddy. Save it for the enemy," said Johnny,

"He was trying to tell me that I didn't win when I won it fair and square," he said, his voice growing louder. "Won three hands in a row, made some of my money back," he said, his hand in his pocket.

"They had me pretty good there until my luck turned around. I've been real lucky lately," said Elric. "Forgot to tell you I got us some work at the Quebec Hotel as soon as we can brush up on our skills."

"Let's get the fuck out of here," said Johnny, tempers flaring, someone else swinging a punch.

"Yeah, let's get outta here," he agreed, following Johnny up the bank toward the road.

"My uncle's house is not far, just on the other side of town. This way, man," said Johnny, leading the way. Elric followed behind, his guitar over his shoulder, everything he owned in two bags, one on his back, another in his hand. Things were working out just the way he wanted.

Johnny was glad for the company. His uncle was gone a lot of the time.

"Just stay out of the house," he had told his nephew. "You got everything you need in there," he said, pointing to the apartment over the garage. He was so grateful to have a place to lay his head. He had been sleeping under the bridge for almost a year now, a life not fit for a dog, he thought to himself, like the other dogs he had to bunk with, more like jackals.

His father had kicked him out when he wouldn't go to school and had started stealing. Things had been really hard until a few months ago, when his uncle gave him a job at his garage and the apartment. He only worked a few days a week, and the rest of the time he still hung out with the gang. He wasn't any better than them, just luckier. It was in his blood, singing, gambling, drinking, fighting, and surviving the best way he knew how.

No more cold nights on the concrete, just a box and a blanket between him and the freezing conditions. He shivered now, thinking of the many nights he went to bed hungry and cold.

George was sitting on the bank of the river, nursing a broken nose, his head back, his undershirt bunched up at his face.

"That fucking son of a bitch. I'll fucking kill that bastard. Who the fuck does he think he is?"

Since Elric had been coming around, the link was changing. He was Johnny's right hand man. Now this kid showed up, Johnny wasn't showing him, his usual respect. Fuck them both, thought George, wondering where he was sleeping tonight.

"This is it, man," said Johnny pointing to a redbrick house with white trim. "The garage is out back. Come on," he said as the garage came into view. Johnny walked to a door on the side of the garage, Elric following,

"Up here, at the top," he said. Elric looked up a narrow flight of stairs.

"It isn't no palace," Johnny said, getting to the top stair, exposing an open A shaped room, a bed to the right and a sink and stove straight ahead. A few clothes were strung on a cord in the corner, beer bottles and cigarette butts strewn about. A shabby looking green tweed couch had cushions showing wear. There was only one space on the floor where someone could put something down. Elric walked over, taking his guitar off his shoulder.

"Shit, man, there is only one bed. We'll have to get one," said Elric, taking off his coat and hat and hanging his coat over the back of a chair.

"Well, it's small, but it's a place to hang your hat," said Elric, looking around. "Hey, you got to clean up this place first before I give you any more money for living here. I like my shit in a clean place, man, that's one thing, I won't stay anywhere that is dirty. Clean is happy, man."

"Sure, man, think you could spot me another twenty? Feels good to have money in my pocket," said Johnny, eyeing his friend.

"Ya, I guess I could, and look, I got something else for you," he said, pulling out the black and gold watch out of his pocket.

"I got a new one." Pulling up his sleeve, show casing the gold and diamond watch.

"Wow, that's a nice watch. Fuck, man, you don't fool around."

"Anyway, that one is yours, and one more thing, I'm going to get your guitar out of hawk. When we get making money, you can pay me back. Right now, it's an investment."

"How old are you again?" asked Johnny.

"Seventeen, going on eighteen," Elric lied.

"Whatever, you are some bright," said Johnny.

"Ah, my old man's a shark, good car salesman and businessman. I guess I take after him."

"Interesting," answered Johnny. "I just turned twenty last month," My father was a fucking drunk, never taught me nothing."

"Sorry to hear that," said Elric, walking over to the bed.

"Tonight I sleep here, is that all right with you?"

"Sure, why not, I'll take the couch," agreed Johnny, grabbing a blanket off the bed.

The guys ate, then drank the rest of the whiskey. They played cards and took turns playing the guitar, harmonizing great together. Johnny was a handsome young man, chiseled features, blue eyes, and sandy blonde hair, and the same height as Elric. They would look good together on stage. They needed a drummer. "Maybe Dean," said Johnny, "and George plays a mean mouth organ."

Now that Elric had punched George in the face, he would have to figure out a way to make it up to him, otherwise he wouldn't want to be in a band called Elric and the Wanderers, thought Elric, chuckling to himself. He knew the way to George's forgiveness would be whiskey and food, and maybe he would give him the other watch, the brown and gold one. That was the plan, he thought. He didn't need it, pleased with his handiwork, pulling up his sleeve, admiring the diamond encrusted watch.

The guys sat up until four in the morning, getting acquainted. Finally, Elric lay down on the bed, closing his eyes, out like a light. When Johnny realized his friend had fallen asleep with his shoes on, he slipped them off, covering him with a light blanket. Going to his couch, he tries his best to get comfortable. He was sure happy he had met this guy. Smart and talented, thought Johnny. Can't go wrong.

Johnny and Elric stayed close to home for most of the week. By the weekend, both of them were getting a little anxious. Do a little drinking, maybe go see that pretty waitress, Sarah. Elric wanted to maybe get to ask her out.

They buzzed around town, going to the guitar shop, picking one out for Johnny deciding his other one was out dated. They walked around town like they owned the place, Elric eyeing a few pretty ladies.

"Let's go to the diner," said Elric. "I saw a pretty thing there the other day."

"Sure, I could eat something," said Johnny, remembering that he had his own money.

Sliding into a booth, Elric eyed the counter.

"Hey, beautiful," Elric said, as she approached their table. "This is my friend Johnny." The waitress and Johnny make eye contact.

"Oh, we know each other," said the girl, Johnny's eyes on Elric now.

"Let's just order our food, man, burger and fries for me, and a strawberry malt," said Johnny.

"Same for me, darlin'," said Elric.

"My name is Sarah," she said boldly, walking away.

"I've had her man. She's a bitch. Her old man's a cop, that Detective Scott."

"I see," said Elric. "Do you mind if I try and talk to her? I don't care for her father. Fuck him. All the more exciting."

"No, but whatever you want, man, just don't bring her around me."

"Sure thing," Elric answered.

"Hey, let's take some sandwiches down to the guys," said Elric, waving the waitress back over.

"Hey, doll, can you get me about ten sandwiches?"

"Sure, what do you really want?" she said, smiling.

"No, really, ten sandwiches, meat and cheese, OK? For some of my friends, that's all."

Johnny stared at Elric.

"That's the nicest thing I think anyone's ever done for those starving bastards," said Johnny, laughing hardily biting into his hamburger.

They ate and laughed, and Sarah brought over the ten sandwiches in two brown bags. "That's it, that will be five dollars," she said. Elric pulled out two fives. "One for you, sweet thing," he said, grinning. "I'll be back to see you."

Smirking she walked away from the table, stuffing the money in her front pocket of her uniform. Peering back at them, as they left the restaurant, wondering where they were going. Realizing he could be one of them, the Riverside Gang.

Johnny and she had history until her father, Detective Scott, put a stop to it. He told her Johnny was a no good bum, telling her to pick better company. Hoping this new hot guy wasn't one of them. She kind of liked him, that baby face and those grey eyes, mmm...

With a bottle of whiskey, and the two bags of sandwiches, Johnny and Elric headed to the bridge to find the guys. They noticed a couple of them standing around the barrel, sparks flying high into the night air. They turned to see their favorite friends, Elric holding up the brown bag with one hand, the whiskey bottle in the other. Howling like wild jackals, they came out of their hiding places, approaching like the walking dead.

"Hey," said Elric, George walking to them.

"Sorry about the other night, man, just had a lot on my mind. Anyway, here's some whiskey and a sandwich."

"Cool," said George, accepting the peace offering.

"I got something else for you too, man, just to show you I'm an honorable guy. Here," he said pulling the last watch out of his pocket.

"You'll need to keep time soon. We got us a gig at the Quebec Hotel."

"Yahoo," shouted George, holding up his new timepiece.

"You know we need you, man," said Elric.

"Sure, buddy," said George, taking the watch from his adversary, his nose still sore, his pride wounded. *Don't kick a gift horse in the mouth,* came the voice in his head. Maybe he wasn't so bad after all.

With two guitars, a cardboard box, and a mouth organ, a new sound was being born.

"We got to go to the Quebec Hotel next week, Saturday," said Elric. "You guys brush up on your skills. Figure we need about ten songs. Are you in or not?

"If we are good enough, we could get regular gigs there, get paid, I mean. You must be sick of going hungry."

"I'm in," said Dean."

"Me too," said George.

"Me three," said Johnny.

"Just want to let you guys know something." All of them staring at the handsome man boy. "I already got hired there. Was in the other day and did a few tunes for the crowd, and the boss man hired me to come back any time. For pay. So I just figured, I'll cut you guys in. I think we really got something here. Never know how big we will get. Just think, the Riverside Gang turned Elric and the Wanderers."

"So we are the Wanderers?" said Johnny, laughing.

"That's right," said Elric, putting the bottle of whiskey to his lips.

"Yeah, I like it. It has a certain ring," said Johnny.

They eyed each other, a new confidence in the air. This kid had brought them some hope and had given them food and whiskey.

They ate and drank their bellies full, Johnny and Elric making their way back to their pad.

Elric had secretly counted his money. He had already spent over five hundred of it, working on the next hundred. The money was going too fast. He was being too generous. He would tighten his belt, make the guys start earning his kindness. *Don't take kindness for a weakness*, he said to himself. No weakness here, he assured himself. Just like to be a good guy, share the wealth, he thought.

The crew had been meeting every day of the week after supper, the darkened night a safety blanket for Elric. He didn't know if the cops were coming for him or not, making him feel like he was being hunted. Or was he? It was stupid. Had his old man given him up?

One evening, the guys are heading toward the bridge, guitars in hand, Elric in the same trench coat and fedora. Scott and his partner had parked next to a bank, watching the evening's goings on. They had a drunk, pushed up against the back of their cruiser, when Scott noticed Elric, who shot a look at them just as Scott turned.

"There's that Schoolcraft kid. I want to talk to him." Leaving his partner standing there, he ran toward Elric, who was moving quickly now, Johnny falling behind him.

"Where the fuck you going so fast?" asked Johnny, looking behind now, a man in a trench coat running after them.

"Stop in the name of the law," screamed Scott, pulling his badge out of his jacket. Johnny stepped out of the way. Scott was hell bent on getting to Elric, who had started running faster now, his guitar holding him back.

"What the hell?" he said, stopping, turning holding his ground.

"What, what do you want?" he asked, staring the detective in the eye, recognizing him as one of the cops at the scene of his father's robbery.

"You are Schoolcraft kid, aren't you?" asked Scott.

"Who the fuck wants to know? Yeah, I am. Elric is my name," he said, turning his head to the side.

By now he knew he wasn't under arrest. The cop was just standing there, looking him over.

"Why were you running, if you weren't hiding anything? You and I both know one thing, Elric. You know you robbed your own father. We know it too, but your old man's got his head in the clouds, wondering what he could have done to bring you up better. You maybe can fool your old man, but you can't fool me. Detective Scott, to you. I am going to wait, bide my time, and I am going to nail you to that robbery. You better watch your Ps and Qs, cause I'm onto you, Schoolcraft."

"Whatever, man, you got no proof of anything. I would not rob my own father. I'm a singer, got my own band. I don't need to rob my old man."

"Just thought I'd let you know I am watching every move you make. Don't make any mistake. I'm taking you down, son," he said as he turned and walked away, pulling his fedora over his forehead.

Walking back to Elric, Johnny is wide eyed.

"What the fuck was all that about?" asked Johnny, thinking of all the money he had seen Elric with lately.

"That's where all that money came from, you robbed your old man?"

"No, I just took what was mine, the way I look at it. He wouldn't pay me so I took it. Not only that, the bastard didn't raise me, my grandmother did. Think he owes me one for that too. Anyway, you had better not repeat any of this, Johnny. I'll fucking kill you man. Do you understand what I just said?"

"Yeah, don't have to fucking threaten me, man, we are brothers, remember. The oath we took with our gang. You got my back, I got yours. I thought he was chasing me. That detective is Sarah's father, you know the chick from the diner.

"What the fuck," said Elric, having a deep hearty laugh. "Well, if that's not justice."

"He threatened to put my ass in jail for spitting on the sidewalk, warned me to stay away from his daughter," said Johnny.

"Really," said Elric. "Well, I got my sights on a piece of that. Fuck him."

The guys had a good laugh and kept on trucking down the road, toward Johnny's uncle's place.

It was a relief to Elric that at least they didn't have enough on him to arrest him. He hadn't planned on getting into any trouble. He wasn't going to ever see that cop again. The band was going to start playing at the hotel soon. They would have money in their pockets. They didn't have to steal anymore, at least he hoped that's how it would go.

The Riverside gang was busy all week, practicing under the bridge some days, attracting an audience, people standing on the bridge, looking down. The rhythm of the guitars and the voices reverberated through the cement pillars, bouncing back and forth, sending the music on the airwaves. In one week they had ten songs, ready for their first gig.

George and Dean were talking. "You see how that Schoolcraft kid just moved in and took over? H tells Johnny what to do now."

"Ah, that's just cause the kids got money," said Dean. "He is buying Johnny's friendship. Can't say I haven't benefited from his generosity myself. Even you, George, you don't mind drinking his whiskey."

"No, he busted me in the mouth, though. I'll get my chance, and I'll fuck him up."

"Let it go, man. He's been hooking us up lately. I kind of like the fucker, tough bastard, that's for sure. And I think he's only sixteen."

"You are kidding, said he was almost eighteen."

"No, man, look at that baby face of his."

"Yeah, baby face, good name for him," said George. "Baby face Elric." They shared a laugh, getting back to stirring the fire of the barrel.

"We'll be playing at the hotel on Saturday," said Dean. "It's fucking exciting."

"Yeah, it is," said George, putting his beer bottle to his lips.

Johnny and Elric were frying up steaks almost every day since Elric moved in. Life was changing for Johnny, since meeting the handsome crooner. With his looks and his voice, Johnny could really go somewhere, and he wasn't bad himself.

Since Johnny had told him that Sarah, the girl at the diner, was Scott's daughter, it made Elric want her more. Today he would go just before closing and coax her into meeting him outside.

Sauntering into the diner, scoping the floor, catching a glimpse of her just coming out of the kitchen with a full tray of steaming food. Not making eye contact, he walked to a booth at the back end of the restaurant, near a window. Seating himself, he took off his overcoat and set it on the seat beside him. Taking off his fedora, he ran his fingers through his black hair, off his forehead.

Sarah spotted a dark haired man with his back to her, a customer she hadn't greeted. She put down her dish cloth and made her way to him.

"Can, I get you a menu, sir?" she asked, Elric smiling up at her.

"Sure thing. Today I am really hungry, how about a waitress on toast."

Giggling she looked behind her, then gave him a welcoming, smile.

"Well, we might be able to arrange something after work," she said. "You are alone today. Johnny isn't waiting around the corner?"

"Ah no. He is not my sidekick. I roll alone. Johnny plays guitar in my band."

"So, you don't belong to the Riverside Gang? I thought you were one of them."

"Hell no. My band is Elric and the Wanderers, and I'm the lead singer and play guitar too."

"Never really heard of you before," she said. "How old are you? You look rather young to be doing all that."

"Just turned eighteen," he lied.

Just then the boss walked out of the kitchen toward where she is standing.

"Better take my order. Your boss is headed this way."

"What was that you wanted?" she asked, pencil to pad.

"I'll have the best steak you got, with a fully loaded baked potato and a vanilla milk shake, please."

"Sure, right away, sir."

As she turned, almost running into her boss, standing within hearing distance.

"Ah, just wondering if this fellow was wasting your time?"

"Oh no, he was just asking about the dinners. Having a steak."

Having a good look at Elric, he turned and headed back to the kitchen.

She liked him. He excited her, a warmth spreading over body, her cheeks getting rosy. Meeting him after her shift, she hoped he would wait for her. Impressed that he ordered the most expensive thing on the menu, and the tips he gave, better than anyone else. Convincing herself that he wasn't one of the Riverside Gang, excited to get to know him better.

Finishing the last bite, he sat back, watching her every move, sucking on his milkshake. Today he would have her, he had decided. She had warmed up to him nicely. This was going to be easy.

Paying for his meal, leaving her a hefty tip, she whispers to him, "All right, just wait for me across the road. Give me a few minutes to close up. I'll meet you there."

"Sure thing," he said, leaving the diner, walking across the street, standing under a street lamp. He watched her coming to him, taking her in his arms, ushering her into an alley, halfway down, he pushed her up against the concrete wall.

"I've been hungry for you," he said, whispering in her ear, raising her dress, his hand slinking up the side of her leg, pulling her underwear to the side. Undoing his pants with the other hand, he pulled out his erect cock. Pushing past the panties, he slammed it into her, she arches her back. Her head went back, letting out an animalistic whine. His face in her thick, golden brown hair, thrusting and thrusting. Sarah let out a few whimpers, finally giving her one last hard thrust of his groin, he stiffened in orgasmic spasms. Unfastening himself from her, he pulled up his pants, surveying his surroudings.

As she put herself together, watching him, looked deep into his cloudy grey eyes.

"You made me crazy for you. Sorry, just couldn't wait to taste your sweet nectar. Hope you liked it."

"Yes," she said, "I've been waiting for you to come for me. Let me know when your band plays. I would love to hear your band."

"This Saturday night, babe. Great, see you there. Quebec Hotel," he said.

Pulling his overcoat around him, his fedora down over his forehead, he walked away from the scene, looking back two times. She had gone the other way. That had been exhilarating, the way he took her almost forcefully, and she seemed to love it. And the fact that she was Scott's daughter made it all the better. *Don't fuck with me, man, I'll fuck your daughter,* he thought to himself with a deep belly laugh. Walking down the road, he felt like he had just won something. A lilt in his step, a feeling of conquest and renewed confidence. Humming a tune, he gets back to Johnny's.

Heading up the stairs, he walked into the open space to see Johnny, sitting on the couch, his feet on the coffee table a beer in his hands.

"Hey, man. I'll talk to you in a minute, got to get into the shower real quick," said Elric.

"Sounds like you might have been pussy hunting, you dirty hound dog."

"You are not far off. Talk to you in a minute."

Peeling off his clothes, they fall on the floor around his feet. Getting in under the hot water, baring his face to the cleansing heat. Soaping his whole body and face, he stood there till it ran warm, then cool, then cold.

Wrapping a towel around his waist, he picked up his clothes off the floor and walked out, past Johnny, to the bed. Throwing his clothes down, he walked back over to where Johnny was sitting. "Man, I just had a great piece of ass. Just guess who?"

"You are kidding me, man. Sarah? Wow, you are really fucking with your life now. If he gets wind of that, he will be all over you like sand flies. He wants your ass already, and you fucked his daughter now? You got more guts than brains, man."

"I don't give a fuck if she was the queen of England's daughter. If I want something, I go for it. And lately I get everything I want."

"You might eat those words if he catches you. When he found out that her and I had been hanging out, he put a stop to that quick. Came down to the bridge one day, him and another dick. Took me aside. Told me that I had better not see his daughter again, or he would put my ass in jail if he saw me spitting on the sidewalk. Threatened to put me away and throw away the key. No pussy is worth all that, man. I would watch myself if I were you, Elric. Just a warning.

"I really just don't give a fuck about that prick, I guess its him and me."

Elric walked over to the bed, sprawling out, laying back closing his eyes.

Johnny looked over at him. What fucking nerve, the bastard had taken over his bed now too. Jealous that he had fucked Sarah, he still liked her. So much for that. Now that Elric had his dick in her, she was used goods. There were lots of hot girls, especially now that the band was going to be playing around the city. He would meet another chick soon. That damn handsome bastard. Even the girl he hadn't met yet, was vulnerable to his new friend. How the hell? Maybe he would have enough respect for him to stay away from the girls he had in his future?

He had been with a lot of pretty girls. There would be more. But from now on, he was going to be more careful. A girl had said she was pregnant with his kid, and just lucky for him, she miscarried. Now he would keep it covered.

Saturday night came quick. The guys dressed in black, Elric ordered. They all had to look the same, his favorite look. Black on black. Dean and George had no black pants or shirts, Elric sprang for them, telling them he would get his money back when they started getting lots of gigs. Inviting them to Johnny's pad, the guys cleaned up nicely. Having a last look at his crew, Elric was satisfied.

"If we sound as good as we look, we are going to win their hearts." Declared Elric, smoothing down the sides of his jet black hair.

"There's no doubt about it," said Dean. "The girls are going to be wild."

"That's the way we want them, wild and hot," said Elric, all the guys having a good laugh.

Walking into the hotel, through the lobby, there were already people moving out of their way, realizing their entertainment had just walked through the door.

Already confident before they hit the stage. Walking into the main lounge with the stage, a loud clapping and hooting, as they are setting up.

Finally, ready for their first song, Elric takes the mike.

"Good evening, ladies and gentlemen. We are Elric and the Wanderers. I'm Elric."

A loud clapping and hooting came from a corner table. Sarah and two friends sitting there, she waved at Elric.

Johnny noticed her and looked away.

"Looks like they are all here tonight, man, let's get this party on," ordered Elric.

The band started with a lively tune. All the bar patrons were glued to the band and the lead singer, Elric. No one spoke, just watched and listened. After the first tune, there was louder clapping and hooting. They had been discovered the first night.

After they played out their set, the owner of the hotel approached the stage.

"Hey, you guys were a big hit here tonight. I would like to hire you for every Saturday night for the next two months. We got another band from

Toronto coming in. If they can't come close to your performance, we will cancel them, and you guys can come every week. That was amazing. And an extra twenty for all of you from a secret admirer," he said, passing out the twenties to the guys.

That night, they had all been stars. Never knowing that kind of happiness, all of them commended Elric on putting the band together. At the end of the night, they are all drunk on happiness and whiskey. Johnny and Elric headed back to the pad, Dean and George back to their campsite under the bridge. With the twenty dollars for the gig, and the extra twenty from some admirer, the guys had enough money to keep them in food and alcohol all week.

Their makeshift home, cardboard boxes to lay on and old blankets they had accumulated over the years, and the barrel for their warmth, like a mother's breast.

Summer was around the corner, and the nights would be warmer. Dean and George had renewed hope for a better life. George was thinking he could maybe talk his grandmother into taking him in again. She just wanted him to have a job and be responsible for himself. Maybe now that he belonged to a band, she would welcome him back.

His parents had separated and left the province, George's mother taking him with her to New Brunswick. She spent most of her time in the bars, taking home different men every night. He soon got sick of the way she was living, leaving him alone most of the time. He packed a bag one day, stealing what money he found in the cookie jar, making his way back to Quebec City. She wouldn't miss him, had never been a good mother to him.

His grandmother had taken him in, finding out quickly he was lazy. Meeting the other vagrants, he fit right in, started stealing and begging to get by. By the time his grandmother got sick of handing out her money to him, she told him to get out.

"Get a job," she had told him. "I can't support you, boy. Get out of my house, grow up, go to work," she had said, throwing his things out in the yard.

Dean never knew his parents, brought up in an orphanage, running away when he was twelve. He would find his own way in life. He hopped on the train, taking a ride into the city. He had been living on the streets for seven years now, stealing mostly to eat and drink.

The money the guys made for one night at the hotel wasn't keeping them in food and booze, most of it running out after one night of gambling. They were back to going hungry and waiting for someone else to bring the booze. Elric seemed to be the only one with money, the others spending theirs quickly.

Everyone loved to see him coming, even Johnny, who had grown accustomed to his generosity, giving him money every month for his lodging.

One night, the guys were sitting around, strumming a few tunes, the bottle passing between them, when there was a loud knock on the door.

"Who the fuck is that?" asked Elric, getting up from the couch. "Don't answer that. Could be the fucking cops?"

"No, man, it's probably my uncle, just coming back from his fishing trip. I'll get it, man. You are paranoid," he said, laughing, going down to the door. Opening it, a show of black and white, Johnny trying to push the door shut in their faces, the cops pushing their way in.

Scott was in a grey overcoat and fedora to match with a black satin ribbon around the base of the hat. A black and white uniformed cop pulled out a badge, showing it to Johnny.

"We are looking for Elric Schoolcraft. We have a warrant for his arrest."

Hearing his name called, he knew it was the cops. He thought right away of his stash of money that he had buried, under the porch in the back of the garage. Really, he had hidden it from Johnny. He was happy now that he hadn't left it in his stuff.

"Fuck," he said out loud, realizing there was no way out. Nowhere to hide.

Johnny held his ground, standing in front of them.

"You got a search warrant, man? I know my rights. Just got a few friends over. We are rehearsing some songs. We are a band."

"Sure," answered Scott, "a band of robbers is more like it. I know each and every one of you personally," he said, a smirk on his wrinkled, handsome face.

"Step aside, son, you don't want to be charged with harboring a fugitive."

Scott led the uniformed cop up the stairs, coming into full view of the guys, George, Dean, and Elric staring at them.

Zoning in on Elric, going in for the kill, he stands in front of him, Elric still relaxing on the couch.

"Elric Schoolcraft, you are under arrest," said Scott. "You have the right to remain silent. Stand up, or do I have to…"

"What the fuck is this all about now? Thought we discussed this shit."

Reaching for Elric's arms, he put the cuffs on him quick.

"We are taking you in to run some fingerprints. We found prints on a piece of wood that was used to break the window, and we need to run you through."

"Whatever, take these fucking cuffs off me man!"

"No, do you want to be charged with resisting arrest? Just give me a reason," said Scott, threatening, looking straight through Elric.

"Where is your stuff?" asked Scott, looking around the apartment. Just then Johnny came up the stairs, the cop pulling his gun.

"Relax, man," said Johnny, putting up his hands. "Just coming to see what is happening."

"We got a search warrant to look through his stuff. What is his?" asked the cop in uniform.

"His stuff is right there," said Johnny, pointing to Elric's guitar and bags, sitting near the bed on the floor.

Scott went to Elric's bags, started to empty them on the bed, searching in all the small pockets. As he watched, Elric getting more pissed off by the minute.

"Leave my shit alone, man, you got no right."

"Yeah, that's what you think," said Scott, still pulling his stuff apart. The guys watched as Scott ripped everything off the bed, then turned the bed upside down, looking through the underside, feeling along the seams of the mattress, padding and prodding on the mattress. Then he went to his clothes, pulling out three twenty-dollar bills.

"That's all you got left, Elric? Spent all that money already? You are a real fool, probably gambled it all away."

"Whatever, what fucking money you talking about? I made that sixty from our hotel gig last Saturday."

"Sure," said Scott sarcastically, "your merry band of thieves. I know you are one of the Riverside Gang now. There is nothing I don't know about you, Schoolcraft."

"Enough small talk, let's go," he said, motioning to the officer to bring him along. The cop reached for the cuffed hands, pulling on his arms. Elric spat in his face. The cop kneed him in the groin.

"Fuckkkkk," whined Elric, buckling over.

"Do as you are told, and come along now, before you really get hurt," said the officer.

"Take these cuffs off me, and talk to me. You wouldn't stand a chance, you old bastard."

The guys watched, saying nothing as Elric is led down the stairs.

"Hey, Johnny," he yelled back. "I'll be back soon. Look after my shit. I just got to get this straightened out."

"Sure, man, I'll be here if you need me."

Johnny sat back on the couch, deep in thought. It was all coming together now. All that cash Elric had been flashing around. Stolen from his father. Hoping that his friend would be back soon, he would look after his stuff. After all, he had paid up-front for two months of rent.

Things just weren't adding up though. All Scott found was sixty dollars. He was sure that Elric had a lot more somewhere. When he went with him to the pawn shop, he pulled out a stack of fifty dollar bills.

Back at the station, Scott personally escorted Elric in.

"Have a seat here, boy," he said, motioning to a metal chair sitting next to a small table.

"I'll find you somewhere to lay your head while I contact your father. In the meantime, we will want fingerprints. If your prints match the ones on the piece of wood, you will go to jail with or without your father's blessing."

After the prints were done, Elric settled into his cell, a single grey blanket, laying on a steel framed single cot.

"It's cold in here, man," he yelled through the steel bars.

"Well, it's no vacation, kid. I'll get you another blanket." The constable looking in at the handsome man boy.

A couple of hours passed by. No sign of Scott. Elric wondered when he was getting out or if his father was coming in to see him.

The officer on duty sitting just outside the cells, kept looking in on the boy. Taking a look at his file. He was fifteen years old, looked like twenty-one. His file reads suspicion of robbery, no charges laid. Scott seemed to hate the kid. Maybe he would show a little kindness and offer him something to eat.

"Hey, kid, you want a sandwich and a drink?"

"Sure," answered Elric, "would me mighty kind of you," he said, figuring he might as well be nice. Maybe get what he wanted.

The tall, thin officer, in his black and whites, pushes the ham and cheese sandwich under the door, handed him a plastic cup, with water.

"How long am I going to be in here? I haven't been charged with anything."

"We are waiting on your father. If the prints don't match, you will be released into your father's care, seeing you are a minor. If he don't want to take you out of here, you will be held here until Detective Scott decides."

Feeling totally vulnerable, and now he had to deal with his old man, one thing he wasn't looking forward to. Relaxing on the bed, he put his hands behind his head and started humming a tune.

Thank God he had hidden his loot. The cops would have found it in his stuff. That would have sealed his fate...jail.

The next day, under the bridge, the gang looked lost and saddened. Everybody's mind was on the handsome crooner, their lead singer and their new recruit.

"Fuck, said George, "he might be an asshole, but he's a smart bastard, and talented too."

"Well, he'll probably turn up sometime soon. See you guys," said Johnny, walking away up the hillside.

Two officers had taken Elric to a little room, where they buttered his fingers with black ink, rolling each of his fingers on the spaces for each finger and thumb. Stupid bastards, he thought to himself, envisioning biting into the side of their necks. A deep sigh. "Are we finished yet? You guys just wasted your time, and mine. I didn't do nothing."

"Look here, kid, shut your face. You wouldn't be in here if Scott didn't think he was onto something. He's the best we got, and he always gets him man. Now that we got your fingerprints, and if you are doing crime, we got you on file. He's the kind of guy who doesn't waste the department's time, or his own. You are only fifteen? You sure don't look fifteen."

"I'm going to be sixteen soon, and I am a lead singer in a band. Don't know why he is messing with me. Hope my father gets here, soon, to straighten this out."

The two cops looked at each other, one of them raising his eyebrows.

Restless, he gets up, pacing the cell like a caged animal, sitting back down, then back up again. He must have asked when he was getting out ten times when the new cop coming in for the night shift walked to his cell.

"Looks like you got the presidential suite for the night. We were not able to contact your father. Scott is going to see him first thing in the morning. I'm sure he will be in tomorrow to see you."

"Damn it," said Elric, grabbing the bars with both hands, pulling on them hard, his knuckles going white. So angry, he could have ripped that cop's ears off his head. Walking back to the slab of a bed he settles in.

Tossing and turning all night, making Johnny's place feel like a luxury hotel. Once the whiskey wore off, the reality of it all came down around his head, hard. Pain in his head and behind his eyes, like his head is in a vise. At the first sight of daylight, through the little window at the top of the cell, Elric got up off his torture slab.

"Hey, somebody, I need a cup of coffee, something to eat. Can anybody hear me?" he shouted.

The cop on duty came out of an office.

"That's enough yelling, young man. Breakfast is served at eight o'clock, not before. Where do you think you are? This is jail, not some camp for wayward kids."

Staring him down, Elric said nothing, instead of what he really wanted to say. Fuck, didn't want to piss these guys off that had the keys for his cage. Instead, he walked back to the cot and sat down, holding his head in his hands.

Finally, after what seemed like forever, his breakfast came, slid under the bars. The cop handed him a steaming paper cup with black coffee.

Eating the scrambled eggs with two pieces of toast, he was still hungry. Washing it down with the black coffee, at least he felt somewhat appeased. "Sure don't give a guy much to eat around here," he commented when the officer came to collect his tray.

"You forget where you are, boy? This is jail. You were lucky you got anything to eat. Your father will be in here before noon to settle your fate. If I were you, I would just sit back like a good little boy, and wait."

What he wanted to say right now, he wouldn't. Better to just shut up and hope for the best.

Detective Scott and his partner had gone to Schoolcraft auto sales and told Earl that his son was in jail. He decided he would make him wait till after his day was over. Let the little bastard feel it. Deep in his heart, he knew, too, that Elric had burned him. With the insurance company paying him back most of the loss, he didn't have a lot of hate for his kid. Just that he didn't want him around anymore, couldn't trust him. The other option was to take him into the bush and put him to work. He had his logging operation up the mountain, and Elric was a strong kid. Surely, he couldn't get into too much trouble, back in the woods.

If he wanted to be wild, the bush would be a good place for him, no place to get alcohol or get himself into trouble. He could see his son was choosing the wrong road in life, thoughts of him, huddled up in some cold place, homeless, leaving Earl with guilt of not raising him.

By the afternoon, Elric was getting hungry again. "Shit, I thought my old man was coming for me. Where the hell is he?"

"Don't ask me," said the cop behind the counter. "We're not mind readers around here."

No choice but to sit and wait, he started singing a song. Both cops on duty listened to the sweet sounding voice coming from the cell. One of the cops gets up and goes to the cell, looked in at Elric.

"Wow, kid, you can sure sing. With that voice, you could really go places. Maybe focus on your talents and stay out of trouble."

"Like I said, I didn't do a thing. I got my own band, too, Elric and the Wanderers. We just played to a packed house, at the Quebec Hotel, last Saturday. We got a steady gig there now."

The cops looked at each other, impressed.

Just then, another officer walked into the cell area, holding the door. Elric watched as his father stepped through the door. Too gentlemanly looking to be in a jail house. Long black trench coat, black and grey fedora, his black shoes with a perfect spit shine.

"Well, well, you guys found him." Staring in at his son, Elric turned and walked back to his cot.

"Oh, he wasn't hard to find. He hangs out with that bad bunch, the Riverside Gang, and looks like they might be recruiting him. If he stays with that bunch, he is sure going to be looking at more time in here.

Earl walked to the cell, staring in at Elric, who didn't look up, just kept his eyes on the cement floor, his hand cradling his chin and mouth.

Getting up from the slab bed, Elric walked to the bars now, looked his dad full in the eyes.

"It's nice of you to come. Can you get me out of here? They got nothing on me. Saying they are holding me on suspicion of the robbery at your car lot. I thought that had already been settled."

"Well, it looks like they are releasing you in my care. The prints on the tire iron did match yours, but like I told the cops, you were using it to change tires."

He knew now that they really had no proof. He would work this all in his favor.

Detective Scott showed in the doorway, looked in at Earl while the officer on duty opened the cell, Elric stepping out.

"Thanks, Dad," he said, walking out past Scott, like he didn't exist. Striding steadily out into the lot, looking for the old man's Cadillac.

Waiting, he saw Scott talking to his dad, who was walking toward him now.

Opening the back door, Elric got in, sliding his way over behind the passenger seat. Stretching his legs out, he leaned his head back into the welcoming softness of the leather seats.

"That was a fucking nightmare," he said out loud.

Pulling his overcoat to the side, Earl slid in behind the wheel, looking back at his son.

"I didn't take your money, Dad, I know how to make my own money. I have a band now. We play every week at the Quebec Hotel."

"At the hotel," said Earl. "You are too young to be hanging out in any hotel. You are only fifteen. You have aged since I saw you, that's what drinking does to you."

"Yeah, I like a drink once in a while, I won't lie."

"Well, as of right now, there is no drinking for you. Drinking will ruin your life boy." Elric rolled his eyes, looking away. Enough said, Earl goes quiet.

Elric closed his eyes, laying back, Earl driving, keeping his eyes on the road, pulling up at the house. Elric remembered his stuff at Johnny's. His guitar, his clothes, and his buried money.

"Dad, I need to get my things from my friend's house. I'll take the car and come right back."

"No, you won't. I'll drive you there tomorrow. Right now, you just get a good sleep, and we'll take care of that stuff tomorrow."

Following his father into the house, he looked around. Everything was the same as he left it. Deciding he would just go to his room; he didn't want any more lectures. Wait to see what his dad had in store for him. If he didn't like it, he would run away again. The cops would have to catch him first.

Laying back in the bed, he thought of Johnny and the gang. What would they do without him? There would be no band without the lead singer. They were nothing without him. Right now, he had no choice; he would have to dance to his father's beat, wondering what his father really had in mind for him? He was probably going to send him into the mountains to work in the bush. Maybe it wouldn't be so bad. Hard work. He was strong and willing. Probably make some good cash. Give the gang a break, stay out of trouble, save some money and buy himself a car soon. Then he could pick up that pretty Sarah, and take her riding. He laughed. Riding, all right.

Waking at the sound of his father's alarm, he sits up, stretching. Today he would get his dad to take him to Johnny's and pick him up after work. He had to tell Johnny the plans. That way, he would have time to dig up his money and put his things together.

Heading out toward the kitchen, he knew he was in for a lecture over breakfast. Earl was already sitting there, having his morning coffee.

"Good morning, Father," he said, buttoning his black cotton shirt, sitting down at the table.

"There's fresh coffee," said Earl, "if you want breakfast, you make it. I've got to get going early today. You will wait until I get home, and we will go for your stuff."

"I'll ride with you as far as the lot, then I'll hitch a ride into town. Can you pick me up on your way home? Johnny lives with his uncle over the body shop. The Williamson place."

"Sure, I know the spot," said Earl. "Sounds good then. Get yourself some breakfast quick. I have to be out of here in twenty.

"So, I'm going to give you a shot working in the bush, with the falling crew. I don't see why you couldn't handle cutting trees, a tall, strong boy like you. A little hard work will get the piss and vinegar out of you. Six days a week. Up at six, in the bush by seven. I'll save your pay for you for six months. You'll have enough to buy yourself a car."

Just the way Earl spoke, he wasn't sure that he had stolen his money. Feeling better about the deceit now, he would try and be cordial with his old man. Really, he wanted the best for him, and he had come to get his ass out of jail. If that fucking Scott had his way, he would put him in jail and throw away the key, chuckling to himself.

A car of his own sounded great. That would sure be worth working for. When he had wheels, he wouldn't have to stay in one place very long. He was a true wanderer and could get the band gigs all over the country. Happy with the sound of that, he settled it in his mind. He would work hard and stay out of trouble.

CHAPTER 58
Six Months in the Bush

Elric went to work in the bush, like his father had ordered. Earl worked him hard and paid him little, saying he was saving his money for him to help him get a vehicle of his own. Days that he did have off, he would steal a ride into the city, spend a few hours getting drunk with the gang.

One morning, hung over, he didn't make it to the job sight in time, his father waiting for him.

"This business can't wait for you. Smarten up, boy. You'll be looking for another place to work. Just because you are my son doesn't give you any right to screw everyone else up. If this happens again, you will be fired."

Do me a favor, thought Elric, getting sick of his father's preaching, making him look bad in front of the other ten loggers, Elric the only teenager.

He had grown taller and was filling out in places, making him more handsome. The hard work was good for him, and he loved being out in the fresh air. If he wanted to scream and yell when a tree was falling, there was no one to hear him but the squirrels or the other men.

He was out of the city, but not out of their minds. His name was in a lot of people's mouths. The bar patrons who came the next Saturday to hear the Wanderers were disappointed. The owner had to hire another band, which didn't thrill them half as much. The gang was lost without the young crooner. No more handouts of liquor and food. Even George said how much he missed him. There was only one person happy to not see him around, Detective Scott.

He had scoped out the Riverside Gang for about a week straight. No sign of Elric. His father must have taken him back in to the fold. He was one of the lucky ones, he thought.

One cold October morning, Elric was using the team of horses, pulling some logs out of the bush to the clearing. The big eyes of the Percherons rolled in their heads, watching him as he rigged up their strappings to their bits, the trailer behind them, dragging on the ground. The fallen trees were stacked liked matchsticks.

The work horses were pushed to their limits, the veins in their chests enlarged like snakes under their skin. Nostrils flaring, their eyes wild. The coldness of the air showed in the stream of breath from their mouths. A kind of madness hung in the air, a light fog showing in the clearing.

"Get up there," he shouted. "Move over, goddamn it. Move over, you son of a bitch!" he said as the big grey Queen, trying to find her footage, stepping straight down on the top of Elric's foot so hard, the moistened earth gave way.

"Holy fuck, oh my God," he screamed, his face drained of blood. Looking down, the top of his foot flattened. Leaning his weight against the horse, the pain running from his foot straight up the leg.

"You son of a bitch!

Limping away now, screaming in pain.

"Fucking son of a bitch," he cursed, walking over to some tools near the horseshoes. He picked up an iron piece of metal used for bending horseshoes. Hobbling back to the horse, both horses now agitated, feeling the energy, Elric cursing and screaming. They pulled away from each other just as Elric slammed the piece of iron, straight on the top of Queen's head. She staggered, her eyes wide in fright.

"You fucker, take that, you fucker," he screamed, hitting the horse again and again, the blood splattering him in the face. Blood trickles down the horse's head, filling her eyes. The assault continued, with him swinging wildly until Queen's eyes rolled back in her head, her legs buckled beneath her, then she rolled over, dead, on the ground.

Pierre, the cook, heard the screaming and came running from the cook house.

First thing he saw was blood splattered all over Elric's face and shirt. Then he saw the horse lying dead.

"Oh my God. What happened here?" he asked, now seeing the murder weapon, a blood crusted piece of iron.

"Fuck off, you French bastard," said Elric, peeling off his boot, the woollen sock stuck to the flesh of his foot.

"It's fucking broken. My foot is broken, man. Go and get my father."

Pierre ran back to the cook house, going straight to where Earl was sitting, having some breakfast.

"You need to come now, sir, something terrible has happened."

Earl left his steaming plate of food and ran behind Pierre, back to the barn.

"What the hell is going on here?"

He took one look at Elric, then the bloodied horse lying dead. The other big Percheron at the other end of the barn, steam rising from its body, its rigging still hanging off its side.

"What happened here, son? You had better start talking."

"Can't you see, the fucking horse broke my foot. I won't be able to work now."

In shock, looking from Elric to his beautiful big mare Queen, her head caked with blood, dead on the ground. Earl had bought her and her brother Bart, as yearlings. Standing eighteen hands, Queen just a little smaller. Two years of training every day, to make them the perfect team, pulling logs out of the bush.

Queen was a dappled grey beauty, with black from her knees down to her hooves. Bart was totally black. Everyone commented on the beauty of the animals. Earl loved them both and had taken a special likeness to Queen, spending quiet time with them in the barns, feeding them apples and carrots. So proud of his team.

Walking past his son, Earl knelt down in the straw, close to the dead horse. Taking a closer look, he saw pieces of her flesh dug out of her head. Overcome with grief, he started crying like a baby. Rubbing his hand over her shoulder, he turned away and started vomiting. Heaving and heaving, until he succumbed to his sadness, lying face down in the straw, a few feet from the horse.

Eying his father, Elric realized he didn't care a bit about his broken foot. He knew that he was going to face some consequences now. A blind rage took over him in his madness. Seeing the dead horse in the straw, and his father weeping, made him feel a bit sorry. What was his old man going to do to him now? Oh shit, I really fucked up!

Earl was picking himself up off the straw, wiping at his face. He turned to Elric now, his eyes wide, his face serious.

"You had better do some talking boy, and fast. What happened to Queen? No, before you start with your lies, let me tell you what happened to her. You killed her. You, you are a killer!" Walking over to where Elric is sitting, Earl takes a swing at him. Elric dodged the fist. "I'm so done with you. You are no son of mine! The money I have been saving for you, forget it now. It will go toward training and buying another horse. You destroy everything you touch. I will have someone take you down the mountain. You make me sick!" he yelled in Elric's face, storming off toward the camp house.

Entering the bunkhouse, all the men came to attention. The air is thick with hate, disgust, and murder. His eyes wide, he summoned six men to load Queen onto the flat bed and haul her up the mountain to her resting place. He asked Ben, a big burly logger, to go and help Elric back to the bunkhouse.

"My son has a broken foot. Would you go and help him into the bunk-house? I have to get someone to help him down off the mountain."

"Yes, of course, sir. What happened to his foot?'

"Looks like one of the big Percherons stepped on him."

Not wanting to answer any more questions, his stomach in knots, the waterworks of tears still hanging behind his eyes. He just wanted to get back down the mountain himself and go home. Reflect on what had really gone wrong with his son.

Wayward. That was it. Never had a mother's love. He could come up with lots of excuses for him, but nothing excused the killing of his horse. Damn kid. Now he just wanted to get rid of him. He would have to let him stay at the house, until he could walk at least. As much as he didn't want to see his face, he would just stay out of his way. Get up early, and avoid him like a leper.

The six men managed to get Queen on her side on the flatbed. Putting a yoke and strappings on Bart, they led him to where his sister lay dead. Bart threw his head and screamed a high pitched whinny, like none of them had ever heard. The men tried their best to quiet and console him, as they hooked him up to the flatbed.

Bart is wide eyed and wild. He pulled hard, the sweat showing in foam between his legs. All the way up the mountain, he screamed his goodbyes to his sister. The men were all caught up in the sadness and the reaction of Bart. So sad, the men just went through the motions, getting the dead horse to an open field. As soon as they had the flatbed where they needed it, one of the men led Bart back down the mountain, the big black turning his head a few times.

The ground was too cold to dig a hole. They would leave the horse's body, for the buzzards and crows. Once spring came, all that would be left would be a skeleton. They could give her a decent burial, then.

The men did what they had to, not saying much. They all knew Elric had an anger problem, most of them staying out of his way. One of the guys had just been joking around, called him Daddy's boy, when Elric punched him square in the face.

The news spread through the campsite quickly that Earl's son had a hair trigger.

He ordered Pierre, the cook, around like he was his own personal chef. *Make me this, make me that.*

The word of the dead horse spread like a bad germ though the camp, all the guys shaking their heads. One of them had been standing not far from Earl when he told his son that he was done with him and that he was sending him packing.

Everyone was happy to get rid of the cocky bastard. The only thing they would miss was his singing.

Nights after work, and at supper quite often, Elric would entertain the guys with a few tunes. They all enjoyed his singing, even though most of them didn't like his arrogance.

There were other reasons, too, that they were all happy he was going. Most of them were on edge, thinking he was there to spy on them for his father. Everything would get back to normal now that the kid was gone.

Sitting on the side of the bed, he tried to get his broken foot into his boot. Wincing in pain, it had swollen to twice the size. The bunkhouse door opened abruptly. Earl stormed in, straight to Elric. Without warning, he punched Elric straight in the face.

"What the fuck," said Elric, his hand going to his mouth. Blood spread across his palm, tasting his own blood.

"That was straight from the horse's mouth, so to speak," said his father. "You had that coming, you son of a bitch!" He yelled in his face.

"Yeah, I guess she was a bitch, all right, fucking the first thing that came along, and then she left your ass and us all alone. You are a fucking asshole," he yelled, glaring at his dad.

"What are you going to do, kill me?" asked Earl, his eyes wide.

Holding his face in his hands, Elric, with his head down, didn't answer his father. He was worried now. Would he make him stay in camp, or let him stay at the house until his foot was better? There was no way he could do anything, with a broken foot.

Earl decided to leave him right there. It was too late to get a doctor there to look at his foot, and he so mad he didn't want to see the likes of him, anymore today.

Ordering one of the guys to hook up Bart to the wagon, to take him down the mountain. Elric could suffer, for all he cared. He needed to feel some of the pain he was feeling.

Going back to the bunkhouse, Earl walked over to the side of the bed, Elric lying flat on his back. Noticing a sheet torn to bits, the remnants tied around Elric's foot.

"It's going to have to do. The doctor is not going to come up here till tomorrow to see if your foot is really broken. Then we can go from there. I've decided you can stay at my house until you can get around, then you are on your own kid. I don't want you working for me anymore, anywhere."

"That's quite OK, Father. I told you, I have my own band and already had steady gigs when all this shit went down."

"Save your foul language for your street friends. Don't use it around me, you hear me, boy? While you are still under my roof, you will dance to the beat of my drum, do you understand? I'll feed you and give you a place to stay, until your foot is better."

The next morning, Pierre carried a tray of breakfast in for Elric, with a steaming hot cup of coffee. Sitting up in the bed, he smiled at Pierre.

"Thanks, man, you are the best. I'm going to miss your cooking. My old man fired me. I'll be leaving as soon as the doc gets here to check on my foot. Thanks for everything."

Putting down the tray on the side table, Pierre bowed slightly and walked out of the bunkhouse.

The doc showed around noon, with his kit of plaster Paris.

The foot was twice the size of the other one, the doctor prodding through the swelling.

"It's broken all right. All the fine bones in the top of your foot. It will be three months before you can get this cast off. I'm going to put one on now, just to the ankle. Try to stay off it, as much as you can," said the grey haired doctor.

"Three months, are you kidding? That's a long time not being able to do anything."

"In a few days, you will be able to walk around, but with crutches. You definitely won't be working up here in the bush, like this." Declared the doctor.

CHAPTER 59

Day in and day out, Earl counted the days until he could get Elric out of his life. He had violated his trust and his generosity. Should have left him in jail, thought Earl, maybe he would have learned a lesson. Now look what he had done, ruined what they did have left as father and son.

Two and a half months later, Elric was getting itchy feet. Actually, his bad foot was itching the hell out of him. He tried sticking forks and other instruments down the side of the cast that ran from his foot up past the ankle. When the itching started driving him crazy, he decided that he would cut the cast off himself. Earl had said that he would take him to the doctor in another two weeks to see if he would take it off early. That was too long to wait.

Picking the sharpest butcher knife he could find in his father's kitchen arsenal, he started sawing down the side of the cast, white plaster of Paris falling away, crumbling to the floor. He cut and cut at it, until the side of it was cut straight through, pulling it away from his foot. Looking down at the foot, pink and scaly, freaking him out. When the cast was all the way off, he put his foot up then tried stretching it. It hurt, but not badly, making him happy that it was healed or almost healed. He could work with this, would just have to wear his work boots, for better support and more room. Today, he was getting out of his father's house. He would wear his work boots.They would give him better support. Nothing was going to stop him from leaving today.

Getting dressed, he grabbed his pack, his guitar, sitting them on the side of the bed. Hobbling out to where his money was buried, he strained to stand on the foot, throbbing now. Fuck, he would have to wait a few more days until he could at least walk. Going back in the house, he rigged up a bandage and wrapped the bad foot. Standing now, it felt better, the tightness of the bandage, taking away some of the pain. Another few days, and he would be out.

Earl preaching to him every day was getting on his last nerve. He had already been living on his own. Why the hell did he insist on him going to work in the bush anyway? By now, the whole county would have known about the band.

He thought about the guys, and how happy they would be to see him. He still had lots of money. Realizing, if he wouldn't have robbed his father, he would be shit out of luck right now, probably have to sleep under the bridge, on a cardboard box. Not happening. If he showed up with food and alcohol, they would let him back into the fold. That he wasn't worried about. They were nothing but a bunch of bums without him.

A week later the foot was feeling a lot better, able to put a little weight on it, and walk, without much pain. Time to make his move.

Hearing Earl getting ready for work, rustling around in the kitchen. With his things pretty much packed, he was ready to make his move. The money was in the same place, hidden in a pile of bricks near the garage. With that, he had enough to get himself settled into the city, until the band started making money. As far as his old man went, he cared less if he ever saw him again. There was bad blood between them now. Earl had turned his back on him.

When he heard the door slam shut, it was his cue to get up and out.

He had one last look around, thinking it might be the last time he saw this room. He was leaving for good this time. Closing the door, walking down the hallway, towards the kitchen.

Leaving a mess on the kitchen table, molasses dripped off the side of his greasy plate.

Ah, leave his something to remember me by, he thought to himself, laughing out loud, going out the door.

Hitting the dirt road with confidence, an air of freedom taking over him.

Taking a deep breath, the sun shining down on him, a cool fall afternoon.

Walking along on the side of the road, his mind cleared. Not a worry in the world, he told himself, a pocket full of money and a nice guitar. What else could anyone ask for?

After a short way, his foot started to hurt. A little way more, and his foot really started hurting. Sitting on the side of the road, he loosened the laces of his boot, then took it right off. He noticed the foot was swelling. "Shit," he said, "can't fucking do this?"

There was no way he was going back. He would just sit and wait, till someone picked him up.

Taking the guitar off his shoulder, he cocked his fedora to the side, strumming and singing, watching down the lonely road. A few cars passed, everyone noticing the handsome kid.

A car slowed and pulled over to the side, near him, having a better look at a woman behind the wheel.

Waving at her, he put his guitar down, hobbling on one foot over to the car.

"Hey, nice car," he said. Then he recognized her. The only car he had sold in his life.

"Well, this must be my lucky day," said Elric, a big smile for the pretty lady. Bonus for him, she was alone, too, her auburn hair pulled back in a French roll.

"Fancy meeting you again," she said. "What might you be doing?" Peering over at his pack, and his guitar, then the boots on his feet.

"A little down on my luck. Was working in the bush for my father and had an accident with a big horse. Broke my foot. I've been laid up for three months. Just heading into the city, to look up my band."

"Oh, you not selling cars anymore?"

"No, I got bigger things in the works. I have my own band, I'm the lead singer. Elric and the Wanderers."

"That sounds exciting. I can see you being a lead singer. Wow, the girls are going to be swarming you. Get in, I just so happen to be going into Quebec City myself. You can ride with me all the way, on one condition."

"And what would that be, pretty lady?"

"You could sing me a couple tunes as we drive. That would be exciting."

"I sure can do that." Answered Elric.

Tossing his stuff in the back seat, his bag and his guitar and the one boot he had taken off his foot, the white bandages showing up to the ankle.

"You know what? I was actually thinking about you the other night. I was in bed, just about to fall asleep. I'm single now, and you know, I was having some fun with myself." Said the pretty lady. "I have to confess, you have been in a few of my fantasies. The day we met, I couldn't stop thinking about you all day, just something about you."

"Well, I have to say, I thought about you a lot that day, I sold you the car too," Elric said, laughing. "Sorry I forgot your name?"

"Joan," she answered, smiling.

He imagined her without her glasses, her thin, tight body her breasts sitting high in her sweater. A little old for him, but she was sexy, and pretty. And she had mentioned she was single. Was that a come on, he wondered, getting excited. The way she was flirting with him gave him confidence that if he wanted her, he could have her.

"You are all grown up, Elric. How long has it been since we met?"

"Over a year ago. I was on my own for a while, then my dad thought it would be good for me to go and work in the bush. Said I am wild, and the bush would tame me," he laughed. "I'm going to be performing full time now," as he combed his long fingers through the front of his hair, pushing it back over his high forehead.

Settling in the comfy leather seat, he extended his legs, giving his foot lots of room. Leaning back into the seat, resting his head back, closing his eyes.

Having a better look at the square jaw and the dimple in his chin, the black shiny hair, long, straight Roman nose. Mmm....she liked what she saw. Sure, he was young, but willing from what she could tell.

Reaching his hand over, he rested it on the top of her bare leg, massaging it tenderly. She didn't pull away but started moaning, the touch exciting her. The moaning was making him hard.

Trying his luck a little further, his hand searched farther up her skirt. Relaxing her thighs, letting him explore.

"Pull this baby over, I've got something to show you," he said, smiling.

Slowing, she watched for a side road. Pulling the Cadillac off the road, she started up a narrow, pot-holed dirt road. A few minutes into the road, turning off the engine.

Sliding over to the passenger side, she pushed herself against his body, deep French kissing him. Wasting no time, Elric's hands started roaming her body, like she was a new present to unwrap.

Slipping out of her blouse, he reached for her bra clasped at the back, undoing it, her breasts bare her nipples pink and erect. The kissing was getting hotter.

"C'mon, let's get in the back," he said.

Opening the back door, she slid in. He had his pants undone and was going for the prize. Without any resistance from her, he pulled off her underpants and hoisted her skirt to her waist. Laying on top of her, feeling for his cock now, guided it between her legs, after a few tries it slipped in. A deep moan from him, a high pitch welcoming cry from her.

Breathing in the essence of her, he rested his head on the side of hers, his face in her thick, beautiful hair.

Going deeper, he thrust fast and hard. Her breath was coming in short gasps now, his quickened and hungry. Ten minutes into the throes of ecstasy, he orgasmed, pulling himself off her. Staring into her eyes; she was happy. She had loved it.

Laughing to himself. Hadn't felt a pain in his foot the whole time, until after the deed.

Pulling herself together, smoothing back her hair, she gets back into the driver's seat, and Elric into the passenger's.

"Was that as good for you, as it was for me?" he asked.

"Let's just say, it's just what I needed. You were fabulous. I think you have a lot of talents, not just singing."

They shared a hearty laugh, their minds and bodies stimulated, the serotonin running thick through their brains. The smooth ride of the Cadillac lulled them into a pensive mood, neither of them saying anything.

Silence for a few minutes, then he spoke.

"Moving back to the city. My old man kicked me out."

"That is terrible. Is there any way I can help?" Thinking of taking him back to her place for a few days. He was so cute and could sing too. Probably not a good idea at all she decided. She was forty-five, and he was eighteen, or so he had said.

"Think you could take me to the Quebec Hotel? Got to get a room there, stay in for a few days until this foot can take me places."

"Sure," she said, "how long you going to be there?"

"For at least a week. Tell you what, help me get my things in. When you get your business done in town, come back and spend the night, I would like that."

"Sure," she said hesitantly, thinking of her obligations. She couldn't come back today but maybe tomorrow or another day.

A sign read Quebec City, fifteen miles. Elric kept his eyes on the road.

Joan pulled the Cadillac up in front of the Quebec Hotel.

The desk clerk's head looked up, as he noticed a nice looking woman carrying a back pack, and behind her, a young fellow he recognized, Elric, the singer.

Booking a room for a week, Elric handed the clerk ten dollars.

"Keep the change," he told the red headed freckled man, with the large black framed glasses.

Joan followed him to the room, carrying his bag. Closing the door, he pulled her to him, kissing her full on the lips.

"Thanks, Joan, come back later if you like. I'll be hanging around here for a while. Our band was playing here before I went to the bush to work for my father. I'll be getting the guys together for some rehearsals. We will be playing here, soon."

"I would love to," she said, walking out of the room.

Elric lay back, comfortable in his private room. He was fine for a couple of hours, until he got an itch for a mickey. The bootlegger hung out not too far from the liquor store. He already knew him. All he needed was money, and he had that too. It was too soon to show up in the bar, to start drinking early in the day, not wanting the bartender or the owner to start barraging him with questions.

Having a shower, he put on clean clothes and fixed his hair, putting all his weight on his good foot. He would have to think of something. What he needed was a crutch. Surely he would find one somewhere downtown.

Not able to get his foot into his boot, he put on a couple wool socks.

This foot was going to slow him down.

Getting onto the street, he looked both ways. Which way should he go? Making his way down toward the bridge, hoping to see one of the guys.

Ten minutes later, Elric noticed an older grey haired man, walking with a cane. Just what he needed. Walking up to the guy, he stopped him.

"Hey, buddy. I wonder if I could buy that cane from you? You see, I have a broken foot, and I need to get around a few places."

"Well, as you can see, I rightfully need my cane to walk. I couldn't part with it."

"Name your price, old man."

"Well, I might part with it for fifty dollars. You got that much?"

"It's a deal," said Elric, excited. Pulling out five ten-dollar bills, handing them to the old man, who looked at the money in shock and happiness?

"Here you go, it's yours," he said, handing Elric the cane. Why, this will keep me fed for a month! My lucky day."

"Ahhh," he sighed, putting his weight on the cane, able to walk much better.

"You see, anything can be bought," he said to himself.

Walking down the street a ways, he turned to see the old man, sitting on the curb.

He thought of Sarah, at the diner. No, he didn't want her to see him busted up. Not only that, he couldn't run from Scott, if he happened to be there having coffee and donuts, laughing out loud to himself at his wit.

After a short time of trying to get around, he decided he should just lay low. Hang around the hotel for a few days, till the foot felt good enough.

Later that day, he went into the bar, a few people recognizing the handsome crooner. Without much encouragement, Elric gave them a couple of tunes. A crowd gathered around him. The owner of the hotel approached him after a song.

"Hey, we wondered what happened to you guys. That next Saturday, you were scheduled to play here, and no show? We had a full house."

"Well, I had an accident, as you can see. I've been laid up for a while. Broke my foot helping my father load some things on a truck. I haven't been in the city for a while. Really sorry for all of that. I'm back now, for good, and would love to get the boys together, say, next weekend?"

"The word around here was you went to jail. You know how people like to start rumors. But listen, kid, the way everyone loved your singing, you have a contract with me for the next year. Every weekend, Saturday nights, it's yours. So don't mess it up, there will be a raise every month. How does that sound?

"Come in to my office in the next few days. We would like to get a few shots of the band, so we can put up posters. We will fill the house every Saturday night."

"Man, why, thank you so much!" Reaching his hand out, to shake on the deal.

"The boys will be thrilled to be back. You can count on us. Saturday night."

That night, a few patrons sent Elric shots of whiskey, no clue that he was only sixteen years old. His singing and his height had them all fooled. Then the bartender gave him a few more shots. By the end of the night, he wasn't feeling the pain in his foot, rather high and mighty, realizing he couldn't do a thing, but go back to his room and go to sleep.

Waking early, it was like a little man with a hammer was knocking him on the brain. Sitting up in the bed, pain behind his eyes, his head killing him.

"Shit, I don't feel good. What the fuck?"

Running to the toilet, bile rising in his throat, heaving until nothing would come but tears.

Going back to bed, covering up, sleeping the day away, waking up hungry, feeling better. Detangling himself from his sheets and blankets, he goes to the window, facing the street. The night was still young, a few people on the streets, tempting him to carouse. Trying to put weight on his bad foot, wincing in pain. Back to the bed, crawling in, resolving to rest one more night.

Getting home from work, Earl walked into the house, looking in the kitchen at Elric's dirty dishes, still sitting on the table. Heading down the hallway, toward his room, he listened but heard no sounds. Opening the door, the bed made, a few pairs of shoes and a couple of shirts hanging in the closet.

Had he taken off? Not even the decency to tell him he was leaving. His guitar and his bags are gone, his overcoat he had given him, and his black dress shoes. Convinced, his son had left for good. Feeling responsible for a minute, driving him away.

His sensible side reasoned with him now. It was better this way, the boy couldn't be tamed. He was wild and dangerous.

The next day in the city, Elric wakes early, the sun streaming in the window, inviting him to wake up to the world. Getting out of bed, his stomach empty, but his foot is feeling a little better.

First things first, he needed some food in his stomach, having not eaten a thing the day before. That whiskey had disabled him for the whole day. At least he hadn't noticed the pain in his foot.

He would go down to the diner, see if that pretty waitress was still working there.

The following Saturday night, Sarah and two of her girlfriends showed up at the bar, thinking they were going to be entertained, only to be told the band had not showed. Sure, she figured, just like she thought. They were using the band to cover for what they really were, a gang of thieves.

A few of the Riverside Gang had come into the diner, hunger in their eyes. When she spotted them, she would ask the other waitress to serve them. Their clothes wrinkled and dirty, smelling like the dampness of the river. The last time she waited on them, one of the guys, smiled at her, his teeth thick with crud, almost making her vomit. That was the last time she would wait on them.

He had said he wasn't one of them, and surely didn't look like them either. Maybe he wasn't lying. Interested in the handsome Elric, she would wait to see him again, maybe give him another chance. Johnny was jealous, of course, telling her Elric was one of the gang, she didn't want to believe that.

Johnny had talked her into coming to his place in the last couple months for hot sex. She liked him. Her father didn't have to know. He told her that Elric went to jail and probably wouldn't be out for a while, about the cops arresting him at his place for robbery.

There was no love between them. The sex was great, and Johnny was a looker, green eyes, big full lips, and muscular body. Mmm, he made her hot. Realizing she was pregnant, skipping her period going on three months now.

Stepping into the diner, his eyes roved the café looking for her. A skinny, dark haired older lady stood at the counter. "Just for one?" she asked, picking up a menu from under the counter.

"Yes," answered Elric, following her to a booth near the back of the restaurant.

"Is Sarah working today?"

"Can I tell her who is asking?"

"Elric," he answered with a big grin.

Watching the waitress go in through the kitchen door. In a minute, Sarah comes out, looking his way, walkng towards him, he stares her way.

"Hi, haven't seen you in a long time."

"I was working for my old man in the bush, cutting logs."

"Really," she said. "That's not what I heard."

"What did you hear, and from who?" he asked, his jaw set.

"Ah, never mind. I just figured it out."

"You been seeing Johnny?" he asked.

"You might say that," she answered, a cute grin on her pretty face.

"Too bad, I was going to ask you out. Couldn't get you out of my mind, girl."

Just then the boss comes out of the kitchen, staring her way.

"Better just get the order. Your boss is watching. I'll have a waitress on toast," he said, laughing now.

"Stop it," she said teasingly."

"OK, give me the deluxe breakfast, steak and eggs. I like my eggs over easy, and rye toast, strawberry jam, sweet cakes."

"Coffee, for you, sir?"

"Yes, and you can be the cream in my coffee?"

They both started chuckling, all the flirting making Sarah's cheeks rosy red. Not sure who the father of the baby is, she says nothing about being pregnant to Elric.

The short Italian, fat boss man had a secret longing for the pretty Sarah. He could get aroused just watching her, bending and being near her in the kitchen. It was all he could hope for anyway.

He had noticed the gangster kid in there before, trying to flirt with her, wasting her time.

Keeping his eyes on her, Tony couldn't help but notice the pink blush running across her cheeks. She liked the kid, he could tell.

Sharpening his ears, he listened to the order.

"Steak and eggs, sunny side up, rye toast, and strawberry jam, please."

The guys came in droves whenever she worked. A pretty face like hers, even if they weren't hungry, they came just to sit and watch her. Tony had to drive them out after sitting there for an hour with only a soda. Just having her there brought men in droves, with lots with money to spend. A definite asset.

Staring at the handsome kid, at the end of the diner, he wondered who he was. He had money for steak and eggs. Hadn't seen him around much?

Tony walked into the kitchen.

"Is that kid bothering you, Sarah?"

"Who?" she asked, knowing full well he meant Elric.

"That kid, with the steak and eggs."

"Oh no, he's a good customer, always orders full meals and tips me well."

"Who is he?"

"He is lead singer of a band, Elric and the Wanderers."

"Ah, OK. That explains a lot." Tony walking back out to the counter, sitting down to enjoy his morning coffee.

With his belly full, Elric decided he would make his way to the bridge, see if Johnny and the guys were around, anxious to get some practicing in, and give them the good news about their steady gig at the Quebec Hotel.

Nearing the bridge, he looks down towards the river, sparks flying into the air from a fire in a barrel, a few silouettes of men standing around. Getting closer, he recognized his crew.

They looked like time had stood still for them, George with the same blue jacket on, Dean with the same raggedy shoes, Elric thinking he would have to get him some new ones. Spring for some new things to make them presentable for the band, considering it an investment.

He would take it out of their share of the money when they got paid. They had to look good, like him. Decided that they would all wear black pants, black shoes, and black shirts. It would be like their trademark, something more for the people to remember them easier. Dean is tall and skinny, blonde hair and freckles. George is shorter than all of them, thick wavy brown hair, Italian descent, wide shoulders, muscular build.

George noticed Elric first.

"What the fuck, man, look what the cat dragged in."

All their heads came up, looking Elric's way as he approached them, limping on one foot.

A big smile for Elric, George walked over to him first.

"Hey, man, where the hell you been, Schoolcraft?"

"Where do you think I was?" asked Elric playfully.

"Heard you went to jail for a while," answered George.

"Ah, shit, that was a long time ago, I've been doing some logging with my old man. I got hurt in the bush, so here I am. Where is Johnny?"

"He hasn't showed up here yet today, but he usually does every day. Man, we've been hurting around here. Didn't know how much I missed you, till just now."

"I'm back, and I got great news. We need a bottle to celebrate. Here." Pulled a ten-dollar bill out of his pocket, handing it to George. "Get us a bottle of whiskey. What do you say?"

A few hoots from the guys welcomed the lost cub back into the fold.

Taking a good look around him, he realized he looked nothing like these guys. Their faces hard, their eyes lacking the lustre of real living. He would try and bring new life to them, get the band up and making money around the country. Turn a band of thieves into a band of singers. At least he was going to give it his best shot.

They passed the bottle till it ran dry. Still no sign of Johnny. The guys were closing in on him, asking for money, food, or whatever he could offer. Knowing he had to get back to the hotel, he pulled out another ten and handed it to George.

"Get the guys some food, man. Don't spend this on alcohol. Go buy some bread and stuff to make sandwiches. Can you handle that? I got to find Johnny. I'll be back tomorrow. We got some serious practising to do. We got a gig, Saturday night, at the Quebec Hotel."

They all cheered, staring at their idol. How could a young kid like him bring that kind of joy to bunch of destitute young men?

Hoisting his guitar over his shoulder, he headed up the hill, toward the road. His foot was still hurting, and worse, now that he was climbing. He'd go back to the hotel and get a good rest, hoping tomorrow it would feel better.

As he walked through the hotel doors, the bartender spotted him.

"Baby face, heard you were playing here Saturday night?"

"That's right." Elric nodded, walking down the hallway toward his room. Baby face. Mmmm, he liked it. Baby face Elric, he laughs to himself.

That wasn't the first person that said he had a baby face. It was a compliment, and he would take it. The world was his stage, and everyone was about to find out the talents he had.

The next day, he woke overwhelmingly motivated. He had to find Johnny and get the plan down. They would get together every day until Saturday, get some songs ready to thrill the crowd, who were already anticipating them coming back. They would not disappoint.

Making his way toward the bridge, he hoped Johnny would already be there. He could see a few guys standing around and what looked like Johnny, standing, talking to a couple of guys, away from the crowd.

Johnny was deep in conversation, didn't notice Elric approaching.

Walking toward where he had noticed George, he wanted to put some distance between him and the strangers.

"Hey buddy," yelled Johnny, "come over and meet these guys."

Elric waved him away, kept heading toward the river. Whatever the deal was, Johnny would fill him in. These guys looked like bad news, either cops or gangsters.

Keeping an eye on Johnny, he noticed the three strangers walking toward the hillside. When they had cleared the hill, and were out of sight, he started walking toward Johnny. He needed to ask him about staying at his pad for a while. Staying in the hotel would eat up his money fast, and anyway the guys had to gig together.

"Who the hell were those guys?" asked Elric.

"They were trying to get us to join their gang. Bank robbers," said Johnny, his eyes wide.

"Not trying to go to jail, anytime soon. They were probably looking for fall guys to go down for them. They looked pretty shady if you ask me," said Elric. "Anyway, we got better things to do. You can do ten to life for a bank job. Pretty serious stuff. My life just started."

"Ya, you are right," answered Johnny, deep in thought. "I guess the fast way isn't the safest or the best way to make money. Too much at stake."

"What did you say their names were?" asked Elric.

"Dennie, Valentino, and the tall guy is the leader, Edward."

"Ah, I see," said Elric.

"Ya, they just showed up here. Said they needed a couple guys for a job. When I asked what kind of job, Edward opened his trench coat and showed me a machine gun strapped to his leg. Holy fuck! I'm like, what you planning on doing with that?"

"He said, 'Going to rob some banks, young man. Do you want in? If not, you had better keep your mouth shut, or I'll come back down here, and kill all of you.'

"That's when I said you might be interested in joining them. He said I should run it by you, and they would come back tomorrow."

"Fuck, that's some serious shit, man. Do you want to rob banks and maybe go to jail for your whole fucking life, or sing in a band and have all the women in the country trying to get a piece of you? I think I just want to keep it light, and nice, and bank robbing isn't in my repertoire right now. Tomorrow, when they show up, I'll tell them myself," said Elric, feeling good about making the right choice.

The next day, Elric was at the river before noon, anxious to do some jamming and rehearsing. He had dressed the part of the lead singer. In his father's trench, his fedora cocked to the side, he looked nothing like the Riverside Gang.

Watching and waiting, he noticed the same three amigos coming down the hillside, a running slide. He alerted Johnny, who was playing a hand of dice up against the cement pillar.

"Those guys, man, they are coming."

"OK, buddy, just you and I go and talk to them," said Elric.

Elric led, Johnny followed close behind.

Walking straight to where the men were standing, Elric stepped up. "Hey, I understand you wanted to talk to me about something."

"Yes," said the tall dark haired fellow." "My name is Edward," putting his hand out to Elric. "You are young boy. Maybe just what I need."

"We will have to discuss the details," said Elric, Johnny wide eyed at what he just heard.

"I make the rules. You listen, everything is ready to roll, just needed a little more manpower. You guys in or not?" asked Edward in a deep menacing voice.

"Not so fast, man," said Elric, looking Edward dead in the eye. "Right now, I'm kind of out of commission. I got a broken foot. But listen, yeah, I want in, just give me a couple of months and come back for me,"

"Sure then, you guys hang tight," said Edward, walking away, his crew falling behind in order of command.

Elric and Johnny headed back over to where the other guys were standing, warming their hands over the fire barrel.

"Those fuckers are serious," said Johnny. "They have robbed banks all around the country, looking for some prospects around here now. They are nobody to mess with, though. Don't let that gentlemanly way he has about him fool you. He'd kill you quick as look at you," said Johnny.

"Ah, fuck them all. I just let on like I was interested so they don't think we are a bunch of pussies around here. Whatever, that's if they don't get killed in a shootout with the cops. Doubt if we will ever see them again," said Elric.

"There are well known, as the Lloyd Gang," said Johnny. "I think that's Edward's last name."

"Ya, he's a cocky bastard, I don't like him," said Elric, walking away.

"Too many ways to split the pot. With him, his two guys, and you and me, that's a five way split.

"Anyway, we have a gig at the hotel on Saturday. Got to get this band sharpened up. Tomorrow we start our practices. We have a week to get about ten songs ready. I'm not trying to go to jail or get killed yet," said Elric.

"Those mungrels are headed for trouble. We don't need in on their shit."

"Wow, buddy, I didn't really consider all of that. Just the way the guy talked about more money than I had ever seen, kind of got me thinking."

All attention is on their gift horse, listening to the plan.

"OK, it's like this," said Elric. "We practice every day at four o'clock, sharp. If you are not here for the practice, you're out. You want to change your lives?"

"Yeah," answered George. "Got to hand it to you, man, without you we were only the Wanderers."

A roar of laughter goes up, with the sparks from the barrel.

"Thanks," answered Elric, tipping his hat. "Oh, yeah, we'll be going shopping for some new threads. We all have to wear the same thing, and look our best, so I am going to lend you the money you can pay me back."

"Yeah," howled Dean, "I'm in like Flynn," he said, shaking his blonde hair, tapping his foot on the concrete.

"It's set then. Here's some money. Get some food in your bellies," said Elric, handing George a twenty.

"Thanks, man, see you all tomorrow," said Johnny, walking away from them, Elric coming up behind him, making their way up the embankment, walking down the road.

"You coming to my place?" asked Johnny.

"No, I got the room for the week. I'll move in next week, OK? Give you time to clean up the place, make room for my shit," said Elric. They shared a laugh, bumping shoulders.

The band got together every day, like Elric had demanded. Passersby would stop on the bridge, looking down on them.

"Just look up," said Elric. "We got fans already." About ten people stopped, a sweet sound reaching their ears.

"Just pretend we are on stage right now, and there's the audience." They laughed, getting into song.

Things were working out great for everyone. One more day to show time.

Elric spent more than enough time in the mirror, getting ready for his star to shine. It was where he belonged, on stage, in the limelight.

Dressing in their black clothes, like a band of vampires, they combed their hair, washing their faces in the cold river water. Standing to the side, he sized up the Wanderers.

"Yeah, just look at that. Everybody looks great. Are you ready? Let's do this," he said, the guys following him up the embankment, walking down the street, toward the Quebec Hotel.

The bar was packed, everyone excited at the four guys in black coming through the doorway.

Jumping up on the stage, dragging his bad foot a bit, Elric grabbed a microphone, taking a bow.

"Just like to introduce my band. We got Dean on drums, George on harmonica, Johnny on base, and I'm Elric, and we are Elric and the Wanderers," he said, his voice reaching a crescendo.

The crowd roared, the tavern filled with happy faces and single women.

At intermission, Elric passed a mickey around, turning their backs to the crowd. The night was great, the revelers howling.

A row of single ladies had gathered at the front of the stage. Elric, loving the attention, putting his hands out to them, turning on the charm. The sexuality in the air is hot and heavy.

At the end of the night, when most of the patrons had cleared out, there was a tall, auburn haired girl waiting to talk to Elric. Stepping up to him, she smiled.

"Hey, didn't I see you here about a year ago?"

"Yes," he answered, looking her up and down. Tall, thick auburn wavy hair past her shoulders, a tight red dress, hugging her curves. Black shiny patent heels, accentuating the tightness of her calves. Her green eyes sparkling, inviting.

She had to be twenty-five. A little old for him, but maybe not. She was just right, in all the right places. He had to know her.

"My name is Loretta," she said. "Will the band be coming back next week?"

"We sure will be. Got a contract for a year. Every Saturday night."

"Great then, see you next Saturday," said the pretty lady. Walking away, she blew Elric a kiss.

With their instruments packed up, the boys head to the bar to have a couple drinks. Confidence and happiness for the lost boys of the night.

Dean and George were overjoyed at their new venue, but for now, both had to go back to the bridge to sleep in their makeshift beds of cardboard and old blankets.

A darkness descended on them as the night came to a close, as they went their ways.

He wanted to tell them to get out of their new clothes and keep them for performing only but didn't have the heart. Johnny and Elric walked with them as far as the bridge, Dean and George descending to the depth of the riverbed.

CHAPTER 60

Elric moved back in with Johnny, the band playing every Saturday night. Picking up another gig entertaining at the candy factory dances in Halifax. The band was so excited about traveling to Nova Scotia, none of them had ever gone anywhere but in Quebec.

The first couple of times they performed there, Dean and Elric both found girlfriends. There were always girls waiting to talk to the band. Even George had a few dates from girls he met. None of them had settled with one girl, Elric taking a different one home every night they performed.

He had been seeing Loretta on a regular basis, moving from Johnny's to Loretta's after two months of dating her.

He had met a girl in Halifax who occupied his mind, a young girl, beautiful, angel like, he thought. She seemed lost, like him. There was something they shared. Wanting to know more about her, he planned secretly that she would be his wife.

She never spoke of her family, only her adopted family, Suzie, and Betty. There were things he would have to do, but right now he was having too much fun. She wasn't going anywhere. When he was ready, he would go for her. He had told her she was his girl. The way Alice had looked into his eyes, melting under the heat of his charm, a helpless girl, he could mould her the way he wanted, and she was a virgin, making her all his.

With the gigs they were getting, once the money was split, the guys were only coming out with enough to keep them in booze and food for a few days.

When their money ran out, they looked to Elric for a handout. His once thick wad of money had dwindled down to the last few hundred dollars, making him feel vulnerable.

They would have to find another way to make money. George and Dean were still living in makeshift box houses under the bridge.

With too much time on his hands, Elric spent hours gambling, usually until all the money in his pocket was gone. When he had consumed too much alcohol, he didn't think twice, gambling till morning, mad at himself all the next day.

Johnny and Elric were talking about the possibilities of getting with Edward's gang.

"You don't need any more than three guys to rob a bank" said Elric. "One to drive the car, and the other two to take it down."

"Yeah, but we don't have the guns and a car, first of all," said Johnny.

"True, but nothing says we can't get them," answered Elric.

Lately, when they were in their liquor, the possibility of them robbing banks was becoming more apparent, the desperation growing in Elric.

"Did you hear the Lloyd Gang had a shootout with the cops, killed two cops just last week? They must be on the lam right now, hiding out somewhere," said Dean."

"Holy fuck, I was right on the money. Remember I told you those fuckers were going down," Elric boasted.

"Ya, don't think they will be coming around here again," said George. "They are wanted countrywide. Everywhere you go, you hear people talking about the last bank they robbed, right here in the city. The Bank of Montreal on King Street got hit, just a few days ago."

"These guys are good, but stupid. Once you start killing cops, your ass is going down. They will hunt them till they kill them all," said Elric.

The more they discussed the Lloyd gang, the more ideas Elric was conjuring up. When face to face with Edward, he realized he looked a lot like him, only much younger. Same tall, wiry build, dark hair. With his hat pulled down over the forehead, and a kerchief over the nose and mouth, Elric looked much like Edward, after taking a good look in the mirror. Would it be possible?

Could they pull it off? They could orchestrate their own bank robbery, and the Lloyd gang would be blamed, just now to perfect the plan.

"I can get the best car for the job. My father's Cadillac. I heard someone say the Lloyd gang uses Cadillacs. At least they are riding high" said Elric, laughing. "I like their style."

As the days went on, the nights getting colder. With the money more sparse, Elric grew unsettled, anxious.

Loretta worked a nine to five nursing, coming home to Elric waiting for her to prepare supper.

Leaving his clothes wherever he took them off, making lots of extra work for her.

Since he had moved in with her, she realized that the novelty of bedding a young crooner had turned into something else.

Tired, after a long day looking after the sick, she came home to nurse a drunken kid.

He had become demanding. Do this, do that. One day, when she didn't respond quickly enough, he grabbed her by the hair and pulled her into the bedroom, ripping off her uniform, raping her. It was exciting while it was happening but disturbing at the same time.

There was just something about him. He had become like an addiction for her. She didn't want to be without him, but her life had become chaotic since he moved in. Only seventeen, and so handsome and talented, and he was her boyfriend.

Every day now, she didn't know what to expect when she got home from work. Said he was rehearsing with the guys most afternoons.

One day after work, she was sitting in the living room, taking off her nurse shoes, then put her feet up to rest when he came storming out of the bedroom, his eyes glassy, his hair disheveled.

"What the fuck you doing? I'm hungry. Where is my supper? How long you been here?"

"I just got in the door, Elric. Can you give me a few minutes, and I'll prepare you something. You were here all day long, nothing to do. Why can't you make your own supper?"

Before the last word was out of her mouth, he grabbed a handful of her thick hair, pulling her to her feet.

"Don't, don't! Why are you hurting me?"

"I'll get you something to eat."

He didn't let go until he had her standing in front of the stove.

Tears of regret stained her cheeks, wondering how she had gone wrong. Through her tears and weeping, she fixed him a steak and potatoes, putting his food on the table. Going into the bedroom, shutting herself in. Lately, she didn't know how he was going to be when she got home.

The next morning, Elric woke at the sound of the alarm, reaching for her. Loretta didn't respond to his touch as he explored her body with his hands. Kissing the back of her neck, he rolled her over, mounting her, making gentle love to her for at least twenty minutes, forgetting about the assault the night before.

It was Saturday morning, Loretta eyeing him as he is getting ready for his gig at the hotel.

"Can we have a talk?" she asked, coming up behind him.

"Sure," he agreed.

"Why do you treat me like dirt? Don't you care about me?"

"Yes, of course I care about you, or I wouldn't be here with you in your bed. Do you know how many chicks I could have? Sorry if I've been uptight lately. It's just that the band is not making enough money. I've been stressed out."

"Maybe you could get a job," she suggested.

"A job. There are no fucking jobs. This depression is killing us. I have a few ideas, quick money ideas, Loretta."

"What? Never mind, don't tell me. I have a feeling I don't want to know."

"Don't ask then," he said, getting back to grooming himself. With a glob of gel in the middle of his hand, smoothing it into his jet black hair.

"Sorry if I hurt you, baby," he said. "I won't do it again." Slipping in behind her, kissing her on the back of her neck, she melts at his touch, like ice cream on a hot day.

The way he held her, the sweet Elric, when he wasn't drinking.

A week later, he spends the whole day near the river, doing what he liked to do best. Drinking and gambling. Lost all his money. Raging mad at himself, he gets another mickey to drown his sorrows.

By the time he made it home to Loretta, he was angry at the world. Knocking on the door, fumbling in his pockets, he can't find the key she had given him. Frustration turns to anger, he starts kicking at the door now.

"Open the fucking door!" he yelled. Loretta awakened by the banging, she sits up straight in bed, her heart in her mouth, it could only be him. What was happening? Pulling on her housecoat, peeking out the window, she can see his overcoat, opening the door, Elric standing there, his eyes bloodshot.

"What took you so fucking long?" he said, storming past her. Loretta locking the door.

"Where is my fucking key? Suppose you took my key. Were you trying to keep me out? Well, let me tell you, if I want in, I'll break in, break the windows, and break you," he said, punching her in the face.

Falling to the floor, covering her face with her hands, blood running from her nose.

Bending, he grabbed a handful of her thick hair, dragging her into the bedroom.

Screaming and crying, he pushed her head first onto the bed. Ripping her nightgown off, he sodomized her, roughly. Her screams muffled, pushing her head into the blankets.

The assault didn't last long, Elric passing out on top of her. Managing to get herself free of him, whimpering, going into the bathroom. Her nose is swollen, a purplish black circled one of her eyes. Oh my God, she couldn't go to work this way. She would have to say she was sick.

Scared, she goes out to the living room, sitting on the couch, thinking of what she could do to get rid of him once and for all. This guy was no good and was going to keep beating and hurting her. Why had she moved him into her life? A kid, a teenager, blaming herself now for being so stupid.

Cleaning herself up, she dresses in a long nightgown, curling up on the couch, she fall asleep. No signs of life from the bedroom; he had passed out cold.

By noon the next day, he still hadn't gotten out of bed. Finally, Loretta goes to the bedroom door, opened it, standing looking at her abuser, his boots still on his feet.

"Hey, you going to sleep all day?"

Stirring in the bed, his hand goes to his head, "ahhhhh fuck, I don't feel good, looking at her now, one eye open, his head pounding, his boots still on his feet.

"What the fuck? You let me go to bed with my boots on?"

"You were shitfaced drunk, punched me in the face and then raped me. I don't think I cared that you had your boots on."

"What! I never laid a hand on you."

"Well, just have a look at my nose. It's swollen, maybe broken, and my eyes are blackened."

Walking away from the door, back out into the kitchen, she decided she would make him some breakfast before he came out and started bitching about no breakfast.

Managing to get himself untangled from the blankets, he unlaced his boots, his one foot still sore, probably from sleeping with the heavy boot on. "Fuck," he said, pushing his hair off his forehead. Taking all his clothes off, he walked out of the bedroom toward the shower.

Standing under the hot water, his usual routine, hogging the warmth of it, until it runs cold. Going to the mirror, having a good look at himself. Staring into his own steel grey eyes, he said, "We got to do a job, and soon. No fucking money. I'm done with being broke. That's not like me to have no money in my pocket." Wondering if he had gambled all his money, heading back into the bedroom, searching through his pants pockets, two hundred dollar bills, the last of his bounty.

Feeling vulnerable and closer to the damp Riverside, broke and hungry. No, that would not be him. Today, he was going to hatch a plan of action. There had to be a way to get some quick money.

Following the inviting smells of bacon and coffee, he walks into the kitchen, a towel around his waist. Loretta is standing at the stove, just about to flip his eggs. "Over medium," he said, kissing her ear.

She turned so he could get a good look at her face.

"Don't touch me! Do you see what you did to me? I can't go to work looking like this. Are you some kind of an animal? I want you to move back in with your friend. You can't live here with me anymore." She starts whimpering.

"Hey, not so fast there. You are just going to kick me out into the cold? I thought you and I had a good thing going, Loretta?"

"I'm scared of you now. You are not the same sweet guy when you are drinking. I can't live like this."

"I'll quit drinking then. I need you, babe. You can't just kick me out like that."

429

"I thought you liked me?" she said, crying harder now, Elric hugging her.

"Oh, sweetie, I am sorry if I hurt you. I won't ever lay a hand on you again. I don't remember doing that to you."

"I don't suppose you remember what else you did to me?"

"Please, babe, just give me a chance to make it up to you, OK? And I promise, I will never hurt you again. If I do, I will walk away myself and never darken your door."

Elric filled his belly, thinking of what he was going to do all day. Had to go see the boys, and get a game plan down. While he dressed, he kept one eye on Loretta, sitting in the parlor, forlorn staring straight ahead.

"I'll see you later," he said, going out, the door slamming behind him.

As soon as he left, she got up from the couch, pacing around, shaking her head. There was no way she could live with this guy any longer, after everything he had done to her.

On his way to the river, he thought he would just take a stroll up King Street to do a little window shopping. That's what it had come down to. No money to buy anything nice. No, this was not how he had planned to live his life, like the Riverside Gang. Going hungry, no place to lay their heads and no money to buy nice things. So far life had been pretty good to him. He had established a style, a way of life, and he liked it. Today, he would figure out the final plan of a bank job.

Walking past a jewellery store, he decided to go back and take a good look at the bounty in the window. Watches, rings, golden things catching his eye. Mmm, he thought. Only a glass pane between him and the loot. Thinking about going in and talking to the clerk, about a ring for his girl, he decided against it. Maybe he would just come back and take it all.

The jewellery store was on his mind all day, reasoning it would be an easy enough job. Put some quick money in his pockets. Gold and diamonds should be easy enough to sell.

It was decided, he would rob the jewellery store, take a few days to case out the joint.

The cops who walked the beat coming towards him, Elric pulling his fedora down, looking at the ground, as they passed by. He wondered whether he should let his friend Johnny in on the job, then decided against it. He could handle it himself.

Lately, the guys weren't as happy to see him. No extra money for booze and cigarettes or food. The little money they were making with the band, one night a week, was spent mostly within one day, then they were broke for the next six. Things were scarce. They were getting mean, like a pack of hungry wolves, fighting over stupid shit, like a butt of a cigarette. It wasn't hard to figure out that Elric's money had run out, his temper flaring easy. One thing they all knew was to stay out of his way when he was drinking and pissed off. Not a good combination. Like walking on a field of land mines. Dangerous.

Fingering his last two hundred dollar bills, he knew he had to spend them wisely. No more Santa Claus shit. The guys had to steal or whatever they had to do to survive, just like he did.

Heading down to the bridge, stopping to get a mickey, he needed to just sit and figure it out.

It was late fall, the coldness seeping into their cardboard box houses, suffering the elements. Johnny was the only one who had a place to lay his head. Now that Loretta was threatening to kick him out, he was one step from sleeping back at Johnny's, or if he didn't get some money soon, on the cold, damp concrete. No fucking way. Not Elric Schoolcraft.

Heading down the embankment toward the river, he could see them, huddled around the barrel, the sparks flying into the air like embers of hope. Taking a better look a few new faces. Fuck, it was hard enough to see the guys that were his crew like this. There was no more time to waste. They were either in, or they could stay and die in the cold.

As they noticed Elric coming, their faces lit up, thinking he might have something to share, like his usual whiskey.

"Hey, what's up," said Elric. "You boys want to come over here? We got something to discuss."

Pulling them away from the barrel, they huddle around him.

Reaching inside his coat, he pulled out the mickey. "Just one shot each, I'm running low, and getting desperate. I got a plan to get us the hell away from this river and into some warm beds for the winter."

Their eyes wide, their ears keen, as the bottle was passed their way.

"Remember the Lloyd gang? The guys who were down here trying to recruit some new talent? Well, they gave me some ideas. As we speak, they are planning a job somewhere. They have been robbing banks all over the countryside, and still the law hasn't caught them. Smart bunch. We don't need to do a lot of bank jobs, just one, at the main branch, right here in town, the Bank of Montreal on King Street. Go big or go home."

"What, you are serious, man?" asked George.

"That's the main branch. They just robbed it a month or so ago."

"Exactly my point. They won't be expecting another robbery in the same bank."

"Do I look serious? I don't talk to hear myself, man. Yes, I'm serious. Either you are in, or you try to stay alive down here all winter. It's your choice."

"Yes, I'm in," said George, then Dean echoed the call.

"OK, I'm going to figure it out. I'll steal one of my old man's Cadillac's, and case out the bank. I'm going to watch it all week and all the goings on. It's all timing. I have to know when the bank manager comes and goes, and when the staff arrive there for their days work. Give me a week or so, and we will set a date. Probably next week. I got no time to waste, and it's getting colder out here by the day. I just got to talk to Johnny about it. I'm sure he is going to be in. OK, it's a deal."

"We are going to make a shit load of money, won't have to worry about a thing for a while."

They bump fists on it, their smiles back, hope in their hearts. The kid was back, and serious.

The cold air biting, Elric wrapped his overcoat around him, passing the bottle between George and Dean, when two other bums tried to join their circle.

"Fuck off. Get your own. I don't know you." Opening his coat, he pulled out a buck knife, waving it their way. "Don't fuck around," Elric threatened.

The strangers retreated, like mongrel wolves backing down from the alpha male, heading back to the barrel, their mouths watering for some of the whiskey.

The plan was set, the last drop of whiskey sealing the deal.

Just being near the river for a half hour, a taste of the cold wind and the helpless feeling for his homeless friends. He thought of Loretta's long legs wrapped around him, her warm bed. Fuck, he had to stop hurting her, or he was going to lose her, she had made that clear. The river at night was like a death sentence, dampness and cold seeping into your very bones.

Heading down the road to Johnny's, they had to lay out the plan for the bank job. Johnny would be in. He just knew it.

Excited to see his friend and share a mickey of whiskey, while they went over the details of the job.

"Good to see you, man. I haven't been down to the river since we last played at the hotel. It's too cold to just hang out, and with the guys all so desperate, no food, no booze, it really isn't like it used to be when we had more money. My uncle said I got to get a job and start paying him some rent, or he wants me out. Fuck, I just don't know what to do, man."

"My luck has run out too, and if I don't make a move on something here quick, I'm going to be laying on a cardboard box with the rest of them desperate fuckers. Which brings to mind why I am here. I want us to hit a bank here in town, like, next week. Fuck, man, my girl is putting me out too."

"What, she is kicking you out cause your money ran out?"

"No, I've been a prick, throwing her around a bit when I get drunk. I just don't know why I do it. I just get angry quick and lash out. Bad temper, but the booze makes it worst. All the stress of things now too, just everything, man."

"The band is great, but people don't have the money to go out to the bars to drink and be entertained. I've gone all over the province, trying to get us work. There just isn't enough money to go around for anyone. This fucking depression is killing us, man."

"I say we hit the main branch downtown, Bank of Montreal. The Lloyd gang has been robbing all the small banks, getting a bit of loot here and there, and they still haven't caught them. I'm talking a big job. I am going to watch every minute of every day, exactly when the manager comes and the tellers. I will know when the armored truck comes around and what times the cops walk the beat around that area. As soon as I have it all down to a science, we are going to hit it. Seeing I look so much like Edward, just a younger version, they will think we are them. Do you see where I am going with this?"

433

"Fucking brilliant, man. Damn it, I got to hand it to you. You got more fucking guts than brains."

They bounced their glasses of whiskey, having a good hearty laugh.

"So everything as planned this week. We play at the hotel on Saturday, then I will case the joint every day. I say we take it on a Friday, when there is lots of traffic downtown, and the cops will be busy with things. First thing in the morning, when they just open the doors."

"You are serious about this, Elric?"

"I'm fucking serious. Look at this face. Do I look like I'm kidding? This is survival. Either we do something quick here, or we join the river rats. Fucking right, I'm doing this!"

"I'm in, buddy. Just let me know what you need me to do."

"I was down to the river and talked to Dean and George. They are in too."

"I'm going to steal one of my old man's cars for the job, probably the big Cadillac. Room for our guns and money, yahoooo," he said, laughing heartily.

Heading back to Loretta's, a long walk from Johnny's, but he needed the cold air to clear his mind. The booze had to wear off before he saw his girl. Would she even let him in after what he did to her?

Stepping up to the door, he tried the door knob, knocking, knocking.

After a few minutes with no answer, he started to lose his patience. He was just about to kick at the door when two policemen in uniform walked by, taking notice of him, his loud voice drawing their attention.

"Hey, do you live here?" asked the short cop.

"What's your name?" asked the taller cop.

"Ah no, my girlfriend lives here," answered Elric, evading the question.

"What is her name?" asked the other shorter one.

"Loretta James," said Elric, seething at having to answer their questions.

"Well, it looks like she is not home."

"You are right," said Elric, backing away from the door, heading down the road, walking, not looking back. Those fucking bastards, he thought, they should mind their own business.

Loretta had heard the voices, had looked out and seen two cops and Elric standing there. She hoped he would just go away, not wanting to let him in. It was already three in the morning. Lately she couldn't sleep soundly, always wondering when he was going to drag himself in. Would he be drunk and want to hurt her?

She really did love him. There was lots to love, but there was something else that took over when he was drinking.

As soon as she noticed he was under the influence, which was more often than not lately, she watched her step. She shouldn't have to live like this, she reasoned.

Johnny would let him in. He walked down the road toward his house. The lights were off in the apartment. He would have to wake up his friend. He stood knocking and knocking, no answer. The cold was biting at his fingers. Elric became agitated, kicking at the door now.

"Come on, buddy, open the door!" he shouted. No answer. Finally, he kicked the door, the door flying open the wood splintering around the lock. Walking up the stairs to the apartment, Johnny jumping out of bed, wrapping his robe around his waist, the sound of his door splintering, waking him. Elric walked past him to the couch.

"Did you break my door? You fucker," he said, looking at Elric taking off his boots.

"I'll break your face if you broke my door, man. My uncle is going to kick me out."

"I'll fucking kill you. Don't threaten me," said Elric, looking him square in the eye. Johnny backed away, going down the stairs, looking at the splintered wood on the floor, the dead bolt hanging off.

What a bastard, he said to himself, walking back upstairs.

"Here," said Elric, handing him a ten spot. "Buy yourself a new lock. I just had to get in, man, its fucking cold out there." Johnny just shook his head, taking the money, walking back to his bed.

The next morning, Johnny awoke to the smell of fresh coffee and bacon, Elric in the kitchen, preparing two plates.

"Good morning," said Elric.

"Yeah," said Johnny, sitting down at the table. "What the fuck got into you?"

"When I went home yesterday, Loretta wouldn't open the door. I started cursing and then the fucking cops came along started asking me questions. Right now, I can't answer no questions. I got lots on my mind, and I don't want to be on their radar. That bitch could have just opened the door, saved me all the aggrevation."

"Oh, that's why you came here, kicking my fucking door in."

"Buddy, I'll fix your door. I'm sorry."

"I don't need no heat on me right now. We are going to do that job soon. Probably as soon as next Friday. A busy day downtown, I figure, better when there is lots going on. Can I hang out here for a few days?"

"Right now, my uncle told me if he doesn't see some money this week, my ass is out on the street too. You got any money so I can give to him to keep him quiet? Then you can hold up here with me, till after the job. Then you will have to find somewhere else, buddy."

"OK, sure, all I got is fifty left to give. You can have it to give to him, so we have time to get our shit together."

Reaching inside his coat pocket, he pulled out a fifty-dollar bill.

"At least you will have a roof over your head too, until we get our money."

"Thanks, man," said Johnny. "You are the best, Schoolcraft."

Hanging tight all day, Johnny gave his uncle the fifty dollars. It would bide him some time. The urgency in Elric's voice told Johnny, time was running out for all of them. A bank job was the last thing on his mind before he met Elric. But the kid was a go getter and the brains behind their survival. It was on.

They had breakfast, bacon and eggs, and fried potatoes, Elric leaving the cleaning up to Johnny. Late afternoon, Johnny watched Elric stealing a drink from a flask inside his coat. Not offering to share, Johnny didn't ask for any. He could see his friend had a lot on his mind.

He watched Elric, who hadn't said as much as ten words since breakfast. Pacing back and forth. By five o'clock, the darkness descending, Elric getting ready to go somewhere, Johnny watching him dress.

"I got a few things to do downtown," he said. "Got to go see if my girl is done with me, or what is going on there. Regardless, I got shit to do, man. I'll be back later."

"Sure, just don't kick down the door, man, I'll leave it open."

Johnny looked Elric up and down. Thick sweater under his overcoat, a grey toque pulled over his head, and a heavy pair of work boots.

"Man, where you going, looking like a lumberjack?"

"Just the reaction I was looking for."

"Don't ask, OK? I just got a couple of things to do and don't want to be recognized."

"You are incognito, all right."

"OK, I see you later tonight."

CHAPTER 61

Walking with conviction, the night cold under a starlit sky, the snow crunching under the weight of his heavy boots. It was a good night, he reasoned, too cold for the cops to be hanging around too long. He would just walk by once, taking in his surroundings, his grey toque pulled down over his forehead, his head down.

There weren't many people on the streets. The steam rose from the chimneys, his breath showed in the air. It was cold, just like his heart.

Walking by the Goldminers jewellery store, he took a second look behind. No one in sight. There were a couple of men walking the opposite direction, coming out of a bar. *Coast is clear*, he said to himself, raising his foot smashing it into the cold glass.

The sound of breaking glass, like a wind chime gone stereo. Glass shattered around his foot, falling to the cement like a xylophone in a silent world. With gloved hands, he pulled away the shards so he could safely crawl through the window. Pulling out the canvas bag out of his coat, he had found in Johnny's uncle's garage.

Slamming the heavy wrench onto the glass case, the jewellery was his for the taking. Watches, rings, diamonds. Within a few minutes, he had it all in the drawstring satchel.

Back out through the window, he started running now, his heart beating like it was coming out of his chest.

A siren sounded in the wind, the wailing getting louder. At the sight of two black and white cruisers speeding down the street, he ducks into an alley. Their headlights illuminated the dark night.

There had to have been an alarm, he reasoned, wondering how they were alerted so quickly.

Back onto the street now, he runs down the sidewalk, his long legs taking deep strides.

Making it to Loretta's door, holding his bounty under his coat, knocking, then knocking louder, when the door opened.

Pushing past her, he tramped straight into her parlor, his boots still on his feet.

"What is wrong?" she asked, looking at the snow that he had tracked into the house.

"Don't start," he said, eyes wide. "I'll take them off. Give me a minute," he said as he nervously threw off his coat and toque, bending down to undo the laces in his boots, leaving snow and dirt around his feet.

Loretta went for the straw broom, cleaning up the dirty snow. As she was bending down to sweep the dirt into the dust pan, she noticed a few splinters of glass mixed in with the dirt.

Walking back out to the living room, Elric headed to the bedroom, closing the door behind him. The frantic look in his eyes told her he was up to no good.

She heard the sirens now and put two and two together. Was he in trouble? The way he had looked at her liked a scared animal. The cop cars were going up and down the street, as if they were looking for someone.

As the beam of their light passed her house, she looked out, the cop car going slowly, shining their lights on all the houses.

Harbouring a fugitive. She had heard the term before. Was she in trouble now too?

Just then, Elric came out of the bedroom.

"If the cops come here looking for me, you haven't seen me in a week. You threw me out."

"Well, they just crawled by with a spotlight on the house. They were shining it on all the houses down the road. Are they looking for you?"

"Look, what you don't know, you don't have to lie about."

She didn't want to aggravate him, after not seeing him for a few days. Without asking him any more questions, she knew in her heart the cops were looking for him.

For the next couple hours, he paced, looked out the front windows a few times, pulling the curtain to the side, careful not to show much more than a fingertip. As the dark of night descended on them, Elric became more playful, happy almost.

She hadn't seen him like this in months.

"Hey, I got you something to make up for things."

Loretta looked his way as he pulled out a gold watch and a solitary diamond ring.

"Oh my God, they are beautiful," she said as he put the diamond ring on her marrying finger. Hesitant, hoping this was not an engagement proposal, she stared at the ring.

"How did you get these things? I thought you didn't have much money?"

Giving her that look, like *don't ask*. Then she put all the puzzle pieces together. The cops, the jewelry, the glass from his boots. He had robbed a jewelry store. The Goldminers store came to mind.

"I know I haven't been the best behaved boyfriend, but I want to make it up to you, babe." Wrapping his arms around her from behind. "The band has a few gigs in Nova Scotia coming up next month, so you won't see much of me. I just hope when I come back, you don't have a new man in your bed."

"No, of course not. I'll wait for you."

He turned her around to him, kissing her deeply. They walked each other to the bedroom, and she shut the door behind them.

After making passionate love for a long time, she falls asleep in his arms. Wow, he could be so sweet when he was sober.

The next morning, they were awakened by a loud persistent knocking at the door. Elric gets up, quickly pulling on his pants.

"Go, peek and see who it is," he ordered as he stepped inside the closet.

"It's the police," she whispered.

"Take off that jewelry, and just answer the door. If you don't answer, they will come back. Just remember what I said. If they are looking for me, say you kicked me out over a week ago and haven't seen me since."

Nervously, Loretta went to the door, pulling her housecoat around her.

Opening the door just a crack, she could see a plainclothes detective and a black and white uniformed cop.

"How can I help you?" she asked with a pouty, pretty face.

"We are checking the neighborhood for a robber. Have you seen anyone hanging around, or anyone trying to sell jewelry? The Goldminers jewelry store was robbed last night. Keep your door locked," said the detective.

"I will, and thank you," said Loretta, an innocent smile for the detective.

Back at the precinct, Detective Scott put together the pieces of the robbery. A large wrench left at the scene was being examined for fingerprints. No prints on the wrench, but a perfect footprint of a boot on the floor. The robber was wearing work boots, size eleven. The only clue they had was the boot. Frustrated by the lack of clues, Scott walked away, leaving it with the rest of them to figure out.

Tuesday, Elric woke with no urge to go out to the world. Loretta had been babying him, making him special sandwiches before bed, asking what else she could do, when he asked her to massage his bad foot. Willing, she settled on a cushion with her lace satin nightie on, her auburn curls around her shoulders, her long elegant legs showing from the knee down. Rubbing his bad foot, she looked up at him.

"Hope you don't stay away too long. How long did you say you were going?"

"Well, I'll be here for a couple of days, then I'm going to hang out with the band, do some rehearsing, and get ready for the gig on Saturday. Are you going to come? Might be our last gig for a while here."

"Yes, of course I will be there. You can count on it. I'm already missing you."

Wow, he thought to himself, give a girl some jewelry, and she was acting so kind and even showing she cared for him.

Amazing how the robbery had changed him back into a gentleman. At least he had something to sell, but he would need to sit on it for a bit. With the bank job on deck, he would just have to sell a watch or two to tide him over. That hopeless, helpless feeling had subsided.

The gang hadn't seen Johnny or Elric for a few days. The guys wondered if they were cutting them out of some scam they were doing.

When the cops showed up down at the bridge, asking the guys questions, they came to the conclusion Johnny or Elric had something to do with the robbery.

The detective seemed rather interested in when they had last seen Schoolcraft. George said he hadn't seen him since their last gig at the hotel. He lied.

Dressing in his black outfit, Loretta watched him from the doorway. Elric standing in the mirror, admiring his profile, then straight on, slicking his hair back over his forehead, then letting a lock of shiny black hang down over his high forehead.

She wanted to tell him how handsome he was but decided against it, knowing his ego was already inflated.

"What time you going to show up, babe?" he asked.

"I'll be there before your last set, OK? I want to make myself the most beautiful for you."

"That's my girl," he said, pursing his lips, kissing the air.

Slipping on his overcoat and fedora, his guitar over his back, his old self, feeling confident again. Reasoning that he shouldn't sell any of his bounty in Quebec City, but he would take it to Nova Scotia, where they wouldn't be looking for the stolen jewellery.

The guys had gone to Johnny's to get showered and ready for their big night. Free booze and lots of women—that part they liked the best.

Women were drawn to them because they were in a band, George had concluded. Couldn't remember ever having that much attention from women. He had always had a complex that he was too short. Since they had put the band together, he was regaining some confidence, moving with a swagger, his wide shoulders and thick curly hair attracting a few sweethearts.

All the guys got attention, but the lead singer had them falling at his feet. Lucky bastard could have any of them that he wanted. The day Loretta had met Elric, she had been talking to George first. He watched her all night, until after the last set, she introduced herself to Elric.

The Wanderers were a big hit, as usual, all of them, feeling happy and sweetened up with free liquor and the girls after the show. Loretta was there but Elric noticed Sarah and a couple of her friends waving at him. Deciding he would make an appearance, he walked over to where the girls are sitting. The other two were drinking, Sarah with a soda.

"Can I talk to you for a minute?" she asked.

Standing up, he noticed right away her rounded tummy, her eyes glossy.

"I'm having a baby, Elric, and I don't know, but it could be yours."

A lump rose in his throat, Loretta coming toward him.

"I'll talk to you after the show," he said, walking away.

For the rest of the night, he just wanted to get finished, and get back to Johnny's. He had his few belongings he would need, and the stolen jewelry in his guitar case.

He didn't tell Loretta where he would be hanging out, just in case someone was asking. Loretta waited and waited for him to come back, but he never did.

Back at the precinct, Scott and his crew were still trying to pull all the pieces together of the latest robbery. He knew that Schoolcraft was back in town, overheard his daughter talking to her friends about the band they were going to see. There was no mistaking it, Elric and Wanderers.

John Scott and his partner decided to visit Schoolcraft auto sales to talk to Elric's father. When Earl saw the cruiser coming, his heart leaped into his mouth.

Getting up quickly from his desk, he walked outside to meet them, wondering if they had bad news about his missing son.

"Good afternoon, sir," said Scott, putting his hand out to Earl.

"Good day, sir," answered Earl. "Is it something about my son?" Anxiety in his voice.

"Well sir, it is about Elric. We have reason to believe that he has robbed the Goldminers jewelry store. We found a foot print, a boot print actually, about a size eleven," said Scott, looking deep into Earl's eyes.

"I have not seen my son in quite a long time now."

"What size is his shoe?" asked Scott.

"Really, I don't know the answer to that question," said Earl. "The boy didn't grow up with me. I don't know much about him. He is like a stranger," he lied.

He knew his shoe size, eleven. They wore the same size.

"Sorry to hear that," said Scott. "Did he leave any of his shoes or boots at your house when he left?"

"No, took everything he owned," lied Earl.

"Well, we won't waste any more of your time, but if you see him, tell him I want to talk to him."

"I will do that. I would like to talk to him too."

"Have a nice day," said Scott, walking back to the cruiser, his partner, getting in behind the wheel.

Earl watched the cops still sitting in the cruiser, looking like they were taking down notes, talking to each other, wishing they would leave. Didn't look good for his business, the cops coming around.

"His old man is trying to cover for him. Right, he lives in the same house, and you don't know his shoe size? That's a little hard to believe," said Scott, the other cop nodding his head.

Earl sat at his desk, a forlorn look on his face. What had he done now? It sounded like something Elric would be capable of.

His son was fearless; he knew that much. He just didn't want to believe that he would steal from him.

The whole day, he was consumed with thoughts of his son going to prison. Maybe that's what he needed to straighten out, before worse things happened to him.

When the guys got back to Johnny's, his uncle was waiting outside of his garage to talk to them.

"The cops have been here looking for you, Elric," said his uncle, trying to look through him. "They said the Goldminers jewelry store was robbed."

"Weird, wonder what they want with me? Probably my dad is looking for me. He wants me to live with him and work for him. I'm done with that. Was in the bush working and broke my foot. I'm a singer, not a lumberjack," answered Elric."

When Johnny's uncle walked into the house, Elric spoke to Johnny.

"I think I'll go to Loretta's for the night. Tomorrow night after dark I'll come back. We have to move fast on this job on Friday. I'll go early morning about four to my old man's car lot and take the car."

"Did you rob the jewellery store, man?" asked Johnny.

"Hell, no. Probably someone that looks like me. Fuck them bastards. They got shit on me. I just don't want to be here, if they come around again. Wasting my time. I got better things to do."

Turning, he walked away from Johnny's, pulling his overcoat collar up, his fedora down over his forehead. His guitar lay across his back.

Thinking hard about their motives, they wanted to know where he was laying his head and where he might have stashed the jewels. That made sense. Fuck, he would have to lay low at Loretta's till Thursday. Let the guys know at their final meeting at Johnny's Thursday night. Have a few drinks, and go over the plan till it was set in stone. There would be no casing out the bank, with the cops looking for him.

Since Scott had visited Earl, he wasn't thinking about Elric. He had bigger fish to fry, the Lloyd gang. The task force was hot on their trail, like bloodhounds. The gang had left Quebec a couple of weeks ago and were headed toward Ontario. They had stopped along the way, robbing a couple of banks as they went. Following the string of robberies on the map, it was easy for the cops to figure out where they were headed. The big city of Toronto. Quebec had been really good to them, but the last job they did resulted in two officers getting killed and one of the robbers.

They were waiting to make their move when they could get them all in one place, where they lay their heads. The gang had been renting flats where they all stayed. They would do the same in Toronto, and Scott was convinced that's where they were going. He could taste the victory, and see his name all over the front pages of the newspapers. Task force headed by Detective Scott, takes down the Lloyd Gang. Yes, he liked it. He could taste the victory.

The gang had been getting sloppy, drinking and carousing in the bars too much.

Brazen killers, making them an easy target for the five-o.

Scott was summoned to head the final showdown. Take them dead or alive, was the order. These guys had been murdering innocent people who got in their way. The whole province of Quebec was stunned by the robberies and the fact that they were still at large.

It was the largest manhunt in history. The Lloyds were holed up in an old farmhouse. A shootout ensued, two officers down, stopping the cops in their tracks. Hitting the road again, they headed into Ontario. Robbing a few more banks as they went in London, Brampton, Barrie.

The front page of the *Quebec Gazette* read Lloyd Gang two cops shot down in cold blood. Still at large.

Stopping by a watering hole, he put back a couple of shots of straight whiskey. Just enough to warm a guy on a cold January night. He told himself just two shots. He was going to see his sweetheart and didn't want any more incidents with her. He overheard a couple of guys sitting at the bar, talking about the Lloyd gang and the shootout at the barn. The cops were hot on their trail, out of province, heading toward Ontario. Perfect, he thought. He couldn't get any luckier if he rolled two sevens on the dice. The planets were lining up for the bank job on Friday. The cops had one thing on their minds now, and it wasn't him, chuckling to himself. They wouldn't be expecting a bank robbery right in the downtown core of Quebec City.

A sadness came over him, his star fading. He had to hold his head down, as if in shame but really just hiding. Running and hiding, he would be doing a lot of that now. He would have to stay a step ahead of the game, the game of life, the game of chance.

Orchestrating the bank job was on his mind. The guys would all wear three piece suits. Surely everyone could borrow a pinstriped suit, fedora, and black shoes. They would fashion themselves like the Lloyd gang.

It was brilliant. If all went well, they would think they were the Lloyd gang. They had lured the cops out of the city, making them think they were leaving Quebec, when they struck one last time, at the main branch, Bank of Montreal.

The guys would have to cover their heads with stockings, just before they went into the bank. He would get some from Loretta's dresser, where he had watched her take out her white stockings she wore with her uniform.

They would meet early in the morning. Mulling the lineup over and over in his mind, deciding, just Dean and Johnny could take down the bank, while he drove the getaway car. Bringing in George, might just upset the applecart, too many in on the job. He would go in the early morning hours and break in to his father's office, taking the key for the 36 Special, getting the car back in time to pick up the boys and be at the bank before it opened.

Loretta would be surprised to see him back so soon on a cold winter's night, the darkness looming over the city. From now on, he would have to move like a night creature. He was being hunted now, with the excitement of the chase. The brightness of his star was dulled by his choices.

Knocking on her door, anxious, he looked both ways down the street. Opening the door, she pulled him in by his coat.

"Hurry, get in here," she said. "The cops have been here twice looking for you. Are you involved with the Lloyd Gang?"

"No, hell no. So, they think I am one of them?"

"I was just wondering, with all the news lately of the bank robberies around the country."

"I'm not that stupid," said Elric, pulling Loretta to him.

"Did you miss me?" Leaning into her, kissing her full on the lips. Holding her tight, he picked her up in his arms, walking her into the bedroom. They made love, for hours.

Getting up early, looking out the window, the sky still dark. The morning would soon steal in, revealing his secrets. He couldn't hang around till daylight. Things to do, places to go, the darkness his cover, he had to move like a vampire now.

Gazing over at her, her reddish curls on the pillow beside him, her complexion clear, pearly pink. She was indeed a beauty, but there were lots of beauties out there. He had to leave her now, with no promise of returning. His mind consumed with her lately, his sweet Alice.

Loretta could never stand in Alice's shoes. She had seen many lovers. It showed in the way she touched him, making love to him with her mouth. Those skills, she hadn't learned from one lover. Tearing himself away from Loretta's beauty, he watched her sleep. Going to her dresser, he pulled on the top drawer, taking out three white stockings.

Going to the kitchen, Elric makes himself a cup of coffee and some eggs. Sitting at the table, thinking of what he would do next. Dressing himself, he looked in at Loretta a few times, then picked up his guitar slinging it over his back. Dressing in a grey toque pulled down over his forehead, a green and black checkered hunting jacket, a pair of baggy pants, and his steel toed boots, looking every bit a lumberjack. Perfect, it being hunting season and all. Taking a last look around, he walked quickly away from Loretta's, down the road toward Johnny's.

He would still be sleeping, thought Elric. He needed to get to his house before anyone spotted him.

Standing outside banging on the door, he looked up at the window over the garage, watching for any sign of Johnny in the window. Growing impatient, he knocked harder, over and over again, his knuckles feeling the abuse. Johnny finally woke,

"Fuck, who the hell?"

Getting out of bed, he wrapped his housecoat around his lean body. Going to the window, Elric standing there, looking up at him. Rushing down to the door, he opened it. Elric stepped in.

"Shit, man, didn't even look like you."

Slipping his guitar off his shoulder, he laid it down on the floor next to the couch. Sitting down, he started to take off his boots. Johnny takes a seat at the kitchen table, watching his partner in crime, waiting to catch up with the plan.

"The cops will think we're the Lloyd Gang. We have three guys, and so do they."

"What, so you are cutting George out?"

"Ya, he's a pussy. I don't trust him to keep his mouth shut."

"I am tall and look like younger version of Edward, so I'll drive the getaway car. You and Dean will take down the bank. It will be smooth. Just one thing: we need some guns."

"Ah, I know where to get some automatic rifles, but it's going to cost, and I got no money," said Johnny.

Pulling his last hundred-dollar bill out of his pocket, he handed it to Johnny.

"Man, you never cease to amaze me. You still have money like this?"

"It's the last money I got. So you see why this job has to go down, I have no other options now. It's go big or go to the river and drown my fucking self, before I sleep on a cardboard box."

"My feelings exactly. I'm down, Elric. You call it."

"You go now and get those guns. I'll have the whole plan of action figured, when you get back. I'll wait till around five a.m. and go get the car, piece of cake."

Pulling the mickey out of his bag, he downed a couple shots, passing it to Johnny.

"Just a mouthful, man, it's the last."

"Friday morning, before the first customers come in, we will be down the road by the time they find them."

"What do you mean, kill them?"

"Hell no, just tie them up, gag them, no harm. No one gets hurt."

"It'll be like taking candy from a baby." He laughed. "I'm not going down for murder."

"I'm going to get the guns, be back soon."

He waited and planned the scenario over and over in his mind. It was easy. The biggest obstacle would be getting in and out, quickly, and out of the downtown before the cops showed up. They wouldn't know what hit them.

Studying the newspaper, the Lloyds were on the front page. Pinstripe suits and fedoras. Dressed to impress.

The pinstriped suit he stole from his father was going to come in handy. The gentlemanly robber.

Two hours later, Johnny showed up at his place, holding two hand guns, one in each hand, pulling a long rife out from under a coat. Coming into the main space, Elric was frying something in the pan. "Got a couple steaks for us, man, and you know what, just because you are my main man, I got you something else too. Something that's going to look real nice when you put on that pinstriped suit, white shirt. I just figure, we are riding in a fucking Cadillac, can't look like a bunch of fucking river rats." Then he turned, with Johnny standing, spread legs, holding one special Weston .38 in each hand. "Fuck, ya!" he said, turning off the stove. He walked over, taking one from Johnny. "I'll handle this one. You got one more for Dean?"

"Oh yes, I do."

"Holy fuck, man, holding this thing makes it all real. This shit is going down. You ain't kidding Schoolcraft."

"Have a good look at this face. Do I look like I'm kidding?"

Reaching into his jacket pocket, he pulled out a gold watch with a diamond face.

"I just wanted you to know that I appreciated everything you did for me, man. You got my back, and I got yours. After this job, I'm going to disappear for a while. I might never see you again, so here." Handing the gold watch to Johnny, his eyes lit like a starry night.

"This is just a little bonus. The big loot comes tomorrow."

"Wowwww," said Johnny, putting the gold watch on his arm.

A sly look crossed his face, and he looked Elric in the eye. There was no sense asking him if he had done the jewelry job. It was a fact, clear as the sparkling diamonds around the watch face.

"Respect, man," he said, shoving his shoulder into Elric, the two of them bouncing fists. "Tomorrow is going to be a big day in our lives."

"Our fate changes tomorrow, big things, places to go and things to do. Fuck, man, we are going to have enough money to just relax and enjoy life for the next few years."

"What, man, I never thought of it that way. I'm freaking right now. I need some whiskey. Actually, I think we better get a couple mickeys, man. Let's get lit before we go. I think it will relax me, man. What do you think?"

"Fuck, man, liquid courage, whatever you want to call it, I'm going to drink a half a fucking mickey before we leave this place. I want to be ready for anything."

"Got ya," said Johnny, the thoughts of the robbery exciting him.

As the night wore on, and the darkness descended, they watched the clock. He would leave at 4:00 a.m. The whiskey was warming his blood, the warrior rising to the surface. The blood pumped fast through his veins, his heart rate elevated. Watching out the window, he waited for Johnny to show with Dean. As soon as the guys got back, he was heading out to get the car.

Pacing back and forth, finally he saw them coming. At the sound of their footsteps up the stairs, Elric stood waiting.

"Hey, good to see you," said Dean. "Thanks for bringing me in. George kept asking what I was doing. Haven't had anything to eat for a couple days." Dean's hollow cheeks and the dark circles under his blue eyes, showing his despair. "I'm sick of living like a dog."

"Go, make yourself sandwich, man. There is bread and some bologna and cheese in there," Johnny said, pointing to the kitchen area.

"Oh, thank you, buddy. You are a life saver."

Johnny pulled out the mickey out of his jacket. Taking a big swallow, he passes it to Elric.

"Sure, I'll take a hit of that. It's fucking cold out there, and I'm leaving in a few minutes. I'll be back with the Cadillac in a couple hours." Looking at his watch: 3:00 a.m.

The guys sit quietly, on the couch, watching and listening to the boss.

"We have to be there when the manager is opening the door, first thing in the morning. As he is unlocking the door, Johnny, you come up behind him, stick the gun in his back and talk to him quietly. Just say, 'Don't make a scene, or you are a dead man.'

"Then Dean, you follow them in. Order him to open the safe. If he refuses, tell him you will kill him. He won't risk his life. The Lloyds have killed so many innocent people with their robbing spree, people are scared. They have done half the job for us already.'" They all have a good laugh.

"Johnny, your uncle got some kind of burlap bags around here? We need something to put the money in."

"Yes, I'll get them," answered Johnny, running down the stairs to the garage.

"Shit," he said out loud. Dean looked up at his friend.

"What, man?"

"Nothing, nothing at all, answered Elric, standing, stretching looking out the window. Light started to creep into the day.

Wearing the same toque on his head, his steel toed boots, and the hunter's coat.

"I figure we got three minutes to do the job, and get the hell out of there. I got this stop watch here, set for four minutes," said Elric, pulling a round golden watch out of his inside pocket.

"I'll be waiting right in front. I expect the two of you and the money back in the car, ready to roll, before the fourth minute strikes.

"Don't fuck this up. We could all end up in jail for the rest of our lives. Timing is the essence, in and out, and down the fucking road in less than five minutes."

"All right, I'm outta here. I'll be back as soon as I can. You boys get dressed to impress. Gentlemanly robbers. See you soon," he said, heading down the stairs.

Out onto the road, he walked quickly, the warmth of the whiskey in his loins, his mind clouded, keeping his eyes open, listening keenly for any oncoming traffic, looking behind him every few minutes.

Noticing the lights of an oncoming vehicle, Elric tried to see past the ditch, jumping across into the bush. Clearing the ditch, he lay flat on his stomach, waiting for the car to pass. "Shit," he said, picking himself up, his left foot hurting.

Getting back on the road, he walked faster. *Just a little ways now*, he told himself, his body cold, the wind cutting into his bare skin, his eye sockets hurting.

His father's car lot came into view, the light on outside the office, the sign Schoolcraft Auto Sales illuminating in the night. Too much light, he thought. He would have to do this fast.

Wasting no time, he walked up to the door to the office. Lifting his right foot, he smashed it into the door, around the lock. The door flew open, splinters of wood falling to the ground.

Stepping in, he tried to focus in the darkened office, walking to the peg board that hung behind the desk. The silver of the keys are illuminated in the dark. He grabbed the keys for the Cadillac, he knew so well.

Deciding to break open the desk drawer, making it look like the robber was looking for money. Using the screwdriver he had brought with him, he pried open the desk drawer, taking a handful of papers and throwing them on the floor. Pulling the door closed behind him, he moved briskly, making his way down the rows of cars. Running his gloved hand over the hood as much to say, *Good car, take me where I need to go.*

Getting in behind the wheel, he pulled the big car out of the lot, down the road, toward Johnny's.

With the daylight just over the horizon, the car would be a heat score sitting in front of Johnny's. They would have to hide it in the garage.

He drove, the road quiet. Too cold for life, he told himself, waiting for the heater to kick in. Making it back to Johnny's, the guys hear the engine, watching out the window.

"Fuck, man, look at the car he has, a fucking Cadillac to boot," said Johnny, his voice raised in excitement.

"That fucker is something else," said Dean. "Where the hell did he get the car?"

"Don't ask stupid questions. Isn't none of your business, is it?"

"I suppose not."

"Well then," said Johnny. Dean put on his fedora, Johnny doing the same. Johnny went down to open the garage door, pulling it shut, once the big car is in safely.

"What do you think of this baby?" asked Elric, Johnny and Dean amazed, checking out the nicest car either of them had ever ridden in.

"I'm going to get me one of these," said Dean, admiring the inside of the car.

"I could live in this thing," he said, laughing.

"OK, get the guns in. We are going to take a little ride around the bank area a few times, scope out the scene. We got two hours before the bank opens. I'm going to get dressed now."

"Johnny, stick the gun to the back of his head, and when you are inside the bank, if he doesn't open the safe right away, stick it in his fucking mouth. Tell him you will blow his head off. He'll open the safe."

"I know he will," laughed Johnny.

"Tie up the old bugger, gag him, leave him face down on the floor in his office. Any questions?" asked Elric, looking at his accomplices.

"How do you know he is old?" asked Johnny.

"Just a calculated guess, is all," laughed Elric.

"I'll get some twine from the garage to tie him," said Johnny.

"Work fast, no time to waste. I'll be right outside of the bank. By the way, you guys look great in those getups. We should dress up more often," said Elric with a hearty laugh.

"Yeah, I kind of like this look myself," said Johnny.

"Let's go in for a bit," said Elric. "I got to get dressed, and we'll have a couple of shots, get the adrenaline fired up." No surprise to Johnny, Elric had another mickey stashed.

"Sounds good to me," said Johnny, following Elric up the stairs to the apartment. Pulling his stop watch out from his pocket, taking a quick look at the time he headed into the bathroom, his clothes in hand. Hanging his suit on the hook behind the bathroom door, standing in front of the mirror, washing his face, combing his shiny black hair, brushing his teeth. Clean, just like this job, clean break. *Outta town, no one any the wiser,* he said to himself, knowing in his heart that if the cops caught them, he was going away and for a long time, with nothing to come back to.

Dressed and ready to roll, taking one last look at himself in the mirror, his fedora cocked to the side. They were a good looking bunch.

Johnny and Dean, sitting on the couch, each with their handguns resting between their legs.

"Get those guns in the car," ordered Elric. "Take mine too, out of sight. Bring a change of clothes so you can ditch those suits as soon as we get out of town. We will go somewhere, split the money, then you guys are on your own."

"I'll take care of that," said Dean, grabbing the guns.

Johnny rifled through a dresser, pulling out two pairs of jeans and two sweaters, handing them to Dean.

Elric took the flask of whiskey out of his pocket, put it to his head.

"One for the road," he said joyfully.

"Here's looking at all that money," he said, his mouth watering, handing the bottle to Johnny, who takes it with shaking hands.

"What, you nervous? You had better not fumble, man. If you fuck up, you will have to deal with me. Can you do this?"

"Oh, yeah, just that I haven't slept all night."

"I see," said Elric, eyeing his buddy. Dean came back up the stairs. "It's all set," he said, noticing the bottle being passed.

"Hey, give me a shot of that." Johnny passed him the bottle, then back to Elric, who put it to his head, draining the rest.

"Ready? Let's do this!" he said, heading down the stairs, the guys following him. They all settled into the big car, Elric at the wheel, Johnny and Dean in the back seat with their guns on the floor.

"When the job is done, we'll drive out of town, find somewhere to stop and split the money, then you guys are on your own. The cops will be looking for three guys in suits and fedoras. So we got to change out of these clothes right away.

"I'm taking off, won't be seeing you bastards for a long time."

"What, what do you mean?" asked Johnny?

"Just what I said, you guys are on your own. Get your own way back home, lay low spend your money however you want. You had better sit on it for a while. The cops will be watching for anyone spending money like they have a money tree."

"I see what you mean," said Johnny.

"Yeah, and if either of you get busted with the money, nobody better mention my name or else I'll come back and kill you," he said staring straight into both of their eyes, his cold grey stare like hardened cement. "Understood?" he said, raising his voice.

The job went just as planned. The old grey haired man ambled up to the bank door. Johnny and Dean, stockings pulled down over their faces, their fedoras pulled down over their foreheads, came up behind him, ordering him in. Johnny pushed him to the ground.

"Don't kill me. I'll give you the money," the old man said, his voice quivering. "You guys the Lloyd gang? I had a feeling you were coming."

Neither Dean nor Johnny uttered a word. Johnny led the old man into the vault, the guys filling their bags with stacks of bills.

In two minutes they had all the money in their bags, then tied up the old man, gagging him with a handkerchief, leaving him face down in the office.

Elric watched as his partners came running out of the bank, their hands full with the loot in four burlap bags. His heart beating fast and hard in his chest, his car ready on the side of the road.

There was a postman walking by, just as they hustled into the car, noticing the bandits. Hiding up against a building until the car passed, taking a good look at the black Cadillac and the three guys in the car.

Fucking Lloyd gang strikes again.

Running to the nearest store, calling the cops. "Robbery at First and King," he said. "Bank of Montreal."

Within five minutes the cops are all over the scene, going into the bank, finding Mr. Diamond, face down, tied up, and gagged.

When they untied him, he sat up, his eyes wide, "It was them, two of them in suits, couldn't see their faces. They had stockings on their heads with guns, and they meant business. The same guys, the Lloyd gang."

Just then, the two female tellers showed at the door, the cops ushering them in.

"There's been a robbery here. Oh my God," said one of the ladies, looking at Mr. Diamond, still sitting on the floor.

The cops searched the bank for clues, fingerprints, anything that could tie the Lloyd gang to the robbery.

There was one thing that was confusing them. The word was that the gang was back in Toronto. There had been a string of robberies in the last week.

"How the hell could they be there, and here too?" asked one of the cops.

"Maybe they split up," answered the other cop.

"Copycat gang maybe? What do you think?" His partner shrugging his shoulders. "You got me," he said.

Pedal to the metal, hitting the highway, they head out of city limits, Elric pulling into the first side road.

"Well, that went smooth. You guys were great," he said, looking back at them, their eyes wide, staring back at him, speechless.

"Now get those clothes off, and let's share out this loot," Elric ordered, getting out of the front seat, joining them in the back.

"Just leave those suits. I'll get rid of them. You don't need nothing tying you to this robbery."

"Fuck, you can buy a hundred new suits, if that's what you want."

They all laughed nervously, as Elric started taking out the stacked bills.

Emptying four bags, a huge pile of money between them on the back seat.

"One for you, one for you, one for me," he counted, until there were ten bundles left.

"The rest is fucking mine. That's for the brains in the bunch," he said, laughing. "Without me, you guys would have fuck all."

They looked at one another, a scowl crossing Johnny's face. Grabbing up his pile of bills stuffing it into his pack, Dean doing the same.

"Don't spend it all in one place," said Elric, laughing out loud. "By the way, you haven't seen me, in a long time, and probably won't see me again," he said, laughing again, louder, maniacal. "It's been a slice.

"I'm out of here. Take it easy. Have a good life."

Johnny gets out of the Cadillac first, Dean following, slamming the back door shut. He used them to get the job done, then threw them out on the road, with a big bag of money.

Putting his money in his pack, he pulled on his toque, getting in the driver's seat.

Watching and waited until the guys were out of sight, then pulled the big car back onto the highway.

That went smooth as warmed butter. *Why the hell didn't I do this long ago? No,* came back the voice of reason, *don't count your lucky stars. Gambling with your life.* What he needed to do right now was get as far away from Quebec, as fast as he could. They would soon be looking for the stolen car and the Lloyd gang.

Looking over at his stack of money, he let out an animal howl.

Heading out along the coastal highway, towards New Brunswick, the car moved smoothly. Without realizing it, he was doing 100 mph, passing a sign reading 70 mph. Knowing he better slow down, and not bring any heat on himself, he settled in at 70 mph.

Getting caught up in his daydreams, he noticed the gas gauge reading on the last quarter of a tank. He would have to stop to refuel, and get some supplies.

A place to hide out was his main concern. Get off the main road, fill up with gas, and head toward the mountains. Find a cabin, even an old hunting cabin would do fine. There should be one somewhere, up in those hills.

Watching the road, the day still young, a few cars passing. Deciding to pull over, he took off his jacket and his pants, putting the hunting outfit back on.

Noticing a sign reading Guysborough, with an arrow, off the main road, Elric following it.

A few miles up the road, he notices a general store and gas station. The sign read Harry's General Store. Pulling the Cadillac up next to the lone gas pump, he quickly goes into the store, asking the clerk for gas.

"Could I get a fill up there, partner?" he said. The older man looked Elric over from head to toe, then out at the Cadillac.

Something just didn't seem right to him, a young fella like him, driving a nice car like that in what looked like a hunting outfit.

"Is that your father's car?" he asked Elric, staring him in the eye.

"As a matter of fact it is," answered Elric.

"What's a young man like you doing in these parts?"

"Going to do some hunting," said Elric, pulling his coat around him. "Lots of deer in these mountains, I've heard," he said, giving the clerk a plastic smile.

Trying to change the subject quickly. "Give me a couple bottles of whiskey," said Elric, walking away from the counter, the clerk keeping a close eye on him.

Grabbing four loaves of bread, matches, ten cans of salmon, five cans of sardines, butter, sugar, coffee, cream and milk, oatmeal, eggs, honey, peanut butter and cooking oil.

"You got bullets, man?"

"What kind of gun you have?" asked the clerk, really interested in this kid now.

"Weston .38 special."

"You got money to pay for all this stuff. Can I see your money?"

Elric pulled out two ten-dollar bills.

Putting all his things in two large paper bags, he gives Elric his change. "Ten dollars gas should fill it up."

The clerk came out of the store and filled the gas tank, as Elric watched him in the rear-view mirror.

Just as he is pulling out of the station, the old man decided to take down the plate number. No plate on the car. Something didn't seem right about that guy, he thought, getting back to what he was doing, the Lloyd gang coming to his mind. And the gun, a .38 handgun, was not exactly a hunting rifle.

"Put out an APB on a black Cadillac, thirty-six special, no plate three men. Looks like the Lloyd gang struck again, suits, fedoras. Armed and dangerous. Take them dead or alive, ten thousand dollar reward," said Scott, putting down his microphone. The cops in all counties, alerted about another bank job.

Loretta peered out her window, an emptiness in her heart. Where was he? Was he all right? It had been so good seeing him for one night. Now she longed to hold him, kiss him. Knowing in her heart that he did rob the jewelry store.

Heading to work and back home, thinking that he might be there waiting, only to find no sign of him. Did they catch him? Maybe she wouldn't see him for a long time. Coming to terms with that possibility, Loretta got back to her life as she knew it, before she had met the stranger, trying hard not to think about him day and night.

Back on the highway, heading out of New Brunswick, Elric followed the coastal road, taking him into the mountains of Cape Breton Island. They wouldn't be looking for him way up here. It would be a safe place to hide his money and spend some time, in the bush.

The darkness fell, his head and body warmed from the whiskey, straight from the bottle. The road started to blur, Elric pulling onto a side road.

The snow was about two feet deep. Guiding the big car up the narrow road, making tracks in the fresh fallen snow.

Making it in about a quarter mile, he gets stuck in a hole, the car's wheels spinning. The car was not moving.

"Fuck," he said, "I'll sleep right here. The cold won't kill me," he told himself, taking another shot.

Glad now that he had brought a blanket from Johnny's. Must have known he was going to be spending a night outside. Pulling the red wool blanket around him, trying to curl up on the back seat, falling asleep, only to wake up a few hours later, and his head killing him, his whole body shaking.

"What the hell?" he said, trying to put his coat over him. Laying back down, falling asleep again, the coat and blanket pulled tight around his body.

Going into a dream of three beautiful women, their large naked breasts warming him, pressing against his chest. They get into a frenzy, scratching him with their long nails, playfully sharing him.

The coldness shakes him out of the nightmare. Sitting up straight, his blood cold, his nose cold, the windows showing a thick fog. Knowing he had to get out of there, and find a warm place to stay, even a motel would do. *Not a good idea*, came back the voice of reason. *Keep the car out of sight, off the road.*

The way the clerk at the store had looked at him, by now the cops would already be looking for the car, or if anyone had noticed it leaving the bank area as well, or his dad could have filed a theft complaint. Regardless, he had to stay out of sight. Just then he felt a stinging on his side, looked down. His shirt is ripped, with three scratch marks running down his side to his waist. What the hell? Shaking his head, "What the hell did I do?" Looking at the reddened flesh wounds,

The same place where he had cut himself on the broken window?

Opening the back door, getting out, the wind howling, a light snow blowing.

"Fuck," he said, getting back into the car, remembering the car is stuck. He would have to get some branches to put under the wheels to give the car some traction. It was still dark, so he would have to wait it out until daylight.

Earl had showed up at the office that morning at seven. Noticing his office door ajar, he looked closer. The door was splintered, the lock hanging off.

"What happened here?" he said out loud walking in farther, taking in the scene, papers scattered around the desk and floor, the top drawer of the desk open. *Well, they didn't get any money*, he said to himself. Just then, his eyes darted to the peg board that held the keys. He knew right away the keys for one of the cars was missing—his favourite Cadillac.

His son was the last one he would suspect. Last he heard his band was playing at the Quebec Hotel.

For a fleeting moment, he was proud of his boy, then all the other things flooded his mind.

Earl called the cops, reporting the break in and the stolen car.

"We'll be down this afternoon, Mr. Schoolcraft. Don't go in the office or touch anything."

"Fine," answered Earl, walking out of his office, thinking of the possibility, of it being Elric.

He remembered how his son had said he wanted a car just like that one. Earl watched the way he walked around it, running his hand over the black shiny paint, a lust in his eye.

No, he didn't want to think that way. With all the talk of the Lloyd gang, they probably stole it for another bank job. That sounded more likely.

Dean and Johnny made it back into town with no incidents. They parted their ways as soon as they hit the city, Dean going to the Quebec Hotel, renting a room.

With some good food and a few drinks, he already felt like a millionaire.

The bartender recognized him as one of the Wanderers, asking about the band and when they would be getting back together.

"I don't think we will be getting together any time soon," he answered. "We had some personal problems, among the guys, couldn't work it out, and things just kinda fell apart," replied Dean.

"Sorry to hear that. Everyone has been asking for you guys. You should really get your own thing going."

"Hey, that's food for thought," said Dean, thinking of Johnny and him. All they would need would be a lead singer to take Elric's place. That wouldn't be an easy task.

The bank job would never be spoken of. He just wanted a good life now.

His mind runs on George, still living under the bridge, deciding he would help him out. They had shared many nights together, cold and hungry. He just couldn't leave him to die in the dampness of the river. When some time had passed, he would go and find him, and give him some money.

Johnny went straight home to his apartment, spreading out the money on his bed. Fuck, there is a lot of money here, he reasoned. He would have to find a good hiding place and just act normal. He wasn't worried about Elric, who was long gone, and Dean he could trust with his life. They had been like brothers. This was the best thing that had ever happened to him, a nervous excitement running through his veins.

What if the cops come here looking for Elric? No, they weren't looking for Elric right now. They had their hands full, with all the bank robberies. Pulling up a couple of floor boards, he hid his money between the insulation, nailing the boards back down. Keeping two hundred dollars, deciding it would last him for a while. Should he go down to the bridge and give George a few bucks, a slight feeling of guilt, that they had cut him out?

Fuck, Elric had already heated up his little place over the garage. Really, he needed to get the hell out as soon as he could. That bastard was smart, got the hell out of Quebec, and he needed to get out too.

Both Dean and Johnny had gone down to the bridge on different occasions, looking for George. Amazed that they both offered him some money, Dean gave him two hundred dollars. "Don't fucking ask," said Dean. "Get yourself a room for a while, live a little man." George gives him a big smile and the once over.

Johnny showed up a few days later, handing him a hundred dollars. "I see," said George, looking deep into Johnny's eyes. "You fuckers went and did it without me. What, I'm not good enough?"

"Not good enough for that fucking Elric. That bastard is going down anyway."

Just then Johnny drove a punch into George's mouth. "Shut your fucking mouth. You are a pussy, just like Elric said, keep his name out of your mouth, or he might kill you."

"Don't kick a gift horse in the mouth, you stupid fuck. Have a good life," he said, walking away.

Holding his mouth, the metallic taste of blood on his tongue, cursing under his breath. One thing for sure, he was no rat. He wouldn't say nothing. After all, they had taken him off the streets for a while. Maybe he would go back to his grandmother's house, give her the money. She might let him back in. It was worth a try.

Good luck to them, he thought. He would hear about Elric, he knew that.

Dean spent a couple of weeks at the Quebec Hotel, laying low, going out to dinner to eat and right back to his room. There was a lot of activity around town, cops crawling all over the place. The Lloyd gang wanted in the latest bank job.

He needed to get out of town, maybe go to Florida for a while and live it up. He had no one to answer to and a pocket full of money. Maybe he'd find himself a sweetheart down there. Dean took the next train out of the country.

Pulling a few branches off an evergreen tree, Elric padded under both tires, taking his time, rocking the big car back and forth. The wheels finally dug into the pine branches, easing it out of the hole, the car freed from the snow. Guiding it out of the road, the car's engine purring. Finding the main road, Elric headed toward the mountains he could see in the distance. Shivering, chilled to the bone, waiting for the heater to kick in.

Driving carefully, not speeding, he followed the highway until he found another logging road. Heading in, it wound up around the mountainside.

Following another narrow, bush ridden road, watching keenly. The snow beaten down with wide deep toothed tires, probably logging trucks, he reasoned, spotting a cabin through the trees in the distance.

Bringing the car to a stop, getting out, trudging in the deep snow towards the cabin. Peering through a small dust-covered window on the front side to the right of the door. Reasoning, there hadn't been anyone there in awhile, no tracks in the snow, a black chimney running up through the roof of the cabin, which meant one thing for sure, there must be a wood stove in there. Looking around the cabin now for any sign of a human occupant. No footprints, only a few animal prints around the side of the cabin, leading into the thick bush.

Grabbing the door handle, he pushed in the wood slat door into a one room cabin. A potbellied black iron stove sitting in the middle. With a few pieces of dry wood, and some smaller kindling he found behind the stove, he set the wood in.

It seems like a hunting cabin, and probably someone had been there not too long ago, a fresh smell of smoke in the air. They had left a few things that he could use to start a fire. Perfect, he thought, as he surveyed the inside of the cabin, dust covering the logs, a few spider webs in the cracks. In places you could see outside, the putty having fallen away from the seam of the logs.

Going back to the car, Elric carried his supplies, his gun, and his sack of money. After putting everything down in the middle of the floor, he struck up a match. Twisting a piece of paper, he put in a few of the small pieces in a teepee form. The smoke started to billow, a flame showing, the dry splinters of the wood catching.

"That's it, baby," he said. "Warmth is what I need right now." Looking over at the single cot up against the other log wall. *Now, if I just had a hot babe to keep me warm. Be careful what you wish for,* came back a voice in his head, remembering the three women who had taken advantage of him in his dream.

A bed, a fire, some food—this would do for a while. He would hide out here, and cover the car with some branches. No one would notice the car way up here anyway. There wasn't anyone around.

He would be ready for them if they came for him, holed up in the log cabin. They didn't have fucking nothing on him anyway, or so he hoped.

Walking outside, gazing up at the mountain that raised into the sky, its peak covered in white, like an altar to something higher, much higher, watching down on him, the sky blue, the air cold.

"This is living," he said. "Good mountain air."

Getting settled, the stove starting to send some warmth from its belly, he lay down on the narrow bed, wrapping himself in the red wool blanket.

Tomorrow, first thing, he would take a trek up the mountain, find a place under a big rock, dig into the frozen ground, and bury his treasure. Nothing was for sure. Might have to leave it there for a long time, he reasoned. Taking out a thousand dollars, putting the rest in the burlap bag, insulated with plastic, using some rope to tie the bag, winding it around and around his treasure. Pleased with his plan, Elric finally fell asleep, the warmth of the woodstove lulling him to sleep.

Waking in the early morning hours, his head pounding, his eyes aching, sitting on the side of the cot. The fire had gone out, the cabin colder than being outside, his breath showing in white billows from his mouth.

Having a look around him at a few fish hooks and memorabilia from previous hunters, a knife stuck in one of the logs near the small window. *Well, whoever it was better stay the fuck away from here. This is my place now,* he said to himself, the pain in his head, making him meaner than a hungry jackal.

He didn't know how long he would have to stay here, but he was going to sit it out for a while, until the dust settled or until they caught the Lloyd gang, whichever came first.

The cops were mulling over the robbery of the Cadillac from Schoolcraft Auto Sales, shaking their heads at the brilliance of the Lloyd gang.

"So, how the hell can you be in two places at once?" asked Scott to his partner. "They were last spotted outside of Toronto the same day. Something just doesn't add up for me," said Scott, rubbing his chin.

There was a footprint on the door, around the doorknob, size eleven boot. The same imprint at the jewelry store. Things were adding up now, Schoolcraft, the wayward kid. The Riverside gang. The singing bandit.

They just needed to find him and get the print from his boots. It would tie him to this robbery and the jewellery store.

Scott smiled to himself. When he found the kid, he would put him away for a while. No doubt in his mind now, he kicked in the door and stole his father's car. Not only that, his daughter had confessed to sleeping with him, and the possibility of him being the father of his grandson, Jude. Johnny Reid or Elric Schoolcraft, she had said. Both members of the Riverside Gang.

Too fucking cocky. The one thing he couldn't deny, he was a good looking bastard, and if he wasn't mistaken, his grandson, had his looks. Shaking his head, he just couldn't believe she would get involved with either of them. Thought he had raised her better. Actually, her mother raised her. He was never around much.

Elric and the Wanderers. The cops taking a good look at the poster, on the wall at the Quebec Hotel, when they went in to inquire about when they had played there last.

"The band of thieves," he commented to the other officer, "all these kids, have done time." Hmmm, thought Scott, he will surface again. He would show up, sometime or the other, and he would nail his ass to the wall.

Putting on his working boots and wool socks, Elric dressed for the elements.

Trudging in the deep snow, his pack on his back, full of money. What he needed now was a perfect place to hide it. Using the tire iron he brought from the car, working it around a big boulder. When he was able to push it out of the hole it had indented in the ground, just enough room to conceal his bounty. Prodding the ground around the boulder, until he had enough frozen dirt to cover the bag of money.

Dropping the money into the mangled dirt, he covered it, then pushed and pulled until the boulder was back in place, like the door to a vault.

It was perfect. No one would find his hiding spot in a hundred years, he thought, laughing to himself, walking back down the mountain. With a limb from a spruce tree, he brushed away his footprints the best he could, getting back to the cabin.

Settling down, he drank some whiskey and sang a few songs, a sudden feeling of lonliness, no money could help, realizing he missed Loretta already.

Gazing out the window, the beautiful sunny day, the whiteness of everything. Mostly he was thinking of Loretta, her warm body, her hot mouth.

Telling himself to forget her now, his next plan of action coming into play. Go and get his sweet Alice. She was still thinking about him, he knew it. Last night he dreamed her in a beautiful dress, her small waist, and rounded breasts. They were dancing, swinging her around, kissing her on her lips, when he awoke, disappointed it was just a dream.

There was just something about her, made him crazy for her.

On the way up the mountain, where he had buried his money, he had noticed some bear tracks and a big pile of wet, shiny bear shit. Bending down to touch the tracks, sunken in the snow. A big one, he thought, from the size of the pads of the paw, too big for a black bear.

Shit, maybe there were grizzlies up here, he thought. Only ever heard of them, never had the pleasure of meeting one. Just then he smiled.

"That bastard will be a rug. Just let me see him," he said, remembering now that he didn't have a rifle, only the handgun. Fucking left the rifle at Johnny's. Shit, and he told the guy at the general store he was going hunting, buying bullets for a hand gun. Busted!

The second day at the cabin, Elric decided to go hunting, get himself some wild meat, maybe a deer or a partridge for dinner. The canned fish he had bought, wasn't going to last long. Deciding to follow the tracks of the deer or find a place to put in a line, catch a few fish. If he shot an animal straight in the head, the handgun would suffice.

465

These were the best times for him. Hunting and fishing, feeling the wildness that ran near under the surface of his blood. The little bit of Indian in him had trickled down from his great grandfather's blood line, giving him that closeness to the bush. The courage of a warrior, with or without the whiskey. He made a trail, pulling a sled he found outside the cabin. Had to belong to the hunter before him.

It was a quiet, crisp, cold day, the sun shining bright against the white of the mountain peaks, like pillars to God. The pine and spruce trees stood like frozen giants, watching him.

Feeling in his inside pocket for his flask of whiskey to keep him warm. It could wait. He needed to be a crack shot, couldn't risk not having a steady hand. If he could shoot a deer, the coldness would keep it. Just hang it in a tree outside the cabin after he gutted it.

The sun was kissing his face, almost as sweet as a woman's lips, feeling like a million dollars, after all, there was almost that much buried in his secret place. What a great feeling, knowing he didn't have to do without anything that he wanted.

As he made his way deeper into the mountain, his mind ran on the Lloyd gang, wondering if they caught up to them yet.

Thing was, he was being hunted too, wondering why he became a suspect so quick, for the Goldminers Jewelry heist. Had he left clues? Thinking hard about what he had taken there, the fucking wrench. No, he had gloves on. There would have been no prints on it? Weird, how could they tie him to that job, they were just fucking guessing.

Crackling of bushes, movement, a deer running ahead, right behind, a big buck. Staying quiet, he watches them. They stopped again, pawing in the deep snow, trying to pull up some roots or branches. It was his perfect opportunity. Holding the thirty-eight with both hands, he aimed for the head of the big bull. Pulling the trigger, the buck fell into the snow like slow motion.

The other one ran for its life, leaping and bounding through the deep crusted snow.

Having fired two shots, one just over his eye, close to the animal now, he fired another shot between the eyes.

Standing over it, he counted its horns. "Five point buck," he said. Not bad for the first day. Now came the question of how the hell he was going to get this beast back to his cabin.

Someone else had heard the shots too. The big grizzly had followed his nose, smelling food, leading him to the cabin. Using his mammoth body, he pushed in the door. Walking like a baby taking its first steps in life, his arms outstretched in front of him on his hind legs, his broad snout in the air.

Going to the cupboards, he ripped them off the hinges.

Reaching in, its giant paw pulling everything out in one swipe. Then he ripped the cupboard right off the wall, and it fell with a hard thump to the floor.

Snorting and sniffing, he smelled the human. Where was he? It was a different one, not the one he had eaten last year. Going back over to the cans and things that he had flung all over the floor, rooting in the bread bag. Getting the honey jar open, he put it to his head, then threw it in the corner. Next he dug his long claws into the peanut butter, licking it from his giant paw.

There wasn't enough here to fill his back teeth.

The shots fired meant two things: human presence and possibly a fresh kill. He would go looking.

Managing to get the great horned head cut off, he worked his buck knife, cutting deep into the warm flesh of the animal. Its blood was still warm, keeping Elric's hands warm as he worked. Cutting the body of the animal into five pieces, he gutted it, the red of the blood on the white snow a shocking horror of kill.

Stacking the fresh meat onto the sled, with just enough room, starting his descent down the mountain.

Looking carefully around him, he knew there were bear up here. That was his only worry. The tracks had told him one thing: it was a big son of a bitch.

Getting closer to the cabin, no sign of smoke from the chimney, the fire must have gone out. Hoping there were still some coals in there to get it going. Approaching from the back of the cabin, he noticed fresh big bear tracks.

"Fuck," he said, letting go of the sled, walking around to the front, the door ajar. Peeking his head in, catching sight of the one room cabin torn up, his food, what he had left of it, scattered. The cupboard splintered into pieces, laying on the floor.

Looking over at his bed, ripped to shreds, a big pile of fresh bear shit right in the middle of it. Something about the whole scene struck him funny. Elric started laughing hysterically, holding his stomach.

Coming to his senses. Fuck, this bear was huge, and probably not far away. Holy fuck, where was his gun? Forget the gun. Wouldn't even sting a big bastard like this.

Well, shit, always did mean money, and he had that already. Would just have to clean up the pile of it and turn over the mattress.

"Come back around here, you bastard, I'll make you into a rug," he threatened out loud.

Picking up the bear shit as much as he could, he threw it out the door into the snow. Then he tried to salvage anything that he could and started the fire.

Putting the dead bolt across the door, peering out the small window. No sign of the bear.

He realized now that all of his foodstuff was gone, and it was not wise for him to go back into town. That guy asked too many questions. He would have to survive on meat alone. Just like a cave man, he told himself. They did it; why couldn't he?

Going back to the window, through a stand of trees, he sees what looks like a big brown bear, bent over his sled, fucking ripping at the deer meat, blood dripping from its wide hairy face.

The bear lifted its mighty head, its snout in the air, shaking his head from side to side.

Fuck, thought Elric, he would be a fool to try and threaten this beast, hoping against hope, the bear would get a bellyful and leave the rest for him. Watching keenly, it looked like the bear had left him a couple chunks of the deer meat. "Mighty kind of you there, big bear," said Elric, laughing.

With no choices now, he would have to go back to the general store for some more supplies, find out the latest on the Lloyd Gang.

Taking the snow laden boughs off the car, he gets in behind the wheel. The car started easily. Backing it out of the narrow road, onto the main road.

Pulling up to the general store, he walked in. The same older man standing behind the counter, like he hadn't left since he was last there.

"How's the hunting going, young man? I didn't realize till you left that you bought bullets for a handgun. Can't hunt very well with that, or do you have a rifle too?"

Fuck, why was he asking so many questions?

"I actually did get myself a five point buck yesterday, only a big bear stole the carcass," answered Elric.

"Really? Sounds like the same bear that ate a guy who was staying in a one room cabin up there. All they found was bones."

"I guess I forgot to bring my rifle. Do you have any for sale?"

"Yes, I got a nice one. You want to take a look at it?"

"Sure thing, I better be ready for that bear when he comes back."

Walking to the back of the store, the old man came back with a rifle in hand. "This costs forty dollars. You got that much?"

Remembering now that all he had was hundred dollar bills, he pulled one out of his inside of his jacket, put it on the counter.

The man stared at the hundred dollar bill. He hadn't seen one in a while, then he stared up at Elric. "How is it that you got that kind of money, young man?"

"My grandmother died and left me a little money is all."

"I see," said the clerk, taking another good look at Elric, heading into the back room to make change.

"You had better watch yourself up there. That bear is rouge all the way and has a taste for human meat."

"He don't know who he is messing with," answered Elric with a good hearty laugh.

The man watched him closely as he brought foodstuff to the counter. "Right, and I'll need some shells for my rifle."

"Have you heard the latest on those bank robbers? The paper said they were back in Quebec, robbed the main branch of the Bank of Montreal, right downtown Quebec City. They did that bank twice now. Brazen, I tell you."

"It's weird the cops haven't caught them yet," answered Elric, smirking under his breath.

The bear had eaten half of the carcass, leaving the rest on the sled. Happy to be able to salvage some of the meat, Elric sliced off a few tender pieces of the loin.

With a full stomach, the deer steak fresh and tender, Elric tries to make himself comfortable. Pulling his lone blanket around him, he remembered his heavy coat in the back seat of the car. Deciding to go out to the car, he heard a crackle of frozen branches. Just left of the cabin, a swaying of trees, the fucking bear coming back for more or maybe him. Rushing back to the cabin, he could just see the back end of the bear, carrying away the rest of the deer he had hung in the tree.

"You fucking bastard," he yelled out the door.

Getting back in the cabin, he went for his rife, but there were no bullets in the chamber. By the time he loaded it, and looks out, the bear was nowhere to be seen.

Thinking of all his hard work, cutting and hauling that big deer down the mountain, only to be stolen by a fucking bear. It had upstaged him, actually made him growl. He realized he was lucky to have an offering for the beast, or it might be his carcass the bear would be ripping apart. Loading the rifle, he put it right next to the bed. He would be ready in case the beast came back. Tomorrow, he would go hunting again.

Coming to the realization he was the one being hunted, by a rogue bear and the cops. Maybe he should get up and out of this place, head toward another city? Maybe Halifax. He could roam around and find a girl. Why was he subjecting himself to this isolation?

The cabin had served its purpose, hiding him away, but the fact that there was a manhunt on right now made him a sitting duck. He had to make a move, and quick.

Gathering all of his things in a spot on the middle of the cabin's roughed in wood plank floor, he sat down on what was left of his cot, thinking of his next move. Surely, they were looking for the stolen car by now, making him a mark. Deciding he should just stay put for a little while more.

Frustrated at his situation, he takes the mickey of whiskey out of his coat, putting it to his head. He had really got himself into a situation he couldn't fix. Should he risk getting busted on the highway, or just stay in the cabin?

The fact was that he had been to the general store twice now, and the clerk had a description of him. If the cops went there asking, they already knew he was in the vicinity. Resolving to just spend the day in the cabin, sing some songs and try and relax. Tomorrow, he would hatch a plan to get rid of the Cadillac.

"They couldn't have gone too far," said Scott to the other detective. "We had road blocks out of the city and at the border to New Brunswick. Those bastards are still around, and I won't sleep till I put their asses in jail," he said with conviction.

The whole country caught up in the excitement of the string of bank robberies and one break out of the Don Jail. These guys were professionals, the public going crazy over their Hollywood like antics. The bad boys, gangsters, the public waiting for the newspapers daily to hear of any capture, a lot of them idolizing the gang as brave and untouchable. Scott kept thinking of Schoolcraft, and the possibilities of whether he could have orchestrated a bank job, no came back his answer, too young, it had to have been the Lloyd Gang.

The police had a helicopter in on the hunt. A stream of smoke billowing from a cabin, deep in the mountains.

Taking a closer look, the pilot could see a small cabin and what looked like a car, covered in spruce boughs. He radioed in to the police station, a fleet of cop cars, headed into the mountains of Cape Breton Island. Two cruisers stopped for some gas, going into Harry's General Store and holding up a picture of the Lloyd gang. Edward in front, a tall, handsome, dark haired fellow.

"Have you seen any guys coming in here, looking like this?" asked the cop.

"No, I can't say as I have, but there has been a fella come in here, twice now, with a nice Cadillac, said he was going hunting and was in here just the other day getting supplies. Think he is staying in an old hunting cabin up there. One thing I did notice, though, is the car had no plates."

"Really," answered the cop, holding up the picture of the Lloyds. "And it wasn't any one of these? You sure now?"

"No, sir, can't say it was. The fella is young, about twenty, and handsome, real handsome, pretty almost."

The cops looked at each other, grabbing a coffee and paying for their gas.

"Thanks for your help," they said, walking back to their cruiser.

With that information, one of the officers got on his two way radio to the other cruisers. The description of the car from the clerk was the same as the stolen Cadillac from Schoolcraft Auto Sales.

When Scott heard the news of the handsome stranger in the car, he just knew they were hot on the trail of Elric Schoolcraft.

Sirens blaring, the police headed into the bush road, toward where the helicopter had led them, finding the car covered in spruce boughs, spotting the cabin, through the trees, smoke coming from the chimney.

Eight police officers, their rifles drawn, slowly made their way to the cabin, following footprints in the deep snow. Kicking in the cabin door to see Elric, passed out on the narrow cot. Shaken by the noise, he reached for his rifle when he saw the four sets of black boots. "Put your hands up!" ordered one of the officers. Elric obeyed, and he grabbed up Elric's rifle, handing it back to one of the others.

"Well, if it isn't the infamous Elric Schoolcraft," said Scott.

"What the hell you want with me? Can't a man hunt in this country anymore?" His speech slurred, the bottle of whiskey, half empty, sitting on the counter.

"What, you just turned into a man overnight? The last time I checked, you were just a kid. And a stupid one too. Why are you hiding way up here? I see you stole another one of your old man's cars."

"Yeah, what about it?" asked Elric, his eyes bloodshot. "I didn't steal shit."

"We will see about it, with your ass in jail for theft."

"He fucking owes me. I work for him."

"That's not what your father told us."

"Really," answered Elric, looked at the eight cops, guns pulled. Not a chance in hell, came back the voice.

Just then, one of the cops picked up Elric's work boots, looked at the bottom of them, Elric watching him.

"What you want with my boots?" A smirk on his face.

"You can just sit down and shut up. You are under arrest. Cuff him now," ordered Scott.

Watching as they pull the cabin apart, one of them searching through his bags, finding a diamond ring and a gold watch.

"Ah, pretty fancy stuff here, Schoolcraft. Where did you get the money for this stuff?"

"I'm a singer. I have my own band."

"Does the Goldminer's jewelry store ring a bell?" teased the tall cop, smirking at him.

Another cop picked up one of his boots, put it in a bag.

"Hey, I need my fucking boots. What are you doing with my boot?"

"Ya, let him put his boots on. He needs to get through the snow to the cruiser," ordered Scott. "We will take them for examination once we get him to the station."

"This is straight bullshit," he yelled. The whiskey in his blood made him want to rip the cops' ears off his head with his teeth.

His thinking distorted, he still knew that he was going down. There was nothing he could do but surrender.

During the search of the cabin, they found seven hundred-dollar bills.

CHAPTER 62

Jail Time

Two police cruisers escorted Elric to the county jail, in Quebec City. One of the cops drive the black Cadillac back to Schoolcraft Auto Sales. There were a few unsolved crimes they wanted to run his statistics against. First things first. They just needed to check the boots out to see if they footprint matched the one they had put together from the broken glass. And the boot imprint on the door of his father's office.

One cop brought in the boot and his money, and the other two held him, each holding an arm, Elric coming along, dragging his feet.

"C'mon, you son of a bitch," said the one officer, tired of Elric pulling against him.

"Book him," said Scott.

Thinking he might just put in a dig to get under the detective's skin, he said, "Can you tell Sarah, I miss her a lot, and want to see my kid."

"You fucking son of a bitch, you stay away from my daughter, or I'll kill you myself."

"Now, now, copper, you guys heard that, threatening my life."

The cops looked at one another and back at Scott, who turns from them sheepishly.

When the preliminaries were finished, another cop led Elric to a cell in the back of the station, next to another drunk.

"You'll be transported to Kingston Penitentiary, if you are found guilty."

"You'll have your day in court Schoolcraft," said the tall cop, pushing Elric into the cell, locking the door behind him.

Elric scoped out the cell, a narrow strip of a bed against the wall, a sink and toilet in the corner.

"I need a pillow and blanket," said Elric, shouting.

"We'll see if we can hook that up," said another cop. The bunch of them huddled together, like a football team, discussing Elric and his charges.

First thing the next morning, John Scott took the opportunity to go and see Elric, rub it in his face that he told him he would put his ass away.

Feeling like he had just won the jackpot, Scott strode into the station, going by the desk, back to the cells. Elric was still asleep, his back to Scott, the rough grey wool blanket pulled tight around him.

"Hey, Schoolcraft," yelled Scott from the outside of the cell.

"Wake up, Schoolcraft, breakfast time." Elric turned, almost falling off the narrow cot. Staring up now at the suited Scott, his fedora cocked to the side.

"Remember me, your worst nightmare," said Scott, laughing. "I just knew we would be joined again," Elric's vision blurring, the pain in his head sharp, his eyes hurting.

"Coffee, how about some coffee? We got to have a talk," said Scott. Elric just watched him, saying nothing. Scott brought coffee, and bacon and eggs, thinking he would feed him and question him afterward. Shoving the tray under the door, he handed Elric the coffee through the bars.

Happy for the offerings, he sat quietly eating the food, drinking the coffee. When he was done, he walked the tray over to the door, pushing it back toward the detective.

"So, Schoolcraft, who helped you with the jewelry job? We know it was you. Your footprint sealed your fate. We will be going to court in the morning. Is there anything you want to tell me? We can see if we can make a deal on your sentence, so who was in on it with you? Do you know the Lloyd gang?" he asked.

"I need to speak to a lawyer," said Elric, clamming up, walking away from the bars, back to his bed.

"Fine, you wanna play stupid, your ass is mine. Tomorrow, the judge will ask for five years. You got it comin', we both know you been getting off easy for too long. No pussy for five years. Just think, Schoolcraft, you might have to get a girlfriend in jail. But the only problem there is, there is only guys where you are going, Kingston Penn. You'll be bunking with your same kind, rapists and murderers. Might teach you a lesson, you fuck," said Scott, walking out of the cell area, a double door slamming behind him.

There were a lot of things he wanted to say to the arrogant cop but spared himself the stress, swallowing his pride. Feeling like a caged animal, now he had to figure out the best way to stay sane, and make things work to his advantage.

After few hours of dead silence, the clock in his head ticking, a strong feeling of anxiety washing over him like a wave, taking him under. The whiskey had cleared, his head hurt, and his mouth is dry, like unbuttered toast.

"I need some water," he yelled, holding on to the bars like a monkey at the zoo.

No one answered to his pleas, the cops out of the cell area.

Pacing now, to and fro, up and down the ten by ten cell. Just yesterday, he was wrestling with a bear, drinking all the whiskey he wanted. Today, he couldn't even get water. Reality was setting in, and the state of his mind without alcohol—he was not a happy camper anymore.

No guitar to keep him company. No women. This life was shit.

Right now, he was really pissed off, not wanting to talk to any cops. The walls were already looking like they were coming in on him. Taking some deep breaths, he paced.

"Hey, boy," said a short stocky cop. "Hear you are a famous singer. What the hell you doing in here?"

"They are trying to pin some robbery on me. I didn't do it and should be out of here, real soon," answered Elric, walking back to the cot. Sitting back down, holding his head in his hands.

Getting more frustrated by the minute, he decided to lay down. Staring into the ceiling, square tiles with pinholes in them. Thought for a minute he saw tiny bugs crawling out of the holes. Fuck, he was losing his mind now. Looking closer—no bugs.

He started to count the tiles now, without realizing it. *Fuck, what am I doing? This place is going to drive me fucking crazy,* he thought.

If I could just get that fucker's keys, I'd lock his ass in here, see how he likes it. Make a clean break. Sure, dream on. It wasn't happening. He would just have to plead with the judge and hope for a short sentence. Sounded like they had enough evidence on him to charge him.

A cold sweat crept over his body, his forehead wet with perspiration. It wasn't cold in the cell. What was happening to him?

His body started to shake, his teeth clattering together, his head feels like its in a vise. What was wrong with him?

Finally, after a couple hours of feeling the worst he had ever remembered, the guard brought in his dinner. Pork chops, mashed potatoes, peas, and two pieces of bread buttered, and a cup of coffee and water.

"Oh, thank God," he said, as the guard slid it under the door. "I don't feel very good."

"No, I bet you don't. This is not a holiday resort. What do you expect? You do the crime, you do the time."

Elric wanted to dig the fork into his fucking forehead, if only he could get to him.

After eating every last bit of food, he lay back on his cot, covering with the scratchy wool blanket. There was no point in fighting the situation. Make the best of a bad situation, he told himself, hoping for a light sentence tomorrow, when he came before the judge.

When the lights went out, that was the toughest. Trying to close his eyes, to pretend he wasn't really there, but the hardness of the cold bed, a half inch slab of a mattress, kept reminding him that this was not Easy Street.

Turning, tossing, getting up off the cot, the hard reality of jail settled in, he stands holding the bars. Feeling regret for getting caught, he started beating himself up in his head. Why the fuck did I just sit there and let them come for me? That was plain stupid, he said to himself, taking a stripe from his character.

It was the longest night of his life. Finally, he heard a few sounds of doors opening, a chair sliding under a desk, the cops back for their next shift. Standing, wide eyed, watching out of the bars. One of the cops, just coming on his shift, walking through the double doors.

"Good morning, sir, you got some coffee? I could sure use one."

A gentlemanly prisoner. This was the kid the other cops were talking about, the singer, his father a rich man.

Earl had been down to the precinct yesterday, signing some papers, not even asking to see his son. In his heart now, he knew that Elric had robbed him, and had stolen the car. As far as he was concerned, he needed to learn a lesson, and he wasn't about to help him in any way. Disgusted, his son had shamed him.

The officer left the cell area, coming back with a whole pot of coffee, some sugar, and milk on a tray. He hooked Elric up with a big cup of fresh coffee, fixing it for him the way he said he liked it, milk and four sugars.

"Looks like you are in here for another day. The judge will hear your case tomorrow morning." After drinking three cups of coffee, eating his breakfast of bacon and eggs, and toast, lying back down on the cot. His mind blank, his body hurting, like he had been wrestling with someone all night, a deep pain behind his eyes.

"Fuck, make it stop!" he said out loud. The cop looked over at him, wondering why he was talking to himself.

By the afternoon, Elric was losing control, his body aching, a sweat breaking out on his forehead. Tryin to curl in a fetal position, pulling the rough grey blanket around him, screaming out loud now.

"What's the matter, young fella?" said the cop, looking through the bars.

"I need a drink, mister, I think I am having some kind of withdrawal. Got any whiskey?" he said, turning to look at the cop.

"You must be kidding. Ah, I don't think so, Schoolcraft, you got to stick it out. You got the DTs," he said, laughing. "I'll get you some more coffee."

The cop went through the door, coming back with more coffee. It was the worst feeling he had ever experienced. Running to the toilet, bile and coffee spewing out of his mouth, his body shivering, a creeping feeling going up his back, like there were bugs all over his body.

Sick to his stomach, his head hurting, his body hurting, he lay down again, staying for hours in the fetal position. No one to come to his aid, no pretty girl to take his pain away, no one to hold him and tell him things would be all right. He had really fucked up.

It had been the worst day of his life. The cops came in and out, the sound of the heavy double doors opening and closing, and the sound of the chair scraping under the desk, driving him crazy.

The lights went out, leaving Elric alone. Another drunk in the next cell was talking to himself.

Waking in the early morning hours, getting up from his cot, stared now into the grey blanket. Snakes, hundreds of them on his bed!

"Ahhh!" he said out loud in a high pitched voice, jumping back, staring at the mass of clumped movement. Something was moving quickly up the walls. What the hell was happening to him? Holding his head in his hands, he looks away, looked back again. No movement on his cot. Running his hands over the blanket. Nothing, no snakes. Fuck, he was imagining it. A deep sigh, he sits back down, his head in his hands.

"Oh my God, that was creepy," he said, still looking for signs of anything moving on the bed. Shit, he was glad he was getting out of here today. The court was set for nine o'clock this morning.

The cops brought him in his clothes he had on when he was arrested, giving him back his boots and coat.

"They will be coming for you soon," said the cop on duty.

Washing his hands and face, running his fingers through his hair, his stomach heaving.

Waiting and watching for the cops who would transport him to the court-house, looking out at nothingness. Quiet, the cop on duty sat with his legs up, his chair back, his hat over his face.

It was like time standing still.

They came, handcuffed him, put his coat over his shoulders, and led him out of the building to an awaiting police cruiser.

"Nine o'clock, court in session," hollered a man outside the courtroom door. Elric stepped in, two officers escorting him. They marched him right up front to the judge's box.

Elric looked up at the judge, a half smile for the old man in a white wig with ringlets to his shoulders. Putting that sad puppy dog look on his face, he said please with his mind, then quickly looked away.

The judge stared hard at him, his pretty boy looks. He knew the type, thought they had the world by the tail and ready to take it all just because he wanted it.

"Mr. Schoolcraft, you have been charged with break and enter, and robbery over five thousand. How do you plead?"

"I am guilty, sir, but with an explanation. If your honor, sir, would give me a few minutes of your time."

He examined the boy's face and the clarity and crispness of his voice. Was he a gentlemanly boy?

"And just what kind of explanation would you have for robbing a jewelry store? I just got to hear this one," he said, smirking. The judge looked at the deputy, who also raised his eyebrows and looked Elric's way.

"Well, sir, it's just that I have a band, and we got a couple of contracts with the Quebec Hotel and the candy factory in Halifax. My point being that if you stick me away in jail for a long time, there are my band member's lives too to consider. They will all be out of work and bumming, like we were doing before we discovered we had talents. If you could find it in your heart, kind sir," he said, softening his steel grey eyes, looking directly at the old judge. The wrinkles around his eyes showing his wisdom in years.

"I have a drinking problem too, sir. It was the alcohol that made me do it," he said, hanging his head shamefully.

"Oh, you mean the devil made you do it is more likely. I've heard that one before. Good try, though," he said, a half smirk on his hardened face. "Well, considering that this is your first offence," said the judge, pausing. "Two years, less a day in Kingston Penitentiary," Smashing his gavel into the oak base.

Any compassion he had for the old bastard drained from his mind, like dirt down a drain. Two fucking years? He would lose his mind for sure. Knowing better than to argue or talk back, really, he wanted to curse the old wrinkled bastard, tell him his face looked like an asshole.

"I don't ever want to see you in my courtroom again, young man. You got off easy, because this is your first charge. Count yourself a lucky fellow today. Make this a learning experience for you, and when you do get out, stay away from the booze. It has ruined many a good man, and what said you, a mere boy."

"All rise."

The judge got up and walked out to his chambers. Two cops escorted Elric out of the courtroom to a holding cell for the night.

CHAPTER 63

Two Years of Hard Time

The first few weeks that he was incarcerated, he went through the usual, getting to know the other convicts, finding out where he fit in the bunch of dysfunctional characters. It didn't take long for them to find out about Elric.

Some guy was looking at him the wrong way one day, Elric busting him in the mouth.

"Don't get in my way. Don't fuck with me, and we'll be fine," he said, walking away, all eyes on him.

He did the everyday thing, cleaned his cell, eating with the guys in the cafeteria, hating all of them, except for one young guy, even singing with him for the other convicts.

His father had bought him a guitar, asked that they give it to him once he was settled. That was the least he could do for his wayward son, hoping some time would heal him. His fancy Fender was left in the cabin for the bear to rip apart or maybe strum a tune. Shit, he regretted not being able to take it with him, and no one else knew he was there. It would surely be gone when he got out.

"Let him have his guitar a few times a week," said the warden. "Maybe he can cheer up the miserable bunch they are."

They would use Schoolcraft for their own good.

Elric barely spoke, kept his eyes open, never turning his back to anyone. Lately it seemed like there were a few too many of them trying to get chummy with him. Asking questions when he would walk away, pretending he didn't hear them.

Fucking informants. He wasn't stupid. He knew how they operated.

One guy was persistent in asking questions. Elric stepped into his personal space, his eyes cold, piercing.

"Just stay out of my business, man, you hear me? And I'll stay out of your face with my fists," he said, thrusting his fisted hands up, threatening like a fierce animal.

"Easy man, easy," said the guy, backing off, walking away.

John Scott had wired Elric's cell to try and find out any more about the robberies or if he was connected to the Lloyd gang. There had been some similarities.

Every day, Elric used his private space and time to visualize the party he was going to have when he got the hell out of there. It was the only thing that kept him going. A new car, a new house, for his new wife, Alice.

Settle down, be a good husband and father, make his father proud of him. Sounded good to him.

This running and hiding and doing time was for dummies, not him. Amazing himself at his brilliance, and lately his head was a clear as the night sky on a frozen day. Good intentions and plans for a better way.

One of the guards gave Elric a calendar. He started right away to mark off the days with a big X.

The first year in jail was a mixed bag, learning a lot about himself, you might say a few lessons. Having to dance to a different drummer made him mad. Do this, don't do that. He hated to take orders from those fuckers, secretly wishing he could kill a couple of them. If he ever caught them anywhere alone when he got out, pity them, he thought.

Singing in his cell, making up new tunes, writing a few songs, trying them out on the guys. Gregory, his newfound friend, was a good singer too. The other convicts egged them on to play. A few fleeting moments dreaming of being that star again, and his band entertaining. Like a bird in the window and right out again.

There would be no more Elric and the Wanderers. He could never be seen with those guys again. He wondered what happened to Johnny and Dean, and if they had spent all their money yet. Both of them were smart players. His secret was safe.

Johnny opened his own body shop with his uncle's help and his money. His uncle did not ask where he got the money from, just happy to go into business with his nephew.

Dean was living large in Florida, champagne, women, gambling, eating out, and room service.

"Shit, this is living," he kept telling himself, happy with his fortune and the new freedoms in his life.

He made up stories about his father being a rich oil man from Texas.

"Don't take your guns to town. Boy. Leave your guns at home," he sang.

"I should have listened to the bastard," Elric sang, the whole cell block breaking out in laughter. Whenever he went into a tune, the brutish, the rapists, the murderers all listened, something sweet in the air taking the edge off, like sharpening a knife on a grindstone.

Even the guards came to enjoy Elric and his gentlemanly manners, always, "Yes, sir, "No, sir."

Knowing it would get him better treatment, after all, they decided his fate, going out of their way to bring him extra coffee, chocolate, and chips when the others weren't paying attention. Not a smoker himself, but he would still ask the guards for cigarettes, which they would buy for him from the money the cops were holding. They couldn't prove that he didn't make the money singing, nor could they prove where it came from, making it still his.

Selling the cigarettes back to the other prisoners at a profit, jail wasn't working out that bad. Might as well make the best of a bad situation, he figured.

His mind clear, his complexion glowing, the handsome Elric looking back at him. The alcohol was stealing his youth and his looks, he reasoned, he was looking a lot fresher, more handsome. No drinking for over a year now. Some of the other prisoners gave him the handle Pretty Boy Elric. That was the second time in his life he was given that handle. It was true. Didn't get much more handsome than him. Work with what you got, came back the voice.

Talk in the prison was that the Lloyd gang had been busted up. Two detectives shot, one dead. They were shipping those guys in, but just for a week or so.

A double hanging for the cop killers, realizing how close he came to joining them, and how they had given him the idea in the first place to rob with his gang.

The whole country had turned on them now, with all the senseless killings. Ready to turn them in, their fame short lived.

CHAPTER 64

Elric Goes Hunting for Alice

A double take on his calendar, one day left until he was a free man, he didn't sleep the whole night.

He heard the train whistle, looked out the small window into a starlit night.

"I'm so lonesome I could cry.

"Hear that lonesome winter bird, he sounds too blue to fly. The midnight train is whining low, I'm so lonesome I could cry. I never seen a night so long, when time went crawling by, the moon just went behind the clouds, to hide its face and cry."

His voice was so sweet, like an angel's kiss.

Both guards came as close as they could to his cell, their ears to the divinity of his voice.

Not being able to sleep a wink, he paced, then lay back down, then paced, until at last he could see the sun's face breaking through the darkness of the night.

Dressing in his black pants and black shirt, he brushed his hair back, looking at himself in the small square mirror.

A hot summer day, the tenth of June. The inside of the cell was sweating, beads of humidity showing on the concrete walls.

"Good day to get the fuck out of here," he said out loud, taking one last look around at what had been his cage for the last two years.

"Hey, Schoolcraft, you getting out of here today," said the guard, watching him sitting on his cot, cleaned up, waiting for his ticket out. His legs spread, his hands held together between them.

The cop on duty brought him his guitar and his bag of things he hadn't seen in two years.

Leading him out the double doors to the main gate, unlocking it. The guards watch as Elric became a free man.

Just outside the main gates, he stopped to pull out the things in his bag, wondering if the money was still there. Sure was.

Making his way to the train station, he had places to go, people to see. Loretta was the first one on the list. The thought of her long legs and her pretty face made him want to have just one more rendezvous, sure that she missed him too.

Hoping she wasn't shacked up with some guy, after all, he had been gone two years.

First things first. He would use up the five hundred dollars he had, before he went back up the mountain to his buried treasure. Hoping to get back in his father's good graces, he would take his old man a few bucks for his troubles.

All that time in jail, he had a lot of time to think of the mistake he had made already in life. When his mind finally cleared from the dirty water, he could think good thoughts, actually waking in the morning with a clear head, no headaches.

Deciding that he would go and look up his mother too and make up for lost time.

Surely she would want to see her son, whom she hadn't seen since she left, that fateful day, the day her love died for her sons. He wasn't old enough to know she was abandoning her twin boys. Then, he would go and find Alice, after he told his mother and father about her, and settle down. Those words, settle down, never really sat right with something in his head. Was he kidding himself?

Spending a few days with Loretta, just like he thought, she was so happy to see him, throwing her arms around his neck, not letting go. The first thing they did was go straight to the bedroom. That taken care of, he asked her to borrow her car, just for a while, until he could get his own. She willingly handed him the keys, saying that she could walk to work. It was fine.

"I got some presents for you, doll," he said.

"How did you get presents for me in jail?" she asked teasingly.

Nothing surprised her about him anymore. She was happy at the thought of presents. He had already surprised her with gold and diamonds.

That day he left Loretta's he failed to tell her that he would be gone for a week or so.

The first two days, Loretta watched out the window after work, wondering when her man would show up with her car. A week went by, still no sign of him. Starting to worry that she wouldn't see her car again, and maybe never see him again neither. No, she couldn't live without him. In the time he had been away, she had a few dates, but nobody did it for her like him.

Taking the long ride along the coast, out of New Brunswick, heading into the mountains of Cape Breton, feeling free and loving it. The happiness was so overwhelming, he wanted to christen it with a bottle.

The thought of the whiskey made his mouth water. It had been so long since he had tasted the golden liquid that fueled his madness.

Pulling into Harry's General Store, for some gas and a few supplies, the same old man at the counter.

"Hey, young fella, aren't you the one the cops pulled out of the cabin, way up in the mountains?"

"Hell no, you must have me mixed up with someone else," he said, pulling his fedora down on his forehead. The old man wasn't sure, but he sure did look a lot like that other guy he met a few years ago. Ah, his age was getting the best of him. He was probably mistaken.

He would go and find the cabin again, spend a few days, let his hair down, relax, and think of his next move. The clerk watched Elric getting into the small car. Definitely not the same guy.

Elric made it back to Loretta's nine days after he had taken her car.

Spending a day with her, mostly in her bedroom, having sex all day. Loretta cooked him a great dinner of steak and potatoes. He handed Loretta a stack of twenties. Shocked, but happy, she ran to her bedroom to hide it.

Before the day was out, Elric had expressed that he was taking her car but would bring it back. "Just got to touch base with the candy factory and get the band working again," he said.

Secretly Elric knew that he was getting the hell out of Quebec, maybe stay in Nova Scotia for a while, show little Alice some life, he thought.

Maybe he would go solo and do a few gigs. No, he needed to stay out of the spotlight. That life was not for him anymore.

Lately he thought about a lot of things to do with Alice. He was going to give her a good life. She wouldn't ever have to work. He would provide for her. With enough money to last for a long time, and all the things she needed, like a house of their own.

Earl owned a few houses. He would ask his father to give him a good deal on a house for them. He would bring Alice to meet his father and his mother, wanting to make up for lost time, be a good son and husband.

The whiskey was already clouding his memory, the good intentions fading away into the recesses of his mind. His intentions, even to himself, seemed cut and dry.

The booze was affecting his moods already, the heat of the whiskey warming his blood, swelling his head, putting a swagger in his walk. Who was he kidding, he was a gangster, and now an ex-con.

Earl was happy to see his son but didn't want to let on. He did get the car back. It had was a couple of scratches up each side, like he had driven it through some rose bramble bush. With just a little paint, it was a good as new. Earl sold the car the day after it was painted.

Hoping that Widdy had learned a hard lesson and was ready for a new start, doing the right things, ready to give his son another chance, looking him over.

"Dad, I just wanted to say how sorry I am for everything. I want to make it up to you."

"Really," said Earl, looking over his tall, handsome son, dressed in a navy blue and white pinstriped suit, dark brown leather suspenders, his fedora, navy with a wide white band around the middle.

Shaking his head, tears coming to his eyes, bending toward Elric, embracing him for a few seconds.

"Come in, son," he said, stepping back into the house, Elric following him in, taking off his hat, hanging it on the wooden hat rack.

Earl led his son to the table in the kitchen. Elric reached into his pocket, took out a roll of hundred dollar bills.

"Well, to start with, Father, I know I owe you, so what do you say, two thousand for your troubles with me?" Earl looked at the stack of hundreds in Elric's hand.

"Figure I owe it to you," said Elric, handing the money to Earl. "Don't say a thing, just take it, OK?"

Earl put it in the pocket inside his coat, smiling at Elric, sitting across from him. Elric returning the smile.

"Oh, by the way," said Elric, "I want to buy one of your Cadillacs. I'm getting married soon and need a nice car for my girl, Alice."

"Who is Alice?" asked Earl, looking at his son's face, the seriousness of the look in his eye making his dad wonder.

Wow, this jail time had sure done something to him. He was going to settle down?

"So, you have money for the Cadillac too?"

"Yes, sir, I got it right here in my pocket," he said, pulling out another stack of hundreds from another pocket on the other side of his jacket. Earl's eyes widened, staring at the money in his hand.

"Son, he said. "Where?"

"Never mind. What you don't know, you don't have to lie about."

Earl just shook his head, a smug look on his face.

"The word around the county is that you were involved with that Lloyd gang?"

"Hell no, the guy just looks like an older version of me, that's all."

"So, my next question is, if I bring a little girl home with me, could we stay here with you? Just until we get settled into a house that you are going to sell me, and I will start working for you again, selling cars, straight up. I want to make a change in my life." Staring at his father, a slight smirk on his face. While saying the words, but deep inside did he really believe himself?

Earl speechless, looking deep into Elric's eyes. The extent of his budget had just grown enormously. He had a feeling that Elric did have all the money he was talking about spending. Eyeing his son suspiciously, realizing he didn't have any problems with the law, or he would still be in jail? Knowing there was a lot Elric wasn't telling him but it was probably better he didn't know.

And where did he find a wife so soon?

Only out of jail a couple of days ago, this son of his didn't fail to amaze him. Now he was getting married?

Whatever, thought Earl. Maybe if he settled down, he could be a real man. The thought of Elric selling cars sounded good to him for a minute, Earl changing his mind quickly. He couldn't have him working with the public, an ex con selling cars. Somehow it just didn't work, and he didn't want any attention from the cops. Elric would bring heat on him. Didn't need anything more to do with the cops, already having to deal with them too much in the last few years since he'd met his son.

CHAPTER 65

Elric spent a week in Quebec City before he headed out of province. His next stop: the candy factory.

Loretta watched out the window, every night before bed. No sign of Elric or her car. Ah, he would come back. He always did, like a cat that couldn't stay away.

Driving along, he watches the waves hitting the shore. The warmth of the sun and his freedom, leaving a permanent smile on his face.

Deep in thought, he takes a swig of the whiskey straight from the bottle, watching out his rear-view mirror, his fedora sitting on the seat beside him.

Without the hat, he looked like the next guy, but when he put the hat on, it made people stare his way. It was good, and it was bad, he thought. Hoping he wouldn't run into any of his fans, didn't want to answer their questions about the break up of the band. Not only that, he wanted to keep a low profile now that he was a free man. Never would he spend another day in jail, he vowed, as he takes another long swig of the whiskey.

Twenty, and he had already learned a lot about life. Thinking hard about Alice. She lived with that friend of hers, Suzie, and her mother, wondering what had happened to her own family. They had a lot in common he reasoned, neither of them having a real family. All he had to do now, was follow the girls' home from work, so he would know exactly where they lived, then get Alice alone, so he could tell her of his plans.

Alice had a feeling that she would see her Prince Charming soon somewhere. Dreaming the same dream a few times of her prince taking her away on his white steed, but she couldn't see his face, covered by something black over his head. Awakening from her dreams, thinking of Elric, each time trying to analyze the dream. Having dreamed things before that came true, she wondered if this was a sign, dreaming the same dream over and over.

Lately her mind was on him a lot, a smile crossing her lips. Suzie caught her friend, in deep thought.

"You are still thinking of him, aren't you?

"Who?" asked Alice?

"I know the singer. You haven't been yourself since the last time you saw him."

Betty kept a close eye on her daughter. The girls busy with Jeramiah, who was almost two years old now and a handful.

There were so many things to do for the baby, the girls hardly had time for themselves even Betty was tired out, at the end of the day.

Alice's life revolved around her new family. Happy to have them, but she longed for a life of her own. He had said that he was going to marry her, and she believed him, with the determination in the way he said it. He was coming for her; it was just a matter of time.

Jeramiah had two grannies who doted on him and two mommies to take care of all his needs. Betty and Roger's mother, Cindy, had become good friends, their grandson bringing them together.

Finding himself standing in the parking lot of the candy factory, he figured he should duck in, out of sight. Parking Loretta's car behind the hall, so no one would notice him. Standing under a tree, not far from the hall, his eyes fixated on the door into the candy factory. Watching like a raven, his eyes keen, sizing up his prey. It was still early afternoon, Elric taking out his flask of whiskey, putting it to his head, shoving it back in his inside pocket.

The girls came out, Elric recognizing Suzie's dark curly hair. Alice was in tow, his blonde haired angel. They head down the road toward their house, Elric waiting until they were well on their way. Getting into Loretta's car, following just behind far enough that they didn't notice him. The girls walked along, chatting, laughing. Making their way off the main road into a long driveway to a red brick house with a porch, a stand of birch trees lining the property.

Pulling up, he watched them from the road until they disappeared into the house. Tomorrow, he would follow them going to work and hopefully get a chance to talk to Alice, tell her he was coming for her, soon.

He didn't have to rush, knowing where she was now. Still wanting to spend some time with Loretta and get that car from his dad. Deciding it was too early to be driving around in a new Cadillac, the car would have to wait for a while at least. After all, he had Loretta's car. She didn't mind letting him use it. Her work was only a walk away. Knowing she had it bad for him, after all, he had given her a few hundred dollars. She wasn't worried about her car, she just wanted him to come back to her.

Trying to get out of Nova Scotia before dark, Elric headed back to Loretta's for some fun and her good cooking.

The bulk of his money was still under the huge boulder, up the side of the mountain, near the cabin where they had busted him. That cabin had served its purpose, but the thought of the bears in that part of the country ran a chill up his spine. *That was close*, he said. Good thing there was a deer for the bear, or else he could have been lunch. Elric laughed again, thinking of the giant bear.

Getting back into Quebec, early in the morning, he pulled Loretta's car in front of her tenement house. Knocking on the door, Loretta hurrying from her bedroom, knowing it must be him.

"Well, nice for you to come back," she said, grabbing him, kissing him passionately.

Spending a week with Loretta, letting her spoil him, run his bath, sometimes joining him in the tub, the both of them ending up on the floor or on her bed.

They drank whiskey, ate, and fucked every day, maybe just not in that order. Loretta was star struck at the gifts that her lover was bringing her, bunches of roses, steaks and lobster, fine wine, and new clothes.

Not having to run and hide anymore gave Loretta some peace of mind. Feeling special, she enjoyed all the spoiling. He was her man. No one could made her feel the way he did. She was crazy in love with him.

He hung his hat at Loretta's, eating and sleeping with her, spending his afternoons playing his guitar, testing the waters, to see if he still had it. Deciding that he would do a little freelancing, he perched himself here and there, throwing down his hat, strumming and singing a few tunes. No one passed him without taking stock of the handsome crooner, his hat soon filled with money. His confidence and the crowds of people grew around him. It was just a show. He hoped that the cops would notice him and see that he was still working for his money. The attention made him feel renewed, his star still shining. The clouds of doubt and secrecy had darkened his star, almost put it out.

"Well, if it isn't Elric Schoolcraft," said Scott to his partner. The cruiser slowing to take a better look. "Looks like he lost his band. Now he is hustling solo. Lucky he is talented, is all I can say. Hope that time in jail straightened him out. The kid's got a lot of talent, if only he could harness it. He's like a wild mustang."

Scott had his own thoughts about Elric, how he had already ruined his father's trust in him. His grandson looked a lot like Elric, but he wasn't telling anyone he could be the father of his daughter's boy, Jude, but in his heart he knew.

"Shit, that kid had it made in the shade, then started stealing from his father. He would have inherited his old man's money, if he knew how to play his cards," said Scott.

Every few days, Elric made his way to his father's lot, looked over the cars, finally settling on a yellow and white coupe, rag top, silver grill, butter yellow Cadillac.

"Wow, this is the one," he said. Going into the office, he announced to his father he had decided on the yellow and white convertible coupe Cadillac.

"Do you want your money up front? I don't want to take it right away. How about in a couple of weeks?"

"What about registration? And a license," said Earl, knowing that his son didn't have one. Getting the car registered in his name might raise some eyebrows, so to speak.

"Can we just keep it in your name? That way, it is your car as far as anyone is concerned."

"I suppose I could do that for you, but you have to go and get your license."

"I will, I promise," said Elric, walking out of his father's office back to Loretta's car.

"Have you thought about giving me some work? I'm going to need to work soon. My savings are going to run out."

"Your savings?" said Earl with a smirk.

"Yes, Dad, I'm going to go broke, the way I've been spending."

"I would consider giving you some work in the bush again, but not at the car lot. If you want to keep your nose clean and want to work hard, I have a position coming up as a faller. You would have nothing to do with the horses. Have you sowed your wild oats, boy?"

"Work in the bush again?" Elric said, thinking hard about it.

"You got a deal that gives me a lot of time to do the things, like get married and settle into a house with my bride. I'm going for Alice soon, and I'll be bringing her back here."

After all, he would have to have some kind of job, might as well work for his father. He didn't mind hard work out in the elements. He loved the fresh air, the clean smell of the bush and freshly cut trees.

"Great, Dad," he said, putting his hand out for his father to shake.

"And one other thing. I want to know where my mother lives. Think it's time she saw me all grown up."

"Why do you want to bother her?" asked Earl. "She has a husband, never had anything to do with your brother, Jack, all these years."

Elric didn't remember his twin brother, just knew he had one. His uncle moved his family to Toronto, Ontario, before Jack turned five.

"If you really want, I'll take you to see her," answered Earl.

"Yes, I would like that," said Elric, bowing out, leaving the office.

Watching out the window, he noticed a nice looking redhead sitting in the passenger seat. That couldn't be the Alice he was talking about, or he would have brought her in.

"Is that the Alice girl you are going to marry?" asked Earl, looking out at the pretty woman, a lock of her auburn wavy hair hanging over her forehead, dark glasses, a colorful scarf pulled tight around her head.

"No, she is just a friend," replied Elric. "Always got to have a spare, you know." Earl just shaking his head.

"See you soon then." Elric walked out of the office, closing the door quietly.

He watched his son get in the driver's seat and pull out onto the road.

"This is your father's car lot?" she asked.

"See the sign? Schoolcraft Auto Sales, and it's not mine," he laughed.

CHAPTER 66

The day had come for Elric to pick up his car and get the hell out of the province for a while. Getting drunk almost every day now, too much time on his hands. The way the cops were watching him made him feel nervous. Did they know more than he thought? Not telling Loretta anything about his plans, their last night together was one that Loretta would remember for a long time, singing to her, and making love to her all night.

Getting up, the darkness still looming, he gets dressed, watching her as she slept. He would miss her, but he had other plans, other conquests. Maybe he would come back some day.

Walking out of the bedroom, taking one last look at the tall beauty, her legs wrapped up in the blankets.

"Goodbye, sweet thing," he said, closing the door behind him.

Walking into the parlor, Elric lay down four hundred-dollar bills on the kitchen table. After all, she had been real nice to him, and he really did like her a lot. Anytime he came calling, she would answer the door.

Slipping on his gold watch and diamond ring, dressing in his best today, celebrating his new car and his journey out of the province. The gold and diamond encrusted cuff links glittered against his black shirt, his black hair combed off his high forehead, shiny slicked back.

Taking one last look in the mirror, cocking his fedora to the side, his pinstriped suit tailored to fit only him.

"Sweet," he said, taking a long look at himself from head to toe, like he was complimenting a lady.

"Can't go wrong," he assured himself, smiling, walking out the door.

He would drive Loretta's car to his father's lot, then phone her and tell her to come and get it. What would he tell her why he left it there?

His father needed him to take the pair of horses up the mountain. That sounded good. She would fall for it.

Loretta woke. No sign of him. Once she was up, she peered into the parlor, and then the kitchen, then looked out the window. He was loading his bags and his guitar into her car. Four hundred-dollar bills on the table, like he was saying, *I won't see you for a while.* Her eyes filled with tears, watching him drive away. Even if he never brought the car back, it was only worth a hundred.

Arriving at the car lot, Earl talking to some gentleman about a car, pointing and gesturing. The two men are laughing and talking.

Walking to his father and the stranger, Elric called Earl to the side.

"Dad," I came to get my car today." Earl looking his son in the eye.

"Yes, of course, I'll meet you in the office. You can just wait till I am finished here. Go and run a soft rag over your new Cadillac," he said, handing Elric the cloth he had in his hands.

When Earl realized the customer was just considering buying a new car, but didn't have the funds right now, he excused himself.

"If you will excuse me, I have a deal to write up. Right now my son is buying one of the best on the lot. He's a singer."

"Fine," answered the tall stranger. "I'll just look around until you come back, give me time to make up my mind."

Walking over to where Elric is running the soft cloth over his car, he beckoned him to come.

"I'm ready now, son, let's do this deal."

"You brought the forty-five hundred?"

"Of course, Father, I have it right here," he said, pulling a stack of hundreds out of the inside of his suit jacket.

Earl watched and counted as Elric peeled off forty-five crisp hundred-dollar bills.

Business had been a little tight for Earl lately, the depression in full swing, not many cars being sold. Only the rich could afford to buy a car.

Happy for the sale, he shook Elric's hand. "Congratulations, son, you are now the proud owner of one of the best Cadillacs money can buy."

"Thank you, Father."

Earl handed him the keys he had already put in the drawer, knowing in his heart his son was not kidding when he first told him he was coming back for the car.

The registration would have to stay in his name, to keep the heat off Elric. He was fine with that, and the feeling he was getting lately was there was a lot he didn't know, nor wanted to know.

"Father, can you call this number and have Loretta pick up her car? Don't tell her where I have gone," said Elric. "Tell her I took the team up the mountain, to start work."

"Sure, whatever," answered Earl, handing Elric the keys. "So where are you going? Do you have a license?"

"Oh Father, if anything comes up, just say I took the car, but I am not getting myself into any more trouble, you can be assured. Jail is not for a fine man like me," he said, holding the corner of his collar.

"Yes, I might say you look like a million bucks. Pretty stylish there, boy."

"Thank you, Dad, kind of what I was going for," he laughed.

"You had better get your license or the cops will impound the car, and you too."

"I will. Right now, I am on my way to Nova Scotia. Got some business to take care of. Going to get my girl, my wife," he said.

"Well, if you are bringing her back here, as you have said, make sure you are married. There will be no illegitimate stuff going on in my house."

"You will love her, Dad. She will cook some good food for you."

Knowing exactly what to say to make it all right. Earl, who was not a cook himself, had been living out of boxed and canned foods, too cheap to eat at diners. The sound of home cooked meals softened him, like butter left out.

Since Blanche left him and shattered his heart, he hadn't taken another woman in. Once a month, if he needed it or not, he would visit the brothel in the city.

CHAPTER 67

The new Caddy hugged the road like it loved it. With his elbow hanging out the window, settling back into the butter yellow leather seat, straight out onto the coastal highway out of Quebec, into New Brunswick.

Although he is a free man he still felt like he was being hunted, having to watch his every move. As soon as he past the Quebec border, into New Brunswick, a new kind of freedom taking over.

Coming into a small town of Edmundston, he notices a general store and a tavern, a few horses tied up outside of the bar.

As soon as he pulled up, a crowd started to gather around the car.

Questions about the car started firing at him, like shots from a rifle.

What make is it? What model is it? How much did it cost?

Prying himself away from the car's fans, he sits at the bar ordering a double whiskey on the rocks.

Paying the bartender, he put the drink to his head.

A crowd had gathered looking at the car. Shit, this was going to cause him too much attention, but after a few minutes, he started to relax, telling himself he wasn't a wanted man anymore.

Walking past the crowd to the general store, he picked up a few things. A bottle of whiskey, a loaf of bread, and some sandwich meat for the road.

As he is pulling away from the tavern, a crowd of onlookers realized that it wasn't just the car, it was the handsome guy with a new Cadillac.

A few days in the city would be fun, he thought. Do a little carousing, a bit of gambling. Get himself a room and a hot girl for the night. With a pocketful of money and not a care in the world, he drove straight into the city of Halifax.

Finding a nice room downtown, he parked his car and brought in his bag.

Watching from his room out onto the street, the car starting to draw a crowd.

Shit, the fucking car was a heat score now, never mind him in a suit and fedora.

Deciding the Cadillac was causing him too much attention, tomorrow he would head up to his private hideaway, and reload his cash reserve.

Giving Loretta some money, and helping his old man out too, made him feel good about himself.

Then he started wondering about Loretta, and whether she had gone to get her car, and if they had discussed him. *Ah, fuck it, don't sweat the small stuff*, came back the voice.

Good intentions were spoiled by the dirty water, whiskey. It took him three days to get out of the city. Waking sick, two mornings in a row, he is not able to get up. Coming to the realization, he needed to get this alcohol thing in check or it could ruin him.

After three days of drinking and gambling, his pocket money had dwindled to just enough for a tank of gas.

Going over the bank robbery in his mind, he thought of the clean break and his new lease on life, a new start with a bunch of money to help him along. It couldn't have been better. Thinking of his friends, living large in the depression.

Realizing he wasn't far from the candy factory, he decided he would take a drive there and watch out for the girls.

He had to see her, and tell her his plans. Would she go willingly? Would he have to coerce her?

The girls were always together, like a knife and fork on the dinner table. There had to be a way to get her by herself and talk to her.

Pulling the big car up near the candy factory, he turned off the engine, leaning back in the seat, watching and waiting, hoping Alice would come out soon. Glancing at his watch; they should be done work any time.

As soon as he saw them, he would offer them a ride home.

There was no way he was leaving without her. Maybe give her a day or so to pack her things, and then he would come for her.

It was in her eyes, the yearning for true love, a deep forest green taking you into her.

The innocence was what he liked the most, pure, still a virgin. No one else would ever have her. He could love her, love her to death, drawing that thought out as fast as it had come.

Spotting them, coming out the door, engaged in conversation. Pulling his car up near the door, staring their way when Alice noticed him. Her eyes grew big, she smiled, then nudged Suzie.

"It's him, look, Suz."

Suzie stared at the pretty yellow Cadillac with the dark haired singer at the wheel.

"Oh my God, it is him, Alice."

The girls rushed over to the side of the car, Elric smiling his pearly whites.

"Thought you girls might need a ride home. I just happened to be in the neighborhood."

They look at each other, smiled, and jumped in the car, Alice in the front seat, and Suzie in the back.

"Sure is nice to see you again. I told you I was coming back," he said.

Alice stared deep into his eyes, like deep pools of grey water, drawing her in.

"So, how's my favorite girl?"

The girls started giggling, a blush running over Alice's cheeks.

"Where do you live, Suzie?" Knowing full well where they lived.

"It's just two miles down the road. I'll tell you when we are getting close."

Suzie couldn't help but notice the connection between Alice and the singer. He kept looked over at her, smiling, Alice excited. She had never seen her friend so happy before.

When they pulled into the yard, Elric asked if he could have a few minutes in private with Alice. Suzie went ahead into the house.

"So, how is my favorite girl in the world? I told you I would come back for you. Come over here."

Pulling her close to him.

Suzie is watching out the window. Elric reaches for Alice, kissing her deep, the warmth of his mouth, almost taking her breath away, exciting everything in her.

Putting his large hand behind her head, he pulled her deeper into him, his tongue exploring her mouth.

It was wet and slippery, snakelike, Alice pulling away.

"You have grown more beautiful," he said, eyeing her breasts through her sweater. "I told you I was coming back for you."

Not knowing what to say to that, she stared straight ahead. What should she do? Was he really here to take her away?

Suzie and Betty had been the only real family she knew. They made room for her in their hearts and their home, treating her better than her own mother ever did. And Jeramiah, who she loved, called her Auntie. Was she ready to give up the only real home she had ever had?

Having daydreamed about this day, and now it was here, she feels scared.

"Well, are you ready to make a life for yourself instead of living with these people who are not your family? You must be sick of wrapping chocolates by now?"

"It's just so sudden. I need a few days to think about all of this. I can't just go and pack my bags and leave now. I have to talk to Suzie and Betty and tell them I have a plan, before I up and leave. It just wouldn't be right."

"OK, sweet thing. I'll give you a couple of days. How about I come back on Friday. Have your things packed and ready to go. Tell your friends you have found your future husband, and it's time for you to make a change in your life."

Staring deep into his eyes, like a bottomless lake, feeling the coolness of the water.

"I will talk things over with them, and you can come on Friday. By then I will know if this is what I want to do."

"I'll be back on Friday. Should I pick you and Suzie up from work?"

"Sure, that will be fine. I better get going now. Suzie has been watching out the window the whole time, worried about me."

"Give me another kiss to hold me over," he said, pulling her close again.

They kissed for what seemed like eternity to her. Pulling away, she tried to catch her breath. It seemed like he was sucking the breath right out of her.

Flushed and feeling scattered, she smoothes her hands over her hair and her dress.

"I've got to go. Goodbye till Friday, then."

Sliding out of the seat, she gets out of the car, heading toward the house.

Elric stared her way until she went in the house and closed the door.

Up until today, she had continually reminded herself, and Suzie, that he said he was coming back for her, but now that he was actually here, it didn't seem real.

"What do you really think, Suzie? I can tell by that look on your face that you are worried for me," said Alice.

"Yeah, well, he disappears for two years, and just shows up now, and expects you to just get up and leave everything. Your job too, Alice. If you just leave, I'm sure that you won't be able to come back. I think you have a good life, right here with us. All you really know about him is he is a singer in a band. I must say, though, he has the prettiest car I ever did see. I've only heard of Cadillacs, and they are the most expensive car almost you can buy. Where did he get all that money to buy that car? Maybe he is rich."

"I really don't know how to think right now. Really, I didn't believe I would ever see him again."

Just then, they heard a few loud honks from a car horn.

"Who could that be? Mother isn't home for another hour. Let me look," said Suzie, running to the window in the parlor, peeking through the chiffon curtains.

"Oh my God, it's him, Alice, back in the yard. What do you suppose he came back for?"

"Ah, let me go and see what he wants," said Alice, going to the door.

Her tight baby blue jeans and her black sweater tight to the chest, running to his car, going to the driver's side, looking in at him.

"Hey, did you forget something?" she said flirtingly.

"That's exactly why I came back. Get in, I have to tell you something quick."

Going around to the other side of the car, she opened the passenger door, sliding into the seat.

"Come over here closer, baby, I'm not going to hurt you."

Moving as close as she could while still being able to look at his face as he spoke. Taking a quick look at the house, Suzie is staring out the window.

"Look, I came here to get you, and tomorrow you will not go to work. You will make an excuse that you are not feeling well. Let Suzie go to work by herself, and when her mother goes out, I will be here to help you pack your things and load them into the car. We'll be out of here in no time flat. Haven't you been waiting for me?" he said, pulling her closer, kissing her softy, running his long fingers through her golden curls. "I've missed you. It's now or never. I got no time to waste. I told you I would get things ready, and now I am here to get you. Don't you want a life of your own, with me? I'll make you the happiest girl in the world. They will say, 'Alice Has a Palace.'"

A weird look came over her face. What did he mean by that?

"You know, you told me you lived in a palace."

"Well, it wasn't really a palace, said Alice, "just a mansion, but to me it was a palace, the most beautiful place I had ever seen."

"You are a princess, Alice, my princess. I'll get you that palace." Searching deep into his grey eyes, like bottomless pools. The stillness tranquilizing her, taking her deeper.

Kissing her again and again, her head swimming. Her heart felt swollen in her chest, its waters cresting, about to go over the edge.

Pulling herself away from him, she backed out of the seat, opening the door.

"I really got to go now," she said, noticing Betty had come to the porch, looking now at the car and the man at the wheel.

"Remember, tomorrow morning after Suzie and Betty leave, I'll be watching and waiting." Alice is waving, walking away not looking back. When she gets to the porch, she tries to avoid Betty's gaze.

"Who is that fellow? Alice? Be careful, dear, remember what happened to Suzie? Boys can change your life overnight," she said, walking back into the house. Thoughts of the grown man, watching him kiss Alice, noticing how flushed she looked.

Running excitedly up the stairs, probably to go and tell secrets to Suzie. Betty knew that the girls kept things from her. Ever since she was surprised with a grandson, she was wary of Suzie seeing other boys. Alice had seemed like she kept to herself and wasn't too interested. Watching them in the car gave Betty a different view of things.

The warmth of his mouth on hers, the sweet smell of his breath, with a hit of something, almost like fresh bread. Holding her blankets to her chest, contemplating how her hand would change if she really left with him tomorrow.

How could she just walk away from her friends, without consulting them? Surely they would discourage her.

Betty voice in her head, continually warning her not to make the same mistake Suzie had made.

Living with them forever, was not an option. It was time for her to have a life of her own, she concluded.

Laying propped up on a few pillows in her big comfy bed, looking adoringly around the room that had been home to her, now for over two years.

All her pretty things, stuffed animals, books, her beautiful dresses hung neatly in the closet.

Even with all of the warmth of the family unit, Alice realized that she was still an outsider. Betty and Suzie had opened their arms and their hearts and she loved them so much.

The thoughts of a new life, the excitement he had instilled in her, helped to make up her mind, she was going to go with him. She would write them a letter, saying she had gone away, to start a new life, hoping they would be happy for her. Getting out a pen and paper, Alice sits at her little desk, gazing out the window, searching for the right heartfelt words to put down.

PART III

Alice and Elric

CHAPTER 68

"Dear Suzie and Betty." The letter already sounding too formal. "I am going away with my boyfriend, Elric. I couldn't find it in my heart to tell you in person, not knowing what you would say, and I don't want to disappoint you.

"I know I am being selfish right now, thinking of myself only, but please try to understand I am grown now and would like a change in my life. Working at the candy factory is great, but it's kind of like the chocolates on the treadmill. That's how I feel, like I am on a treadmill of life, going nowhere.

"I don't want to grow old there.

"Suzie, you know I love you like a sister, and Betty, I love you like the mother I never had. Please love each other for me. Kiss Jeremiah for me. I couldn't say goodbye to him without breaking down. Pray for me, love always, Alice.

PS I am getting married and will come back to visit as soon as I can."

Looking back over the note, Alice started to cry, her tears falling on the note, staining out some of the words. *Why does love have to hurt?* She said to herself, folding the note, putting it in an envelope. Her tears had blurred out the word *married*, the ink and the tears mixing together, bleeding down the page.

Turning off the light, she gets under the covers, her mind racing. Feeling all alone for some reason, she should be excited and happy about leaving with him.

Lighting a candle, she packed her bags in the dark, shadows filling the room.

Hardly sleeping all night, tossing and turning, when finally she went into a deep sleep, and started dreaming. She was in a small boat, in a deep, dark body of water, the sea convulsing, sending her boat up against a rock cut. Holding on for dear life, her fingers clinging to the sides of the boat, her knuckles white.

Vicious waves battered the small boat, tossing and heaving it. Holding tight, her eyes closed, cold water washed over her body, and the boat started to fill with water. Looking down at her feet, the water getting deeper, she starts screaming for help, but no sounds could come out of her mouth.

Awake, in a cold sweat, sitting up, staring into the dark, shadows dancing on the walls, by the light of the moon. What looks like a large beast with fangs, scaring her, she pulls the covers over her head.

Lying in a fetal position, she recanted the dream, more like a nightmare. Falling back asleep, she is awakened by the sound of Betty's alarm. Everyone would be in the kitchen soon, expecting her to help prepare the breakfast.

When the breakfast was ready, bacon and eggs, and toast, they all sat down, Betty giving thanks, the girls quiet. Betty noticed that Alice didn't seem like herself this morning.

"Is everything all right, dear?" asked Betty, looking straight at Alice, who had not made eye contact all morning.

"Oh, yes, ma'am," she answered. Betty is surprised she had called her ma'am. They had lost that formality a long time ago.

Suzie looked up at her friend, noticing the redness around Alice's eyes, like she had been crying.

Suzie hadn't confided in her mother about Elric and the connection with him and Alice. Was Alice really going away with him? Would she really just up and leave with this stranger?

"I really don't feel well today. Maybe it's my monthly. I am going to stay home from work. My belly really hurts," lied Alice, putting down her fork.

"That is fine, dear," said Betty. "Suzie will tell them at work that you are not well.

"Thanks," she replied, getting up, taking her plate to the sink.

The deception made her feel terrible, her stomach churning. There had never been any secrets between her and Suzie. Should she tell her?

No, she couldn't, came back the voice.

Suzie stood at the door, watching Alice, still at the sink, doing the dishes. "See you after work," she said, going out the door.

Betty went to her room to get ready for work. Alice finished up in the kitchen and made her way back to her room.

She listened for when Betty went out the door, watching from her upstairs window, Betty backing her car out of the driveway.

Looking over her belongings, knowing she couldn't take them all.

Packing her special things, her pretty dresses, her jewellery, picking up the emerald and gold necklace. Where would she ever wear such a gem, almost afraid to put it on?

Her life had changed so much, deciding she would leave it for Betty as a thank you for all the wonderful things she had done for her.

Taking the necklace, she laid it in the dark green velvet-lined box. Walking into Betty's room, she put it down on the dresser.

Going back to her room, she wrote another note.

"To a very special person, just want to show you how much I love you. Alice." Taking it back into Betty's room, she put it under the long slim box.

Waiting until she thought Betty was long gone, Alice came out of her room, suitcase in hand, down the stairs.

Going up and down the stairs carrying all her things she could get into three bags, leaving the rest behind.

What would she do with stuffed toys? Suzie would give them to Jeremiah. She was grown now, a young lady.

No sooner had she got her three suitcases to the bottom steps when Alice looked out the picture window. The yellow and white Cadillac was coming up the driveway. Her heart jumped in her chest, beating fast.

CHAPTER 69

Opening the door, she looked out, and there he was. Pulling the big car up in front of the house. Wasting no time, he came up the stairs to the house, Alice with the door open already.

"Good girl," he said, bending to kiss her. "Let me get these things," he said, grabbing two bags. "You just go and wait in the car," he said, putting the last bag in the trunk.

With Alice sitting up front next to him, Elric looked over at his prize. Things were going just as planned.

"Sure nice to see you, sweet cheeks," he said, looking over at her.

"So you ready to start a new life?" Her life so far flashed in her mind's eye. "I suppose I am," she answered shyly, her voice childlike.

"You won't have to work anymore, my princess," he said. "We are leaving this province in a few days."

"Where are we going?" asked Alice, holding her small clutch purse in her lap.

"Where my father and mother live. I want you to meet them, and we will probably stay with my father for a while, until we get our house."

"A house?" said Alice, raising her eyebrows, looking at his perfect profile.

Elric looked over at her. "Yes, our house, Alice. Like I said, I am going to marry you, girl," Grabbing for her, pulling her close to his side, the lightness of her body giving him a thrill.

She warmed up to him, his body warm, comforting her.

"It's you and me now, babe. The world is at your feet, and I am the happiest man in the world," he said, grinning, driving away down the road, destination unknown.

"We'll be going over the border of Nova Scotia into New Brunswick, stay in a hotel for the night, and the next day drive through to Quebec."

"Is it a long way?" she asked.

"Yes, it is, but we are in no rush. We are just going to have some fun, take it easy, and enjoy each other's company," he said, kissing the top of her head.

She didn't answer, just looked up at him, her prince. He had come for her, just like he had promised.

Making her feel special, a new freedom coming over her. No more working, no more chocolates going by all day long, the reality of it all settling.

Heading out to the ocean front, Elric drove, singing a tune, serenading his conquest.

"So, you said that you were all over the country singing. Where did you go?"

"Let's not talk about it right now," he said. "How about we stop for a picnic? I got some bread and cheese, and a nice bottle of wine I picked out especially for you."

"Oh no, I don't drink. I'm only sixteen," she replied.

"Really, well, you might as well know I like to have a drink once in a while, its fine, if you don't want to."

Reaching under his seat, he pulls out a flask of whiskey, putting it to his head, taking a deep swig.

"Ahhhh," he said, putting the top back on the bottle, pushing it under the seat.

At that moment, Alice feels frightened, his eyes taking on a sheen.

Sitting quietly, lost for words, Elric starts to sing again, pulling her so close to him there isn't enough room for a piece of paper. Giving into his touch, her body excited, she feels happy again, and free.

They were going on a trip, in the most beautiful car, Alice looking into the back seat, large enough for two people to do whatever they wanted, thinking of the unthinkable.

Suzie had tried to talk to Alice about sex. The thought repulsed her after what Charlie had done to her. Anything associated with the act felt like a violation. She couldn't imagine liking it.

Elric runs his hand up her bare leg, the baby blue and white dress tight at the waist, low in the front, showing her cleavage.

His eyes roam her rounded breasts, thinking of licking them, sucking on the nipples. Oh, yeah, he would later, and a lot more things on his mind.

Pulling the car over to the side of the highway, overlooking the ocean, the water cresting, glistening under the sunbeams. Silent rippling of the waves beating the shoreline.

"Wow," she said, getting out of the car standing on the cliff, overlooking the magnificent ocean. It looked like the water stretched to the ends of the earth, as far as her eyes could see.

Looked back to see if he was coming to join her, she notices him reaching for something, bent down.

Pulling out his flask of whiskey from under the seat, turning his back to her taking another shot. The burn on his tongue, the golden fluid hitting him, a sudden warmth in his chest.

Walking over to Alice, he held her from behind. "So did you believe I was coming back for you?"

"Yes," she answered. "I dreamed of you many times."

"Really," he answered, holding her tight, turning her around to him now, placing his big hands under her armpits, he picks her up, kissing her, holding her off the ground.

"Put me down," she insisted, his hands pinching her skin under her arms, her dress pulled up in the back, Alice looking around to see if there were any other cars coming.

"Don't worry, I won't hurt you, little one. You are mine now, and I'll take good care of you."

"Thanks," said Alice, when her feet hit the ground, trying on a meek smile, letting him touch her. Kissing her deep, holding her tight to him.

"So, Alice, it is your first time, right?"

"First time?" she said, a squeak in her voice.

"You know what I mean. Don't play stupid." Looking her square in the eye.

"Yes and no," she answered. "There was an accident, sort of," she said, tears coming to her eyes.

"What! You had better tell me the whole story," said Elric, taking her hands in his, pulling her to sit on the front of the car.

"Well, my mother sent me to work for an old man, and he took advantage of me one day when he was drunk."

"You mean he raped you?"

"Yes," said Alice, tears running down her cherub cheeks, holding her hands over her face.

Pulling her tiny hands from her face, he studied her, looked into her forest green eyes, the truth written on her sad face.

"Don't cry now, darling, it's OK. At least you told me the truth, and that is what our life together will be. No lies." he said. "You have to be true to me," he demanded, looking softly into her eyes.

"I will," she agreed.

"Dry those tears now. You are still my angel," he said, "just a little damaged, like a broken wing. You will mend and fly again."

Gazing deep into his grey eyes, like deep grey clouds on a rainy day. Not so sure she wanted to be compared to an angel with a broken wing.

Spreading a blanket on the ground, he laid her down, the sun high in the sky, warming the lovers. Pressing his chest into hers, kissing her deep.

"I am going to take you tonight, Alice, is that all right?" he whispered softly, nuzzling her ear.

"Take me where?" she asked.

"I'm going to make love to you. It won't be anything like what that old man did to you, I promise that."

Staring into his eyes, searching his face. He wanted to have sex with her. What could she do? She was with him, and she didn't want to disappoint him. There was no turning back now.

Oh no, what about getting pregnant? She didn't want to get pregnant, not right away, thinking of what she could say to discourage him from doing it, until she could get some pills. Betty told the girls, just one pill a day, would stop a girl from getting pregnant, warning Suzie that if she was to get another boyfriend, she would need to go to the doctor and get some of them.

"But I don't take the pills, so it is probably not a good idea. I am not ready for a baby."

Looking at her, he did understand what she was saying, but what was stopping them from having a baby? That was part of settling down, wasn't it? Tonight he would have her, no matter what she thought of it, take his chances and claim what was rightfully his. Surely she wouldn't get pregnant from just once, or twice, or all night, he thought, laughing to himself.

Enjoying some of the bread and cheese, Elric taking a few hits off the bottle of wine. When they had finished with their picnic, Alice picked up the remainder of the cheese and bread, putting it back in the bag.

"Let's hit the road," he said. "We have all of our lives together. Now we need to get going."

Sitting quiet, she thought of Betty and Suzie, getting home realizing that she was gone.

They had already found her note. Suzie would be crying when she found out, Betty stunned at the beauty of the emerald necklace.

"Where did Alice get such a beautiful necklace?" she asked Suzie, holding it up for her to see.

"The millionaires that she worked for gave it to her," answered Suzie."

"Oh my God, she gave it to you, Mom? You see what a kind heart she has. I love her so much, but I am worried sick already."

"We don't know anything about that guy, and neither does Alice," said Suzie, the two of them sitting in the parlor together, holding each other.

Feeling the whiskey, his appetite for Alice was already too much for him to handle. Leaning into him, her prince taking her away to another place and time.

It didn't feel real to her, as she watched out the window, new scenery, new places to go, a man who wanted her, a new life. Why didn't she feel happier?

It was all wrong, the way she had left her friends, feeling like she had betrayed them, lied to them.Trying to drive those thoughts out of her mind, they would understand.

Pulling the car to the side of the road, then turning the car around, headed back the way they came, then turning off the highway, up a narrow, dusty road.

"Where are we going?" she asked, panic in her voice.

"Don't worry, darling, I just got something I got to do, and we will be back on our way."

Watching him now, the look in his eyes frightened her. Why was he going on this old road? Just in a ways, stopping the car, the highway out of sight. Elric opened his door, then slid into the back seat.

"Come back here, and join me, sweetie," he said, touching her arm.

Knowing she couldn't refuse, alone with this stranger, and he had the upper hand. After she slipped into the back seat, he pulled her dress up and off.

Undoing his pants, Alice noticed a long hardness making a tent in his trousers.

"See what you do to me? I want you now. I just can't wait. I've been waiting for almost two years for this, since we met," he said staring deep in her eyes.

Without answering, she lowered her eyes, Elric taking over, slipping her panties off laying her back on the soft leather seat. Holding her head in his hands, her eyes closed, he pressed his body to her, his mouth searching hers, a hardness against the side of her leg. Pushing her legs apart with his leg, his hardness found the wet, warm place. Alice's body tensed.

"No, no, relax, honey. I won't hurt you. You will like it after a while," he said, tucking Alice's head into his chest, thrusting his groin into hers.

A wail escaped Alice's lips, her eyes wide. Slowly, he pushed the whole length of it into her hot body, the stiffness of him in her, his body searching hers.

Penetrating her deeply, Alice letting out another high-pitched half scream. Gently putting his hand over her mouth, thrusting slowly now, as he kissed her neck, sucking gently on her skin, his tongue exploring the warmth of her mouth.

The pain mixed with the pleasure, Alice's body feeling things she had never dreamed of, the two of them reaching ecstasy together, Elric letting out a low growl.

Getting up off her, he put his clothes back on, as she tried to put herself back together.

At first it had been painful, but after a while, she didn't notice it quite so much, relaxing her body, giving in to him. Hoping they would reach their destination soon, with the immediate need to take a shower.

Sitting quiet, the thoughts of what they had done, feeling a heartbeat in her private place, a feeling of pressure between her legs. It had been totally different when the old man did it to her.

"We need to get into New Brunswick before dark," he said, putting his foot to the pedal, the car accelerating. Alice becomes nervous, the car moving so fast, things by the wayside, going by too quickly.

"Don't worry, sweetie, I'm a good driver."

"Please slow down," she asked. "I am scared. I haven't been in many cars," her eyes pleading with him.

"Fine, sweetie, are you happy?"

"Yes," she answered, Elric slowing the big car.

Staring at his handsome face, his full lips her body knowing him now. *Is this what love feels like?* She asked herself. Did she love him?

"I love you, Alice," he said, his grey eyes softened, a smile on his face.

Thinking of getting his story straight, Elric decided that he would lie to his father, tell him Alice was seventeen. What would it matter?

Earl would ask too many questions when he saw how small she was, just over five feet tall and tiny, maybe ninety pounds. The size of her excited him again, his cock getting hard, trying to put it out of his mind. She was his forever. He didn't have to eat it all in one sitting, his hard-on subsiding.

Growing tired and weary from the long drive, Alice asked if she could go in the back seat and lay down.

"Sure, sweetie," he said, pulling over. Getting into the back seat, he put his coat over her. Tucking a sweater under her head she falls asleep.

Enjoying the drive in the stillness of the night, a sky full of stars. Romantic, he thought, gazing out into the dark.

Crossing the border into Quebec, in the early morning hours, Alice still asleep in the back seat.

Making it to his dad's house, he pulled up in the yard.

Looking back at her, still sleeping, putting his arm over the seat nudging her.

"Wake up, sweetie, we are here at my father's."

Sitting up, she looked out the window. A white house, the morning sun coming over the horizon.

"What time is it?" she asked, rubbing her eyes.

"You've been sleeping for about ten hours now. This is our stop. My father is expecting us."

Getting out of the car, he went around, opening the door for her. Stepping out, straightening her dress, smoothing down her curls with her hands.

Staring at the house, noticing the kitchen light just coming on, a man standing looking out the window. Earl doing his ritual morning coffee and yesterday's paper, he sits back down, waiting for Elric to come to the door.

Leading Alice up the steps, Elric knocks on the door. Earl comes to the door, his grey flannel house coat tied around him.

"Good morning, Father," he said, waiting for his father to step out of the way.

"This is Alice, my fiancée," he said. Alice looking up at Earl.

"Good morning, sir," she said in her childlike soft voice, a welcoming smile.

"Come on in. I suppose you are tired from the long trip. Elric tells me you live in Halifax."

"Yes, just outside of the city."

"My goodness, but you are a tiny one. How old were you?"

"Almost seventeen," she lied. A stern look on Elric's face made her feel as though she had said something wrong. Shit, he thought, watching his father's face, reading his thoughts.

"Alice, make yourself comfortable, in the kitchen," said Earl, staring hard at his son. "I need to talk to you, son, and right now, in the parlor."

Walking into the kitchen, she takes a seat at the table. Admiring the bright kitchen, a big window looking out onto a nice lawn, and cement driveway. Feeling hungry, she wanted to get up and fix herself something to eat, but now she was a stranger in Elric's father's house, knowing she would have to wait for the green light to even move from the table. With her hands folded in front of her, waiting for the men to come back out to join her. She could hear Earl's voice raised, no sound of Elric's.

"You are going to marry that girl? She is sixteen years old .Do you have her family's permission?"

"Yes, of course, talked to her father myself," he lied. Earl eyed his son. What a small girl? Why did he want to marry a mere child?

"Look here, boy, I told you not to bring that girl here until you two were married. There will be no sleeping in the same room in my house."

"But, Father, we drove all night, and half of yesterday to get here."

"That's fine. She can have the guest room, and you can sleep on the couch, until you decide what you are doing."

"I want you to sell me one of your houses, and then we will move to our own place."

"Really, you have money for all of that?"

"Yes, Father, I wouldn't joke about such a thing. How much will it cost me, twenty thousand?"

"What did you do? Rob a bank or something? My God, boy, I don't want to know where you got all of this money, but we won't be able to put anything in your name. I will have to keep it all in my name for now.

"Sure, whatever works?"

"Fine, Elric, we will talk about it when I come back from work today. So you and Alice make yourself at home, let her get something to eat, and remember what I said. She takes the guest room, you make your bed on the couch."

"Yes, Father, I understand," said Elric, walking away from him towards the kitchen.

Earl walked to the coat rack, put on his overcoat and fedora, taking another peek into the kitchen at the small girl. Her bright green eyes had taken his heart already. Where had Elric found her?

A real little angel, for a minute he is worried for her. Elric could be so changeable. Looking at the two of them together, anyone would think that Alice was still a child. At six foot tall, Elric towering over her.

All day at work, Earl thought about the new situation that had unfolded at his house that morning. Tonight after work, he would sit down with her and get to the bottom of the story.

Walking Alice down the hall to the guest room taking her bags in, Elric told her what his father had said about them not being in the same room. That was fine with her, taking the first opportunity to have a shower and put on some clean clothes.

Elric helped himself to the kitchen, making bacon and eggs, and rye toast, the aroma of the freshly brewed coffee filling the house.

Standing under the hot water of the shower, Alice thinking of all the new developments in her life. Putting on her housecoat, wrapping her hair in a towel, walking back out to the kitchen, Elric setting the table.

"Have a seat, sweetie, I fixed us some grub." Alice looking at the breakfast spread of bacon and eggs, and brown toast. "Yum," she said. "I am sure hungry." Sitting down across from him, eating slowly, smiling sweetly at him, feeling his eyes on her every move.

Deciding she would make something good for dinner. Show his dad thanks for letting them stay there. It was indeed a beautiful house, nothing like the Olsenses' house, but nice oak trimmed doors and windows. A clean bright kitchen, everything white, the floor, black and white squares like the hallway at the Olsenses'.

Loving the house, going through the downstairs rooms, dusting with a wet dishcloth, Elric sitting in the parlor, his feet up, a glass in his hand, drinking that stuff again, she thought.

Was all of this really happening to her, so fast?

Thinking of Betty and Suzie and what they were doing this morning.

She could see them, sitting around the table in the kitchen, her name on their lips, worrying for her. Trying to put those thoughts aside and be happy. It was her decision to leave with him, now she had to make the best of it. He was smart, handsome, and talented, and had a rich father. That was a good start, she thought to herself, thinking of the nice life she was destined to have. So far, so good, she thought, whizzing around the house, her denim overalls on, a bright pink blouse underneath, bringing in the hue of her rosy cheeks.

Taking time to put on a little lipstick, and blush, lining her green eyes, with a smoky grey liner, staring at her reflection. "Who wouldn't want a beauty like me?" she said playfully, tossing her golden curls, shaking her head.

Getting married sounded so final. She had no family to be part of a wedding. Was it just going to be like the ones she had heard about? The shotgun type, go to the judge, get a paper, and say I do. That was probably what was going to happen, she thought, the way Elric had rushed into taking her away, talking of marriage right away, an urgency in his tone.

★★★

The hand she had been dealt had some high cards, a couple of aces, and a few low cards that hadn't been turned over, yet... Like a big cat, the steel yellow one clawing its way up the hillside, its steel spines raking along, the mud clinging to the bottom, the monster machine rolled along, taking with it mud, the earthy smell. Raindrops fell like God's tears from the earth, back to the earth.

The game went on, the final toss of the cards by the Almighty.

CHAPTER 70

Earl showed in the doorway, looking in his house, a warm inviting smell of something baking. "Mmm," he said, his nose leading him to the kitchen, little Alice standing at the oven, Earl's eyes glued to her behind, the tightness and smallness of her. A fresh loaf of banana bread sits on the counter.

"Thought I would surprise you with a nice cake."

"Thank you," he said, putting his coat over the back of the chair, taking off his hat, he pulls out a chair, sitting down.

Elric had fallen asleep on the couch, not hearing his father come in. Earl noticed his son, stretched out on the couch.

Watching Alice stirring a pot of something, then bending down, opening the oven. A roast of beef in a pan with some potatoes and carrots. "I made a roast too," she said. "Elric took it out of the freezer, told me to cook it."

"Indeed," said Earl, "it's been a long time since I came home to a cooked meal. Can't remember the last time.

"Come over here, dear, for a few minutes. We need to get acquainted a little."

Turning, she looked at the gentleman with the kind voice, tall, just an older version of Elric. Long straight nose, the same colored eyes, only a little grey on the sides of his hair, slender build like his son too. Nice looked for an older man, she thought.

She couldn't help but notice a nice gold watch and gold cufflinks in his shirt with a suit.

"I own a car lot, and I have a logging company. What kind of work do you do?"

"I worked at the candy factory for nearly two years, and I worked as a maid for a doctor's family."

"I see," said Earl. "That's where you got those cooking skills from," he said, looking at her pretty face. "Don't mind if I say, young lady, you sure are pretty."

"Thank you, sir," she answered, her eyes lowering.

"No, you call me Earl, and I'll call you Alice. How about that?"

"Sure," she answered, smiling softly at him.

Earl went on, asking her questions. Alice starting to grow frustrated, when the questions, involved her family.

"So where do your parents live?" he asked. Just then, Elric arose, walking into the kitchen. Earl stopped the questioning, motioning for his son to sit down.

"Should I put out the dinner now?" she asked, looking over at Elric and then at Earl.

"Of course," said Elric. "Two hungry men to feed. I'll help you get the plates and things."

Earl watched his son from behind getting the plates down, helping Alice bring the feast to the table. Earl spooned some coined carrots on his plate, a few slices of the roast beef. Perfect, just like he liked it: mashed potatoes, the brown gravy sitting in a bowl by itself. He started eating.

The young couple arranging their dinners on the plate, Elric sitting at the opposite end of his father.

Winking at Alice, mouthing, "I love you." Earl picked his head up from his plate in time to see the exchange.

Dinner was great. Earl took Elric into the parlor to discuss the house he would let them have. Elric agreed to give him ten thousand dollars by the end of the month.

"I have to go and do some business, and I will bring back the money."

Earl looked at him, questioning.

"Don't worry, I have it. I wouldn't drag Alice across the country on false promises. I'm going to marry her, Dad. Do you like her?"

"She is everything a man could want, son. I just can't figure out how you got so lucky."

"I'm just a lucky guy, Dad."

"Sure looks that way," said Earl, walking away.

The next day for breakfast, Alice made strawberry crepes and fresh coffee, Earl and Elric sitting at opposite ends of the table.

"Do you think you could come to the lot today, and clean up a few cars?" Asked Earl, picking up his head from his breakfast.

"Oh, Father, I am still tired from the trip. How about tomorrow? I'll gladly come down and help you."

"Sure, then," answered Earl, finishing up his breakfast, saying his good-byes to Alice, walking out the door to his awaiting Cadillac.

Elric had plans for the afternoon. He wanted to start where he had left off in the back seat of the car. Earl was no sooner out of the driveway, taking her by the hand, leading her to the guest room, closing and locking the door.

"Take off your clothes," he said, looking deep into her soft eyes. "We have some unfinished business to take care of."

"What?" she said giggling? Pushing her down on the bed, without much foreplay, he gets down to business, his body over her, his erection already at the spot, pushing hard. Pinned beneath him, her face in his chest, wrestling to get her head where she could breathe, as he heaves his body in long, deep strokes. It seemed like forever to her when finally a deep growl indicated the last stroke.

Rolling off her, Alice's hair messed up, looking down at her naked self, running to the bathroom, getting in the shower right away.

Getting up and out of the room, Elric heads back into the kitchen, finishing up his breakfast.

Coming back out to the kitchen, going to the sink, Alice finishing the dishes she had started.

"That was great," he said. "There are just some things a man needs, and now it's you and me."

Starting to wonder how often this was going to happen to her, standing quiet, not knowing what to say back to that. It hadn't been painful, like the last time with him, but it still didn't feel great, the way Suzie had described it. How could she talk to him about getting some pills?

Standing with her back to him, a lot of things going through her mind. The force with which he had taken her, leaving her feeling vulnerable. He could just take what he wanted, when he wanted. Too small to fight him, if she didn't go willingly, he would get angry. What they were doing was for married people, making Alice feel ashamed, guilty.

Betty reminded the girls there would always babies when there is a lot of lovemaking. You have to be ready for these things, she had warned. It was all out of control, Elric making the rules now. Dazing into the kaleidoscope of colors in the dish water, Alice's mind going back to her life with the Olsenses, staring into the bubbles.

Wishing she could still be there. Life would never be like that again. Better to have lived it than never have, came a voice in her head.

Sometimes, especially lately, when she thought back to those wonderful times, it was almost like a fairy tale she had conjured up.

By the time Earl made it home for supper, Elric had been laying in the parlor all day, a blanket pulled over him. Alice made a wonderful dinner again, this time a lemon meringue pie to go with the main course: baked chicken, stuffed with ham and cheese, Cordon Bleu, Pierre called it, a big hit on the Olsenses' menu.

Having made it for Betty and Suzie with rave reviews, she would try it on the men in her life now.

Serving out their plates, Alice watched as they examined the foreign dish, both of them caught up in the wonderful tastes, *mmm* sounds coming from the table. Sitting down to join them, a small piece of chicken, and two roasted potatoes, browned and perfect.

Earl had noticed the lemon meringue pie when he came in. After eating his dinner, he asked Alice for tea and a piece of the pie in the parlor.

Elric ate his piece of pie and finished his dinner with a cup of tea, going to the parlor to relax. Alice thought she would join him in the parlor, bringing in her pie and tea, and a book she had started reading. Earl had also sat down, across from Elric, who was taking up the whole couch. Alice pushed her way onto the couch at the end where Elric's feet were, Earl telling his son to make room for her.

"Get up, boy, can't you see that the little lady is trying to sit down?

"Yes, of course, I am moving," he answered, glaring at his father.

"How is the pie?" she asked in a high pitched, sweet voice, trying to mend the rift.

"It is so good, I would marry you myself," said his father, smirking. Elric stared straight at his father, saying nothing, mad underneath that Earl would say something like that to his girl. Better to keep his mouth shut, came the voice in his head.

Alice ate her pie slowly, drinking her tea in between bites. When she had finished, she took the two small plates from Earl and Elric, walking them back into the kitchen.

Washing up the dishes, she heads back into the parlor to relax, picking up her book. Elric had lay back down, making room at his feet for Alice to sit. Pulling her legs up under her, her feet on the couch, her book perched on her knees.

Earl couldn't help but notice the tightness of Alice's pants, and the way that they had formed a camel toe shape between her legs, shaped like a heart, his eyes glued to her crotch. Elric turned around on the couch, noticing his father staring at Alice's crotch area.

Kicking Alice in the side of the leg with his foot, just hard enough to make her knees come together. His father catches himself, looking back at the newspaper.

"Go to your room now," Elric ordered, sitting up now. Alice's eyes grew large. What had just happened? Getting up from the couch, she walked slowly, her head lowered, out of the parlor toward the guest room, her book still in hand.

Waiting until she was in the room, Elric walked out of the parlor, down the hallway toward, the guest room.

Earl noticed him going into Alice's room, where he had told him was off limits to him. He would let them talk, his boy wasn't going to disobey his house rules.

Walking in, he slammed the door behind him. Earl's ears tuned to the loud bang of the door, looking the way the sound had come. Had he really slammed his door? Not in his house!

Walking over to where Alice is sitting on the bed, she looked up at him, fear in her eyes. Elric grabbed a handful of her hair, pulling up hard, almost lifting her off the bed.

"So you are teasing my old man now? You have only been here two days, and the old man has a hard-on for you already. Why are you showing him your pussy?"

"Oh my God," cried Alice. "I didn't do anything, please," she said, putting her hand over his big hand, her little fingers trying to pry his fingers from her hair, her eyes wide, like a frightened animal, caught in a leg hold trap.

Yanking her around the room by her hair, Alice whining louder now.

"Shut up, you stupid bitch," he said, throwing her in the corner like she was a rag doll.

Just then Earl opened the door, noticing Alice on the floor, her hands over her face. Earl glaring at his son.

"Just stop right there, son. There will be none of that in here. Leave her alone."

"Get the hell out of this room! This is Alice's room, get out, I said."

"Or you can pack your bags. Alice will stay here."

"No, she won't," came back an angry, deep voice. "She is my wife, and she leaves when I leave." Alice peeked through her fingers, the spit flying, both men enraged.

Thank God Earl had come in. She didn't know what he was going to do to her. All of her admiration for him drained from her, hating him now for hurting her. He had promised to look after her, not hurt her.

A flood of sadness came over her, like the waves that washed over her little boat. Oh my God. It was in my dream, remembering the danger in the small boat.

She dared not move a muscle. Elric stormed out of the room, going for his coat, leaving the house. Earl stood in the doorway, watching Elric back the car out, the dust flying.

I should have known better, he said to himself, closing the door, going back to the room to talk to Alice.

"What happened, dear?" he asked, putting his hand out to her. Alice looking up, afraid to accept his hand.

"He is gone. Come here, darling," Earl said, picking her up off the floor, a few strands of her curls on the floor.

"Come on, dear, we will have some tea and have a talk. We have a problem, that Widdy is a wild one, always has been. He's like trying to tame a wild mustang. Don't know how he got so bad. Guess it might have something to do with the way he was raised without a mother and father. His granny brought him up. Let him get away with anything his little heart desired until she died, leaving him without anyone. That's when I took him in, been trouble ever since. I don't know my son."

Listening to him, a blank, lost look in her eyes. She had seen the other side of him, the evil prince. *Ohhhh,* came back the thoughts in her head, the faceless prince in her dreams. He was an imposter prince in his new clothes and car, his voice deceiving even Alice.

What could she do now? So far from home, she had already disappointed Suzie and Betty, who were probably worried sick about her. She was going to marry, this guy. *Oh no, I just can't,* she thought.

"What is it, Alice? Are you going be all right? Did he hit you?"

"No," she answered, started to cry again. "He just pulled my hair, hard." Putting her tiny hand up to her head, a handful of hair coming away in her hand. "Then he threw me down on the floor."

"Oh my God," answered Earl, holding Alice to him, hugging her like a father.

Elric came back in the door, standing in the doorway, watching his father, with his arms around Alice. It made him so angry, he held his back teeth together, wanting to scream at him to get his hands off of her.

Instead, he took off his coat and hat and went into the parlor, laying down, seething at the position he was in. He had to get her out of here, and quick. He couldn't be the man he wanted to be around his father. Too many chiefs, he thought. Earl was the man of the house, and he had to get out of his father's house, and right away.

Earl noticed his son back in the parlor, going in. Sitting there, across from him, he looked at him with disgust.

"So, you are starting your stupid shit again, I thought you learned a few things in jail."

"Actually I did, learned how to speak French, do some mechanics, and got better at math. As for learning anything else? No, I don't think so."

"With that cocky attitude, you will not go far in life, son, and if you ever put your hands on Alice again, I will turn you into the police. Do you understand me? It's easy to hurt such a small girl. Does that make you feel good?"

Hanging his head, mad at his father's intrusion into his private affairs.

"Look, Father," said Elric. "I know that Alice and I are visitors in your house. Do you think we could hurry things along, and get us into our own place? I'm not trying to move in on you with my new wife."

"Yes, the house that I'm thinking about for you needs some painting and a few other minor things done. We will get working on it, right away."

Sitting in the room, under the dark sky, Alice lay in the bed, her eyes wide, thinking of any way to escape this man who had taken her away, so far away, she couldn't walk back.

She had saved some money and had it stashed in her little purse. Putting on the light, making sure the money was still there. Four hundred dollars, enough to get a bus or a train back to Halifax. Tucking her money back into the side of her suitcase, Alice goes back to bed, finally falling asleep.

As soon as the sun came over the horizon, shining in the window, the warmth filtered by the sheer curtains, Alice gets up, going to the window, looked out at the new place, the unfamiliar landscape.

CHAPTER 71

In the next days that followed, Elric tried to make up to Alice, apologizing for hurting her. Alice is caught up in the excitement of her new house. Going shopping for new furniture and the biggest bed, she had ever seen, Elric being extra sweet, kissing her every chance he got.

"We'll be spending lots of time in that bed," he said teasingly, Alice's cheeks growing warmer. As the new furniture arrived, Earl and Elric put the finishing touches on the house, new flooring in the kitchen, new carpeting in the parlor and in the bedroom.

They had planned to move in the following week. Alice, being a good wife to be, made dinner every night, catering to the guys. Everyone was seemingly happy.

Elric took her shopping for new curtains, dishes, and everything else she needed for her new house. Looking through the department store, Elric joked about needing a baby's bed sometime soon.

"We can come and get that when we need to," he said. "We'll make the smaller bedroom into a nursery."

A baby, oh my God, thought Alice. A whirlwind of thoughts and anxieties, Alice realizing she might be in a bad situation, the fairy tale of her prince charming, taking on a whole different story.

Afraid of him now and permanently tied down to him. Said, his father's attention on her, made him insanely jealous, the reason for getting angry, and lashing out.

Buying her everything she wanted for the house and some new clothes, and anything else her heart desired.

Every afternoon now, while Earl was at work, the young couple made love in the guest room. If she was the perfect wife, he wouldn't hurt her, throwing away the tight, skin colored pants that had caused the problem.

CHAPTER 72

Life with Elric

Hold on tight. You are in for the ride of your life, not in the pretty Cadillac. The candy coating, the fairy tale life, was over for Alice, the highlights replaced by dim lights, and then no light at all.

The darkness loomed over her head, never knowing when the storm would burst through to take her sunshine away with the fury of a tropical storm.

She would have to tread lightly as though walking through a field of land mines, watching every move. The suffering and pain he inflicted on his victim, my dear mother, Alice, will chill you to your bones.

She lived to tell the tale, as I tell it to you.

CHAPTER 73

Earl and Elric put the finishing touches on the little house. There had only been one other family that lived there, a man, his wife, and five kids, and the woman's father, of ninety years. The old man died in the house, so the family moved shortly afterward, for a new start.

They moved to the city, and Earl picked up the bungalow for a good price, five thousand dollars.

Earl was enamoured by his future daughter in law, her childlike body and her beautiful face. His son did not deserve such a beauty, but he knew he should keep his two cents' worth out of his affairs.

Whitewashing everything in the house with bleach, the way her mother had instilled, the bleach effect. Smiling at her handiwork, her kitchen pretty, sky blue curtains up to the window, new sheer lacy curtains up to the picture window in the parlor, the new furniture in the house making everything look beautiful. New things for her new life.

When it was all ready for them to move in, Elric stood in the middle of the kitchen floor, holding on to Alice, kissing her.

"We will have a good life, Alice, just like I promised. Do you love me?"

Looking up at him, his grey eyes pools of darkened water, inviting her into the deepness of the whirlpools lurking behind.

"Yes, I do," she said, hanging her head. Elric put his index finger under her chin, lifting her face to him.

Picking her up off the ground, he held her tight to him, turning her around and around, making her dizzy,

"Alice has a palace," he chanted.

"Let me down. You are silly. Why do you say that?"

"I know everything is new to you, Alice. I don't expect you to love me right away, but I will show you how to love me."

Not knowing how to answer that statement, Alice said nothing, giving into the big hug.

Earl helped the young couple bring in their bags, happy they were leaving his house. There would be peace again: he liked it when he locked his door, knowing there was no one in his personal space. He had worked too hard all his life to have his wayward son bring any drama into his life. The boy would learn about life as he went, he thought. He could not teach him everything in one day.

"Today is the first day of the rest of our lives," Elric said, holding her to him, Earl leaving the two lovebirds to their new home. Alice watched her future father in law walking away, wishing that he was moving in with them.

The first few days in their new house, Earl came every day after his work day at the office.

"Just wondered what's for dinner," he would say, inviting himself into the house, sitting at the kitchen table.

At first, it was fine, but by week's end, Elric started to get pissed off.

"Don't answer it," he said, a loud knocking on the door. "It's my old man again, he needs to fuck off and get his own fucking wife," he said angrily, after Earl had walked away from the door, trying to peer in the window, Alice and Elric hiding in the bedroom.

"He sure does love my cooking," said Alice, which was the wrong thing to say.

"Yeah, I think he loves something else about you, always wearing lipstick and stuff to attract him."

"No, I don't wear it for him. I like to look nice for you," she replied.

"Well, that's it, no more dressing fancy and putting on makeup when you are just here, cooking and cleaning. From now on, no more makeup unless we are going out. I want you to look beautiful for me only, Alice. Do you understand what I am saying?"

"Yes," she answered quietly, knowing there was no other way. Keep him happy so he wouldn't hurt her, came the voice.

The day they finished up the painting, they went into the master bedroom. A picture of the Virgin Mary holding baby Jesus, squared on the wall over their bed.

Earl's and Elric's eyes met, Alice commenting on the picture.

"Why didn't they take their picture?" she asked, neither of them answering,

"I don't mind having a picture of Jesus in my room," said Alice, smiling, Earl smiling back at her. Elric did not comment, just walked out of the room.

Alice took the picture down so they could paint. Earl walked up behind her, talking quietly.

"Listen, Alice, if Widdy doesn't treat you right, you can come back and live with me anytime, OK?" he said, looking into her green eyes. "Just don't tell him I told you that."

"I won't," said Alice, wringing her hands nervously. Alice looked toward the door, Elric standing there, watching Earl whispering to her. Backing away from the door, he goes into the parlor, sitting down, pissed.

Standing at the sink, Alice started thinking of the people who had lived in the house before them, wondering if they were religious people, and the guilt she was feeling about the sex they were having, a lot lately.

The picture in the bedroom was making her feel uneasy when they were doing it. It all felt so wrong. They were getting married soon. Elric had reminded her. Next week Friday, he had said.

Gazing out at the thicket of pine trees, not far from the house, a large field of green, the grass blowing in the wind, like it was waving to her. *Sure is pretty around here*, she thought. *I love the country.* It reminded her of her own childhood home, vast fields of green, grey and red barns dotting the landscape, black and white dotted cows. Other things were reminding her of her childhood too, bad things.

Elric came up behind Alice, grabbing her, turning her head slightly resting her head on him.

"I love our new house, honey," she said. "I will keep it clean for you, and cook you nice dinners every day." Looking down at her suspiciously.

"What was my dad whispering to you? I saw that," he said.

"Whispering? I don't remember what he said," she lied.

"Oh, by the way, Alice, I went down to the justice of the peace and got our marriage application. It's right here," Pulling a folded piece of paper out of his pocket.

"Next Friday," he said, "then it will be official. You will be mine. We'll be man and wife," he said, determined.

"What will I wear?" she asked.

"I will take you to buy the nicest wedding dress you can find," he answered, hugging her to him, kissing her deep.

"Oh, thank you," she said, wrapping her tiny arms around him.

CHAPTER 74

The days leading up to her wedding day had gone by too fast for her. Rushing around on Thursday, going from store to store to find a special dress to fit a girl, not a woman.

They eventually had to take a dress to a seamstress to hem it and make a few other adjustment. Finally pleased with a white dress, with an overlay of flowers in silk. It was beautiful and cost a pretty penny, the most expensive in the whole store.

The lady who helped her pick it out was star struck, watching Elric out of the corner of her eye, thinking of them together, this small girl getting married. "I am just small for my age," Alice told her.

Later that day, Alice and Elric tied tin cans to the back of the yellow and white Cadillac, Alice making some plastic flowers she had learned to make at the Olsenses'.

The car looked great. Just Married was spelled out on the trunk of the car, the two of them laughing, kissing, Elric chasing her around the car, grabbing her, kissing her hard.

A few days before they got married, Earl had been over for dinner and commented that Alice looked a little pale.

"Haven't you been eating?" he asked. "You don't look like your old self." Elric now eyed his bride.

She had thrown up two days in a row in the morning, thinking it was just the wedding jitters everyone talked about.

Earl had agreed to stand for Elric and Alice, picking out his best suit for the occasion. They were all dressed and ready to go by noon on Friday, the time set for one o'clock at the justice of the peace.

Feeling anxious, Elric dressed in his finery, watching his little bride dressed in her beautiful dress they had picked out together, her hair pinned up on her head, a few tendrils of hair hanging down the sides of her cheeks.

"You look so beautiful," he said, watching her in the mirror putting on the finishing touches, rouge and some pink lipstick.

"You look like a real princess," he said to her, leaning down, kissing her on the top of her head.

She felt a weird, almost disconnected feeling. Why always the princess and the palace? It was fun when it was just her and Suzie, laughing about her life, with the Olsenses, but why was he carrying on with the fairy tale?

A sudden feeling of sadness passed over Alice, thinking that none of her friends were here to share in what was supposed to be the biggest day of her life.

Who was she kidding? It was not the best day of her life. She was scared to death, the fear sitting close to the surface.

"What is the matter?" he asked, noticing the smile fading.

"I was just thinking I don't have any friends to see me on this special day."

"What do you need with them? I am the one who keeps you warm at night and gives you everything you need. What have they done for you lately?"

"Nothing, just that... Oh, never mind."

"My father is going to give you away and then that's it, over. You will be mine, sugar," he said, hugging her close again.

He looked at his reflection in the mirror, standing behind her. They looked so handsome together. Alice is thinking the same thing, then the voice....Looks can be deceiving.... throwing that thought to the wayside.

Feeling anxious, Elric sneaked in a few shots of whiskey. They waited and watched for his father who should arrive any minute, then Elric spotted the long black Cadillac coming down the road.

Earl gets out of the car, looking dapper in a pinstriped grey suit with a black fedora, a grey silk ribbon adorning around the base.

Opening the door, he welcomed his dad. "You look great, Dad."

"Just look at your beautiful bride, and I have to say, you look quite handsome too, Elric."

"It's the biggest day of my life. I want to look my best."

Earl noticed the gold and diamond cuff links, set off by the black and white of the tuxedo.

"You two look like the most handsome couple I've ever seen."

At the clanging of the tin cans, Alice watched out the back window, a billow of dust flying.

Standing before the justice of the peace, Elric held her hand as he reads the vows.

"Do you, Alice, take Elric to be your lawfully wedded husband, to have and to hold, for the rest of your life?

"I do," she said, in a small, hushed voice.

"And do you, Elric, take this woman to be your lawfully wedded wife, to have and to hold, till death do you part?"

"Yes," he answered, looking down at his perfect wife.

"I now pronounce you man and wife," said the justice minister. "You may now kiss your bride."

Earl watched the kiss, hard and long, Elric coming up for air.

"Yahooooo," he yelled, jumping up, picking Alice off the ground, in his arms.

Could have done without that, thought Earl to himself, walking out of the office toward his car.

He watched as Elric, with Alice in his arms, walked her back to the car, like you see them do in the movies. Only usually it was over the threshold of the bedroom door.

Well, he is happy today, thought his father, but he was already worried for his daughter-in-law. Trying to get those thoughts out of his head, Earl got in the car, waving back at Alice, who was waving at him. The two love birds get into the butter yellow Cadillac, the cans rumbling down the road behind them, a billow of dust kicking into the air.

Driving fast down the road, Elric pulled up at the general store a few miles from the house.

"Do you want a soda or something?" he asked, looking over at his blushing bride.

"No, thank you," she answered, Elric going into the store and straight to the liquor.

Now came the celebration.

When Elric came back to the car, Alice asked him, "Where are we going today? I would sure like to show off my dress. It is so beautiful."

Driving straight home, not answering her question, pretending he didn't hear it. Elric picked her up again, carrying her in the door in his long arms. Feeling overwhelmed with all the excitement, Alice started for feel a bit woozy, telling him she had to lie down for a little while.

Turning her around and around, he chanted, "Alice has a palace, Alice has a palace," finally letting her down.

Sitting still, trying to get her sea legs, she felt queasy, then vomited all over the front of her dress, then she started to cry, tears staining the bodice. "Oh my God, I've ruined my dress. Ohhhhh nooo," she cried, Elric coming to her.

"Ah, just take the stupid thing off. It won't be worn again anyway, might as well throw it in the garbage. Stop your crying now. No way to be acting on our wedding day. Here, let me help you get it off."

Undoing the back of the dress, he slipped it off her shoulders and carefully let it pool around her legs, while she stepped out of it. Rolling it into a big ball, he took it out of the house to the shed, throwing it in a garbage pail. Heading back in the house, Alice is already in the bedroom, looking for something to put on, when he comes up behind her. "The dress needed to come off any way, honey," he said, leading her to the bed, helping her out of her bra and panties, he undressed himself, joining her. They made love for a couple of hours. Alice's head is light with ecstasy, clouding her better judgment. She loved him. And now she would be the best wife in the world. The warmth of him made her feel wanted and loved. Safe in his embrace, they fell asleep.

Awakening, he looked over at his princess, her eyes still closed the rhythm of her soft breathing soothing him.

Getting out of the bed, he goes into the kitchen, where he had put the two bottles of whiskey. Grabbing for one of them, he thought it was his time to celebrate.

Thinking of his bride, in there asleep, he would just let her relax while he had a party.

One swig turned into another. Elric pretty much downed the whole mickey before she awoke, showing herself in the doorway, looking at him, sprawled on the couch in the parlor. He glanced her way, his eyes glossed over, the power of the dirty water, his senses numbed.

"Come over here to your husband," he said, motioning to her. Alice, in her nightgown, walked to him, sitting own. Throwing a heavy arm over her shoulder. "Well, sweet cheeks, it a done deed, you and me." Alice looked at him, wondering what he was saying. "You are now mine, forever."

Searching his face, his eyes bloodshot, the way he said mine squeezing her arm for a second. The heavy smell of the spicy liquor from his mouth almost made her sick to her stomach. A nauseated feeling crept into her chest and head, she tried to get up. "I really don't feel good. Sorry, I think I am going to get sick again."

"Go and lay down for a while, I'm right here. Don't think we are going anywhere. I drank a little too much," he said, almost falling off the couch.

"Too much excitement for you in one day, my love."

Just then, a bright light went on in her mind, remembering Suzie getting sick. Oh my God, she was pregnant. A panic filled her little body. That's what it was making her sick, a baby.

Disappointed they didn't go anywhere special. Was this what it was like when you went to the justice of the peace, quick, the paper signed, take off the dress, and then what? No special dinner or dancing, thought Alice. It just didn't seem right, and the way that Earl had left right away after the I dos.

Putting on her overalls and a pretty blouse, fixing a nice dinner, steak and baked potatoes, with some corn on the side. Joining her at the table, he ate his in five minutes. She watched as he headed to the bathroom, not coming out. Alice, already finished with her dinner, put the plates in the sink. He had still not come out.

Walking down the hallway toward the bathroom, Alice stepped in, Elric slicking his hair back off his face, looking like he was going somewhere. "Are we going somewhere?" she asked him.

"Yes, actually, I am going out for a little while. Got to go and let some of my friends know I got hitched today. You had better stay home and rest. After all, can't have you getting sick again. Just relax, and I'll see you in a bit, OK, sweetie."

Really, she didn't feel like going anywhere, and he was right, she should just stay home. It was his wedding day, and he wanted to share it with the world.

"But you shouldn't drive," she said, watching him swaying, standing in front of the mirror.

"What do you mean? I can do whatever I want to, and don't tell me what to do. I am the man of the house, I'll tell you what to do," he said glaring at her.

The tone of his voice told her not to question him anymore. Backing out of the bathroom, she heads back to the kitchen, sitting at the table. Tears sting her eyes. No, she wouldn't cry. He might get upset if he saw her crying.

Watching for any sign of him coming out to her, she told herself she couldn't cry, not now, the water receding back, her emotions on hold.

Making his way to Alice, his over coat on his arm, he put on his fedora. Bending down to kiss her on the forehead. "I won't be long, love," he said, kissing her now on the lips.

"Just wait for me. We'll have some more fun when I get back. Got a little celebrating to do."

"Sure," she answered, watching him go to the door, not looking back at her, the screen door slamming behind him.

Going to the window over the sink, watching him get into his car, driving backward out of the driveway to the road. As he peeled away down the road, the dust flying. No sign of the cans that had told the world they were just married. The plastic flowers were strewn all over the lawn, like he had pulled them off and thew them there.

Sitting at the kitchen table, holding her face in her hands she started weeping, the tears falling like rain, staining her cheeks.

Where had he gone? Why did he leave her alone in this house? When would he come back?

All the uncertainty of what she had just done hit her hard in the face. Married now, and she was the only one that knew about it, other than her father in law. Betty and Suzie would be shocked if they knew what had happened to her already.

Nothing, no special dinner and dancing. Her marriage day had been one she would remember and regret forever.

Finally, falling asleep in the big bed, she slept lightly, every little sound awakening her, thinking it was him coming back. She swore she heard a faint voice talking. Sitting up in the bed, looking at the picture overhead, the Virgin Mary. It seemed the voice had come from the picture, a soft woman's voice.

"I am here with you," said the voice, Alice pulling the covers over her head, laying in a fetal position. A few times she got out of bed and went out into the parlor to see if he was sleeping out there.

Finally, the sun started coming up over the horizon. Still no sign of Elric, now she starts to worry. Making the bed, she readies herself, putting on a pretty dress, fixing her hair, sitting at the kitchen table waiting for the sound of an engine.

Noticing a car approaching the house, looking out the window, its Earl, in the black Cadillac.

Straightening her dress, she goes to the door, looking out. Earl gets out of the car, a large bouquet of flowers in his hands, walking up the stairs. Opening the door for him, Earl handing her a fragrant bouquet of pink roses.

"These are for you, dear, I wanted to give them to you yesterday, but Widdy just kind of got in the way. Where is that hombre today? I didn't see his car."

"Oh, he went out last night and never came back," said Alice, a look of worry on her face.

"Really," said Earl, stepping into the house. Looking around the kitchen, Earl grabbed her hand, leading her to the table.

"Don't worry, dear, I am sure he is fine. So you say that he has been gone all night?"

"Yes, he left here, drunk, got into his car, all dressed in his wedding suit, leaving me all alone."

"I am sorry, dear. That Widdy is something else. Look here, Alice, this is a gift to you." he said, handing Alice an envelope, a thick feeling between her fingers.

"It is just a little something for you. Elric has lots of money. Hide it away, and use it as you like, from your new father-in-law," he said, bending to kiss Alice on the cheek.

"Thank you," she said, putting the envelope down on the table.

Earl couldn't believe what he was hearing. Elric had left his new bride on her wedding night, not returning. Thinking the worst had happened. Maybe he ran off the road, killed himself, thought his father.

"Do you think you could throw a little breakfast together for a hungry man?" he asked, looking Alice's way, her eyes glossy.

"Yes, of course," she said, glad to get up from the table. Feeling like her tears would come again, like a dam that had burst, waiting to cascade over and drown her heart.

CHAPTER 75

L eaving his new bride that day, he was drunk, not thinking wisely, the dirty water clouding his better judgment. The road ahead blurred, as he struggled to keep the big Cadillac on the road, a couple times hitting the soft shoulder.

Getting to the city, he headed straight to the Quebec Hotel, parking the car right in front.

Sitting at the bar, the bartender recognized him right away. Walking to him to get his order, he realized that Elric was already drunk. Taking a good look now, he understood. A celebration was in progress, Elric in a tuxedo.

"Looks like you just came from a wedding?"

"Yes, sure did. My wedding,"

"Is that your car out there?"

"No, it's my father's. He just let me use it for my big day."

John Scott and his partner were in the area, checking out some disturbance, a couple of drunks fighting on the street. Putting them both into the back of the paddy wagon, Scott noticed a familiar face staggering out of the Quebec Hotel, getting behind the wheel of the nicest car he had ever seen.

"Hey, buddy, that fellow right there, he is drunk. Him and I have some catching up to do," said Scott to his partner, getting out of the cruiser, going over to the window, looking in at Elric, who is fumbling to find the key hole.

Grabbing the handle of the door, Scott opened it, Elric glaring up at him.

"And just where do you think you are going? Get out of the car," Scott ordered.

Recognizing Scott right away, Elric smirked.

"What the hell you guys want with me? It's my wedding night," he announced, his words slurred.

The cops looked in him over. "In that case, just go back to your new wife, and no driving tonight for you. If you get behind the wheel again, you will be arrested."

"Shit," said, Elric realizing that he had better walk away or go to jail. These guys weren't fooling around.

Walking back toward the hotel, the cops watched Elric mount the stairs, back into the bar.

Those fuckers, he said to himself. *I'll just wait a bit, until they were gone, and do what I got to do*, he told himself, now watching the cops, moving off in the cruiser.

"Did you check that car out? Where the hell did that kid get that new Cadillac?" asked the grey haired cop.

"Ah, probably back in his father's good graces. His dad never wanted to admit his son was a hoodlum. Stupid bastard, that Elric, thinks the world revolves around him, had an easy time in the pen. Got out early on good behavior."

"Really," said his partner, the guys settling in, pulling up behind a row of cars, watching to see if Elric would dare to defy them.

"Just give the kid a bit. He'll be right back at the wheel, and then he's going down. Let's just wait right here," said Scott, putting his head back, relaxing, the other cop eying the Cadillac.

Sure enough, about twenty minutes later, Elric staggered out of the hotel, his legs weary beneath him, almost missing a step. Going to his car, he opened the door and got in.

"Just watch what I said, that fucker trying to drive."

"Let's go for him," said Scott. The other cop put on his siren, pulling out, now following a few feet behind him.

Hearing the sirens blaring behind him, fucking the cops on his tail.

Deciding he would give them a run, he stepped on it, leading them through a couple of streets, then he pulled up abruptly behind a building, turning off the engine.

The cops go flying by.

When they are well out of sight, he gets the big car back on the road, heading toward Loretta's, just a few minutes away.

Making half stops, squealing his tires, feeling the wildness of the whiskey, his blood hot. Pulling up to a stop outside of Loretta's house, the cop car pulling up behind him.

He didn't notice the cops behind him. Getting to Loretta's door, he knocked loudly. Awakened by the knocking, Loretta came to the front window, looked out onto the steps. Noticing the police cruiser, she decided she better open the door.

Tying her housecoat around her, she opened the door, peering out, Elric standing there in a full tuxedo.

"Hey, sweetie," he said. Just then Scott grabbed a hold of his arm, trying to put the cuffs on him.

Pulling his arm out of his hold, he jerked away. "Fuck off."

Trying to wrestle his way out of the cops' hold on him, the uniform cop hit him over the head with the billy club. His knees buckled, and he falls down hard on the wooden steps.

"Oh my God," she said, watching as he started to come to, staggering to get up now, blood trickling down his forehead.

"You are under arrest. Drunk driving, open liquor in the vehicle," declared Scott.

"Do you know this guy?" asked Scott's partner.

"Yes, I do," she answered. "We are friends."

Taking a good look at him, the fancy suit. Where was he going dressed like this?

"Can't a guy even have fun on his wedding night?" he said. Loretta is stunned. What was he doing coming here if he just got married? She thought, slamming the door, leaving the cops to do what they might to him.

Peeking out the window, she watched them handcuff him, leading him to the cruiser, a nice Cadillac parked in front of her house. When they had him in the cruiser, they came back to Loretta's door, knocking again.

"Was he bothering you, ma'am?" Scott asked.

"No, haven't seen him in a while."

"Fine then, he won't be bothering you any more tonight. He will be sleeping it off in jail."

Closing the door on the cops, Loretta went to her bedroom, throwing herself on her bed, face down, crying herself to sleep, hating him for leaving her for another woman. She never wanted to see him again, deciding that she would never let him in again. It was over.

CHAPTER 76

The next morning, the bright lights in the cell woke him.

"Shit," he said, sitting up on the cot, his head pounding. The pain behind his eyes like a knife, digging in. "Fuck, can a guy get a coffee in this place?" he asked out loud. The guard looked over at him. Still in the suit, his shirt wrinkled, his pants wrinkled, he looked a mess.

Things were starting to come back to him, in bits and pieces. He had been arrested. What happened before that? Oh right, Loretta, remembering her coming to the door, staring at him in his tuxedo. Had he told her he just got married? Ah, shit, he was busted, all the way around. And, oh fuck, what did he do with the car?

"Whose car were you driving?" asked the uniformed cop.

"My old man let me use it for my wedding day. I suppose that's a crime too," he said, the pain in his head making him less than cordial.

"You stole one of your father's cars before, so it seems that we are waiting for your father to come and claim this one and straighten things out before you are going anywhere, young man. Did you really get married yesterday? Not a good way to start a new life. Where is the bride?"

He was so fucking mad right now, he wanted to pull the cop's tongue out of his head.

Earl noticed the cops coming, driving into the lot, parking near the office. He met them at the door, thinking of the worst.

"Your boy has been up to no good again, Earl. We got him down at the jail, waiting for the word from you on the car. Is that your car? Did he steal it?"

"No, it's mine. I let him use it for his special day. So, he's OK?"

"Yeah, just a little hung over," said Scott. "We caught him last night, drunker than a skunk, open liquor in the car. He could have easily killed himself, or someone else. Good thing we caught him."

"And the car?" Earl asked. "It is in one piece?"

"He left it at a girl's place, Loretta is her name. Does that name sound familiar?"

"Oh yes, we have met, a red headed dame," answered Earl.

"Fine then, Mr. Schoolcraft, if you can just come down to the precinct and sign the paperwork saying the car is yours."

"I'll be there after work today. Let his ass stay in there for a while."

"OK then, see you downtown," said Scott, leaving Earl with his thoughts, the cops getting back in the cruiser, going their way down the road.

Sitting at his desk, contemplating the new scenario. He hadn't sold any cars today. He would go and tell Alice what was going on and get something to eat. Then he would go and get his son out of jail. What the hell was he doing at Loretta's on his wedding night? Shaking his head, thinking of little Alice, alone in the house, waiting for word.

Grabbing his coat, Earl locked the office door, getting in his car, heading down the road.

Having done all the housework, pacing back and forth, looking out the window every once in a while. Where had he gone?

Drinking her fourth cup of tea, sitting at the kitchen table, trying not to think the worst.

Earl pulled up in front of the small white clapboard house. Hearing the sound of the car's engine, Alice gets up quickly, going to the door, looking out. Earl is getting out of his car, heading to the door.

"Hi there," he said. "Let's go in. I have news on Widdy."

Alice walked to the kitchen table quickly, waiting for Earl to spill the story.

"Well, it's not as bad as I was thinking," he said. "The stupid fool ended up in jail. The cops caught him drunk driving with open liquor in the car. Now he is sitting in jail downtown, waiting for me to sign him out. They thought the car was stolen and came to my office to tell me the news."

"Really," said Alice. "Can we go and get him now?"

"You want to come too?"

"Yes, please," she said.

"Fine, throw on your coat, meet me outside," said Earl, heading out the door.

Driving along, Alice watched out the window. Earl was quiet. "Really, I should just leave him in there. That boy just won't learn. It is terrible, Alice, your wedding night he spent in jail."

"I know," she said. "We didn't even go dancing."

"Oh my God," he said, looking into her sad green eyes. "That is terrible. I just don't know what to say to make it any better."

"Hey, copper," said Elric, standing up, holding on to the bars. "Where the hell is my old man?"

"Look here, you will address me as Constable. Maybe you would like to stay in here for a while?"

Just then, the double doors opened, Earl and another detective walking in, going to the desk. Handing Earl the paper to sign, Earl jotting down his signature, turning looked at his pathetic son, still dressed in his tuxedo.

"You look like something the cat dragged in," said Earl, staring hard at his son, Elric saying nothing.

The cop came up behind Earl, opening the cell door. Elric jutted out, past his father, through the double doors, walking out the main door onto the street. Searching for his father's car, Alice sitting in the front.

Fuck, he said to himself, why did he have to bring her?

Walking to the car, he pulled open the door, sliding into the back. Alice turned, looked him over, his crumpled suit, his eyes bloodshot.

"I am sorry," he said, looking into her eyes. "Shit just happened, drank too much, and I am sicker than a dog right now," he said, leaning his head back on the cool leather seats.

Turning back around, she stared out the window, watching Earl coming to the car.

Getting in, he looked in the rear view mirror at his son.

Earl drove. No one spoke, Alice happy to be with them and not at home alone.

Earl thought about jumping down Elric's throat, but he looked over at her. He would spare her the indignation.

She watched out the window, not knowing where the road would lead her, hating the insecurities of this new life, not knowing.

When the car pulled up at the house, Elric realized that his car was still at Loretta's.

"Father, did they give you the keys to the car?"

"Yes, they did," Earl replied, handing the keys to his son. "If you keep drinking and driving, you won't have that car long or maybe even lose your life."

"Don't talk like that. I am not stupid."

"We'll see how smart you are, Widdy. Keep making mistakes like that one last night, and you won't have anything for long." Looking over at Alice, who hadn't turned her head, only listening to the men talking.

"Whatever, Father, it was my wedding day. A guy's bound to get a little lit up."

"Fine, just thought I would mention it."

Pulling the big black Cadillac into the driveway, he turns off the engine, looked over at Alice.

Without a word spoken, Elric got out of the car and straight into the house. Heading to the bedroom, he slipped out of his crumpled clothes. Naked, he crawled into the big bed, the coldness of the sheets soothing his hangover for a minute.

Walking into her house, noticing the bedroom door shut. Wanting to go to him, she decided against it. Earl walked into the house, heading straight to the kitchen, where he sat at the table.

"Can you fix me something to eat, Alice? Anything really will do."

"Of course," she answered, going to the refrigerator. Finding a cold roast of beef with just a few strips off it. "How about a roast beef sandwich?"

"That sounds just great," he answered, "and some tea would be nice."

Standing at the counter, she fixed the sandwich and made a pot of black tea. Not hungry herself, she decided she would pour herself a cup of tea and sit with Earl while he had his sandwich.

Finishing up his sandwich and tea, he thanked her, then left.

The house quiet, she wondered what she could cook for him that would make him feel better when he woke. Soup, she decided.

Getting a half a chicken out of the freezer, she chopped it into soup size pieces, adding water and a whole onion, some carrots and celery, and a few spices.

The soup boiled, filling the house with a wholesome home feeling.

Trying to busy herself, she cleaned the kitchen again. Sitting down to read her book, no sounds from the bedroom.

Darkness settled over her little house. Still no sounds from the bedroom. He was sleeping the whole day away.

Getting into bed next to him, she closed her eyes, falling asleep.

Awakened by the light of the sun's rays beaming in the window, she sits up. With a sudden nauseated feeling, she hurries to the bathroom, throwing up again. It could only mean one thing. She was pregnant.

Suddenly she was scared. Would he be mad that she was pregnant?

She wasn't ready to have a baby, and he didn't give her time to get the pills. Oh no, she thought, starting to cry now. Feeling helpless, with no one to talk to, she would have to go to a doctor to make sure.

She would have to tell Elric. What she was thinking? Later, maybe tomorrow. Oh no, what would she do?

The rest of the week, he stayed close to home, getting things done, having Earl drive him to Loretta's to pick up his car. He just looked toward her house but decided he wouldn't go and bother her, knowing she probably didn't want anything to do with him now that he was married.

The newlyweds spent long days together, cooking together, enjoying each other's company. He hadn't had a drink in days, feeling fresher and clear minded. When he was boozed up, he realized he was getting himself into trouble. Not wanting Alice to think she had married a drunk, he decided to lay off the shit for a while.

That taste of jail had been enough for him. Never again, he told himself.

Earl had been coming for dinner almost every night, a few times Elric telling Alice to not answer the door.

"Just stay in the room until he is gone. Maybe he'll think we are getting busy. It's just not right that he invites himself here so much for dinner."

Alice felt bad about her father in law walking away from the house, knowing they were in there, the car in the yard.

One day when he had come for dinner, he looked at Alice hard. "Are you all right, dear. You look a little pale. Have you been eating right?"

"Haven't had much of an appetite lately," she said, "and I've been getting sick too." Elric's head came up quickly from his plate, looked over at his wife.

"Oh, dear," answered Earl. "If I'm not mistaken, you are with child, a child having a child," he said, looking at his son accusingly.

"What are you looked at me like that for? If she is, she is my wife, and we are married."

She looked from Earl to Elric, both men with their faces in their plates, leaving her with her thoughts.

"I will take you to the doctor," said Earl when he was leaving that day. "Be ready tomorrow by nine o'clock in the morning. Doc Thompson, he delivers all the babies in the county."

"Sure, I'll be ready," answered Alice, Elric listening to the plan.

"So, Alice, do you think that you are pregnant?" asked Elric.

"I don't know, but I have felt different the last week or so."

"Things are happening so quickly, wasn't thinking of having children right away."

"Remember I told you I needed to get those pills."

"Couldn't wait for all of that. You drive me crazy, sweet cheeks, I want to have you right now."

"Not right now, I don't feel very good," she answered.

"Fine then," he said, walking away from her.

The next morning Alice was up early, made Elric some breakfast, and cleaned herself up, waiting, watching out the window for Earl to take her to the doctor.

They get to the doctor's office, Earl waiting in a small room, the doctor taking Alice in to his examination room. Doing an internal examination, feeling around her uterus. Nodding his head, telling her to put her clothes back on. "Well, you will be a mother soon, Alice. You are pregnant," he said, tears coming to her eyes.

"Are you happy or sad?" he asked.

"I don't know," she answered, walking out to Earl, who was waiting for the news.

"I am going to have a baby," she said, looking at him pitifully. Earl put his arms out, hugging Alice to him. "It will be all right. I am here for you, and I am sure Widdy will be happy."

Getting back to the house, the car is gone, the house quiet. Earl let Alice off, leaving to get to his office. Sitting down at the kitchen table, she thought hard about the news. A heavy sadness engulfed her, scared and uncertain of her future. Should she tell him? Maybe she wouldn't bring it up unless he did, or she would wait for the right time to tell him.

Later that week, Earl had come by the house for dinner, the guys getting into a conversation about Elric starting work soon. He wouldn't be handling the horses and was told to stay away from the barn. Elric turned away from his father as soon as he mentioned the team.

He was a good faller and loved the machine, the chain saw, its mighty teeth in his hands, ripping through trees, working the limbs, cutting them off, the hard work making his muscles sore, his body tight. The roar of the chainsaw engine reverberated in his brain, no thoughts, just eyes on the tree, watching overhead. Which way will it fall? Get clear of it. The possibility of a falling tree, could take your head clean off.

The schedule Elric followed was five days in, two days off, his choice. He decided to work Monday to Friday, leaving the weekend to do fun things with Alice.

CHAPTER 77

Everything was working out, Elric finally settling in, no more partying for him, thought his father, safely stowed away, back in the bush. The camp was a twenty mile trip into the Laurentian Mountains, a narrow logging road up the side of the mountain to the campsite. A row of bunkhouses, and the main house, the cookhouse, where all the men ate their breakfast and dinner. Lunch they took with them.

Elric realized the seriousness of the work schedule. Having counted his money the last time he had gone to get his father the money for the house. Fifteen thousand dollars, leaving him with only five thousand left. Where had he spent all of the money? He knew he had gambled away a lot of it, but had no clue he was down to the last five thousand. When that ran out, he would have to depend solely on the job with his dad.

The day Alice got the news that she was pregnant, Elric stayed away most of the day, coming in late when she was already sleeping. Drunk, he didn't make it past the parlor, where he passed out. In the morning, he had forgotten everything about Alice going to the doctor, not asking her anything, Alice not offering any news. Waiting on him hand and foot all day, while he nursed his hang over, Alice not ready to tell him.

Watching out the window, Elric loaded his father's old Studebaker, the car that they drove up into the mountain with. Looking over at his baby, the pretty Cadillac, deciding to just drive it on special days, when he would take Alice shopping, or times he wanted to have to himself. Go to the city and have a little fun. *All work and no play makes Elric a dull boy,* came the voice in his head.

Putting his chain saw in the back seat, his work clothes, and boots, everything ready for the morning. With one last day at home with Alice he wanted to make it fun for both of them.

"Come on, get a picnic together. We are going for a drive along the coast, spend the day together. I have to leave tomorrow to start working. Won't be seeing you for almost a week." he said, pulling her close to him, kissing her.

That day they had a wonderful time together, the sun shining: a perfect day for a picnic. Alice made sandwiches and brought some chocolate cake that was left over from the day before. It was wonderful. They ate and lay on the blanket, Elric holding her to him, kissing her, until he decided that he would make love to her right there.

There was no one around. They had pulled off the main road, over-looking the ocean. When they were finished, Alice put her clothes back on, wanting to tell him the news. "Elric, there is something I need to tell you," she said.

He looked deep into her eyes. "What is it?"

"Well, I am going to have a baby. The doctor said I am pregnant."

"That's great news," he said, laughing out loud. "A baby, well, better sooner than later," he said, holding her tight. To Alice he seemed happy, maybe she could be happy too? After all, a baby would make them a family.

The next morning, Elric is up with the alarm. The dutiful wife, makes him a breakfast of bacon and eggs and rye toast, Elric slathering the toast with honey. Getting up from the table, putting on his work boots, his heavy coat, going out the door. Alice stands in the doorway, waving to her husband. "See you on the weekend," he said. "You are not to go to my father's while I am gone. Stay home and wait for me. If he asks you, just say no. Do you hear me?" he said, his eyes wide.

She didn't answer, just waved one more time, going into the little house, watching the car pull away. Realizing he would be gone for five days: what would she do with all of her time alone? There was only so much housework she could do. Why didn't he want her to go to his father's? Alice wasn't alone like she figured. There was unseen company that kept letting her know just that. The picture had talked to her again. "You are not alone," it had said again, in a breathy whisper, scaring her.

Shadows crept across the bedroom when the lights were out, frightening her, reminding her of when she was a little girl, in the room after Pearl had died. Unable to sleep in that room in the dark, she left the lights on, pulling the covers over her head.

Earl came every day after work, bringing things for Alice to cook, sitting with her for a while after dinner. It was wonderful having Alice, he thought, bringing her little gifts, enjoying the wonderful things she was cooking. Having to make dinner every night gave her lots to do, preparation and cleaning after, taking her mind off being alone. They played cards and talked about the baby. "Soon, we will have to go and see Blanche, Elric's mother."

"Yes, I would like that," said Alice, thinking of having someone to talk to, other than him.

Elric had been gone for a few days when one night, just as Alice was putting on her nightgown, feeling alone, a faint voice came from over her bed. "Don't cry," the whispering voice said. "No harm will come to you."

"Oh my God," said Alice, looking up at the picture. She knew for sure now the voice was coming from the picture. Chills ran up her spine, the hair on her arms standing straight up. Was she going crazy? Did it have something to do with being pregnant? Was she hearing things?

For the rest of the week, Alice made her bed on the couch in the parlor. The picture was scaring her, but she couldn't understand why something Godly would be frightening her. She should feel comfort, but the voices? Wondering if she should tell Earl about the voices, but no, he might think she was going crazy.

It was Saturday, the day Elric would come home from the bush. Alice got up early, thinking of making everything special for him. Fixing a lovely dinner of whitefish, mashed potatoes and green peas. Picking some wildflowers she found in the field behind the house, arranging them in a glass jar, sitting her bouquet on the table.

Everything was perfect, so she waited, watching out the window, waiting. Growing weary from sitting and waiting, she decided she would wash a few things. Going into the bathroom, she scrubbed some of her undies and a few things on the washboard, her face flushed from the scrubbing, her hair slightly disheveled. Hearing the screen door slam, she gets up from the washboard, walking out toward the door. Trying to straighten out her hair, running her fingers through her curls, hurrying to the door. Elric strode through the door, looked straight at Alice, his eyes wide. "What have you been doing?" he asked.

"Oh, I was just scrubbing some clothes," she said, wiping her hands on her apron. The look in his eyes frightened her. Moving back, away from him, his dirty boots spilling out sawdust from the tops of them as he walked, every step leaving dirt on her floor. Scared to say anything, just feeling remorse for her freshly cleaned and waxed floor.

Watching him walk towards the bedroom now, opening the door, staring in. Froze in place, an uneasy feeling filling the air, no hugs no kisses. Deciding to follow him in there, wondering what he was doing. Bending he is running his hands over the bed. What was he doing? Coming up behind him, she said, "What is the matter?"

Elric turned his eyes glaring, grabbing a handful of her hair in his big hands, pulling hard, not letting go.

"Who the fuck has been in this bed?" he demanded, fury, in his voice.

"What do you mean?" Her eyes wide in fright. Twisting his hand around, he pulled on her hair harder. Alice started screaming. "Stop, stop, please, what are you doing? I haven't done anything," she said. "No one has been here. What are you saying? Please," she begged. Pulling her around the room as he looked under the bed and in the closet, then pushing her hard up against the wall, Alice falling to her knees on the carpet.

Bending her head down low, like a beaten dog, whimpering, she did not look up at him, Elric standing over her. All she could see was his big dirty boots. Finally, after what seemed like forever, he left her alone in the room, slamming the door behind him.

Staying in one place, trembling like fallen leaves on a windy day, she wept silently, wiping at her tears. Finally picking herself up from the floor, looking down at her knees, bloodied. Sitting on the side of the bed, the mortar in her cement world shattering, leaving her broken and scared.

What have I done to deserve this treatment? Feeling so lost, and vulnerable, her world not her own, her master deciding her fate.

Afraid to leave the room, she refolded her clothes in the dresser, rearranging her things on the top. Wishing Earl would come now, but to no avail. No noise from the kitchen, no door opening, alone with him.

Eating his dinner, he left the dirty plates on the table. Taking off his boots, the rest of the sawdust scattering across her clean floor. Going into the parlor, he lay down, falling asleep.

Standing in front of the mirror, over the dresser, she dried her tears, running the brush through her curls, a clump of hair stuck in the spines of the brush. Listening hard for any sound from the kitchen, she finally went to the door, peeking out no sign of him. Slowly trudging up the hallway toward the kitchen, she noticed the boots sitting on the floor near the door, clumps of mud dropped like shit on her clean whitewashed floors. Walking slowly into the kitchen, she could see him lying on the couch, fast asleep.

Watching for any movement from him, she gets out the broom, cleaning up the mud, following the footsteps down the hall and into the bedroom. The carpet in the bedroom, a light rose color. Getting on her hands and knees, she scrubbed the dirt out with a brush. Her knees hurt, but the pain in her heart overshadowed all. Crying, her tears fell, mixing with the soapy solution. Finally, all the mud was cleaned up, the floor washed. Taking the boots outside, shaking the rest of the dirt off emptying them of the sawdust that was packed right to the toes.

Carefully swabbing the cuts on her knees, she put bandages over both of them, finding some comfortable pants to hide the telltale signs.

Looking in at him every once in a while. Going to the bedroom, getting a blanket, laying it over him, his face turned from her.

Later that day, when he woke, he searched Alice out. She was hanging up some of his shirts she had just ironed perfectly. His little wife, taking care of his shirts. He felt sorry for what he had done. In his mind, he knew he was wrong. The whole time away from her, he imagined that someone had come to the house, maybe a fuller brush salesman, seeing his beautiful wife. She might be lonely, let him in, and...all in his stupid head, he told himself. Going to her, hugging and kissing her, saying he was sorry, then taking her to bed, making love to her over and over again. Alice's emotions are on a treadmill, not knowing how to feel or what to say, just going along for the ride, so to speak, happiness was so far away now, like a sinking sunset. Thinking of a baby growing inside of her made her cry herself to sleep.

The rest of the weekend, he tried in his own sick way to make her forget the assault. Taking her shopping, walking in the field behind the house, holding her hand and even rubbing her belly while they sat on the couch together. The mixed emotions that were running through her head were making her dizzy with confusion to cry or laugh.

Sunday night dinner, they sat quietly at either end of the table. Meatloaf, with string beans and mashed potatoes and a brown gravy, the way Pierre had taught her to make. He ate greedily, devouring every last crumb, complimenting her on the meatloaf. Feeling her staring at him. "Don't watch me," he ordered, "eat your dinner." Pushing himself away from the table, he walked to the bedroom, closing the door behind him.

Cleaning up the kitchen, she settled on the couch in the parlor to read her book.

"Get in here," he ordered, his voice assaulting her peace. Going to the bedroom, she opened the door, looked in. He was stark naked, his penis standing straight up.

"Come in here," he said. Alice going to him. Pulling her on top of him, greedily taking off her clothes. Making her sit atop him, like she was riding a horse.

CHAPTER 78

Blanche

Lately, always worried, Alice started noticing some changes in her body, her breasts sensitive to the touch, Elric's big hands all over her, her nipples sore to his caress or kiss.

Earl was started to notice changes in his daughter in law. Still making regular trips to her house for dinner, most nights when Elric was in the bush. When he came home for the weekend, Earl made himself scarce.

The following week at work, Elric worked hard, his mind on his wife and the baby coming. Something deep inside of his constitution wanted to be a good husband and father. Now that she was pregnant, he should stop drinking, noticing that his moods were altered. She sidestepped him, scared of him now, the way she watched him, examining his talk, searching his eyes, for that look that told her to tread lightly. When he called to her, she came running, a look of alarm on her face. Deciding he would try hard to lighten up, stop drinking. The way his father looked at him lately too made him feel less a man. He had to change all of that.

Standing in the mirror, she runs her hands over her once tight stomach, a show of roundness from the sides. Her breasts had grown larger too. Thinking back to Elric, holding her, caressing her stomach, telling her he was sorry for hurting her, the tears came again. "I will be a good husband and father from now on," he promised. Looking into his grey eyes, bottomless pools of deep muddy water. Did he think that his kisses and promises could wipe away the hurt? Brushing her hair, she noticed a bald spot in the front of her head, just above her ear, pulling some other stands over, covering the spot, worried that Earl would notice.

The next weekend home, Elric was the picture perfect husband, helping to get the little bedroom ready for a nursery. They went paint shopping, buying a pale yellow, the color of buttercups, buying all the things the nursery needed. A crib, dressing table, and a large dresser to put all the baby's things in. He helped her pick out blankets and stuffed toys, and anything else she thought they needed.

It was one of the best days she had spent with him yet, staying close to her side, kissing her, holding her, singing to her. While they sat in the parlor, he put his head down near her stomach, pretending he was singing to the baby, making her giggle. Earl showed up with a special surprise for the nursery.

"This is for my grandchild," he said, handing Alice the wrapped box, heavy, with a big bow on the top. Alice put the box on the kitchen table, while the guys watched her undo the package, pulling out a mink blanket. Black, shiny fur. "Is this real fur?" she asked, running her hand over the silky shiny surface.

"Only the best for my grandchild," said Earl proudly, hugging Alice. The three of them sat down to a lovely dinner of roast beef and mashed potatoes. Thanking Alice for the dinner, he left as soon after he had eaten.

Feeling more secure now, Elric was so caring, staying home with her the whole weekend, leaving her with a false sense of security.

They were taking long road trips in the pretty Cadillac along the coast, Alice loving the water, the peacefulness of the beauty abounding. Earl was starting to feel different about his son too, Elric working hard, putting in twice as much work as the regular fallers. With his son working with the crew, they were on time, keeping their eyes on the aggressive young man, the boss's son, Earl getting more work for his dollar.

Almost every time that Earl visited lately, he brought presents for the new arrival and little things for Alice, fresh fruit, chocolates, and food items. One evening, as they ate, Earl mentioned Blanche, Elric's mother.

"She lives close to the border of New Brunswick, a little rural town called Hope Town," he said. "It would be the best part of a day driving."

Blanche married a man shortly after she left Earl, trying to put the thought of her twins out of her mind. Feeling the guilt of leaving them, she had no hope to see them again or them wanting to see her.

Blanche and her husband, Tom, were sitting on the porch of their house, when they noticed a car coming up the driveway. A yellow and white Cadillac, stopping right in front. Blanche got up from her rocking chair, trying to make out the woman and man in the car. Walking slowly, with her edema filled ankles, she held on to the railing, her wide hips taking up the width of the steps. Slowly making her way to the bottom of the steps, Elric noticed his mother. Getting out of the car, walking to her.

Looking deep into his eyes, feeling a connection right away. It was her son, Elric. Holding his arms out to her, Blanche going to him.

"Hello, Mother," he said. "Thought it was time we met." Blanche started crying now, standing back looking into his softened grey eyes.

"Elric?" she said.

"Yes, Mother." They hugged for a long time, Blanche trying to put all those years of yearning into one hug. "Mother, I had to come to see you. I just got married and thought it was time that you met your new daughter in law, Alice."

"Oh my," she said, putting her hands up to her face. Alice had opened the door and was standing beside the car, watching Elric with his mother. Alice noticed her labored walking, going to her. "Nice to meet you, dear," said the heavy set lady, a tight, dark curl close to her head. Puffy cheeks, deep wrinkles under her blue eyes. Age had not agreed with Blanche, her extra weight hiding any beauty she had left.

"Come in the house," she said, waving Alice in. Her husband, Tom, was a tall, thin, slightly stooped balding man with a walking stick, following them in.

"Tom, this is my son, Elric, and his wife, Alice."

"Nice to meet you," he said, holding out his hand to Elric. Shaking hands, they followed Blanche to the kitchen table. "Well, we got lots of time to make up," said Blanche, smiling from her grown son to his wife. "You will be a grandmother soon, too. Alice will have a baby in February."

"Oh, my dear," said Blanche, looking Alice over. "If you don't mind me saying, you look like a child yourself."

"Yes, I am just small for my age. I'm sixteen."

"Now that you two are here, I'll make up the guest room. You can stay a spell."

"Thanks, Mother. We will stay the night so you and Alice, can get acquainted."

"Come and help me fix some dinner, Alice," said Blanche, going to the refrigerator. Alice stood next to her, waiting for instruction.

Together they made mashed potatoes, with steaks for everyone. Eating in silence, the thoughts of times gone by infecting Blanche's mind. Could she make it up to him for all the time they had lost? She would do her best and already wanted to be part of her grandchild's life. This was the perfect time to make up to her son, and the thought of a grandchild made her happy. There was no running away anymore. She could hardly run from herself, a prisoner of her fat body.

Blanche ushered Alice into her room, closing the door. "Come over here, dear, I would like to talk to you." Sitting down on a yellow plush chair, Blanche sat on the side of her bed. "Where did you meet my son?" she asked.

"We met when he was playing in a band at the candy factory in Halifax. I worked there for two years," replied Alice.

"Can you keep a secret, dear?"

"Yes," said Alice.

"I went to one of those dances just so I could see him, all grown up and so talented. I left when he was very young."

"Don't worry. I won't say a thing."

"I would like to make up for lost time, Alice. I want to be here for you and your baby."

"Thank you, ma'am," said Alice, slipping into Blanche's open arms, pressed against her rounded stomach, her large breasts softening the hug. "It's so nice to have you. Let's go and join the guys."

Going back to the kitchen, Tom had walked outside to the porch, Elric going to the car, bringing in the small bag with the things that Alice had packed for the trip.

"Just take your things to the guest room," said Blanche, pointing down a narrow hallway toward the back of the house.

Elric went in, closing the door, laying on the bed, wanting to have some private time. It was overwhelming meeting her. She was not well. He could tell that by the way she struggled to move her body. *She is so fat*, he thought to himself, *and ugly*. Not wanting to talk anymore, he stayed in the room until Alice came to bed. The one handshake between him and Tom had been the only exchange of words, Elric passing him in the hallway, Tom's head down not making eye contact.

Blanche didn't let Alice get a word in edgewise, standing behind her as she stood at the sink, washing the dishes from dinner, wanting to make her new mother in law know that she wouldn't take advantage of her kindness.

"Come in here, dear, when you are done. We need to get acquainted. The guys have both gone to bed. It's time for us women to get to know each other. Did you meet Elric before he went to the pen?" she asked. Alice looked at her, confused.

"You know what I mean? My boy just got out of jail. Been in there almost two years. Does he treat you right? His father has been filling me in on all the details, his wild carousing and antics."

The blank frightened look on Alice's face answered her question. She didn't know everything.

Putting her hand to her mouth, Alice looked deeply into Blanche's blue grey eyes, not knowing what to say, just shocked at the news she had just heard.

"Well, dear?"

"Actually no. He just came and took me away with him about four months ago now." Blanche searched her daughter-in-law's face for the truth. Alice looked away from her direct stare, trying to change the subject. "We have only been married for three weeks now," said Alice.

"My God, dear, everything is happening so fast for you. A baby on the way already? Are you ready for all of this?"

"No," said Alice, her eyes filling full of tears, the dam holding them back from falling.

"Listen here, now that you and I are acquainted, you can come here any time. When the baby comes, you can leave the child with me, give you a break."

"Thank you," said Alice, starting to wonder if Elric was sitting up waiting for her. Something told her she had better excuse herself and join her husband.

He was sitting on the side of the bed, wanting to go and take her by the arm and lead her into the room. His mother seemed too friendly, all too soon. What were Alice and her talking about? He wanted her to come now and join him. Just as he was going to go out and call her, Alice came through the door, walking to him. Putting out his long arms, accepting her into his chest, pulling her close.

Taking her quietly, Alice tried not to make any noise. They fell asleep in each other's arms, love in the air.

Awakening the next morning, Alice went to the kitchen to help Blanche make the breakfast. Blanche complained about pain in her back and legs if she stood for more than two minutes. Alice took over the job of cooking for the four of them, bacon, eggs, and strawberry crepes, and fresh brewed coffee. Tom sat quietly, looking from his wife to the young couple. Pushing away his plate, he picked up the morning paper, closing them off. Elric got up, went to the room and packed their bag. Alice tried to have a few bites, then got up to clean the kitchen, without help from anyone, her back hurting her.

They said their goodbyes to Blanche and Tom, the young newlyweds off, down the road toward their new home. An hour's drive from Quebec City in the countryside.

As they drove, Alice is deep in thought about the new developments, and the things Blanche had told her about Elric being in jail. Everything was making more sense now, all the money he had been spending since the day he had picked her up at Suzie's, probably stolen, she figured. Elric broke the silence, his voice loud.

"So, what was my mother saying to you? She seemed to have a lot to say. I don't even know the bitch. She left me when I was just a baby."

Alice looked over at him, staring blankly ahead. "I am sorry," she said, putting her tiny hand on his arm.

"I was better off without that cunt, and look at that no mind she married. Just like her, no fucking mind."

Afraid to say the wrong thing, she said nothing at all.

CHAPTER 79
A Baby Girl

Getting through a couple of weeks of night sweats, irritability, and the shakes, at the end of two weeks, he was feeling like himself again. Wanting to be the perfect husband, waiting patiently for the birth of his first baby. This time, coming off the booze had been light compared to his jailhouse time.

The symptoms had subsided, leaving a calm, smiling, caring Elric, with good intentions.

The dirty water clouded his good thoughts, awakening a monster that even he couldn't control, someone else at the helm, driving him over the edge…insanity.

When he questioned himself about hurting Alice, he figured he hadn't done any real damage. Just she didn't trust him anymore, sometimes catching her watching him like a frightened animal.

She was the best girl he could have ever found to be a mother for his child and a good wife. Determined not to hurt her anymore, he told himself. He was a changed man.

Alice is well on in her pregnancy, the baby due in one month.

The baby making it hard for her to sleep and eat, always with heartburn.

"I'll take you to my mother's," Elric suggested, "pick you up in a few days, OK? At least I know you are safe there."

Complaining about the sex being uncomfortable irritated Elric.

The longing for a good drink was more than he could handle. Going to the city, he picked up a pretty girl at the bar and took her back to a hotel room he rented for the night.

He was taking Alice every weekend now to his mother's so he could get away and let loose.

One night, sitting at the Quebec Hotel, Elric is hitting on a hot blonde girl when her boyfriend walked up behind him, telling him to back off. Taking a swing at the guy, too drunk to keep his balance, he fell backward, hitting his head on the floor. The guy walked out of the bar, cursing the fool. The bartender helped Elric to his feet, telling him he had to leave now. No more drinks for the night.

Going back to his room alone, he slept off the drink, sleeping all the next day, a hangover like no other he had experienced.

He hadn't put his hands on Alice since the last time that he had falsely accused her of having someone else in his bed. His father had threatened him, and he needed his job, now that his money was all but spent. The pay he was getting from his father was putting food on the table and gas in the car. He felt good about being a father and wanted to give his wife and baby the best.

Trying to make up for lost time every chance Blanche had, she would hug Elric. Distant, she didn't feel any love connection between them, his heart hardened against her.

Blanche had become a big part of their lives now, always talking about her grandchild and how she was going to help Alice with everything, assuring her she didn't have to be alone with a new baby.

When she got close to her due date, Elric took the week off work, staying close to home, getting her meals, helping any way he could.

Watching the man that had seemingly changed, she tried to put the bad things, out of her mind.

On a cold February morning, the first day of the month, Alice awoke with a surprise, a gush of warm water wetting the bed. Sitting up, she called to him. Elric came running into the bedroom.

"Is it time?" he asked, Alice nodding, looking down at her enlarged stomach, the baby moving inside of her.

"Yes, we had better go to the doctor," she said. "He told me this would be a sign the baby was coming."

Rushing to her, helping, putting a coat over her shoulders, getting the car started, helping her into the back seat.

Driving quickly down the frozen road, they made it to Dr. Thompson's office just as the doc was coming out the door.

Rushing out of the car, he walked toward the doctor.

"Good morning, Doc. Alice is going to have the baby. Her water broke," he said.

"Get her in here now," ordered the doctor, looking back at the car.

Elric helped her out of the car into the office. The doctor ushered Alice into the examination room, telling Elric to sit outside the door.

The pains of labor wracked her stomach, making her cry out, the pain unbearable.

Wiping her forehead, trying to relax her, Elric heard her cries and opened the door to the examination room.

"Can I come in and help?" he asked.

"Sure, here, put this on," the doctor said, handing him a white coat. "Wash your hands and you can help deliver your own baby."

Excited, Elric did exactly what the doctor said, watching Alice's reddened face, the pains coming every few minutes now.

"It won't be long now," said the doctor. A few more stabbing pains in her back, pressure between her legs, the baby's head showing.

"Push now, dear, push, push hard," the doctor ordered, the baby's head coming out, then the rest of the body sliding out.

"A perfect baby girl," the doctor announced. Elric was in shock, seeing the blood and a paste covering the baby's face.

The doctor cleaned the baby off, then wrapped her in a soft pink blanket, handing her to Alice, who watched in awe at the miracle of life, staring into the blueness of the baby's eyes, her baby.

Hugging Alice and kissing her on the forehead, Elric beamed as a proud father.

"If you would just go to the waiting room now, I have to talk to Alice about some private things."

He instructed her on postnatal care and about the stitches where he had to cut her.

"You guys are fine to go home with your new baby girl," said the doctor, leading Alice out of the examination room carrying her baby.

Elric staring at his new daughter, her skin the color of peaches. Running his hand gently along her cheek and down her arm. For a brief moment, he felt joy like he had never before.

I really have something to live for now, he thought, feeling a renewed closeness to his little wife. She had given him a daughter to love.

"I'll hold her till we get to the car. You go ahead, sweet thing."

The loving Elric made her cry happy tears of joy, watching him with his daughter, hoping things would stay this way. There was more to worry about now, keeping her daughter safe as well as herself.

Sitting together in the parlor, Elric watched the baby suckling Alice's breasts, which had become engorged with milk. Playfully he put his lips around the other nipple, a squirt of warm breast milk in his mouth.

"You are silly," she said, watching his antics. They laughed and played with the baby, taking turns holding her. "What will we call her?" asked Alice.

"Well, we could call her Blanche after my mother." He no sooner got that mouthful out when he said, "No, we will call her Brenda."

"That is pretty," said Alice, nodding her head. "Her name will be Brenda Rae, after her great-great-grandfather Henry, the brains in the family line." Announced Elric.

"Who was your grandfather Henry?" asked Alice.

"He was a great man, an explorer and a scientist, and a writer of many books. Maybe she will be just like him," he said. "We might have a genius on our hands."

"Wow," she answered, "that would be great." Elric can't take his eyes off his beautiful daughter, saying her name. "Brenda." The baby's sea blue eyes opened discovering her new world, the sounds coming to her plainly, her mouth searching out her source of life, her mother.

CHAPTER 80

The first week at home with the baby had been hard on both of them, Alice waking every few hours to feed her, Elric awakened by the crying.

The excitement and happiness was short lived.

"Shut that kid up," he would yell, causing Alice to panic, taking Brenda in her arms, trying to feed her.

Being nervous, and worried, Alice's milk started drying up.

"We will have to get her something more to eat. My milk is drying up," said Alice at the breakfast table one morning.

"What is wrong? What kind of mother are you that you don't have enough milk for the baby?"

Not knowing how to answer that, feeling like a bad mother now. No milk for the baby.

Blanche had mentioned that it happens often to new mothers, the stress of the new baby drying up the milk. She told Alice about a formula that they gave babies that didn't get the pleasure of breast milk. Some mothers decided not to feed their babies from their breasts for cosmetic reasons.

Those babies miss out on a lot, assured Blanche. *At least you gave her a few weeks of breast milk.* That made Alice feel better. Already getting a complex that she wasn't a good mother, she put Brenda on formula.

Earl brought cases of it. The baby settled into its new life, the sounds of the world already affecting her.

"She is such a good baby," Blanche said, looking down at her perfect granddaughter. "Now that she is on formula, you can leave her with me."

At first Elric told her no, but later on he was happy to drop the baby off, taking Alice shopping or just spending time with her alone, feeling jealousy toward the baby.

When the baby was a week old, Elric started back to work in the bush, cutting trees. Getting away in the bush gave him the peace he needed so desperately, the baby getting on his last nerve.

He had been short with Alice, yelling at her, the baby crying harder, the sound of his voice scaring Brenda already.

Coming home to Alice and the baby on weekends, he felt shorted, the baby taking centre stage, Alice always busy, using the baby as the reason she tried to stay away from him, her baby her main concern.

"You don't have time for me anymore," he complained. "I need breakfast too," he said, sitting at the table, fork and knife in hand like a spoiled child.

"I need food, now!" he ordered. Alice had to put the baby down, rushing to get him his breakfast.

When he left for work Monday morning, Alice was relieved, happy to see him leave. She could spend every minute with her baby girl, her soft blonde hair, her blue eyes that followed her mother's every move.

In the months that followed, Elric made excuses to go into the city on Saturday, lots of times not showing up for the whole weekend. Earl noticed Elric was mostly gone on weekends.

"He hardly stays around now," she had told Earl, relieved at having her time with her baby, but his absence making her feel vulnerable again.

Waking in the middle of the night, she sat up in bed, not being able to go back to sleep. She'd sit in the parlor, listening for any sound of a car engine, wondering where her husband was. In her heart she knew he was drinking and carousing again, the telltale signs coming home just in time to get ready to go back to work.

Washing one of his white shirts one day, she noticed a streak of red lipstick on his collar. It put all those nagging questions to rest. He was having affairs with other women, but she knew better than to blame him, mentioning it to Blanche, his mother.

"Please don't say anything to him," said Alice, Blanche recognizing the look of fear on her face.

"That Widdy is just no good, Alice. Sorry you had to end up with him. Didn't your mother tell you to watch out for guys like him?"

"My mother never told me anything," said Alice. "The day that I started my period, I thought I was bleeding to death. My mother was never there for me."

"I am sorry," said Blanche, holding her daughter in law in her warm, squishy arms.

The happiness with her new baby was overshadowed by the constant reminder Elric was like a time bomb, watching her step and everything she said to him, taking orders and trying her best to be a good wife.

Lately, he had taken to verbally abusing Alice, coming up behind her when she was doing dishes, grabbing at her little extra flesh on her stomach. "Looks like you are getting a little fat," he said. "Don't get fat like my mother, or I'll put you out to pasture, like that fat cow."

Lately, when he was home, she would prepare his dinner and take hers into the parlor, making excuses she had to do something with the baby.

Making her feel insecure of the little extra weight she had gained, Alice eating only small portions, the extra baby weight falling off her, and more, making her look gaunt.

Blanche had commented that she was looked skinny, putting large portions of food in front of Alice.

"Come on, dear, eat," she would say, watching Alice pick at the food. A few times she yelled at her.

"Why are you starving yourself? You have to keep up your strength, you have a baby to look after."

Elric stopped teasing her about being fat, noticing too that Alice had grown thin.

"My God, girl, you don't look like more than eighty pounds soaking wet," teased Blanche, setting a big piece of chocolate cake in front of her. Taking one bite of the cake, Alice leaves the rest on the plate. Blanche grumbled under her breath. "Wasteful," she said.

When the subject came up of taking the baby to Blanche's, Alice would decline, making excuses of why she didn't want to go.

The constant food forcing issue was making her feel uneasy, Blanche becoming agitated, Alice feeling more abuse. Watching Blanche eat was enough to ruin her appetite, devouring huge heaps of food, looking at the fat dimples on the flesh of her arms and legs.

CHAPTER 81

Keeping her little house spic and span, washing Elric's and the baby's clothes on the washboard. Earl surprised her one day with a washing machine that had an agitator, swishing away the dirt and a contraption that looked like two rolling pins together, where Alice would run the clothes through to wring out the water.

The new washing machine, was making Alice's life much easier, especially for the three dozen cloth diapers she had for Brenda. Earl helped by hanging a clothesline just outside the door, fastening it to a nearby tree, Alice hanging all the freshly washed clothes to dry. All the little things Earl was doing for her and her baby girl, Alice made sure to thank Earl, and make him special things he liked for dinner.

Going back through the bedroom a few times, smoothing down the bedspread, until it looked like even she didn't sleep in the room, even looking for imaginary foot prints on the carpet.

The counting things was happening again, like she did when she was a child, as she hung up the baby's things, counting as she went, or going down the steps to the outside of the house, to the frozen ground.

Winter was in full swing, Alice keeping the belly of the woodstove full, and burning hot. Carrying in the wood that Earl had cut and stacked in the shed, just outside of the house. He still came for dinner, and sometimes breakfast, but only times when his son was up the mountain working in the bush.

Elric knew that his father was going to his house. The wood pile was stacked with fresh cut pieces. It made him angry and jealous, his father enjoying his wife's cooking while he was in the bush, eating the camp food. They had a good camp cook who took care of the men, everything made fresh, keeping the guys happy. After a day cutting trees, the bitter cold, their fingers freezing. Fresh homemade soup every day and a hearty meat and potatoes dinner.

Elric had started making demands of the chef, ordering what he wanted for dinner, Earl not any the wiser. The food bill had gone up, but it was all figured into their pay, taking so much out for their food and lodging.

Being jealous of his father's time with Alice, he told her that she was not to go anywhere with Earl. She should wait for him to take her shopping or whatever she needed. His father was becoming a thorn in his heel, spending too much time with his wife.

The times that Elric was away working were peaceful, but as Friday approached she started to become anxious. Lately, it had been verbal abuse toward her.

The little digs were like stabbing her with a dagger, ripping small tears in her heart. Frustration with the baby crying had frightened Alice. The way he screamed, "Shut it up, do this, do that."

Looking over at her pretty baby girl, she feared for her now, as well as herself. The storm had calmed for her in the last while, but she knew in her heart that the eye of the storm was always watching. The reality was, she was worried for her helpless baby and herself.

Brenda was nearing six months of age, her straight platinum blonde hair like tendrils of wheat, her eyes blue, like a clear blue sky. The baby would squeal when she saw Elric coming through the door.

"Happy to see me," he would say, going to the baby, rubbing her head hard, his big hand fitting over the baby's skull. Now that the baby was eating solid foods, like mashed potatoes and vegetables, she was sleeping through the night, crawling around on the floor, following her mother here and there.

The playpen that Earl had bought was great, keeping Brenda in one place, playing with all her toys, sometimes falling asleep with her favorite soft blanket in the playpen. Earl was so taken by his granddaughter, he couldn't wait to see her almost every day when Elric was away, trying to make up for the not so perfect husband and father.

Lately, his son was coming in Mondays to work hung over, staying in the bunkhouse sometimes half the day.

"You can't be pulling this around here, Widdy, I've got a business to run. You are supposed to set an example for the others. You are my son."

Earl was nobody's fool. He had seen the signs of alcoholism on others that had worked for him, sometimes catching them drinking straight from the bottle while out in the bush, putting everyone's life in danger.

"It doesn't agree with you, son. Why do you have to drink now? You have a wonderful wife and baby."

"Ya, ya," he answered, his head pounding, his father's voice like a sledgehammer on the top of his skull.

The week that Alice had to herself and the baby was becoming a favorite time for her, taking care of her little house, the smell of bleach, the house gleaming.

It was a hot summer, Brenda and Alice spending a lot of time outside, Earl picking Alice and the baby up, taking them to his house and shopping or whatever Alice wanted to do. Although Alice tried to make excuses why she shouldn't go to his house, Earl insisted that there was no harm in her going.

Not expecting Elric home until early Saturday, Earl had come to pick them up early in the day, taking them to his house. While Earl played with his granddaughter, Alice lost herself in the rows and rows of books in the study, books on everything she could imagine.

Alice loved the cooking books, copying down new recipes.

Earl lent Alice a few books to read, Alice taking a bag of them home, not thinking that she would have to answer to Elric about them.

Getting caught up with reading, Earl played with his granddaughter, the time escaping them, darkness looming.

"Well, we had better get you guys home," said Earl, looking at the clock. Ten o'clock, the big round said. Dressing the baby, she stood in the doorway, waiting for Earl to pull the big Cadillac up to the step. Earl got out, helping them into the back seat.

It was a beautiful night, the sky a dark purple velvet, lit with stars, like jewels.

Alice sat nervously watching out the window at the night sky.

Earl noticed first the Studebaker parked in front of the house. "Looks like he is home," said Earl, looking back at Alice, her face going stark white, her eyes wide.

"He wasn't to be home until tomorrow," she recanted, a chill running through her.

"Can you come in with us? Please, can you come in and talk to him?"

"What? What is the matter, Alice?" he asked, pulling up to the house, getting out, helping her and the baby out.

"Please," she begged, "he told me that I wasn't to go to your house when he was away."

"What!" said Earl. "That is ludicrous. He is away, and I am here to help you when you are alone. What is wrong with his head? That boy needs a talking to."

"No, no," said Alice, her eyes glossed over, holding the baby close to her, the weight of the growing baby, Alice straining to hold her.

"Here, let me take Brenda, and we will go in and face him together," he said.

Pushing open the door, Alice walked in, her eyes jutting around the house. No sign of Elric. He was probably in the bedroom, she concluded. Earl stepped in, put the baby down, looking around to come face to face with him: no sign of him.

"Just sit a spell," she said, going to the bedroom, opening the door quietly. Elric is covered, his back to her.

"Elric," she said, in a quiet, small voice. No answer, no movement. "Are you sleeping? Your father is here, wants to talk to you."

Still no movement, his eyes wide open.

"He must be sleeping," she said to herself under her breath. Going back out to the parlor, Earl waited to see his son coming.

"He's sleeping," she said. "Thank you for coming in. We'll be all right," she said, picking up Brenda, taking her toward her room. Covering the baby, kissing her on the forehead, Alice pulled up the sides of her crib. "Good night, angel," she said, walking out, the baby's eyes closed tight.

Earl walked toward the door, put his arms out to hug Alice. Reluctant to go to him, she stood back. Earl got a weird feeling.

"OK then, sweets," he said. "See you guys tomorrow maybe," he said, knowing full well he wouldn't visit when Elric was home.

The car engine, the final sounds of the wheels on the hardened dirt, leaving, the drawl of the engine, going, going, gone.

Standing up now in the parlor, a frightened feeling creeping over her, she is afraid to wake him. Sitting on the couch, she grabbed at the bag of books she had brought with her from Earl's.

Getting comfortable on the couch, she pulled her legs up under her, picking out one of the books, *Life and Times of Sam Ragee*, opening it to the front page. Just then, she heard a noise from the bedroom, the door opening. Laying the book down, on the coffee table, knowing that he was awake. Alice sat there, like a scared animal, her heart beating fast in her chest like a million wings of doves.

Standing now, one arm holding the door jam, still, staring in at her.

"Did I hear my father's voice?" he asked, his lips tight, glaring at Alice.

"Yes, he brought us home. He came early today, wanted to take Brenda to the fair," she said, her words running together like two cars colliding.

Walking over to her, peering down at his helpless victim. Grabbing a big handful of her hair, he ripped at it, pulling her to her feet.

"You stupid bitch, you won't learn, will you? I told you to stay away from him, to stay home and be a good wife, but no, you are too stupid for that. You like being with him, don't you?" he screamed.

"Oh no. Please, please," she begged as he pulled her alongside him, his hand wrapped firmly around her hair, Alice trying not to resist him, hoping it would stop, on her tiptoes.

The babies' cries reached her ears, mingled with her own cries.

"Let her cry," he said, pulling Alice into the bedroom, letting his grip go from her hair, shoving her onto the bed.

"You are my wife, not his, but you don't listen. I told you." Rushing over to her, punching her with a closed fist in the face. Alice falls onto the bed, blood gushing from her nose, Elric continues his assault, punching her in the back of the head.

Her little hands held tight over her face, the blood seeping between her fingers. Her nose started to swell.

"Oh my God," she screamed now, Brenda screaming now too, standing up in her crib, her little eyes red, waiting for her mother to come, but to no avail, crying herself to sleep, hugging her teddy, sucking the corner of her blanket.

"I will fucking kill you, you stupid bitch," he screamed. "I work my ass off to get you and the baby things, keep my household running, and you are gallivanting all over the country like you are on some holiday."

Somehow, she had managed to get to the corner of the room, the blood dripping into a white towel she held tight to her face.

The damage done, he stares over at her, curled up in a ball. All he could see were her little feet.

Storming out of the room, he goes out to the parlor, seeking out the bottle he knew he had stashed last week when he was home.

In a state of shock, she lay on the floor all night. In the morning, her head felt twice the size, her little hands feeling the lumps all over her head where his fists had pummeled her.

Hearing his voice, kind, happy, talking to the baby. Pulling herself off the floor, she looked down at a white towel, soaked in blood, just a few spots of white.

Feeling her face now, her nose swollen, sore to the touch, a shooting pain.

She had to tell someone what he had done to her, worried now that he was going to kill her like he had said. With nowhere to go, only to Blanche's, where she felt like every move she made was under the microscope. Telling Earl would cause more trouble.

There was nothing she could do. Remembering that she had money stashed away in her suitcase, she went to the closet, pulling the red suitcase out, listening to make sure he wasn't coming. Her little hand felt around the secret pocket where her money was. The little wallet was gone.

There was no doubt in her mind, he had stolen it. For a minute she thought about taking the money and getting a train into Halifax, and she would look up Betty and Suzie. They would help her. But now, with no money to run away, she was afraid to tell Earl and the only other solution to go to Blanche and tell her what he had done to her.

Would he really kill her then, when his mother was mad at him?

Confused and dazed, she walked out to the kitchen, Elric holding Brenda over his shoulder, the baby reaching her arms out to her mother.

"Well, finally, you get up. We've already had our breakfast, and we're ready to go for a ride."

Looking from him and his Cheshire grin, and back to her baby. Walking straight to him, Elric gazing down at his pathetic wife, her nose swollen, black bruising under both eyes, her hair uncombed.

"Go and fix yourself up," he said, handing the baby to her. Keeping her eyes on Brenda, saying nothing, she walked away like walking on glass.

The baby seemed fussy today, not wanting Alice to put her down. Elric paced around the parlor now, looking out at the beautiful day, at his Cadillac waiting for him to take a ride, trying to avoid looking at her, the reminder of what he had done.

Deciding that he would go by himself, he needed time to think.

Staying in the baby's room, she washed her, holding her to her chest, trying to calm her, rocking her back and forth, back and forth, closing her eyes, pretending it was just a bad dream that she would wake from any minute.

The sound of the engine brought Alice to the window over the sink, as she watched the pretty Cadillac back out of the driveway, until there was no sign of him. Where was he going now? Really, she didn't care. She wouldn't have to side step him or stay in the room away from him altogether.

Putting the baby down in her playpen, finally going to look in the mirror at the damage she could feel her fingers telling her. It was a different Alice staring out at her, dark purple under both of her eyes, swollen lids, bloodshot in the corners of them, her sad green eyes with blood specs in the whites of them.

Was he trying to beat the beauty out of her? He had sure done a good job of it.

Starting to weep out loud now, Brenda looked up at her mom, her little mouth quivering, her big blue eyes filled to the brim. Realizing she needed to stop crying; the baby feeling her anguish. Touching the bump on the top of her nose, a sharp bone showing through her pale skin, the pain searing, "Owwwww" She cried.

Reaching for a washcloth, running it under the hottest water she could get out of the tap, holding the cloth to her face, the pain subsiding a bit. What would she do? She couldn't go anywhere looking like this, and what if Earl came to visit? Should she open the door or hide in the room with the baby? She knew there would be hell to pay for Elric when Earl saw what he had done to her face.

Driving straight to the city, he headed to the Quebec Hotel.

Missing all the attention when he was lead singer, when strangers would recognize him, giving him star treatment, it made him feel good, remembering how much attention he got from the women especially. The bartender always sent him a few free drinks, in exchange for a couple songs for the bar patrons.

One whiskey after another, Elric started singing, a few people gathering around him, a pretty lady perching herself next to him on a stool. The alcohol blurring his better judgment, slapping her on the ass as she got up to go to the bathroom. A man came up behind Elric, giving him a shot to the back of the head.

Turning around quickly, Elric took a swing at him, the strangers' friends coming to his aid. Grabbing Elric by the neck, the other three guys hauled him out of the bar onto the street, where they started to put the boots to him.

Down on the ground, his face bloodied, the kicks still coming. Drunk as he was, he knew he should protect his face and not move. When they figured they had taught him a lesson, they walked away, leaving him on the sidewalk, beaten, hopefully not dead.

Still watching as they walked out of sight, Elric didn't move. When he thought they were long gone, he pulled himself up. Standing up now, his nice clothes ruined, a blood stain on the front of his shirt, remembering for a minute, the white towel filled with Alice's blood. Did he have it coming for hurting her? Just a fleeting thought, right out the other side.

His head hurt where they had kicked him. Putting his dirtied hand up to feel the bumps. *Fucking bastards*, he said to himself. *I'll kill them all, those fuckers.*

Staggering back to his car, with no sign of any cops, Elric started up the Cadillac, heading down the road toward the countryside, back to his little wifey. He would go home and be a good boy, and make love to his little Alice. That would make her feel better.

Driving fast now, his foot to the pedal, the Cadillac moved along. Elric passing a few cars, getting too close to the oncoming traffic, almost hitting one car head on. Swerving to avoid hitting another car, causing his car to careen to the soft shoulder, sending the Cadillac into the ditch, the front end connected with a hydro pole, splitting the pole, the car almost tore in half.

Slamming his head on the steering wheel, knocking him out. Bleeding now from a new cut, smoke rising from the car. Another car coming along the other way stopped in time to pull him out of the car before it exploded, going up in flames.

The events of the night sobered him quickly. With sirens blaring, the cops arriving on the scene. Elric stood helplessly, watching his baby going up in smoke.

Recognizing him, Scott got out of the cruiser, walking over to one of his favorite conquests.

"Hey, boy, did you steal that car too? You are sure in trouble now. That was your father's car. Your ass is grass," he said, grabbing him by his wrist, cuffing him, leading him to the cruiser. Morning comes, his head pounding, the sunlight bleeding through the little window in his cell, he was fucked, remembering bits and pieces of yesterday, like his worst nightmare, come alive.

The morning guard held out a cup of coffee to Elric, telling him breakfast was coming soon. "I'm getting the hell out of here. Call my old man to bail me out."

"Sure, whatever," answered the guard. "You aren't going nowhere. A doctor will be in this morning to take a look at that gash on your head, and until the judge decides your fate, two drunk driving charges doesn't look good. You could be doing some time," said the guard, who hated the cocky, nice looking prick.

"Fuck you," Elric said under his breath, going back to his hard bed, trying to cover with the itchy grey prison blanket.

Earl noticed the familiar sight, a cop car coming to his office again. What now? He said to himself. Getting up from his desk walking out of the office.

Standing, waiting for them to get out of the cruiser. Two officers gave Earl the news.

"Your boy is up to no good again. Your yellow and white Cadillac is a write off. Wrapped it around a hydro pole."

"Oh my God," said Earl, putting his hand to his head. "And what about him? Is he hurt?"

"Yeah, he's busted up pretty good, lacerations to the head. He could have a concussion, head injury for sure."

"Oh no," he answered, thinking of little Alice. He would have to go and bring her the bad news. Fuck the bastard, thought Earl. Now that the cops were charging him with the busted up hydro pole, and it was his car as far as they knew. That Widdy was causing him more problems, and he was sick of the cops coming to his business to bring news of his foolish son. What the hell was he going to do now? No car. He would have to let him use the Studebaker full time. The old car was good enough to go up the mountain to work, good enough for him to ride anywhere else too.

That boy had no appreciation for nothing. He was disgusting him, shaking his head, trying to shake him off altogether. His mind on Alice, he told the cops he would come down later to bail him out. "That's if the judge lets him out," said the uniformed cop. "He might do time. It's his second offense. He will definitely lose his license, and probably a hefty fine, at best."

Earl shook his head, walking back into his office, sitting down at his desk, thinking of what to do next. *Go and see Alice and the baby*, came back the words, in his head.

Putting on his coat and fedora, Earl closed his office door, locking it, checking it again. It was locked. He would go and see Alice and the baby, call it a day.

Going straight to the house, Earl pulled into the driveway. No lights on in the house. She had to be there. He hadn't taken them with him. "Thank God," he said. Knocking at the door now, he stood waiting. No answer. He knocked again. Alice was holding her baby, going to the nursery, closing the door, tears coming now. She couldn't open the door, and she knew it was not Elric. He wouldn't be knocking.

Peeking out the window, she noticed it was Earl's car and decided she had better go to the door. It was getting near dark, and Elric was still not home. Maybe she should tell him what he had done to her. He would help her, maybe take her to stay with him or with Blanche. She had to tell him the truth. It was her only hope for safety for her and her baby.

Just as Earl was getting back into his car, Alice opened the door. Earl noticed her, standing with the baby in her arms. Walking to her now, he came up the steps, noticing Alice's face black and blue, her face swollen, her eyes red.

"What has happened to you, dear?" he said, taking Brenda from her, kissing his granddaughter on the cheek.

Trying to hide her face from him, Alice walked to the table in the kitchen. Earl sat down, Brenda on his knee.

"Looks like you were in a car accident," he said. "You weren't with Elric, were you?"

"Oh no. What are you saying?" asked Alice, trying to hide her broken nose with her little hand.

"Did he do this to you, dear?"

Alice started crying out loudly, Brenda watching her mom, the baby started to cry too.

"No, baby, don't cry," urged Earl, holding her close to him, Alice wiping at her eyes.

"He beat me because I went to your house, and he burned the books in the stove, the books you loaned me."

"Are you kidding me? That fool, he is no son of mine. Oh my God, dear, let me see your face. You might need to go to see Doc Thompson." Looking closer at the bone sticking up on the top of her nose.

"Get yourself and the baby ready. Bring enough clothes for a week. We are going to do something about this now, before it's too late. As for him, he can rot in there. He's in jail, wrecked the car, and has to face the judge tomorrow, drunk driving again. He won't be hurting you anymore, dear, not on my watch," said Earl, feeling so bad for the little girl, woman. "He doesn't deserve you. I knew that all along."

Helping Alice get the baby's things together, Alice packed a suitcase with the baby's clothes and a few outfits for herself.

They closed up the house, turning off all the lights, Earl helping them into the back seat of the car, driving down the road toward his house. "Tomorrow, I will take you and Brenda to stay with Blanche," said Earl, looking back at Alice in the rear view mirror. "You will be safe there until we figure out what is going to happen to him."

Holding the baby close to her, Brenda fell asleep. Alice laid her down on the seat next to her, looking at her little princess. All the hurt that had been inflicted on her, she would die to protect her little one. Would he really hurt her baby? She didn't know, and the not knowing was scaring her more than anything.

The next morning, Earl decided it was time to go and find out what they were going to do with Elric and when he would be getting out of jail. He talked to the cop on duty, who looked over his notes and told Earl that there was going to be a hearing for Elric, and it wasn't until next week Monday, today being Sunday. He would have to spend a whole week in jail before he came before the judge. Earl wondered if he should come to his aid, tell them that he had been working for him in the bush and that he had a wife and baby to look after. Whatever, Earl thought to himself, he wasn't doing anything of the sort. Elric was on a real collision course, with everything and everyone in his way. Leaving the police station, heavy hearted, without asking to see him.

Should he really take Alice to Blanche's house? Alice didn't seem too thrilled about the idea. He could just let her stay at his house, or she could go back to her house, seeing that Elric wasn't going to be home for a while. Regardless, he should probably let Alice decide.

Getting the baby some breakfast, Alice tried to have something to eat herself. Running to the bathroom, she threw up, her stomach upset, her nerves on edge. Not thinking there was anything really wrong, she cleaned herself up, managing to get some tea down without getting sick again. Being too embarrassed to tell the doctor what he had done to her, she decided she would tell Earl she was fine and didn't want to see the doctor.

Her face was swollen, her eyes black, her nose twice the size as usual, frightening her when she looked at her reflection, getting away from the mirror quickly. Not wanting anyone to see her like this, she decided she would ask Earl to let her stay at his house. Blanche would want to know all the details, and Alice was trying to avoid any more drama.

Waiting for Earl to return, she kept the baby quiet, giving her some toys. Alice went back to the study, looked over some of the books, trying to get into someone else's world, hers falling apart around her.

Hearing the sound of the Cadillac engine, Alice watched out the picture window to see Earl getting out of the car, approaching the house. As she waited near the door, Earl walked in, taking off his boots, looking at his daughter in law, pity written on his face.

"We have to talk about Widdy," he said. "Come on, let's have some tea."

"I just had tea," she answered, going to the kitchen, putting the kettle on the stove.

Sitting at the table, she waited to hear the outcome. Earl looked up at her, tears in his eyes. "I hate to see you like this, dear. What do you say you stay here for a while? Elric is not getting out of jail for at least a week. He's been in an accident. The car is totalled.

"What?" she said.

"He is pretty banged up too, probably has a concussion, but they are not letting him out of jail until he comes before the judge. They have charged him with drinking and driving again. He will surely lose his license and a hefty fine probably, that's if he is lucky. Maybe he will do some time, we will just have to wait and see."

Blindly staring at Earl, not saying a word, thinking of what was going to happen to her baby and her. "Don't worry, dear, you can either stay here with me, or go back to the house."

"Oh no, please, I don't want to go back there alone."

"Fine then, it is decided. You and Brenda will stay here with me."

"Thank you," she said, tears coming to her eyes, Earl reaching for her, holding her tight.

"Don't cry now, you and Brenda are welcome to stay here with me forever, if needed. I think we ought to get you to see the doctor, Alice, what do you think? How about tomorrow?"

"Oh no, I am fine. My nose is really sore, but it looks better already," she said. Earl surveying her bruised face, realizing why she didn't want to go.

"Fine then. We got to get Elric straightened around, if that is at all possible."

Relieved that she didn't have to see him for a while, Alice settled into the guest room, putting Brenda's things in the dresser, unpacking the suitcase and arranging her few clothing items in the closet.

The next day, Earl went to the office for a few hours, the baby and Alice on his mind. He closed early, heading home. There was a nice dinner on the table, Earl sitting down to enjoy a home cooked meal with his daughter in law. Brenda sat at the table eating mashed potatoes with some gravy and a few small pieces of chicken. "When we are finished, I'll take you to the house to get the rest of your things."

"Thank you," she answered, getting up to clean up the dishes, putting things away.

Loading them into the car, Earl headed toward the little house, about fifteen minutes on the highway, deep into the countryside.

Pulling up in front, there is no sign of life or lights in the house. Earl went in first, Alice and Brenda coming up the stairs. An eerie feeling in the air, even Earl feeling it.

"I am right here. Go ahead, get what you need. I'll play with Brenda while you get your things together."

Walking into the bedroom, she noticed the picture of the Virgin Mary face down on the floor, glass sprayed around the frame, a blood stain showing near the picture.

"Oh my God," she said out loud. Earl running to the room, noticing the red stain, and a picture on the floor, glass everywhere.

"What is it, Alice?"

"Just the picture. It has fallen, and is broken."

"Wonder what happened there?" he said, walking out of the bedroom, Alice trying to pick up the glass. Walking back in to see if she is all right, he noticed her bent down, picking up the splinters of glass.

Alice tried to clean up the blood stains from the carpet, even after scrubbing with soap and a brush, a faint outline of red.

"Just leave that for now, Alice. You can clean it up when you come back."

"OK," she said, leaving the picture, going to the dresser, taking out the things she wanted.

Heading to the baby's room, filling the diaper bag, taking one last look around, glad that she was leaving this house. There was just something she couldn't put her finger on, a creepy feeling, like someone was watching. And the picture, how had it fallen?

Walking quickly back out to the kitchen, Earl grabbed up the bags that she had brought out. Alice took Brenda's hand, leading her out of the house, down the steps to the awaiting car.

Wasting no time, Earl made it back to his house, helping them in. Alice and the baby settled into the guest room. Walking toward his own room, he opened the guest room door and looked in.

"Good night Alice," he said.

"Good night," she replied. Holding the baby close to her, Brenda going to sleep right away, Alice laying awake for a long time, the events going through her mind like a whirlwind. Feeling like she had been to hell and back, sick to her stomach, with a baby to care for. The dark clouds in her world had all but taken her sunshine away. Feeling her baby close to her, the only ray of light she had to hold on to. Not knowing what tomorrow would bring, she prayed to God to give her the strength to go on for her little one. Finally, she fell asleep, her arms wrapped around her angel.

The week was almost up, Alice started worrying about Elric coming out of jail soon.

The morning of the court hearing, Earl went to the courtroom, speaking for Elric. "He is my son, and he has a job with me and a wife and child to support."

"I will release him in your care," said the judge.

"Don't let me see you before me again, Elric, or you are going away for a long time," the judge said, ending the hearing,

Earl took him back to the house, going in with him.

"Where is Alice and the baby?" asked Elric, looking around, the house cold, no sign of his family.

"They are staying with me right now, and they will stay with me until I see fit."

"What does that mean, exactly? She is my wife."

"She is not your wife to mistreat. What is wrong with you? I will put you back in jail myself, if you ever hurt her again, and another thing, she will come to my place any time she wants."

"Whatever, I want my family back home with me! When are you going to bring them back?"

"You are going back to work tomorrow. I will bring them back when I think it is safe for them to be around you. I'm just not sure when. The judge let you out in my care, and any little thing, your ass is going back there for a long time. Do you get it?"

Mad, he walked away from his father, going into the bedroom. The picture was still on the floor. Bending down, he picked it up, a shard of glass stuck in his hand.

"Fuck," he said, blood dripping from his hand onto the rose colored carpet, noticing the blood stain, near the picture. "Fucking dumb picture, never did like this thing."

Picking it up, he heads to the door, throwing it out in the yard. Earl watched his son storming to the door. "Bad luck shit," he said, going back to the bathroom, looked for a bandage for his hand.

Earl had to watch his step, going out, glass shards on the step, he shakes his head at the aggression of his fool son. What would he do with him?

By the next day, the cut on Elric's hand is infected, yellow puss showing in the gash a few inches in length. "Shit, didn't know it cut me like that," he said, going for the alcohol to cleanse the cut.

With his hand bandaged now, he gets into bed, turning off the light. In the middle of the night, he is awakened by a high pitched scream. Thinking he must have been dreaming, turning on the light. "What the fuck was that?" He says to himself. Getting up now, he looked around the house, deciding to lay down on the sofa to sleep. Coming to the conclusion, he must have just imagined the screaming.

The next morning, he gets up, ate breakfast, put on his work clothes, waiting for Earl to come for him. His father arrived shortly after nine, seeing the picture of the Virgin Mary on the lawn outside, deciding to take it to the shed, behind the house. Taking a closer look, the glass completely broken out, a scrape down the side of Mary's face leading from her eye, making it look like a stream of tears.

"Oh my God," said Earl to himself, turning the picture toward the wall, heading back into the house, standing at the door.

"Let's get this day on the road. Got to get you up the mountain. You have disrupted my life too, son. Now I am looking after what is supposed to be yours."

Walking toward his father, his chainsaw in hand, his pack over his back. "I'm ready," he announced, trying not to make eye contact. "When can I see my family?"

"When I bring you home, we will see if Alice wants to come home to you." Elric shook his head, mad that his father was interfering with his family.

"They are not yours to hurt, Elric. Can you get that through your head? You will lose them too, if you don't change your ways." Elric goes quiet, thinking of actually losing his wife and baby. They were his, and his father could not keep him away from them.

The whole way up the mountain, Earl lectured his son until Elric wanted to cut him up in little pieces, with the big toothed monster that sat next to him. Thinking of his car, what car? There was no car left, totalled, they had said. With nothing much left of his savings, he would have to drive the old Studebaker to and from. Surely his father would let him use it.

"You will stay in camp until I come to get you."

"What do you mean?"

"You need some time to think about where your life is going, time to think about what you have done."

"Whatever," he said under his breath.

"There will be no car for you to use, either. I will come and get you when I see fit." Not answering his father, he waited until the car pulled up to the campsite, taking out his things, walking to the bunkhouse, not looking back.

The next morning at the campsite, Elric heading into the cookhouse for some breakfast, not making any small talk with the other guys. Going back to the bunkhouse, heading up the mountain, chainsaw in hand. His hand hurt him so much, he had to use his left hand to hold the heavy machine, all day, his hand throbbing with pain. Noticing blood seeping through the bandage, he cursed the picture, all day long.

It was a long hard week for Elric, thinking of what he had done, his family now taken from him, his father his warden. The more he thought about the situation, the madder he got, the more trees he cut down. Working like a son of a bitch, he cut down more trees in one week than the rest of the crew did in a month.

When his father came to camp, he realized that his boy was working hard. Taking him aside, telling him he wanted to talk to him. "Look, Elric, I am not sure what is wrong with Alice, but she is getting rather thin, and she has not been eating. Not only that, she has been throwing up again, and you know what that means. She is probably pregnant again. I don't know what to do. She didn't want to go to the doctor, so I am taking her to your mother's for a while. Maybe Blanche can figure out what is wrong with her."

"How is the baby?"

"She is fine, Alice looks after her well. It's Alice I am worried about. Her face has all but healed up, no thanks to you.

"I tell you, son, if you ever lay another hand on her, it will be all over. I will banish you from my life forever, and I will see to it that you lose your little family you pretend to care about."

"I do care about them. I love them! They are mine," he said.

"Whatever, Elric that is all I have to say to you right now. You will stay in camp another week. I'll ask Alice is she wants to see you."

In the next few days, Earl decided that he would go to Blanche and fill her in on the new developments, maybe ask her advice. Taking her aside, Tom trying to hear what Earl was saying. Blanche held her hand to her mouth, saddened by the news.

"Just bring her and the baby here. They are better here with me. I can help Alice with Brenda, and I will get Alice to the doctor. Maybe it is just her nerves making her sick."

He agreed he would bring the baby and Alice there the next day, giving him some relief, and his quiet house back.

Wide eyed, she listened intently to the new hand she was being dealt.

"You and the baby are better off with Blanche for a while. She can help you with the baby, and she misses seeing you and Brenda."

"OK then," answered Alice, weary. "If that's what you think is best."

"For right now, it is. We'll give Widdy some more time by himself. Maybe he will straighten out, that's all we can hope for."

"Sure," answered Alice, going to the guest room, starting to pack up the baby's things.

Waiting for Earl to take the bags out to the car, Alice sat with Brenda, thinking of the new hand she was dealt. Her life wasn't her own anymore, she just had to go with the flow.

Blanche welcomed them with open arms, getting the guest room ready before they arrived. Not saying a thing about what Earl had told her, she pretended everything was fine, not wanting to remind Alice of the terrible things that Elric had done to her. "You don't look well, my dear," she commented at the dinner table. "I think we should go to see old Doc Thompson. What do you think, dear?"

"Sure," answered Alice, knowing there was something wrong with her. Suspecting what she feared the most, another baby growing inside of her. With one to look after, and a husband who had turned out to be the enemy, thoughts of another child saddened her, making her feel weak and helpless.

Blanche did everything she could to make Alice and the baby feel welcome, telling Alice she could stay as long as she liked. Inside she was seething. Her son was a woman beater. She hated him now, realizing they had a real problem on their hands.

Tom watched Brenda while Blanche and Alice went to see the doctor.

"Well, how are you, my dear?" asked the doctor. "You look a little pale. Have you been eating?"

"Not much, have no appetite, and I am throwing up almost every morning now."

"Come over here. Just sit up there, and I will examine you." Noticing the bump on her nose, he asked her, "What had happened there?"

"Oh, just banged my face on the cupboard door," she said, thinking quickly. The doctor put his finger on the bone that showed slightly on the bridge of her nose. "Looks like you might have broken it, but it is healed. Can't really notice it," he said, trying to make her feel better.

Upon examination, telling her to put her clothes back on, he went to his desk to make some notes. "Have a seat here, dear," he said, looking into her sad green eyes. "It's what I suspected. You are expecting another baby."

"Oh no," she said putting her hands up to her face, crying now, the tears flowing like rain water down a windowpane.

"Don't cry, dear, it happens. We will get you on some pills when this baby comes, so you won't be having one every nine months. Some women just keep having them. I see it all the time. Here, now, wipe those tears. Come and see me when you start showing, and we'll check to see that everything is all right. You have to try and eat though, dear. You are mighty thin. A baby won't get any nourishment if you don't eat."

"Yes, Doctor," she said, walking out of the office, Blanche waiting for her in her car outside.

"Well, are you pregnant?"

"Yes, ma'am," answered Alice. Blanche noticing her tear stained face. "It will be all right, dear. I will help you, any way I can."

"Thank you," Alice replied, settling into the seat, staring out the window as Blanche drove back to the house. Blanche tried to make small talk, noticing that Alice was far off, her eyes wide a blankness overshadowing her.

Earl left his son in camp for three weeks before he decided that he would let him see his wife and baby. He dressed, had breakfast, happy to see his family again. Deciding he would smarten up, his world falling apart around him, and it was all his fault. After he promised Earl that he would never lay another hand on Alice, Earl gave him the keys for the Studebaker, leaving Elric alone at the little house.

Making a fire in the woodstove, he looked around the little bungalow, all alone, realizing he needed to stay straight, go and get his family and bring them home.

Blanche and Brenda were sitting on the porch when the old Studebaker pulled up in the yard, Blanche getting up, going into the house, holding on to Brenda's hand and leading her in. "Alice, Alice," she shouted. "Widdy is here." Hearing Blanche's announcement, Alice swallowed hard, looking out the window of the guest room. There he was, trudging slowly toward the house. The screen door slammed, Elric standing in the foyer. Everyone had scattered, no sign of anyone when Tom showed up in the hallway. "I suppose you are here to see Alice?" he said, moving toward Elric, cane in one hand, his spectacles sitting on the end of his nose.

"Yes, can you get them for me?" asked Elric.

"Just a minute," said Tom, walking to the kitchen where Blanche sat with Brenda on her knee. "Come in here," Tom said, heading toward the kitchen. Elric took off his boots and walked to the doorway, looked in at his baby and his mother. Brenda looked at him, wide eyed, no smile. Elric smiled. "It's Daddy," he said in baby talk. Brenda turned her face to her grandmother now, hugging in closer, dropping her head into Blanche's chest. "Fine then," he said, Blanche motioning to him to come and sit.

Before she could say a thing, Elric spoke. "OK, Mother, I know what I have done is wrong, and I am so sorry to have hurt my little wife, but I am a changed man, and I promise I will never hurt her again."

Blanche looked at her son, a blank look on her face. Alice appeared in the doorway now, gazing at her husband, who looked softly her way, putting out his arms to her. "Come here, little one," he said. "Please, come to me." Her eyes filled with tears, Alice walking to him, Elric sitting her on his lap. "Can we start over? Please," he begged.

Searching into his softened grey eyes, like clouds, on a rainy day.

"I'll leave you guys alone," said Blanche getting up from the table, Brenda hanging on to her legs. "Go see your Daddy," she said to Brenda. Elric put his arms out to the baby. Brenda stared at her father, walking slowly to him, looking into his eyes, searching for love.

Elric was so overwhelmed, he put his head on Alice's shoulder and started to cry. "Sorry, guys," he said, picking up Brenda now, setting her on the other knee. "How about a kiss for Daddy," he said, holding his baby close to his chest, kissing her on her cheek. "You got bigger," he said. Brenda trying to go to her mother now. "Oh, I see how it is. Don't love me anymore?"

"She just hasn't seen you in a while, Elric," said Alice.

"Come on, baby," said Blanche from the doorway. "Let your mom and dad have some time to themselves," she said, holding her arms out to her granddaughter.

"I need you guys to come home now. The little house is so quiet without you and Brenda, and I hear that you have some news for me. Are we having another baby?"

"Yes," she answered quietly, Elric hugging her close to him. "It is going to be all right, you will see. Can you just give me one more chance?"

Before the day was out, Elric had packed up his little family, taking them back to the house, Alice getting the baby settled in, putting the clothes and things back in the dressers, attempting to scrub out the memories of the beating in the bedroom, still a visible stain.

Blanche had watched from the porch with mixed feelings. She hoped that everything would be all right, but something deep inside of her made her heart bleed for Alice. Her son was some kind of monster. She hated him.

Things got back to normal, Elric working hard in the bush, coming home to his little family, spending time with them. Alice started to feel loved again. There hadn't been any more incidents of abuse. Alice looked forward to the days when he would come home from work, even the baby loving the time spent with her dad. Watching Elric with Brenda made Alice's heart glad. He was a good father, as long as the old Elric didn't come back to them. She was getting on with her pregnancy, her stomach rounded, six months now, keeping a close check on the calendar Dr. Thompson had given her. The doctor had told her to come for a checkup around then, and she told Elric she had to go to see the doctor. "I'll get my father to take you during the week," he said, Alice's eyes growing wide. "Its fine, I know that he still comes around here when I am not here, but after all, he is the grandfather to our child, and with another one coming and all." Really he was trying to get into his father's good graces again, thinking of trying to make a deal on another car, hoping his dad would give him one on credit, and take so much out of every pay.

Getting up the nerve to ask his father about a car on credit, Earl turned him down flat.

"What do you need with a fancy car? The Studebaker gets you from A to B, seems to me you just want to show off. That's why you have been staying close to home, ashamed of the old car, are you? Got nobody to blame but yourself." Earl chastised.

'Fuck you," Elric said under his breath. His father, hearing the curse words, walking away from him.

"You can't fool me. You haven't changed a bit. Think you can fool Alice, but I see you for what you are, a maniac. You don't deserve little Alice. It's just too bad she ended up with the likes of you."

Just staring his father's way, not saying a word, he knew he was better off. Without his old man, he wouldn't have a job, and now with another baby on the way, he needed his job more than ever. He would find a way to get another car, with or without his father.

Earl had been by, visiting, telling Alice that Blanche wanted to see her and the baby, maybe the next weekend when Widdy was home from work. Mentioning it to Elric, he agreed to take them to see his mother. Alice dressed in a loose fitting dress, fixing her hair, putting on a little rouge and lipstick. When Elric put Brenda in the back seat, he looked over at his wife, the makeup on her face enraging him. "You look like a fucking whore with all that makeup on your face."

Alice's smile soon faded. Reaching into her purse for some tissue, tears in her eyes, wiping at the lipstick, her mascara running in dark rivers down her cheeks.

"Stop your fucking crying, or I'll give you something to cry about," he threatened. Alice's nerves on edge, the baby in her belly tossing around, a tightening feeling in her stomach. *Relax, relax*, she told herself, rubbing her tummy. Elric got in behind the wheel.

"Please, Elric, don't upset the baby," she said, looking over at him.

"Don't think you can use that one on me. Fuck the baby," he said, his eyes wide, his movements quick, pulling the car out onto the road, staring ahead. Brenda sat quiet, watching and noticing the changes in their voices, Elric's voice loud, scaring her. Starting to whimper now, Elric turning to her.

"Shut the fuck up! Shut up!" he yelled. Brenda scared now, reaching her little arms toward her mother. Turning around, he shoved her back onto the seat. "Sit down, and shut up," he ordered. Brenda goes quiet, her big blue eyes the size of saucers. Alice too scared to say anything, the baby in her moving, uneasy.

The ride to Blanche's was the longest ride of Alice's life, praying that he wouldn't hurt them, his voice raised, the monster at the wheel.

When the car finally pulled into the yard, Alice was relieved they had arrived unharmed. Blanche noticed right away that there was something wrong. Alice's eyes bloodshot, the baby agitated. "Is everything all right?" she asked Alice.

Elric walked past her, bringing in the baby's bag, then walked back out of the house. "Yes, we are fine," said Alice, watching Elric walk back out the door.

"You guys are just in time to have some lunch with us, tuna fish sandwiches and pea soup," Blanche said, Elric hearing the menu. From the minute he stepped into that house, he wanted to leave but decided he would wait until they had some lunch, and then he would make an excuse to leave early.

While the women put the finishing touches on the lunch, bringing things to the table, Elric paced around the outside of the house and then back in. He said a few things to Tom, who just nodded, sticking his nose back in his paper. "Stupid old fucker," said Elric under his breath, "must be senile." Tom watching him out of the corner of his eye.

"Lunch is served," said Blanche, going to the porch to get Tom. Alice helped Brenda up to the table, Elric taking a seat next to the baby.

Everyone ate in silence. Blanche couldn't help but notice Alice picking at her food. Elric ate his food fast, getting up and away from the table. Cleaning up the table, doing the dishes, Alice felt tired all of a sudden, and she sat back down for a breather. The baby was larger this time, taking up a lot of space under her rib cage. Just then, Elric appeared in the doorway.

"Get the kid ready. I want to go home." Looking from him to Blanche, and then back to the baby.

"Sure, I'll just finish up the dishes, and we'll get ready to go."

"Fine," he said, walking back out of the house. Blanche walked over to Alice.

"What is wrong with him today?"

"I think it started when he had an argument with his father. Asked him to give him a car on credit, and Earl flatly refused. Then he got mad at me, because I was wearing makeup," she answered nervously.

"That is so foolish. Women like to look pretty," she said. "Don't worry, dear. Remember, you can't be getting upset. You have a baby in your belly who knows and feels everything." Just then, Alice felt the baby kick, holding her stomach, her emotions on a roller coaster. Trying to stay happy for her baby, but how could she when she was scared of him. That look in his eye today reminded her that the monster was still alive.

As she dressed Brenda in her little coat, Alice started to worry about the ride home. Should she refuse to leave and let him go home alone to stew in his anger? Regardless, she got herself ready, walking out to the porch, Elric already sitting in the front seat of the old car. Blanche watched with a keen eye, the son she didn't know and hated, taking his little family away again. Worried for them now, Blanche couldn't get her mind off the state he was in. "Just like a time bomb, that boy," she said to Tom, who just looked up from his paper, saying nothing.

"Stupid men anyway," said Blanche, going back into the house.

They were just a ways down the road when Elric spoke, Alice listening intently, holding Brenda in her arms. "Don't ask me to take you to that fat bitch again any time soon," he said, looking over at Alice. Brenda just falling asleep in her mother's arms.

"That's fine, I won't," she agreed in a whispered voice, looking down at the baby. "I noticed that you are not comfortable there, and if you are not, I can't be either."

"Really, didn't know that you cared."

"Well, you hardly said boo the whole time we were there," said Alice.

"I just don't like that bitch of a thing. She asks too many questions and is trying to come between us."

"No one can do that," answered Alice, thinking fast, looking for the right thing to say. Looked back over at her, he shrugged, watching intently out the window, driving his family home.

Getting home before dark, he helped Alice and the baby into the house, then went back out to the car. Watching him, Alice noticed that he had changed his jacket and had combed his hair before leaving the house. Before she had time to ask him where he was going, he was already long gone, down the driveway. About a half an hour later, she heard the door open, and in stepped Elric with a few cartons of take-out food. "Thought I would bring dinner, so you wouldn't have to prepare it," he said putting the boxes down on the kitchen table. With a sigh of relief, Alice sat Brenda down, joining her husband and baby, enjoying the Chinese take-out food, noodles, and some kind of meat and vegetables.

"Thank you for dinner," she said, getting up to clean the table.

"Just leave it. I will clean up. Let's just go into the parlor and relax."

Taking a double take at the change that had come over him, Alice ushered Brenda into the parlor, setting up some blocks for her that Earl had brought for his granddaughter. Elric joined in, helping Brenda build a few towers and a boat, and a few other things that didn't resemble anything. They all had a good laugh about the building block creations, Brenda laughing right along with her mom and dad.

They spent a few hours together, until Brenda's eyes started to get sleepy, Alice excused herself, going to the nursery, taking her baby in, covering her, kissing her good-night. It had been such a lovely evening, just the three of them, wishing they had more times like these, not being able to remember the last time she was so happy. Elric waited for her in the parlor, pulling her to him, hugging and kissing her, falling asleep on the couch, his head in her lap. Trying not to wake him, she slowly slipped away, going for a blanket to cover him, making her way to the bedroom to put away some clothes and things. Rolling down the sheets, she thought she would go and wake him, get him into bed, where he would have a much better sleep. Doing just that, Elric followed her into the bedroom, Alice joining him, laying with her back to him so she could feel him close. It wasn't long before they were fast asleep. Alice turned over, trying to get herself comfortable. Before long, she went into a dream.

She was in the bathroom of the house they lived in now. When she turned on the water, the water turned to blood, her hands and arms covered now in thick, sticky blood. "Noooo," she screamed in her dream. No noise came out. Looking around now, a white towel hanging on the towel rack over the sink, the same picture of the Virgin Mary watching her. Ripping at the towel, she wiped her hands as she watched the sink fill to the brim, blood spilling all over the floor.

Looking down at her feet, her shoes filling full of blood, her hands and arms and legs stained in the thick, dark red blood. Trying to get out of the bathroom, she fell down, her clothes now bloodstained.

Struggling, the floor slimy, trying to get up, she fell again, this time face down, her hair, her face, her whole body stained blood red, screaming and screaming. Finally, she woke herself from the dream, sitting straight up in the bed, her eyes bulging like a night owl.

Elric was also awakened by the screams. He looked over at her, staring into space.

"Ae you all right? You were screaming. Were you dreaming?"

"Yes, just a nightmare," she said, her eyes glazed. Slipping his arm over her rounded stomach. "It's OK now, honey, no one can hurt you. I am here. The screams that were coming out of you were blood curdling. You scared me too."

"Weird actually, this house is really freaking me out. When you were away at my father's, I heard screams like that in this house. In this bedroom too. It was so loud, it woke me."

"Oh my God," she said, turning to face him now, "I didn't want to tell you, but the picture spoke to me more than once when I was here alone, and she was in the dream, watching me. It was so scary, oh, oh," she said, holding him tight.

"This fucking place is haunted," he said. "That's why my old man was so quick to sell it to me, and at a great price too."

"I don't want to believe that," she answered, closing her eyes, falling asleep in his arms.

It had been a great weekend, all but the terrible dream that kept coming back to her again and again. Dreaming had become an open book for Alice lately, she realized. Her dreams were trying to tell her something. All that blood, oh my God. Cupping her hands on her stomach, the baby moving inside her. No, it couldn't mean anything. It was just a dream, she tried to tell herself over and over.

The fact that he had hurt her a lot already, and the last time he had threatened to kill her, bringing the dream back in three dimensions.

Was it telling her something? Warning her of some impending danger? Terrible things were running through her mind. Was Brenda in danger? Was her unborn baby in danger? Thinking realistically for a few minutes, she summed up her fears. The one who professed to love her could turn on her in a heartbeat and rip her heart out, literally. Her mind racing, her heart beating too fast, the baby inside turning somersaults. *Relax, don't think bad things,* she told herself, rubbing her stomach.

Watching Elric pack the Studebaker with his chainsaw and tools, dressed in his heavy work clothes, waving from the car. Alice, held Brenda, now peering out the window. "Wave to Daddy," she said, Brenda just keeping her eyes on his every move. With Elric long gone, Alice made Brenda some breakfast, oatmeal with raisins and some toast, making herself some eggs and toast. They sat quietly, eating, watching each other, Alice smiling at her beautiful baby, Brenda at ease, finishing her porridge.

It was a perfect sunny day, a good day for them to take a long walk down the country road, maybe pick some wildflowers. Taking the calendar off the wall, she sat down at the table, thinking of when the new baby would arrive. Late January or early February. Remembering the doctor had said to come back for a checkup, she would ask Earl to take her to see Dr. Thompson.

With all the housework done, Alice dressed the baby, put her in the push along stroller, getting herself ready and off they went down the road. It was a beautiful autumn day, the sun still warm in the sky, a pretty bouquet of fallen leaves on the ground, Brenda pointing to the leaves, Alice picking up a few for her to hold while they walked along. Happy, she reflected on the wonderful day they had spent with Elric yesterday.

Something had come over him since they left Blanche's. Going from madman to lover, all within a few hours. So changeable, she thought. Really she never knew what to expect from him anymore, making her so nervous all the time.

Remembering how frightened she had been on the ride to his mother's brought back the fear that sat so close to the surface, looking down at her baby girl. Things had sure changed for her, and quickly, her large rounded stomach in front of her reminding her, of more changes to come. Would he finally settle down? Be a good father and husband to her? She could only wish. Tears tried to come. Wiping at her eyes, enjoying the walk with her baby girl, the late fall flowers lining a ditch, a few pretty horses in a field. Stopping to let Brenda look at the horses. "Horsie, horsie," she pointed, laughing. "Maybe Daddy will get you a horse one day, sweetie," she said, not believing the notion herself.

Getting back to the house, she made a light lunch, put Brenda down for her afternoon nap. Sitting in the parlor, she picked up a book she had started reading. The house was silent, only the hum of the refrigerator. Gazing around at the perfect little house, loving it when it was cleaned with the bleach effect. Elric just wanted to say something about his father selling him a haunted house. He never had much to say about Earl, hardly ever anything nice, and if it wasn't for him, they wouldn't even have a house. Without him, they wouldn't have anything, she thought.

Just then, she heard the familiar sound of a Cadillac engine. It was Earl. Getting up from the couch, she heads to the window over the sink, watching Earl approaching the house, his arms filled with parcels. Opening the door, she greeted him with a kiss on the cheek.

"Hi there, thought I would drop in, was just in the neighborhood," he said, walking past her with his hands full of wrapped presents. Putting them down on the table, he looked over at Alice.

'How are you, dear?"

"I am fine. Why do you ask?"

"Well, I happened to be in the vicinity of Blanche's and stopped in to visit her and Tom. She mentioned that Elric was acting weird yesterday when you and him were there, something about you wearing makeup."

"Oh, it was nothing. He just doesn't want me to wear makeup, said it was too much, so I just rubbed it off, and then everything was fine."

"Don't know what we are going to do with that boy. His moods are like the shifting sands in the desert, never knowing if your foothold is good or not."

Alice just looked at her father-in-law, knowing that what he was saying was true. Hugging her hard, Alice lingering in the hug. "My goodness, the little one is sure growing. Can hardly get my arms around you." She laughed and went for the kettle to make some tea.

The whole week was glorious, Earl taking them shopping, Brenda getting anything she pointed at, Earl spoiling his granddaughter and loving it.

"So what do you think you will have this time, Alice?"

"Pretty sure it is a boy," she said. "He kicks real hard, and look at how much bigger I am."

"Should we pick out a name for him?"

"Well, Elric might have something to say about that," she answered.

"Whatever, surely you could name your own child. Let's call him Henry Earl, after his grandfathers. What do you think?"

"Actually, I like the sound of that name," she said smiling.

CHAPTER 82

Keeping his nose to the grindstone, rather, chainsaw, all week, he put out more logs than three men. Working diligently, the chainsaw in his big hands, his back strong his leg muscles aching after a long day in the bush. The noise from the chainsaw drowns out away all his thoughts. Just hold tight and watch overhead, another one down, then he ripped at the limbs with the sharp toothed beast destroying everything in its path. It was when he had settled into the bunkhouse for the night that the thoughts would come. What was she doing right now? Who might have dropped by? Was his father eating and laughing and spending time with his wife? It was driving him crazy, being away from her for the whole week not knowing what was going on. By the end of the week, he was growing anxious. Earl had left the Studebaker with him, so he could take himself back down the mountain at the end of the work week. Packing up his things in the car, he decided he would wait until early morning and get back to his little family.

First thing in the morning, he headed out to his car, a sigh of relief. No work for two days. He hadn't been to town now for a couple of months, the thought of tying one on giving him some reprieve from his duties. Work, and then his other responsibilities, a wife and baby, and another on the way.

Earl hadn't budged about letting him have another nice car, making him mad. *I work my ass off= for that son of a bitch, and he can't find it in his heart? Fuck him,* he said to himself. Deciding that he needed a night on the town, he would go and spend the day with Alice and Brenda and take off early in the night, go and let loose for a while. This tied down life was making him old. Missing the attention when he had the band, now he was just another pretty face.

Noticing the car pulling up the driveway, Alice and Brenda stood in the doorway, watching Elric come into the house.

"Hey, sweet cheeks," he said, grabbing Alice, looking at the rounded stomach keeping them apart.

"My God, look like you swallowed an elephant," he said. They laughed at that comment.

"Yeah, I think we have a son this time. I am much bigger than with Brenda."

"Probably just eating too much," he said.

"No, actually, haven't been eating a lot."

"Must be all those chocolates that Earl brings around here. Not good for Brenda's teeth. Going to tell him to eat them himself."

Just then, Alice noticed the tone of his voice had changed, walking away from him, going to do something in Brenda's room.

Elric hadn't made any demands of her. Alice fixed him some lunch, salmon sandwiches and a big cup of steaming coffee. Noticing a change in his demeanor, finding him in the bathroom, fixing his hair, a fresh white shirt on, his black dress pants and shiny black shoes.

"Are we going somewhere?" she asked, quietly, standing in the doorway.

"You are not going anywhere with that big belly. You had better stay home and put up your feet."

"Oh no, please, can you take Brenda and me out somewhere, maybe just a ride in the country?"

"You want to ride in that piece of shit car? Where is your head, woman? In the clouds, I would say. Isn't it enough that Earl sports you and Brenda around all week in his big Cadillac? Think you would have had enough driving around," he said, still fixing his hair in the mirror, having not turned to talk to her.

"Go and do something with yourself. You look pale and fat," he said. Alice walked away from him, going to the bedroom, closing the door. Throwing herself on the bed, burying her head in the pillow, the tears flowing, staining the pillow case.

Hearing the door slam, she gets up to go and look out the window, just in time to see him backing out of the driveway, gone down the road.

"Great, I hate him," she said out loud, surprised at her own voice. "I hate you!" she screamed, Brenda waking up. Standing up in her crib, she started to cry too now, her little chubby arms outreached to her mom.

Before Alice realized it, the darkness was looming. No sign of Elric. Feeling nervous, not knowing where he was or what he was doing, she decided that she would bake him his favorite chocolate cake.

Getting the baby to bed, taking one last look in, Brenda sound asleep. Alice went back out to her little kitchen, taking the chocolate cake out of the oven, making a white icing for the top, raspberry jam in the middle between the two layers. Icing it perfectly, she sat it in the middle of the table.

Going from the parlor back to the kitchen, she walked down the hallway, looking in at Brenda again, fast asleep, and then back to the picture window, staring out at the black sky, no stars to light up her night. Trying to settle down in the parlor, she picked up a book. Not being able to concentrate on the story, she put it back down, pacing some more. "Oh my God," she cried out loud. "Where is he?" The nights were getting a little chilly. Alice deciding to make a fire in the round potbellied woodstove that sat between the parlor and kitchen, stoking the ashes. A few pieces caught fire, and soon a good warm fire warmed the air and her heart.

Sitting down at the kitchen table, silence, only her breathing in her own ears, the baby inside of her active, rolling, and kicking. Realizing she had better relax, her baby feeling her nervous energy. Going back to the parlor with a cup of tea, putting her feet up, laying her head back on the cushions, closing her eyes. A high pitches scream separated the silence, she sits up quickly, looking through the doorway into the kitchen. Sure it was a woman's screaming. *Oh no*, she said to herself, it's what Elric had told her that he had heard. "Please, God, bring him home," she said. Gazing up at the clock now, two o'clock in the morning, and still no sign of him. Trying to lay down on the couch, covering with a light blanket, her eyes wide open, her ears perked for any sound of the car engine.

Finally, she heard a loud engine roar, the Studebaker coming in the driveway. Getting up, as quick as her enlarged stomach would allow, going to the window, watching, the car coming to a stop. No sign of Elric getting out. Watching and waiting for what seemed like forever, she heard the car door slamming shut.

Going to the door now, she opened it, waiting for him to come in. Elric staggered up the stairs, almost falling in the door. Backing away from him, recognizing that dazed look in his bloodshot eyes, a strong smell of whiskey on his breath.

"What are you looking at, fatso," he said. Trying to get out of his way, scared, thinking of the cake, she goes to the kitchen. Picking up the cake, taking it back to where he is still standing, wobbling, holding onto the door, trying to get his balance. "Look what I made for you," she said in a small scared voice, looking up at the monster that had just come through the door.

"Aren't you fat enough?"

"Oh, I made it for you, honey," she said. "It's your favorite, chocolate."

"Really," he said, his eyes widened, taking one step toward Alice, with one swipe of his large hand sending the chocolate cake into the wall. Alice watched as her beautiful creation slid down the wall onto the floor. Bending now to pick up the pieces, he lurched for her, grabbing her by her hair.

"No, no, please, I haven't done anything, Elric, please. The baby." Leading her into the bathroom by her hair, Alice screaming, her stomach tightening, the baby bunched up in a ball, frozen in terror.

"Look at your fat face," he said, holding the back of her head, staring into the mirror, barely the top of her head showing.

"You disgust me, you fat bitch," he screamed, throwing her into the wall. Falling down now on the ground, she held her stomach, her words coming out, but no noise in her ears as he started kicking her in the back, her screams muffled. Grabbing at her, with both hands, shoving her head into the bathtub, kicking and kicking her, for what seemed like forever to Alice. Feeling herself going under, face down on the floor, no movement. Elric backed away from her, looked at her through his alcohol dazed eyes, a pool of blood started to form around her body.

Coming to, Alice realizes she is in trouble. Trying to stand up now, holding herself against the wall, her head fuzzy, blood dripping from her nose, something wet on her feet, looking down her shoes filling with blood.

"Oh my God," she screamed, crying. Elric comes back to the doorway, looked through his fog, noticing the blood. Going to her now, in his drunken stupor, slips and falls into the pool of blood, his hands and white shirt telling the tale of what he had done.

"Oh my God, my baby," she cried, the blood still gushing down her legs. In his dazed condition, the sight of all the blood struck something in him. He was in big trouble. Picking himself up, he tried to help Alice to the door and to the car.

"The baby," she cried. "No, no!" Her screams trailing off to nothingness. Passing out in his arms, he shoved her into the back seat of the Studebaker, getting behind the wheel now. The drunken fog started to lift, realizing he had better get her some help. Driving straight to his father's house, he made it to the front door, pounding and pounding on the door until Earl appeared. Earl opened the door, the sight of the blood on Elric's shirt and hands making him panic, the stench of whiskey on his breath, his eyes bloodshot.

"What has happened to you? Oh my God," he said, looking his son over from head to toe.

"No, it is Alice," said Elric. "She had fallen and is in the back seat of the car."

"What? What are you saying?" Earl screamed, bypassing Elric, almost knocking him off the stairs. Running to the car now, he opened the back door, looked in, Alice's face stark white, blood all over her, her eyes shut.

"What have you done? You monster," he said, leaving Elric standing there in the yard. Getting behind the wheel of the car, he backed out quickly, straight to Doc Thompson's, going to the door, knocking as hard as he could. The old doctor showed in the window, then came to the door, Earl standing there, looking like he had seen a ghost.

"It is Alice. She had had an accident, fell down the stairs. Oh my God, please help her!" He cried, tears falling down his face.

"Get yourself together now, I need you to help me get her in here and now," the doctor ordered. The doctor took one look at all the blood on her legs and her shoes drenched in the thick red blood.

"Oh my God, hurry, she could be dying." Earl went into a state of shock, standing there, pointing, tears running down his face.

"Come on, help me," screamed the doctor, pulling Alice from the back seat. Getting her into the examination room, he took her pulse, a faint showing of life.

"My God, she is dying. We need to get her to the hospital! I don't have the necessary things here to save her. Hurry, help me get her into my car. I will take her to the Quebec hospital. You follow me in your car."

Helping the best he could, they managed to get Alice into the back seat of the doctor's car, covering her with a blanket, the doctor wasting no time, speeding down the highway at breakneck time, pulling into the emergency entrance. Two paramedics hurry out to help bring in his patient. Earl stood at the reception desk, his legs wobbly under him his hands to his face. In his tearstained house coat, he gazed down at his feet, his slippers still on. Giving the reception all the information he could, he told them what Elric had told him, she had fallen down the stairs. The nurse on duty writing all the information down, telling Earl he should take a seat and wait for the news. Just then, he remembered his granddaughter, Brenda. Where was she? Had Elric left her all alone at the house? Worried now for his grand-daughter, Earl left the hospital, speeding toward the little house. He had to know if Brenda was all right. Deciding to try the door, he opened it, walking into the baby's room.

Brenda is standing up straight, holding on to the side of her crib, a soaking wet diaper, her eyes stained with tears, whimpering, putting out her little arms to her grandpa. Getting her out of the crib, he laid her on the change table, putting a fresh diaper on her, and a warm sweater. Tucking her back into her crib, he gives her a warmed bottle of milk. Heading to the bathroom, he opened the door to the bloodbath. Handprints in blood on the walls, blood pooled on the floor and in the bathtub. Putting his hands to his mouth, he started projectile puking. Running back out, he picked up the baby, taking her out of the crib. He knew now that Elric had beat Alice half to death and killed the baby.

"What am I going to do with you, sweet thing?" he said, looking deep into Brenda's sea blue eyes. "Wanna go with Grandpa, go bye-bye?" he said, a smile coming to her lips.

"Fine, that's the plan. Just give me a few minutes to gather your things. You and Grandpa are going to leave this godforsaken place. If Alice dies, I will keep you little one, don't worry." Brenda watched as her grandpa packed some things in a diaper bag, grabbing more things out of the dresser that held her little T-shirts, overalls, shoes, and anything else he could stuff in another bag. When he figured he had everything he needed, her bottles, a stuffed bear, and the bags, he dressed her in her little coat and hat and shoes.

Brenda in his arms, the bags over his shoulder, he walked out of the house, not looking back. *I would dare him to try to take this baby from me. He doesn't deserve this baby, or Alice, or anything. He has ruined his little family. He's a killer, no son of mine. I don't know him.*

Earl put Brenda in the seat next to him, in the front, pulling the seat belt around her, Brenda quiet, pensive, looking at the dashboard, all the silver gadgets, watching her grandpa start the car, backing out of the driveway, getting away from the house of horrors and his killer son. *Think again,* came back the voice, *he isn't going anywhere.* Where was he really going? Hopefully to jail, forever. *Whatever,* said Earl to himself. He couldn't stand the sight of him anymore. It was over, this fake father and son relationship. Time to cut all ties to Elric.

Thinking of Alice, Earl's eyes filled full of tears. What if, what if… "Oh my God, don't let her die," he said out loud, looking over at his pretty granddaughter, who hadn't said a word since he'd picked her out of the crib.

All that blood didn't look good for the unborn baby, Earl knowing in his heart the baby must have died. It would be a miracle if both of them had survived. What did he think, that he was stupid? That was no accident. The truth was written on the wall. The bloodstained handprints. Blood all over the bathroom floor, no fall down the stairs could cause such bleeding. There was no doubt in his mind what had happened.

The next morning, Elric woke on his father's couch. Noticing his shoes and clothes still on, bloodstains on his white shirt, remembering that he had been pretty drunk. Flashes of what had happened last night started coming back to him. Oh my God, something about Alice. He was remembering now that he had driven her to his dad's house, and that's why he was here, but where were they?

"Oh my God," he said out loud, getting himself up off the couch. What the hell happened? He had to get back to the house.

Walking and walking, his head pounding, the reality of what might have happened coming down on him hard, he started to cry, putting his thumb out for a ride. The first car coming down the road a truck, carrying a load of wood. It pulled over. The driver noticing a man in distress, blood on his shirt.

"What happened to you, young man? Where are you going?"

"Please, if you could just give me a lift. I have to get to my house. It's about fifteen minutes from here down the highway."

"Sure, get in."

Letting him off at the roadside, Elric running to the house. Looking frantically through the rooms, opening the bathroom door, stepping in, slipping in a congealed pool of blood. Trying to get up, he slipped again, blood all over his pants and hands and arms. Holding on to the toilet now, he ripped at his clothes, throwing them in the corner, realizing he was in a possible murder scene. Now he starts screaming, "Oh my God, what have I done?"

Frantically washing himself, he looked down at his feet, the water stained red. Getting out, he ran to the bedroom, opening the door. Not a thing out of place, the bed made perfectly. Going now to the nursery, he threw open the door, Brenda gone. Oh no, where was she? Whimpering, tears running down his face, his head pounding. He could hear a faint crying. "Shut up!" he screamed at the top of his lungs. Where the hell was that screaming coming from? *Am I going crazy? What the hell is going on here? Where is my family?* Just then he remembered that he had put Alice in the car and taken her, to the doctor, or no, he had taken her to his father's, his dad taking her to the doctor.

"Shit," he said out loud. Was he in trouble? *Without a doubt*, came back the voice of reason, *you really fucked up this time*. Not my little Alice, he said, holding his head in his hands, the biggest worry was that he might have killed her. *Fuck, I'll be looking at years in the pen. What have I done?* Sitting for what seemed like eternity to him, not knowing, was driving him crazy. Should he go to his father's? No, that might not be a good thing right now. He just had to know where his family was. Sitting still, he stared ahead, worried about what was ahead for him. He had really done it this time.

The doctors put Alice on a twenty four hour watch, an emergency surgery, as soon as they brought her in, taking out her dead fetus, a fully formed baby boy, with no sign of life. Alice's life hung on by a thread, as fragile as a spider web. She had lost so much blood, the doctor ordered two blood transfusions. Finally, her heart began beating more regularly, life coming back to her. Alice had not awakened since she was admitted. The nurses took turns, every half hour checking her feeding tube and the heart monitor that told them one thing: she was getting stronger but still on life support. The doctors concern was she might have brain damage. The injuries did not add up with a fall down some stairs, as had been reported by her father in law, Earl Schoolcraft.

The doctors who worked on her resuscitated her, taking out her dead baby, making notes about the condition she was in, bruising around the spine area, lower back abrasions, cuts to her hands, and a cracked rib on the right side. The doctors looking at her X-rays, concluding one thing: she hadn't fallen down the stairs. The rib that was cracked was near her waistline, close to her spine. Writing their notes about her condition, the report read possible attempted murder, six month old baby, fully formed, taken by C-section, fetus dead. Alice Schoolcraft, swelling on the back of her head, bruising all over her back, blunt trauma to the body, including legs and back. Had she been brought in ten minutes later, she would have died, having lost too much blood. Given two blood transfusions, her condition was stabilizing. Serious condition, must have around the clock watch. Signed Dr. Johnson.

The nurses checked on Alice every half hour. Still no sign of her regaining consciousness. On the third morning, Alice came to, stirring in the bed, a fuzzy feeling in her head, opening her eyes, the bright overhead lights forcing her to close her eyes quickly. There was a monitor connected to her bed, alerting the nurses of movement, Nurse Betty, ran to her room, going to the bed. Taking Alice's little hand in hers, she spoke softly. "Alice, Alice," she said, noticing some movement in her fingers, squeezing her hand tight now. Alice moaned, opening her eyes again. "It's OK, sweetie, I am here with you. I am your nurse." Trying hard to see through the fog, her whole body hurt, she started to weep. The nurse rubbed her arm. "It's OK, Alice, you are safe here."

"Where am I?" she asked in a hushed voice?

"You are in the hospital, dear, you had an accident." She watched Alice's little hand going down the sheet, feeling for her baby, her stomach flat.

"My baby, where is my baby?" she screamed. Trying to lift her head off the pillow. "Relax, my dear. I am sorry to say the baby didn't make it."

"Oh no. No!" she cried, trying to sit up, he nurse gently pushing her back down. "You have to be still, dear. You are still not in the clear. You have been fighting for your life now for three days. Just rest now, dear, we are trying to contact your husband."

"No, no," screamed Alice. "Not my husband. I don't have a husband." The nurse wondered if she was delirious, telling her to quiet herself and rest.

"You need rest, dear, please."

"Call my friend. His name is Earl."

"You mean Earl Schoolcraft?" asked the nurse.

"Yes," she answered faintly, her eyes closing again.

"He's the one who brought you here, said he is your father-in-law."

No movement from Alice, losing consciousness again, the nurse covering her, walking back out to the nurses' station.

Consulting with the head nurse on her shift, Nurse Betty told her what she suspected. "After talking to her for a few minutes, I get the feeling that her husband beat her and killed the baby. When I said that we were trying to locate her husband, she became agitated, denying him, saying she didn't have a husband. She is either delirious, but my feeling is that she is scared to death." The head nurse made notes of what they had concluded, put the file back in the cabinet. "She asked that we notify Earl of her condition"

"Fine," answered the head nurse. "We will decide whether we should bring this to the police's attention. In the meantime, she is still on twenty-four-hour watch."

"Yes, ma'am," answered Nurse Betty.

Waking at his usual six o'clock, Earl looked in on his granddaughter, stirring in the bed.

"Good morning, pumpkin," he said, sticking his head in the door. Thinking of what he should do next, he went in, rolling the blankets down and seeing a large wet stain on the bed.

"Oh my goodness, I guess I didn't do something right," he said, realizing that he forgot to put the plastic pants on over the diaper. "I have never done this before, sorry." Taking off the soaking wet diaper, pinning another on, slipping the plastic pants on over the bulky cotton. Starting to dress her in a pair of overalls, trying to find a pair of socks. No socks. "Oh, my goodness" he said. Brenda looking up at her grandfather.

"I think I will have to take you to Blanche. I am new to all of this." Trying his best to dress her, he sat her at the table, making soft boiled eggs and toast. She ate up, making a mess. "It's OK," Earl said, wiping the table, trying to help Brenda with the glass of orange juice, spilling half of it, laughing.

"I guess I could use some lessons with babies," he said, putting her coat and shoes on with no socks, taking her to the car.

"Grandma will know what to do," he said, strapping her into the front seat beside him. She watched everything out the window, while Grandpa drove to Blanche's house, pulling up in the yard.

Glancing at his watch. Eight o'clock, it read. He wondered if they were out of bed yet and ready for the morning newsflash they were about to get.

Lovingly grabbing baby up in his arms, Earl walked toward the house, up the front steps onto the porch.

Just then, Tom was coming out, with his newspaper in one hand, his cane in the other.

"Good morning," said Earl. "Well, actually, it isn't a good morning. Where is Blanche?" Pointing to the door, saying nothing, Tom took his place on one of the rockers. Earl walked into the house, noticing Blanche standing at the sink in the kitchen. Startled, she turned to see Earl holding her grandchild.

"Hi," she said in a high pitched tone. "Sorry, you startled me," she said, a questioning look on her face. "Where is Alice?"

"Well, that's what I have come about. You had better have a seat," he said, pulling out one of the chairs for himself. Gazing down at his granddaughter, her eyes wide, listening to everything, thinking he should take her to the parlor, with something to play with while he filled Blanche in.

"Here, sweetie," he said, handing her the brown teddy bear he had brought along, sitting her on the couch. Going back into the kitchen, Blanche stared blankly at him, waiting for the news. "There has been a terrible accident, Blanche. It's Alice. She is in the hospital, and it's bad. She might not make it."

"What? What?" said Blanche, her face tightening in a frightful look. "What are you saying?" The tears started to come to Earl's eyes.

"Elric brought her to me two nights ago in the back of his car, unconscious, full of blood, on the back seat of the Studebaker, said she had fallen down the stairs, but I tell you, Blanche…"

She stared, wide-eyed, not saying a word, her mouth agape.

"Alice did not fall down the stairs. I think he beat her. No, I know he did. Went to the house to get Brenda, found blood all over the bathroom floor, on the walls. Oh my God, Blanche, it was the worst thing I have ever seen," Crying now, Blanche put her hand on his arm.

"Oh my God! Is she OK? That monster!"

"He was dazed and drunk when he brought her to me. I took her to Doc Thompson, who drove her straight away to the emergency. When I realized that Brenda was at home alone, I went back there and found little Brenda soaking wet, whimpering in her crib. At that point, I took what I could and brought her home with me." Letting out a big sigh, his head hanging, Blanche stared straight ahead.

"Listen," she said, without quivering, "you leave Brenda here with me, and go and find out if Alice is all right. Oh no," she cried out loud. "The baby is probably dead, oh my God." Blanche starts to cry now too, the tears running down her fat cheeks, walking away from Earl to her granddaughter, picking her up in her arms, holding her close, kissing the top of her head, sitting down on the couch, talking to her, Brenda clutching her brown bear to her tightly.

"It's going to be all right, sweetie. Grandma is here," she said, kissing her on the cheek.

"Got a kiss for Grandma?" she said, turning her cheek and bending toward the baby, Brenda kissing her grandma.

So many things were going through Blanche's mind right now, the first being what would they do if Alice died? Who would keep Brenda? She would love to keep the little angel, sitting quiet, looking up at her, but she could hardly care for herself, her arthritic knees, and her husband, who she had to care for. It would be too much for her, she discerned. "Please, God, let Alice be all right. Please, God."

Earl walked into the parlor, excusing himself, telling Blanche that he would be back with the news as soon as he knew. Earl walked out of the house, Tom did not look up from his paper, Earl walking by him, not saying anything. There had been so much going on, Earl was overwhelmed, deciding he just couldn't go to the office today, but he needed to go back home and get some rest before he took the trip to the hospital. Afraid of what he might find out, he tried to put the sight of Alice out of his mind. She just had to be all right. He was sticking with that thought.

On the drive back to his house, he thought about all of the possibilities. What was Elric going to do when he realized that both his wife and baby were gone? He wouldn't dare to come around, threatening him, or he would go to the police and tell them what he suspected, put him in jail, where he belonged. Regardless, he dreaded the talk that he would have to have with Elric, telling him that he didn't want nothing more to do with him, and he didn't have a job with him anymore. What would his son do then? The thoughts were coming faster than Earl could figure them out, making him weary, tired.

The fact that they hadn't called him from the hospital was good news. No news is good news, he recanted trying to reassure himself she would be all right.

Alice had regained consciousness, the nurses taking her in hot soup and tea. They tried to give her other food. Alice refused to eat. The head nurse had sent the others in, trying to find out the truth of what had happened to her, Alice giving one, one story, then contradicting herself with another nurse. Things just weren't adding up, the nurses making notes of the things she told them. When Nurse Betty mentioned her husband, Alice's face went stark white, her eyes large. "No, please, don't tell him I am here. I don't want to see him, never, never," she said, starting to cry.

"It's OK, Alice. Don't worry, we won't tell him anything." That was all she needed to seal the case. Her husband had done this to her. Alice needed time to rest, and heal, said the head nurse.

"When she is better, and ready to leave us, we will notify the police of our findings," said the head nurse. "Let's not bring any more stress on her right now." The other nurses in agreement.

Elric had spent the whole day in the house, going over and over in his head what he was going to do. Who was going to clean the crime scene? It was driving him crazy, not knowing what had happened to Alice. The only way he was going to find out was go and face his father, the last thing he wanted to do but the only way, he figured. Remembering that his father had taken the Studebaker, with Alice in it, he had no car to get anywhere, frustrating him even further.

Searching through all the cupboards, he finds a mickey of whiskey he had hid from Alice, put it to his head, the burn on his tongue warming him, straight to his stomach. Relaxing back on the sofa, putting up his feet. By the time the mickey was finished, Elric was feeling anxious again, thinking of how he could get to his father's. Probably walk, he thought, changing his mind, hoping his father would come to him with some news, one way or the other. It had been one of the longest days of his life, pacing, the liquor wearing off quick, trying to make something to eat leaving a big mess in the kitchen. Unable to go back into the bathroom, he went outside to piss. Finally, the darkness came down on him, trying to get comfortable in the parlor, stretching out on the couch. The stillness of the night, the silence freaking him out. Feeling all alone in the world, no one to love. Just as Elric was drifting off to sleep, he recognized the familiar screaming, far off, like it was down the road but coming through the windows, under the crack in the door. "Make it stop. Fuck off, fuck off," he yelled, over and over, putting his hands over his ears, not knowing if he was going crazy, or if he had guests.

Earl had decided that when he found out if Alice was all right, he would go and talk to his son and give him the lowdown, not wanting him to show up at his place of business. Elric would get a serious tongue lashing, never to show up at his home or business again. Bringing down shame on Earl, like a heavy ash from a volcano, suffocating any love that could have been there. Having not had any sleep in almost two days, when Earl dropped off to sleep, he didn't awaken till the next morning. First things first, he needed to get to the hospital, to see about Alice.

Making his way to the reception desk, Earl waited in anticipation of the news of his daughter in law. "What is your name, sir?" asked Nurse Betty. "There are no visitors allowed in at this time," she said, looking at him suspiciously.

"I am the one who brought her in. My name is Earl, Earl Schoolcraft," he said. .The nurse searching his eyes.

"Fine then, just a few minutes. She is still in intensive care."

"You mean, she is all right?"

"Well, she has regained consciousness but is still very fragile, and she lost the baby." Putting his hand to his mouth, his eyes started to gloss over.

"Follow me. I will take you to her room."

The nurse led Earl down the hallway, to the room, opening the door quietly, Earl stepping in, the nurse reminding him only a few minutes. Going to her side, he sits in the chair, pulling it up to her bedside, touching her hand softly. Staring into her face, ghostly pale, as the sheets on the bed.

"Alice, Alice." Her eyes opened, noticing Earl sitting there. "Shh." He put his finger up to his lips. "Just be quiet, dear, I just wanted to come to see you for a few minutes and tell you that Brenda is safe with her grandmother."

Before Alice could respond, the nurse was back at the door, motioning for Earl to leave. "That is all, Mr. Schoolcraft, for today. Visiting hours are over, and..."

"Fine," he said, getting up, kissing her on the forehead.

"I'll come back tomorrow, after work, OK? See you then," he said, smiling, his eyes loving, backing out of the room, the nurse turning off the lights.

Wanting to share the good and bad news with Blanche, Earl heading toward Blanche's house. Pulling up in the yard, Blanche was just walking out the door, Brenda in her arms. Standing, she watched Earl getting out of the car. "It's Grandpa, sweetie," she said to Brenda, Earl coming to the porch, taking Brenda from Blanche, who was struggling with her bad knees, handing the baby to him right away.

"Well," she said, looking deep into his eyes. "Any word yet?"

"Yes, I just came from the hospital. She is in stable condition."

"Oh my God," said Blanche, putting her hand to her mouth, waiting for the news, that she was afraid was imminent. Earl's face, his lips quivering, told the rest of the story. Blanche reached her hand out to him, touching his arm.

"Let's go inside, Earl. We will have some coffee. I've got some pancakes too, if you are hungry.

"Sure, sounds good to me." Letting Brenda down, she toddled away, toward her pile of toys Blanche had placed in the middle of the room, finding anything she thought the baby would play with, a hair brush, a pot, and a spoon, her fuzzy teddy bear in the middle of all of it. Going to her toys, Brenda entertained herself.

"The baby," Earl started to say.

"No, just let it go. I already know the rest. What's important now is we figure out what we will do with the baby and Alice when she is released from the hospital. One thing for sure, there is no way I will let this baby or Alice go back to that house, to that creep. My son, I never knew him, and I don't want to know anything about him ever again," she said, raising her voice. "He is dead to me," she said her voice loud.

"I feel the same way, and my next stop is I am going to tell him just where he fits in in this family, and that's out. I am firing him. He will have no way to make any money. I just don't know what is going to happen from here, but going to see him today is the last thing I want to do. After what he has done, I can't even look him in the eye. He is evil, Blanche. I have washed my hands of him."

"I am here for Alice and the baby," said Blanche.

"That's wonderful. I will give you an allowance to take care of everything they need. It's just that I have a business to run and no time to watch them every minute. Just don't know how Widdy is going to react to all of this."

"He doesn't really have a choice, does he? Surely the hospital has called the police already. He is probably in jail as we speak."

"That's a big possibility," answered Earl, going quiet for a few minutes, thinking of his next move.

Eating a few bites of the pancakes, finishing the coffee, excusing himself, setting out on his encounter with the devil.

Arming himself with all the muster he could get in him, the thoughts ripped his heart out. Banishing him from his life forever, that's what he had to do.

As he pulled the car up in front of the house, Elric is outside, swinging an ax, piling wood up in a pyramid. Oh shit, thought Earl, this was definitely not a good time. Elric put the ax down, staring toward his father, no sight of his beloved family in the car.

Standing straight, he watched his father getting out of the car, Earl walking toward him slowly, coming face to face with him. "Widdy, we need to talk. Let's go inside."

"No, you can say what you have to say right here." Earl eyed the ax leaning against the house. Taking a deep look into Elric's grey eyes, Earl fumbled with the words he was trying to find.

"First things first, son," he said, glaring into his eyes now. Elric turned his head from his father. "You and I both know what you have done. There is no point in you denying it. You have killed your unborn son, and your little wife is laying in the hospital right now, fighting for her life,"

Elric put both of his hands over his face, bending down now, almost losing his foothold. Walking to the side of the house, he leaned into it, making no sounds. Earl watching his son coming apart at the seams, silent tears falling down his shirt.

"Sorry to bring bad news, but I am sure that you knew it wasn't good news. While I am at it, I might as well tell you the rest. Your family will not be coming back here to live with you. It's over, Elric. Alice and the baby will be staying with Blanche, and if I was you, I wouldn't be going anywhere near them, or Blanche will call the police, and..."

"Shut up, you fuck," he said, opening his eyes wide now, glaring at his father, taking a quick look at the ax, Earl's blood running cold.

"There is nothing you can do, Elric, but I would advise you to make yourself scarce. The cops are probably going to be coming for you anytime."

"What for? I haven't done nothing. It was an accident."

"Sure, whatever, Elric. You and I both know the truth."

"Just shut up, old man, fuck you and the cops," said Elric, getting mad now. "They can't keep me away from my family. Over my dead body," he said, eyeing the ax again.

"I don't know what you are going to do, boy, but I have your last pay-check, I'll bring it for you. Don't come around my business or my house. Do you hear me?" Earl walking away toward his car. Before he could get his door closed, Elric running to the car.

"Look, I want to get out of here. This house is of no need to me. Can you give me back my money? I have nothing now, no job no family. I need cash to get the hell out of this province and the hell away from all of you."

Earl sat quietly, watching his agitated son, thinking of what he could do with the house. He knew full well he could just say no, the house was in his name, but something in him told him to try to come halfway with his foolish son.

"I will tell you what, I will come tomorrow with ten thousand dollars, cash money. You clean up the mess in the house, and I mean everything," said Earl, pursing his lips, remembering the bloody sight of the bathroom.

"I will be here after work tomorrow with the money. You can have the Studebaker to go where you need to go." Elric just listened, not responding.

"Have the house spic and span, that's the deal. If there is one thing out of place, the deal is off. Do you understand what I just said?"

"Sure, whatever, I'll clean it up. What time are you going to be here?"

"Right after work tomorrow, say, six o'clock."

Elric walked away from the car, as Earl backed out of the driveway.

Just as soon as the darkness came, the screaming started again, Elric getting up from the couch, agitated. "Can't stand this fucking shit," he said out loud, taking his blanket, throwing his coat on, getting out of the house.

Staring into the darkness, realizing that he couldn't go anywhere. No car. Heading back into the house, an eerie feeling of someone watching him.

"I'll burn this son of a bitch to the ground," he yelled, the screaming stopping abruptly. "Right," he said, going back to the couch, thinking he had made a deal with the ghost.

Just as he had promised, Earl showed up at the house the next day, Elric sitting on the steps. The thought of all that cash made his mouth water for a party, go to town, get a sweetie, tie one on, forget about everything, and plan his next move. At least his father was giving him the old car. He could get where he needed to go. Having cleaned up the blood in the bathroom, his tears falling the whole time, bile rising in his throat, tears of regret, missing his little family, trying to erase the thoughts that he had killed his unborn son. The reality of what he had done made him hate himself. He was really a monster. Passing the mirror, he quickly turned away, the sight of his own face disgusting him. Busying himself, he walked past the nursery, not looking in, packing up his clothes in Alice's red suitcases, taking one last look in at what was left of his life with her and his baby girl, who he missed terribly. He had to get on with his life now, get some work in the city maybe try to get the band back together.

With all that money, he didn't really have to worry about where he would lay his head. Maybe look up Loretta. Lost in the thoughts of what he would do in the city, he is overshadowed by regret. What he needed mostly was to lose himself in a mickey of the dirty water, blurring his thoughts and feelings right away.

"Well, son," said Earl, "let's step in the house." Elric went in first, standing at the door, watching his father go from room to room, the house perfect.

"You kept your end of the bargain, so here it is," he said, handing Elric a fat envelope. "Your final pay is in there too. Got enough money there to go wherever you want, and hopefully far away as you can get."

Not saying another word, Earl walked back out of the house.

"Oh, you have to get me back home," said Earl. "I have no time to waste, not anymore."

Earl got in behind the wheel, Elric getting into the passenger seat. Driving without words, Earl pulling up in his yard, slipping out of the driver's seat, the engine still running.

"This is goodbye, son. Hope you can find some peace in your life sometime. Get as far away as you can, that's my advice to you."

"Save your advice," said Elric. "It's a little too late, don't you think?"

"You made your bed. Now lie in it," said Earl, angrily walking away, not looking back.

"Fucking bastard," said Elric under his breath, backing out of the driveway, getting away from him and everyone, dust billowing behind the car, Earl watching until he was out of site.

Going straight back to the house, wasting no time getting everything he owned in the Studebaker, taking one last look before driving away, "Fuck you bastards too," he said, eyes on the road, leading to nowhere.

CHAPTER 83

A New Home for Alice

It had been exactly a week. The doctor went in the morning to see Alice.

"Today, you can go home, dear, but, there are a few things you have to adhere to. No heavy lifting, no standing for long periods of time, and you have to get your appetite back. You are a mere eighty five pounds, my dear. My twelve year old is heavier than you."

"Yes, sir," answered Alice in a childlike voice.

"Your father is here to get you. He is waiting outside the room."

"My father?" she said.

"Oh, I mean your father-in-law," recanted the doctor.

"Must be, my father has been dead for years," said Alice, a sliver of a smile for the doc.

"Sorry, miss," he said, walking out of the room. The nurse on duty helped Alice get dressed, taking one last look around the room. Earl stepped in, grabbing up Alice's bag. She had come in with nothing but was leaving with a big bag of presents, mostly from Earl, who came every day after work.

"Blanche and Brenda are waiting for us," he said, a smile crossing her pale lips.

Starting to cry now, Earl wiped at her eyes. "Don't cry no more. You need to be strong for your little girl. I told her you were coming home today."

"Home?" Alice said, thinking of her new living arrangements, wanting to ask Earl where he was, deciding against it. What had happened to him?

The cops had been in visiting her, asking her questions. She just couldn't tell them the truth, the officers getting frustrated with her.

"We know he did this to you. Why are you protecting him?" Fear, that's what it was, afraid of what he might do if she told them the truth.

"We'll put him away for a long time," one of the officers said, another plainclothes officer, just listening.

"What did I tell you?" said Scott to his partner. "I see this kind of thing all the time. The woman will protect them until they kill them. I know who we are dealing with, and I know he did it. Elric and I will meet again. It's just a matter of time," said Scott, closing his notebook, onto the next case.

Pulling up into the yard, they saw Blanche, Tom, and Brenda sitting on the porch.

"Mommy is here," yelled Blanche excitedly. Brenda looked out at the big black Cadillac, Earl getting out first, going to the door, giving Alice his hand. They walked together up to the step. Blanche put her arms out for Alice, hugging her close to her huge breasts. Brenda stood looking up at her mommy, her arms outstretched to her. Alice went to bend down to pick her up, a dizzy feeling sweeping over her head.

"I can't, honey. Let's sit over here," she said, going to the wicker settee, Brenda getting up beside her mom, touching her face, looking into her sad eyes, a connection only a mother and daughter could have, Blanche watching the exchange of love between them. They sat, Alice hugging her little girl, Brenda crooning over her mommy, twisting her fingers in her golden curls, talking baby talk, Alice lost in the love of her daughter.

Blanche ushered Tom into the kitchen, setting him at the table. Tom had taken to long periods of no talking, staring off blankly, Blanche realizing that there was something wrong with him. Being that he was seventy now, a little hunched over, and had become somewhat antisocial, Blanche accepted the fact there was something not right in his head. She had seen it before in older people, never expecting it to happen to him. He had become her patient, the doctor diagnosing, Alsheimer Disease.

With the baby and Alice, life came back in the old homestead and love in her heart. It would all work out, she told herself. With the money from Earl, things might even be a little better for her and Tom, both of them living off a pension alone.

They could have the spare room, all they needed was a bigger bed. Earl would get anything for them that they needed, making her feel like they could do this together.

Within a few days, there was a new schedule in the house, Blanche enjoying having her granddaughter, giving her a new purpose in life. In a way, she was trying to make up for leaving her own children, her granddaughter getting all the love now.

Elric had done exactly what he had planned. Went to the Quebec Hotel, paying for a room for the week, hiding the Studebaker behind the hotel, trying to not let anyone see him getting in the car. From an ace to a deuce, he couldn't live with the fact that he had been such a huge hit not long ago.

Now he was all alone, just another drunk at the bar. Thinking of asking for some work, he changed his mind. Didn't have it in him anymore, too much on his mind, consumed with the thoughts of his wife and baby. They were his, and he wasn't going to just leave them behind. Consumed with the thoughts of finding a way to get them back.

It wasn't long before Blanche started in on Alice about the food issue, noticing how thin she was. Alice tried to eat, but just birdlike servings, Blanche rolling her eyes, mad almost every day that she wouldn't eat a whole plate full. Finally, after a few weeks, Blanche blurted out at the dinner table.

"Eat something, girl. Are you afraid of getting fat like me? It took years for me to get this fat," said Blanche, insulting herself. "Don't worry, you will probably never look like me."

"Don't say that. You are just fine."

"Save your lies. You know I am as fat as a pig." A saddened look on Alice's face, pushing away from the table.

Things were fine, except for the fact that Alice was started to feel like a guest in Blanche's house. Trying to do all the housework to keep Blanche happy. Waiting on Tom hand and foot, Blanche dragged her heavy body up the stairs, stopping to get her breath. Having trouble walking, the pain visible on her face, Alice feeling sorry for her.

Brenda was happy, all the attention from her mother, grandma, and Earl, who came every second day to take them for rides and ice cream. The sight of the big Cadillac made Brenda scream with glee, the others laughing at her excitement. There was no sign of her missing her father, who she hadn't seen now long enough for her to forget him.

Problem was, Elric had not forgotten, trying to drink away his memories of them, only making the urge to go and get them more desperate.

Having relations with about a dozen women over the course of a few weeks. The bartender was getting sick of telling him, "No more, go to your room," cutting him off. Elric woke with a hangover almost every morning, finally deciding to lay off the alcohol, get his shit together, and go and get his family, any way he had to. It became his nagging obsession. They had no right to try and keep his family away from him. Planning on how he was going to steal them away, he would hide and watch. Surely there was times when Alice and Brenda were alone. That's when he would make his move and take them.

The cops had been watching Elric, every move he made. "Looks like he has turned into a drunk," said Scott, walking through the Quebec Hotel, noticing Elric sitting at the bar. *Where the hell have I seen him before?* Elric staring hard at the detective in his long overcoat and fedora.

The last night at the Quebec Hotel, Elric picked himself up two mickeys, deciding to have a night in, no women, nobody to tell him there was no more, he had more than enough. After tonight, he decided to leave the dirty water alone, it was ruining him. Settling down, he picked up his guitar, strumming a few chords. No real music in his heart, laying his guitar down, his star all but fizzled out.

Taking the last shot of the first mickey, he paced now, back and forth, his wife and daughter taking up every last thought. *Tomorrow, I will go and get them*, he decided, no matter what. He would die trying. They were all he had left, and wasn't letting anyone take them away from him. Tossing the empty mickey across the room, going to the bed, almost falling off of it, the room spinning, he passes out with all his clothes on, even his shoes.

Waking, a little man with a hammer, on top of his head, trying to dig a hole. Fuck, the pain in his head making him dizzy, his mind foggy. Getting up, peeling off his clothes, jumping in under the shower, thinking of what he had to do. Determined, today was the day. Bile rose in his mouth, spewing puke all over the bathtub and on his feet. Disgusted with himself, getting out of the shower, grabbing for the big towel, rubbing his head first, the pain in his head worse than the pain in his heart. Surveying the room, his bag unpacked, clothes strewn all over the place. Anger at himself, he starts stuffing everything into his suitcase, noticing a half of bottle of whiskey sitting on the night table. "Fuck that," he says.

Picking up the bottle, he smashed it into the wall, glass and whiskey spraying the room. "Enough is enough." He had to get his life back. The alcohol was ruining him and everything he touched. If he was going to get his family back, he would have to give it up once again. Knowing it wasn't going to be easy, but he had a strong mind, he reasoned. If he had done it before, he could do it again. Feeling around in his pants pockets, he fingered the wad of hundred dollar bills that he had separated from the rest and nine thousand dollars in the secret compartment of the suitcase.

Remembering now that he had played a few games of dice, losing two hundred of it already, and the money he had spent in the hotel all week. Pulling out the wad, he counted what he had left. Five hundred dollars. Shit, it could go quickly if you weren't watching what you were spending it on. With still lots left, he would go and get his family, get the fuck out of dodge, and find them a nice place to live. If it wasn't now, it would be never, he reasoned, the money running through his fingers like sand. Getting himself ready, combing his black hair off his forehead, taking one last look in the mirror. "Going to get my family," he told the mirror. "Good riddance," he said, slamming the hotel door, walking down the hallway toward the back door.

Making his way toward Blanche's house, Elric thought about the possibilities. Would everyone be there? Would he be able to get to them? Would Blanche call the police, like Earl had said? Whatever, he had to try. He just had to see them, even get a glimpse of them. Not knowing was driving him crazy. He just had to go.

Pulling up in the yard, there is no sign of anyone, nothing moving. Blanche noticed a car approaching, looked hard out the window. Alice and Brenda were in the guest room. She looked over at Tom. No use, he couldn't help her. Taking a better look, she recognizing the driver, Elric. He was here. What was she to do? A fleeting thought of calling the police, with Elric now a few steps from the house. Going to the closet instead, pulling out her shotgun, holding it up against her shoulder, ambling to the door, slowly pushing open the front door, Elric just about to take his first step onto the porch.

"I wouldn't, if I were you, boy. Just turn around, and get the hell out of here, I will shoot you right where you stand. You are a wanted man. They will give me a medal for killing you. Don't make one more move, or I'll let you have it," she warned, in her best deepest voice, not a quiver in her speech, her one eye closed, the other with Elric in her scope, right between his eyes. Frozen in his steps, he was just about to open his mouth when Tom came through the doorway, swinging his cane, nothing coming out of his mouth. Without saying a word, Elric backed down the step, keeping his eyes on his mother, who meant business. "Just keep on going," she said. "I will use this thing. Don't try me." Turning, he walked back to the car, like a beaten dog, retreating, his tail between his legs. Getting back behind the wheel of the Studebaker, watching now from the car, Blanche still holding her ground, her rife poised, until he disappeared out of site.

Just when she was walking back into the house, rifle still in hand, Alice had emerged from the guest room, coming out, saying something when her words froze as she noticed the rifle.

"What, is everything all right?"

"You just go back in with Brenda now. Lock the door, and stay in there." Alice's eyes grew large, knowing in her heart that he had been there to try and take them back. As she sat on the side of the bed, staring into space, Brenda came to her mom, noticing the change in her mother's demeanor.

"Mommy, Mommy," she said, Alice snapping out of her stare.

"Come here, sweetie," she said, picking her up, holding her close.

That fucking old bitch thinks she can hold my family hostage from me. She's got another thing coming. I'll be back. I don't give up that easy, he said to himself, backing out of the driveway.

Driving away from the house, the Studebaker engine choking, and sputtering, Elric put his foot to the medal, madder than hell. *I'll just sit and wait, give them a few days, and I'll be back. That old bag has to leave the house some time, and that old man can't even talk. He won't be any problem at all.*

Getting back into the city, Elric decided he would go and look up Loretta, just for the hell of it. The sweet golden fluid was calling him too, and right now, the way he felt, he could put a whole mickey to his head. Better not do that, came back a voice in his head. Might want to go back and kill that old bitch. She was no a match for him when he got going.

Don't want to get myself in any more trouble, he thought deciding that he would tough it out. "No whiskey," he said out loud.

Cruising slowly by Loretta's, he noticed a man and woman walking up to the door. It was Loretta, looking back, recognizing those long legs. Fuck, she has a new man, the two of them walking into her house. A little late, thought Elric. After all, he hadn't seen her now in a long time.

Oh, well, what now? Concluding to go and hide in the bushes near Blanche's house and watch for them to go out. Her car was in the driveway, and by the looks of things, Tom wasn't doing any driving.

Turning the car around, he headed back the way he had come to Blanche's. Parking the car about a mile from her house, he walked down the road, his fedora pulled down over his forehead, wearing his long grey overcoat. Getting closer to the house, he could see the porch from where he was standing in the bushes. Making himself comfortable on a tree stump, he eyes glued to the porch and the front door. After about an hour, Tom came through the door, newspaper in one hand, settling down on one of the rockers. Putting his cane down, getting into his newspaper. A few minutes later, Alice and Brenda walked out. Alice put Brenda up in the seat next to the old man, giving her a teddy bear and her bottle. Elric's eyes fixated on his little angel, her wheat blonde hair like a bright light.

A steady stare at every move she made, getting up from the seat, walking back and forth across the porch, then walking down the stairs, throwing a ball around in the front yard. *I could just go and snatch her, right now,* he reasoned, but with the car so far away, he surely wouldn't get far without Blanche's driving to catch them.

Deciding he needed a better plan. Just wait until Blanche made her move and went somewhere in her car. Time passed, the sun started to retreat. Elric was getting cold but was determined to stay, until the time was right. Tom and Brenda had gone back into the house. Elric gazing at his watch: six o'clock. Must be dinnertime, he thought, his stomach rumbling, his eyes glued to the door. Just then, Blanche came out of the house with her coat on, waving to Alice, who had come to the doorway. He could almost hear her words, talking to Alice. His beautiful little Alice. There she was.

He watched now as Blanche walked to her car. *That's it, that's it. Get the hell out of there, bitch.* His heart beat fast in his chest, watching as she got in behind the wheel, backing out of the driveway. Thinking she must just be going down to the general store that was about ten minutes away, Elric knew he would have to act fast.

Waiting until the car is out of sight, he ran to the house, knocking on the door. Alice was just spooning out peas and carrots on her plate when she heard the loud knocking. It's probably Earl, she thought, going toward the door. Just before she opened it, a lump rose in her throat. What if it was him? Tom came up behind her, also hearing the knock, motioning for her to open it, Alice opened the latch, the door flying open, Elric stepping in, flying by Tom, knocking him to the ground, going straight to the kitchen where his little girl is eating. Picking her up in his arms. "Hey, sugar," he said. "It's Daddy." Alice came flying up behind him. "Put her down. Put her down now, or I am calling the police." Running to the phone, she just got it off the receiver when he knocked it out of her hand.

"Look here, little woman, get your bag, and now. You and Brenda are coming with me. Don't make me hurt you or her. I mean business."

"Why, why would you hurt your baby?" Alice screamed, watching the fright in Brenda's eyes now.

"I said let's go! I have no time to waste. Either you come now, or you will never see your baby again." Tom is struggling to pick himself up off the floor, standing now, his cane wobbly, trying to say something, gibberish coming out of his mouth. "Get out of my way, old man, or I'll…just get out of my way!" he said, rushing by him, the baby in his arms, Alice watching as he headed toward the door.

"It's your last chance to ever see your baby again. Come with me now, or…"

Just then, Alice rushed to the guest room, grabbing up her diaper bag and her bag, stuffing everything she could into it, pulling a few blouses off the hangers, crying now, her vision blurred. Running out to the door, Elric was already down the steps. "OK, OK, here, get these bags, I will go."

Turning to see her standing there with the bags, he quickly went up the steps, put the two bags over his shoulder, the other suitcase in hand still holding Brenda close to his chest.

"You won't regret this, sweet cheeks. I can't go on without you guys. Come on, let's hurry. We got a ways to go to get to the car." Tom stood in the doorway, waving his cane, garbled sounds of nothing coming out, his eyes bulging out of his head.

Hustling them as fast as he could go down the road, Alice trying to keep up, Elric's strides just short of a run.

"Hurry," he said, looking behind. "If that old bag comes after us, I'll have to hurt her."

"No, no," Alice cried. "She has been good to us."

Brenda had gone quiet, her two front fingers in her mouth, her eyes wide, Elric holding her tight. Laying her head, on his chest as they made it as fast as Elric could go to the Studebaker. Wasting no time, he laid the baby in the back seat, covering her with the blankets he had taken from the house, Alice settling into the front seat next to him, her heart strings bouncing around. Gazing over at him, her captor, the killer, her husband.

"Where are you taking us?"

"Never mind. We sure as hell are not going back to that haunted house. Those fucking ghosts drove me crazy. That's what happened, the ghosts made me do it."

"What?" asked Alice?

"I just went crazy that night." Turning her face from him, the tears just beneath the surface. She had cried so much, the river of tears had all but dried up, replaced with regret and anger. An emotion she didn't really know, but when she thought of what he had done, the feeling grew stronger than any other. Never had she known anything called hate, an emotion her heart couldn't find.

Irene had been so mean to her, yet she never could find hate in her heart toward her. It turned into pity, watching her mother in her madness. Fear was the deciding emotion in her today, not wanting him to steal her baby away, maybe never see her again. Glancing at Brenda asleep on the back seat of the car.

Elric put his long arm out toward Alice, pulling her closer to him.

"I couldn't live without you and Brenda. You guys are my world and everything I have."

"What about the house and all of our things?"

"I brought all your clothes and Brenda's things. They are in the back." Alice looked way back in the rumble seat, a blanket covering a large lump of things.

"Sold the house back to my old man, and I got a pocket full of money. We'll get another house. We just go to get the hell out of here, out of Quebec. I've decided we will drive to Ontario and start a new life."

Knowing, whatever she said, wouldn't make a difference, she didn't say one word, just listening.

"I've got enough money to get us a place, and a little time to make things up to you, sweetie. I don't want to have to say I am sorry, and I will never hurt you again. I know you probably don't believe me, but as of right now, I am a changed man, quit drinking too."

The statement, *I will never hurt you again*, she didn't believe. Not one cell in body believed it, more like a record skipping, saying the same thing over and over.

"Really," said Alice, looking at him now, wanting to believe that statement was true. The times that were good was when he had given up drinking.

"Too much water under the bridge," he said, Alice not understanding what that meant.

"I am going to be a good husband and father, you will see. Now come over here, and give me a kiss," he said, pulling her to him. Alice's eyes looked down, Elric kissing her on the forehead.

The Studebaker made its way down the highway, Alice noticing a sign saying Ontario Quebec border, two hundred and fifty miles.

Blanche had come home to Tom, still standing on the porch, his eyes bugging out of his head, trying to tell her what had happened. Waving his cane in the air, as she searched his face for clues, walking into the house, something not right. No sounds of the baby, no noises from the kitchen.

Hastily walking from room to room, opening the guest room, things strewn all over the bed, the baby's things gone, Alice's bags gone.

"Oh no," she started screaming. "He was here, oh no! Oh, God please," she begged, running to the telephone.

"Police, police, I want to report a kidnapping."

"Slow down, ma'am. Who kidnapped who?"

"Alice and the baby, they are gone. Elric, my son, killed the baby, must have taken them when I was at the store."

The operator took down the information, sending it through to the police. The police were at Blanche's door in about twenty minutes, taking a statement from her. She told them about Elric and what she suspected, kidnapped Alice and the baby, and gone. They looked from one to the other, the name Schoolcraft, one that they couldn't forget. They put out an APB on a 1930 Studebaker, white, with red roof and trim, man and woman, and a baby. It came over the airwaves, Scott picking up the trail.

"That fucker is mine," he said, getting into his cruiser, not knowing where to start. Before long, he gave up the search. No sign of him anywhere in the city or outlying areas, scoping out the countryside, around the little white house.

"Give up the ghost," he said over the airwaves. "No sign of Schoolcraft anyway, probably wasting our time. These domestic violence cases usually don't go anywhere."

Driving and driving, Elric stared out into the dark night, like a vampire. Where was he going? All he knew was he wouldn't let anyone take them away again. Glancing over at Little Alice, who had fallen asleep, her head resting on a blanket, leaning on the door, his baby girl sound asleep in the back seat, a feeling of calm coming over him.

The first town he came to, Elric pulled off the TransCanada highway at a sign reading Blind River. It was far enough from Quebec and small enough they would never find them here. Not only that, he had heard some of the other fallers talk about a big lumber company called Bereyhauser that was hiring fallers. They paid twice what his old man was paying, deciding it was the perfect place to find a house, and get his family settled in. A new start was what they needed.

Brenda woke, hungry, whining a little, sitting up. Elric looked back at her. "Hey, you, bet you are hungry." Just then Alice started to stir, sitting up now, looking out the window, the sun just starting to come over the horizon.

"Where are we?" she asked, looking back at her baby girl, who is wet and hungry. "We have to stop, Elric, the baby needs feeding and changing."

"That's why we are here. We'll find a room and settle in for a few days. Give me time to look for a house to rent and get a job."

Just listening to what he was saying, hearing it but not sure of anything, only that Brenda and her were along for the ride, not knowing, making her feel helpless. Trying to put on a smile for Brenda. At a sign reading River's Inn, Elric pulled the car up to the office, going in. A thin older lady came out from the back, a tight perm stuck to her head, reminding Elric of a grey wool hat he wore in the bush, deep wrinkles around her eyes and mouth. "Can I help you?" she asked.

"Yes, I need a room for a week for my wife and baby, and me."

"Sure thing, just fill out this for me. I'll see what we have."

Coming back to the counter, she handed him a room key. "There is a stove and fridge in there, and two beds. Is that fine?"

"Sure, we will take it," he said, handing her forty dollars, telling her to keep the change.

"Thanks, sir." Stuffing the money in her apron pocket. Elric went back out to the car, sticking his head in, announcing they had a room for a week. Parking the car outside of the room, bringing in the things they needed, getting Alice and the baby in. Brenda walked around the small room, looked at the old pictures on the wall and the room that would be their home for the next week. Baby stepping into the bathroom, then back out, then around and around the room, Elric yelling to her to sit down.

"We won't be here long, sweets. Give the kid something to play with," he ordered, looking at Alice.

PART IV

Brenda

CHAPTER 84

Blind River

The river knows, the river flows,
It winds, it roars,
It takes you,
It wakes you.
It can break you.
If you lend your ear to the wrath of the river,
You will hear of ruined lives,
Promises broken.
Darkness and shadows of the river,
It calls you, it becomes you,
It will consume you.
The river only knows,
The secrets that have been told of a family broken to pieces by the storm,
The river can blind you,
The river can swallow you up in its treacherous waters.
Still waters run deep,
Reflections distorted, time distorted, love distorted,
All on the river of darkness.
Beware of the spirit of the river,
It can swallow you whole, or break you into pieces.

By Brenda Rae Schoolcraft

CHAPTER 85

My Life Six Years Later

S o many things had happened to us, trying to sweep the bad memories, under the carpet, far away, in the deep recesses of my mind, only to crawl back out eventually, haunting me in every aspect of my life.

By now, I had two siblings, Roderick and Lillian. Mother had so much scar tissue from the lost baby that the doctors told her she would probably never have any more children. Good thing in a way, or we would have had a new one every year, Elric forbidding my mother from taking the pills.

At the time that Roderick was born, Elric had taken to emotionally abusing all of us. Mom was probably just about a hundred and ten pounds. Calling her fat, pinching at her abdomen, teasing her, making her feel insecure. Mom went days without eating. Dad had taken a job at the big lumber giant, making pretty good money. He spent most of what he made gambling, the money gone in no time at all. We were now living in a rented house behind a hall they called the teen town. There was a big problem with rodents, and I mean big ones, rats.

Frightened to go to sleep at night, my mom set traps for them, hearing them clicking hard, the sound becoming familiar, killing one almost every day.

We realized they were coming from under the hall. There was nothing we could do but trap them until we had caught them all, which never happened. They kept breeding under the teen town, as fast as we were catching them. I remember one morning waking, looking through my sleep filled eyes at a rat chewing on my fingernails. I screamed bloody murder, the rat scurrying under my bed, my father running into the room.

"What the hell is going on here?"

"A rat was chewing on my fingernails."

"Ah, you must be seeing things. I don't see no rats in here." I remembered that Roderick and I had stolen a few donuts from my father's lunch bucket and had gone to bed, without washing my hands. The rat was feasting on the sugar on my nails. After that night, I washed my hands good before going to bed.

One thing I did know was that we were all being tormented by Elric, each in our own way. He continued to drink, mostly hiding booze, coming home to us drunk. I would notice my mother pacing, looking out the window. That's when my heart would start beating fast too. I would go to her, hugging her close, asking her when he was coming.

Mom had become hardened to the abuse, finding ways to avoid him when he came home drunk or getting us all together, walking down the road, nowhere to go. A couple of times, I remember her taking us to a lady's house, a Jehovah's Witness who would drop in on some days. One day, my drunken father invited her in.

While we all watched from our conspicuous places, he invited her to sit down at the kitchen table. Even Mom wouldn't come out of the bedroom, afraid that Elric would embarrass her, and so he did. He asked the lady if she wanted a cup of tea, to which she said yes. My father brought it to her in a bowl. Looking into the bowl, she had a surprised look on her face at the tea bag floating. Not saying a word about it, she added milk and sugar that he brought to her from the counter. Then he joined her and started flirting with her but in a sick way. He was like, "Look at those big tits you have. I bet your husband has fun…"

Before he could get the rest out of his mouth, she pushed away from the table and walked out the door. She came back one other time, and my mom let her in, apologizing for his ignorance.

A loving concern in the woman's eyes, taking my mom aside, she whispered in her ear, "If you ever need to come to my house, I just live down the road a ways, a redbrick house with blue curtains in the living room window." Mom made a mental note of the safe house, as she called it, taking us there a few times, once in the middle of the night.

We all had strict orders that we were not to go to the door if someone knocked. He told us to go to our rooms and hide until the knocking stopped. I think he was worried that the cops were still looking for him, or for whatever reason, we weren't to answer the door.

When he did come home to us drunk, we would all scurry away, like scared animals to our cages, hiding under the beds or under the covers, hoping that he would entertain himself with other things than us.

I had just turned seven years old when my brother, Roderick, was born, and then the next year Lillian, and the year after, my baby sister, Gwen. I noticed that Mom would stand up to him, especially the next day after he had abused us, never letting him forget the worst thing he had done to her. "You are a baby killer," I heard her say more than once, my mother confiding in me about what he had done. From that day forward, I had a secret loathing for him. Sometimes I prayed that he would die and never come home.

When Dad was sober, he wouldn't even argue back, just walk out of the house or go sharpen his chainsaw blades. It was a source of stress and disappointment when he would bring the big saw into the living room and work on it in front of all of us. Mom would be so distressed, worried that he would get grease on her freshly scrubbed and waxed floors.

I remember her working hard from sun up to sun down, keeping our house clean. No matter what it looked like on the outside, the inside was clean from top to bottom, the bleach in effect.

Days when he was in a drunken rage, we became the object of his torment, leaving Mom alone, at least for a while. We would run outside sometimes to try and get away from him. Whatever, he made sure that we all got our equal share of his abuse.

After living in the house, behind the teen town, for two years, Dad decided that he wanted us closer to him where he was working at the bush camp, a trailer court not far away where a lot of the other guys who worked for the same company lived. Coming home to us, just days before we had to pay the rent, moving us into the trailer in the middle of the night, cursing about the fucking landlord, expecting us to live in a rat infested house.

"Fuck him, he isn't getting another penny out of me," he said. By morning, we were all so tired, they kept us home from school to help put away some of our things.

Walking from one end of the trailer to the other, a sick feeling came over me. I hated it. It felt like I was in a long box or a cage. There was a wooden step up to the front door, which opened to the living room. Next to the living room, just a little farther down the box, was the kitchen, then it went through a narrow hallway to a small bedroom, with a double bed, a few shelves built into the wall, and then another small room, farther down the hallway, with two sets of bunk beds on either side of the hallway, and then a smaller room, just big enough for a single bed, at the very end of the trailer, which they told me would be my room. Looking around, I wondered where I would put all my books, and things. There was a door there too, not far from my room, between my room and the middle room. Immediately, I felt a pang of happiness with my own door to come and go, without having to encounter him. A way out too, if I had to escape for whatever reason.

The only source of heat was a small square woodstove, a narrow black pipe running up through the roof of the trailer.

"It's just temporary," he told us, noticing our disappointment. Mom sat at the little kitchen table, staring straight ahead. "At least it's a roof over your heads," he said, walking out the door to his car.

CHAPTER 86

We Became the Hunted

We had just been living in the trailer for a while when something awful happened to us that I will never forget.

He had come home from work on a Friday night and had started drinking while Mom made us supper, probably some kind of wild meat. My father was always out looked for something to kill, whether it was in season or not. There was a freezer sitting outside the back of the trailer, where he kept his catch, frozen partridges, fish, moose meat, and deer. Those were the only things I remember eating as a kid, but the odd time, he would bring home beef steaks, Elric getting the most of the steak, the rest of us sharing one, Dad getting a whole one.

He had just stepped through the trailer door, walking into the living room with his muddy boots on, sawdust spilling out of the tops of them. Looking over at the mud droppings to where he was sitting now, Mom started to cry about her clean floor.

"I bring the money home, keep you guys fed. Shut up, before I shut you up," he said, everyone feeling the heat, the tension rising in the air. I tried to help my mom clean up the mud, Elric ordering me to take off his boots and put them near the door, where there was a plastic boot holder. I did as he ordered, Mom watching, Elric pulling a mickey out of his bag. Well, we all knew it was all downhill from there. My eyes darted to my mother's eyes and told me we would have to be ready for anything. Resuming making the supper, my father sat on the couch, quiet, drinking one drink after another, until his eyes started getting that faraway, glossy, madman look. I was sitting at the table, reading or doing some homework, trying to block him out, when he yelled at Mom.

"Hurry up with the fucking supper. I am starved. What the hell you been doing all day that I have to wait so long." I watched from my perch as he got up from where he was sitting, came to the table, my eyes on him now. Mom had just put down the gravy bowl on the table, bending over now, pulling the moose roast out of the over.

"All you ever want to do is bitch cause you are a bitch," he said, slapping her hard on her behind, sending Mom's head into the oven, causing her to fall in front of the stove. The moose roast hit the floor, the hot juices splashing out, burning her legs and feet.

"Now look what you have done!" Picking up the gravy bowl off the table, he poured it over her head. At this point, I was screaming, and so was Mom. I looked to see where the other kids were, Roderick and Lillian playing outside, waiting for supper, and Gwen sitting on the floor playing with some blocks. Quickly, I made a beeline for the door, my father catching me by my hair, ripping me back into the house.

"Go to your room, you stupid brat," he said. "Get, before I..." he screamed, my mom covered in the hot gravy, crying now, her head down, whimpering. Gwen started to cry too, the familiar sounds of the monster scaring her. Running toward the back of the trailer, I tried the door, pulling, struggling, to no avail. It wasn't opening. Thinking of what I should do next, I ran back out to the kitchen, Mom still on the floor, Elric raining down punches on her head.

"Stop, stop!" I yelled, picking up a big butcher knife off the table. He turned from my mother, seeing the knife, reaching for me. Stepping out of his reach, I screamed now, "Leave her alone or I will kill you."

"Why, you little bastard," he said, trying to grab for me, slipping in the gravy, falling down now. Mom made it to the door, running out with Gwen in her arms.

"C'mon, let's go," I yelled to Rod and Lillian, who were already on their guard, running behind Mom, who was struggling with Gwen, trying to get away. It had just started to get dark, a light mist of rain falling, the sky grey darkening quickly.

"Hurry, hurry," Mom urged, all of us running now for our lives, the knife still in my hands. The other trailers were quite a ways from ours, but we weren't wasting no time, trying to alert someone, just kept running down the road.

A series of loud sounds ripping through the air over our heads. Oh my God, he was shooting at us. I looked back to see him in the distance, through the fog, laughing like the devil himself, shooting the gun into the air.

Finally, down the road about a half a mile, no other houses in sight, we found an abandoned car, all of us piling in. Nestling into it, Mom and Gwen in the front, Roderick, Lilly, and me in the back seat. Withno time to stop for coats, all we had were the clothes on our backs, not enough to stay warm for the night. Regardless, we did what we could, huddling close to each other in the back, as Mom cradled Gwen in her arms, singing a soft lullaby. Mom's hair was stuck to her head, a raised bump on her forehead where she had hit the oven door, a bright red burn mark on the side of her face, and forehead from the scalding gravy. I noticed that while Elric was punching her, she held her head in her little hands, guarding her face from him. It struck me as something she had learned from being beaten so many times. She had become a seasoned fighter.

Sleeping off and on, through the cold damp night, all the windows fogged from our warm breath, we seemed to all awake at the same time, the sun just coming up. It was early, but we knew one thing: he had probably passed out. It was reasonably safe to go back home now, the bunch of us piling out of the old car, happy to have had somewhere to hide the night out.

Getting back to the trailer, no movement or sign of him. Stepping up quietly to the door, the kids' eyes widened, I went in the door first. I still had the knife just inside of my sweater, trying to get up the gumption to use it if he threatened us again. Mom and the kids stepped in quietly, their eyes searching. Elric was sitting at the small kitchen table that was right up against the wall, putting molasses on his bread, a plate of bacon and eggs sitting in front of him.

"If I knew you were coming, I would have made breakfast for you all," he said, eyeing us quickly, my eyes meeting his, his eyes lowering from mine to his plate.

The air had settled, Mom going past him to the bathroom. The kids sat around the table, looked at his plate. "I'll get you guys some breakfast," I said, getting out the eggs and bacon, putting some bread in the toaster. All morning, he never once mentioned where we had gone or anything about the night before. Mom emerged from the bathroom with a towel around her head, her housecoat on, walking past Elric like he was an invisible man. As soon as he had finished his food, he got up away from the table, leaving us with our peace, not coming back the whole day.

As I watched from the window, he put some of his tools in the back seat of the car and a can of worms. I had a feeling of relief. He was getting away from us, at least for a while.

After the incident of the shooting, Elric didn't come home to us for over a month. When he did show up at the door, we were all in anticipation of another brutal episode. Mom had made a special dinner, like she knew he was coming, put on a pretty bright red dress. Earlier in the day, I watched her put rollers in her hair, dabbing a little rouge on her cheeks. He had probably told her that he was coming that day, but she didn't announce it to us, and I can understand why. None of us would jump up and down, happy to welcome our absent father back home. It was more like she would have to tell us that the boogeyman was coming to our house.

I had my nose in a book, my favorite pastime, when the door opened, Elric stepping in. Roderick and Lilly were somewhere together playing, only a year apart in age. Gwen was sitting quietly, playing with her toys, a quiet baby, large blue eyes, always watching and listening to her world that had been nothing but chaos since she was born. Sometimes I would watch her, thinking she didn't know whether to laugh or cry. We all turned our gaze to him. Taking off his boots at the door, he deposited them in the plastic tray that sat near the door, walking in gently, looking at my mom.

"Hey, sweet cheeks," he said, my mother's eyes lighting up. With a deep sigh of relief, I went back into my book and into another world. Sitting down on the couch not far from where I was sitting, he called Roderick and Lilly to him. The kids were all over him, the smiling happy father they hadn't seen in over a month.

Gwen crawled over toward him, near his feet. I watched every move he made from my perch, the big chair that sat on the other side of the box.

That whole weekend was utter bliss to me, no angry voices, no screaming, mom seemingly happy. It was a scene right out of a normal family movie. I wished that I could freeze it in time, the picture never changing would have been too much to ask. Having been through too much drama already, at my young age, and whatever love I should have had, was squeezed right out of my heart, like there was a vise grip holding it closed to him. I knew that the happiness they were experiencing was just a ploy, a sweet treat to catch the rat, and get it in the trap. The trailer did feel like a trap to me, especially that I couldn't get that back door open. One day, I investigated it from the outside. He had hammered a few long nails right through the tin into the wood, around the latch. God knows, he didn't want us to have an easy escape route.

Roderick had developed a nervous twitch, blinking his eyes over and over. My father thought it was some kind of bad habit, finally telling him he would spank him if he didn't quit it. Well, it wasn't something he could control, getting spanked a few times, Elric realizing the spanking wasn't working, possibly making it worse. "Leave the boy alone," I would hear my mother saying. "He has to go to the doctor." My father finally gave up the threats. Lilly was a pretty baby, dark wavy curls, big blue eyes, and a happy baby. Dad seemed to pay more attention to her, maybe trying to make me jealous, which I was not. "You are Dad's favorite," he would say and then laugh, watching the rest of our faces. Really, I didn't care if he had one iota of love for me. There was no love lost on my part. He had become the enemy in my mind, and nothing was going to change the way I felt.

The baby, Gwen, only knew the changes in the voices, stirring her little world, crying or laughing, responding to the sounds from the family around her.

After the weekend, we waited for Dad to pack up his things to go back into the bush, announcing to us that he had been laid off and would be staying home for a while, at which point my world was shattered. I became very nervous and sullen.

For the first week, he seemed quite happy, hanging around the trailer, helping Mom prepare some meals, playing with the kids while I watched from afar. "Come over here, and give your old man a kiss," he had said to me. Taking one look at him, I walked out of the trailer, telling Mom I was going to see my friend from school.

"Get your ass back in here. You aren't going nowhere," he said. Going back into the trailer now, I headed down the hallway toward my room at the back of the box, closing my door. I stayed in there almost all day, until my mom asked me to help her fix some dinner. Mom had become very distant emotionally, trying to stay away from him, Elric trying to rub himself up against her. I watched my mother push away.

"Why don't you take the kids out to play," Elric said to me after dinner. "Your mother and I have some things to talk about." Well, I knew full well what that meant. I had heard their lovemaking through the walls of the trailer, sickening my stomach. If that was what it was all about, I wanted nothing to do with it.

Elric was getting restless, I could see it in him. One thing I have to say in his defense was that he didn't mind hard work. The only problem was, when he did get paid, most of it was gone before my mother saw any of it, still gambling and drinking most of it away. Mom had confided in me that she was getting a welfare check to put food on the table, the company taking the rent for the trailer out of his check. Good thing, or we wouldn't had a place to lay our heads.

Elric had discovered a gold mine. A couple of ladies he had met at a department store in town became easy prey for him. Walking in there, all dressed up one day, his hair slicked back off his high forehead, a swagger in his walk, his fedora cocked to the side, real movie stuff. Both of the ladies looked up from what they were doing, noticing the handsome stranger.

"Good afternoon," he said, tipping his hat to them. Both Martha and Gilda blushed, a show of pink on their fat cheeks.

"You are sure looking good today," he said, smiling his Cheshire grin, showing his pearly whites. They are so smitten by the handsome stranger, they didn't notice that while he walked the aisles of the store, he was filling up the inside of his long overcoat. Stopping to buy a cigar, on the way out, he thanked them for their time, wishing them a good day, walking out thirty pounds heavier.

He didn't make any bones about showing us what a good thief he was, coming home, unloading his kitty, emptying the contents of his oversize overcoat on the kitchen table, saying the words as he pulled out things from the secret pockets. "Lobster, steak, butter for the steak," he would say, laughing as he went, pulling out food from one side, and then slacks for Mom and a few things he picked up for each of us.

Those were the days, we might end up with a chocolate bar. If there was only one steak, he would hoard it for himself, making us eat whatever else there was. We were doing without many necessary things, like lunch bags for school. It showed on us at school, in the clothes we wore and the meager lunches, usually just a molasses sandwich, or a meat sandwich if we were lucky. On good days, we might have an orange to accompany the dried out sandwich.

The other kids laughed at us, noticing our sandwiches wrapped in brown paper and the clothes that we wore over and over again, making us a target for the mean kids at school.

I overheard the conversations, when Elric had gambled his pogie check, demanding that Mom give him some of the welfare money that she always said she had spent on food, sometimes hiding a few dollars for a rainy day.

Elric had gone down to the department store one too many times, when the ladies father noticed him one day, from the back room, standing talking to his spinster daughters, who were nothing short of fat and ugly. Why was he being so nice? Deciding there was something amis about this character, he started watching Elric.

David, the girls' father, had noticed that his inventory and the money in the cash were not adding up, knowing there must be a thief, either his daughters, which he knew wouldn't take him for a penny, or shoplifters, knowing he would have to keep a closer eye on his store.

Watching from the back room, a finger holding the heavy grey curtain, he noticed Elric put something inside of his long overcoat. Waiting until he went to the cash register with nothing to claim, walking out the door, waving to the women. David came running out of the back room, chasing Elric outside of the store, waving his hands in the air.

"Stop, thief!" he shouted, Elric taking to running, his long legs getting him out of the area before David could catch up with him. Well, that gold mine had been closed down to Elric, making him have to look for other ways to feed and clothe us.

Dad would soon be going back to work, he had told us. The ground started to dry up, the logging crew able to get back into the deep woods with their machinery. It had been a rainy spring nearing four months since he had worked.

Without anything to do, he started constructing a house outside just behind the trailer made out of roughed in timbers. "A place where I can take my boots off in the middle of the floor if I want," he had said. He asked me to come out to help him, which I did with gladness, thinking it was a great idea. A place for him to be, away from us made my heart glad. If only he knew how much I wanted him to stay away from us altogether. It was the one thing that I prayed about every night, that he would just somehow magically disappear, and my mom and I, and the kids, would be finally free of him. In my mind he was a monster. Passing him the hammer, I helped him hold the timbers upright, as he secured them. I was amazed, after one week he had constructed a small one room log house, a tree running up the middle of it. That seemed funny to me, but to him it was the cement that held the whole thing together.

It was too much to hope for that he would move into the cabin and just come into the trailer when it was time to eat. Right, not. He would just go out there to brood and to plot his next terror attack, or so I thought. I had grown not to trust his intentions. Even when they were good, his smiles and his hugs were just tricks and could turn into hell on earth. After a few drinks, I would watch him transform right before my eyes, in no time flat. He could go from the caring, doting father to the enemy that hated us all. I often wondered if the whiskey was just an excuse to hurt us, or if it was something else.

The days were getting nicer, and I had heard him telling Mom that the guys were going back in the bush next week. "Why don't we take the kids fishing?" he asked, Mom excited about the thought of a picnic, cooking some fish, at the water's edge. Happy about an outing, she got the kids ready, packing everything we would need into the back of the car. We all settled in, Dad at the helm. The fishing hole he had in mind was a good ten miles up an old logging road, the road winding through some mountainous terrain. Everyone was excited, the sun making it a great day for an outing. Even I was blinded by the happiness of fishing and spending time near the water. He had taken us on a few fishing trips that had been wonderful, the few times I remember actually having fun, gutting and cooking the fish right there, my dad fixing me a line of my own, catching a few, was exciting.

We all loved car rides and had enjoyed a few nice days driving through the countryside, or stopping to enjoy a picnic next to a pretty place. I would watch my father and listen intently, trying to figure out what was in for us.

That particular day, he had spent the most of the early morning in his cabin, gutting some partridges, building a few shelves, lining the roughed in logs. I hadn't noticed any changes in him, feeling safe about the drive into the bush to go fishing.

We started on our journey, Mom and Gwen in the front seat, with me and Rod and Lillian settling into the back, watching out the window, Dad turned off the main road onto a narrow dirt road, going in quite a ways until we reached the designated spot where we would settle and put our lines in the river.

Getting our things out of the car, Mom settled down near the river's edge, putting down a blanket, letting Gwen crawl around, the sun high in the sky, a perfect day for our perfect family. Dad made us fishing poles from some young poplar switches he cut off some nearby trees, attaching a line and hook, making us put on our own worms. "If you don't put on your own worm, there is no fishing for you," he said, watching us, our faces strained, sticking the worm with the sharp hook, blood and guts spewing from the worm. That was the worst part for me, sickening my stomach. He watched in enjoyment at the disgust in my eyes, trying not to look at the mangled worm. Rod and I made a bet to see who would catch the first fish. Rod caught the first one, a yelp of excitement from him, Mom laughing and playing with Gwen from the shore. Having spent most of the day catching a few, Mom rolling them in cornmeal, cooking them right there. I hadn't noticed that Elric had a mickey in his coat pocket, probably sneaking a drink when we weren't watching.

Noticing some changes in him, his voice raising, laughing hysterically about nothing. Worrying that there was something I hadn't noticed, until I saw what would be the end of my happy fishing trip, watching him put the bottle to his head, drinking the last of the whiskey then throwing the bottle in the bushes.

"Get your fucking asses in the car," he ordered, the monster in full view now, my heart sinking. Mom's face went stark white, picking up Gwen, holding her close, as though she could shield her from the monster. I watched Mom, her movements robotlike, her eyes connecting with mine a few times, the pain and fright in them making me want to vomit. We had to get back home, and we were a long ways in. Remembering the winding road up to the fishing hole is when I really started worrying, wishing I could just take off running, but run where? I had to be there for my mom and the kids. Mom had put Gwen in the car, going back to pick up the blanket and some toys that she had taken for the baby. I watched as Elric went over to where Mom was, ripping the blanket out of her hands, sending the little toys all over the ground. "Just leave that shit. I want to get back. It's getting fucking dark." Roderick and Lillian stood near the car, frozen in their shoes, watching and listening to the goings on.

"Get in the car. We don't have all day!" he shouted, the rest of us piling in, me in the back with Rod and Lilly.

"Hey, Alice, how about you get that driving lesson I've been meaning to give you." All of a sudden, all my hair stood up on my body.

"No," I said, Elric swinging his arm back, backhanding me in the face. Too afraid to cry, I held my face, sitting back farther now. Mom's eyes started to water. I didn't dare say another thing, the kids squeezing in next to me as far away from the long arm of the monster.

"Actually, Elric, it's not a good idea. We have all the children with us, and the roads up here aren't the best," she said with pleading eyes.

"You are gutless!" he shouted, the rest of us knowing we were in trouble and a long ways from home. I dared not to lose my composure, my mom depending on me for moral support, the kids huddling into my body, frightened now, Lillian, whimpering, Rod's eyes blinking too fast. Dad passed Gwen back to us, as he ordered Mom behind the driver's seat, Elric going around the other side of the car, slamming Mom's door hard, as though he was closing a prison door on us. A sick quiet enveloped us, trying not to breathe too loudly.

"Now, just put it in gear, and put your foot on the gas pedal," he ordered. "I am right here. Everything will be fine," he assured her.

Yeah, just about as fine as walking on glass, I thought. With my eyes glued to the back of my father's head, like watching a stranger, who had kidnapped us, fearing for our lives. "Grab a hold of the wheel," he demanded as he put the car in gear. It jerked onto the hardened dirt road as the car inched along. "C'mon, put a little step on it," he said, as he put his big foot down on top of Mom's foot, sending the car faster, dust spewing from the back wheels.

"No, Dad," I cried. "Not so fast, the kids are scared. You are scaring us!" I screamed, the monster, not looking back.

"Shut up, you big cry baby," he said, looking back at us, the eyes of the devil himself. Mom started crying now too, begging him to let her stop driving.

"Please, not today," she begged.

"You will do as I say," he bellowed, backhanding Mom with a closed fist, into her face. Letting go of the wheel now, he grabbed for it, the kids screaming, my eyes bugging out of my head, wanting to get out of the car and run for my life, but he would surely come after me and probably kill me. "That is what you need, you stupid bitch. You don't want to learn anything! You are too fucking dumb!" he screamed, staring her way. At that point, I had the kids as close to me as possible, covering their ears, the monster in full effect.

"Get the fuck out of the seat," he said, hitting her again. Mom's hands up to her face, as he continues to punch her in the body, slamming her into the car door, the door opening, sending her out of the car, onto the road, the car careening around a corner, as he grabbed the wheel, the car barely gripping the road, close to the ditch.

"You fucking dumb whore! Now look what you've done, trying to kill yourself," he said as he looked around at us, frozen, his steel grey eyes like a dagger, going straight through our hearts.

The kids were all screaming. I had just gone numb, trying to look out the window to see where Mom was, Elric jerking the car to the side of the road. Without thinking, I flew out of the car to my mom, who was still on the road, trying to pick herself up. "Oh my God, Mom," I said as I bent down to help her, the side of her face scraped, blood showing in the scrape lines, dirt and gravel in the cuts. Elric had just emerged from the car now, walking towards us with a heavy gait. When he got close enough, I just looked up at him, as much to say, stay away from us.

"Get away!" I shouted, crying at the same time. "You are a murderer. I hate your guts."

"Whatever, you stupid brat," he said, kicking gravel in my face. He waited in the driver's seat, watching us approach the car, through the rear view mirror. I opened the back seat door, telling mom to get in with the kids, I got in next to her. Staring straight ahead, he started up the car, the kids crying, trying to get close to mom, blood caked on her mouth, I wanted to scream, or just kill him. He drove, his eyes glued to the dirt road, driving too fast, the gravel spitting out from under the wheels. At that point, he couldn't hurt us anymore than he had already, the erratic driving not bothering me. I wrapped a blanket around Mom, and she put her head on my shoulder as I wiped the dirt from her bloodied face. When he rounded one of the bends, I thought for sure it was the end of all of us, for a moment thinking we would all be better off dead.

I don't remember how we got home, only that we did, Elric pulling up outside the trailer. He looked back at us, his victims the booze draining from him. I thought I saw a single tear fall from his cold cement eyes. That's when I lost it.

"Look here!" I shouted, tears still falling, "If you ever hurt Mom again, you are going to have to kill me. I am going straight to the cops and tell them all your dirty little secrets."

"Why, you little bastard," he said, his eyes narrowing. "I will fucking kill you, and I will kill all of you if you ever go to the cops to squeal on me. The only good rat is a dead one," he screamed, his eyes bloodshot, his mouth dried at the corners.

Leaving us all to pick up the pieces, he went straight to his cabin, not emerging for the rest of the day. Getting Mom into the trailer, I helped her sponge off her face, dabbing on some ozonol, putting a large gauze bandage on the worse side.

I watched her, the rest of the day, Mom not saying much, just talking to me, with her eyes, the sadness of them ripping my own heart out. The greenness of them like the news baby shoots of grass, Mom trying hard to hold on to her life, for us.

Our minds and hearts were a lot more broken after that day. One thing for sure, I would never fall for the fishing trip, trap, again, trying hard to stay away from him altogether, speaking to him only when spoken to.

The kids got settled in, had some dinner, and I put them all to bed. Mom sat in the tub for a long time, calling me in to talk to her. "I know you are the oldest one, and the one who understands me. Somehow the Lord will get us through this, dear," she said, the sadness in her eyes overbearing. Her little knees were scraped, the reddened flesh showing. Her face was swollen, one of her eyes with blood specks in the white of it. "It will be all right, honey," she said, as she turned her bruised face from me.

The day came for Elric to go back into the bush to work. It was such a sigh of relief for all of us. Mom had healed up, the black under her eyes almost gone, the raw flesh of her knees healed over. Her heart would never heal,

I thought. Mom had lots of time to think about her life and how her hand had changed. You could tell by the way she looked at us that she was sad for the way we were suffering too. I can just imagine in her prayers, what she was saying to God. I think it would go something like this.

"Why, God, why is this happening to me and my children? Why was this the hand I was dealt? What have I done to deserve this, Almighty God? If not for me, please protect my little family. I love them so."

Elric stayed away from us for a couple of months that time, not wanting to face us, especially me, who had become his true enemy. Mom was able to put her welfare check to good use but with no frills. She made casseroles and cooked the wild meat that Dad had stored in the freezer. It seemed to me that he was always killing something, piling the dead meat on top of one another.

He was the real white hunter, something in him driving him to kill and kill some more. Sometimes he would insist I accompany him on his trapping trail, picking up rabbits that he had caught in snares, strangling them with the thin wire. He took me hunting with him, a few times, making me shoot the rifle, which was a heavy thirty six he called it. "Here," he said, the first time he made me shoot it. "Just hold it tight against your shoulder," Backing away, he said, "Now, pull the trigger." The gun went off with a big bang. I went flying one way and the gun the other way. Standing back, laughing his head off, as I lay on the ground, watching the pleasure in his eyes. Picking myself up off the ground, I felt a sharp pain in my shoulder.

With Elric away at work, we all settled into a routine that was pleasing. A nice hot meal after a long bus ride home from school. Mom would be waiting for us, her apron on, the sweet smell of fresh buns wafting out the cracks of the trailer, our hearts warmed by the smells and the smiles of our precious mother. I was getting good grades at school, amazingly so, usually with my mind on other things, like when he was coming back home, praying that he never would.

CHAPTER 87

Four Years Later

E lric had tried on and off to stop drinking. When he was sober, he could handle situations better. He knew full well the damage he had done to his family. I suppose he could see it in our eyes. I believe he loved us in his own sick way but rarely showed it. When he was feeling like expressing his love, he would say, "I love you little rascals" as he was on his way out the door, but when he was drunk, we went from rascals to "you little bastards."

Mom had survived so many beatings from him, which left her with some damage in one eye and a cracked bone over one cheek, and the healed broken nose, from years before. Her love for us had grown, but there was no love lost between them. She would threaten to go to the police if he kept hurting us and tell them all the things he had done, including killing his unborn son. I noticed that she liked to torment him with that, only when he was sober. It was the one thing that shook him. He would grow sullen or just walk out of the trailer. Maybe he really did feel remorse over what he had done. "You are nothing but a nag," he would say in retaliation.

At ten years old, I had grown tall and lean and looked a lot like my dad. He seemed proud to tell strangers, "This is my oldest. Doesn't she look just like her old man?" People would look and smile, a doting father, how nice.

Dad was still handsome, but the drinking was starting to wear on him, showing in the tiny lines around his eyes and the sagging of his skin around the jowls. Still, he never passed a mirror without taking time to admire himself. One thing for sure, he seemed to love himself, even if he couldn't find it in his cold heart to love us the way he should.

All the information he had willfully told us, my brother and me, I kept stored in a secret place, able to pull it out if I needed to use it. One day, when he had had a few, he took Roderick and me out to his private cabin, sitting us down, passing the bottle of whiskey to us, telling us to take a swig. "Just one swig. No one will know," he said, Roderick taking it first, putting it to his lips, making a face. "Yuck," he said, passing the bottle to me. My father watched as I too took a small sip of the liquor, a sharp burning taste on my tongue, passing it back to him. This was the drink that had all but ruined his life, and ours as well, making me hate the smell of it and the thought of it. He tried to pass it back to us. We both refused while he continued to take a few more swigs, as he called them, tucking the bottle away in a coat pocket.

I knew now that he was hiding his brew out here, where Mom wouldn't notice it, where he could have his private drink away from us.

That same day, we sat listening to his stories, so we would say, "Wow," or "Holy," surprised at the violence and the gangster in him that lay just beneath the surface. He went on to tell us that he had made his own whiskey in the hills in Quebec, and the cops had run him out of the province because of it. That didn't sound likely to me, but I listened with a keen ear for the rest of the stories. "Hell, your old man has robbed banks, and I killed a couple men in cold blood." Roderick and I looked at each other, shocked but not surprised, Elric being no stranger to us.

When he said, "In cold blood," he outstretched his wide, long fingered hands that stretched out twice the size of any hand. It reminded me of the sting on my flesh when he had beaten me on my buttocks, arms, or anywhere else that was bare skin.

I remember an incident that will stay with me and has my whole life. Gwen was about three years old when she found a pack of matches and snuck into my dad's car, sitting there, striking the matches, until the whole package caught on fire. Frightened, she threw them down on the seat of the car. The cloth upholstery started to burn. Elric was in his shack when he walked out, noticing the plume of grey smoke coming through the cracks in the car. Running to the car now, he opened the door, the car seat on fire. By that time, we had all run outside to see what was on fire. My father yelling, "Fire, fire." Gwen had just come out of the car, wearing a white eyelet lace cotton dress she insisted on wearing, everyone commenting on the pretty baby in the white dress. Elric went for a pail of water, dousing the fire, then put the pail down, ran into the trailer, looking for Gwen, who was hiding behind my mother on the couch. He strode straight to my mother, who pleaded with him, "Don't hurt her, she is just a baby," as Elric plucked her out from behind my mother, Gwen's eyes bulging out of her head, Elric with his big hand, grabbing her by the head, holding her by her hair, pulling her outside. We all watched as he gave her the worst beating of her life. He was hitting her about the head like she was some kind of punching bag, when my mother grabbed for her, taking a few of the loose fists to her head. Elric snapped out of his madness, Gwen's nose bleeding all down the front of her pretty white dress. The blood against the white of it was like a sacrificial lamb. Afraid for my little sister, I was in shock.

I watched him from afar, promising him in my mind that his time would come. He couldn't get away with hurting us like this. Walking back into the trailer, I went to my room, crying myself to sleep.

After the attack, Gwen was never the same. A clump of her baby hair, lay on the floor. She had started talking, but after that, she forgot the words she was starting to form, regressing back to baby talk. The weird thing was, whenever Elric walked through the door, Gwen would run to him and want to sit on his knee. This was too much for me. The whole family had gone nuts, me included, not able to concentrate on the important things, always in a war zone, looking for that place of comfort and peace.

CHAPTER 88

Bad Dreams for Alice

When Elric was away, Mom spent a lot of time with us, gathered around her, telling us the stories of her childhood, whether it was to ease the pain of our own lives or to entertain us. We sat quietly, listening to every word she spoke. Even the stories that she had already told us, we listened to, wanting to hear them over again.

"When I worked for the Olsenses," she said, "I had my own driver, and he took me home to my mother and picked me back up in a couple of days, escorting me back to the palace, oh, I mean the mansion. You see, I had never been in such a beautiful house before, and to me, it was what a palace would be like."

I could see my mom as a real princess in a palace. When she told the stories I envisioned my own fairy tale. Never seeing her as the lowly, forgotten child she really was made me happy for the child, Alice. Her stories gave me hope for my own life, and I know now why she always told us the stories, over and over.

The other thing that totally fascinated me were the stories of her dreams, and how she would dream things, and then in the near future, the dream would all but come true, or it would have symbolic meaning, like the one she would love to tell us about her Prince Charming, a faceless rider of a horse that flew through the air. We would laugh at that one, knowing the prince was our father, Elric. "I really think it is the Lord, trying to warn me of impending danger," she had said.

"If only I would have heeded the warning," she said, then looked at us lovingly. "But then, if I had listened, I wouldn't have all of you. I would have never gone away with him."

It was Mom's love that was keeping us going, because without that force in our lives, there wasn't much else to live for.

Elric had been away from us for two months when she announced one morning at breakfast that we could expect our father any time soon. Before we got up from the table, she also said she had something to tell us. We all watched and listened as she described a dream. When she said it was a bad dream, my hair stood on end. The other kids just listened, not digesting it. I was already scared before she revealed the dream to us.

"I dreamed of a loud knocking," she said. "In the dream, I was awakened by a clinking noise, like a nail on glass. When I looked up at the window, a hand but a skeleton's hand, just bones, knocked on the glass, disappearing as fast as it had come. I have dreamed the dream twice now," she said, every hair on my body standing now. The kids started to move away from the table while I remained seated, wanting to hear more. |"And that's all, Mom, that's all you saw?"

"Yes," she answered, a faraway look in her eyes. I wouldn't tell her what I was thinking, just looked deep into her loving green eyes, inviting me in like walking in tall grass.

A few days later, low and behold, Elric pulled up to the trailer in his car. I watched from the picture window as he unloaded the back seat, taking out his chainsaw, his tools and extra work boots, and things. It was great he had the log house, where he could take his gas smelling chainsaw, his dirty boots, and other dirty things, instead of throwing them in the middle of the floor for us to step around, and for Mom to complain about. I watched him closely now, for any signs of the monster. He looked up at me, watching him, smiling at me. "Hello, Brenda," he said, as I read the movement of his lips.

I announced, "Dad is home," like I was ringing a dinner bell, Mom coming from the back of the trailer, looking out now, too, Elric coming to the steps. Coming in, Mom stood there, looking at him. He reached for her, hugging her close to him.

"Missed you, sweet cheeks," he said, kissing her on the lips. Surprised at his kind voice and his gestures, I stood back, watching from the doorway.

The other kids had emerged from their rooms, also looking out now at him. Elric put his arms out for them to run to, Gwen the first one, then Lillian, then Rod, all getting their hello hugs. He looked directly at me, watching. "Suppose you are too big to give your old man a hug." I just hung my head, trying not to make eye contact with him or give him a reason to call me to him.

"Hey, I got all kinds of things for you guys. Come outside and see" he said, walking outside, the kids going in earnest to see what gifts he came bearing. Really, I didn't want anything from him, knowing that it was just a buffer for what he had already done to us, and really, there was nothing he could have given me that would make everything all right. I stood in the doorway, watching the kids going to the trunk, where he was pulling out his offerings, handing them each a few things. A new scarf, a new hat, a baseball bat for Rod, and a glove and ball. Handing Lilly a big bag of black licorice and a Barbie doll, still in the package, and a big rag doll for Gwen that was a large as her with soft legs and arms with a raggedy red head, with braids to its shoulders, wearing a pair of jean overalls. Mom was standing next to me when she became quite excited. "Oh my God," she said. "That is just like the doll, the one that I pretended was my sister, Pearl. Remember, Brenda? I told you about that doll."

"Yes, Mother," I answered, watching Elric pulling more things from the trunk. "And here," he said to Mom, looking up at her. "A new knife set for you. Tired of watching you trying to cut up things with those old dull knives you got."

That's when my blood ran cold. Mom's eyes met mine. I'm sure the same things were going through our minds. I decided that I would bide my time, and hide them, all of them, away from the kids, I said to myself, knowing full well why I had to hide them.

The first few days he was home, everything was peachy keen, just too perfect, making me watch every move he made, planning my escape route, if I had to, just like a soldier in a war game. My nerves were raw. Every little thing made me jump, especially the sound of his voice, if it changed its octaves. Mom had not mentioned the dream again. I think she just erased it from her thoughts. "What's the use in worrying?" she would say.

About a week of being home, I was waiting for the announcement, like we had won a big prize. He would be going back to work. Taking his good old time, he eventually told Mom that he had been laid off again, and he was going to be looking for a new job. Truth was, he had been fired, the foreman catching him with a stolen chainsaw that had been brought to his attention, which belonged to another company, Elric stealing it off one of their trucks. Elric said he had bought it from someone, but couldn't come up with the rest of the alibi, like who and where they were now, so they couldn't confirm the story.

"There is a better company, just farther north of here hiring fallers," he said. "Better money too," he said, all of us feeling more insecure now.

Did that mean that we would be moving? I wondered, but didn't bother to ask. What was the point in asking? Whatever was going to be decided would have nothing to do with what any of us wanted. We were just along for the ride. The air in the house-trailer had become stifling, Mom walking around, uncertainty taking up her mind, probably the dream, coming back to remind her. The not knowing made her uneasy, insecure. The clincher was that the job wouldn't start for another two months. That sounded like an eternity to me, and probably like the end of the world for Mom. Without saying much, I could see her thoughts in her eyes, the way she walked, the way she doted on the baby, not saying much, trying to be the best mother she could be to all of us. I lay in my room that night for hours, not being able to sleep, thinking of running away. I would just pack a bag, put on some comfortable shoes, and just start walking, wherever the road took me would be better than in this cage, fighting for survival, trying to side step the bombs, trying hard not to fall through the cracks. The only problem was, I needed to be there for them. We all had to hang together. My mom would never be all right without me.

The way I felt about my father, I'm sure he could tell. The way I watched him from afar, the way my lips were slow to find the urge to smile his way.

At least there was hope now, a new job for Elric, possibly a better place to live than in this long box, much like a coffin for me. I was really dying inside, in many ways, too many things to think about and worry about, losing myself in my books, my wonderful books, where I could be the princess in the story if I wanted to, like my mom, or on my way to a tropical island, where the breeze blew warm air all the time, where time stood still and there was only happiness. Just a dream, but for a little while it was worth every word and moment, in a faraway land.

A week or so after that, Elric became restless, headed into town to get a few things, stopping for a few drinks. Roderick and I went to play with a friend we had met at school. Beatrice Frankoure, her name was. She spoke French. She had a disabled brother who sat in a wheelchair. A few times, when I was at her house, I saw him pick his nose and eat it, disgusting me. I couldn't even look his way and tried not to walk near his wheelchair. Another time, I watched him pull something out of his head, mom said it was probably lice. The sickest thing was they had a tall pail in the bathroom, about three feet high, where everyone went to the bathroom, and it seemed really full all the time, the whole bathroom stinking badly, the smell leaching out into the hallway, dispersing into a lighter stink through the whole house. Everything about the house was gross. Mrs. Frankoure was not a good housekeeper, like Mom.

Mom said we could stay until seven o'clock, so I watched the clock closely, knowing that my father was home too. I went to find Rod, who was playing with his new bat and ball with his friend Johnny. We were nearing the trailer when I heard the familiar sound of my mother's screams. I ran to the door, throwing it open, Roderick coming up fast behind me. I looked over to see my mother down on the floor, Elric standing directly over her, punching the top of her head, slamming her head between the refrigerator door. Sitting in her own blood, her head bowed, her little arms trying to protect her face. Elric's eyes on us now.

"Get the fuck out of here, now, you little bastards, before I kill all of you. Get out now!" he shrieked, his face contorted. The devil himself glaring at us. I tried hard to see if Mom was still alive, her head hung low, barely moving.

"Oh my God. Stop it, stop, stop!" I screamed, crying hysterically now, Lillian and Gwen hiding under the table, hugging each other, their faces buried in each other's necks. Rod took off, down the road, as fast as his legs would take him, running aimlessly into the bushes.

All I knew was that I had to do something, and fast. He was still punching her, her body not moving anymore. I ran for the stove and picked up the cast iron frying pan, Elric so dazed that he didn't notice me coming up from behind him, bringing the cast iron frying pan into the back of his head with all my might. His knees gave way, going down hard into the floor. I tried to get to my mom, shaking her now. "Mom, Mom, please, Mom, help! Help!

Somebody!" Blood running from her nose, the girls frozen in fear under the table, whimpering.

Running outside now, trying to see through my tears. Where was I going to run to? I couldn't leave her. I went back in the house now, Elric unconscious sprawled out on the floor, Mom moaning. Trying with all my might, I pulled her battered body to the bedroom, pulling her up on the bed, running hot cloths to put to her face, talking to her, holding her head in my hands, her eyes swollen shut. She had lost a lot of blood, but finally I had held her nose up and stuffed it with some tissue, the blood crusted around her lips. Rocking back and forth, her head in my lap, I cried my whole heart out to her, it falling in pieces, tattered at her feet.

I could still feel a faint show of life, her pulse under my fingers. Sitting there with her, for what seemed like days, no one coming to the door all night. I knew Rod had come back home at some time, must have seen Elric passed out on the floor, blood splattered around the floor, near the refrigerator. Said he found Lillian and Gwen, together in one bed, the covers pulled over their heads. Roderick walked into Mom's room, looked over at us, not saying a thing, backing out of the room, closing the door behind him.

The next morning, I woke up cramped and tired. I had held Mom all night, not leaving her side, even to go to the bathroom. My mind didn't go on Elric once, hoping in a way, he was dead. I heard the door handle turn. Elric walked in, looked our way. "Get out, get out!" I screamed. He kept coming toward the bed. Frantic now, my eyes buldging out of my head.

"Is she OK?" he asked, a frightened look of concern on his face.

"She needs to see a doctor. I think she might die, and you did this to her!" Staring now at my mom's face, swollen, and bruised, like he knew nothing of what had happened, rubbing the back of his head.

"I hate you. You are a monster, not my father, ever, ever!" I screamed at him. "Get away from us. Haven't you done enough?" I cried. At that point he walked away from us and out of the room.

Before long, he came back into the room, announcing that we were not going to school today and that I had better get out to the kitchen, and make my brother and sisters some breakfast. I kept my eyes on him as he spewed out the same orders again, only this time his voice raised, his eyes glaring at me. Afraid of what he might do to me, or Mom, I slowly got up from the bed, trying not to disturb Mom, who hadn't moved or made any sounds yet. Standing his ground, he watched me navigate around him, like he was a leper, out the door to the kitchen.

The kids had already seated themselves, watching me, as I emerged into the kitchen, their haunting eyes watching me. I smiled gently at them, telling them I was going to make some breakfast. Not being able to think straight, I grabbed a box of cereal out of the cupboard and put some bowls and the milk on the table, the kids pouring their own while I sat and watched, not being able to find my appetite.

Noticing that he hadn't come out of the room, I decided to sneak back there, not worried that the monster would attack again. He was sober, the reality of what he had done shocking him. I peeked in the door, Elric bending down, pulling the covers back gazing at Mom. He was saying something. I put my ear to the crack. I heard him say, "Don't die, Alice, and if you do, I am going to bury you out in the marsh. I've already dug your grave" Shocked at what I had just heard, he was a killer, in every sense a killer. Had he planned on her murder?

He kept us home the whole week from school. On the seventh day, someone came from the school, knocking on the door. Elric watched out the small window, whispering to us, "Don't answer the door." I recognized the fellow from the school office. They were checking to see if we were all right.

Mom hadn't been out of bed, only to use the bathroom, and that was painful for her. Her sides hurt, she said, and she had finally opened her eyes but told me she couldn't see anything.

"I am blind," she told me, tears running down her bruised face. I was so sad for her, I had hardly eaten all week. I cried so much, my eyelids were swollen. The sight of him made me sick. He went to her bedside every day and sat there, just looking at her. "I am so sorry for hurting you, little one," I heard him say. "I never deserved a great woman like you." I watched secretly every time he ventured near her, tears actually rolling down his face. There seemed to be some remorse in what he had done? Had he seen the light? Was he just sorry for himself or scared that she would die, and he would go to prison forever?

"I am going back to work soon in a few days. You had better get out of the bed soon and look after these kids," he said, Mom turning her back to him.

"Can you please just leave her alone?" I said, walking in the room, looking him square in his cold grey cement eyes.

"Look here," he said. "I am leaving for camp tomorrow, and you have to take care of your brother and sisters."

"I know that already," I said. "Mom can't see out of her eyes. She is blind." Turning from him, I walked out of the room.

Doing the best I could, I fed and made sure the kids were bathed, Roderick helping me with Gwen. Mom had showed me, where she hurt, running her hands over her face, wincing when she touched different places. She looked up at me through a fog, her eyes bloodied in the whites of them. "Don't worry, Mom. As soon as he leaves, I am going to go for help and get you to the hospital."

We watched in anticipation of him leaving us, gathering his tools and his best friend, his chainsaw, loading them in the back of his car, watching in ernest as he put on his hard toed boots, the final sign he was actually leaving us. What a relief, finally, he would leave us in peace, and I could get Mom the help she needed.

No sooner was he out of the yard, I started planning the next step. "Look, Rod, you stay with Lilly and Gwen. I am going for help," I told him, Rod shaking his head, blinking in agreement.

I rushed down the road toward my friend's house like a freed animal, running as fast as my legs could carry me, the tears falling hard my heart beating out of my chest. By the time I got to Beatrice's house, I was really a mess, hardly able to get the words out. It was Sunday, everyone home, having lunch. Knocking hard, one of the boys answered the door. I went flying in, Beatrice's mother coming to me right away. "Sit down, girl. Take a deep breath. Now what is wrong?"

"Please, please, my mom, she needs to get to a hospital right away. She is hurt badly." Her husband John, drove me back to the trailer, the kids all watching intently, as we loaded mom in the back seat, covering her with a blanket. She hadn't eaten anything in a whole week, except for the broth of chicken noodle soup I had warmed from a can. Beatrice's father picking her up, like she was a featherweight.

Pulling up to the emergency entrance of the hospital, Beatrice's dad, went in for help. They whisked Mom in quickly in a wheelchair. Following close behind, they ushered me into another room. The nurse told me I would

have to wait here until the doctor examined Mom. That's when I wished
I had brought a book along, my mind clouded with sadness, needing to
escape the reality of what was happening.

Not knowing was killing me. Walking near the room, I went in, the
doctor and a nurse standing over my mom. "Alice Schoolcraft," the doctor
said. "I am Dr. Jones. Can you open your eyes, dear? Can you see me?"

Mom shook her head, talking softly. "I can only see shadows," she said.

"Can you tell me what happened to you?"

"Yes," Mom replied, without thinking hard. "I was in a car accident."
The doctor looked down at her swollen black and blue face, holding up
two fingers.

"How many fingers do you see?" he asked.

"I can't see anything," she replied. I bit into my lip, and tears started to
flow again, like I had an endless flow of sadness.

"It's OK, Alice," the doctor said, giving me hope. "You will be all right,"
he said, touching her arm gently.

Sitting down now, near her bedside, I heard the doctor talking to the
nurse. "No sight in either of her eyes, a splintered cheekbone, but it looks
like an old injury, lacerations to her upper body not conducive with a car
accident. Also, brain swelling and hemorrhage, further X-rays will reveal
the damage to her eyes and other tissue or bone damage.

"I want a twenty-four-hour watch on this woman. She is to have no
visitors," he said, "and I want someone to interview her daughter." Looking
over at me.

"Maybe we can get the whole story and the truth of what really happened
to this poor woman. My guess is that her husband beat her," he said, looking
me straight in my eyes,

the truth written on my tear stained face. I hung my head in admission.
I would tell them the truth, the whole truth.

I could never let this happen again and was ready to tell it all, sparing
nothing, hoping he would go to jail forever, and leave us in peace.

The nurse came and took me to another room, where it was just her and
I. "Can you tell me what happened to your mom? It will be just between
you and me," she assured me, waiting for me to spill the story. "The doctor
needs to know the full truth so he can treat your mom and get her better."

"Yes, I know," I answered. "She was not in an accident. My father beat her. I watched him punching her in the face, slamming her head between the refrigerator door. He beats her often and has threatened to kill all of us. If he knew that I said anything, he would want to kill me too," I cried. She came to me, hugging me.

"Listen Brenda, we already knew the truth. We just needed you to confirm what the tests have already revealed. We have to report this to the police, this is a serious matter. Your mom is hurt badly and is blind." Hearing her say the word *blind* cut into me, like a knife.

"No, no," I cried, holding my head in my hands, wailing, just letting it all out. The nurse doing the best she could to comfort me.

Cozying up in the chair next to my mom's bed, the nurse brought me a couple of books. I lost myself in the words and the lives of others, waiting for any news on my mother. The whiteness of the room and the bright lights were hurting my eyes, thinking of my poor mother, who couldn't see at all. Reaching for her, I uttered, "I am here, Mom. I am not leaving you. The kids are at Beatrice's house. Her mom said they could stay there until I come back for them." Mom's little hand reached out for mine, squeezing me, the love from her spreading warmth from her fingers to my heart.

I sat in the chair all day, reading the most of one book. Finally, when all went quiet in the hospital, the nurse came to turn off the light, and I crawled up beside Mom in her hospital bed, putting my arm around her. The night nurse, noticing me, said she wouldn't tell anyone, but it wasn't allowed.

The next day the doctor came in, asking Mom how she was feeling. "And what about you, miss? Shouldn't you be going to school?"

"Not until my mom is out of here. I can't leave her. I am all she's got."

Touching her hand, he spoke. "We will be operating on your eyes tomorrow, Alice. The retinas in both eyes are damaged, but there is a good chance we can fix them, and you will see again."

"Oh, thank you, Doctor," I said, hope in my heart. Mom was quiet, just listening.

"Just be still now, get some rest. Tomorrow is a big day," he said, leaving us alone in the white room, my mom's breathing, the only sound in my ears.

"It's going to be all right, Mom. I told them everything, the truth." Not saying a word, just keeping her eyes closed. I think she was relieved. She had taught us not to lie, and the lies were breaking her. The truth would set us free.

Early morning, I had fallen asleep on the chair, my body cramped, the nurse bringing in a breakfast platter for me. Mom couldn't even have a drink, her operation scheduled for this morning. I watched as they put her on a stretcher, telling me it would be a couple of hours, and why didn't I go outside for a walk or go home and come back. There was no way I could leave her. I just asked for another book to read while I sat in the waiting room, looking out the window, praying hard that God would give her back her eyesight.

Finally, the doctor emerged from the double doors, coming straight to me. Pulling away the white mask, he bent down to talk to me quietly. "We have operated on your mother's eyes, and it went well, she should be able to see your pretty face by tomorrow."

Overwhelmed and happy, I thanked him, and got up and hugged him. "Thank you, thank you," I kept saying over and over.

The rest of that day, I lost myself in the book they had given me, coming back to reality just long enough to hold her hand and kiss her on the cheek, and then back to my book. Watching keenly for any sign of her awakening. As she started to stir, getting up now, close to her. Opening her eyes, I stared straight into them, the green of them glossed over.

"Mom, Mom, wake up, Mommy. I am here. Can you see me, Mom?" Trying to sit up. I helped her, putting a pillow behind her back. I waited for her words, like waiting for the best present anyone could ever give me.

"Yes, honey," she said, pulling my face close to her. "I can see you, my beautiful princess," she said, tears flowing again like healing water.

Later that afternoon, two constables walked in, in blue uniforms. I knew what was coming next. One of them walked to my mom's bedside. "Are you Mrs. Schoolcraft?" he asked, the other one sitting in the chair next to me.

"Yes, I am," my mother answered in a small voice.

"What happened to you, ma'am?" asked the tall slim policeman.

"I am Constable Bell, and this is my partner, Constable Billy. We have a report here that says you were in some kind of accident, ma'am?"

"Yes, I was," answered my mom, my heart sinking. She was still going to lie for him? I just couldn't believe it! The other constable stared my way, my eyes lowered to the floor. The officer who was eyeing me said to his partner, "Let her rest now." He beckoned to me to come out of the room. I got up slowly, looked over at Mom, who was trying to make some kind of gesture to me. Looking away from her quickly, I followed the cops out of the room to a chair outside the room.

"What is your name?" asked the policeman with the soft brown eyes, a pen and pad in his hand.

"Brenda," I answered.

"Can you tell me what happened to your mom?"

I started crying and told the story over again to him. "But please, don't tell him I told you. I am scared for our lives, please," I begged.

"Don't you worry your little head," he answered. "You just stay by your mother's side. She needs you now."

CHAPTER 89

Elric's New Plans for His Family

D ad had settled into his new job, making a good impression with the foreman, doing the job of two men, wondering how everyone had made out at home. He wouldn't see his family for a while, just wanting to make lots of money to take home, make Alice and the kids happy. His mind took him back to the terrible state he had left us in, the hatred in Brenda's eyes. Had he ruined everything? He worked faster and harder, trying to drive the thoughts of them back into the deep graves of his mind.

Deciding that he would move his family out of Blind River. Too much water under the bridge, and too much danger for all of us, like the large dark sturgeon fish that trolled the bottom of the river that was said could swallow a man whole, he thought.

They all needed a new start. Get the kids into a new school. Too many questions. Just then, he thought of the possibilities that Mom might have died, and the cops were looking for him right now. No, if that was the case, they would have already come for him. Everything was all right, he assured himself. The new job had taken him a few hundred miles from us, and he would just find us another place to live, closer to where he was working now, near Sault Ste. Marie.

On his days off, he drove around, trying to find a new home for us.

CHAPTER 90
Alice Leaves the Hospital

Mom had to stay in the hospital a few more days after her operation but became restless, wanting to get back to the kids. I was so excited the day she would be released, bringing her fresh clothes. The doctor said her eyes had healed up well and that she should just take it easy.

"I will help her do everything," I said, the doctor reminding me that I should be in school. When I walked into the trailer, the dampness seeped into my bones, the memory of the events still hanging fresh in the air. I hated this place and never wanted to come back, but where else would we go? *You have nowhere else to go,* came back the voice of reason.

I ran all the way back to the hospital, hurrying to mom's room. She was sitting on the side of the bed, her housecoat and slippers on her feet.

"Are you ready to get out of here?" I asked, excitement in my voice.

"Sure am, let's go and get the kids and bring them home."

"No, Mom. You will go home, and I will go and get the kids."

"All right," she said, stepping down from her bed, slipping into her slacks and the soft red wool sweater, I had brought her.

We took the bus most of the way home and then walked about a half a mile to the trailer. As we approached, no sign of life in the yard. Getting in, I put a few sticks of wood in the stove getting a fire started. Helping Mom straighten out a few things, I watched her eyes, going to the place where she had almost lost her life. No sign of the struggle, the blood cleaned up. Pulling a frozen rabbit out of the freezer, she put it in the sink to thaw.

"We will have rabbit provincial," she said with a slight giggle.

"What is that?" I asked.

"Its' rabbit cooked in whiskey," she answered, pointing to a half full bottle sitting on the counter. There was something that just struck me funny. I started laughing hysterically. Using his poison in our rabbit dinner. Mom tried to laugh, but it hurt her, but I could see the relief and happiness to be home with the ones she loved.

"Here, you cut up the onion, and I'll do the rest." I hugged up close to her, the smell of her sweet breath on my face, the warmth of her love permeating me to my bones.

With Mom home cooking dinner, I went to get my brother and sisters. I watched their faces when the saw Mom standing in the kitchen with her apron on. Like time had stood still for them, not telling them anything, the kids just fell into place, like a happy family puzzle.

It was the best day ever, having her back. We sat eating dinner together, the spot at the head of the table empty. None of the kids asked where he was.

CHAPTER 91

Back to School

The next day, Monday, we all got up early, getting ready for our first day back to school. Gwen would be at home with Mom, keeping her company. Roderick and Lillian were excited, just like the first day of school for them. They were ready, with their lunches, waiting for me to go catch the bus.

The principal called me out of class, asking me why we hadn't been to school in ten days.

"My mother was in a terrible accident," I lied. "I had to stay home to look after everyone. My father was away at work."

He just looked at me and rolled his eyes.

"If this keeps up, your brother and sister will be kept back a grade. You are just lucky your grades are good. You are an A student," he said.

"Well, I don't know what I can do about it now," I answered. "There are just some things in life you have no control over."

I wondered where that had come from. Anyway, it sounded good to my ears.

"All right then," he said, a short, stout man with a flat face and big fish eyes.

"Go back to class, and try not to miss any more school." He was the teacher, the principal, and the bus driver, teaching all the grades, from one to eight, all in one big classroom.

The next couple of months were great. We were doing without things, but at least we hadn't seen Elric in a long time. Mom rarely brought him up, like he had just disappeared from our lives forever. Knowing that wasn't realistic, I became anxious, knowing in my heart he was coming back. The question was when.

The police had been keeping their eyes out for him too. I noticed a cruiser parked just down the road from us, more than once. It worried me a lot, knowing that he might find out I was the one who had told his dirty little secrets.

"Domestic abuse cases rarely go to court," said one of the cops to the other. "These women won't testify. Either they are scared to death, or they just get used to living that kind of life. The abuser usually walks away a free man, just a waste of the court's time," he explained, shaking his head, watching for any movement near the Schoolcraft trailer.

Mom and I were outside raking leaves around the trailer when a car approached from the road. It was Elric, in an older Chevy. Getting out of the car, his eyes directly on Mom, not even looking my way. Walking over to her, Mom dropped her head. Pulling her to him, my stomach churning, my eyes burning holes into him.

"Good to see you. Are you alright?" he said.

"No thanks to you," I muttered under my breath.

"What did you say?" he asked, staring at me now.

"Come in the house, dear," he said, taking my mother's hand. "I have some good news."

I really had to hear this. I walked in behind them, Dad taking Mom to the couch. They both sat down, Mom with her gaze towards the floor.

"Tonight, we are packing up and getting the hell out of this place. I have found us a new place to live. You are going to love it. Its' called the Black Spruce Resort. It's a place that's owned by an old German man, just about an hour from Sault Ste. Marie." He went on, Mom just listening, not saying a word.

"Things are going to be different. I've had lots of time to think it through, and you have my word. I have quit drinking, haven't had a drink since I left here two months ago."

Mom slowly raised her head, looked into his face, a blankness in her eyes.

"Well, come on," he said, like we were supposed to get up and start dancing.

"Don't have all day. We got to pack up everything that will fit into the car, and the rest, leave it behind. We got a nice house with a lawn and everything. You guys are going to love it. And Brenda," he said, looking over at me, "I got you a job already. You will be able to make your own money."

That was the best news I had ever heard. A job, a real job. "Doing what?" I asked, anxious to hear the rest.

"Our new house is just two minutes from a huge chalet, with lots of rooms that need cleaning. I already talked to the owner about you, and he said that you could clean the rooms. And just guess what, Alice? I got you a job too," he said, Mom now searching his face, waiting for him to spill out the rest of his plan. "You can do some cooking at the resort. There are lots of tourists, in the summer especially, and we will be living right there." A faint smile crossed Mom's face. She was probably thinking the same thing I was: safety. There would be lots of other people around. Hope shined in her face and eyes, her eyes meeting mine.

Without further ado, I got up and went back to my room, gathering up the things I absolutely couldn't live without, packing up my books first, my clothes and my school supplies.

That day was such a turning point in our lives. It went by with such a blur, like the changing scenery as we drove and drove, the car packed to the hilt. I watched my father struggling to close the trunk, everything we owned in the back seat. The kids and I sat high up on the blankets and other soft things, like clothing, they stuffed into the car until it was like a fully filled, pail of water, with no room for one more drop.

CHAPTER 92

A Few Moons Later

My next birthday, I would be twelve. Two bumps had appeared on my sweater, and daily, they seemed to be growing. I was working every day now, cleaning units for the boss, Peter, a German man, originally born in the Black Forest in Germany. His beautiful wife, Johanna, kept herself busy in the kitchen of the resort, creating German delicacies, like apple strudel. There were other German foods that excited my taste buds, like liverwurst that I had never eaten before. Deep, dark rye breads, German mustards, and pickles. I was loving this new experience so much. Johanna insisted that I wear a special dirndl dress when I was working out front in the dining area, making me feel like an authentic German girl, Johanna mentioning that I looked German, with my blonde hair and blue eyes. Waiting on tables and taking their money when they were ready to pay for their meals, I was loving it.

These new happenings in my life were lifting the dark blanket that had hung over my heart and soul most of my life. Mom, seemingly, was much happier too.

Elric was gone most of the time, and when he did come home lately, he was hanging out with Peter, helping him pour and mix cement for the new foundations he was putting in expanding his already famous resort.

Travellers were coming from Germany, some just pulling in off the Trans-Canada highway, the huge sign reading the Black Spruce Resort, attracting tourists. Lake Superior loomed in the backdrop, like a sea of forever water. We went down to the lake to explore, Roderick and I, and Lillian in tow, picking agate rocks, putting our feet into the ice water. Even when summer came, the water remained cold, but a respite of the hot weather. Rod and I ran in fast and came back out, our skin taking on a purple tinge.

Johanna had invited Mom down to help her in the kitchen a few days, letting Mom take home some of the leftovers that didn't get sold that day. Well, that was a God's blessing right there, Mom getting so excited, unwrapping the foiled packages that she had meticulously wrapped, bringing them home to us. The kids were enjoying all the food, especially the Black Forest cake.

Whipped topping with cherries in the middle, it became my favorite cake. I would buy my own piece with a cup of coffee, after a long day in the dining room.

Peter had taken me all around the resort, in his Beetle bug, he called it, a green Volkswagen with large round lights in the front that really did look like beetle's eyes. I loved the car, and within a few weeks of meeting him, he let me drive around the resort, sending me on errands to go and get him this from his wife or go and get some nails. I couldn't believe it, I was driving and loving the little green Beetle car.

We had only been there a few months when Peter told us that his wife was going home for a visit, giving both Mom and I more designated jobs. I would be cleaning all the units now, and Mom would be full time cook.

Overjoyed at our new duties, Mom and I planned a big shopping trip into Sault Ste. Marie, where we would buy some new things for everybody. This was the first time in my life that I remember getting new clothes, mostly they came from handouts, or the free things that the church gave away. Mom and I planned our shopping trip for a whole month. I was getting really good with the tourists, knowing just the right words to say so they would leave me a big tip. Some days, I was making fifty dollars in tips, the wages of most of the men working in the bush. At first it seemed like there was too much money, so I started hiding it all over in my room. At one point, I pulled up few floorboards in my closet and stuffed about five hundred dollars down there. I think I was mostly hiding it from you know who, but whatever, I was working for this money and was going to enjoy the fruits of my labor.

Working hard that whole month, Mom and I were anxious to take our shopping trip, waiting for the word when Peter's wife would return, letting us get back to our light duties.

The work started showing on Mom, too tired after a whole day cooking for the tourists, bringing us home leftovers every day now, which we didn't mind, all kinds of good stuff.

Peter took us aside one day, announcing that his wife had left him. We were sad for him, Mom trying to make the special things, finally having to get a German cookbook to make the schnitzel, Black Forest cakes, and strudel.

Dad had been home a few times, staying far away from me. My top lip was trained in a snarl that I used for him if he tried to hug or kiss me.

"Oh, you are too big to get a hug from your old man, ah?" I wondered why he called himself the old man, when in truth he looked really young and still nice looking. I couldn't help but notice how strange women looked at him, yearning in their eyes. If only they knew what a monster he was, I thought, laughing inside.

You could sure fool the people with that face, I would think. The devil can be such a deceiver. To me, he was the devil walking, and I secretly wished that the Lord would bind him in an abyss, just like it was promised in the last book of the Bible.

I read the bible in earnest, with all its promises of a new world, with only love and happiness, where death would be no more, where you could feed a lion as if it were a kitten. Those passages really intrigued me, taking me there. It was so wonderful there, closing the book of promises, keeping them close to my heart. It was the book I watched my mother hugging to her chest so many times, the book I loved the best.

Peter had taken to fixing large platters of crackers and liverwurst, and special cheeses. He was always full of compliments, telling me that I looked just like the girls in Germany with my wheat blonde hair and blue eyes. Before long, I felt a different friendship building between us. It had changed from boss and worker to friend and confidante. He let me decide whether he would pay me by the hour or by the room, and I chose by the room, and five dollars a room was a lot in those days. Seemingly very happy with my work, he sometimes followed me from room to room, which made me feel uncomfortable. I didn't always want to talk to the short little man with the large bulbous nose, reminding me of a big leprechaun.

Dad was staying in the bush for longer periods of time, and to me, it seemed like we were on some kind of holiday, eating good, the kids with a big yard to play in. Forty acres to be exact, trails and small roads that led us all over the resort.

There was a creek separating the property, where Rod would go fishing, always bringing home something. He was the great white hunter in training, I thought to myself, laughing one day he even shot a big fish out of the creek.

Dad had displayed his guns in one section of the house. At first it creeped me out, worrying that he would use them on us, but lately there was no reason for worry. When he did come home to us, he was the perfect gentleman, trying to cozy up to Mom, but I noticed that she tried to keep her distance from him too. I'm sure he knew in his hard cold heart that he had done a lot of damage to her, and underneath I wondered how he could expect her to ever love him again.

Especially the first day when we had arrived at the resort. Arriving there in the middle of the night, Dad taking us to one of the suites. He told us it was OK. He had it all arranged. Opening the door onto a full suite with two double beds on one side and two single beds on the other, perfect for all of us to sleep. The next day, we would move into a brand-new house.

Excited about a brand-new house, I softened my heart toward him a little, just slightly, thinking that he was trying to make our lives better.

I watched as the final things were carried into the house, which was fully furnished, with four bedrooms. Gwen and Lilly had to share one. I had my own bright room, with a big picture window, looking out over a bit of a meadow to a large, dark stand of spruce trees. It was absolutely beautiful, the house brand-new, and everything in it.

Pinch me, I thought. Was this just a dream I would wake from any minute? Going back out to the living room, all set up with a television and everything Mom would need to cook. Fresh towels hung in the bathroom, which had a shower and a bath. My heart was glad. Walking back out to the living room now, my mom and dad were standing there. All of a sudden he picked her up off the floor, twirling her whole body around, her dress ballooning around her, chanting, "Alice has a palace, Alice has a palace." Mom started laughing hysterically. I don't know if it was because she was really happy, or was it that chant that had become a sick kind of thing for my father.

Thinking back, when he took us to the trailer, he didn't do that. Never mentioned any palace. Was it because he knew in his heart it wasn't a home but a coffin? Had he planned on killing us there? It reminded me of the stories he told Roderick and me of him killing a few men, like he was talking about skinning a beaver. Sick, that's what he was. I finally figured it out, he was crazy.

The four bedroom cottage was part of the whole resort idea, another five more just like it. Ours sat on a hill, a perfectly manicured lawn surrounding the house, a few rose bushes in front. Mom got so excited about the rose bushes, more excited than she was about the house. The kids walked from room to room, looking through like they were in a candy store, the three of them fighting about which room was going to be theirs. Mom and Dad's room was the same size as mine and exactly the same. I hoped that it would mostly be Mom's, now that we were seeing less of him. When he did come home, he seemed to be laying off the liquor, but I did notice him having German beer with Peter once in a while. Watching him from afar, I really believe that he wanted us back in his life, but like something he would have said, "Too much water under the bridge."

Settling into our respective schools, I went fifty miles every day on a bus into Sault Ste. Marie, and the other kids went to a school about twenty miles the other way, also catching a bus on the highway every morning. Things were unbelievably happy. I would rush home from school and go straight to the resort for something good to eat, then get busy cleaning the rooms that had been rented the night before. Peter was giving me small gifts, like a pendant, a gold chain, things I thought that maybe belonged to his wife. I felt bad about taking them, but nonetheless happy for the trinkets.

Mom had told me secretly that Elric wasn't giving her any money lately, and she suspected that he was spending time in the village on his days off at an Indian settlement called Batchewana Bay. It had one store, and one bar.

"Whatever, I don't care," she told me. Between her and me, we were making good money and doing without nothing.

I think that Peter was letting us stay in the house for free because we were part of a team, keeping his resort running, and he loved having me around to look at and dream about at night.

Being so far from the city, the resort was rather isolated. He would have had a hard time getting someone else to work there, unless they drove from far. It was perfect.

Mom had been spot on when she said that Elric was probably spending time in the village. Someone told her they had seen him with an Indian woman called Julie, sitting at the only bar in town.

When she confronted him, he tried to make out as though it couldn't have been him, saying he was away in the bush working, but Mom knew in her heart it was true. He was having an affair and carrying on with some other woman. Knowing better than to start something that she couldn't finish, she never brought it up to him again, making me wonder, but I was happy that it wasn't really bothering her much.

CHAPTER 93

Shocking Changes

One day, we had just got home from school when a police car drove into the yard with an ambulance following it. I was the first one to notice them from my picture window, and yelled to Mom to come and look. We watched together from the window, as two paramedics in their uniforms went to the back of the ambulance, taking someone out on a stretcher. I knew right away it was my father, my heart sinking.

"It's Dad," I said out loud.

"Oh my God," my mother said, running to the door, opening it wide, the cold fall air seeping in. They brought Elric up the steps strapped to a stretcher, a contraption running right around his head, two pronged things that looked like they were growing out of the sides of his head connected to the other steel plate.

With his eyes wide open, he looked straight up. It was something out of a horror movie, especially with him, the scary character.

"What happened to him?" my mother cried, her hands up to her face, her eyes full of tears.

"Your husband was hit by a tree, ma'am. He has a broken neck and a few broken vertebrae in his back. They did all they could for him at the hospital. He will be laid up for a few months, until everything heals. He is best here, at home with his family. He will have to remain on his back the whole time, needs bathing in bed and feeding."

"Yes, yes, of course," my mom said, looking over at me, our eyes talking without saying.

I stared down at my father, his eyes now focused on me.

"Hi, Brenda," he said, his grey eyes softening, like a fluffy grey cloud.

"Hi, Dad," I answered. "I'm sorry," I said, walking away. The paramedics laid him down on Mom's double bed. We watched as they put him down gently, pulling the blue soft blanket up over him to his waist.

They walked out of the room, leaving Mom and I, one on either side of the bed, staring at each other.

Something unbelievable had just happened. He was delivered to us on a platter, I thought, my mean side taking over.

I looked at him from across the room, seeing new opportunities for my father to get to know me.

One of the paramedics called Mom out to give her instructions on how to feed and bathe him, as I listened to every word. The other kids were out playing somewhere. I was glad that they didn't see them bring him in. They would find out soon enough.

Really, I didn't feel the least bit sorry for him and was secretly laughing inside, happy to see him suffering. A vision of my poor mom, her head on my lap, fighting for her life, showed in my mind's eye.

For a minute, I felt guilty. Did all my prayers and bad wishes do this to him? I didn't want to go with that thought, but my heart was overflowing. It was time that he felt the wrath of God. How could he have hurt us so much and get away with it?

Mom had told us God saw everything, and that he could be an angry God. I wondered what was taking him so long to bring Elric to his knees, having grown to hate the sight of him or the mention of his name. The facade that he put on for us since he had brought us here was temporary too, just waiting for the storm to come. I looked at him, helpless now, giving me a new power over him. He would get to know the daughter who hated him.

Mom and I took shifts looking after Elric. Mom was so tired after all day at the resort, then had to come home and bathe him. I could see that she had pity for him, but it seemed she was just going through the motions, not much love spent. When it was my turn to get him soup or water, I would deliberately wait or pretend I forgot.

He would start yelling from the room. "C'mon in here, you little bastard. I'll fix you when I get out of this thing," he threatened, his threats falling on deaf ears.

Watching from the doorway, he would try to pick up the stick he had asked Rod to bring him so he could reach for things. Waving it in the air like the madman that he was, I laughed to myself, amused by his helplessness.

Sometimes, I would walk by the room slowly so he could see me, but just keep walking, then he would start screaming. The other kids were all going to him, to try to get him what he needed but they couldn't make tea or heat up soup. Elric was my patient.

One afternoon, I brought in a large bowl of almost boiling chicken soup, accidentally spilling it all over his bare chest. "You stupid fucking whore!" he yelled, his eyes bugging out of his head.

Really, I am that, I thought. I had purposely spilled the steaming hot soup on him, wanting him to hurt, to feel just a little of the pain he had inflicted on us. As I walked out of the room, he started screaming bloody murder, the door closed in his face like a kick in the ribs.

After about an hour, I went back to clean the noodles off his chest and dress his burn. Watching me, I felt his eyes on me, like a hot poker, burning my flesh. It really did look like an accident, Elric dropping the spoon from his mouth, the spoon sending the soup, all over him.

CHAPTER 94

O
ne weekend in late October, the cold of winter threatening, the snow deep already. The kids were all at home playing, Roderick keeping watch, being the older one, eight years old now, Lillian seven, and Gwen five. I was cleaning up to ten rooms a day now, plus my duties with Elric, and trying to fit my homework in somewhere, which made for busy, hurried days. My grades were good, and I barely had to study for a test to attain honor grades right through. That made me feel good about myself, and thank God I had some smarts. Trying to survive a war zone took brains and guts.

Mom, and I had been working all morning, Mom sending me to the house to check on the kids. I walked in, calling Rod's name. No sign of him, so I walked into Dad's room to see if he was in there. What I saw sickened me. Lillian sprawled out on top of his chest, bare naked, Elric touching her private parts. When he noticed me, he quickly took his hands off her, trying to push her down. Gwen was playing with something at the foot of the bed.

"Hey, Brenda. It's about time you showed up to help your old man."

"What do you want, and what was Lilly doing, laying on your chest?" Tryiing to turn his face from me, as I got closer, close enough that my breath was blowing in his face.

"You are just what I've known all along, a sick bastard. I know what you were doing. Don't think I am stupid."

"Ah, she crawled up here herself. I wasn't doing anything."

Looking him straight in his steel grey eyes, I spat right in his face, the spittle flying, dropping on him like many insults.

"You are a low life," I screamed. "I don't feel one bit sorry for you. If I ever see you touching my sister again, I will go to the police and report you. You think you can get away with hurting us over and over, well, you can't! Not anymore," I screamed, "and I am going to tell Mom about this!"

"Fuck you, you stupid bitch," he said, foam around his dry, cracked lips, his greasy hair stuck to his head.

Roderick had just came through the door with an armful of wood to feed the little woodstove that was backup heat for our oil furnace.

"Dad sent me outside to chop wood," he said, putting the pieces of the puzzle together for me.

"Convenient," I said.

"What did you say?" asked Roderick.

"Never mind," I answered, summing up the situation.

I took some leftovers to the house, fixing the kids some dinner. The door to Elric's room remained closed. I could hear him in there, shuffling around, trying to get up to use the bathroom, which was just off the room. He needed my help to get him up, and I decided he would just have to make out the best way he could.

Mom came home from work, tired and weary, going in to get ready to wash him up.

"That fucking Brenda wouldn't help me to the bathroom. I'm sorry," I heard him say. He had pissed the bed. Feeling so bad that my mom had to clean up the mess, but not wanting to go near the room.

That night, after she finished cleaning him up, feeding him some soup, she came back out to join me at the table, doing some homework. I explained what I had seen him doing to Lilly.

"The Lord will always have the last say. Sometimes he may seem slow to his promises, but he is a person of his word. He never forsakes the ones who love him and whom he loves." I went to her, and we hugged.

Mom had made her bed in Roderick's room, letting him take over the living room, the big couch, comfy for a little skinny guy. Rod was quite happy to have a different room for a while. His blinking was getting better, only noticing it when he was stressed about something, talking too fast, then his eyes would start fluttering.

One day, Peter had followed me into one of the rooms I was cleaning, asking me if he could talk to me privately. It made me a little uneasy, but I had grown to like and trust him. After all, he was the source of all our plenty right now, like we had never known.

"Come over here," he coaxed, separating his knees, meaning that I should sit on his knee. I really didn't see any harm in it, going to him.

He told me about his failed marriage, and how they had tried to have children, his wife a barren woman. They had been married ten years, and without a child. She had become withdrawn from him, his ranting about a child turning her away from him altogether in the bedroom department.

"A man had needs," he said in his heavy German accent. "I could make your life really good," he said, a sparkle in his blue eyes.

"How about ten dollars a room, but there is something you would have to do for me." Waiting for him to tell me the rest, I tried to relax on his short, stubby knee.

"No one would have to know," he went on. "It would be our secret," he said as he put his gnarly hand on my breast. At first it felt disgusting, but after a few minutes, I didn't really mind, keeping my mind on the money I would be making, and all the new clothes and things. I could even buy my mother dresses, and my brother and sisters… My mind far away as he continued to fondle my breasts. It was definitely weird, but when I looked into his eyes, I saw the needs of a lonely old man. If that's all I had to do, it was fine with me.

After about ten minutes, I noticed that there was something growing between his legs, Peter put my hand there. "See what you have done to me, made me happy," he said, getting up now, walking out of the room not wanting me to see the wet spot on the front of his pants and the tent that had grown under his baggy pants.

About once a week now, Peter would seek me out in the privacy of the room I was cleaning, and go through the ritual of rubbing my breasts until they felt tender to the touch. It started to bother me, but the money was always on my mind while he fondled me, thinking of all the nice things I could buy.

One day, when he was getting a little too excited, he started running his hand up and down the hardness in his pants, finally letting out a low growl, throwing back his wide, large head, his beady blue eyes closed, a final grunt, like a stud boar running through the bush.

I guess Elric had told my mom that I was not doing my share when she was working. Mom took me aside, asking me to be more understanding, telling me that he had bedsores all over his bum and back and was in a lot of pain, making my heart glad.

"He might want to hurt you when he gets better, Brenda," she said. "You had better try harder to help him." With my mother's urging, I really did put more effort into helping him, hating every minute of it.

In my rebellion, I told her I couldn't stand the sight of him, and wished that he would die right there, so we could be rid of him forever.

Staring into my eyes, saddened by my words. "Brenda, two wrongs don't make a right. Don't be like him, God would not like that."

With that said, I changed my perspective, trying to be more considerate. Pity, that's what it was, not love, pity for a helpless person.

"It's really hard on me," she explained. "At least get him some food and water, and help him to the bathroom," to which I agreed.

"I am doing it for you, Mom, not for him," I explained.

I don't know how we managed, but Elric had been a prisoner in that bed for three months straight. It was getting close to the end of March, spring starting to show itself in the buds on the trees. Lately he was talking about going back to work and getting out of the contraption that had become his hell on earth. I went to him every day now, knowing too that he would soon be up and moving, and I was worried in the back of my mind that he would take out all of his frustrations on me.

One day, when I was feeding him some soup, he said to me, between gulps, "You don't like your old man, do you?" Waiting for an answer.

I said, with much hesitation, "Actually, Dad, I really don't know who you are. I don't like you at all. Can you really blame me?" I asked, to which he didn't answer.

"I will make it up to you guys," he answered, not making eye contact with me.

Sure, I thought. Nothing he could do or say could take the pain away that he had inflicted on Mom and us. My heart was hardened towards him a long time ago, and I personally did not feel the hurt, trying to shield Mom and the kids. I had to be strong for them.

As the days grew longer, the snow started melting, spring starting to loosen the hold of winter that had kept us inside most of the time. It had been a long cold winter, and colder in my heart, with the constant needs of him.

The birds were singing, making their nests, the bears were starting to come out of their caves, showing themselves in the nearby trees of the resort. We spotted a few baby bears, the tourists trying to get close enough for some pictures, and some of them trying to feed the hungry bears. Big mistake.

We were watching one day when a man approached a young bear in a tree, the bear reaching out with its massive paw, swiping its long nails across the man's face opening up long gashes. Holding his face as the blood spilled from his open cuts, he ran to the dining room, asking for help.

Peter was having a coffee break. Getting up quickly, he cleaned and bandaged his face.

That incident made us afraid of the cuddly bears, bringing the warning, they were wild and dangerous.

We were awakened one morning by the cries of a baby. I looked out the window to see a brand new baby bear, halfway up the tree in front of the house. I called my mom and the kids to the window to watch, as the mama bear came to our window, opening her great jaws, showing us her long teeth, like ivory tusks in her mouth.

Frightened, we backed away from the window. The danger was apparent. We would watch for them now, and run like hell if there were any around.

Our lives had sure changed since we reached the Black Spruce Resort, the short, thick man, Peter, like our savior. Mom and I both had extra savings, still planning on our one day that we would go to the Sault and shop all day, and go out to eat at a Chinese restaurant, something we had never done.

Dad was feeling a lot better, and his scheduled trip to the Sault was soon, to get the contraption off his head, letting his neck settle back into place, giving him his freedom again.

Having him there, no threat to us, relying on us for everything, gave me renewed power in my mind. Hopefully he had learned some humility while he was bedridden, having to dig deep into his cold heart and show us some appreciation. When I changed my attitude toward him a bit, I noticed that he too tried to be nicer in the things he would say.

"My, you are growing into a beautiful young woman," he had said. Not knowing how to take that statement, I wondered if he had noticed the bumps that seemed to me to be growing daily, making me self-conscious.

One thing for sure, when I was working around Peter, I would try my best to wear loose fitting blouses. When I had to wear the dirndl dress in the dining room, making me look like an authentic German girl from the Black Forest, the rise of my chest couldn't be hidden. That's when I would catch Peter staring at my bumps, talking to my chest instead of talking to me. Knowing the extra money I was making, due to the fact, he loved to play with them, giving me a kind of a power over him.

After a while, I started to embrace my new womanhood, even taking a liking to a boy who came around the resort with his father to help Peter with the electrical work for his new units.

His name was Ray. We took a few walks into the bush together, started out on a mission for Peter, with Ray coaxing me into the bushes, kissing me.

It was great that a boy liked me. I started to feel excited around him, my hormones kicking in, looking forward to his visits.

Ray was a tall, good looking boy, with a cleft in his chin and big blue eyes. He became my secret crush.

Lately, the kids were doing better at school too, especially Roderick, who had written an essay about why Mom was the best mom on earth. To our surprise, he won the contest that would grant Mom a trip to Sault Ste. Marie to meet the mayor and be the guest of honor at a special ceremony.

Along with a great dinner and a day on the town, being the mayor's guest for the day, she received a plaque on a piece of dark wood in copper that read, Mother of the Year, with her name on it in thick black letters on the bottom.

How had I missed that in him? I guess I was just too busy trying to survive, his brightness overshadowed by the dark cloud that followed us most of the time.

We were so proud of him, Mom making a special dinner in his honor, his favorite, perogies with onion and fried bacon, with real sour cream and Black Forest cake for dessert.

After dinner, we all clapped and cheered him on, Elric still a prisoner of his bed, getting some of the dinner fed to him by my mother.

Peter took the whole day off to take my father into the Sault to get his contraption off his neck. Dad came home to us, walking straight, showing us how he could turn his head, the doctor giving him a clean bill of health to go back to work whenever he was ready.

The going back to work part made me happy. The less we saw of him, the better. Spending a couple of weeks around the house, Mom and I kept busy at the resort. Dad enjoyed a dinner with Peter and a beer on occasion. Watching him, to make sure that he had only had one, I tried to stay close to their conversations. Bringing out some food from the kitchen, I overheard my father say my name, "Brenda," smiling, then Peter got a funny look on his face, trying not to look my way. It made me wonder what my father had said to him, but I forgot about it until a few days later, when Peter and I met for one of our visits.

"Do you know what your father said about you? He said he would sell you to me for half of my resort."

I was so shocked, I didn't know what to say.

Peter went quiet, gazing at me, a wanting look in his beady eyes, making me shudder.

"Oh gosh," I said. "My father is a funny man sometimes. I am sure he was just kidding."

In my mind, I put the contraption thing back on his head, wishing that his tongue was cut out of his head too. How dare he, try to sell me to this old creepy ogre of a man!

I was finding out lots of things about Peter, spending time in his private study. He was a fan of Hitler and had a stack of books on him and his propaganda.

One day, after finishing my shift at the resort, I went back to get something I had forgotten there. Going in the kitchen back door, I looked through the window where the food came out and saw a man standing in the middle of the room. I later found out his name was John Beatty. He was proud to tell us he was in our history books as the leader of the Canadian Nazi Party.

There were about ten men in the dining room, all sitting around, listening to him speak. My jaw dropped when I noticed my father sitting there with the same dark grey shirt on like the rest, wearing a swastika armband.

Roderick sat in the chair next to my father. Why would he have my brother there, and what were they doing?

It didn't look like the time and place to present myself, but I continued watching from the kitchen window, a full out Nazi party meeting, just thinking leave it to my father to find us a sanctuary in the middle of a Nazi camp.

The man who was leading the meeting, I had noticed helping Peter with odd jobs. He had taken notice of me a couple of times, staring too long, and the last few days, he chose the same seat in a corner, reading a book or newspaper.

Things were starting to come together now, but there was no way I was going to be a Nazi's bride.

The night before my father would go back into the bush, he insisted on all of us sitting down to a dinner together. I think he had prepared a speech for us, because as soon as we all sat down, he held his head down for a bit, sitting at the head of the table. I sat directly across from him, Mom and Gwen on one side and Roderick and Lillian on the other.

"Well, kids, I know it's been pretty hard. Everything, I mean, but I want to say I am going to be a better father. You just have to give me the chance. Tomorrow, I am going to go back to the bush, and I just want you guys to be happy here. Brenda, you help your mom with your brother and sisters."

I regarded him, sitting there in a freshly ironed black cotton shirt, a nice pair of dress pants with silver cuff links at the wrist. Throwing his head back, pushing his black hair off his high forehead.

"Now that we have a great place to live, and both you Brenda and Alice have work with Peter, everything will work out. So let's eat. It might be the last dinner I have with you in a while. I'm really not sure when I'll be back. There is a lot of work cutting slashes and skidder work. Shit, if I land a job driving skidder, I'll be making good money, get you guys anything you want."

I held my head at that moment, not wanting to show him that I didn't trust anything he said. Mom watched him, glancing at me and then at each of them, taking time to make eye contact. We ate dinner without much else said, Mom deep in thought. I was thinking about Ray. I was supposed to meet him later, near unit number ten, the one closest to the deep black forest. It was shaping up to be the best spring and summer of my life.

The next morning Mom was especially cordial to Elric, making him a hot breakfast before she attended to Gwen, Lillian, and Roderick. Fixing myself a bowl of porridge, spooning on a heaping teaspoon of brown sugar, and straight cream, from the resort, I sat at the table, taking in the goings on, Dad coming in from outside with a completely different look than he had yesterday. Sitting there across from him reminded me that if he was one thing, I had to hand to him, he was a nice looking man, like some of the Hollywood actors I had seen on television. I could just see him on stage, the way he told us about those days when his star was shining bright. What had really happened to him? How had he grown bad over the years, and progressively got worse, up until now?

Was it just another facade, or did he really mean well, bringing back the vision of my sister, sprawled across his bare chest, his hands on her body.

No, he was an imposter, just like Mom had called him her imposter prince. He couldn't pull the wool over my eyes, not now, not ever.

CHAPTER 95

D ad stood in the doorway, a grey touque, he called his hunting hat, a green and black checkered shirt and heavy, dark camel colored pants, with his signature steeled toed boots on his feet.

"Well, here's seeing you guys," he said, Gwen going to him first.

"C'mon, all you rascals," he said. "Come and give your old man a hug. Won't see you for a while." The other kids went to him quickly, Mom and I staring at the floor to see which would go first, Mom taking a step toward him. Reaching his long arms around us all, bending down to my mom, kissing her on the forehead.

It was a kiss I will remember all my life. Mom looked up at him, her broken heart trying to find somehow to put it back together, the longing in her eyes and his made me turn away.

OK, let's get on with it, I thought in my mind. *Can you please get the hell away from us?* I wanted to scream from the highest hill.

Watching him gather his things and pack them away, then one last wave, as the car went out of sight.

I took a deep sigh. It was going to be a great day, and I was excited about meeting Ray in unit number ten.

Elric had been gone for two months, and needless to say, we had settled in nicely, even if it was a secret Nazi camp, with me the new fraulein of the resort.

The head of the Nazi party had a complimentary suite and free food, as far as I knew, although he spent a lot of time in the dining room. He sat in the corner, near the wide open windows of the chalet that looked out toward the highway, always with a book or magazine. Sometimes I would feel his eyes on me, looking his way, his eyes darting back to his reading.

Yuck, this place was getting a bit creepy for me, but for now, it was working in a lot of ways. The kids were loving time at the water's edge, picking agates from the shore of Lake Superior. Ray, and I had taken to long walks along the shoreline, the spring sunshine warming our hearts and our bodies.

We did some deep necking a few times, I can recall, on the warm sand. Forbidden love at thirteen. I forgot to mention he was seventeen and very much a man. Mom had met Ray a couple of times and didn't seem to worry when we took off for walks on the beach, trusting me, after having a couple of the talks that made me shy away from her eyes. Said she just wanted me to be happy, but to never end up in the same predicament that she had, as a young woman.

The new spring grass was showing itself around our perfect white chalet. It was pretty, indeed, all the bulbs shoving their heads out to the world. Mom loved the brand new house, keeping it immaculate the bleach in effect.

I watched her bloom into a whole new woman, a smile on her beautiful face mostly now. Mother's Day was coming up, and I got the kids together and told them we would give Mom a surprise party, which I had planned would be the best party of her life. Secretly, I had bought a few balloons and a crown I had found in a party store, Why not? *It will be fun, she is my queen*, I thought. I could see the smile on her face when I put the crown on her head, just as Roderick would bring in the big cake. Remembering her stories of the birthday party in the palace, when she was a princess for a day, now she would be queen.

Chocolate, her favorite, with raspberry jam in the middle with white perfect icing on the top to make it look like lots of little waves. It would be perfect.

I mentioned it to Peter, who said he would take me to the Sault to buy all the special things for our party, secretly having a couple of meetings with Roderick, Gwen, and Lillian.

I had never been to a party and couldn't remember ever having one, only one time, when one of my friends from school brought me a big piece of her birthday cake, surprising me with it at lunchtime.

Tomorrow was Mother's Day, and the kids and I had finished up our preparations, the beautiful cake hidden at the resort in the back of a cooler, where Mom wouldn't see it. We would whisper, just short of her hearing us, trying to tease her or give her an inkling of the surprise. Making her laugh a few times, Mom was trying to figure out what we were up to, catching me wrapping a present in the kitchen at our house. "Is someone having a birthday?" she asked.

Having nothing to say about a birthday, I just walked into my room, hiding the present, a beautiful red velvet dressing gown with white silk on the collar. The lady at the dress shop helped me pick it out, it was the most beautiful one, and the most expensive. I chose a pretty floral silk scarf for Roderick to give to her and a nice pair of leather gloves from Lillian, and a pretty pink blouse from Gwen, and a thin gold necklace with a heart pendant.

Bringing the kids into my room, I let them wrap their own presents, and we all joined in making Mom a homemade card that was about fifteen inches by fifteen inches, with lots of pictures on it that we drew with colored pencils. Roderick drew a horse, and Gwen drew a sunshine, and Lillian made some flowers. I put in a rainbow and a few hearts, with our names in the middle. It was beautiful, and I knowing the way mom was, she would display it close to her, probably in her room, where she could admire it every day. We were her reason for living and fighting the fight.

Without her, we would have been nothing. She kept us going, put food on the table when there was no one else. My mother, my queen, indeed, she would wear the crown, and we were going have the best party, ever. The kids had arranged all the special soda, Gwen getting up on a stool to put the ice cream in the freezer. Peter knew that I was planning the party, not expecting me there to help in the dining room. Mom had been at the resort all day, preparing things. Not seeing me since the morning at the kitchen table, she started wondering where I had been all day, and she walked back to the house to check on us, still dressed in her uniform, from the resort. Stepping in the door, streamers and balloons on the walls and ceiling, a spread of food on the table, and our big card displayed near the cake.

Glancing around at all of us standing there, in our Mother's Day best, Lillian and Gwen with ribbons in their hair, matching the ribbons on our decorations. Roderick, tall and skinny for his age, a bright light complexion, his sandy blonde wavy hair, long to his shoulders, wearing a white shirt, a fresh pair of black dress pants, a big smile on his full lips.

We all ran to her, hugging her hard, saying, "Happy Mother's Day," as if in a song, all of us settling around the table, Mom disappearing into her room for a few minutes, coming out to us with a pretty baby blue dress on, her soft golden brown hair pulled back off her pretty face. Sitting down at the table with us, she gazed at all of us in succession, smiling.

"Well, kids," she said, "this is the best surprise I have had in a long time, and being with all of you is the most wonderful gift of all. Thank you. Now let's have cake," she said, looking at the beautiful cake we had prepared. I watched Mom, examining the cake. As she is bringing the knife through the moist cake, stopping, frozen, staring at the raspberry centre and the deep chocolate of the cake, like she had just cut into a mouse.

"What is it, Mom?" I asked, watching the sheer terror look on her face. Quickly, she snapped out of it, continuing to cut the pieces perfectly, the kids digging into theirs right away, vanilla ice cream on the side. We ate and sang songs, and Mom was the queen of the ball. Slipping into my room I brought out the crown gently placing it on her head. The kids' eyes lit up, and so did Mom's. It was the cutest, the kids getting the biggest kick out of calling Mom a queen.

We were just going to start opening the presents when there was a loud knock at the door. Looking around at us, then she rose to go to the door, forgetting she is wearing the plastic jewled crown. Our eyes on the door, I wondered if it was Peter, wanting to wish Mom a happy Mother's Day, when Mom opened the door. I went to my mother right away, the kids following. Two police officers standing there. At the surprise of the police at the door, Mom pulled the plastic crown off her head.

"Sorry, are we interrupting something, a party?" said one of the cops. Mom nodded her head. I had a gut feeling it was something about my father.

"Are you Mrs. Schoolcraft?" asked the taller constable.

"Yes, I am," answered Mom, hesitation in her voice.

"Well, this is really not the best news to give you, ma'am, on Mother's Day, but your husband, Elric, is dead."

I watched my mother, in what seemed like slow motion, fall to the floor on her knees, her hands covering her face, the rest of us in shock now. Roderick and Lillian started crying, Mom whimpering.

I stood there in the middle of the room, looked up at the ceiling, the ribbon streamers like happy thoughts caught on pretty paper, looking back at them, at the doorway. Everything went silent for a few minutes. I ran to Mom now. The policeman was now sitting on the couch, with Mom on the chair.

Gwen got back to the table, digging into her big piece of cake. Roderick dried his few tears quickly. Lillian had her cake, on her fork, keeping her eyes on the policeman. I sat next to Mom on the side of her chair, while they poured out the information about our father.

"Your husband was in a bad accident in the bush," one of them said, not wanting to go into details to ruin or celebration.

As far as I was concerned, the celebration had just begun. The thought of not having Elric in my life excited me. A sense of real life and freedom took over me.

Trying to conceal my happiness at this time, I tried to console Mom, who had run to the bedroom. I followed her in, watching her throw herself on the bed, face down. Going to her, I rubbed her back and said, "It will be all right, Mom. Don't you see we are better off without him? Do you forget all the terrible things he did to you and us? Mom, don't cry for him. Cry tears of happiness for us. We are free now, Mom, don't you see?"

Pulling herself up off the bed, turning to me, hugging me tight.

"Yes, Brenda, I know, we are finally free." We sat embracing for a few minutes, then headed out to join the kids. The neat little cucumber and cream cheese sandwiches I made were untouched. A casserole of roasted chicken and potatoes was also still in the oven. Mom took one look at them, ice cream all over Gwen's face, and started laughing, almost hysterically. We hugged and got on with our celebration.

"Is Dad really dead?" asked Roderick to Mom, looking her straight in the eyes.

"Yes, God must have come for him," she answered, rubbing his shoulder.

"You mean that God took him to heaven?" he asked. Waiting to see what she would answer, she went quiet for a minute and then answered his question.

"Well, God might come back for him later, but right now he probably has to go somewhere else first."

"What do you mean, Mom?" he said, drawling out his last two words.

"We had better just leave that to God. He knows all. He is from ever-lasting to everlasting, so whatever he decides is how it is."

I liked her explanation, but knew that she would have never said he was going to heaven, or else I might have had to interrupt.

Lillian ran to the picture window, pointing out at something. We all went to look at two officers getting out of a cop car. "The police are back," I said, going to the door, opening it.

"Yes," I said, looking at them, noticing that they were not the same ones.

"Can we please come in?" one of them said. I looked at Mom, who was standing on the other side of the door.

"Yes, let them in," she said. One of them had a piece of paper in his hands, reading something.

"We have an arrest warrant for one Elric Schoolcraft," read the redheaded cop. My mother looked at him, surprised, while I spoke.

"What? There were two other policemen here not long ago, telling us that our father is dead, died in an accident."

"Really," the other replied, looking at his partner.

"Just a minute," said the one, leaving the house. He went out to his two-way radio. The other policeman kept talking to Mom.

"Your husband is wanted in connection with an attempted murder in the case of one Julie Jamieson, who is laying in ICU right now, in a coma."

"Oh my God," said Mom, putting her hands to her face.

"Who is Julie Jamieson?" she asked.

"A Native woman, from the Batchewana Bay reserve," he replied. "She was last seen with Elric Schoolcraft at the bar there." Mom held her head, closing her eyes.

"If this woman dies, he will be charged with first degree murder."

"And how do you know it was my husband?" The other cop coming through the door.

"It is true. We came too late. He is a dead man."

The other one closed up his notebook, taking one look at our party celebrations, wondering if we just got started.

Mom and I just stared at each other, Roderick trying to make heads or tails of it, Lily and Gwen, back at the table getting into some of the little sandwiches.

Elric had beat the forty-year-old Native woman so badly, she had suffered a stroke. Holding up a picture she took from her purse, a picture of Dad with his band, his name on the back of it: Elric and the Wanderers. There was no doubt in Mom's mind he had done it.

CHAPTER 96
The Final Hand for Elric

The way I see it, Elric played his last hand of cards of his life. The Lord sat at the head of the table and dealt the last, deciding hand. Elric toyed with our lives, like we were dice, throwing us around, like life was just a gamble, and we were at his hand. He had lost the game of life, only fitting for the destructive path he took, dragging us with him. God sees and knows everything, even what is in your heart. There is nothing he doesn't know, even the slightest thought. If only Elric would have known the Lord.

He was led along by the adversary, the devil, making Elric one of his pawns, using his weakness to infiltrate his mind, doing the devil's deeds, Elric an instrument of evil. The Lord would have to bind him in an abyss, the way he had planned for the devil himself.

God will bring fire and brimstone down on those who hurt his own, so it says in the good book. What, said Elric? Woe be it, to the ones who are doing the devil's work.

★★★

It had been a rainy morning, Elric anxious to get his day started. He was waiting for a couple of other guys from the camp who were supposed to go into the woods with him, the sky heavy with wetness. Deep grey clouds hung overhead, a light, misty rain falling. Getting anxious, he waited some more, no sign of them. Deciding he would head into the bush without them, convincing himself that it wasn't that wet out, he could at least pull a few of the downed trees out before they got to the site.

Sitting in the seat of the big skidder, he had a sip of hot coffee from his thermos, eating a bacon and egg sandwich. Starting his ascent up the narrow logging road, the big machine pulling along, digging its deep spines into the softened ground, taking with it large chunks of mud, stuck to the rudder of the machine. Elric watched carefully, navigating it up the hill, the hillside right there on the left, glancing down from where he was now sitting on a steep cliff.

The rain dripped down from a hole in the roof of the skidder, like God's tears, wetting Elric's face. Trying to wipe the water from his face, he takes off his hard hat, his hand slipping off one of the controls. Forging on, the skidder started to slide a bit now. A tight grip on the controls, trying to move it over from the side of the steep hillside, but the ground is slick, slippery, wet, the big cat slipping more now, towards the cliff. Trying to adjust his weight in the seat, the skidder slowly edging off the cliff. Without any warning, the big cat tipped slowly, as Elric is thrown out the open skidder door. Looking up, but with no time to get out of the way, the skidder coming down on top of him, pinning him under ten thousand pounds of metal.

A sudden rush of pain through his body, his head like it is exploding, the feeling draining from his legs quickly, going under now, one last breath, one last word: "Please, God," he said, but God was busy on the other line, with someone he knew quite well. God looked over at one of his angels and said. "Please take a message. I am sorry, I never knew that person." Click.

Elric lay alive for four hours, the blood slowly draining from his body.

His dead body was discovered later that day. When he didn't come back to the cookhouse for dinner, a couple of guys went looking for him, finding the machine turned on its side, no sign of him until they saw a boot hanging out from under the big yellow cat. Its fangs showing in the big spines of its claws, mud caked to the bottom of it. The ground sucked the machine, and Elric, deep into the mud, like hell opening up its gates.

The guys on the crew were pretty shaken and had to take a few days off. The foreman urged them to wait, until the ground dried up a bit.

★★★

The abuse that we all suffered at the hands of Elric impacted us greatly, all the rest of our lives, in more ways than I can say. The cycle continued on in the family, but nothing like the life we endured, but in other ways it manifested itself.

It made me a survivor, and I grew stronger, trying to get off the treadmill. It wasn't easy, taking more than a conscious effort many times, abuse raising its ugly head. Our lives were never perfect, but we made it through.

We stayed at the Black Spruce Resort for the next five years. My mother remarried a kind soul who couldn't live without her cooking. I left the resort when I was fifteen with a boy I had met from Toronto, going there with him for a visit, never to return to the Black Spruce Resort.

Mom and the kids stayed there, Peter moving them into a different house after Mom married the poor fellow from the village. He was everything Elric wasn't, not good looking, seldom spoke, sweet with kind ways, and his favorite book the Bible.

When I found out all of those things about him, I knew in my heart Mom would be all right. Peter sent away to Germany for a mail order bride after I left, a young, pretty, willowy blonde with big blue eyes. Her name was Angelica. Mom told me it lasted a while, but she thought that the girl just came to see what she could take from Peter, going back to Germany only after a few short months.

Our foundation as a family was weak, like cement that hasn't cured properly before setting, falling apart, Mother trying to patch it up with her love.

As we grew older, falling by the wayside, like wildflowers scattered by the wind, growing wild. The family as we knew it grew apart, with them not knowing my Mom the way I did, her love for me overbearing for them, at times.

My dear brother Roderick died at a young age of forty of cancer. He had four children with two different women.

None of us went to the funeral, which was held in Thunder Bay, Ontario, where my brother ran his own logging business. We were pretty much all scattered around the Toronto area, my mom and Russell moving closer to the Sault.

Russell died later in life, leaving Mom a widow. She is eighty four as we speak, sound of mind and heart, and waiting for the end of this book to finally put some closure to her life of pain, and to realize her dream of one day having a palace.

My sisters Gwen and Lillian have families of their own and will also be able to connect the dots when the story is finally spoken, helping them to pick up the pieces, trying to make sense of things.

We speak once in a while, mostly just to say, "Hey, I'm still alive," trying to catch up on years lost, in a hurried conversation.

My dear mother Alice, passed away suddenly, after suffering from Cancer. Up until she took her last breath, it was never about her, asking the nurses every day, how they were, trying to make them happy. I knew the day I walked into her hospital room, and the nurse on duty's name was Angel, written on the blackboard in the room. Mom died that day, peacefully, waiting for God to take her home.

Free at Last

Free, free, at last,
Release the chains that bind me, I cry onto the wind,
The words of this story, like a magical chant,
Unleashing my heart and soul,
Soaring high, on angel's wings.
Running free as a child, weightless,
My burdens lifted, swooped up in an eagle's wings,
Dropped into a deep, forgotten sea.
Like my mother's bleach effect,
My heart and soul lightened.
The grey blanketed sky that hung over our heads,
The storm always threatening to unleash it fury.
The greyness, like my father's eyes, gone, gone, gone, like him.
The sky opening up, the sunshine bleeding through,
The warmth of my mother's love,
Like the sunshine kissing my face,
Hopes and dreams renewed,
Lost in my mother's green eyes,
Like the fresh new grass of spring.

Hallelujah!

The fate of Elric was in the cards, so to speak. The Lord, would deal the last hand.

This book is based on the true life story of Brenda Rae Schoolcraft.
To forgive is to be forgiven.
I forgive you, Elric. Your daughter, Brenda.
It was a story that begged to be told. I wanted to share with the world, to help others who may be suffering the same kind of abuse or to alert innocent victims of the warning signs, to safeguard them. With my mother's blessing, a percentage of the proceeds of this book and possible motion picture will go to a chosen organization for abused women and children.

May God be with you and yours.

Love from Alice and Brenda.

My readers will see and feel the truth in this tale. My brother deceased, and my two other siblings are still alive. They know of the story, but it is not their story, it is mine. The abuse stunted my life and kept me from dreaming too big. There will be those who will deny my story, but like I said, it is my story, not anyone else's. I show you how this kind of dysfunction affects children and how it impacted my life in many negative ways. Abuse destroys lives and stunts the growth we all deserve. This story is based on the true life of Brenda Rae Schoolcraft.

Mom now knows her full story. When she was alive, I let her read the first hundred pages, refusing to let her go through the pain all over again. Alice is the queen of my heart and will always be in God's embrace, now an angel watching over me.

The End.

FEB 09 2024

Made in the USA
San Bernardino, CA
14 August 2019